Kundalini Tantra

Swami Satyananda Saraswati

Yoga Publications Trust, Munger, Bihar, India

© Bihar School of Yoga 1984

Published by Bihar School of Yoga
    First published 1984
    Reprinted 1992, 1996

Published by Yoga Publications Trust
    Reprinted 2000, 2001, 2003, 2004, 2006, 2007, 2009, 2012

ISBN: 978-81-85787-15-2

Publisher and distributor: Yoga Publications Trust, Ganga Darshan, Munger, Bihar, India.

Website: www.biharyoga.net
        www.rikhiapeeth.net

Printed at Thomson Press (India) Limited, New Delhi, 110001

Dedication

*In humility we offer this dedication to
Swami Sivananda Saraswati, who initiated
Swami Satyananda Saraswati into the secrets of yoga.*

Kundalini Tantra

WORLD YOGA CONVENTION 2013
GANGA DARSHAN, MUNGER, BIHAR, INDIA
23rd–27th October 2013

1963–2013
GOLDEN JUBILEE

Contents

Introduction to Kundalini and Tantra   1

Kundalini
1. Ye Man, Tame the Kundalini   9
2. What is Kundalini?   13
3. Kundalini Physiology   21
4. Kundalini and the Brain   31
5. Methods of Awakening   37
6. Preparing for the Awakening   48
7. Diet for Kundalini Awakening   59
8. Risks and Precautions   64
9. Kundalini and Madness   72
10. Four Forms of Awakening   76
11. The Descent of Kundalini   81
12. The Experiences of Awakening   86
13. The Path of Kriya Yoga   93
14. Vama Marga and Kundalini Awakening   101

The Chakras
15. Introduction to the Chakras   113
16. Evolution through the Chakras   119
17. Ajna Chakra   127
18. Mooladhara Chakra   137
19. Swadhisthana Chakra   146
20. Manipura Chakra   156
21. Anahata Chakra   162
22. Vishuddhi Chakra   173
23. Bindu   180
24. Sahasrara and Samadhi   189

Kundalini Yoga Practice

25. Rules and Preparation   197
26. Posture   201
27. Chakra Sadhana Course   209
28. Practices for Ajna Chakra   211
29. Practices for Mooladhara Chakra   219
30. Practices for Swadhisthana Chakra   226
31. Practices for Manipura Chakra   229
32. Practices for Anahata Chakra   238
33. Practices for Vishuddhi Chakra   245
34. Practices for Bindu   251
35. Practices for Integrated Chakra Awareness   259
36. Your Sadhana Program   277
37. Kundalini Kriyas of Kriya Yoga   279
38. The Kriya Yoga Practices   284

Kundalini Research

39. Introduction   319
40. Kundalini, Fact not Fiction   324
41. Defining the Nadis   330
42. Controlling the Nadis and the Brain   338
43. Evidence for the Existence of Nadis   350
44. Neurophysiology of the Chakras   358
45. Evidence for the Existence of Chakras   370
46. The Cosmic Trigger   380
47. Cross-Cultural Evidence   395
48. Analysis of the Chakras from a
    Psychophysiological Viewpoint   402

Appendix   427
Glossary   433
References   446
Index of Practices   451

Introduction to Kundalini and Tantra

I have been travelling the world for the last three decades in order to pass on the message of yoga, and I find that yoga has influenced the course of human thinking tremendously. Initially of course, there was some doubt about it as many people thought that yoga was a type of religion, witchcraft or mysticism. This particularly happened because man believed matter was the ultimate point in the evolution of nature. The materialistic world did not understand yoga for some time, but as scientists dived deep into the mysteries of matter, they came to understand and realize that matter was not the ultimate in the evolution of nature.

If that is so for one form of matter, it applies to every form of matter. This external experience, the perception you have through your senses, is a product of matter. Even your thoughts, feelings, emotions and cognitions are products of matter. Therefore, they cannot be absolute and final. This means there must be another realm of experience, and if there is another realm of experience, it must be possible to transcend the present limitations of the mind.

The mind is also matter; it is definitely not spirit. Therefore, the mind can also be transformed and made to evolve. Many people have begun to realize and experience this fact in the last few decades. In my opinion, this marks the end of one era and the beginning of another. For those who have some knowledge of science and the nature of

1

matter, it is not difficult to understand exactly what inner experience is.

An inner experience is the manifestation of a deeper level of oneself. Dream, of course, is an experience. Your dreams may be schizophrenic, but that is an expression of your own self. Thought is also a concept or expression of your own self. A piece of music is an expression of your self, whether you compose it or just admire it. A painting or sculpture is a concept of your self whether you create it or just admire it. That means the external world is a manifestation of your inner experience, and you can improve this experience to any extent. You can also bring about deterioration of this experience. When everything is hopeless outside, that is your experience of yourself, and if everything is beautiful outside, that is also your experience of yourself.

In the last few decades, yoga has helped millions of people to improve their self-concept. Yoga realizes that man is not only the mind, but the body as well. Therefore, one does not experience happiness only through the mind. The body is also real and it is a part of one's personality. Just improving the condition of the body, however, will not necessarily enable the mind to experience happiness either. This is because man is not only the body and mind, but emotion and desire as well. He is something beyond the mind or psyche. Therefore, yoga has been designed in such a way that it can complete the process of evolution of the personality in every possible direction. That is why yoga has so many branches – hatha yoga, karma yoga, bhakti yoga, raja yoga, jnana yoga, kundalini yoga, and so on.

A combined, integrated practice of yoga in one's life will definitely ensure a better quality of experience within you and without. Every seeker and practitioner on the path of yoga must remember that the various paths of yoga are to improve the quality of head, heart and hands. However, yoga does not end with the development of the personality. One level of the personality is dependent on this mind, this body and these emotions, but there is another deeper part of the personality which you have to develop with another kind of mind and emotion. This requires a special process, and that process is known as kundalini yoga.

Objective experience is not the ultimate

Kundalini yoga is a part of the tantric tradition. Although you may have already been introduced to yoga, it is also necessary for you to know something about tantra. Since ancient times, the wise have realized that the mind can be expanded and that experiences do not necessarily depend on an object. This means that if somebody is playing music, I can hear it, and if somebody has painted a picture, I can see it, but I can also see if there is no picture, and I can hear if there is no music. This is also a quality of the personality which has been ignored in the last one hundred and fifty to two hundred years.

Tantra says that the range of mental experience can be broadened. With the help of the senses, your mind can have an experience based on an object. There can be an experience within the framework of time, space and object, but there can also be an experience beyond the framework of time, space and object. The second form of experience can happen when the present mind expands beyond its given definitions and borders, and when this experience occurs, energy is released from yourself.

For hundreds of years, people have been talking about an experience called nirvana, moksha, emancipation, self-realization, salvation or liberation, without understanding it properly. Yogis call this experience samadhi. Although many people think that in samadhi or nirvana everything is completely finished, it is definitely not a process of quitting the world. Nothing finishes, only one level of experience ends, but then another begins.

Since the dawn of creation, the tantrics and yogis have realized that in this physical body there is a potential force. It is not psychological, philosophical or transcendental; it is a dynamic potential force in the material body, and it is called kundalini. This kundalini is the greatest discovery of tantra and yoga. Scientists have begun to look into this, and a summary of some of the latest scientific experiments is included in this book. We can see from this research that science is not actually going to discover anything new in this field. It is only rediscovering and substantiating what yogis discovered many, many centuries ago.

A universal event

The seat of kundalini is a small gland at the base of the spinal cord. With the evolution of the natural forces in man, this gland has now come to a point where man can explode it. Those people who have awakened this supernatural force have been called rishis, prophets, yogis, siddhas and various other names according to the time, tradition and culture. In India the entire cultural set-up was once organized to facilitate this explosion, but today things are a little different because materialism is a very powerful force, and for the moment it has even stupefied the Indian mind.

For the awakening of kundalini, not only the practices of yoga are required. If this awakening is to become a universal event, then the entire social structure has to be reorganized and millions of people all over the world have to be told the purpose of their existence. The whole of life from the time of conception to the moment when you leave the body, each and everything has to be reoriented. You will see in this book how even the instinctive and emotional interaction between men and women must be revised and refined, so that it can lead us not away from, but towards this ultimate awakening. This reorientation has to be undertaken with the purpose of expanding the mind and opening new doors of experience.

Today we are living in a world where everyone is more or less satisfied. We have all the comforts and everything we need and do not need. There will come a time, however, when man will be prepared to throw off these comforts. Luxury and comfort weaken the will and keep one under constant hypnosis. Alcohol and drugs are not as dangerous as total slavery to luxury and comfort. Man cannot pull himself away from them. It is impossible unless he has become aware of something more than that which his parents and society could give him.

Formerly there were only a few seekers, but now millions and millions of people in the world are striving for a higher experience. This higher experience is known as knowledge. When, through yoga and tantra, the awakening of kundalini takes place, a process of metamorphosis occurs in the realm of nature and in the realm of spirit. The elements of both the physical and the mental body also change.

It may be difficult for people of today to understand the whole concept, but soon humanity will comprehend it all. Matter will become unnecessary and insignificant. Behind the matter and behind the mind there is energy and there is an experience of that energy.

Proceed slowly, sensibly and systematically

Yet, you should not try to realize and experience these things abruptly. You will find here detailed instructions on the gradual preparation of your mind and body for the arousal of kundalini, and advice on elementary precautions to be observed in order to avoid unnecessary risks and obstacles. Do not try to influence your mind directly, because the mind is nothing but an extension of the body complex. Start systematically with the body, the prana, the nadis and chakras, according to the scheme outlined in this book. Then see how you evolve.

Many people, encouraged by a type of hurried philosophy, take to drugs, chemicals and other things they consider to be speedy alternatives. They are very serious people I believe, but they are not practical and systematic because they think they can transcend the role of the body in the realm of evolution. In the final evolution of mind, matter and man, you cannot ignore either the body or the mind. You cannot even ignore the nose, the stomach or the digestive system. That is why this transcendental philosophy begins with the basic considerations of diet and yogic physiology that you find discussed here.

The discovery of the great energy began with matter. Did nuclear energy descend from heaven? No, it evolved from crude matter. Where does the experience generate from? From heaven? From the sanctum sanctorum? No, from this body and this nervous system. That is how you should be practical and sensible.

This book presents a systematic and pragmatic approach to the awakening of kundalini. It begins with an expanded understanding of the true role and potential of the body and nervous system, moving through an exhaustive examination of the different methods of awakening suitable for different personalities and conditions. You will find clear and direct instructions on the actual yogic and tantric techniques to be practised towards this goal, together with a map of possible experiences you may encounter as the practices mature, so that you can sustain this great awakening and integrate it into a more conscious and creative way of life.

We have included here a systematic schedule of practice, within the context of a philosophy that is both pragmatic and transcendental, to prepare you in every way for this great adventure in consciousness.

Kundalini

1

Ye Man, Tame the Kundalini

When I was six years old I had a spontaneous spiritual experience during which I became completely unaware of my body for quite a long time. Again, when I was ten, the same thing happened, but this time I was old enough to think and rationalize, and I told my father about it. At first he did not understand what had happened and he wanted to take me to a doctor, but fortunately there were no doctors in our area at that time. Had there been, perhaps I would have ended up in a mental hospital, but things being what they were, I did not have to undergo treatment and was left unattended.

My father had great regard for the Vedas and for his guru. One day this guru happened to visit my home town, so my father took me to him and asked his advice about me. The sage told him that I had had a spiritual experience and therefore should be instructed to lead a spiritual life. My father obeyed his guru and arranged for me to be trained accordingly. Thus at an early age I was dedicated to the spiritual quest.

My family was Hindu, and in Hinduism there are two traditions: one believes in the worship of idols, and the other that God is formless. My family belonged to the latter, but still I often looked at the pictures of all the different deities and wondered at them. Durga was mounted on a lion; Saraswati on a swan; Vishnu lay sleeping on a huge cobra;

Kali was completely naked, standing on the body of Shiva; Tara too was naked and Shiva was drinking milk from her breast. I could not understand what it all meant. Why did Shiva ride upon a bull and have so many snakes wrapped around him; how could the Ganga flow from his hair; why was Ganesha, with his enormous elephantine head and pot belly, riding on a small rat? I thought that there must be some symbolic meaning behind all this, but I only began to understand it through kundalini yoga, which I started practising at the age of fifteen, while still at school.

Around this time I had another experience. I was sitting quietly when suddenly, without any effort, my mind turned inwards. I immediately saw the whole earth with its oceans, continents, mountains and cities, crack into pieces. I did not understand this vision until a few days later when the Second World War broke out. This really made me begin to wonder. How could I have seen this future event symbolically in meditation when living in a remote area? I had neither heard nor read about it previously, nor had I any way of knowing that it was coming.

A new life begins

By the time I was seventeen, I was asking questions which nobody could answer. I wondered about things like the difference between perception and experience. I talked a lot about such topics with my maternal uncle and younger sister, but this did not quench my thirst and I knew I had to go out and discover the answers for myself. I postponed my departure from home until one day my father pushed me out with ninety rupees in my pocket. Thus my wandering life began.

During my travels I met a very old swami who invited me to stay in his ashram. He had a wonderful knowledge of tantra and taught me many things. Though I knew I would never forget him, he was not my guru and after nine months I left his ashram and continued wandering. Soon after I arrived in Rishikesh, where I heard about Swami Sivananda. I went to him and asked how to experience the highest consciousness. He told me to stay in his ashram and he would guide me. So I followed monastic life, but still, for a long time I was puzzled about the purpose of my existence. I felt that man was a seeker, yet I really did not know what I was seeking and was often left with the terrifying question that man asks himself regarding death.

The awakening of kundalini

Sometime later I had another experience while sitting on the banks of the Ganga. I was thinking of something mundane when my mind spontaneously started going in and in. Suddenly I felt as if the earth was slipping from under me and the sky was expanding and receding. A moment later I experienced a terrible force springing from the base of my body like an atomic explosion. I felt that I was vibrating very fast, the light currents were terrific. I experienced the supreme bliss, like the climax of a man's desire, and it continued for a long time. My whole body was contracting until the feeling of pleasure became quite unbearable and I completely lost awareness of my body. This was the third time it had happened.

After returning to consciousness I was listless for many days. I could not eat, sleep or move, even to go to the toilet. I saw everything but nothing registered. The bliss was a living thing within me and I knew that if I moved, this wonderful feeling would cease; I would lose the intensity of it all. How could I move when bells were ringing inside? This was the awakening of my kundalini.

After a week or so I returned to normal and then I started to study tantra and yoga very seriously. At first I was still a bit weak and sick, so I practised hatha yoga to purify my whole system. Then I began to explore the fantastic science of kundalini yoga. What is this power which awakens in mooladhara chakra? My interest was aroused and I put much effort into trying to understand this marvellous force.

With the awakening of kundalini, the greater intelligence is aroused from its sleep and you can give birth to a new range of creativity. When kundalini awakens, not only are you blessed with visions and psychic experiences, you could become a prophet, saint, inspired artist or musician, a brilliant writer or poet, a clairvoyant or messiah. Or you could become an outstanding leader, prime minister, governor or president. The awakening of kundalini affects the whole area of the human mind and behaviour.

Kundalini is not a myth or an illusion. It is not a hypothesis or a hypnotic suggestion. Kundalini is a biological substance that exists within the framework of the body. Its awakening generates electrical impulses throughout the whole body and these impulses can be detected by modern scientific instruments and machines. Therefore, each of us should consider the importance and the benefits of awakening kundalini, and we should make a resolve to awaken this great shakti.

2

What is Kundalini?

E verybody should know something about kundalini as it represents the coming consciousness of mankind. Kundalini is the name of a sleeping dormant potential force in the human organism and it is situated at the root of the spinal column. In the masculine body it is in the perineum, between the urinary and excretory organs. In the female body its location is at the root of the uterus, in the cervix. This centre is known as mooladhara chakra and it is actually a physical structure. It is a small gland which you can even take out and press. However, kundalini is a dormant energy, and even if you press it, it will not explode like a bomb.

To awaken kundalini you must prepare yourself through yogic techniques. You must practise asanas, pranayama, kriya yoga and meditation. Then, when you are able to direct your prana into the seat of kundalini, the energy wakes up and makes its way through sushumna nadi, in the central nervous canal, to the brain. As kundalini ascends, it passes through each of the chakras which are interconnected with the different silent areas of the brain. With the awakening of kundalini there is an explosion in the brain as the dormant or sleeping areas start blossoming like flowers. Therefore, kundalini can be equated with the awakening of the silent areas of the brain.

Although kundalini is said to reside in mooladhara chakra, we are all at different stages of evolution, and in some

13

of us kundalini may have already reached swadhisthana, manipura or anahata chakra. If this is so, whatever sadhana you do now might start an awakening in anahata or some other chakra. However, awakening of kundalini in mooladhara chakra is one thing, and awakening in sahasrara, the highest centre of the brain, is another. Once the multipetalled lotus of sahasrara blossoms, a new consciousness dawns. Our present consciousness is not independent, as the mind depends on the information supplied by the senses. If you have no eyes, you can never see; if you are deaf, you will never hear. However, when the superconsciousness emerges, experience becomes completely independent and knowledge also becomes completely independent.

How kundalini was discovered

Right from the beginning of creation, man witnessed many transcendental happenings. Sometimes he was able to read the thoughts of others, he witnessed somebody else's predictions coming true, or he may even have seen his own dreams manifesting into realities. He pondered over the fact that some people could write inspiring poems or compose beautiful music whereas others could not; one person could fight on the battlefield for days together and another person could not even get out of bed. So he wanted to discover why everybody seemed to be different.

During the course of his investigations, man came to understand that within every individual there is a special form of energy. He saw that in some people this energy was dormant, in others it was evolving and in a very small minority it was actually awakened. Originally, man named this energy after the gods, goddesses, angels or divinities. Then he discovered prana and called it prana shakti. In tantra they called it kundalini.

What the various names for kundalini mean

In Sanskrit, *kundal* means a coil, and so kundalini has been described as that which is coiled. This is the traditional belief, but it has been incorrectly understood. The word *kundalini* actually comes from the word *kunda*, meaning a deeper place, pit or cavity. The fire used in the ceremony of initiation is kindled in a pit called a kunda. Similarly, the place where a dead body is burned is a kunda. If you dig a ditch or a hole, it is called a kunda. Kunda refers to the concave cavity in which the brain, resembling a coiled and sleeping serpent, nestles. (If you have the opportunity of examining a dissection of the human brain you will see that it is in the form of a coil or snake curled up upon itself.) This is the true meaning of kundalini. The word kundalini refers to the shakti or power when it is in its dormant potential state, but when it is manifesting, you can call it Devi, Kali, Durga, Saraswati, Lakshmi or any other name according to the manifestation it is exhibiting before you.

In the Christian tradition, the terms 'the Path of the Initiates' and 'the Stairway to Heaven' used in the Bible, refer to kundalini's ascent through sushumna nadi. The ascent of kundalini and, ultimately, the descent of spiritual grace, are symbolized by the cross. This is why Christians make the sign of the cross at ajna, anahata and vishuddhi chakras, for ajna is the centre where the ascending consciousness is transcended and anahata is where the descending grace is made manifest to the world.

Whatever happens in spiritual life, it is related to the awakening of kundalini. And the goal of every form of spiritual life, whether you call it samadhi, nirvana, moksha, communion, union, kaivalya, liberation or whatever, is in fact awakening of kundalini.

Kundalini, Kali and Durga

When kundalini has just awakened and you are not able to handle it, it is called Kali. When you can handle it and are able to use it for beneficial purposes and you become powerful on account of it, it is called Durga.

Kali is a female deity, naked, black or smoky in colour, wearing a mala of one hundred and eight human skulls, representing the memories of different births. Kali's lolling tongue of a blood red colour signifies the rajo guna whose circular movement gives impetus to all creative activities. By this specific gesture, she is exhorting sadhakas to control their rajo guna. The sacrificial sword and the severed head held by the left hand are the symbols of dissolution. Darkness and death are by no means the mere absence of light and life, rather they are their origin. The sadhaka worships the cosmic power in its female form, for she represents the kinetic aspect, the masculine being the static aspect which is activated only through her power.

In Hindu mythology, the awakening of Kali has been described in great detail. When Kali rises in red anger, all the gods and demons are stunned and everybody keeps quiet. They do not know what she is going to do. They ask Lord Shiva to pacify her, but Kali roars ferociously, throwing him down and standing on his chest with her mouth wide open, thirsty for flesh and blood. When the devas hold prayers to pacify Kali, she becomes calm and quiet.

Then there is the emergence of Durga, the higher, more refined and benign symbols of the unconscious. Durga is a beautiful goddess seated on a tiger. She has eight hands representing the eightfold elements. Durga wears a mala of human heads to symbolize her wisdom and power. These heads are generally fifty-two in number, representing the fifty-two letters of the Sanskrit alphabet, which are the outer manifestations of Shabda Brahma or Brahma in the form of sound. Durga is the remover of all evil consequences of life and the giver of power and peace that is released from mooladhara.

According to yoga philosophy, Kali, the first manifestation of the unconscious kundalini is a terrible power; it completely subdues the individual soul, represented by her standing on Lord Shiva. It sometimes happens that due to mental instability, some people come into contact with their unconscious body and see inauspicious, ferocious elements – ghosts, monsters, etc. When Kali, the unconscious power

of man, is awakened she goes up to meet the further manifestation, being Durga, the superconscious, bestowing glory
and beauty.

Symbolic representation of kundalini

In the tantric texts, kundalini is conceived of as the primal
power or energy. In terms of modern psychology, it can be
called the unconscious in man. As we have just discussed, in
Hindu mythology, kundalini corresponds to the concept of
Kali. In the philosophy of Shaivism, the concept of kundalini
is represented by the shivalingam, the oval-shaped stone or
pillar with a snake coiled around it.

However, most commonly, kundalini is illustrated as a
sleeping serpent coiled three and a half times. Of course,
there is no serpent residing in mooladhara, sahasrara or
any other chakra, but the serpent has always been a symbol
for efficient consciousness. In all the oldest mystic cults of
the world you will find the serpent, and if you have seen
any pictures of images of Lord Shiva, you will have noticed
serpents girdling his waist, neck and arms. Kali is also
adorned with serpents and Lord Vishnu eternally reposes
on a large coiled serpent. This serpent power symbolizes the
unconscious in man.

In Scandinavian, European, Latin American and Middle
Eastern countries and many different civilizations of the
world, the concept of the serpent power is represented in
monuments and ancient artefacts. This means that kundalini
was known to people from all parts of the world in the past.
However, we can conceive of kundalini in any manner we
like because actually, prana has no form or dimension, it is
infinite.

In the traditional descriptions of kundalini awakening,
it is said that kundalini resides in mooladhara in the form
of a coiled snake and when the snake awakens it uncoils
and shoots up through sushumna (the psychic passage in
the centre of the spinal cord), opening the other chakras
as it goes. (See Sir John Woodroffe's *The Serpent Power*.)

17

Brahmachari Swami Vyasdev, in his book *Science of the Soul*, describes the awakening of kundalini in the following way: "Sadhakas have seen the sushumna in the form of a luminous rod or pillar, a golden yellow snake, or sometimes as a shining black snake about ten inches long with blood red eyes like smouldering charcoal, the front part of the tongue vibrating and shining like lightning, ascending the spinal column."

The meaning of the three coils of the serpent is as follows: the three coils represent the three matras of Om, which relate to past, present and future; to the three gunas: tamas, rajas and sattwa; to the three states of consciousness: waking, sleeping and dreaming; and to the three types of experience: subjective experience, sensual experience and absence of experience. The half coil represents the state of transcendence, where there is neither waking, sleeping nor dreaming. So, the three and a half coils signify the total experience of the universe and the experience of transcendence.

Who can awaken kundalini?

There are many people who have awakened their kundalini. Not only saints and sadhus, but poets, painters, warriors, writers, anyone can awaken their kundalini. With the awakening of kundalini, not only visions of God take place, there is dawning of creative intelligence and an awakening of supramental faculties. By activating kundalini you may become anything in life.

The energy of kundalini is one energy, but it expresses itself differently through the individual psychic centres or chakras – first in gross instinctive ways and then in progressively more subtle ways. Refining of the expression of this energy at higher and more subtle levels of vibration represents the ascent of human consciousness to its highest possibilities.

Kundalini is the creative energy; it is the energy of self-expression. Just as in reproduction a new life is created, in the same way, someone like Einstein uses that same energy in a different, more subtle realm, to create a theory like relativity. It is the same energy that is expressed when someone composes or plays beautiful music. It is the same energy which is expressed in all parts of life, whether it is building up a business, fulfilling the family duties or reaching whatever goal you aspire for. These are all expressions of the same creative energy.

Everybody, whether householder or sannyasin, must remember that the awakening of kundalini is the prime purpose of human incarnation. All the pleasures of sensual life which we are enjoying now are intended only to enhance the awakening of kundalini amidst the adverse circumstances of human life.

A process of metamorphosis

With the awakening of kundalini, a transformation takes place in life. It has little to do with one's moral, religious or ethical life. It has more to do with the quality of our experiences and perceptions. When kundalini wakes up, your mind changes and your priorities and attachments also change. All your karmas undergo a process of integration. It is very simple to understand. When you were a child you loved toys, but why don't you love them now? Because your mind has changed and consequently, your attachments have also changed. So with the awakening of kundalini, a metamorphosis takes place. There is even the possibility of restructuring the entire physical body.

When kundalini awakens, the physical body actually undergoes many changes. Generally they are positive, but if your guru is not cautious, they can be negative also. When the shakti wakes up, the cells in the body are completely charged and a process of rejuvenation also starts. The voice changes, the smell of the body changes and the hormonal secretions also change. In fact, the transformation of cells in the body and brain takes place at a much higher rate than normal. These are just a few observations. However, scientific researchers are still taking their first steps into this field.

Why awaken kundalini?

If you want to take up the practice of kundalini yoga, the most important thing is that you have a reason or an aim. If you want to awaken kundalini for psychic powers, then please go ahead with your own destiny. But if you want to awaken kundalini in order to enjoy communion between Shiva and Shakti, the actual communion between the two great forces within you, and if you want to enter samadhi and experience the absolute in the cosmos, and if you want to understand the truth behind the appearance, and if the purpose of your pilgrimage is very great, then there is nothing that can come to you as an obstacle.

By means of kundalini awakening, you are compensating for the laws of nature and speeding up the pace of your physical, mental and spiritual evolution. Once the great shakti awakens, man is no longer a gross physical body operating with a lower mind and low voltage prana. Instead, every cell of the body is charged with the high voltage prana of kundalini. And when total awakening occurs, man becomes a junior god, an embodiment of divinity.

3

Kundalini Physiology

Kundalini or the serpent power does not belong to the physical body, though it is connected to it. Nor can it be discovered in the mental body or even the astral body. Its abode is actually in the causal body, where the concepts of time, space and object are completely lost.

How and where is the concept of kundalini related to the supreme consciousness? The serpent power is considered to arise from the unconscious state in mooladhara. This unconscious awareness then has to pass through different phases and becomes one with the cosmic awareness in the highest realm of existence. The supreme awareness of Shiva is considered to be seated in sahasrara, the superconscious or transcendental body at the crown of the head. In the Vedas, as well as the Tantras, this supreme seat is called *hiranyagarbha*, the womb of consciousness. It corresponds to the pituitary body, the master gland situated within the brain.

Immediately below this centre of supreme consciousness, there is another psychic centre – the third eye or ajna chakra, which corresponds to the pineal gland. This is the seat of intuitive knowledge. This centre lies on top of the spinal column, at the level of *bhrumadhya*, the eyebrow centre. Ajna chakra is important because it is simultaneously connected with the seat of supreme consciousness in sahasrara, and with mooladhara, the seat of the unconscious, at the base of the spine, via sushumna, the psychic passage within the spinal column. Therefore, it is the connecting link between the lowest unconscious seat of power and the highest centre of illumination within the individual.

Kundalini yoga is not abstract. It considers this very physical body as the basis. For a kundalini yogi, the supreme consciousness represents the highest possible manifestation of physical matter in this body. The matter of this physical body is being transformed into subtle forces – such as feeling, thinking, reasoning, remembering, postulating and doubting, in the gradual process of evolution. This psychic, suprasensory or transcendental power is the ultimate point of human evolution.

The chakras

The literal meaning of the word *chakra* is 'wheel' or 'circle', but in the yogic context a better translation of the Sanskrit word is 'vortex' or 'whirlpool'. The chakras are vortices of psychic energy and they are visualized and experienced as circular movements of energy at particular rates of vibration.

In each person there are myriads of chakras, but in the practices of tantra and yoga, only a few principal ones are utilized. These chakras span the full spectrum of man's being, from the gross to the subtle.

The chakras relate to physiological as well as psychic centres whose structures correspond more or less with the traditional descriptions. These nerve centres are not situated inside the spinal cord itself, but lie like junctions on the interior walls of the spinal column. If you cut the spinal cord transversely at different levels, you can see that the grey matter in the cross section resembles the lotus shape and the ascending and descending tracts of nerve fibres correspond to the nadis. These communicating nerve fibres control the different physiological functions of that portion of the body. Many books state that the chakras are reservoirs of power, but this is not true.

A chakra is like a centrally placed electricity pole from which electrical wires are run to different places, houses and street lights in the vicinity. This arrangement is the same for each one of the chakras. The nadis which emerge from each chakra carry prana in both directions. There is a forward and backward pranic motion in the nadis, which is analogous to the flow of alternating current in electrical wires. The outgoing communication and the incoming reaction enter and leave the chakra in the form of this pranic flow in the corresponding nadis.

There are six chakras in the human body which are directly connected with the higher unillumined centres of the brain. The first chakra is mooladhara. It is situated in the pelvic floor and corresponds to the coccygeal plexus of nerves. In the masculine body it lies between the urinary and excretory openings, in the form of a small dormant gland termed the perineal body. In the feminine body it is situated inside the posterior surface of the cervix.

Mooladhara is the first chakra in spiritual evolution, where one goes beyond animal consciousness and starts to be a real human being. It is also the last chakra in the completion of animal evolution. It is said that from mooladhara chakra right down to the heels there are other lower chakras which are responsible for the development of the animal and human qualities of instinct and intellect. From mooladhara chakra upwards lie the chakras which are concerned with illumination and evolution of the higher or super man. Mooladhara chakra has control over the entire range of human excretory and sexual functions.

The second chakra is *swadhisthana*, located at the lowest point or termination of the spinal cord. It corresponds to the sacral plexus of nerves and controls the unconscious.

The third chakra is *manipura*, situated in the spinal column exactly at the level of the navel. It corresponds to the solar plexus and controls the entire processes of digestion, assimilation and temperature regulation in the body.

The fourth chakra is *anahata*, and it lies in the vertebral column behind the base of the heart, at the level of the depression in the sternum. It corresponds to the cardiac plexus

23

Location of the Chakras

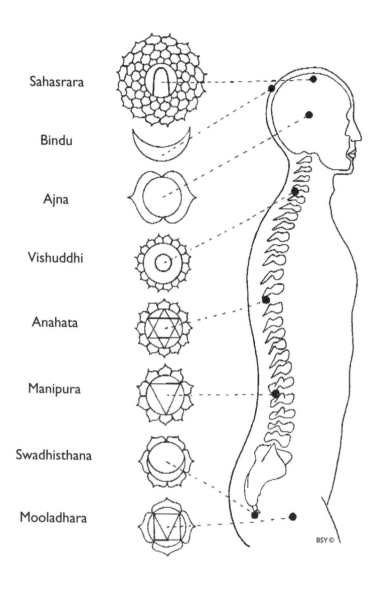

Sahasrara

Bindu

Ajna

Vishuddhi

Anahata

Manipura

Swadhisthana

Mooladhara

BSY©

of nerves, and also controls the functions of the heart, the lungs, the diaphragm and other organs in this region of the body.

The fifth chakra is *vishuddhi*, which lies at the level of the throat pit in the vertebral column. This chakra corresponds to the cervical plexus of nerves and controls the thyroid complex and also some systems of articulation, the upper palate and the epiglottis.

Ajna, the sixth and most important chakra, corresponds to the pineal gland, lying in the midline of the brain directly above the spinal column. This chakra controls the muscles and the onset of sexual activity. Tantra and yoga maintain that ajna chakra, the command centre, has complete control over all the functions of the disciple's life.

These six chakras serve as switches for turning on different parts of the brain. The awakening which is brought about in the chakras is conducted to the higher centres in the brain via the nadis.

There are also two higher centres in the brain which are commonly referred to in kundalini yoga: bindu and sahasrara. *Bindu* is located at the top back of the head, where Hindu Brahmins keep a tuft of hair. This is the point where oneness first divides itself into many. Bindu feeds the whole optic system and is also the seat of nectar or amrit.

Sahasrara is supreme; it is the final culmination of kundalini shakti. It is the seat of higher awareness. Sahasrara is situated at the top of the head and is physically correlated to the pituitary gland, which controls each and every gland and system of the body.

Nadis

Nadis are not nerves but rather channels for the flow of consciousness. The literal meaning of *nadi* is flow. Just as the negative and positive forces of electricity flow through complex circuits, in the same way, *prana shakti* (vital force) and *manas shakti* (mental force) flow through every part of our body via these nadis. According to the tantras there are 72,000

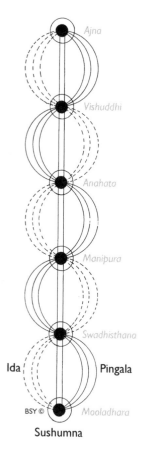

Ajna

Vishuddhi

Anahata

Manipura

Swadhisthana

Ida

Pingala

BSY ©

Mooladhara

Sushumna

or more such channels or networks through which the stimuli flow like an electric current from one point to another. These 72,000 nadis cover the whole body and through them the inherent rhythms of activity in the different organs of the body are maintained. Within this network of nadis, there are ten main channels, and of these ten, three are most important for they control the flow of prana and conscious-ness within all the other nadis of the body. These three nadis are called ida, pingala and sushumna. *Ida nadi* controls all the mental processes, while *pingala nadi* controls all the vital processes. Ida is known as the moon, and pingala as the sun. A third nadi, *sushumna,* is the channel for the awakening of spiritual consciousness. You may consider these three nadis as pranic force, mental force and spiritual force.

As sushumna flows inside the central canal of the spinal cord, ida and pingala simultaneously flow on the outer sur-face of the spinal cord, still within the bony vertebral column. Ida, pingala and sushumna nadis begin in mooladhara in the pelvic floor. From there, sushumna flows directly upwards within the central canal, while ida passes to the left and pingala to the right. At swadhisthana chakra, or the sacral plexus, the three nadis come together again and ida and pingala cross over one another. Ida passes up to the right,

26

pingala to the left, and sushumna continues to flow directly upwards in the central canal. The three nadis come together again at manipura chakra, the solar plexus, and so on. Finally, ida, pingala and sushumna meet in the ajna chakra.

Ida and pingala function in the body alternately and not simultaneously. If you observe your nostrils, you will find that generally one is flowing freely and the other is blocked. When the left nostril is open, it is the lunar energy or ida nadi which is flowing. When the right nostril is free, the solar energy or pingala nadi is flowing.

Investigations have shown that when the right nostril is flowing, the left hemisphere of the brain is activated. When the left nostril is flowing, the right hemisphere is activated. This is how the nadis or energy channels control the brain and the events of life and consciousness.

Now, if these two energies – prana and chitta, pingala and ida, life and consciousness, can be made to function simultaneously, then both hemispheres of the brain can be made to function simultaneously and to participate together in the thinking, living, intuitive and regulating processes.

In ordinary life this does not happen because the simultaneous awakening and functioning of life force and consciousness can take place only if the central canal, sushumna, is connected with kundalini, the source of energy. If sushumna can be connected in the physical body, it can reactivate the brain cells and create a new physical structure.

The importance of awakening sushumna

Sushumna nadi is regarded as a hollow tube in which there are three more concentric tubes, each being progressively more subtle than the previous one. The tubes or nadis are as follows: *sushumna* – signifying tamas, *vajrini* – signifying rajas, *chitrini* – signifying sattwa, and *brahma* – signifying consciousness. The higher consciousness created by kundalini passes through brahma nadi.

When the kundalini shakti awakens it passes through sushumna nadi. The moment awakening takes place in mooladhara chakra, the energy makes headway through sushumna up to ajna chakra.

Mooladhara chakra is just like a powerful generator. In order to start this generator, you need some sort of pranic energy. This pranic energy is generated through pranayama. When you practise pranayama you generate energy and this energy is forced down by a positive pressure which starts the generator in mooladhara chakra. Then this generated energy is pushed upward by a negative pressure and forced up to ajna chakra.

Therefore, awakening of sushumna is just as important as awakening of kundalini. Supposing you have started your generator but you have not plugged in the cable, the generator will keep running but distribution will not take place. You have to connect the plug into the generator so the generated energy can pass through the cable to the different areas of your house.

When only ida and pingala are active and not sushumna, it is like having the positive and negative lines in your electrical cable, but no earth. When the mind receives the three currents of energy all the lights start working, but if you remove the earth wire the lights will go down. Energy flows through ida and pingala all the time, but its effulgence is very low. When there is current flowing in ida, pingala and sushumna, then enlightenment takes place. This is how you have to understand the awakening of kundalini, the awakening of sushumna and the union of the three in ajna chakra.

The whole science of kundalini yoga concerns the awakening of sushumna, for once sushumna comes to life, a means of communication between the higher and lower dimensions of consciousness is established and the awakening of kundalini occurs. Shakti then travels up sushumna nadi to become one with Shiva in sahasrara chakra.

Kundalini awakening is definitely not fictional or symbolic; it is electrophysiological! Many modern scientists are working on this, and Dr Hiroshi Motoyama of Japan has developed a unit by which the waves and currents of energy, which accompany the awakening of kundalini, can be recorded and measured.

When the roots of a plant are watered properly, the plant grows and its flowers bloom forth beautifully. Similarly, when kundalini awakening occurs in sushumna, awakening occurs in all the stages of life. But if awakening only occurs in ida or pingala or in one of the other centres, it is by no means complete. Only when kundalini shakti awakens and travels up the sushumna passage to sahasrara is the entire store of higher energy in man unleashed.

The mystical tree

In the fifteenth chapter of the *Bhagavad Gita* there is a description of the imperishable tree which has its roots at the top and its trunk and branches below, growing downwards. One who knows this tree knows the truth. This tree exists in the structure and function of the human body and nervous system. One must know and climb this paradoxical tree to arrive at the truth. It can be understood in this way: the thoughts, the emotions, the distractions and so on are only the leaves of this tree whose roots are the brain itself and whose trunk is the spinal column. One has to climb this tree from the top to the bottom if one wishes to cut the roots.

This tree seems to be completely topsy-turvy, yet it contains the essence of all occult truth and secret knowledge. It cannot be understood intellectually, but only through a progressive spiritual awakening, for true spiritual understanding always dawns in a way which is paradoxical and irrational to the faculty of intellect. This same tree is known as the 'Tree of Life' in the Kabbalah and as the 'Tree of Knowledge' in the Bible. Its understanding forms the basis of both the Christian and Judaic religious traditions, but unfortunately it has been completely misunderstood, by and large, for a very long time.

So it is that everybody who is trying to move from mooladhara to sahasrara is climbing to the root every time, and the root is at the brain, the sahasrara. Mooladhara is not the root centre at all. So if you are moving from swadhisthana to sahasrara or from manipura to sahasrara, then you are climbing to the root, which is at the top in sahasrara.

The Mystical Tree

4

Kundalini and the Brain

The awakening of kundalini and its union with Shiva is immediately and intimately connected with the whole brain. To explain it simply, we can say the brain has ten compartments, and of these, nine are dormant and one is active. Whatever you know, whatever you think or do is coming from one-tenth of the brain. The other nine-tenths, which are in the frontal portion of the brain, are known as the inactive or sleeping brain.

Why are these compartments inactive? Because there is no energy. The active portion of the brain functions on the energies of ida and pingala, but the other nine-tenths have only pingala. Pingala is life and ida is consciousness. If a person is living but is unable to think, we say he has prana shakti but not manas shakti. Similarly, the silent parts of the brain have prana, not consciousness.

Therefore, a very difficult question arises, which is how to awaken the sleeping compartments of the brain? We know how to awaken fear, anxiety and passion, the basic instincts, but most of us do not know how to awaken these dormant areas of the brain. In order to arouse the silent areas of the brain, we must charge the frontal brain with sufficient prana, with sufficient vital energy and consciousness, and we must awaken sushumna nadi. For both these purposes we must practise pranayama regularly and consistently over a long period of time.

31

Lighting up the brain

In kundalini yoga it was discovered that the different parts of the brain are connected with the chakras. Certain areas are connected with mooladhara chakra, others with swadhisthana, manipura, and so on. When you want to turn on an electric lamp, you do not have to touch the lamp itself, you operate it by means of the switch on the wall. Likewise, when you want to awaken the brain, you cannot deal with it directly, you have to flick the switches which are located in the chakras.

Modern science divides the dormant area of the brain into ten parts, whereas in kundalini yoga we divide it into six. The qualities or manifestations of the brain are also sixfold, for example, the psychic powers. These manifest in different individuals according to the degree of awakening in the corresponding areas of the brain. Not everybody is clairvoyant or telepathic; some people are talented musicians. Anybody can sing, but there is a centre in the brain where transcendental music expresses itself.

Total and partial awakening

A genius is one who has awakened one or more of the dormant areas of the brain. People who have flashes of genius are those who have had a momentary awakening in certain circuits of the brain. It is not total awakening. When the total brain wakes up, you become a junior god, an incarnation or embodiment of divinity. There are various types of geniuses: child prodigies, inspired poets, musicians, inventors, prophets, etc., in whom a partial awakening has occurred.

Sahasrara is the actual seat of kundalini

Although the classical descriptions place heavy emphasis on the awakening of kundalini in mooladhara chakra, there is a widespread misconception that kundalini must be awakened there and made to travel through and awaken all the chakras in turn. In fact, the seat of kundalini is actually sahasrara. Mooladhara is only a manipulating centre or switch, like the other chakras, but it happens to be easier for most people to operate this switch.

Each of the chakras is independent; they are not connected with each other. This means that if kundalini shakti awakens in mooladhara, it goes directly to sahasrara, to a particular centre in the brain. Similarly, from swadhisthana the shakti passes directly to sahasrara, from manipura it goes straight to sahasrara and so on. Kundalini can be awakened in an individual chakra or it can awaken throughout the whole network of chakras collectively. From each chakra, the awakening shock moves up to the top of sahasrara. However, the awakening is not sustained and those centres in the brain return to dormancy. This is what is meant by the return of kundalini to mooladhara.

If kundalini awakens in an individual chakra, the experiences which are characteristic of that chakra will be brought into consciousness. This may also occur when one does the practices for an individual chakra. For example, swadhisthana practices will raise joy; manipura practices will increase self-assertion; anahata stimulation will expand the love; vishuddhi practices will awaken discrimination and wisdom, and ajna practices will increase the flow of intuition, knowledge and perhaps extrasensory abilities and so on.

If the nervous system is highly aroused, we may have other faculties opening because of the general arousal of the brain. This probably results from stimulation of an area in the lower end of the brain called the *reticular formation*. The function of this area is to rouse the whole brain or to relax it, as in sleep.

The reticular formation and related areas have an inherent rhythm which is responsible for our sleeping/ waking cycles, but it is also largely activated by sensations from outside – by light, sound, touch, etc., and from inside via the autonomic nervous system. It is the latter which seems to account for the more general arousal caused by the kundalini practices and other powerful yoga practices such as kumbhaka or breath retention.

Kundalini – energy or nerve messages?

There are a number of schools of thought as to what kundalini really is. Many yogis say that kundalini is a flow of pranic energy along an esoteric pathway (sushumna) associated with the spinal axis. They consider that it is part of the flow of prana within the meshwork of the pranic body and that there is no anatomical counterpart. Other yogis relate their perceptions of kundalini to the flow of messages along the nerve fibres. These arise in the networks of the autonomic plexuses and ascend along tracts in the spinal cord to definite anatomical centres in the brain.

These schools of thought use different descriptions to convey the experience of kundalini, but they all agree that the experience of kundalini is a total psychophysiological event which centres around the spinal cord. Within the spinal cord there is a very important fluid, the cerebrospinal fluid. When, through practices such as pranayama, awakening occurs in mooladhara chakra, this fluid gets excited. We cannot really say what happens to it because even the scientists are not exactly sure, but by studying the experiences of kundalini awakening, one thing is apparent. When the cerebrospinal fluid moves through the vertebral column, it alters the phases of consciousness and this is a very important process as far as evolution is concerned.

It is the chitta or consciousness which undergoes evolution in man. Chitta does not have a location point in the body, it is psychological in nature, but it is controlled by the information supplied by the *indriyas* or senses. While chitta is being constantly supplied with information, its evolution is blocked, but if you prevent the passage of information from the indriyas, chitta will evolve very quickly. That is to say, if you isolate chitta from the information being relayed through the eyes, nose, ears, skin and tongue, chitta is then compelled to experience independence. When the cerebrospinal fluid is affected during pranayama, the senses become dull and their messages are relayed to chitta very slowly. Sometimes, when the cerebrospinal fluid is highly stimulated, all sensory

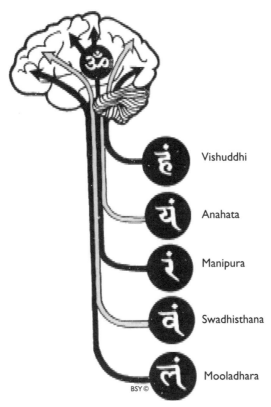

हं	Vishuddhi
यं	Anahata
रं	Manipura
वं	Swadhisthana
लं	Mooladhara

Arousal of Different Brain Centres

impulses are suspended and experiences take place within the chitta. Sometimes these experiences are fantastic, you might see light, feel the whole earth trembling or experience your body as if it were as light as a piece of cotton. These and others are the experiences of chitta as a consequence of the cerebrospinal fluid's reactions.

One world-renowned scientist, the late Itzhak Bentov, put forward the theory that kundalini is an effect caused by the rotation of nerve impulses around the cortex of the brain during meditation. He considered that this is caused by rhythmical pressure waves which result from the interaction of the heart beat, breathing, and the fluid inside the skull,

35

thereby causing the brain to oscillate up and down, which stimulates specific nerve currents in the brain.

Unlocking the storehouse of cosmic consciousness

Although there are varying views about kundalini, one thing is certain – kundalini has the ability to activate the human consciousness in such a way that a person can develop his or her most beneficial qualities, can enter a much more intimate relationship with nature and can become aware of oneness with the whole cosmos.

All the great miracles of the remote and recent past, and the ones yet to come, have sprung from what is known as the storehouse of cosmic consciousness, the golden egg, the golden worm, the hidden hiranyagarbha within the structure of the human brain. This particular centre in us is not sleeping or inactive, but it is unconscious, only because we are not conscious of it. What came as a revelation to the ancient rishis, to Newton and Einstein and to many other great seers, exists in us also, but it came to their conscious plane while it does not come to ours. This is the only difference between an inspired artist and an ordinary person.

The aim of kundalini yoga is not really to awaken the power of man, but rather to bring the power down to earth or to bring the power of the unconscious or higher consciousness to normal consciousness. We have no need to awaken the consciousness, for it is ever awake. We have only to gain complete control over our higher conscious forces. By means of kundalini yoga we just try to bring the centres from mooladhara to ajna into operation so that the higher knowledge will be gradually revealed to us.

Today man has mastered the material dimension, the energy of prakriti, and discovered the mysteries of nature. Now, through the process of kundalini, man should become master of the spiritual dimension.

5

Methods of Awakening

According to the tantras, kundalini can be awakened by various methods which can be practised individually or in combination. However, the first method cannot be practised because it is awakened by birth. Of course, it is too late for most of us to take advantage of this particular method, but some of us may be instrumental in producing children who have awakened kundalinis.

Awakening by birth

By a favourable birth, if your parents were highly evolved, you can have an awakened kundalini. It is also possible to be born with an awakened sushumna, ida or pingala nadi. This means that from the time of birth your higher faculties will be operating either partially or fully. If a child comes with partial awakening, he is called a saint, and if he comes with full illumination, he is known as an incarnation, avatara or son of God.

If one is born with an awakened kundalini, his experiences are very much under control. They take place in him right from the beginning in a natural way, so he never feels that something extraordinary is happening to him. A child with an awakened kundalini has clarity of vision, a high quality of thinking and a sublime philosophy. His attitude to life is somewhat unusual as he has total detachment. To him, his parents were only his means of creation, and therefore he is unable to accept the normal social relationship with them. Although he may live with them, he feels as if he were just a guest. Such a child exhibits very mature behaviour and does not react emotionally to anything in life. As he grows he becomes aware of his mission and purpose in life.

Many of us may wish to give birth to a yogi or an enlightened child but it is not such a simple matter. Every marriage or union of partners cannot produce a yogi, even if the man and woman practise yoga morning and night. It is only under certain circumstances that a higher being can be produced. In order to usher a highly evolved soul into this world, one has first to transform one's gross desires into spiritual aspirations.

It is very difficult to convince people of the West that a child can be born in an enlightened state, because they have the moral attitudes of a particular religion deeply ingrained in their minds and their faith. For them, the union between a man and a woman is sin. If you explain to them that a yogi can be produced as a result of sexual union, they say, "No! How can a yogi be born out of sin?"

It is possible that a new generation of supermen and women will be produced in this way. Through the practices of yoga you can transform the quality of your genes. If genes can produce artists, scientists, inventors and intellectual geniuses, then why not awakened kundalinis? You have to transform the quality of your sperm or ova by firstly transforming your whole consciousness. Neither drugs nor diet will transform your genes, but if you change your consciousness, you can then affect the elements of the body and ultimately change the quality of the sperm or ova. Then you will have children with awakened kundalinis. They will become the yogis and spiritual masters of the house who set things right for you. They will say, "Mummy, you are not the physical body." "Papa, drinking is no good."

Those of you who choose to enter married life should go into it keeping in mind that the purpose is not just pleasure, or to produce offspring, but to create a genius. All over the world, people who marry for progeny should try for higher quality children.

Mantra

The second method of awakening kundalini is through steady regular practice of mantra. This is a very powerful, smooth and risk-free method, but of course it is a sadhana which requires time and a lot of patience. First you need to obtain a suitable mantra from a guru who knows yoga and tantra, and who can guide you through your sadhana. When you practise the mantra incessantly, it develops in you the vision of a higher force and enables you to live amidst the sensualities of life with indifference to them.

When you throw a pebble into a still lake, it produces circular ripples. In the same way, when you repeat a mantra over and over again, the sound force gathers momentum and creates vibrations in the ocean of the mind. When you repeat the mantra millions and billions of times, it permeates every part of your brain and purifies your whole physical, mental and emotional body.

The mantra must be chanted loudly, softly, on the mental plane and on the psychic plane. By practising it at these four levels, kundalini awakens methodically and systematically. You can also use the mantra by repeating it mentally in coordination with the breath, or you can sing it aloud in the form of kirtan. This creates a great potential in mooladhara and awakening takes place.

Closely related to mantra yoga is awakening through sound or music – nada yoga. Here the sounds are the beeja mantras and the music consists of particular melodies corresponding to particular chakras. This is a most tender and absorbing way of awakening.

Tapasya

The third method of awakening is *tapasya*, which means the performance of austerities. Tapasya is a means of purification, a burning or setting on fire so that a process

39

of elimination is created, not in the physical body, but in the mental and emotional bodies. Through this process the mind, the emotions and the whole personality are cleansed of all the dirt, complexes and the patterns of behaviour that cause pain and suffering. Tapasya is an act of purification. It should not be misunderstood to involve standing naked in cold water or snow, or observing foolish and meaningless austerities.

When you want to eliminate a bad habit, the more you try, the more powerful it becomes. When you abandon it in the waking state, it appears in dreams, and when you stop those dreams, it expresses itself in your behaviour or manifests in disease. This particular habit must be destroyed at its psychic root, not only at the conscious level. The samskaras and vasanas must be eliminated by some form of tapasya.

Tapasya is a psychological or psycho-emotional process through which the aspirant tries to set in motion a process of metabolism that will eradicate the habits that create weakness and obstruct the awakening of willpower. "I must do this but I can't." Why does this difference between resolution and implementation arise in the mind of the aspirant? Why is it so great? It is due to a deficiency of will, and that weakness, that distance or barrier between resolution and execution can be removed through regular and repeated practice of tapasya. Then the willpower makes a decision once and the matter is finished. This strength of will is the fruit of tapasya.

The psychology of austerity plays a very important part in the awakening of man's latent power. It is not well understood by modern man who has unfortunately accepted that man lives for the pleasure principle, as propounded by Freud and his disciples. The psychology of austerity is very sound and certainly not abnormal. When the senses are satisfied by the objective pleasures, by the comforts and luxuries, the brain and nervous system become weak and the consciousness and energy undergo a process of regression. It is in this situation that the method of austerity is one of the most powerful and sometimes explosive methods of awakening.

40

Here the manifestations are tremendous and the aspirant has to face his lower instincts in the beginning. He confronts a lot of temptations and the assaults of the satanic and tamasic forces. All the evil or negative samskaras or karmas of many, many incarnations rise to the surface. Sometimes fear manifests very powerfully or attachment to the world comes with a great force. In some people, sexual fantasies haunt the mind for days together, while others become lean and thin, or even sick. At this juncture, siddhis can appear. One develops extrasensory perceptions, one can read the minds of others, and can suppress others by a thought, or one's own thoughts materialize. In the beginning, black forces manifest and all these siddhis are negative or of a lower quality. Tapasya is a very, very powerful method of awakening which not everybody can handle.

Awakening through herbs

The fourth method of awakening is through the use of specific herbs. In Sanskrit this is called *aushadhi*, and it should not be interpreted as meaning drugs like marijuana, LSD, and so on. Aushadhi is the most powerful and rapid method of awakening, but it is not for all and very few people know about it. There are herbs which can transform the nature of the body and its elements and bring about either partial or full awakening, but they should never be used without a guru or qualified guide. This is because certain herbs selectively awaken ida or pingala and others can suppress both these nadis and quickly lead one to the mental asylum. For this reason, aushadhi is a very risky and unreliable method for awakening.

In the ancient vedic texts of India, there are references to a substance called soma. Soma was a juice extracted from a creeper which was picked on special days of the dark lunar fortnight. It was placed in an earthen pitcher and buried underground until the full moon. Then it was removed and the juice was extracted and taken. This induced visions, experiences and an awakening of higher consciousness.

The Persians knew of another drink, homa, which may have been the same as soma. In Brazil and some of the African countries, people used hallucinogenic mushrooms and in the Himalayan regions marijuana or hashish were taken with the thought that they might provide a shortcut in arousing spiritual awakening. From time to time, in different parts of the world, other things were also discovered and used, some being very mild in effect and others being very concentrated.

With the help of the correct herbs, purified aspirants were able to visualize divine beings, holy rivers, mountains, sacred places, holy people and so on. When the effects of the herbs were more concentrated, they could separate the self from the body and travel astrally. Of course, it was often illusory, but sometimes it was a real experience as well. People were able to enter a state of samadhi and awaken their kundalini. In this particular field of awakening, the sexual instinct was completely eliminated. Therefore, many aspirants preferred this method and have been trying to discover the appropriate herbs for many centuries.

With aushadhi awakening, the body becomes still and quiet, the metabolism slows and the temperature drops. As a result of this, the nerve reflexes function differently and in most cases the aushadhi method of awakening is no longer practised because it was misused by ordinary people who were neither prepared, competent nor qualified. As a result, knowledge of the herbs was withdrawn and today it is a closely guarded secret.

Everyone is craving kundalini awakening, but few people have the discipline and mental, emotional, physical and nervous preparation required to avoid damage to the brain and tissues. So, although no one is teaching the aushadhi method of awakening today, its knowledge has been transmitted from generation to generation through the guru-disciple tradition. Perhaps some day, when the nature of man changes and we find better intellectual, physical and mental responses, the science may again be revealed.

Raja yoga

The fifth method of inducing awakening is through raja yoga and the development of an equipoised mind. This is the total merging of individual consciousness with superconsciousness. It occurs by a sequential process of concentration, meditation and communion; experience of union with the absolute or supreme.

All the practices of raja yoga, preceded by hatha yoga, bring about very mild and durable experiences, but they can lead to a state of complete depression, in which you do not feel like doing anything. The raja yoga method is very difficult for the majority of people as it requires time, patience, discipline and perseverance. Concentration of mind is one of the most difficult things for people of today to achieve. It cannot be undertaken before the mind has been stabilized, the karmas deactivated and the emotions purified through the practices of karma yoga and bhakti yoga. It is the nature of the mind to remain active all the time, and this constitutes a very real danger for people of our time, because when we try to concentrate the mind we create a split. Therefore, the majority of us should only practise concentration up to a certain point.

Following awakening through raja yoga, changes take place in the aspirant. One may transcend hunger and all addictions or habits. The sensualities of life are no longer appealing, hunger and the sexual urge diminish and detachment develops spontaneously. Raja yoga brings about a slow transformation of consciousness.

Pranayama

The sixth method of awakening kundalini is through pranayama. When a sufficiently prepared aspirant practises intense pranayama in a calm, cool and quiet environment, preferably at a high altitude, with a diet only sufficient to maintain life, the awakening of kundalini takes place like an explosion. In fact, the awakening is so rapid that kundalini ascends to sahasrara immediately.

Pranayama is not only a breathing exercise or a means to increase prana in the body; it is a powerful method of creating yogic fire to heat the kundalini and awaken it. However, if it is practised without sufficient preparation, this will not occur because the generated heat will not be directed to the proper centres. Therefore, jalandhara, uddiyana and moola bandhas are practised to lock the prana in and force it up to the frontal brain.

When pranayama is practised correctly, the mind is automatically conquered. However, the effects of pranayama are not that simple to manage. It creates extra heat in the body, it awakens some of the centres in the brain and it can hinder the production of sperm and testosterone. Pranayama may also lower the temperature of the inner body and even bring down the rate of respiration and alter the brain waves. Unless you have practised the shatkarmas first and purified the body to a degree, when these changes take place, you may not be able to handle them.

There are two important ways of awakening kundalini – the direct method and the indirect. Pranayama is the direct method. The experiences it brings about are explosive and results are attained very quickly. Expansion is rapid and the mind attains quick metamorphosis. However, this form of kundalini awakening is always accompanied by certain experiences, and for one who is not sufficiently prepared mentally, philosophically, physically and emotionally, these experiences can be terrifying. Therefore, although the path of pranayama is a jetset method, it is drastic and is considered to be a very difficult one that everybody cannot manage.

Kriya yoga

The seventh method of inducing awakening is kriya yoga. It is the most simple and practical way for the modern day individual as it does not require confrontation with the mind. Sattwic people may be able to awaken kundalini through raja yoga, but those who have a tumultuous, noisy, rajasic mind will not succeed this way. They will only develop more tensions, guilt and complexes, and may even become schizophrenic. For such people kriya yoga is by far the best and most effective system.

When you practise kriya yoga, kundalini does not wake up with force, nor does it awaken like a satellite or as a vision or experience. It wakes up like a noble queen. Before getting up she will open her eyes, then close them again for a while. Then she will open her eyes again, look here and there, turn to the right and left, then pull the sheet up over her head and doze. After some time she will again stretch her body and open her eyes, then doze for a while. Each time she stretches and looks around she says, "Hmmm." This is what happens in kriya yoga awakening.

Sometimes you feel very grand and sometimes you do not feel quite right. Sometimes you pay too much attention to the things of life and sometimes you think everything is useless. Sometimes you eat extravagantly and sometimes you do not eat for days together. Sometimes you have sleepless nights and at other times you do nothing but sleep and sleep. All these signs of awakening and reversion, awakening and reversion keep coming every now and then. Kriya yoga does not create an explosive awakening. However, it can bring visions and other very mild and controllable experiences.

Tantric initiation

This eighth method of awakening kundalini through tantric initiation is a very secret topic. Only those people who have transcended passions, and who understand the two principles of nature, Shiva and Shakti, are entitled to this initiation. It is not meant for those who have urges lurking within them or for those who have a need for physical contact. With the guidance of a guru, this is the quickest possible way to awaken kundalini.

There are no extraordinary experiences or feelings and there is no neurosis; everything seems quite normal, but at the same time, without your knowledge, awakening is taking place. Transformation takes place and your awareness expands, but you do not know it. In this particular system, awakening and arriving at sahasrara are the same event. It takes just three seconds. However, who is qualified for this path? Few people in this world have completely transcended the sexual urge and overcome their passions.

Shaktipat

The ninth method of awakening is performed by the guru. It is called shaktipat. The awakening is instant, but it is only a glimpse, not a permanent event. When the guru creates this awakening you experience samadhi. You can practise all forms of pranayama and all asanas, mudras and bandhas without having learned them or prepared for them. All the mantras are revealed to you and you know the scriptures from within. Changes take place in the physical body in an instant. The skin becomes very soft, the eyes glow and the body emits a particular aroma which is neither agreeable nor disagreeable.

This shaktipat can be conducted in the physical presence or from a distance. It can be transmitted by touch, by a handkerchief, a mala, a flower, a fruit or anything edible, depending on the system the guru has mastered. It can even be transmitted by letter, telegram or telephone.

It is very difficult to say who is qualified for this awakening. You may have lived the life of a renunciate for fifty years, but still you may not get it. You may be just an ordinary person, living a non-spiritual life, eating all kinds of junk foods, but the guru may give you shaktipat. Your eligibility for shaktipat does not depend on your social or immediate conduct, but on the point of evolution you have reached. There is a point in evolution beyond which shaktipat becomes effective, but this evolution is not intellectual, emotional, social or religious. It is a spiritual evolution which has nothing to do with the way we live, eat, behave or think, because generally we do these things not because of our evolvement, but according to the way we have been brought up and educated.

Self-surrender

We have discussed the nine established methods of awakening kundalini, but there is a tenth way – do not aspire for awakening. Let it happen if it happens: "I am not responsible for the awakening, nature is accomplishing everything. I accept what comes to me." This is known as the path of self-surrender, and in this path, if you have a strong enough belief that your kundalini will indeed awaken, twenty thousand years can pass in the twinkling of an eye and kundalini will awaken instantly.

Effects of the different methods of awakening

When the awakening of kundalini takes place, scientific observations have revealed different effects. Those who have awakened kundalini from birth do not register any emotional changes. They are like blocks of wood. Those who have awakened kundalini through pranayama have a great quantum of electrical charges in the spinal column and throughout the body, and momentarily they could manifest schizophrenically in an individual.

Karma yoga and bhakti yoga are considered comparatively safe and mild methods of awakening, but the tantric methods are more scientific than the non-tantric methods, because in tantra there is no scope for suppression or dispersion of energy. In non-tantric methods there is antagonism; one part of the mind wants it and another part of the same mind is saying no. You suppress your thoughts, you want to enjoy, but at the same time you think, "No, it is bad."

I am not criticizing non-tantric methods. They are the mild methods which do not bring you any trouble. They are just like beer, you drink a little bit and nothing happens. If you drink four to ten glasses not much will happen. But tantric methods are like LSD, you have a little and it takes you right out. If something is wrong, it is wrong; if something is right, it is right.

6

Preparing for the Awakening

Without a guru you can practise any form of yoga, but not kundalini. This is an extremely powerful system. Kundalini yoga does not start suddenly or with fits. You do not have to make any substantial changes in your way of life, but you must begin to practise.

Do not start with advanced practices; you should train and prepare the physical body for some time, then go to the mind and gradually explore the deeper levels. Before commencing the practices which bring about the actual awakening of kundalini, you must prepare yourself step by step on the physical, mental and emotional planes. If you are patient and prepare correctly, awakening of kundalini will definitely take place.

Adequate preparation is necessary to ensure that one has the strength to bear the impact of full awakening of the mighty potential force within. Most of us do not even have control over our physical manifestations and behaviours. If you were given a sleep inducing injection, you would become drowsy whether you wanted to or not. This is because you have no control over the processes and actions of your brain and you do not know how to control sleep. Similarly, if you have a headache, you are unable to exert control over it. When physical manifestations such as sleep and pain are not under your control, what would happen if other manifestations began to occur in your brain? You would not be able to control them. Therefore, before kundalini awakens, it is important that you are able to manage the mind.

If you can maintain a balanced mind in the face of mental and emotional conflicts, and you can endure anger, worry, love and passion, disappointment, jealousy, hatred, memories of the past, sufferings and sorrows, you are ready for the awakening. If you can still feel joy when the scales are heavily loaded against you, you are an aspirant for kundalini yoga. Before you bring into use a generator of five megawatts, you must have a factory ready to utilize the energy. In the same way, before you awaken kundalini shakti, you must be able to merge yourself with the higher spirit and you must know how to utilize the creative energy of kundalini.

So if you want to follow the path of kundalini yoga, it is absolutely essential to have a guru with whom you feel intimate. Many people say the guru is within, but are they able to communicate, understand and follow the intricate instructions? If so, it is possible to proceed with this internal guidance, but few people have such a relationship with the inner guru. They need an external guru first who will connect them with the inner guru. If you have a guru, he will help you to prepare for kundalini awakening. He will be there if you need any advice and he will guide you through the crisis of awakening.

Usually, because we are religious minded people, our relationship with the guru is based on a sort of formality. To us he is worshipful, respectable, superior and supreme, but at the time of awakening, all these attitudes to the guru must be set aside. At this time you must evolve a more intimate attitude, as if your relationship was based on love, not merely devotion and worship. When you serve your mother you do so with an attitude of love, not respect and veneration. With this same attitude you should serve the guru, then his direct influence is upon you. Then, if there is excitement in any chakra, the relationship with the guru will balance it.

The relationship between guru and disciple is the most intimate of relationships; it is neither a religious nor a legal relationship. Guru and disciple live like an object and its shadow. The guru is the best thing in spiritual life, and if you have a guru you are very fortunate. However, it is sometimes difficult to find a guru. If you do not have a guru, you can cultivate a mental picture of him, try to feel his guidance and continue practising faithfully. You will surely succeed.

The time factor

Preparation is not the job of one lifetime. Man strives spiritually lifetime after lifetime. In fact, this body is given to you only for that purpose. For eating, sleeping and sexual interaction a human body is not necessary, so in our lower stages of evolution we had an animal body. However, even with this human body, we still have animal in us, so these natural urges follow us. Let them, but remember this body is not for their fulfilment alone. In this human body the consciousness is the most important point. Man is aware of his awareness and he does not only think, he knows that he thinks. The evolution of awareness has been going on life after life. And what you have been practising for your spiritual life in the last five to ten years is in addition to what you have already done.

Supposing your children are studying in primary school and you are transferred to another city. Where will your children begin their education in the new city? Right from the beginning? No, from the point where they left their studies. The same thing happens in reincarnation. That is why, even though you may have brothers and sisters born of the same mother and father, they will be different from you. In your previous incarnation your preferences were different from theirs. Maybe after a few incarnations they may come to the point where you are now. So we cannot say how long preparation takes, because this life is one of those milestones and you have left behind many, many milestones.

However, if you are eager to awaken kundalini and the chakras, you should not be in a hurry. Set apart twelve years of your life for this purpose. This is not to say that the awakening cannot be brought about within one, two or three years – it can be. Total awakening can even take place in a month, or the guru can give you awakening in one day, but you will be unable to hold and sustain the awakening. When one is in possession of a weak mind which cannot sustain even a little bit of cheerfulness or excitement, or bear the death of a spouse or separation from a loved one, how can one sustain the tremendous force of an awakened kundalini? Therefore, the twelve years are not for the actual awakening. The twelve years are only for preparation so you can hold and sustain the awakening.

Where to begin

The practices of kundalini yoga are intended to create the awareness, not necessarily to awaken kundalini. First of all, we have to decide whether kundalini is already awakened. It may already be on the way and you are opening the garage and there is no car because it is already on the highway. When you go to satsang, do some kirtan or lead a yogic lifestyle, you begin to have experiences and you realize something is happening to you. Then, when you discuss kundalini and the chakras with a guru you start to understand.

The practices that you do develop your awareness and help you to remember your connection with your past evolution. They remove the veil which separates this current incarnation from the previous one. I will give you a very gross example.

There was a boy who was the only son of a very rich man. The boy went crazy and was sent to a mental hospital. He ran away and used to go from house to house begging for food. He did not know that his parents had died and he had inherited a large estate, cars and shops and a lot of money in fixed deposits. One day his uncle found him and had him treated properly. The boy recovered from his mental illness and remembered everything about his heritage. Similarly, there is a process of remembering, and when it takes place, you know exactly where you stand.

So, practices are necessary to remove the veil in front of the consciousness which separates the two lives. Once you know that your kundalini is already in the process of transition, then practices are of no real use. If you are practising, it is because you are forced to, and if you are not practising, it is because you are forced not to. During the period of transition of kundalini the practices are not useless, but your efforts to practise them are of no use. However, if there is no awakening, if kundalini is in mooladhara or swadhisthana or in between the two, then that is the time for the practices which are enjoined in the books.

It is very important that you awaken sushumna nadi before kundalini. This essential point has not been stressed clearly in any books, but Swami Sivananda hinted at it in his writings. If sushumna is not opened, where will the shakti go? It will pass through either ida or pingala and complications will arise.

You must also undergo purification of the tattwas or elements, and purification of the chakras and nadis. Otherwise, when kundalini awakens there will be a traffic jam. Asanas, pranayama and the hatha yoga shatkarmas provide the best means of purification. Surya namaskara and surya bheda pranayama purify pingala nadi and the shatkarmas and pranayama will purify and awaken sushumna. There are specific asanas that are very important for purifying the nadis and inducing a mild awakening in the chakras. So, start with purification of the tattwas by the hatha yoga cleansing techniques. Take up asanas next and then pranayama. Later you can practise mudras and bandhas and then begin kriya yoga.

Awakening before preparation

If experiences commence before you are properly prepared, you should immediately start to prepare yourself. The first thing to do is start fasting or switch to a light diet. You should also live quietly and avoid social interactions, reading books and magazines. Of course, during this period you must not take any drugs or medicines and you must guard against introducing any chemicals into the body.

If you minimize your interactions with the world outside, the experiences will subside after five or six days and you can resume your normal life. You should then start searching for someone who can give you further guidance.

Proceed to an ashram

When you know that kundalini is arousing, as soon as you can, you should retire to a congenial place. As far as I know, the only congenial place is an ashram, where you can be with a guru and like-minded people. An ashram is a community where the inmates have plenty of work, no attachments, no hatred or prejudices, a simple life, little to eat, no comforts or luxuries, only the bare essentials. There are no social expectations and pressures in an ashram, no fashion, no show, no useless conversations, no interference and gossip.

If you live in an ashram, the awakening of kundalini can be streamlined and if a mental crisis occurs, you are free to experience whatever happens. If you do not want to eat, it is okay; if you cannot sleep and you just want to sit, it is all right; if you have emotional problems or no emotions at all, people will understand and leave you alone.

If you stay with your family during the crisis period, they may send you off to a mental hospital. If you do not feel like eating, they will say, "Not eating today?" When they see you have not eaten for a few days, they will say, "Something is wrong with her," and they will try to get you to see a doctor or psychiatrist. Or if you are married, when your behaviour seems a little strange, your partner might be ready to divorce you. So it is much better to get away from such places. That is why there are so many monasteries and ashrams all over the world today.

What to practise in the ashram

In the ashram you should practise purification of the physical body through the shatkarmas to balance the acid, wind and mucus in the body. Physical and mental purification will also take place on account of the pure and simple ashram diet. The physical body must be kept very, very light and made sattwic and entirely free of toxins.

If you are a bhakta by temperament, spend your time in prayer, singing kirtan or bhajan. If you are an intellectual, then read books, talk minimally, practise hatha yoga and fast from time to time. If you are a very active person, work hard and dedicate yourself to karma yoga.

It is also necessary to perfect the sitting posture, as you must be able to sit comfortably in one of the three postures: siddhasana/siddha yoni asana, padmasana or vajrasana. The best and most powerful of these postures is siddhasana/siddha yoni asana.

Some people think they should practise a lot of meditation or pranayama when kundalini is ascending so it will go straight to sushumna. However, I do not think meditation is necessary anymore, because when kundalini is in the process of transition, you can do nothing with your mind. If your mind is agitated, you can do nothing about it because that is the effect of the awakening of kundalini. It is not the effect of your practice.

The movement of consciousness during the transition of kundalini is spontaneous, whether it is depression, a state of trance, an experience or vision, a feeling or sensation in the body; you cannot alter any of them. They will continue because they are forced on you, they are evolving in you because you are passing through that stage. But if you live in the non-agitating ashram environment and partake of ashram food and share in the karma yoga, there will be no disturbances in your experiences.

Regarding pranayama or kriyas, when the experience is moving onwards, pranayama happens by itself, you do not have to think about what to do. Sometimes kevala kumbhaka takes place, or you automatically begin to practise bhastrika or ujjayi. Moola bandha or vajroli mudra happen by themselves, or you begin to do asanas spontaneously. So you do not have to worry, just follow the flow of experience and take care of your environment and food, and make sure nobody disturbs you.

The role of karma yoga

Karma yoga is a very important part of spiritual life. Even if you practise austerities or mantra, use herbs, practise pranayama, undergo tantric initiation or get shaktipat, or are born with an awakened kundalini, if you do not follow the path of karma yoga, your evolution will definitely be retarded at some point.

If you have a good, strong, reliable automobile but the road is bumpy and covered in rocks, pebbles and marsh, try to accelerate and then see what happens. It is very important that the mind is prepared and the personality is rendered ready. Samskaras, positive and negative, must be exhausted, awareness must be extended to every level, dedication or consecration must be perfected and your attachments, illusions and infatuations must be spotted, scrutinized and analyzed. All that is not possible without doing karma yoga.

Karma yoga is not directly responsible for the awakening of kundalini, but without its practice, kundalini cannot budge even one centimetre. Therefore, you can understand how important karma yoga is in the life of a disciple. You must read a lot about karma yoga in the Bhagavad Gita, for perhaps that is the only philosophical and yogic explanation of karma yoga.

The need for discipline

Some people who have awakened kundalini look quite abnormal, and they behave in a peculiar way. They are very disorganized, unsystematic and totally confused, and you cannot understand what they are doing. Therefore, in yoga you are advised to discipline yourself right from the beginning, so that when kundalini wakes up you remain disciplined. Otherwise you might go out to the street and just lie down there in a heap.

Sometimes I used to feel like this. When I was living in Rishikesh with my guru, I decided to visit the Ganga each morning and cross it five times, swimming through the icy cold water. One day Swami Sivananda called me and said, "Are you going to continue with your swimming or am I going to put you out of this ashram?" This brought me back to my senses.

Life has to be disciplined so that when kundalini awakens you can remain unconfused. You have to discharge your responsibilities. You have to go to the office, bank, shops, and drive a car as well. Not everybody can become a swami or stay in an ashram.

Specific recommendations

If the awakening of kundalini takes place through birth, pranayama, tantric initiation or shaktipat, you do not have to know anything. In these situations everything is beyond control; whether things go right or wrong; you are helpless. But when awakening takes place through the other methods, there are certain steps to take.

Except in tantric initiation, sexual obligations have to be kept at bay. Food should be minimal, light and pure. One must have a guru and seek his guidance. Isolation from people is also very important.

Often when kundalini awakens the person develops some sort of power. Some aspirants can materialize things, see clairvoyantly, hear clairaudiently or read the minds of others. When you are amongst many people, it becomes a great temptation to exercise these powers. This can be dangerous. Whereas some people will not care if you can read their mind, others will feel it is a great impingement on their privacy and may even want to shoot you. People get scared at the exhibition of siddhis, so if you are facing any psychic manifestations, you will have to control them by force.

The great Tibetan yogi, Milarepa, learned certain forms of magic, and when he developed powers, he took revenge on his uncle and relatives. He created hailstorms that destroyed crops, huts and even lives, because he was then an ordinary man with love and hatred, friends and enemies. As long as you have likes and dislikes, you must not know what psychic powers you have. Milarepa had to perform penance for his misdeeds and suffer a lot at the hands of his guru.

Awakening by mantra and the need for seclusion

When awakening takes place by mantra, you will have to adjust your diet and retire from sexual obligations, not permanently, but for a while. From time to time it is also beneficial if you enter total seclusion. Twice a year is sufficient. In the beginning, start with one complete day, then increase to three days, and when you are used to it, extend to a maximum period of nine days. It is preferable if you practise seclusion when it is neither too hot nor too cold.

During your first day of seclusion, observe silence and eat very light food and very little. Do not meditate or try to concentrate. From morning until evening, with a few breaks here and there, only practise your mantra on a mala. Do not do it with exertion or strain, and if you become introverted, stop it. Maintain your mental concept with the external experiences; do not aspire for an introverted meditative state. If introversion forces itself, keep your eyes open. Practise this for twelve hours, but not in one stretch. For the last hour you must sit in meditation.

Next time you go into seclusion, do so for three to nine days. During this period devote as much time as possible to the repetition, resolution and reflection of the mantra. On the last day, at the end of the process, sit quietly for one hour of meditation.

Seclusion is actually recommended for all who are undergoing awakening of kundalini. At that time it is best to retire from active life and family environments for at least forty-five days. Unless you are in semi-seclusion from the world at the time of awakening, as well as having strange experiences and hallucinations, you may have peculiar doubts, fears, anger and strong passions.

57

Sadhus always live in seclusion because when there are interactions with people, so many thought currents move in the mind. Mixing with people, talking and gossiping create crosscurrents of love, hatred, infatuation, likes and dislikes, restlessness, worry and anxiety, desires and passions. Therefore, if you are practising a lot of sadhana, or you are facing the awakening of kundalini, do not have very much interaction with people. You will then be spared a lot of mental turmoil.

7

Diet for Kundalini Awakening

When the awakening of kundalini takes place, it is important to have the correct diet, as food influences the mind and your nature. At the time of awakening, certain physiological changes occur in the body, particularly in the digestive system, and the digestive process is frequently disturbed, or hunger vanishes completely. Therefore, a kundalini aspirant has to be very careful about his diet.

Scientific observations have shown that the awakening of kundalini is generally accompanied by a state of nervous depression. The inner body temperature undergoes erratic changes and drops so much that it becomes much lower than the outer body temperature. Metabolism slows down and sometimes it even stops completely. Consumption of oxygen also falls. Therefore, when you are experiencing kundalini awakening your diet must be very light and easy to assimilate.

The best diet for a kundalini yogi is boiled food. Crushed wheat, barley, lentils and dal are excellent foods, particularly when they are in a liquid form. Fats and greasy foods should be avoided and protein should be kept to a minimum. This will take any strain off the liver, because when the mind undergoes a crisis, the liver is overtaxed.

It is advisable to increase the carbohydrates in your diet, for example, rice, wheat, maize, barley, potato, etc., because carbohydrates help to maintain the inner body temperature and they do not require much heat to digest. Eggs, chicken and other heavy foods do not produce much heat themselves, but they require heat for digestion.

The yogic diet is macrobiotic, simple, plain and relatively bland. From time to time, fruit and roots can also be taken, but they are not essential.

Dietary misconceptions

A great misunderstanding has taken place in the last twenty to thirty years, which is that a yogi should only take milk, fruit and raw vegetables. On the basis of personal observation, trial and error, I cannot accept that this is correct. There are certain foods which are not meant for the human body at all.

If you analyze your digestive and salivary secretions and the durability of the mucous membranes in the alimentary canal, you will find that they are not really meant for digesting meat and uncooked foods. Whereas carnivorous animals have short intestines so that their food can be expelled quickly, before fermentation takes place, we have very long intestines (thirty-six feet in length) and our food should take eighteen hours to pass through the body. As well cooked vegetarian food is less likely to ferment, and we can keep it in our intestines for a full eighteen hours, it is the best for the human digestive tract.

Of course, this is not to say that people who have a non-vegetarian diet cannot awaken their kundalini, as history indicates otherwise. There have been many Christian, Tibetan and Sufi saints who awakened their kundalini although they had a meat diet, and we cannot say what Christ, Moses, Mohammed and Buddha ate. However, from scientific observations made in the event of kundalini awakening, we know what is likely to occur in our body. At certain periods we may not be able to digest raw foods and there may be days when the body cannot even accept water. Therefore, during the period of kundalini awakening, please have a diet which can be easily assimilated and eat the bare minimum for existence. Do not live to eat, but eat to live.

The essence of food

The food we eat is not merely to satisfy our taste. Every food item has an essence in it, and in yoga we call this sattwa. Sattwa means the ultimate essence of food, but please do not mistake this for vitamins or minerals. Sattwa is the more subtle form of food. When you eat for the sake of taste or enjoyment, instead of extracting the sattwa you only get the gross things. This is why the yogis and saints of all traditions have always lived on the minimum possible amount of food during periods of sadhana.

When we overeat we create a burden for the digestive system, and when the digestive system is overburdened we are unable to extract the sattwa from the food. Sattwa is a substance which nourishes the thoughts and nervous system. When the thoughts are fed with sattwa they are more refined and pure, and one is able to live in higher consciousness. Therefore, it is beneficial for a sadhaka to fast from time to time. When the body is kept light and pure, it is far more capable of extracting the sattwa from food.

The use of condiments

In the diet for kundalini aspirants, condiments have a very important role to play. Condiments such as coriander, cumin seeds, turmeric, aniseed, black pepper, green pepper, cayenne, cloves, mustard seed, cardamom, cinnamon and so on are also called digestives, as they aid digestion. These substances are not spices for taste; they are condiments which have the same properties as the enzymes in the body, and by helping to break down the food for digestion, they conserve vital energy and help to maintain the body's internal temperature.

When we talk about diet, let us not do so in puritanical terms. We must remember only one point in this case, to be sure the body is capable of digesting all the food. Having made a thorough study of natural foods and having tried them on myself, I have come to the conclusion that a combination of natural and macrobiotic foods is best. I have

61

also discovered that instead of cooking the food in your stomach, it is best to cook it properly in the pan. Five or six condiments should be added during cooking to liberate the enzymes and chemicals which enhance digestion. The combination of heat, condiments and enzymes breaks down the food into smaller and more basic components, making it easier to digest.

Yoga and diet are independent sciences

Although diet is an independent science, it is definitely related to every system of yoga. Of course, the ideal diet varies from yoga to yoga. A hatha yogi who has been practising shankhaprakshalana will not be able to eat lots of red peppers and black peppers or he will die. The diet regime for a karma yoga, a bhakta yogi, raja yogi, hatha yogi and kriya yogi will not be the same.

A bhakta yogi can eat all types of sweets and confectionery, consume cheese, butter, milk, etc. and he can eat and eat because his metabolism is very fast. Similarly, a karma yogi can take cheese, coffee, raw food or cooked food, and even a little bit of champagne, because he is working hard physically and his metabolism is also very fast. But in raja yoga and kundalini awakening, the metabolism becomes slow and you have to be very careful about your diet and how much you consume.

Over the years I have done a lot of work on food because I run ashrams where I have to manage all the affairs in relation to money, labour and the spiritual welfare of the ashram inmates. As it is not possible to provide different types of diets for the various aspirants of yoga, I have evolved two wonderful foods which suit everybody. One is for those who like rice and the other is for those who prefer wheat. You either cook the rice with dal (pulses such as lentils), vegetables and a few condiments, or you pound the wheat, add all the same ingredients to that and cook it well. I call this 'integrated khichari'. You can add anything to it and it is all right. This is the cheapest and most nutritious of all the foods I have eaten in any part of the world. You can also eat as much khichari as you want without any fear, because it digests so smoothly. This diet is suitable for all yoga practitioners and it is ideal for those who are ranging high in spiritual life and are about to merge into the ultimate state.

For one who is serious about yoga practices and spiritual aspirations in life, diet is as important as yoga, but if you are only worried about your diet and are not practising yoga, then you may be called a fanatic.

8

Risks and Precautions

The awakening of kundalini is a very important, pleasant and historical experience in a person's life. If you can see and experience something more than what you can generally see and experience through your senses, you are indeed fortunate. However, at the same time, if you have such experiences without adequate preparation, you may be startled, frightened and confused. Therefore, before the actual awakening of kundalini occurs, it is better to experience some mild awakenings in the chakras first.

Nowadays, if you travel by motor car at a very high speed, you do not really feel anything unusual, but if a person did it a hundred years ago when there was no adaptation to speed, he would have felt very giddy. Similarly, if a sudden awakening takes place and you are not used to the experience, you may become disoriented. You will not be able to cope with the radical changes in perception or with the contents of the unconscious mind welling up into the consciousness. But if you have been practising hatha yoga and meditation, and have experienced slight awakenings previously, you will be better able to cope with it.

When the body in totality is purified by the practices of shatkarma and hatha yoga, when the mind is purified by mantra, when the pranas are brought under control through the practices of pranayama and the diet is pure and yogic, at that time, awakening of kundalini takes place without any danger or accident. But with those who are in a hurry to awaken kundalini and who take to any practice in a haphazard manner without going through the preliminaries, and who do not take care of their diet, there will be some problems because they do not know how to control and utilize the fantastic energy they are unleashing.

The question of risk

There are so many whispers about the dangers of awakening and dark hints about people going crazy or developing disturbing powers, but everything in life is risky and there are far more dangers in ordinary daily life than you will encounter on the path of kundalini. Every time you walk across the street or travel by car or plane, you take a risk. In the pursuit of desires, passions and ambitions, people take great risks every day without thinking twice about it. Yet they allow the relatively minor risk of kundalini to deter them from pursuing the supreme goal of higher consciousness.

When a woman discovers she is pregnant, does she think it might be dangerous for her to have a child? She might die! She may have to have a caesarean! She may lose her figure for life! She may become seriously ill! Does a woman think like this and decide she does not want a child at all? No. Then why think like this about kundalini?

Awakening of kundalini is the birth of Christ, Krishna, Buddha or Mohammed. It is one of the greatest events of human life, just as for a mother to have a baby is one of the major and happiest events of her life, no matter what the consequences. In the same way, awakening of kundalini is one of the greatest events in the life of a yogi. It is the destiny of mankind, so why not go ahead with it?

Without involving yourself in a risk, nothing great in life can be achieved. Every great yogi, scientist, explorer and adventurer has faced risks and in this way has invented, discovered or made progress. People who think and talk about risks are cowards, and should not even practise yoga. It is better they eat, drink, be merry and die unenlightened.

Kundalini practices are certainly no more dangerous than many activities people engage in for the sake of thrills, sport or altered states of consciousness. The risks are not nearly as great as those associated with LSD, hashish, marijuana and alcohol, which are used by many people every day. Those who practise kundalini yoga are assured of attaining states of expanded consciousness which are safer, smoother, more comprehensible and longer lasting than anything that can be obtained through the use of psychedelics.

The science of kundalini yoga has its own inbuilt safety mechanisms. If you perform asanas or pranayama incorrectly, nature will immediately send a warning and compel you to stop practising. In the same way, when kundalini awakening takes place and you are not prepared to face it, nature puts obstacles in your way. If ever you become scared and want to stop the process of kundalini awakening, all you have to do is revert to a gross lifestyle. Just revise all your passions, dreams and worldly ambitions.

Unless you are an extremely introverted person, you can proceed along the path of kundalini yoga without fear. If you are hypersensitive, have difficulty communicating with others and live within a sort of fantasy world, you will find kundalini yoga upsetting and dangerous. Such people should not practise kundalini yoga or any techniques for exploring the inner world until they have developed the ability to strike fearlessly and confidently through the outer world. This also applies to timid and dependent people. For all these individuals, karma yoga is the way. They should lead a life of unselfish service in the world and develop non-attachment and maximum awareness.

Fear of mistakes

Some people worry about kundalini ascending through the wrong nadi, but there is no danger here because if kundalini enters through any other nadi, the whole circuit will fuse. If kundalini has awakened but a chakra is blocked, say swadhisthana, then the kundalini will only roam about in mooladhara and all the instincts of that chakra will develop. You will become a high class animal for a while and may develop some siddhis. If there is any obstruction in the chakras beyond that, the energy will be blocked for a long time, affecting the psychological constitution. If kundalini enters into the pranic nadi, pingala, it could set the whole brain into turmoil. However, this does not usually happen. Nature intervenes, and unless sushumna is clear, the chakra will not open and the energy will not be able to move further.

Mistakes do occur, but not in average individuals because they are scared of something wrong happening somewhere. If they are practising and suddenly feel they are going crazy, they will discontinue their practices immediately. So, every individual possesses a sort of fear. Before anything wrong can happen totally, man takes care of himself. However, there are some blockheads and very stuffy people who plod on no matter what happens. They do not care about the consequences and these are the people who generally get themselves into trouble.

Kundalini awakening and illness

If you take care of all the requirements, then no illness will come to you. However, many people are very hasty and impatient. When they want to make money, they want to make it overnight, quickly, and the same psychology is transferred into spiritual life: quick money and quick realization. With this impatience, sometimes we will overstep the necessary prerequisites.

Some people develop weakness of the lower limbs because they have not trained their body through hatha yoga. Some develop digestive disorders because they have not understood the relationship between food and the temperature of the body. Therefore, the prerequisites have to be observed. Those who suffer do so not because of the kundalini awakening, but because they have not harmonized the nervous system.

Through hatha yoga you must create a balance between the two forces in the physical body, the pranic and the

67

mental. Even in modern times we say that a balance between the sympathetic and parasympathetic nervous systems is absolutely essential to develop the higher faculties of the brain. When there is an imbalance between these two forces, that is, if one is predominant and the other subservient, then you are supplying one energy in excess and the other energy is deficient. This inevitably leads to sickness.

Airing the unconscious

In the course of your practices there may be isolated awakenings in ajna chakra, in which the awareness enters the realms of the unconscious mind and you see figures, symbols and even monsters or benevolent beings. You may hear or experience many inexplicable things, but they are all simply products of your own unconscious mind and should be regarded as nothing more. With the awakening of psychic consciousness, the symbols belonging to your own personality come out. When this happens you may have a problem under-standing it, but just remember that these kinds of expressions are simply parts of your being which have been lying in reserve and they have to 'come out for airing'.

You should not fear kundalini awakening, but you must be prepared for the events that may occur. Otherwise, if you have a weak mind and are confronted by fear, it could lead to mental derangement. So, before you attempt kundalini awakening you should undergo a process of thought purifica-tion and develop understanding of your way of thinking.

When the prerequisites for kundalini awakening are followed properly, psychological and psycho-emotional symp-toms do not occur. In fact, all these things happen before the actual event of kundalini awakening. But of course, when the awakening takes place, an aspirant who is not maintaining the proper discipline that is required is bound to get into some psychological cobwebs.

The awakening of kundalini should never be equated with obsessions or neurosis. When an explosion takes place it brings out whatever was in you. If you have a personality full of obsessions and mental blocks, then it is going to explode. Therefore, before one attempts awakening of kundalini, one must have arrived at a point of purity of consciousness or clarity of mind, chitta shuddhi.

Purity of consciousness is not religious terminology. You may have pure thoughts in your mind, but you may not be pure at all. You may be thinking about purity, chastity, compassion, charity and generosity, but in the subterranean plane of your personality there may be conflicts or other unresolved mental problems. When the mind enters into meditation or samadhi, this subterranean level comes up to the surface. You begin to see all the debris and you feel it and enact it. This can happen at anytime, when you are dreaming, when you are in a state of craziness and when kundalini is waking.

That is why a relentless effort should be made to render the mind free from all the disturbing archetypes or samskaras before you try to handle this project. An integration of karma, bhakti and raja yoga, tempered with hatha and jnana yoga, must be adopted first.

Purity and impurity

Although I recommend chitta shuddhi, I know that many people have an obsession about purity and impurity. They keep thinking they are impure and therefore they should not try to awaken kundalini. But when the sun rises, what happens to the darkness? Purity and impurity are ethical and moral concepts created by society and religion. Awakening of kundalini is the awakening of the great light within mankind. It rises like the sun, and when it can be seen on the horizon there will be no darkness, no pain, suffering, disappointment or impurity.

Siddhis and the ego factor

When one has been practising kundalini yoga for a couple of years and suddenly starts having beautiful experiences, one tends to think oneself superior to everybody else and may

69

even consider oneself as godly. To protect yourself from this, you must place yourself in the calibre of chela or disciple. A disciple remains a disciple, there is no promotion. Many people think that after twelve years of discipleship they will be promoted to guruhood, but this is not so.

In the path of kundalini yoga it is very important that you live the life of a disciple even after the awakening of kundalini, and not only after that, but even when Shiva and Shakti have united.

The path of kundalini yoga is the means for attaining supreme awareness and enlightenment, but if you get lost in the beauty of kundalini, you may not reach enlightenment. When, at a certain stage of awakening, the mind becomes very efficient and siddhis such as telepathy, clairvoyance, hypnotism, spiritual healing and so on manifest, some aspirants take that to be a divine accomplishment and begin to think, "Now I am God." Then, in the name of doing good to everybody, they start performing all sorts of funny magic. This feeds the ego, and in the course of time, their ignorance becomes very great.

There is extreme danger here and many aspirants get caught. Their ego becomes tremendously gross and they develop a strong feeling of grandeur. And that is as far as they get. Although there is nothing really wrong with psychic powers, those whose seek them must know that they can completely destroy their spiritual consciousness if they are not disciplined. You can become lost in these powers, just as some people get lost in money, beauty, intellect and so on. These parapsychological attainments are momentary; they live with you for only a short period of time and then you lose them. They are only additional properties to be experienced and left behind in the wake of the dawning of supreme awareness.

It is important to remember what Maharishi Patanjali has said in the *Yoga Sutras*: "All these psychic manifestations are obstacles which block the free flow of consciousness towards samadhi."

Two opposing forces

In the realms of higher consciousness, there are both divine and demonical forces. Both these forces can be brought down to earth by the same techniques. Without higher awareness, when the awakening of the chakras begins, the knowledge and destructive energy of the atom bomb might be unleashed, rather than the wisdom and spiritual power of the rishis. When kundalini awakens in a person with no dispassion and discrimination, who does not seek liberation and does not know the reality of this world, the consequences can be disastrous. Ultimately, that person will destroy himself, and possibly many others in the process.

Therefore, a kundalini aspirant must constantly work towards the development of higher awareness. To be conscious of the unconscious is very difficult. When your awareness is heavy and burdened with tension and confusion, it cannot survive for long in the unconscious state. But when your consciousness is light and clear, it can penetrate into the unconscious like a sharp and speedy arrow, successfully navigating past all the danger zones and emerging with higher knowledge.

Anyone who has the urge to expand his or her awareness is a pioneer. In this we are emerging from the confines of a mental prison within which the human race has been incarcerated for millennia. It is the privilege of each one of us to participate in this historic adventure, and we must be prepared for any eventuality. Kundalini yoga, if practised with dedication, patience and appropriate guidance, is the safest and most pleasant way of awakening that can ever take place in our lives.

With the awakening of kundalini, life becomes smooth. Plans and projects become clear, decisions become accurate, and the personality becomes dynamic and powerful. Therefore, do not be afraid of any risk. Once the awakening takes place, all your limitations will be overcome, because darkness can never exist in the face of kundalini.

9

Kundalini and Madness

Many individuals who experience the awakening of kundalini behave in a peculiar way; they think in a different style or pattern. They may see auras and visions, feel peculiar in the body, hear strange sounds and talk about things which seem to be all sorts of nonsense.

In society our brains are structured in a certain way; there is discipline and control which inhibit us from expressing ourselves freely. When the awakening of kundalini takes place, this conditioning is withdrawn and the lid is completely lifted from the mind. That is why the actions and words of those people who are undergoing kundalini awakening appear so nonsensical, deviant and oftentimes mad to the ordinary person.

During kundalini awakening and madness, people may manifest the same symptoms, but on closer examination a difference can be detected between them. Similarly, if you film one person laughing out of madness and another person laughing with friends, they will look almost the same but actually they are different. Most of us have probably read stories about the avadhootas and fakirs of India, and the Sufi and Christian mystics. Externally, these God-intoxicated ones looked crazy, but if you were with them they would have appeared and proved to be very clear. The inner consciousness of such people is absolutely lucid, organized and disciplined.

A great misunderstanding

Mystics throughout the ages have been persecuted for their experiences, which to the normal mundane consciousness are insanity, yet to the sage are ecstasy. Socrates was poisoned because he did not behave normally. Christ was crucified on the cross because his teachings were not understood. Al-Hallaj, the Sufi saint, was skinned alive because he spoke the truth without fear of society. Joan of Arc and the witches of Salem were burned at the stake, as were many others. All have been persecuted and harassed by the mundane populace for their vision, which arose as a result of inner work. Due to this lack of understanding, many of the esoteric doctrines were hidden from the majority of people.

Of course, this was long ago. We live in a more enlightened world today, far from the barbarous atrocities of the past, or do we? War and poverty still exist, as do insanity and madness. People who are shown to be crazy, relative to the norms of our society, are locked up until they are 'better'. Yet, by what criteria are they judged insane? How do we know the difference between insanity and the ecstasy of enlightenment? Is it by the superficial external appearances that we sense with our limited sensory apparatus, or is it by some deeper inner fear that we are motivated to judge others insane because they do not behave like the majority? Some of the people in the west who are locked up as insane would be recognized in the east as having undergone higher spiritual experiences. Therefore, it is now up to modern science to determine some definite, concrete and reliable ways to differentiate between the broken, insane mind and the opening, enlightened mind.

Spiritual experiences in the East and West

Knowledge of spiritual experience has been lost in the West. During the last few centuries, many unfortunate people whose kundalini had awakened were sent to mental hospitals and given drugs, electric shocks and other inappropriate treatments. The scientists and doctors believed that the awakening was an abnormal kind of behaviour, and no one was able to accept or handle it, not even the person's immediate family or closest friends. That is why in the last two hundred years, there have been so few great personalities in the west; they have all been committed to mental hospitals or they have remained quiet to avoid that fate.

In India, the situation is quite different. There, when an individual expresses some abnormal symptoms, makes some very peculiar gestures or speaks of extraordinary dreams, it is understood that he is experiencing events beyond the mind. The Hindu belief is that the consciousness is not the finished product of nature, but is subject to evolution, and between one state of being and the next, there is a crisis. When strange symptoms occur in someone, it is believed that his consciousness is undergoing evolution. If a child's total personality is devoted to God and he can experience things beyond the mind, then his whole family is purified and such a child is universally respected.

A spiritual awakening or madness?

Though the process of spiritual awakening usually occurs without incident or interruption, it may happen that block-ages and impurities in the body create symptoms which mimic various neurological and psychiatric conditions. These problems necessitate careful diagnosis to differentiate kun-dalini arousal and pathology.

It is very simple to distinguish between a mental or psychic phenomenon and a mental sickness, however many of the symptoms may overlap; mental illness never develops in people who are free from conflict. If a person is undergoing a problem in his personal life, perhaps due to a death, loss of property or emotional breakdown, psychotic behaviour can develop. Fantasies can take form and one's own psychological volition can manifest in the form of psychic energy. On the other hand, if there are no conflicts, anxieties or strong crosscurrents in a person's life, he cannot possibly have any mental disease. Suppose you have no apparent problems, no personal or social difficulties, but still you are having some strange supra-sensual experiences. In a case like this, there should be no doubt about what is taking place.

A mad person does not have a constant and consistent flow of experience and his awareness is very dissipated. He is both disorganized externally and completely blinded internally. On the other hand, the awareness of a person who is awakened is constant and consistent. Whereas a person with an awakened consciousness can make accurate decisions and judgements, a crazy person cannot. Madness and spiritual awakening may both be characterized by a certain lack of control, but the spiritually awakened person is guided by a higher consciousness while the mad person is not.

When some supra-sensual experience is taking place, it is important to consult an experienced person who has knowledge of illumination and also knows about madness. A guru can make the correct judgement and determine whether the brain has begun a process of regression or is actually progressing along transcendental lines. If there is some organic damage in the brain, it can be treated, but if the symptoms are spiritual, the person is initiated and given something to practise so his behaviour is streamlined. He or she will not be forced into married life or any other of the social roles which are unsuitable. Instead, he will be exposed to saintly personalities and teachings.

If this type of guidance and support for the experience is not obtained, it is very easy to end up in a mental hospital, or even a prison. However, scientists are now broadening their description of the spectrum of human behaviour and they are discovering that behaviour can be psychic or spiritual in origin as well as psychological or physical. Everybody should understand one very important point. Awakening of kundalini should never be equated with abnormal psychological behaviour, because awakening of kundalini is a process of jumping out of the mind.

10

Four Forms of Awakening

When we talk about awakening we should not confuse awakening of kundalini with other forms of awakening. Awakening of the chakras is completely different from awakening of kundalini. Awakening of sushumna is also quite a different event, and awakening of mooladhara chakra is not awakening of kundalini. Even if all the chakras from mooladhara up to ajna are awakened this does not mean that kundalini is awakened.

In the systematic process of awakening kundalini, the first step is to purify ida and pingala nadis and create harmony in their functioning. Next, all the chakras have to be awakened. Then sushumna nadi is awakened, and when there is a clear pathway for its ascent, kundalini can be awakened.

If the first three steps have been taken, awakening of kundalini will only have positive effects, but if they have been neglected and kundalini awakens, there will definitely be some negative results. Supposing you have awakened kundalini before sushumna awakening has taken place, then the shakti will not find a channel towards Shiva. It will remain obstructed in mooladhara chakra and will create tremendous sexual and neurotic problems. This is a negative result because you wanted to unite with Shiva and have higher experiences, whereas now you are experiencing the grosser things. If the chakras are not awakened before kundalini, the shakti will get blocked in one of the chakras and remain stagnant, possibly for years. Some siddhis may develop and you may not be able to transcend them at all. This is also a negative effect.

Each form of awakening has its own psychic potential. Every nerve and fibre of your body is psychic; it is capable of producing psychic manifestations. There is a possibility of awakening the entire physical body. Every cell of the body is one individual. You are the macrocosmic body for that microcosmic individual.

Step 1: Disciplining ida and pingala

Ida and pingala nadis are responsible for the mundane existence. Pingala conducts the life that is in your body and ida conducts the consciousness. These two nadis respectively feed the two hemispheres of the brain, which in turn control every activity of the body. It is not awakening of these nadis we aim towards, but discipline. As you know, ida and pingala function alternately and directly influence the temperature of the body, digestive and hormonal secretions, the brain waves and all the bodily systems.

Ida and pingala function according to a natural cycle, but on account of poor eating habits and inharmonious lifestyles, the natural cycle is often disturbed. Sometimes one nadi predominates and the other is suppressed, which leads to mental and physical imbalances and generally results in disease. Therefore, ida and pingala must be disciplined or made to function according to the laws of nature. Only when there is harmony between these two nadis can sushumna be awakened.

So, through the practices of hatha yoga, pranayama and raja yoga, the nadis should be purified and disciplined. The best practice for this is nadi shodhana pranayama, the nadi purifying pranayama.

Step 2: Awakening the chakras

From incarnation to incarnation the yoga we have been practising may have already awakened the lower chakras.

Although most of us try to awaken mooladhara, swadhisthana etc. it may not be necessary to awaken them because we may have evolved even beyond manipura on account of our efforts in a previous life. It is even possible that kundalini may have ascended through the chakras, but we do not know it because we have not noticed any symptoms. However, in any case, it is essential that all the chakras must be awakened before we make an attempt to awaken sushumna.

If the chakras are not purified, then purification of the nadis will not serve any purpose. If the electrical junctions are not connected or properly organized, even if you have the best wiring available, how will the electrical energy be distributed? The chakras are the junctions from which the nadis, like cables, transmit the energy to different parts of the body.

Every point, speck or fibre of the body is directly related to one of the chakras. If you experience pain in any part of the body, the sensation will go to the chakras related to that particular area. This means your whole body is connected to the chakras. For example, the urinary, excretory and reproductive systems are fed by swadhisthana chakra. Besides this, the sexual organs are connected to mooladhara chakra. The digestive system, small intestine, large intestine, appendix, pancreas, duodenum, stomach and liver are all connected to manipura chakra. The heart and lungs are fed by anahata chakra.

However, in most people, the chakras beyond manipura are dormant. Because mooladhara chakra is the highest chakra in animal evolution, it is already functioning in most people. That is why everybody has a very acute sexual awareness and sex has become one of the most important events in man's life. Therefore, most of our social traditions are based upon this particular human requirement. The mere fact that today's society is utilizing the five tattwas of tantra (meat, fish, wine, grain and sexual interaction) in everyday life means that in most people, kundalini is somewhere between mooladhara and swadhisthana. Once kundalini leaves swadhisthana and ascends to manipura and anahata, you no longer need the five tattwas.

If you are stuck in mooladhara or swadhisthana chakra, you will need to purify the higher chakras and bring them into operation. There are many ways of doing it. For those who are strong in mind, there are some higher practices. By concentration on bhrumadhya you can awaken one chakra, by the practice of uddiyana bandha you can awaken another, by practising mantra, your mantra or any beeja mantra, you can awaken almost all the chakras one by one, and as a result of this awakening, you can have very good psychic experiences which you can easily handle. In my opinion, it is safer to awaken the chakras by the mild methods.

The asanas are intended to create mild awakening in the chakras. For example, sarvangasana will awaken vishuddhi, matsyasana will awaken anahata, and bhujangasana will awaken swadhisthana. By awakening the chakras mildly, you will not have any jolting experiences. Sometimes, when a chakra awakens suddenly, you can have the experience of lower lives. This means you can be assailed by fear, anxiety, greed, passion, depression, and so on.

Each chakra is symbolized by a certain animal, indicating a type of animal consciousness, and if sudden awakening of a chakra takes place, you may exhibit some of the animal emotions in either a mild or very strong way. For instance, fear is not a human emotion, nor is infatuation or violence. Of course, man is trying to expel the animal from himself, but at the same time he is maintaining it. Therefore, care must be taken not to give an explosive manifestation to the awakening of the chakras.

Step 3: Awakening sushumna

In order to purify and awaken sushumna, a lot of work has to be done and you must be ready to cope with experiences that are more intense than those associated with chakra awakening. These experiences are beyond logic. They are not even real and they cannot be explained or properly understood. If the chakras are awakened, ida and pingala are balanced and the other nadis are also purified, but there is an obstruction in sushumna, then the awakening of kundalini will not fulfil its purpose.

Actually, I do not believe that ida and pingala nadis are inferior to sushumna. Awakening of pingala nadi will awaken one portion of the brain and awakening of ida will awaken another portion. However, when kundalini enters sushumna, it affects the whole brain.

In the ancient texts of tantra it has been clearly indicated that it does not matter if kundalini enters another passageway. If there is an awakening in pingala, one becomes a healer or a siddha, one who has control over nature, matter and the mind. When there is awakening in ida, one can predict things; one becomes a prophet. But when sushumna awakens, kundalini ascends straight to sahasrara and one becomes a jivanmukta, a liberated soul.

So, hatha yoga and pranayama are prescribed for the awakening of sushumna. There are also other ways, but kriya yoga is the best, particularly the practices of maha mudra and maha bheda mudra. For awakening of sushumna, ida and pingala have to be suppressed. Thus you can see the importance of practising kumbhaka, breath retention. When both nadis are suppressed in kumbhaka, immediately after you will find that both nadis are flowing simultaneously. It is at this time that kundalini should awaken.

11

The Descent of Kundalini

Everybody talks about the ascent of kundalini, but few ever discuss the descent. When the descent of kundalini occurs, it means the lower mental plane of the human being is no longer influenced by the ordinary mind, the supermind takes over instead. This higher form of consciousness rules the body, mind and senses and directs your life, thoughts and emotions. Kundalini is henceforth the ruler of your life. That is the concept of descent.

The whole process after union

When Shiva and Shakti unite in sahasrara, one experiences samadhi, illumination occurs in the brain and the silent areas begin to function. Shiva and Shakti remain merged together for some time, during which there is a total loss of consciousness pertaining to each other. At that time a bindu evolves. Bindu means a point, a drop, and that bindu is the substratum of the whole cosmos. Within that bindu is the seat of human intelligence and the seat of the total creation. Then the bindu splits into two and Shiva and Shakti manifest again in duality. When ascension took place it was only the ascent of Shakti, but when descent takes place, Shiva and Shakti both descend to the gross plane and there is again knowledge of duality.

Those who have studied quantum physics will have a better understanding of this as it is difficult for everyone to understand from the philosophical point of view. After total union there is a process of coming down the same pathway you ascended. The gross consciousness which became fine, again becomes gross. That is the concept of divine incarnation or avatara.

The non-dual experience of samadhi

When one attains the highest pinnacles of samadhi, purusha and prakriti, or Shiva and Shakti, are in total union and only adwaita, non-dual experience, exists. At this time, when there is no subject/object plus distinction, it is very difficult for one to differentiate. He may look like an idiot and not know it, or he may appear to be a great scholar and not be aware of that. He does not know whether he is talking to a man or a woman, he sees no difference between them. He may even be associating with spiritual or divine people without being aware of that, because at this point of time his consciousness is reduced to a level of innocence just like that of a baby.

So, in the state of samadhi you are a baby. A baby cannot tell the difference between a man and a woman because he has no physical or sexual distinction. He cannot distinguish a scholar from an idiot and he may not even see any difference between a snake and a rope. He can hold a snake just as he holds a rope. This only happens when union is taking place.

When Shiva and Shakti descend to the gross plane, that is, mooladhara chakra, they separate and live as two entities. There is duality in mooladhara chakra. There is duality in the mind and senses and in the world of name and form, but there is no duality in samadhi. There is no seer or experiencer in the state of samadhi. There is nobody to say what samadhi is like because it is a non-dual experience.

Why Shiva and Shakti both descend

It is very difficult to understand why Shiva and Shakti both descend to the gross plane after having attained the highest union. What is the use of destroying the world and then creating it again? What is the point of transcending the consciousness if you have to come back to it again? Why bother to awaken kundalini and unite with Shiva in sahasrara if you have to come down to mooladhara again? This is something very mysterious and we can well ask, "Why awaken kundalini at all?"

Why build a mansion if you know you will have to burn it down when it is completed? We actually create a lot of things that are ultimately going to be destroyed. So why do it at all? It seems so crazy! We do so much sadhana to transcend the chakras and ascend from earth to heaven. Then, when we reach paradise and become one with that great reality, we suddenly decide to come back down; and not all alone, we bring the great one with us. It would be easier to understand if Shakti came back alone and Shiva remained in heaven. Maybe when Shakti is about to leave, Shiva says, "Wait, I'm coming with you."

A new existence on the gross plane

When kundalini descends, you come down to the gross plane with a totally transformed consciousness. You live a normal life, associating with everybody and discharging your worldly obligations just like other people do. Maybe you even play the game of desires, passions, cravings and such things. Maybe you play the game of victory and defeat, attachment and infatuation, but you are just playing a game. You know it; you do everything as an actor. You are not involved in it life and soul.

It is at this time that the genius or the transformed consciousness manifests through you. You do not have to think or plan how to perform miracles. You have to remember that you have come down as a transformed quality of consciousness. You must remember that you are now connected with those areas of the brain which were previously silent. You must also remember that you are linked with those reservoirs of knowledge, power and wisdom which belong to the realm of the higher cosmos.

Until the descent is complete, such a person lives a very simple life, unnoticed and unattended. Once the descent is complete he begins to play the game and people recognize him as a divine incarnation. They see he is something special compared to everybody else and they call him a guru. Such a person is actually a junior god.

Dealing with the issues of reality

When Shiva and Shakti descend to the gross level of awareness there is again duality. That is why the self-realized person is able to understand pain and all the mundane affairs of life. He understands the whole drama of duality, multiplicity and diversity. Sometimes we ordinary mortals are at a fix to understand how this person with the highest attainment is able to cope with the hopeless dualities of life.

When I was about thirteen, I was also puzzled by this question. There was a great lady saint who was supposed to have attained the very highest state and I used to visit her with my elders. I used to hear her discussing all the mundane and ordinary things of life – "How are you? How is your child? Is he sick? Are you giving him medicine? Why do you fight with your wife?" I used to think, "If she is an enlightened lady, she shouldn't talk about duality. How can she understand duality if she is in unity?"

I never got an answer, but everyone has his moments of experience in life and I have not been an exception to that. I came to understand that Shiva and Shakti live on both planes and that this gross plane of duality is an expression and manifestation of the correlation of Shiva and Shakti. This is precisely the reason why the great saints and mahatmas talk about charity, compassion, love, and so on. However, there is a period when they do not understand these things and they do not care what happens to the world. They do not even know what is going on, who is happy and who is suffering. Finally, however, there is a great transformation. Shakti rules matter and Shiva rules consciousness, and when they descend to the gross plane Shakti continues to rule matter, and Shiva, being consciousness, gives an understanding to the whole world.

Therefore, if we ever see a self-realized person discussing the trivialities of life and dealing with the issues of reality, we should not be surprised.

12

The Experiences of Awakening

The awakening of kundalini is like a great explosion which transports a person into another plane of being. No matter which spiritual path you follow, you must eventually reach this domain. Ordinary consciousness and transcendental consciousness cannot be maintained at the same time; it is necessary to pass through an intermediate zone of change, where perceptions, feelings and experiences undergo a transformation. The adventure is always the same; it is a journey through the border region between the known and the unknown.

At this time it is very important to recognize that this explosion signals a profound alteration in consciousness. The complete process of awakening is comprised of several stages, as the kundalini rises and passes through the various chakras. It takes quite some time to become fully stabilized, but if one has a good understanding, the transition process can be managed without any serious difficulties.

The preliminary awakening of kundalini is followed by the experience of light in bhrumadhya. Usually this develops in a very mild way over an extended period of time and, therefore, does not precipitate any sudden agitation or disturbance. After some time, the appetite for food and sleep gradually decreases and the mind becomes quieter.

There is another prior warning which heralds the awakening of kundalini. In yoga and tantra it is very clearly indicated that when ida and pingala flow simultaneously for a long period of time, and sushumna begins to flow, then it is time to prepare for a spiritual event. Therefore, one should be conversant with swara yoga, the science of the breath cycle, and keep a close watch over the breathing process. The breathing pattern in the nostrils normally changes every fourth day, according to the cycles of the moon, but when both nostrils have been functioning equally well for at least fifteen days, that is an advance warning of an impending spiritual breakthrough.

An onslaught of experiences

When the actual awakening occurs there is an explosion in the realm of experience and there are symptoms which are sometimes very difficult to understand. The most unique and common experience is the release of energy like an electric shock from the bottom of the spinal cord, as if it were connected to an electrical power point. This may be accompanied by a burning sensation in mooladhara chakra and energy passing up and down through sushumna. Sometimes you hear drums, flutes, bells, birds, celestial music, or you may even think you can hear peacocks singing. You may have a very momentary sensation of sitting outside in the middle of a monsoon shower, and there can also be the sensation of dark clouds in continual movement overhead and the sound of thunder.

At times your body feels so light and you may even visualize your spinal cord as fluorescent light. It is common to feel illumination from within, as if hundreds of little lights were burning inside your body. This is one side. The other side is that all the anger, passions and suppressions come out. Sometimes you are so filled with fear that you cannot sleep, sometimes for days together you have nothing in your mind but sex, at other times you think of nothing but food. However, all these symptoms pass within a few days or weeks.

Some people obtain psychic powers: clairvoyance, telepathy, clairaudience, psychotelekinesis, the ability to heal, etc., and this brings a lot of temptations. However, this is a phase and it will pass away.

Sometimes you do not feel like eating for days. You may not have any appetite for fifteen to twenty days, and even if people try to force you to eat, you cannot. There is sometimes a feeling of nervous depression, and you may just want to sit, or you may feel restricted and closed in. There is a detachment from the normal emotions of life; for days you may live a life of utter dispassion. Nothing is interesting in life and everything and everybody seems as dry as a desert. But at the same time, the mind becomes very dynamic and appears to be formless. Various sensations, poetic emotions and artistic perceptions also occur, such as visions of angels and divinities. All kinds of things can emerge from the depths of the mind. However, these are just a few of the symptoms you may experience, but all of them pass away quickly.

The storm always settles and then the yogi lives a very normal life. Externally his life seems the same as anybody else's, but his inner awareness is far greater and more vast.

Headaches and insomnia

Some aspirants experience terrible headaches when kundalini is awakening, however, this does not mean that all headaches are related to kundalini, and not everybody will have headaches. Generally, those who have had a married life do not have this experience. It is usually only those who have not had any kind of sexual interactions who experience headaches with the advent of kundalini awakening.

There is also another explanation about headaches. One-tenth of the brain is active and nine-tenths are not. In some cases, when the silent areas of the brain begin to wake up, the first symptom is headache. People have equated this experience with labour pain. Just as a woman experiences labour pain when she is about to give birth to a child, when the silent areas of the brain are about to become active and you are giving birth to spiritual consciousness, there is also pain. Therefore, one has to bear with this pain for some time, but it will inevitably settle down. Of course, you can reduce the pain by adjusting your diet and lifestyle, but under no circumstances should you use sedatives, aspirins or pain relieving pills.

It is also likely that an aspirant will experience insomnia. However, yogis do not call it insomnia. They say, "Why should I sleep?" If you love a person very much and he stays with you and does not allow you to sleep, will you call that insomnia? So, not all those who do not sleep are yogis. There are yogis who do not sleep and are happy about it because yogis have an entirely different attitude. They say one-third of life is wasted in sleeping.

So, when kundalini awakens in a yogi and consciousness is constant and consistent, and there is no waking, sleeping and dreaming, they are very happy about it. Therefore, insomnia does not usually bother a person who has awakened kundalini. However, if you are disturbed by your inability to sleep, you should never resort to sleeping pills or tranquillizers. It is also not necessary that you practise yoga to induce sleep. Just accept your sleeplessness and enjoy it. You can do japa or meditation or just do some spiritual reflection. If this is not possible, just lie down and let it happen as it will.

Experiencing the threefold awakenings

Each of the three forms of awakening – nadis, chakras and sushumna is accompanied by its own set of experiences. Many aspirants have psychic experiences and think that these indicate the awakening of kundalini, but this is not so.

When the chakras are awakening, the experiences one has are not so frightening and critical. They are usually of a fantastic nature, very pleasant, hallucinatory and comfortable. Even if you have an experience of fear or terror, it does not shake your mind. When you have experiences of your ishta devata or guru, or you have some experience in meditation or during kirtan, and it feels very nice, that represents chakra awakening and not kundalini awakening.

When you experience a chakra awakening it is rather beautiful and leaves a comfortable or blissful feeling. That is to encourage you to go further.

When awakening takes place in sushumna, you may feel or see a rod of light, or your spinal cord may seem to be fully illumined from within. Such experiences are described by saints of different religions in their poems, songs and stories, which are unfortunately understood by very few people today.

The awakening of sushumna can also bring some mind exploding experiences which are sometimes very confusing. You can smell pleasant and unpleasant odours, you will hear shrieks and screams as if ghosts are crying, and there is a feeling of heat, creeping sensations and pain in different parts of the body. You may get a high fever or manifest the symptoms of some common disease or some baffling illness which medical experts find difficult to analyze.

At the time of sushumna awakening, the quality and experience of the mind begin to change. One has the experience of depression, anorexia and loneliness. You begin to realize the inner essence. Matter appears to be nothing, and even your body feels as if it were only made up of air. Or you may feel that you are not part of this physical body, you are someone else. When you look at people, animals and the objects of nature – the flowers, trees, rivers and mountains, and so on, you feel a communication with them.

At this time, you also experience prophetic vision, but your visions or forewarnings may not be clear and you only foresee the bad things – imminent perils, accidents, disasters and catastrophes. Throughout the awakening one generally has an aversion to work and cannot really apply oneself to anything. It is actually best if an aspirant is near his guru at this time of awakening so he can explain what is happening. The sadhaka is not merely making a transition from one state of mind to another, he is actually jumping from one state to another. It is also very difficult for even an expert guru to handle these matters unless the disciple has totally accepted him as his guru.

Differentiating the experiences

You must remember that when you have certain visions and fantastic experiences, they do not necessarily represent the awakening of kundalini or even sushumna nadi. They may indicate chakra awakening or they may just be the expression of your archetypes or samskaras. Because of your sadhana, concentration or one-pointedness, you may be allowing an outlet for your deep-rooted samskaras to express themselves.

These experiences and those that accompany chakra awakening do not mean anything when you try to assess them. I will give you an example. Many years ago, I was meditating on the bank of the Ganga in Rishikesh and suddenly I had a very vivid experience. I saw the whole earth split into two. It was a very clear vision, and I remember it even today, but this vision had nothing to do with reality; I just had it. This was an experience of chakra awakening.

When the actual awakening of kundalini takes place, it is a great event. Every experience has a tangible proof, whether it is awakening of extrasensory perceptions or the awakening of a particular kind of genius. It may be in the form of a philosophy you are able to deliver to people, a transformation in the physical elements of the body that you are able to materialize, or a magnetic influence that you can cast over the masses of people as a politician, musician or saint.

The awakening of kundalini has tangible, positive and concrete proof. You cannot believe your kundalini is awakened if you have no proof, because when the awakening of kundalini takes place, you completely transcend the normal categories of mental awareness and the scope of your knowledge becomes greater.

A scientist who jumped beyond the mind

There was a scientist named Eddington, who observed the determined laws of electrons and tried to formulate a system, a law. He succeeded, the result being the law of determinacy. However, once when he was studying the electrons, his vision changed entirely. He found that the electrons were behaving in a very anarchical manner. There was no logic, system or hypothesis behind their behaviour. That was his vision, and he called it the law of indeterminacy.

Once he was asked, "What is this law which you have discovered behind the mathematical and logical behaviour of electrons?" He replied, "It cannot be explained." Someone asked, "How can you say that a movement in matter cannot be explained?" Eddington answered, "It can be explained if you can jump over the mind."

The process of transition

There is a natural process of transition in which a person's consciousness evolves over the course of millions of years. It takes place in the same way that a baby develops into a child, a child into a young person, a young person into a middle-aged person, a middle-aged person into an old person. Suppose a child of five suddenly transformed into an old person and found he was tall, grey haired and speaking like an old person. It would be very difficult for him to handle the situation and to connect both the areas of his life. This is what generally happens with those who awaken kundalini.

Their experiences are often imbalanced and extremely difficult to understand. Just imagine how it would be if you felt your whole body burning as if it were in flames, or you kept feeling that a snake was crawling through your body. Imagine what it would be like to look at somebody's face and instead of seeing the person you see a ghost. You would start to think you were crazy! These are just a few of the bizarre experiences you could be confronted with. However, with the awakening of kundalini, there is also an awakening of vairagya, detachment. And when vairagya develops the turbulence settles, the awakening becomes peaceful and the transition is smooth.

13

The Path of Kriya Yoga

Awakening of kundalini is very difficult. You can try the various yogic and religious practices that have evolved throughout the ages, but they require a lot of self-discipline and demanding austerities. There are so many do's and don'ts that the average person finds unpalatable. Therefore, the rishis of the tantric tradition evolved a series of practices that could be easily adopted by every type of aspirant regardless of lifestyle, habits, beliefs, and so on. Of course, there are many practices belonging to tantra, but of them all, kriya yoga is considered to be the most powerful and suitable for a modern day person who is enmeshed in this world.

For many years, knowledge of this system of yoga was revealed to very few. The practices were mentioned in the tantric texts, but they were never clearly defined. Through a tradition, the practices were handed down from guru to disciple. They were given to both householder and monastic disciples, who soon discovered that through these techniques, kundalini became a real experience in their lives.

The ultimate purpose of kriya yoga is to create awakening in the chakras, to purify the nadis and, finally, to awaken the kundalini shakti. The kriyas are intended to awaken the kundalini in stages, not abruptly. When kundalini awakens abruptly, the experiences you have are very difficult to handle and you cannot understand what is happening to you. The techniques of kriya yoga offer a smooth and relatively risk-free means of expanding your awareness and awakening the dormant areas of the brain. This system of kriya yoga also provides a means whereby you do not have to tackle the mind directly. Its practices are based on hatha yoga, which aims at controlling the prana. Mind and prana interact with each other and therefore, by controlling the prana, we can gain control of the mind.

Kriya yoga offers a unique approach

Kriya yoga means 'the yoga of practice, movement of action.' Unlike the various religious, mystical or yogic practices which demand mental control, the special instruction in the system of kriya yoga is: "Do not worry about the mind." If your mind is dissipated or if there are distractions in your mind and you are not able to concentrate even for one second, it does not matter. You have only to continue with your practices, for even without confronting, controlling or trying to balance the mind, you can still evolve.

This is an entirely new concept in spiritual life, and most people have probably never even considered it. When they take to a religion, commence spiritual practices or go to gurus, the first thing they are told is to control the mind. "You should think like this. Don't think like that. You should do this. Don't do that. This is good. This is bad. That is evil. Do not sin," and so on.

People think that the mind is the greatest barrier in spiritual life, but this is a very wrong and dangerous concept. The mind is a bridge between this and that, so how can it be a barrier? An idiot thinks it is a barrier and he tries to destroy that bridge. Then when he has destroyed it, he wonders how he will get to the other side. This is the ironical fate of most people, and unfortunately it is religions, ethics and morality that are responsible. People who are less aware of ethics and morality have no mental problems. They are very good, happy-go-lucky people.

The seers and rishis of kriya yoga have said, "Control of the mind is not necessary. Just go on practising the kriyas and let the mind do what it wants. In the course of time, the evolution of consciousness will take you to that point where the mind will no longer trouble you."

Dissipation of mind is not necessarily the fault of the mind. Distractions can be due to hormonal imbalances, bad digestion, low influx of energy in the nervous system and many other things. Never blame the mind for its restlessness, and do not consider yourself to be an impure, bad or inferior person because your mind jumps all over the place, thinking negative things and what you consider to be evil thoughts.

Everybody has negative thoughts and distractions of mind, even a compassionate and charitable person, a peaceful person, a chaste and pure person. Dozens of factors could be the cause of a distracted mind. Suppressing the mind and calling it back again and again is not the way to concentrate the mind, it is a way to the mental hospital. After all, who suppresses or calls back who? Are there two personalities or two minds in you? Is there one bad mind which keeps wandering off and one good mind which tries to bring back the bad mind? No, there is only one mind and you should not create a split by antagonizing the mind. If you do this, one part of the mind becomes the dictator and controller and the other part becomes the victim. Then you will become totally schizophrenic.

It is necessary to understand this point very well, because our religions, philosophies and ways of thinking have not been very systematic, loving and tender in their approach to the mind. We have always been led to believe that the mind is very mischievous, but this is a grave mistake. Therefore, please try to redefine the mind and approach it scientifically.

The mind is not a psychological construct, nor is it a thought process. The mind is energy. Anger, passion, greed, ambition, and so on are waves of that energy. Through kriya yoga you are trying to harness the energies of the mind, but you should not try to suppress this energy because it will explode. And the more you suppress this energy the greater will be the ultimate explosion.

Kriya yoga is very clear in its approach to the mind. It emphasizes that you do not try to do anything with the mind. If your body protests about maintaining a fixed posture, change it. If your mind objects about closing the eyes, keep them open. However, you must continue with the kriya yoga practices because they have a direct effect on the deeper processes of the body which are responsible for the state of your mind. Remember that the body affects the mind and the mind affects the body.

We should not consider the techniques of kriya yoga as practices of concentration or meditation as their aim is not mental control. The beauty of kriya yoga is that you have only to remain relaxed and let the mind move naturally and spontaneously. Inner awareness will then awaken, and in time, your mind will automatically become one-pointed.

A path for all

As you know, we are all aspirants of a different calibre. Some of us are tamasic, some are rajasic and a very small number are sattwic. Of course, we are not purely sattwic, rajasic or tamasic. We are predominantly one of these, but we retain traces of the other two gunas. The tamasic mind has traces of rajo guna, and as it evolves, it retains traces of tamas, but it is now predominantly rajasic. It also develops traces of sattwa. As it evolves further, it becomes more rajasic and may or may not have traces of tamas and sattwa. Next, it becomes predominantly sattwic, with traces of rajo and tamo gunas here and there. Then in its fifth stage of evolution, the mind becomes totally sattwic, manifesting rajo and tamo gunas very rarely.

These five stages are like rungs on a ladder, representing the evolution of chitta or the mind. The lowest rung is known as the inert mind. The second rung is the scattered mind, the third is the oscillating mind, the fourth is the one-pointed mind and the fifth is the controlled mind.

Now, if you belong to one of the first three categories, and most of us do, after practising hatha yoga, you should take to kriya yoga. If you belong to one of the last two categories, then after hatha yoga, you can take to kriya yoga if you wish, or you can follow the path of raja yoga or any other path which asks you to concentrate through willpower. When you are at the sattwic level you can deal with the mind through the mind. At the tamasic or rajasic level, if you try to deal with the mind through the mind, you will cause a mental crisis.

In this world, there are very few sattwic people. Most of us have very restless and distracted minds, and we find it impossible to focus on one object or theme for very long. You know what happens if you light a candle when the wind is blowing? The same thing happens when most people try to concentrate. The fluctuations of the mind totally annihilate the one-pointedness. So, the kriya yoga practices were designed for those people who are unable to control, concentrate or stabilize their mind and for those who cannot sit in one posture for a prolonged period of time.

Whether you are sattwic, rajasic or tamasic, the practices of hatha yoga should be taken up first. A tamasic person needs hatha yoga to awaken his mind, body and personality. A person who is rajasic needs hatha yoga to balance the solar and lunar energies in his body and mind. A person who is sattwic by temperament needs hatha yoga to help awaken kundalini. Hatha yoga is for everybody. If you have been practising asanas, pranayama, mudras and bandhas consistently for two years or more, then you are ready for kriya yoga. Hatha yoga is the basis of kriya yoga.

The practices

There are many kriya yoga practices, but a combination of twenty is considered very important and powerful. These twenty practices are divided into two groups. One group, comprised of the first nine practices, is to be done with the eyes open, and the other group, comprised of eleven practices, is to be done with the eyes closed. For the first group of practices, the central instruction is, "Do not close your eyes." Even though you feel very relaxed and have a tendency to go within, you must not close your eyes. You can blink, you can rest, you can stop the practices for a minute, but each practice must be done with the eyes open. This is a very important instruction for kriya yoga practise.

The first practice in kriya yoga is called vipareeta karani mudra. Vipareeta means reverse and karani means action, therefore, vipareeta karani mudra is a method for creating a reverse action. In *Hatha Yoga Pradipika* and in the tantric texts, there is a wonderful statement regarding this reverse action: "From the moon the nectar emanates. When the sun consumes the nectar, the yogi becomes old. His body decays and he dies. Therefore, by constant practice, the yogi should try to reverse the process. The nectar which is flowing from the moon (bindu) towards the sun (manipura chakra) should be reversed and sent back to the higher centres." What will happen then? *Hatha Yoga Pradipika* continues: "When you are able to reverse the flow of amrit or nectar, it will not be consumed by the sun. It will be assimilated by your pure body."

When your body has been purified by hatha yoga, pranayama and a pure diet, this nectar is assimilated by the body and, as a result, you experience a high mental state. When the nectar returns to its source in the higher centres of the brain, and is not consumed by the sun, you begin to feel a sort of calmness and quietness. Even if your mind was distracted, confused, wandering and vacillating a few moments before, suddenly all these activities come to an end and you feel total brightness. Your eyes are open, you can hear sounds and see everything around you, but the mind does not move. It appears as if time, space and object have ceased and the whole universe has stopped functioning.

The main hypothesis or contention here is that you can influence the structures of the body; you can create a change in the energy forces. By creating a change in the physical secretions, by altering the chemical and energy proportions in the body, you can create an effect on the mind which you may call shanti, dharana, dhyana or samadhi. This means that even when your mind is totally undisciplined and you cannot handle it for a second, if you are able to create the correct proportion of secretions in the different areas of the body/mind, then the higher state can be achieved.

You know what happens if you take a dose of ganja (marijuana)? Take a few puffs and see what happens to your mind. It slows down and the brain waves change from theta to beta, from alpha to delta. Suddenly you feel calm and quiet. What happened to your mind? You did not fight with it. I am not advocating the use of ganja, I am just giving you a very gross example of how kriya yoga works on your mind. By infusing ganja or some hallucinogenic drug, the chemical properties of the gross body change. The heart slows down, the breathing rate changes, the brain waves alter and the mind becomes calm and still. Is it not possible to arrive at the same point through kriya yoga? Yes, this is exactly what is accomplished through kriya yoga.

The various practices of kriya yoga, particularly vipareeta karani mudra, amrit pan, khechari mudra, moola bandha, maha mudra, maha bheda mudra, etc. regulate the nervous system. They harmonize the pranic forces in the body and equalize the quantity and effects of the positive and negative ions. More than that, they help you to attain a state of peace and tranquillity without beating, kicking and abusing the mind. All this is a result of having induced the flow of certain unused and natural chemicals of the body. Amrit is one of those chemicals and through a practice known as khechari mudra, it can be made to flow.

Khechari mudra

Khechari mudra is a simple but very important technique which is utilized in most of the kriya yoga practices. It involves folding the tongue back and placing it against the upper palate. In the course of time the tongue becomes elongated and can be inserted into the nasal orifice. Then certain glands which are connected with the cranial passage and bindu are stimulated and, as a result, amrit or nectar begins to flow. When amrit is released you experience a special type of 'high' or intoxication.

It might take you a few years to perfect khechari mudra and to stimulate the flow of amrit, but it is well worth the effort. When you sit for meditation the mind is perfectly still, it cannot move and you cannot think. There is shoonyata, an experience of total nothingness. If you are practising mantra, you feel that somebody else is practising and you are only witnessing it. This is considered a very important experience because it puts you in touch with the external and internal experiences at the same time and you are completely aware of yourself. You attain a state where you are simultaneously aware of the world of mind, senses and objects, and the world of inner peace, tranquillity and relaxation. When there is perfect harmony in the nervous system, coronary behaviour is in inertia, body temperature is low and alpha waves are predominant in the brain, how can the mind move? This is the philosophy of kriya yoga.

Readiness for kriya yoga

If through the yoga practices you have been doing, you have reached a point where you find that although concentration has been achieved, inner peace has been experienced and you can maintain total quietness of body, mind and spirit for a prolonged period, but still you feel there is something more to achieve, you are definitely ready for kriya yoga.

Peace of mind, relaxation and proper understanding, which are the fruits of spiritual life, are not an end in themselves. The ultimate purpose of yoga is to change the quality of experience and to change the quality of the mind and its perception. What man has aimed at achieving through yoga is expansion of mind and liberation of energy and, in essence, that is tantra, and that is the ultimate goal of kriya yoga.

14

Vama Marga and Kundalini Awakening

Sexual life has always been a problem for mankind. From the beginning of history, the primal energy has been misunderstood. Religious teachers and moralists have denounced it, but still sexual life has continued, not because man respects it, but because he needs it. He may want to give it up, but he cannot remove it from his mind, for this is one of his most powerful urges.

In the context of yoga and tantra the common definition of sexual life has no relevance. It is absolutely unscientific and incorrect. This definition has created a society of hypocrites. It has led thousands of young people into mental asylums. When you want something which you think is bad, all kinds of guilt complexes arise. This is the beginning of schizophrenia, and all of us are schizophrenic to some extent.

Therefore, the yogis have tried to give a correct direction to the sexual urge. Yoga does not interfere with sexual life. Normal sexual life is neither spiritual nor aspiritual, but if you practise yoga and master certain techniques, then sexual life becomes spiritual. Of course, if you lead a celibate life, that is spiritual too.

Left hand tantra

The science of tantra has two main branches, which are known as vama marga and dakshina marga. Vama marga is the left path which combines sexual life with yoga practices

101

in order to explode the dormant energy centres. Dakshina marga is the right path of yoga practices without sexual enactment. Previously, due to the barriers in sexual life, the path most widely followed was dakshina marga. Today, however, these barriers are rapidly being broken, and the path most sought after by people everywhere is vama marga, which utilizes sexual life for spiritual development.

According to tantra, sexual life has a threefold purpose. Some practise it for procreation, others for pleasure, but the tantric yogi practises it for samadhi. He does not hold any negative views about it, he does it as a part of his sadhana, but, at the same time, he realizes that for spiritual purposes, the experience must be maintained. Ordinarily this experience is lost before one is able to deepen it. By mastering certain techniques, however, this experience can become continuous even throughout daily life. Then the silent centres of the brain are awakened and start to function all the time.

The energy principle

The contention of vama marga is that the awakening of kundalini is possible through the sexual interaction between man and woman. The concept behind this follows the same lines as the process of fission and fusion described in modern physics. Man and woman represent positive and negative energy. On a mental level they represent time and space. Ordinarily, these two forces stand at opposite poles. During sexual interaction, however, they move out of their position of polarity, towards the centre. When they come together at the nucleus or central point, an explosion occurs and matter becomes manifest. This is the basic theme of tantric initiation.

The natural event that takes place between a man and woman is considered as the explosion of the energy centre. In every speck of life, the union between the positive and negative poles is responsible for creation. At the same time, union between the positive and negative poles is also responsible for enlightenment. The experience which takes place at the time of union is a glimpse of the higher experience.

This subject has been thoroughly discussed in all the old scriptures of tantra. Actually, more important than the energy waves that are created during the mutual union, is the process of directing that energy to the higher centres. Everybody knows how this energy is to be created, but nobody knows how to direct it to the higher centres. In fact, very few people have a full and positive understanding of this natural event which almost everybody in the world experiences. If the conjugal experience, which is generally very transitory, could be extended for a period of time, then the experience of enlightenment would take place.

The elements that are brought together in this process of union are known as Shiva and Shakti. Shiva represents purusha or consciousness and Shakti represents prakriti or energy. Shakti, in different forms, is present in all creation. Both material and spiritual energy are known as Shakti. When the energy moves outwardly it is material energy and when it is directed upwards it is spiritual energy. Therefore, when the union between man and woman is practised in the correct way, it has a very positive influence on the development of spiritual awareness.

Retaining the bindu

Bindu means a point or a drop. In tantra, bindu is considered to be the nucleus, or the abode of matter, the point from which all creation becomes manifest. The source of bindu is actually in the higher centres of the brain, but due to the development of emotions and passions, bindu falls down to the lower region where it is transformed into sperm and ova. At the higher level bindu is a point. At the lower level it is a drop of liquid, which drips from the male and female orgasm.

According to tantra, the preservation of the bindu is absolutely necessary for two reasons. Firstly, the process of regeneration can only be carried out with the help of bindu. Secondly, all the spiritual experiences take place when there is an explosion of bindu. This explosion can result in the creation of a thought or of anything. Therefore, in tantra, certain practices are recommended by which the male partner can stop ejaculation and retain the bindu.

According to tantra, ejaculation should not take place. One should learn how to stop it. For this purpose, the male partner should perfect the practices of vajroli mudra as well as moola bandha and uddiyana bandha. When these three kriyas are perfected, one is able to stop ejaculation completely at any point of the experience.

The sexual act culminates in a particular experience which is reached only at the point of explosion of energy. Unless the energy explodes, the experience cannot take place. However, this experience has to be maintained so that the energy level remains high. When the energy level falls, ejaculation takes place. Therefore, ejaculation is avoided, not so much to preserve the semen, but because it causes a depression in the level of energy.

To make this energy travel upwards through the spine, certain hatha yoga kriyas have to be mastered. The experience which is concomitant of energy has to be raised to the higher centres. It is only possible to do this if you are able to prolong and maintain that experience. As long as the experience continues, you can direct it to the higher centres, but as soon as the energy level undergoes depression, ejaculation will inevitably take place.

Ejaculation brings down the temperature of the body and, at the same time, the nervous system undergoes depression. When the sympathetic and parasympathetic nervous systems undergo depression, the brain is affected, which is why many people have mental problems. When you are able to retain the semen without ejaculating at all, the energy in the nervous system and the temperature in the whole body are maintained. At the same time, you are free from the sense of loss, depression, frustration and guilt. Retention of the semen will also help to increase the sexual frequency, and that is better for both partners. The sexual act does not have to create weakness or dissipate the energy, on the contrary, it can become a means of exploding the energy.

Therefore, the value of retaining the bindu should not be underestimated.

In hatha yoga there are certain practices which must be perfected for this purpose. You should begin with asanas such as paschimottanasana, shalabhasana, vajrasana, supta vajrasana and siddhasana. These are beneficial as they place an automatic contraction on the lower centres. Sirshasana is also important because it ventilates the brain so that all of one's experiences will be healthy. When these postures have been mastered, shambhavi mudra is perfected in order to hold the concentration steadily at bhrumadhya. Then vajroli mudra has to be practised together with moola bandha and uddiyana bandha with kumbhaka. Practise of kumbhaka is necessary while the ejaculation is being held. Retention of the breath and the bindu go hand in hand. Loss of kumbhaka is loss of bindu, and loss of bindu is loss of kumbhaka.

During kumbhaka, when you are maintaining the experience, you should be able to direct it to the higher centres. If you are able to create an archetype of this experience, perhaps in the form of a serpent or a luminous continuity, then the result will be fantastic. So, in spiritual life bindu must be preserved at all costs.

The female experience

In the female body, the point of concentration is at mooladhara chakra, which is situated at the cervix, just behind the opening of the uterus. This is the point where space and time unite and explode in the form of an experience. In ordinary language that experience is known as orgasm, but in the language of tantra it is called an awakening. In order to maintain the continuity of that experience, it is necessary for a build up of energy to take place at that particular bindu or point. Usually this does not happen because the explosion of energy dissipates throughout the body through the sexual orgasm. In order to avoid this happening, the woman must be able to hold her mind in absolute concentration on that particular point. The practice for this is known as sahajoli.

Sahajoli is actually concentration on the bindu, but this is very difficult. Therefore, the practice of sahajoli, which is the contraction of the vaginal as well as the uterine muscles, should be practised over a long period of time.

If girls are taught uddiyana bandha at an early age, they will perfect sahajoli quite naturally with time. Uddiyana bandha is always practised with external retention. It is important to be able to perform this in any position. Usually it is practised in siddha yoni asana, but one should be able to do it in vajrasana or the crow posture as well. When you practise uddiyana bandha, the other two bandhas – jalandhara and moola bandha, occur spontaneously.

Years of practice will create a keen sense of concentration on the correct point in the body. This concentration is more mental in nature; however, since it is not possible to do it mentally one has to start from some physical point. If a woman is able to concentrate and maintain the continuity of the experience, she can awaken her energy to a high level.

According to tantra, there are two different areas of orgasm. One is in the nervous zone, which is the common experience for most women, and the other is in mooladhara chakra. When sahajoli is practised during maithuna (the act of sexual union), mooladhara chakra wakes up and the spiritual or tantric orgasm takes place.

When the female yogi is able to practise sahajoli for say five to fifteen minutes, she can retain the tantric orgasm for the same period of time. By retaining this experience, the flow of energy is reversed. Circulation of blood and sympathetic/parasympathetic forces move upward. At this point, she transcends normal consciousness and sees the light. That is how she enters the deep state of dhyana. Unless the woman is able to practise sahajoli, she will not be able to retain the impulses necessary for the tantric orgasm, and consequently she will have the nervous orgasm, which is short-lived and followed by dissatisfaction and exhaustion. This is often the cause of a woman's hysteria and depression. So sahajoli is an extremely important practice for women. In

106

uddiyana, nauli, naukasana, vajrasana and siddha yoni asana, sahajoli comes naturally.

The practice of amaroli is very important for married women. The word amaroli means 'immortal' and through this practice one is freed of many diseases. Practising amaroli over a prolonged period also produces a hormone known as prostaglandin, which destroys the ova and prevents conception from taking place

Tantric guru

Just as in the scheme of creation, Shakti is the creator and Shiva the witness of the whole game, in tantra the woman has the status of guru and the man of disciple. The tantric tradition is actually passed on from the woman to the man. In the tantric practice, it is the woman who initiates. It is only by her power that the act of maithuna takes place. All the preliminaries are done by her. She puts the mark on the man's forehead and tells him where to meditate. In ordinary interaction the man takes the aggressive role and the woman participates, but in tantra they switch roles. The woman becomes the operator and the man her medium. She has to be able to arouse him. Then, at the right moment, she must create the bindu so he can practise vajroli. If the man loses his bindu, it means that the woman has failed to carry out her functions properly.

In tantra it is said that Shiva is incapable without Shakti. Shakti is the priestess. Therefore, when vama marga is practised, the man must have an absolutely tantric attitude towards the woman. He cannot behave with her as men generally do with other women. Ordinarily, when a man looks at a woman he becomes passionate, but during maithuna he should not. He should see her as the divine mother, Devi, and approach her with an attitude of devotion and surrender, not with lust.

According to the tantric concept, women are more endowed with spiritual qualities and it would be wise if they were allowed to assume higher positions in social affairs.

Then there would be greater beauty, compassion, love and understanding in all spheres of life. What we are discussing here is not patriarchal society versus matriarchal society, but tantra, particularly left hand tantra.

Path of yogis not bhogis

In tantra, the practice of maithuna is said to be the easiest way to awaken sushumna because it involves an act which most people are already accustomed to. However, frankly speaking, very few are prepared for this path. Ordinary sexual interaction is not maithuna. The physical act may be the same, but the background is totally different.

In the relationship between husband and wife, for example, there is dependency and ownership, but in tantra each partner is independent. Another difficult thing in tantric sadhana is cultivating the attitude of passionlessness. One has to virtually become brahmacharya so as to free the mind and emotions of the sexual thoughts and passions which normally arise.

Both partners must be absolutely purified and controlled internally and externally before they practise maithuna. This is hard for the ordinary person to comprehend because for most people, sexual interaction is the result of passion and physical or emotional attraction, either for progeny or pleasure. It is only when you are purified that these instinctive urges are absent. According to tradition, this is why the path of dakshina marga must be followed for many years before the path of vama marga can be entered. Then the interaction of maithuna does not take place for physical gratification. The purpose is very clear – awakening of sushumna, raising the kundalini energy from mooladhara chakra, and exploding the unconscious areas of the brain.

If this is not clear when you practise the kriyas, and sushumna becomes active, you will not be able to face the awakening. You will not be able to control the passion and excitement because you have not tranquillized your brain. Therefore, in my opinion, only those who are adepts in yoga

108

qualify for vama marga. This path is not to be used indiscriminately as a pretext for self-indulgence. It is meant for mature and serious-minded householder sadhakas, who are evolved, who have been practising sadhana to awaken the energy potential and to attain samadhi. They must utilize this path as a vehicle of awakening otherwise it becomes a path of downfall.

The Chakras

15

Introduction to the Chakras

The subject of chakras is not going to be an easy one. Many scientists and philosophers are confronted with a great difficulty when it comes to accepting and explaining the existence of the chakras. They do not know whether the chakras are to be found in the physical body or in the subtle body. If they exist in the physical body, where are they? And, of course, the subtle body is not the subject of modern anatomical science.

In the past, doctors and scientists used to ask me, "Why, when we have witnessed many operations, have we never seen the chakras?" At the time, the only reply I could give them was, "Can you show me the sound waves in a transistor radio? I have opened up radios but I have never found the BBC there." This reply answered their questions, but it did not really satisfy them. Scientists want a scientific explanation and, for this, new areas of research are being developed.

An eminent Japanese scientist, Dr Hiroshi Motoyama, has invented sensitive machines for measuring the vital energy of the body. One apparatus measures the functioning of the nadis and their corresponding body organs, and this machine is now being used in some Japanese hospitals to diagnose disease tendencies before they actually manifest. Another invention is 'the chakra machine', which records the impulses that emanate from the psychic centres in the spinal cord. On this machine it is possible to register definite impulses from these areas in individuals who have been practising yoga for many years, and who have awakened their psychic faculties. For example, when a subject practises pranayama with kumbhaka and maha bandha – contraction of the perineum, abdomen and thyroid, the machine registers changes in the impulses emanating from the psychic centres. This research shows that energy is definitely activated by the yoga practices. However we still have a lot of research to do in order to provide more scientific explanations.

There are many different interpretations of the science of chakras. Of course, the differences are not that great, but they are there. The thinkers of Theosophical movements and their predecessors have their own interpretations of the chakras, their location points, their colours, and so on. The Rosicrucians and others may say something completely different and the tantric texts may also present entirely different concepts.

Chakra perception

The chakras, kundalini and the mind have subtle aspects on all levels of vibration. This is extremely complicated and most of the realization at these levels must be very personal. Even then, different people see these occult aspects from different points of view. For instance, if they have realizations about the chakras, these will be coloured by their own personal tendencies. Some concentrate on their more subtle mystical aspects, some on their energy and pranic manifestations, some on their functional reality, some on their psychological effects, and still others on their physical concomitants. These are usually all correct and when various authorities get together, they find that they are talking about the same things but from different points of view. If we look at a person through binoculars, he looks large. If we look at him with ordinary vision, he looks the usual size. If we view him through an X-ray screen, we see his skeleton, and if we look through a gastroscope, we see the inside of his stomach. Same person – different viewpoints.

In the same way, whereas a mystic or yogi will describe the chakras in a spiritual or symbolic way, the surgeon may describe the chakras as bunches of nerve fibres making up what he calls the plexuses, and a clairvoyant will describe the energy manifestations of the chakras in yet a different way. These people may have disagreements, but actually they are seeing the same thing from different viewpoints. Discrepancies are largely semantic due to differing cultural, educational and personal understandings. This is a common problem amongst people when they try to communicate any idea or experience in words.

Whereas I have great respect for the tantric concept, I have my own experience and, therefore, in my description of the chakras I will make references to both. However, rather than trying to understand the chakras through the written or verbal description of others, you must experience them for yourself and gain your own personal knowledge. Tantra is essentially a practical science rather than an intellectual one and only practise leads to true experience and real understanding.

Chakra symbology

If you are practising kundalini or kriya yoga, you will need to know the different colours and symbols of the chakras. They are very beautiful and form an intrinsic part of the awakening of the individual chakras. Each chakra has a particular colour, mantra, situation and range of experiences.

Whereas the various esoteric cults and spiritual systems use different symbols to represent the chakras, in tantra and yoga the chakras are symbolized by lotus flowers. As a symbol, the lotus is very significant. Man must pass through three clear stages in spiritual life, which represent his existence on three different levels: ignorance, aspiration and endeavour, and illumination. The lotus also exists on three different levels – mud, water and air. It sprouts in the mud (ignorance), grows up through the water in an effort to reach the surface (endeavour and aspiration) and eventually

115

reaches the air and the direct light of the sun (illumination). Thus the lotus symbolizes man's growth from the lowest states of awareness to the higher states of consciousness. The culmination of the growth of the lotus is a beautiful flower. In the same way, the culmination of man's spiritual quest is the awakening and blossoming of human potential.

So each of the principal chakras can be visualized as a lotus flower with a specific colour and number of petals:
1. *Mooladhara* – four-petalled deep red lotus
2. *Swadhisthana* – six-petalled vermilion lotus
3. *Manipura* – ten-petalled bright yellow lotus
4. *Anahata*   – twelve-petalled blue lotus
5. *Vishuddhi* – sixteen-petalled violet lotus
6. *Ajna* – two-petalled silver-grey lotus
7. *Sahasrara* – one thousand-petalled multicoloured or red lotus

In each chakra six aspects are combined:
1. the chakra colour
2. the petals of the lotus flower
3. the yantra or geometrical shape
4. the beeja mantra
5. the animal symbol
6. the higher or divine beings.

The animals represent your previous evolution and instincts, and the divine beings represent higher consciousness.

In my exposition of the chakras I may say a chakra is a particular colour, but if you are a good yogic aspirant and in your concentration on that chakra you realize another colour, that is the truth for you. Your experiences are just as valid as mine, but one thing is definite: as you move up through the chakras, the frequencies of the colours become more subtle and more powerful.

Chakra kshetram

In many of the practices of kundalini yoga we must concentrate or focus our awareness on the chakra trigger points in the spinal cord. However, many people find it easier to concentrate on the chakra kshetram located on the front surface of the body. In kriya yoga particularly, the chakra kshetrams are utilized in many of the practices. The kshetrams can be regarded as reflections of the original chakra trigger points, and when we concentrate on them it creates a sensation which passes through the nerves to the chakra itself and then travels up to the brain.

Mooladhara does not have a kshetram, but swadhisthana, manipura, anahata, vishuddhi and ajna have physical counterparts directly in front of them on the same horizontal plane. Swadhisthana kshetram is at the level of the pubic bone in the front of the body, just above the genital organ. Manipura kshetram is at the navel, anahata kshetram is at the heart, and vishuddhi kshetram is located on the front surface of the throat pit, in the vicinity of the thyroid gland. Ajna kshetram is bhrumadhya, the mid-eyebrow centre.

The granthis

There are three *granthis* (psychic knots) in the physical body which are obstacles on the path of the awakened kundalini. The granthis are called *brahma, vishnu* and *rudra*, and they represent levels of awareness where the power of *maya*, ignorance and attachment to material things is especially strong. Each aspirant must transcend these barriers to make a clear passageway for the ascending kundalini.

Brahma granthi functions in the region of mooladhara chakra. It implies attachment to physical pleasures, material objects and excessive selfishness. It also implies the ensnaring power of tamas – negativity, lethargy and ignorance.

Vishnu granthi operates in the region of anahata chakra. It is associated with the bondage of emotional attachment and attachment to people and inner psychic visions. It is connected with rajas – the tendency towards passion, ambition and assertiveness.

Rudra granthi functions in the region of ajna chakra. It is associated with attachment to siddhis, psychic phenomena and the concept of ourselves as individuals. One must

117

surrender the sense of individual ego and transcend duality to make further spiritual progress.

Conversion centres

Besides functioning as control centres, the chakras work as centres of interchange between the physical, astral and causal dimensions. For instance, through the chakras, subtle energy from the astral and causal dimension can be transformed into energy for the physical dimension. This can be seen in yogis who have been buried underground for long periods of time. Through activation of vishuddhi chakra, which controls hunger and thirst and enables one to subsist on subtle energy in the form of amrit or nectar, they have been able to maintain their existence.

It is further contemplated that physical energy can be transformed into subtle energy through the action of the chakras and that physical energy can be converted into mental energy within the physical dimension.

Thus the chakras are seen to be intermediaries for energy transfer and conversion between two neighbouring dimensions of being as well as facilitating the energy conversion between the body and mind. As the chakras are activated and awakened, man not only becomes aware of the higher realms of existence, but also gains the power to enter those realms and then, in turn, to support and give life to the lower dimensions.

16

Evolution through the Chakras

All life is evolving and man is no exception. Human evolution, the evolution which we are undergoing relentlessly, both as individuals and as a race, is a journey through the different chakras. Mooladhara is the most basic, fundamental chakra from where we commence our evolution, and sahasrara is where our evolution is completed. As we evolve towards sahasrara, outer experiences come our way in life, and inner experiences come to us in meditation, as different capacities and centres awaken progressively within the nervous system. This occurs as energy flows at higher voltages and rates of vibration through the different nadis in the psychic body.

Mooladhara is the first centre in human incarnation, but it is the highest chakra that animals have the capacity to awaken. It is their sahasrara. The higher chakras beyond mooladhara are not present in the psychic physiology of animals and their nervous systems reflect this relative deficiency.

Below mooladhara there are other chakras, known as patalas, which represent the evolution of the animal kingdom. These chakras are only related to sense consciousness and not to mental awareness. When your consciousness was evolving through these chakras your mind was only associated with sense consciousness. There was no individual awareness and no ego; it began from mooladhara. These lower centres are no longer functioning in human beings because we have transcended them.

In the animal body, these inferior chakras are situated in the legs, and so are the nadis. The nadis flow to their confluence point at mooladhara chakra, just as the nadis in the human body flow to ajna chakra. The names of the lower chakras are *atala, vitala, sutala, talatala, rasatala, mahatala* and the lowest is *patala*. Just as mooladhara is the lowest chakra in the human body, patala is the lowest in the animal kingdom. It is the dimension which represents total darkness, where nature is not functioning and matter is completely dormant and static.

Above sahasrara there are also other chakras, or we can call them *lokas*, which represent the higher divine consciousness. So mooladhara chakra is the highest in animal evolution and the first in human evolution. Sahasrara is the highest point in human evolution and the first step in the highest divine evolution.

As you read more about the chakras, you will come to realize that kundalini actually controls every affair of life. When this shakti was passing through the animal stages of our evolution, it was influencing the whole species with *avidya* or ignorance. On account of its influence, the animal kingdom was compelled to follow the instinctual path of eating, sleeping, fearing and mating. This represented the tamasic phase of evolution. From mooladhara onward we pass through the rajasic phase and from sahasrara onward we enter the sattwic phase of evolution.

Spontaneous and self-propelled evolution

Up to mooladhara chakra evolution takes place automatically. Animals do not have to practise pranayama and japa yoga. They do not have to find a guru, take sannyasa and become disciples. They do not have to do anything and they can eat whatever they want. Nature controls them completely. Because they do not think, nature is benevolently responsible for every phase of their evolution.

However, once kundalini reaches mooladhara chakra, evolution is no longer spontaneous because a human being is not completely subject to the laws of nature. For example, animals will only mate in particular seasons. At other times, even if they live together, they will not mate. But, because man is free from the laws of nature, he can mate whenever he chooses.

Man has awareness of time and space, and he has an ego. He can think, he can know that he is thinking and he can know that he knows that he is thinking. This is due to the evolution of ego. If there is no ego, there will be no double awareness. Animals do not have double awareness. If a dog is chasing another dog, it is under nature's compulsion. It does not know that it is running. It runs because instinct compels it to.

So, man has a higher consciousness, and once he has it he has to work towards its evolution. That is why it is said that kundalini is sleeping in mooladhara chakra. It cannot progress beyond this point unless it is pushed.

Discovering your point of evolution

Of course, when the shakti awakens suddenly in mooladhara, it cannot rise immediately. It may wake up and sleep again many times. In the morning you usually have to wake your children several times because they keep going back to sleep. Kundalini behaves in the same way. Sometimes it even ascends to swadhisthana or manipura, only to return to mooladhara again to sleep. However, once the shakti goes beyond manipura chakra there is no going back. Stagnation in a chakra only occurs when there is an obstruction in sushumna or one of the chakras. Kundalini can remain in one chakra for many years, or even for a whole lifetime.

Sometimes, when kundalini gets blocked in a chakra during transit, you begin to exhibit some of the siddhis or psychic powers associated with that chakra. At that time you may not have self-control and understanding of the fact that you are only on the road. When one attains siddhis one is tempted to display them. One may think one is using them for the good of humanity, but this only feeds the ego and clouds one in a thick veil of maya or ignorance, hindering further progress.

If one is manifesting siddhis, one can assume that one has evolved to the chakra which is associated with those siddhis. However, siddhis do not usually manifest when kundalini passes through all the chakras quickly and, if they do, they will not stay long. For a few days you may be able to read the thoughts of others, but then that ability will pass away. For a few days you may be able to heal people, but that will also pass. Psychic powers usually only linger when kundalini gets blocked in a chakra.

Of course, some of our lower chakras may already be functioning without our knowledge. We are all at different levels on the scale of evolution and, therefore, it may not be necessary to start the process of awakening from mooladhara. We say that kundalini is in mooladhara in order to explain the whole concept, but due to your progress in previous lives, or the sadhana your mother or father may have done, you might have been born with your kundalini in manipura. If that is the case, the ascension must take place from that point. However, as you cannot remember your previous life, similarly you have also forgotten about the state of your kundalini. That is why the gurus teach that kundalini is sleeping in mooladhara. It may be in anahata, but I will always tell you it is in mooladhara and make you do the practices from mooladhara. You might not have any experience of kundalini there. You may go to swadhisthana and manipura and not have any experiences there either. But the moment you go to anahata you suddenly start having experiences.

So before you commence the practices of kundalini yoga, you should try to find out at which point your ascension will actually start. In order to do this, the best method is to concentrate on mooladhara daily for fifteen to thirty minutes, then swadhisthana for fifteen days, manipura for fifteen days and so on up to sahasrara. You will soon discover your point of evolution.

Some people will find concentration on anahata easiest, so that is likely to be their centre. Others will find ajna chakra very powerful and attractive to them, whereas other people will find it easiest to relate to mooladhara, while the higher chakras seem almost impossible to locate. Ultimately you will be able to decide which is your most sensitive chakra, and you will be ready for the next step, which is awakening.

However, there is one important point to be added. Even if a higher chakra such as anahata has awakened at random, you must try to awaken the lower chakras also. The purpose of awakening kundalini and ascending it through all the chakras is to awaken them and their related parts of the brain. Therefore, in order to awaken the whole brain, all the chakras must be awakened.

Awakening the chakras

Awakening of the chakras is a very important event in human evolution. It should not be misunderstood for mysticism or occultism, because with the awakening of the chakras, our consciousness and our mind undergo changes. These changes have significant relevance and relationship with our day to day life.

Our present state of mind is not capable of handling all the affairs of life. Our love and hatred, our relationships with people, are the consequences of the quality of our present mind. It appears that our sufferings, our agonies and frustrations are not so much due to the circumstances of life, but more to the responses of our mind. Therefore, the purpose of awakening the chakras, sushumna and kundalini should be related to our day to day life

Thousands of people are born with awakened chakras and kundalini, and these people virtually rule the whole world. I am not talking about governing or ruling a country; I am saying that they are superior people in every aspect of life. They are the great thinkers, musicians, artists, builders, scientists, research scholars, inventors, prophets, statesmen, and so on.

There are many children born with awakened chakras and kundalini and as they grow up they show different manifestations. However, our materialistic societies consider these manifestations as abnormal and those who display them are subjected to psychoanalysis and psychological scrutiny and treatment.

It is not regarded as abnormal if you undergo personal conflicts in relation to family or work events, but as your mind and consciousness expand, you become very alert and sensitive to all that is happening in your mind, your family, colleagues, society and country, and you cannot ignore even the tiniest things of life. This is not regarded as normal by ordinary people, but it is a natural consequence that follows awakening of the chakras. One's consciousness becomes very receptive because the frequencies of the mind change.

The manifestation of higher qualities

Every form, sound and colour has a certain frequency. All sounds, colours and forms do not have the same frequency. In the same way, every thought has a frequency, some are of a low frequency and some are of a high frequency. I will give you an example of a high frequency idea.

Once the great scientist Isaac Newton was sitting in a garden and he watched an apple fall from a tree. We may have also seen apples fall from trees and because it does not seem strange to us, we have not given any thought to the process. But Isaac Newton had what we could call philosophic attention. This was a quality of his mind and personality and because of it, when an apple fell before him, he discovered the theory of gravitation.

Why shouldn't you tell lies? Maybe you think there is no harm in it if you can make money, rule a nation or suppress people. The whole contingency depends on the frequency of your consciousness. At a lower frequency of consciousness you will say there is no harm in telling lies, but when the frequency is raised the mind operates at a different level and you cannot really accept that any more. Many people ask the question, "Why shouldn't we kill? After all, when we kill an animal we may be liberating it and enabling it to get a better birth quicker." Our attitudes and way of thinking are a result of the quality of our mind and the particular frequency at which it is functioning.

Once Lord Buddha went hunting with his cousin Deva-datta. Devadatta shot an arrow at a pigeon and it fell, injured by the arrow. Lord Buddha felt the pain of that bird and immediately rushed to remove the arrow. But Devadatta did not feel the pain; he was very pleased with himself because he had struck his target. Buddha's consciousness had attained a higher frequency vibration, as a result of which he was sensitive to the bird's pain and was therefore manifesting compassion.

Therefore, the higher qualities of love, compassion, charity, mercy and so on are the expressions of a mind which is influenced by awakened chakras. This is precisely the reason why so much importance is given to the awakening of anahata chakra. Of course, every chakra is very important and each chakra confers certain abilities, but you will find that all the scriptural texts place great emphasis on the awakening of anahata, ajna and mooladhara chakras. Yogis emphasize ajna and mooladhara chakras and all of mankind gives emphasis to anahata chakra. When anahata is awakened, we have a sublime relationship with God, with our family members and with every being.

When the chakras are awakened, the mind automatically changes. Your values in life also change and the quality of your love and relationships improve immensely, enabling you to balance out the disappointments and frustrations in life. Therefore, you are able to live a little higher than you do now, and your attitude towards yourself and towards this life is much better.

If awakening of the chakras can bring about unbreakable unity in your family, what more do you need? Do you need a happy family or another husband or wife? Frankly, man needs a happy mind and a happy family. It does not matter what he does or what his children are. Does it really matter if there is little to eat? Happiness and inner contentment are above all, and as far as I can see, true contentment can only be gained by a systematic awakening of the chakras.

17

Ajna Chakra

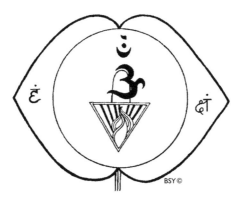

Our reflection on the psychic centres, begins from ajna chakra. According to tradition, mooladhara chakra is generally designated as the first chakra since it is the seat of kundalini shakti. However, there is another system in which consideration and study of the chakras commence from ajna.

Ajna chakra is the point of confluence where the three main nadis or forces – ida, pingala and sushumna, merge into one stream of consciousness and flow up to sahasrara, the crown centre. In mythology, these three nadis are represented by three great rivers – Ganga (ida), Jamuna (pingala) and Saraswati (a subterranean current which represents sushumna). They converge at a place called Prayag or Triveni, which is near present day Allahabad. Indians believe that every twelve years, when the sun is in Aquarius, if one

127

takes a dip at the point of confluence, he or she will be purified. This place of confluence corresponds symbolically to ajna chakra.

When the mind is concentrated at this conjunction, transformation of individual consciousness is brought about by the merging of the three great forces. Individual consciousness is mainly comprised of ego, and it is on account of ego that we are aware of dualities. As long as there is duality, there cannot be samadhi; as long as you remember yourself, you cannot get out of yourself.

Although there are experiences of trance in the other chakras, there is no merger of the individual ego with the cosmic ego. All throughout you find you are trying to assert yourself behind all the experiences you are having, but when ida and pingala unite with sushumna in ajna chakra, you lose yourself completely.

By this I do not mean that you become unconscious. Your awareness expands and becomes homogeneous. The individual awareness falls flat and you completely transcend the realm of duality. Therefore, ajna chakra is a very important centre, which you must experience in order to bring about purification of the mind. Once the mind is purified, the experience and awakening of the other chakras can proceed.

There is a certain problem with the awakening of the other chakras. Each of these chakras contains within it a store of karmas or samskaras, which may be both good and bad, positive and negative, painful and pleasant. The awakening of any chakra will bring to the surface an explosion or an expression of these karmas, and not everybody is prepared or ready to face them. Only those who are equipped with reason and understanding can cope. Therefore, it is said that, before you start awakening and manifesting the great force, it is best to purify the mind at the point of confluence. Then, with a purified mind, you can awaken all the other chakras. Therefore, we begin our exposition of the chakras with ajna.

The centre of command

The word *ajna* comes from the Sanskrit root which means 'to know, to obey or to follow'. Literally, ajna means 'command' or 'the monitoring centre'. In astrology ajna is the centre of Jupiter, which symbolizes the guru or preceptor. Amongst the deities, Jupiter is represented by Brihaspati, the guru of the devas and preceptor of the gods. Therefore, this centre is also known as 'the guru chakra'.

Ajna is the bridge which links the guru with the disciples. It represents the level at which it is possible for direct mind to mind communication to take place between two people. It is in this chakra that communication with the external guru, teacher or preceptor takes place. And it is here that the directions of the inner guru are heard in the deepest state of meditation, when all the sense modalities are withdrawn and one enters the state of *shoonya* or void.

This is a state of absolute nothingness, where the empirical experiences of name and form, subject and object, do not penetrate. In this completely static state, the light of the mind is extinguished; the consciousness ceases to function, and no ego awareness remains. This void state is the same as the death experience, and in order to traverse it the voice or command of the guru must be heard in ajna chakra.

Of course, if you are new to spiritual life you will not be facing this problem yet, but when it comes you will find it very difficult to manage. At the moment your problems are just mental – dispersion of mind, worries, anxiety, restlessness, etc., but when the night is dark and you have gone very deep in meditation, losing your individual awareness, the only thing that can guide you at this point is the instructions or command of your guru heard through ajna chakra.

It has also been called 'the eye of intuition', and it is the doorway through which the individual enters the astral and psychic dimension of consciousness. Perhaps the most common name for this chakra is 'the third eye', and the mystical traditions of every age and culture make abundant references to it. It is portrayed as a psychic eye located midway between the two physical eyes and it looks inward instead of outward.

In India, ajna chakra is called *divya chakshu* (the divine eye), *jnana chakshu* or *jnana netra* (the eye of knowledge) because it is the channel through which the spiritual aspirant receives revelation and insight into the underlying nature of existence. It is also called 'the eye of Shiva', for Shiva is the epitome of meditation, which is directly associated with the awakening of ajna chakra.

It is interesting to note that ajna chakra is more active in females than in males. Women are more sensitive, psychic and perceptive and they are often able to predict coming events. However, in most people this inner eye remains closed, and though they see the events of the outside world, knowledge and understanding of truth cannot be gained. In this sense, we are blind to the real possibilities of the world, unable to view the deeper levels of human existence.

The location point

Ajna chakra is located in the brain, directly behind the eyebrow centre. It is at the very top of the spinal cord, at the medulla oblongata. Initially it is very hard to feel the exact location point of ajna, so we concentrate on ajna kshetram, at the mid-eyebrow centre, bhrumadhya. These two centres are directly connected. That is why it has always been an Indian custom to place tilaka, chandan, sindoor or kumkum on the mid-eyebrow centre. Sindoor contains mercury, and when it is applied to the eyebrow centre, a constant pressure is exerted on the nerve which runs from bhrumadhya to the medulla oblongata. Maybe the original purpose for applying these substances has been forgotten by most people today, but it is not a religious mark or even a beauty spot. It is a means by which you can maintain constant conscious and unconscious awareness of ajna chakra.

It should also be mentioned here that the pineal gland is the physical concomitant of ajna chakra and the pituitary gland of sahasrara. Just as the pituitary and pineal glands are intimately connected, so are ajna and sahasrara. We could say that ajna is the gateway to sahasrara chakra. If ajna is awakened and functioning properly, all the experiences happening in sahasrara can be managed well.

The pineal gland acts as a lock on the pituitary. As long as the pineal gland is healthy, the functions of the pituitary are controlled. However, in most of us, the pineal gland started to degenerate when we reached the age of eight, nine or ten. Then the pituitary began to function and to secrete various hormones which instigated our sexual consciousness, our sensuality and worldly personality. At this time we began to lose touch with our spiritual heritage. However, through various yogic techniques, such as trataka and shambhavi mudra, it is possible to regenerate or maintain the health of the pineal gland.

Traditional symbology

Ajna is symbolized by a two-petalled lotus. According to the scriptures, it is a pale colour, light grey like a rainy day. Some say it is white like the moon, or silver, but actually it is an intangible colour. On the left petal is the letter *ham* हं and on the right *ksham* क्षं. Ham and ksham are inscribed in a silvery white colour and are the beeja mantras for Shiva and Shakti. One represents the moon or ida nadi and the other the sun or pingala nadi. Below the chakra the three nadis merge – ida on the left, pingala on the right and sushumna in between.

Within the lotus is a perfectly round circle which symbolizes shoonya, the void. Within the circle is an inverted triangle which represents shakti – creativity and manifestation. Above the triangle is a black shivalingam. The shivalingam is not, as many people believe, a phallic symbol. It is the symbol of your astral body. According to tantra and occult sciences, the astral body is the attribute of your personality, and in the form of the shivalingam, it can be one of three colours, depending on the purification or evolution of your consciousness.

131

In mooladhara chakra, the shivalingam is smoky and ill-defined. It is known as *dhumra lingam*, and we can compare this with our state of consciousness when we live an instinctive life. We have no real concept of ourselves or what we are. Ajna chakra has a black lingam with a very consolidated outline. It is called the *itarakhya lingam*. Here, in ajna, the awareness of 'what I am' is more sharply defined and various capacities are being awakened. In sahasrara, the consciousness is illumined and therefore the lingam there is luminous. It is called the *jyotir lingam*.

When a person of unevolved mind concentrates, he experiences the shivalingam in the form of a smoky column. It comes and then disperses, comes again and disperses, and so on. With deeper concentration, as the restlessness of the mind is annihilated, the lingam becomes black in colour. By concentrating on that black shivalingam, the jyotir lingam is produced within the illumined astral consciousness. Therefore, the black lingam of ajna chakra is the key to the greater spiritual dimension of life.

Over the shivalingam is the traditional symbol of *Om*, ॐ with its tail on top and the crescent moon and bindu above that. Om is the beeja mantra and symbol of ajna chakra, and above its form can be seen the *raif*, the trace of sound consciousness. Paramshiva is the deity of ajna chakra and he shines like a chain of lightning flashes. The goddess is the pure minded Hakini whose six faces are like so many moons.

Each chakra is considered to possess a *tanmatra* or specific sense of modality, a *jnanendriya* or organ of sense perception, and a *karmendriya* or organ of action. The tanmatra, jnanendriya and karmendriya of ajna chakra are all considered to be the mind. The mind is able to gain knowledge by subtle means, rather than by the input of sense data from the various sense organs, which are the jnanendriyas of the other chakras. The mind perceives knowledge directly via a sixth or intuitive sense, which comes into operation as ajna chakra awakens. This sense is the jnanendriya of the mind. Similarly, the mind can manifest actively without the aid of the physical body. This is the faculty of astral projection, which manifests with the awakening of ajna chakra. Therefore, mind is considered to be the karmendriya of ajna. The mode of operation of this centre is purely mental and so the tanmatra is also the mind. The plane is *tapa loka*, where vestiges of imperfection are purified and the karmas burned away. Along with vishuddhi chakra, ajna forms the basis for *vijnanamaya kosha*, which initiates psychic development.

Often the experience one has when awakening takes place in ajna is similar to that induced by ganja (marijuana) or any other drug of that type. He who meditates on this awakened chakra sees a flaming lamp shining as the morning sun and he dwells within the regions of fire, sun and moon. He is able to enter another's body at will and becomes the most excellent amongst munis, being all-knowing and all-seeing. He becomes the benefactor of all and is versed in all the shastras. He realizes his unity with the Brahman and acquires siddhis. Different results accruing out of meditation on the various centres are collectively realized by meditating on this centre alone.

Ajna and the mind

So, ajna is essentially the chakra of the mind, representing a higher level of awareness. Whenever you concentrate on something, whether it is mooladhara, swadhisthana or manipura chakra, or you concentrate on an external object or an idea, ajna is affected, sometimes mildly, sometimes powerfully, depending on the degree of your concentration. When we visualize or when we dream at night, the inner vision that occurs is through ajna. If you are eating, sleeping or talking and you are not aware of it, then ajna is not operating, but if you are talking and one area of your awareness knows it, this knowing, this awareness is the faculty of ajna.

When you develop ajna, you can have knowledge without the aid of the senses. Normally all knowledge comes to us by means of information the senses conduct to the brain, and a process of classification, logic, and intellect that takes place in the frontal brain. However, the smaller brain, where ajna chakra is situated, has the capacity to acquire knowledge directly without the aid of the indriyas or senses. If it is a very cloudy day, you can know, through logic that it will rain. But if there are no clouds in the sky and still you know beyond a doubt that it will rain, this means your intuition and perception are very acute, and ajna chakra is functioning.

When ajna is awakened, fickleness of the individual mind disperses and the purified *buddhi* (subtle intelligence or higher perception) manifests. Attachment, which is the cause of ignorance and lack of discrimination, drops away, and *sankalpa shakti* (willpower) becomes very strong. Mental resolves fructify almost immediately, provided they are in accordance with individual dharma.

Ajna is the witnessing centre where one becomes the detached observer of all events, including those within the body and mind. Here the level of awareness is developed whereby one begins to 'see' the hidden essence underlying all visible appearances. When ajna is awakened, the meaning and significance of symbols flashes into one's conscious perception and intuitive knowledge arises effortlessly and one becomes a 'seer'.

This is the centre of extrasensory perception where various siddhis manifest according to one's samskaras or mental tendencies. For this reason, ajna chakra is said to resemble a knot directly on top of the spinal cord. According to tantra, this knot is called *rudra granthi*, the knot of Shiva. This knot is symbolic of the aspirant's attachment to the newly developed siddhis which accompany the awakening of ajna. The knot effectively blocks spiritual evolution until attachment to psychic phenomena is overcome and the knot in consciousness is freed.

Understanding cause and effect

Until ajna chakra awakens we are under delusions, we view things incorrectly and we have many great misconceptions about love and attachment, hatred and jealousy, tragedy and comedy, victory and defeat, and many other things. Our fears are unfounded, so are our jealousies and attachments, but still we have them. Our mind is functioning within a limited sphere and we cannot transcend it. Just as we dream at night and our dream experiences are relative, we are also dreaming in our waking state and our experiences are relative. In the same way that we wake from a dream, when ajna awakens, there is also a process of waking up from this present dream we are living, and we can fully understand the relationship between cause and effect.

It is necessary for us to understand the law of cause and effect in relation to our lives, otherwise we are depressed and sorrowful about certain events in life. Supposing you give birth to a child and it dies shortly afterwards. Why did it happen? If a child was meant to die straight after birth, why was it born at all? You can only understand the reason if you understand the laws of cause and effect.

Cause and effect are not immediate events. Each and every action is both a cause and an effect. This life we have is an effect, but what was the cause? You have to discover it, then you can understand the relationship between cause and effect. It is only after awakening of ajna chakra that these laws can be known. Thereafter your whole philosophical attitude and approach to life changes. No events of life affect you adversely, and the various objects and experiences that come into your life and fade out of your life do not disturb you at all. You participate in all the affairs of life and you live fully, but as a detached witness. Life flows like a fast current and you surrender and move with it.

Moving on from ajna to sahasrara

To reach ajna chakra requires sadhana, discipline, firm belief and persistent effort. With our present state of mind it is not possible to know how to reach sahasrara, but once ajna chakra becomes active, you develop superior perception and you realize how sahasrara can be reached. It is like setting out on a journey from Munger to Marine Drive, Bombay. The

135

most important stage of the journey is the long train trip to Bombay. Once you are there, reaching Marine Drive is no problem. It is easy to find the way, you just take a taxi and go there. So, in my opinion, it is not important for us to know how to reach sahasrara from ajna chakra, but it is essential for us to know how to awaken ajna.

18

Mooladhara Chakra

The Sanskrit word *moola* means 'root' or 'foundation' and that is precisely what this chakra is. Mooladhara is at the root of the chakra system and its influences are at the root of our whole existence. The impulses of life rise through the body and flower as the widest expansion of our awareness in the area known as sahasrara. It seems a great paradox that this earthiest and most basic of the chakras guides us to the highest consciousness.

In Samkhya philosophy, the concept of mooladhara is understood as *moola prakriti*, the transcendental basis of physical nature. The whole universe and all its objects must have some basis from which they evolve and to which they return after dissolution. The original source of all evolution is moola prakriti. Mooladhara, as the basis of moola prakriti, is responsible for everything that manifests in the world of name and form.

In tantra, mooladhara is the seat of kundalini shakti, the basis from which the possibility of higher realization arises. This great potential is said to be lying dormant in the form of a coiled serpent. When aroused, it makes its way upward through sushumna nadi in the spinal cord until it reaches sahasrara where the ultimate experience of enlightenment occurs. Therefore, the awakening of mooladhara is considered to be of great importance in kundalini yoga.

The location point

The seat of mooladhara in the male body is located slightly inside the perineum, midway between the scrotum and the anus. It is the inner aspect of that nerve complex which carries all kinds of sensations and is immediately connected with the testes. In the female body, mooladhara chakra lies on the posterior side of the cervix.

In both the male and female bodies, there is a vestigial gland at mooladhara chakra which is something like a knot. In Sanskrit, this is known as *brahma granthi*, the knot of Brahma. As long as this knot remains intact, the energy located in this area is blocked, but the moment the knot is opened, shakti awakens. It is only when the individual awakens to the possibility of divine consciousness, to a greater force and purpose than that of instinctive animal life, that the brahma granthi begins to loosen. Consciousness begins to be liberated from the root centre as the individual's aspiration awakens.

Many people feel hesitant and shy about believing kundalini that is in mooladhara chakra and claim it to be in manipura, because they do not want to associate this holy kundalini shakti with the unholy sexual system. However, scientific investigation shows that this tiny gland in mooladhara chakra contains infinite energy and that many psychic and spiritual experiences originate from mooladhara.

Just because mooladhara is situated in the sexual region, this does not make it an impure centre.

Traditional symbology

Mooladhara chakra is traditionally represented by a lotus flower with four deep crimson petals. On each petal is a letter: *vam* वं, *sham* शं, *sham* षं, *sam* सं, written in gold.

In the pericarp is a yellow square, symbol of the earth element, surrounded by eight golden spears, four at each corner and four at the cardinal points. These spears are said to represent the seven Kula mountains on the base spear of the earth.

The golden yellow square, yantra of the earth element, is supported by an elephant with seven trunks. The elephant is the largest of all land animals and possesses great strength and solidity. These are the attributes of mooladhara, a great, dormant power, resting in a completely stable, solid place. The seven trunks of the elephant denote the seven minerals that are vital to physical functioning; in Sanskrit they are known as *sapta dhatu*. The seven-trunked elephant is the vehicle of the great mind, the great creativity.

Riding on the elephant's back, in the centre of the square, is a deep red inverted triangle. This is the symbol of shakti or creative energy, which is responsible for the productivity and multiplicity of all things. Within the triangle is the swayambhu or dhumra linga, smoky grey in colour. Around this lingam, which represents the astral body, kundalini is coiled three and a half times, her lustre being that of lightning. Three represents the three gunas or qualities of nature in an individual. As long as the three gunas are operating, individuality is functioning within the confinements of ego. The half represents transcendence.

In tantra, this serpent is known as *mahakala*, meaning great or endless time. Here kundalini is lying in the womb of the unconscious, beyond time and space. When kundalini begins to manifest, it enters the dimensions of personality and individuality, and becomes subject to time and space.

That is the awakening of the great serpent power within the individual form, frame and consciousness of man. However, in most people it is dormant. In its awakened state kundalini shakti represents our spiritual potential, but in its dormant state it represents that instinctive level of life which supports our basic existence. Both possibilities lie in mooladhara.

Resting on top of the inverted triangle is the beeja mantra *lam* लं. Inside the bindu, over the mantra, reside the elephant deva Ganesha and the devi Dakini, who has four arms and brilliant red eyes. She is resplendent like the lustre of many suns rising at the same time. She is the carrier of ever pure intelligence.

The tanmatra or sense associated with mooladhara is smell, and it is here that the psychic smells manifest. The jnanendriya or sensory organ is the nose and the karmendriya, organ of activity is the anus. Mooladhara awakening is often accompanied by itchy sensations around the coccyx or anus, and the sense of smell becomes so acute that offensive odours are difficult to bear.

Mooladhara is the direct switch for awakening ajna chakra. It belongs to *bhuloka*, the first plane of mortal existence and it is the chief centre of *apana*. Mooladhara is also the seat of *annamaya kosha*, the body of nourishment, connected with the absorption of food and evacuation of faeces.

By meditating on kundalini in mooladhara chakra, a man becomes lord of speech, a king among men and an adept in all kinds of learning. He becomes ever free from all diseases and he remains cheerful at all times.

Balancing the nadis

Mooladhara is the base from which the three main psychic channels or nadis emerge and flow up the spinal cord. It is said that ida, the mental force, emerges from the left of mooladhara; pingala, the vital force, from the right; and sushumna, the spiritual force, from the centre. According to tantra, this emanation point is highly volatile. When the positive and negative forces of ida and pingala are completely balanced, an awakening is sparked off here which arouses the dormant kundalini. Usually, this state of balance between ida and pingala nadis can only be achieved sporadically and for short durations. This may be sufficient to trigger off a mild awakening, in which kundalini rises as far as swadhisthana or manipura and then drops back to mooladhara again.

Therefore, the hatha yoga practices, particularly those of pranayama, are very important in kundalini yoga, because they purify and rebalance the psychic flows. Once the state of balance between ida and pingala becomes steady and ongoing, the awakening engendered in mooladhara becomes explosive, and kundalini rises with great force, overcoming all obstacles on its path until it reaches its ultimate destination in sahasrara.

Pranotthana versus kundalini

Many people have experiences in meditation when they feel the shakti rising through the spinal cord from mooladhara to the brain. However, in most cases, this is not the awakening of kundalini, but a release of pranic force called pranotthana. This preliminary awakening starts from mooladhara and ascends the spinal cord via pingala nadi, only partially purifying the chakras, until it reaches the brain where it is usually dispersed.

In this type of awakening the experience of shakti is rarely sustained. However, it does prepare the aspirant for the eventual awakening of kundalini, which is something altogether different and more powerful. After the awakening of kundalini, the individual will never be the same again. Here there is an ascent of force accompanied by a psychic awakening which is permanently accessible. Even though it may fall back again, the potential will always be there.

Mooladhara and sexual expression

Awakening of mooladhara chakra is very important, firstly, because it is the seat of kundalini and, secondly, because it is the seat of great tamas. All of the passions are stored in mooladhara, all the guilt, every complex and every agony has its root here.

This chakra is physiologically related to the excretory, urinary, sexual and reproductive organs. It is very important for everybody to awaken this chakra and get out of it. Our life, desires, actions and accomplishments are controlled by the sexual desires, and whatever we do in life is an expression of that lower chakra. Our lower samskaras and karmas are embedded there and, as in lower incarnations, our whole being is founded on the sexual personality. Dr Sigmund Freud has also emphasized this point. He said that our selection of clothing, food, friends, home furnishings, decor, etc., are influenced by our sexual awareness.

All the schizophrenics, neurotics and crazy people who are ridden with guilt and complexes are people who have not been able to get the shakti out of mooladhara chakra. As a result their lives are imbalanced.

Sexual fulfilment and sexual frustrations control our life. If sexual urges are removed from life, everything will change. Often we react to sexual life on account of bitter experiences and we vow not to follow the same path again. We are fed up and on account of that we say, "No more." But this is no solution, it is only a reaction and not the permanent structure of our mind.

Unless mooladhara chakra is purified, its corresponding centre in the brain will always remain tamasic. We can live the same type of life as we do today, but we can make it much better. Sexual relationships are not a sin, but the conscious-ness must awaken and the purpose of the whole act must be transmuted. It is clearly stated in tantra that the purpose of the sexual act is threefold, and these threefold purposes depend on the level and frequency of one's mind. Some people practise it for procreation, others for pleasure only, because that is the level of their mind. Some practise it to open the window to samadhi. They do not care for procrea-tion or the fulfilment of passion; they are only concerned with awakening an experience and sublimating it.

Through that experience they open the higher centres. So those who practise the normal sexual act must awaken mooladhara chakra first. Also, through the sexual act, a female can awaken mooladhara and swadhisthana chakras if her partner is a yogi. Generally for these chakras to awaken in a man's body, he will have to practise kriya yoga and techniques such as vajroli.

There is another important thing we should all understand. A person who has controlled his lower impulses, a yogi who is practising higher sadhana, does not have to give up his or her partner and the marital relationship. If you think that to be a yogi you must give up sex, why don't you also give up eating and sleeping? Yoga has nothing to do with giving up these things; it is only concerned with transforming their purpose and meaning.

The greatest mistake mankind has been making for thousands of years is that man has been fighting with himself. He wants to renounce sex but he has not been able to do it. Therefore, it is important that mooladhara awakening takes place. Then you can make your mind totally free.

Managing mooladhara awakening

When awakening takes place in mooladhara as the result of yoga practice or other spiritual disciplines, many things explode into conscious awareness in the same way that an erupting volcano pushes to the surface things that were hidden beneath the earth. With the awakening of kundalini, there is simultaneous awakening of things from the unconscious field of human existence which one may not have had prior conscious knowledge of whatsoever.

When mooladhara awakens, a number of phenomena occur. The first thing many practitioners experience is levitation of the astral body. One has the sensation of floating upward in space, leaving the physical body behind. This is due to the energy of kundalini whose ascending momentum causes the astral body to disassociate from the physical and move upward. This phenomenon is limited to the astral and

143

possibly mental dimensions, and this differs from what is normally called levitation – the actual displacement of the physical body.

Besides astral levitation, one sometimes experiences psychic phenomena such as clairvoyance or clairaudience. Other common manifestations include movements or increasing warmth in the area of the coccyx, or a creeping sensation, like something moving slowly up the spinal cord. These sensations result from the ascension of shakti or the awakened kundalini.

In most cases, when the shakti reaches manipura chakra, it begins to descend to mooladhara again. Sometimes the practitioner feels that the energy ascends to the top of the head, but usually only a very small portion of the shakti is able to pass beyond manipura. Repeated earnest attempts are necessary for the further ascension of kundalini, but once kundalini passes manipura chakra, serious obstacles are rarely encountered.

However, when kundalini is ascending from mooladhara to swadhisthana, the sadhaka experiences a crucial period in which all his repressed emotions, especially those of a more primal nature, express themselves. Passions mount during this period and all kinds of infatuations ensue, making the sadhaka extremely irritable and unstable at times. He can be seen sitting quietly in contemplation one moment and hurling objects at someone the next. One day he may sleep deeply for hours together, another day he may get up at one or two in the morning to take a bath and meditate. He becomes very passionate, loud and talkative, while at other times he is silent. At this stage the sadhaka often expresses a great fondness for singing.

During this period of intense psychic and emotional upheaval, the guidance of a qualified and understanding guru is essential. Although some people may regard this emotional turmoil as the indication of a great fall, the guru will assure each and every aspirant that it is an essential part of spiritual life which will accelerate their evolution. If this explosion does not take place, the same purging process will still occur, but very slowly, as problems arise and work themselves out life after life.

Mooladhara is one of the most important and exciting, but also disturbing of the psychic centres which are awakened through the practices of kundalini yoga. For this reason, the awakening of ajna chakra should always accompany mooladhara awakening. The mental faculties of ajna chakra give the practitioner an ability to witness the events of mooladhara awakening objectively, with greater understanding. This makes the whole experience less disturbing and traumatic.

When ajna is awakened, you will find that mooladhara is the easiest of chakras to awaken. The gross mind can concentrate on this centre and manipulate it with ease. As your body and mind begin to break their animal bonds, your awareness expands and you are able to envision the greater possibility of your creative potential.

19

Swadhisthana Chakra

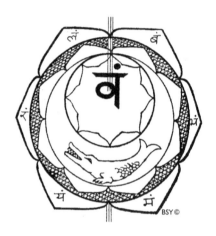

The Sanskrit word *swa* means 'one's own' and *adhisthana* means 'dwelling place or residence'. Although mooladhara occupies a very important place in the scheme of the chakras, swadhisthana, which is located very near to mooladhara, is also involved in and responsible for the awakening of kundalini shakti in mooladhara. In fact, it is said that previously the seat of kundalini was in swadhisthana, but there was a fall and subsequently mahakundalini came to rest in mooladhara.

The location point

Swadhisthana corresponds to the reproductive and urinary systems in the gross body and is physiologically related to the prostatic or utero-vaginal plexus of nerves. The location of

146

swadhisthana is at the base of the spinal column, at the level of the coccyx or tailbone. This is a small bony bulb which can be felt just above the anus. It is anatomically very close to mooladhara chakra in both the male and female bodies. Swadhisthana kshetram is in the front of the body at the level of the pubic bone.

Traditional symbology

Swadhisthana chakra can be experienced as black in colour, as it is the seat of primary ignorance. However, traditionally it is depicted as a six-petalled vermilion or orange-red lotus. On each petal there is a letter: *bam* बं, *bham* भं, *mam* मं, *yam* यं, *ram* रं, and *lam* लं, written in the colour of lightning.

The element of this chakra is water, symbolized by a white crescent moon within the pericarp of the lotus. The crescent moon is formed by two circles which engender two further yantras. The larger has outward turned petals and represents the conscious dimension of existence. On the inside of the crescent moon is a similar petalled but smaller circle with petals facing inwards. This is the unconscious dimension, the store of formless karma. These two yantras are separated by the white crocodile in the crescent moon. The crocodile is the vehicle which carries the whole phantom of unconscious life. It symbolizes the subterranean movement of the karmas. Seated on the crocodile is the beeja mantra *vam* वं, stainless and white.

Within the bindu of the mantra reside the deva Vishnu and the devi Rakini. Vishnu has four arms, his body is a luminous blue colour, he is clothed in yellow raiment and he is beautiful to behold. Rakini is the colour of a blue lotus and she is clothed in celestial raiment and ornaments. In her uplifted arms she holds various weapons and her mind is exalted from drinking nectar. She is the goddess of the vegetable kingdom and, as swadhisthana chakra is closely related to the vegetable world, the observance of a vegetarian diet is said to be an important practice for the awakening of this chakra.

147

The loka for swadhisthana is *bhuvar*, the intermediate plane of spiritual awareness. The tanmatra or sense connected with this chakra is taste. The jnanendriyas or senses of knowledge are the tongue. The karmendriya or sense of action is the sexual organs, kidneys and urinary system. The chief vayu of swadhisthana is *apana*, which courses throughout the body, and swadhisthana and manipura are the seat of *pranamaya kosha*.

It is said that he who meditates on kundalini in swadhisthana chakra is immediately freed from his internal enemies: lust, anger, greed, etc. His nectar-like words flow in prose and verse and in well-reasoned discourse. He becomes like the sun, illumining the darkness of ignorance.

Home of the unconscious

Swadhisthana is regarded as the substratum or basis of individual human existence. Its counterpart in the brain is the unconscious mind and it is the storehouse of mental impressions or samskaras. It is said that all the karmas, the past lives, the previous experiences, the greater dimension of the human personality that is unconscious, can be symbolized by swadhisthana chakra. Individual being takes root in the unconscious mind, and the many instinctive drives that are felt at the level of this chakra bubble up from the depths of the unconscious.

In tantra there is the concept of the animal, and the master of the animal. In Sanskrit, *pashu* means animal and *pati* means master. *Pashupati* is the master or controller of all the animal instincts. This is one of the names of Lord Shiva, and it is also one of the attributes of swadhisthana chakra. According to mythology, Pashupati is the total unconscious. It has absolute control over mooladhara chakra and the animal propensities during the first milestone of human evolution.

The unconscious principle of swadhisthana should never be considered as an inactive or dormant process. Rather it is a far more dynamic and powerful process than the normal consciousness. When the shakti enters swadhisthana chakra there is an overwhelming experience of this unconscious state. It is different from mooladhara, which is the manifest expression of that unconscious. In mooladhara, the karmas of the lower stages of our evolution are manifested in the form of anger, greed, jealousy, passion, love, hatred and so on. There we work out that karma, manifesting and expressing it overtly. At the level of swadhisthana, however, there is no conscious activity or manifestation. This is hiranyagarbha, the universal womb, where everything exists in a potential state. The *Rig Veda* says: "In the beginning of creation there was hiranyagarbha, then came all the living beings, all the beings that exist, and He was the protector of all."

In the collective unconscious, the samskaras and the karmas exist in a seed state. For example, yesterday you may have had a pleasant or a painful experience. That experience has become a subconscious process or force which is acting on and colouring your conscious awareness today. There are many experiences like this from the past which we do not consciously recall, but nevertheless they are playing a part in determining our daily behaviour, attitudes and reactions. There are many karmas influencing us in this way, but we remain completely unaware of them.

According to tantra, each and every perception, experience and association is recorded. If you have a quarrel or bitter exchange, that is a very strong registration. However, if you happen to pass someone on the path, look at him and walk on, this is also registered. Many things come within your range of association, and they are all automatically registered. They are not analyzed, but simply filed away in some layer of the mind. All those insignificant and unimpressive karmas, which have been registered automatically in our consciousness, form the total unconscious.

In kundalini yoga, swadhisthana is often regarded as a hindrance in the sense that these karmas lying embedded in the unconscious do not allow the rising kundalini to pass through. After the initial awakening, kundalini returns to dormancy time and time again, solely due to the karmic block at swadhisthana. These karmas are beyond the range of analysis. They have practically no form but they are a great force. To give a crude analogy, suppose there is a big water tank into which you drop all kinds of things. If you were to empty the tank five years later and examine the contents, you would no longer find those same objects which you put in. The matter would still be there but its form would have changed. The collective karma of the unconscious exists in swadhisthana as a form or force somewhat like the matter in this tank.

Therefore, the awakening of swadhisthana presents many difficulties for the sadhaka. When the explosion takes place and swadhisthana begins to erupt, the aspirant is often confused and disturbed by the activation of all this unconscious material. It is absolutely impossible for one to understand these impressions, which are attributed to a disturbed mental condition.

Although the sadhaka may be duly apprehensive about entering this stage of awakening, it is absolutely necessary for his spiritual evolution. Provided he has a competent guru or spiritual guide who knows how to avoid all the pitfalls of this area, swadhisthana can be traversed safely and without any problems.

Swadhisthana and purgatory

When kundalini is residing in swadhisthana chakra, the last vestige of karma is being thrown out and all the negative samskaras express themselves and are expelled. At this time you may be angry, afraid or full of sexual fantasies and passion. You may also experience lethargy, indolence, depression and all kinds of tamasic characteristics. The tendency to procrastinate is very strong and you just want to sleep and sleep. This stage of evolution is known as purgatory, and if you read the lives of many of the great saints, you will find that most of them encountered great turmoil and temptations when they were passing through this stage.

When Lord Buddha was sitting beneath the bodhi tree waiting for enlightenment, he was visited by Mara. Mara is a demonical mythological force, the same force which the Bible refers to as Satan. Just as Satan is a tempter, so Mara is a temptress. This demonical force is not external; it is an internal force which can be found in everybody. It is situated at a very great depth of our personality and is capable of creating illusion. In the Buddhist tradition Mara is represented by a big snake, a grotesque looking person with big teeth and a horrible face, or as beautiful naked women hovering around waiting to embrace an aspirant who is involved in his sadhana. These are all mythological symbols no doubt, but they are realities.

Only those who are fearless and of strong willpower can survive through the temptation. Every great person and every saint has had to undergo this peculiar experience, which is like the ultimate explosion of the seed of life. It seems that the seed of man's cycle of birth and rebirth is situated in swadhisthana chakra. Although most people confront difficulties when they are moving through the terrain of swadhisthana, if one has the grace of guru, indomitable and invincible willpower, has been sincere and not hypocritical in one's spiritual pursuits, is very clear about one's goal and understands what these experiences of purgatory are, then one can face these difficulties properly and overcome them.

If one fluctuates even slightly, kundalini will return to mooladhara and the real awakening will be more difficult. Therefore, in the first stages of sadhana and awakening, one must have a supreme kind of vairagya (detachment). It should not be intellectual vairagya, but the outcome of a thorough analysis of the situations of life. Where is the end to the pleasures of life? Can you ever satisfy your desires? Even when you reach the age of eighty or ninety and your body can no longer enjoy pleasures, the mind still dwells on them constantly. You can leave all the sensual pleasures, but the taste will remain in the mind.

If the sadhaka understands this truth, that desires can never be satisfied in one lifetime, or even in thousands of lifetimes, then kundalini can pass through swadhisthana safely and relatively fast, and make its way to manipura chakra. Without this understanding, swadhisthana becomes like an impenetrable iron curtain and perhaps only one in thousands can transcend it. Many people awaken kundalini quite easily, but passing the swadhisthana border is another thing; you cannot get through without a visa.

The sexual crisis

I remember reading a book written by a well-known swami* who had experienced difficulties getting through swadhisthana. He wrote that he was sitting all night and nothing but sex and sensual thoughts came to his mind. He dreamed of many women presenting themselves in their naked form, and his whole body was becoming hot and cold, hot and cold. Ultimately he got a headache, and at one point, he thought that my heart would collapse.

Throughout the crisis, his guru's face used to come like a glimpse. The guru's face was stern and expressionless and that used to bring his temperature back to normal. However, this confrontation with the powerful side of his mind continued until morning. At last, when morning came he breathed a sigh of relief. But then, when he sat for meditation in the evening he had mixed feelings – there was fear in his mind and confidence as well.

Day in and day out the mind played its tricks on him. Then one night Parvati came to him. Parvati is the shakti of Lord Shiva, and she is the Divine Mother. He knew she was Parvati, but because she looked so beautiful and she was wearing almost transparent clothing, he began to desire her. Rather than remembering that she was the Divine Mother, his mind was more aware of the form behind the transparent apparel.

*Swami Muktananda, *Chitshakti Vilas*, 1971, SYDA, South Fallsburg, New York.

Like a flash of lightning the guru showed his face and he regained his senses and prayed, "Mother, withdraw your maya. I can't face these experiences. You are the giver of liberation and you are the creator of illusion. You have the power to cast me back into the cycle of birth and rebirth and you have the power to lift me from this quagmire of ignorance."

As he prayed, tears rolled down his face and he felt a cool breeze passing through the interior of his body. The whole panorama vanished and he understood that kundalini had passed through swadhisthana and was now heading towards manipura.

Transforming the primal energy

When no sexual desires of any kind manifest in an aspirant any more, and when there is no more personal attraction, that means kundalini has passed beyond swadhisthana chakra. However, when you are dealing with the subject of sex, your understanding must be very thorough. Although you may not have any sexual awareness at the moment, that does not mean your desires have been exterminated. They might be in a suppressed state. There is an automatic process of suppression in the human constitution, and that is inherent in our own mental being.

Indian rishis have stated that sexual awareness and desires can manifest at any stage of evolution. They are very acute and clearly expressed when one is in swadhisthana and having continual fantasies, but sexual awareness never really dies because it is fuelled by the primal energy which is present all throughout. Sex is only an expression of that, and therefore it can manifest at any stage, and one should never think that one has transcended it. It is even present when one is in the highest state of consciousness. The only difference is that in swadhisthana it is in a very disturbed state, whereas in the higher centres of evolution it is in a seed form. After all, what is bhakti or devotion; what is union? They are the sublimated pure form of sexual energy.

153

Energy at different levels is known by different names. At the highest level it is called spiritual experience. On the emotional level it is known as love. On the physical level it is known as sex, and at the lowest level it is known as avidya or ignorance. So therefore, when you talk about sex, you must understand that it is only a particular formation of energy. Just as curd, butter and cheese are different formations of the one thing – milk, energy has different manifestations. Matter is the grossest manifestation of energy; in the ultimate state, matter is energy. Therefore, energy and matter are intra-convertible. A thought is an object and an object is a thought. This body is consciousness and consciousness has become this body. In the same way that you understand this, you have to reanalyze and redefine sexual awareness.

The rishis say that the same energy which flows through passion, when channelled, manifests as devotion. Channel this same energy again and it manifests as spiritual experience. That is why spiritual aspirants love God in various manifestations. Some picture him as a father, a mother, a child, a friend, husband or lover. In this way, they can sublimate the form of their emotional energy and even transform the primal energy into a divine experience.

Psychic propensities of swadhisthana

At a higher level swadhisthana acts as the switch for bindu. This is the point where primal sound originates. Any awakening in swadhisthana is simultaneously carried up to bindu, where it is experienced in the form of the sound body, which is an important psychic attribute of this chakra.

According to the tantric texts, there are many other psychic propensities gained through the awakening of swadhisthana chakra. These include: loss of fear of water, dawning of intuitive knowledge, awareness of astral entities, and the ability to taste anything desired for oneself or others.

It must be remembered that up to swadhisthana, the consciousness is not yet purified. Due to ignorance and confusion, the psychic powers awakened at this level are often accompanied by the maleficent mental attributes. What happens here when the aspirant tries to manifest or express himself through the psychic medium is that more often than not it becomes a vehicle for personal and lower tendencies, rather than for the divine.

The sum and substance is this – awakening of kundalini is not a difficult task, but to get beyond swadhisthana is. For that, you must improve the general background of your psycho-emotional life. Once you pass swadhisthana you will not have to face any explosive traumas again, but there will be other difficulties further on. Kundalini is unlikely to descend again as it is destined to move on, but the problems you will confront will be concerned with siddhis, and they are more difficult to subdue.

20

Manipura Chakra

Manipura is derived from two Sanskrit words: *mani* meaning 'jewel' and *pura* meaning 'city'. Therefore, manipura literally means 'city of jewels'. In the Tibetan tradition, this chakra is known as *mani padma*, which means 'jewelled lotus'.

Manipura is a very important centre as far as the awakening of kundalini shakti is concerned. It is the centre of dynamism, energy, willpower and achievement and it is often compared to the dazzling heat and power of the sun, without which life on earth would not exist. In the same way that the sun continually radiates energy to the planets, manipura chakra radiates and distributes pranic energy throughout the entire human framework, regulating and energizing the various activities of organs, systems and processes of life.

When deficient, it is more like the glowing embers of a dying fire rather than a powerful intense blaze. In this state the individual is rendered lifeless, vitality deficient and devoid of energy. He will be hindered by poor health, depression and lack of motivation and commitment in life. Therefore, the awakening of manipura is an important precedent, not only for the sadhaka, but for anyone who wishes to enjoy life more fully.

The location point

Manipura chakra is located directly behind the navel on the inner wall of the spinal column. The kshetram is situated right at the navel. This chakra is anatomically related to the solar plexus, which controls the digestive fire and heat regulation in the body.

Traditional symbology

Manipura is symbolized by a ten petalled bright yellow lotus. Some of the tantric texts say the lotus petals are the colour of heavily laden rain clouds. On each petal one of the ten letters: *pham* फं, *dam* डं, *dham* ढं, *nam* णं, *tam* तं, *tham* थं, *dam* दं, *dham* धं, *nam* नं, *pam* पं, is inscribed in the colour of the blue lotus. In the centre of the lotus is the region of fire, symbolized by an inverted fiery red triangle which shines like the rising sun. The triangle has a bhupura or swastika in the shape of a T on each of its three sides. In the lower apex is the ram, vehicle for manipura, symbolizing dynamism and indomitable endurance. Seated on the ram is the beeja mantra of manipura – *ram* रं. In the bindu reside the deva Rudra and the devi Lakini. Rudra is of a pure vermilion hue and he is smeared with white ashes. He is three-eyed and of an ancient aspect. Lakini, the benefactress of all, is four-armed, of dark complexion and radiant body. She is clothed in yellow raiment, decked with various ornaments and exalted from drinking nectar.

The tanmatra of manipura is sight. The jnanendriya or organ of knowledge is the eyes, and the karmendriya or organ of action is the feet. These two organs are closely linked in the sense that vision and wilful action are inter-dependent.

Manipura belongs to *swaha loka*, the heavenly plane of existence. This is the last of the mortal planes. Its guna is pre-dominantly rajas (activity, intensity, acquisitiveness), whereas the lower chakras are predominantly tamasic (lethargic and negative). The tattwa is agni, the fire element, which is very important in kundalini yoga. Its vayu is *samana*, which digests and distributes the essence of food to the entire system. Manipura and swadhisthana chakras are the seat of *pranamaya kosha*.

In the yogic scriptures it is said that the moon at bindu secretes nectar which falls down to manipura and is consumed by the sun. This results in the ongoing process of degeneration which leads to old age, disease and death. This process can be reversed in the human body by adopting certain yogic practices which send the pranic forces in manipura back up to the brain. Otherwise the vitality is quickly dissipated and lost in the mundane affairs of life.

It is said that meditation on manipura chakra leads to knowledge of the entire physical system. When this centre is purified and awakened, the body becomes disease-free and luminous, and the yogi's consciousness does not fall back into the lower states.

The centre of awakening

According to the Buddhist tradition and many of the tantric texts, the actual awakening of kundalini takes place from manipura and not from mooladhara. In some tantric tradi-tions, mooladhara and swadhisthana are not referred to at all, as these two centres are believed to belong to the higher realms of animal life, whereas from manipura onwards, higher man predominates. So mooladhara is the seat of kundalini, swadhisthana is the abode, and the awakening takes place in manipura. This is because from manipura the awakening becomes ongoing and there is practically no danger of a downfall or devolution of consciousness. Up to this point, kundalini may awaken and arise many times, only to recede again, but awakening of manipura is what we call a confirmed awakening.

To stabilize the awareness in manipura and sustain the awakening there is not easy. The sadhaka must be very earnest and persevering in his effort to bring about further awakenings. I have found that in sincere sadhakas, kundalini is mostly in manipura. If you are exposed to spiritual life, practise yoga, have a keen desire to find a guru and to pursue a higher life, side by side with the work you are doing, it means kundalini is not in mooladhara. It is in manipura or one of the higher centres.

Union of prana and apana

In tantra there is an important branch known as *swara yoga*, the science of the breath, which is used to bring about the awakening of kundalini. According to this system, all the pranas in the body are classified into five dimensions, *prana, apana, vyana, udana* and *samana*. At the navel region, there is an important junction where two of these vital forces, prana and apana, meet.

The prana moves upwards and downwards between the navel and throat, and the apana flows up and down between the perineum and navel. These two movements are normally coupled together, like two railway carriages, so that with the inspired breath, prana is experienced moving up from the navel to the throat, while apana is simultaneously moving up to the navel centre from mooladhara. Then with exhalation, prana descends from the throat to the navel and apana descends from manipura to mooladhara. In this way prana and apana are continually functioning together and changing direction with the flow of the inspired/expired breath.

This movement can be readily experienced through relaxed breath awareness in the psychic passages between the perineal region, the navel and the throat centres in the front of the body. By gaining control through particular kriyas,

159

the apana is separated from prana, and its flow is reversed to bring about the awakening of the chakra. Whereas the apana normally descends from manipura during expiration, the flow is reversed so that prana and apana both enter the navel centre simultaneously from above and below, and are joined. This is the union of prana and apana.

It is said that when kundalini wakes up in mooladhara it begins to ascend spirally, like a hissing snake. However, the awakening of kundalini in manipura takes place like a blast, as the prana and the redirected apana meet in the navel centre. It is like two great forces colliding with each other and then fusing together at this pranic junction, manipura kshetram. As they fuse together, they create heat and an energy or force which is conducted directly back from the navel to the manipura chakra within the spinal cord. It is this force which awakens manipura chakra. The force of sadhana has caused a total reorganization of the pranic flow in the body, so that mooladhara is transcended and the new base of kundalini is manipura chakra.

Manipura in perspective

Human evolution takes place through seven planes in the same way that kundalini awakens in the seven chakras. When the consciousness evolves to manipura, the sadhaka acquires a spiritual perspective. He gets a glimpse of the higher lokas or planes of existence.

From mooladhara and swadhisthana, the higher planes cannot be seen. Therefore, the limitations of perception in the lower planes are responsible for the misuse of siddhis or powers which begin to manifest there. Only when the sadhaka reaches manipura is he able to visualize the infinite state of consciousness which is no longer gross and empirical. It stretches before him endlessly, full of beauty, truth and auspiciousness. In the face of this vision, all his views are completely changed. The personal prejudices, complexes and biases drop away as the endless beauty and perfection of the higher worlds dawn within the consciousness.

As long as the evolution is in the planes of mooladhara and swadhisthana, one has mental and emotional problems and sees the whole world correspondingly, but as soon as one transcends these planes and goes to manipura, all the bliss, noble views, perfect ideas and greater possibilities of human consciousness are seen. Then, naturally, whatever one thinks and does will be influenced by this higher vision.

This is why the psychic powers that come to the sadhaka after having awakened and established the kundalini in manipura are really benevolent and compassionate, whereas those which manifest in mooladhara and swadhisthana are still tinged by the dark aspect of the lower mind.

The powers gained through the awakening of manipura chakra are the ability to create and destroy, self-defence, the acquisition of hidden treasures, no fear of fire, knowledge of one's own body, freedom from disease and the ability to withdraw the energy to sahasrara.

21

Anahata Chakra

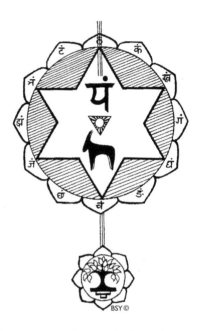

In kundalini yoga, anahata chakra is a centre of great importance. This is because although awakening from manipura is constant, kundalini has to remain in anahata for quite a long time. It is said that in this present age, the consciousness of mankind is passing through a phase of anahata. This means that in many people anahata chakra has started to function. However, there is a difference between functioning and awakening. In most people, anahata is not completely active, but it functions slightly. Mooladhara, on the other hand, is very active and almost awake in the majority of people today.

The word *anahata* actually means 'unstruck' or 'unbeaten'. This centre is known as such because of its relationship with the heart, which throbs, beats or vibrates to a constant unbroken rhythm. It is said in many of the scriptures that there is a sound which is non-physical and non-empirical, which is transcendental in nature, and this sound is endless and unbroken in the same way that the heart beats faithfully and continuously from before birth up until death.

The location point

Anahata chakra is situated in the spinal column on the inner wall, directly behind the centre of the chest. The kshetram is the heart, and although anahata is known as the heart centre, this should not be misinterpreted to mean the biological heart. Although its physiological component is the cardiac plexus of nerves, the nature of this centre is far beyond the physiological dimension.

In yoga the heart centre is also known as *hridayakasha*, which means 'the space within the heart where purity resides'. This chakra is a very delicate centre, for it is directly connected with that part of the brain which is responsible for all the creative sciences and fine arts such as painting, dance, music, poetry, and so on.

Traditional symbology

Although most of the tantric texts say that anahata is a shining crimson colour, like that of the bandhuka flower, my experience is that it is blue in colour. It has twelve petals and on each petal a letter is inscribed in vermilion: *kam* कं, *kham* खं, *gam* गं, *gham* घं, *ngam* ङं, *cham* चं, *chham* छं, *jam* जं, *jham* झं, *nyam* ञं, *tam* टं and *tham* ठं.

The inner region is hexagonal in shape, representing the air element, *vayu* tattwa. It is made up of two interlaced triangles, symbolizing the union of Shiva and Shakti. The inverted triangle is the symbol of creativity, Shakti; and the upright triangle represents consciousness or Shiva. The vehicle, located within the hexagon, is a black antelope, which is known for its alertness and fleetness of foot. Above it is situated the beeja mantra *yam* यं, which is dark grey in colour. Within the bindu of this mantra is the presiding deva, Isha (Lord in an all-pervading form), who is lustrous like the sun. With him is the devi Kakini (benefactress of all), who is yellow in colour, three-eyed, four-armed, auspicious and exhilarated.

In the centre of the pericarp of the lotus is an inverted triangle, within which burns the *akhanda jyotir*, unflickering eternal flame, representing the *jivatma* or individual soul. Some of the tantric texts say there is a shivalingam inside the triangle. It is called the *bana linga* and is like shining gold.

Below the main lotus of anahata is a subsidiary lotus with red petals, which contain the *kalpa taru* or wish-fulfilling tree. Many saints have recommended visualization of the kalpa taru or of a still lake within the anahata hexagon. Upon this lake there is a beautiful blue lotus. You may have seen this symbol because it is utilized by several ashrams and spiritual missions.

Anahata belongs to *maha loka*, the first of the immortal planes. Its vayu is *prana*, which passes through the nose and mouth, and its tanmatra is feeling or touch. The jnanendriya is the skin and the karmendriya is the hands. Anahata represents *manomaya kosha*, controlling the mind and emotions.

Vishnu granthi, the second psychic knot, is located at this heart centre. It represents the bondage of emotional attachment, the tendency to live one's life making decisions on the strength of the emotions and feelings, rather than in the light of the spiritual quest. Vishnu granthi is untied as the emotions harmonize and enhance, rather than oppose, the spiritual awakening.

It is said that he who meditates on the heart lotus is foremost among yogis and adored by women, that he is pre-eminently wise and full of noble deeds. His senses are completely under control and his mind can be engrossed in intense concentration. His speech is inspired and he has the ability to enter another's body at will.

Fate and free will

Tantric scriptures say that in anahata thoughts and desires of the individual are materialized and fulfilled. There are basically two ways of thinking: dependently or independently. Up to manipura chakra the first approach holds true, but once the shakti pierces anahata, the second approach takes precedence.

As long as the consciousness is centred in the lower chakras, you will remain completely dependent on what is already enjoined for you, your fate or destiny, *prarabdha karma*. Even the awakening of the lower chakras does not make much difference. Once the consciousness ascends through manipura, you become master over some of the situations of life, but you are still influenced and bound by your prarabdha karma. You know that you can escape it, but you do not know how.

The lower chakras belong to the empirical world of body, mind and sense. People who accept their fate as inevitable have not yet transcended mooladhara and swadhisthana chakras. Manipura is still considered earthly, although it lies at the boundary between mortal and immortal planes. Those who actively shape their own destiny through strength of will channelled in a positive direction, which leads to realization and achievement, are in the realm of manipura.

Anahata chakra is almost completely beyond these empirical dimensions. Here, one realizes that fate is of course real, but still one can go totally beyond its dictates. It is like throwing something into the sky. If you are able to hurl that object right out of the gravitational field, then it will no longer be pulled down by the earth's magnetic forces. Just as a rocket is launched at tremendous speed in order to go beyond the gravitational pull of the earth, so the consciousness is accelerated in anahata to the speed of free will in order to transcend the pull of latent samskaras.

It is only when you reach anahata chakra that you become a yogi. Up until then, whether you are in mooladhara, swadhisthana or manipura, you are a yoga practitioner. In anahata you become a yogi because you are completely established in yogic consciousness and you depend solely upon the power of your own consciousness, rather than on anything that is external or concerning faith.

Wish fulfilment

In anahata chakra, the freedom to escape from a preordained fate and to determine one's own destiny becomes a reality. According to the tantras, at the root of anahata there is a wish-fulfilling tree known as the *kalpa taru* or *kalpa vriksha*. When this tree starts to fructify, whatever you think or wish comes true. Ordinarily we have many wishes, but they rarely assume more than the air of a daydream. However, if they were all to become realities, we would quickly start to question whether we want our wishes fulfilled at all. Most people prefer to depend on fate rather than take responsibility for creating their own destiny, and well they should. There is a fine story which is often told to illustrate this.

Once a traveller was sitting underneath a tree. He was feeling very tired and wanted to have a drink. So he thought of a clear stream, and immediately he heard the trickle of water flowing beside him. After drinking some water, he thought he would like to have a little food to satisfy his hunger, and that appeared beside him also. Then, as he was feeling tired and thought he would like to rest, there appeared before him a nice bed, and so he went to sleep. The foolish man did not know that he had come to rest beneath the wish-fulfilling tree. In the evening when he awoke, the sun had already set and night had fallen. He got up and the thought came to his mind: "Oh, it is terribly dark, perhaps the tigers will come and eat me," and so they did.

This is what can happen to anyone who awakens the wish-fulfilling capacity without sufficient preparation. If the consciousness awakens in anahata, but you do not know the powers of your mind, or you possess negative, pessimistic attitudes, dark approaches to life, apprehensions, fears and many other negative mental tendencies, then you will immediately fall prey to them. If this happens, you risk the possibility of falling back from anahata. And if you fall from anahata, there is hardly any chance of making a second start. To avoid a downfall at this point, it is necessary to always remain as alert as the antelope, which is sensitive to each and every sound. The antelope is the vehicle of anahata for this reason; it is not the symbol of restlessness, but of alertness.

When whatever you wish for comes true, you are very happy, but at the same time, it is necessary to constantly analyze your attitude towards yourself and others. You have to be careful of doubts. For example, if you develop a few palpitations of the heart and think: "Perhaps I am developing angina pectoris," or a pain in the abdomen and think: "Now I have appendicitis or gall bladder disease," such thoughts may bring many problems and disorders in their wake. You must also guard against doubts concerning others: "Maybe that man is my enemy," "My son is sick, maybe he will die," "My friend has not contacted me, he must have had an accident." It is important to have a firm and alert control over the mental tendencies and fantasies of the mind.

Thoughts concerning the body, husband, wife, children, family, social, economic or political situations come to us all the time. If kundalini is asleep, these thoughts have no power, but when kundalini awakens in anahata chakra, all these thoughts suddenly become realities. Unless we are ever alert at this stage we will place our own destructive hand on our head.

In the tantric text *Saundarya Lahari*, this wish-fulfilling process is aptly described as the *chintamani*, or wish-fulfilling gem. Here *chinta* applies to the 'process of selective thought' and *mani* means 'jewel'. Therefore, chintamani means the 'jewel' of correct and positive thinking. In this text, anahata is described as the garden of devas. At the centre is a small divine lake inside which is the chintamani. It is not necessary

167

to obtain this jewel; as long as you can realize your proximity to it that is enough, then whatever you think comes true.

Develop a new way of thinking

When anahata chakra blooms and awakens, you must have very good *sangha*, associations. You should never associate with people who depend on their fate. Rather, you should always associate with those who depend on faith. You must have unswerving faith in the power of your own will. Even in the face of tremendous odds, be unflinching, then you will succeed. Willpower is never the outcome of suggestion. If you are ill and you say a hundred times, "I am well, I am well, I am well . . .," this is called autosuggestion. It is not will. Will is something more than this. "Even if my son is suffering from the worst disease and medical science has declared that he is about to die, I know he will not." This is how you have to think and use your will.

The first preparation, therefore, with regards to awakening anahata is to change your entire way of thinking. If you are the type of person whose thoughts and wishes often come true, even when conditions seem to be opposed to that outcome, then it is necessary to develop a certain amount of caution along with a new way of thinking.

You must become extremely optimistic and positive, always full of hope. You must never dwell in the negativity of the mind. Physically, mentally and spiritually you must be completely at peace with yourself, others and the whole community at large. Though the world is full of conflicts, contradictions and deep animosities, you have to always feel deep peace throughout your being. Never be negative about any situation. Even if you meet a murderer, a hopeless gambler or a debaucher, to you he is still a good person.

Every situation is a good one for you and the future is always bright. In all circumstances this must be your attitude. It makes no difference whether you are amidst poverty, suffering, disease, conflict, divorce, emotional crises and discord. It is all part of the good, therefore you accept it.

168

You have to think only one thought resolutely: "The whole world is in me," or "I am in everyone." When you are able to develop this universal sort of attitude, the kundalini will shine forth and pierce the fifth chakra – vishuddhi, the centre of immortality. This is the importance and significance of anahata. Perhaps the best mantra for the heart centre is Om shanti. *Om* is the universal cosmic vibration which permeates the whole creation and *shanti* means peace.

Love without expectations

Anahata chakra awakens refined emotion in the brain and its awakening is characterized by a feeling of universal, unlimited love for all beings. Of course, there are many people in the world who practise kindness and charity, but they have selfishness. Their charity is not an expression of anahata chakra and spiritual compassion, it is human compassion. When you have human compassion you open hospitals and feeding centres or you give clothing, money and medicine in charity, but that is human charity.

How can we tell the difference between human charity and spiritual charity? In human charity there is always an element of selfishness. If I want to make you a Hindu by giving you things, this is a manifestation of human charity. Or if I want to make you my followers I can show you great kindness, but that is human kindness. However, when anahata awakens all your actions are controlled and ruled by unselfishness and you develop spiritual compassion. You understand that love does not involve bargaining; it is free of expectation.

Every form of love is contaminated by selfishness, even the love you have for God, because you are expecting something from him. Perhaps in this world, the love with minimum selfishness is a mother's love. Of course, it is not totally unselfish, but because a mother's sacrifices are so great, her love has minimum selfishness.

The qualities of anahata chakra can be awakened by many methods. The symbol of anahata chakra is a blue lotus, and in the centre are two interlaced triangles. This lotus represents the opening of one's heart. Music, art, sculpture, literature and poetry are all important aids to the development of anahata chakra. And when anahata opens, your understanding of all beings changes a lot. There is a story about it.

In India there is a traditional pilgrimage in which sadhakas go north to the source of Ganga, take some water from there and carry it across the continent to South India. Here they go to a temple and pour the holy water over a shivalingam. The distance they have to cover in this pilgrimage is almost three thousand miles.

Once a saint had almost completed this pilgrimage and he was carrying a container full of Ganga water. As he entered the precincts of the temple where he was to bathe the shivalingam, he found a donkey which was desperately pining for water. Immediately he opened his can and gave water to the donkey. His fellow travellers cried out, "Hey, what are you doing? You have brought this water such a long way to give a bath to Lord Shiva and here you are giving it to an ordinary animal!" But the saint did not see it that way. His mind was working at a different and much higher frequency.

Here is another example: Once Lord Buddha was going for an evening walk. He came across an old man and he was greatly moved by the sufferings of old age. Next he saw a dead person, and again he was moved very much. How many times do we see old people? Are we moved in the same way that Lord Buddha was? No, because our minds are different. Awakening of a chakra alters the frequency of the mind and immediately influences our day to day relationships with people and our surroundings.

Love overcomes ego
Anahata chakra can be aroused and awakened by the practice of bhakti yoga, in which there is no place for egotistical consciousness. Your devotion can be for God or guru. It is easy to practise devotion to God because he does not check your ego, or even if he does, you do not know it. But when

you practise devotion to the guru, the first thing he does is 'egodectomy'. So when you direct your devotion to guru, you have lots of difficulties. If you only meet your guru from time to time, the problems are invisible, but if you live with him, the problems are greater. Therefore, many people think it is safer to have a guru who is no longer living.

Not only is ego an obstacle on the spiritual path, it is also the greatest barrier to harmony and cordiality in family and social life. Therefore, in order to treat the ego there are two very important paths. One is karma yoga and the other is bhakti yoga. Ego can never be removed by intellectual persuasion. It can never be subdued or eliminated unless you develop the highest form of love. Just as the sun removes darkness, love removes ego. These two can never coexist.

So, in order to induce anahata awakening we should definitely practise bhakti yoga. When kundalini is established in anahata there is absolute devotion and even a confirmed atheist will change. However, awakening of anahata is not only a way to God or guru, it is also a way to complete unity and harmony in family life. Therefore, in India, most Hindu women are initiated into bhakti yoga at a very young age. When they are four to six years old they are taught to practise devotion to Lord Shiva, Krishna, Rama, Vishnu, Lakshmi, Durga and so on, because it is easier for women to develop anahata chakra. For this reason, women are also told to use anahata as their centre for meditation, whereas men are generally advised to concentrate on ajna chakra. Anahata is the seat of human love and the seat of divine love. They are not two things, they are one and the same.

Psychic propensities of anahata chakra

Prior to the awakening of anahata there may be frequent pain in the chest or irregular functioning of the heart, such as accelerated pulse. However, rather than feeling ill, one feels healthy and active and requires little sleep. One obtains complete emotional balance and the ability to communicate externally as well as internally. Voices or sounds coming from other realms may be heard, and buzzing or humming sounds and the music of a flute may be experienced.

The sadhaka may become an inspired poet, artist or singer. He may manifest clairvoyant/clairaudient or psychokinetic ability, or he may be able to conquer people by the immensity of love he emits. A person in anahata is generally very sensitive to the feelings of others and his sense of touch is strongly developed. He also has the ability to heal others, either by touch or by generating his own spiritual energy to other people. Many people who perform miraculous healings do so through the agency of anahata chakra.

With anahata awakening one develops non-attachment to worldly things and a constant feeling of optimism, understanding that good and bad coexist, but there is also a world beyond this duality. After ridding oneself of attachment, the mind becomes relaxed, free and peaceful. And with the discovery of true freedom, pleasures of dualistic life become meaningless.

22

Vishuddhi Chakra

Vishuddhi chakra is known as the 'purification centre'. The Sanskrit word *shuddhi* means 'to purify', and in this chakra the purifying and harmonizing of all opposites takes place. Vishuddhi is also known as the 'nectar and poison centre'. Here, the nectar which drips down from bindu is said to be split into the pure form and the poison. The poison is discarded and the pure nectar then nourishes the body, ensuring excellent health and longevity.

Vishuddhi represents a state of openness in which life is regarded as the provider of experiences that lead to greater understanding. One ceases to continually avoid the unpleasant aspects of life and seek the pleasant. Instead there is a flowing with life, allowing things to happen in the way that they must. Both poison and nectar are consumed in vishuddhi chakra, and they are understood to be but parts of a greater cosmic whole. Proper understanding and true discrimination dawn out of this equal acceptance of the dualities and polarities of life.

The more abstract aspect of vishuddhi is the faculty of higher discrimination. Hence any communication received telepathically can be tested here for its correctness and accuracy. Similarly, vishuddhi allows us to differentiate between realization coming into our consciousness from the higher levels of knowledge, and the mere babblings of our unconscious mind and wishful thinking.

Vishuddhi chakra is often treated as an insignificant chakra in the scheme of kundalini yoga. People are more concerned with mooladhara, anahata and ajna, and therefore the significance of vishuddhi is easily disregarded. In fact, the reverse attitude may even be more appropriate.

The location point

Vishuddhi chakra is in the cervical plexus directly behind the throat pit. Its kshetram is in the front of the neck, at the throat pit or thyroid gland. The physiological concomitants of vishuddhi are the pharyngeal and laryngeal nerve plexi.

Traditional symbology

Some tantric texts say vishuddhi chakra is represented by a dark grey coloured lotus, however, it seems to be more commonly perceived as a purple lotus of sixteen petals. These sixteen petals correspond to the number of nadis associated with this centre. On each petal one of the Sanskrit vowels is inscribed in crimson: *am* अं, *aam* आं, *im* इं, *eem* ईं, *um* उं, *oom* ऊं, *rim* ऋं, *reem* ॠं, *lrim* लृं, *lreem* लॄं, *em* एं, *aim* ऐं, *om* ओं, *aum* औं, *am* अं, *ah* अ:.

In the pericarp of this lotus is a circle which is white like the full moon, representing the element of ether or *akasha*. This ethereal region is the gateway to liberation for one whose senses are pure and controlled. Within this moon

174

shape is a snow white elephant, also symbolic of the akasha element. This is considered as the vehicle of consciousness of this plane, and the aspirant may picture himself upon its back. The beeja mantra is *ham* हं, also pure white, which is the seed sound or vibration of the etheric element.

The presiding deity of vishuddhi is Sadashiva, who is snow white, three-eyed and five-faced, with ten arms and clothed in a tiger's skin. The goddess is Sakini who is purer than the ocean of nectar that flows down from the moon region. Her raiment is yellow and in her four hands she holds the bow, the arrow, the noose and the goad.

Vishuddhi belongs to the fifth loka, the plane of *janah*. Its vayu is *udana* which lasts till the end of life and rises upwards, and along with ajna chakra, vishuddhi forms the basis for *vijnanamaya kosha*, which initiates psychic development. The tanmatra or sense is hearing and the jnanendriya or organ of knowledge is the ears. The karmendriya or organ of action is the vocal chords.

In nada yoga, the branch of kundalini yoga concerned with sound vibration, vishuddhi and mooladhara are considered to be the two basic centres of vibration. In nada yoga the ascent of consciousness through the chakras is integrated with the musical scale. Each note of the scale corresponds to the vibratory level of consciousness of one of the chakras. This scale, often chanted in the form of mantras, bhajans and kirtans, is a very powerful means of awakening kundalini in the different chakras.

Mooladhara is the first and vishuddhi is the fifth level of vibration in the scale. They produce the basic sounds or vowels around which the music of the chakras is constructed. These vowel sounds, pictured on the sixteen petals of the yantra, are the primal sounds. They originate from vishuddhi chakra and are directly connected to the brain.

By meditation on vishuddhi chakra, the mind becomes pure like the akasha. One becomes a great sage, eloquent and wise and enjoys uninterrupted peace of mind. Amrit can be felt as a cold fluid flowing into the chakra and the aspirant becomes free from disease and sorrow; he is compassionate, full of bliss and long lived.

Nectar and poison

In the tantric scriptures it is said that within bindu at the back of the head, the moon is secreting a vital fluid or essence known as nectar. This transcendental fluid drips down into the individual consciousness from bindu. Bindu can be regarded in this context as the centre or passage through which the individuality emerges from cosmic consciousness in sahasrara.

This divine fluid has many different names. In English it can be termed ambrosia – the nectar of the gods. It is also known as amrit – the nectar of immortality. In the Vedas it is known as soma and in the tantras it is referred to as madya (divine wine). Many of the great Sufi poets refer to the sweet wine which brings instant intoxication. The same symbolism is contained in the Christian rituals where wine is consecrated and sacramentally imbibed. In fact, every religious system and mystical tradition concerned with awakening higher consciousness has its own symbolism for the unspeakable and indescribable feeling of bliss.

Between bindu and vishuddhi chakras there is another smaller psychic centre known as *lalana chakra* or *talumula*, and it is closely related to vishuddhi chakra. When the nectar trickles down from bindu it is stored in lalana. This centre is like a glandular reservoir, situated in the back of the naso-pharynx, the inner cavity above and beyond the soft palate into which the nasal passages open. When you perform khechari mudra you are attempting to turn the tongue up and backwards into this cavity to stimulate the flow of nectar.

Although this fluid is known as ambrosia, it actually has a dual nature which can act as poison as well as nectar. When it is produced in bindu and stored in lalana, it remains undifferentiated, neither poison nor nectar. As long as vishuddhi chakra remains inactive, this fluid runs downward unimpeded, to be consumed in the fire of manipura,

176

resulting in the processes of decay, degeneration and finally death in the body's tissues.

However, by certain practices such as khechari mudra, the ambrosia is secreted from lalana and passes to vishuddhi chakra, the purifying and refining centre. When vishuddhi is awakened, the divine fluid is retained and utilized, becoming the nectar of immortality. The secret of youth and regeneration of the body lies in the awakening of vishuddhi.

There is a wonderful story from the mythology of India which concerns the nectar and poison of vishuddhi. It is said that in the primordial past, the devas and the rakshasas, symbolizing the forces of good and evil, were continually fighting each other. Each was seeking to dominate and destroy the other. Eventually Vishnu attempted to resolve the conflict. He suggested they stir up the primordial ocean (representing the world and the mind), and said they could divide the contents equally between them.

This seemed a fair solution and Vishnu's plan was agreed upon. The ocean was churned and many things came to the surface for sharing and distribution between the devas and rakshasas. In all, fourteen things arose, including the nectar of immortality side by side with the worst poison. Of course, both the devas and the rakshasas wanted the nectar, but nobody wanted anything to do with the poison. Ultimately only the devas got the nectar, because if it had been given to the vicious rakshasas they would have become immortal. The poison could not even be discarded, for wherever it was thrown it would cause harm. A great dilemma arose and eventually Vishnu took the poison to Shiva to ask his advice. Shiva swallowed the poison in a single gulp. From that time onwards, one of the names of Lord Shiva has been Nilakantha, the blue-throated one, and he is often depicted in this way.

This story signifies that even poison can be readily digested when vishuddhi chakra is awakened. It means that at higher levels of awareness, vishuddhi and above, even the poisonous and negative aspects of existence become integrated into the total scheme of being. They are rendered powerless as concepts of good and bad fall away. At this state of awareness the poisonous aspects and experiences of life are absorbed and transformed into a state of bliss.

In this chakra it is possible that not only internal poisons but also external poisons can be neutralized and rendered ineffective. This is one of the siddhis associated with vishuddhi chakra, and many yogis have possessed this power. It depends on the awakening of the throat centre and bindu in the brain, to which it is directly connected.

The potential of vishuddhi

Vishuddhi is the centre responsible for receiving thought vibrations from other people's minds. This actually occurs through a minor centre which is closely connected with vishuddhi. It acts somewhat like a transistor radio tuning into a radio station, allowing the yogi to tune into the thoughts and feelings of people both close by and far away. The thought waves of others are also experienced elsewhere in the body, in other centres such as manipura, but the actual reception centre of thought waves and transmissions is vishuddhi. From vishuddhi they are relayed to the centres in the brain associated with the other chakras, and in this way they enter into the individual awareness.

Associated with vishuddhi is a particular nerve channel known as *kurma nadi*, the tortoise nadi. When it is awakened, the practitioner is able to completely overcome the desire and necessity for food and drink. This capability has been demonstrated by many yogis in the past.

Vishuddhi is actually the legendary 'fountain of youth'. It is said that when kundalini is in vishuddhi one enjoys eternal youth. When it awakens by the practices of hatha yoga, kundalini yoga or tantra, then a spontaneous physical rejuvenation begins to take place.

There is a point in life, usually in the second or third decade, when the rate of degeneration of the cells of the body surpasses the rate of regeneration. It is from that point that decay, old age, disease and death come to the fore in man's experience. In certain disease states such as some forms of leukaemia, the degenerative and destructive forces develop even more rapidly. The rejuvenation effected by vishuddhi chakra on the tissues, organs and systems of the body is in contradistinction to this ongoing ageing process, which is man's normal condition.

The powers attained through awakening vishuddhi include imperishability, full knowledge of the scriptures and also the knowledge of the past, present and future. The sense of hearing becomes very sharp, but through the mind and not the ears. One frequently experiences shoonyata, the void, and one overcomes all fear and attachment. One is then able to work freely in the world without being attached to the fruits of one's actions.

23

Bindu

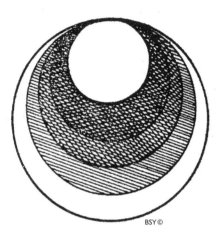

BSY©

Bindu, the source of creation, is beyond the realm of all conventional experience and, therefore, even in the tantric texts, there is very little written about it. It is the storehouse of all the karmas of man from his previous life. Not only are these karmas in the form of vasanas, they are also in the form of memories.

The word *bindu* means 'drop' or 'point'. It is more widely termed *bindu visarga*, which literally means 'falling of the drop'. Bindu is represented by the crescent moon and a white drop, which is the nectar dripping down to vishuddhi chakra. It is the ultimate source out of which all things manifest and into which all things return. In *Kama-Kala-Vilasa* (verses 6–9) it says, "... (bindu) is the cause of the creation of word and meaning, now entering and now separating from one another." ". . . from that (bindu) came ether, air, fire, water, earth and the letters of the alphabet."

Bindu is interconnected with vishuddhi chakra in the same way that the minor centres of the digestive system are connected with manipura, and those of the uro-genital and reproductive systems with swadhisthana and mooladhara chakras. Similarly, the minor centres of the respiratory and circulatory systems are integrated into anahata chakra and so on. In each case, the connection is mediated by the particular group of nerves associated with that chakra. Bindu and vishuddhi are connected via the network of nerves which flow through the interior portion of the nasal orifice, passing through lalana chakra, which is found at the uvula or palate. Therefore, when awakening takes place in vishuddhi, it simultaneously takes place in bindu and lalana.

The ten paired cranial nerves which emerge along the brain stem from their associated centres or nuclei are considered to actually have their initial origins within this tiny centre, so that the whole visual, nasal, auditory and tasting systems are ultimately manifestations from bindu.

The location point

The seat of bindu is at the top back of the head, exactly at the spot where Hindu brahmins leave a tuft of hair growing. Although this custom is still being followed today, its original purpose has been completely forgotten. In Sanskrit that tuft of hair is called *shikha*, which means 'the flame of fire'. Here, the word 'flame' stands for the flame of vasanas or the hidden karmas belonging to the previous life.

In the Vedic tradition, during *sandhya*, the hour of conjunction when the daily practices are performed by one who has undergone the thread ceremony and been initiated into mantra, a child was taught to practise with the tuft tied and tightened as much as possible. When the tuft was tightened and the child practised mantra, he developed a powerful and continuing awareness of this bindu point.

181

He felt tightness rather than pain at that point. This is one traditional way of gaining contact with bindu.

Tantric physiology

According to tantric tradition, within the higher centres of the upper cortex of the brain there is a small depression or pit which contains a minute secretion. In the centre of that tiny secretion is a small elevation or point like an island in the middle of a lake. In the psychophysiological framework, this tiny point is considered to be bindu.

The actual isolation of such a miniscule structure within the anatomy of the brain has never been reported or verified by medical scientists. However, such a study could prove both interesting and rewarding, in the same way that modern research into the mysterious pineal gland has verified that it is the anatomical and functional concomitant of ajna chakra, as described in the tantra shastras. However, it is easy to imagine that such a delicate and minute structure as the bindu would undoubtedly be disrupted during post mortem procedures. Certainly the tiny amount of fluid could hardly be expected to remain localized for easy extraction and analysis, when it is well known that other more plentiful neural and glandular transmitters and secretions degenerate and disperse into the tissues at the time of death. Nevertheless it is certainly a possibility to be considered.

Traditional symbology

In the tantric scriptures, the symbol of bindu is a crescent moon on a moonlit night. This symbol is very rich in meaning. The crescent moon indicates that bindu is closely related to the *kalas* (phases) of the moon, as are the endocrine, emotional and mental fluctuations of human beings. The immensity of sahasrara is gradually unveiled through ardent yoga practice in the same way that the full moon is progressively revealed from the time of the new moon to full moon each month. The background of the night sky also symbolizes the infinity of sahasrara beyond

182

bindu. However, sahasrara cannot be fully experienced while individuality remains.

The symbol of *Om* ॐ also contains the representation of bindu in its uppermost part, which is a small point above a crescent moon. In fact, all the chakras are symbolized within the body of the Om symbol, as are the three gunas or qualities of the created world: tamas, rajas and sattwa. These chakras exist in the realm of prakriti and its gunas. In the Om symbol, bindu, however, is placed separately from the main body to indicate that it is transcendental and beyond the fetters of nature.

Bindu belongs to the seventh or highest loka of satyam, the plane of truth, and it also belongs to the causal body, or *anandamaya kosha*. It is said that when bindu awakens, the cosmic sound of Om is heard and one realizes the source of all creation, emanating from the bindu point and crescent moon above the symbol of Om.

The seat of nectar

In many of the tantric texts it is written that bindu, the moon, produces a very intoxicating secretion. Yogis can live on this ambrosial fluid. If its secretion is awakened and controlled in the body, then one needs nothing more for survival. The maintenance of the body's vitality becomes independent of food.

There have been many reports of people who have entered into states of hibernation or suspended animation underneath the earth. This phenomenon has been verified many times under strict scientific observation. This human hibernation has been witnessed for periods as long as forty days. Not all cases have been genuine, but when authentic, they have been carried out exactly in the following manner. Initially pranayama is practised assiduously, until kumbhaka (retention of the breath) has been perfected. At this stage, khechari mudra is performed. This is not the simple form of khechari as performed in kundalini yoga sadhana, but the practice from the hatha yoga tradition in which the root or frenulum of the under surface of the tongue is gradually cut and the tongue is slowly elongated and inserted into the nasopharynx. It blocks off the passage as a cork seals a bottle. The whole practice is perfected over a two year period.

By this practice, the drops from bindu fall to vishuddhi and subsequently permeate the whole bodily system. These drops of nectar maintain the nutrition and vitality of the bodily tissues while simultaneously arresting the metabolic processes of the body. When the metabolism of the cells and tissues of the body is suspended in this way, oxygen is no longer required and cellular wastes are not produced. Therefore, the person who hibernates can live without breathing for quite an extended period of time. Even the facial hair does not grow during the period of hibernation.

The poison centre

Besides producing nectar, bindu is responsible for the production of poison. The poison gland and the nectar glands are almost simultaneously situated. You may wonder if by awakening bindu there is any danger in stimulating the poison glands. If bindu and vishuddhi are stimulated at the same time, there is absolutely no danger, because bindu controls the nectar glands and vishuddhi has a bearing on both nectar and poison. As long as nectar is flowing, the poison can do no harm. Furthermore, if a yogi has purified his body through hatha yoga and the practices of dhyana and raja yoga, the poison glands are utilized for the production of nectar.

The origin of individuality

Bindu is considered to be the origin of creation or the point where oneness first divides itself to produce the world of multiple individual forms. This aspect of bindu can be traced to the Sanskrit root *bind*, which means 'to split' or 'divide'.

Bindu implies a point without dimension, a dimensionless centre. In some Sanskrit texts it is termed *chidghana* – which has its roots in the limitless consciousness. Bindu is considered to be the gateway to *shoonya*, the state of void. This void should not be misinterpreted as a state of nothingness. Rather, it is the state of no-thingness – the state of pure, absolute and undifferentiated consciousness. Bindu is mysterious. It is an ineffable focal point within which the two opposites, infinity and zero, fullness and nothingness, coexist.

Within bindu is contained the evolutionary potential for all the myriad objects of the universe. Bindu contains the blueprint for creation. Evolution here refers to the vertical, transcendental process by which life, objects and organisms arise from the underlying substratum of existence. This evolution is not at all the same as the scientific concept of Darwinian evolution, which is but an historical trace of the changes over a period of time in the form, function or appearance of particular manifestations of individuality, such as the species of plants or animals. That evolution is an historical record over time, whereas the evolution and dissolution of consciousness into and out of individuality is in the realm of the timeless.

There is an individuating principle that generates the myriads of objects in the universe. In Sanskrit it is called *kala*, that which causes the potential inherent in the underlying consciousness to accumulate at bindu. From this point or seed an object, an animal, a human being or whatever can arise and manifest. Each and every object has a bindu as its base. This bindu lies within the *hiranyagarbha*, the golden egg or womb of creation. That which was previously formless assumes shape through the bindu, and its nature is fixed by the bindu as well. The bindu is both the means of expression of consciousness and also the means of limitation.

Some of the centres of manifestation from bindu possess consciousness, such as man. However, most centres are unconscious, such as the elements, stones, and so on. The potential to be conscious or unconscious depends only on the nature and structure of the individual object, and this is also determined by the bindu. Man has the apparatus that allows him to be a conscious centre.

Every object, conscious or unconscious, is linked to the underlying essence of consciousness through the intermediary of the bindu. Every object evolves into material existence through the medium of the bindu and every object is withdrawn back to the source via the bindu as well. Bindu is a trapdoor opening in both directions. It is the means through which conscious centres such as man can realize the totality of sahasrara.

There are essentially only two types of human beings: those who are on the *pravritti* path and those who are on the *nivritti* path. A man following the pravritti (outward) path looks away from bindu towards the outside world. He is almost entirely motivated by external events. This is the path of most people today and it leads away from self-knowledge and into bondage. The other path, the nivritti (reversed) path, is the spiritual path, the path of wisdom. On this path the individual begins to face the bindu, turning in towards the source of his being. This path leads to freedom. The path of evolution is the pravritti path of manifestation and extroversion. The path of involution leads back along the path that has produced your individual being. It leads back through the bindu to sahasrara. In fact, the whole purpose of yoga practice is to help direct your awareness along the involutionary path.

The power of the point

There is tremendous power ensheathed within the infinitesimal point. For example, one theory about the origin of the universe suggests that an infinitely dense point of matter exploded in a 'big bang' to form the entire cosmos. Similarly, research in subatomic physics has revealed that vast amounts of power are found concentrated within the multitudinous and different subatomic particles existing in the space/time continuum. Physics is now moving into the realms of the ineffable bindu.

In molecular biology, the essence of bindu can be found in the DNA and RNA molecules, each one of which contains the complete genetic blueprint for the entire organism. This

186

is another illustration of the great intelligence and potential which can be condensed and expressed in the confines of a tiny point. In fact, the deeper science delves into nature and the structure of the universe, the greater the power and complexity it uncovers. Within the tiny dimensions of these points vast potentials of meaning are contained.

The power of the point or bindu has been known to mystics throughout the history of mankind. In tantra, each bindu, each particle of manifested existence is regarded as a centre of power or shakti. This shakti is an expression of the underlying substratum of static consciousness. The aim of the tantric system is to bring about a fusion of Shakti – the individual manifested power, with Shiva – the inert, underlying universal consciousness.

The red and white bindu

The bindu is the cosmic seed from which all things manifest and grow. It is often related to male sperm because from the tiny bindu of a single spermatozoon, joined with the minute female ovum, a new life grows. The act of conception is a perfect symbol of the principle of the bindu. In fact, bindu is explained in these terms in many of the texts of tantric kundalini yoga. In the *Yogachudamani Upanishad* (verse 60) it says: "The bindu is of two types, white and red. The white is *shukla* (sperm) and the red is *maharaj* (menses)."

Here the white bindu symbolizes Shiva, purusha or consciousness, and the red bindu symbolizes Shakti, prakriti or the power of manifestation. The white bindu lies in the bindu visarga and the red bindu is seated in mooladhara chakra. The purpose of tantra and yoga is to unite these two principles so that Shiva and Shakti become one.

The text continues (verse 61): "The red bindu is established in the sun; the white bindu in the moon. Their union is difficult." The sun represents pingala nadi and the moon represents ida. The two bindus symbolize the merging of the world of opposites, in terms of male and female. Out of their union results the ascent of kundalini. Again the text continues (verse 63): "When the red bindu (Shakti) moves upwards (the ascent of kundalini) by control of prana, it mixes with the white bindu (Shiva) and one becomes divine."

All the systems of yoga control the prana in one way or another to bring about this union. In some cases it is through direct control, as in pranayama, while in other cases it is less direct. Nevertheless, the meeting of these two polarities, Shiva and Shakti, leads to superconsciousness. Verse 64 states: "He who realizes the essential oneness of the two bindus, when the red bindu merges with the white bindu, alone knows yoga."

Sahasrara

24

Sahasrara and Samadhi

Sahasrara is not a chakra as is often thought. Chakras are within the realm of the psyche. Consciousness manifests at different levels according to the chakra that is predominantly active. Sahasrara acts through nothing and yet again, it acts through everything. Sahasrara is beyond the beyond (*parat-param*) and yet it is right here. Sahasrara is the culmination of the progressive ascension through the different chakras. It is the crown of expanded awareness. The power of the chakras does not reside in the chakras themselves, but in sahasrara. The chakras are only switches. All the potential lies in sahasrara.

The literal meaning of the word *sahasrara* is 'one thousand'. For this reason it is said to be a lotus with one thousand petals. However, while literally meaning one thousand, the word sahasrara implies that its magnitude and significance is vast – in fact, unlimited. Therefore, sahasrara should more aptly be described as a lotus with an infinite number of petals, usually said to be red or multicoloured.

Sahasrara is both formless (*nirakara*) and with form (*akara*), yet it is also beyond, and therefore untouched by form (*nirvikara*). It is shoonya, or in actual fact, the void of totality. It is Brahman. It is everything and nothing. Whatever we say about sahasrara will immediately limit and categorize it, even if we say it is infinite. It transcends logic, for logic compares one thing with another. Sahasrara is the

189

totality, so what is there to compare it with? It transcends all concepts and yet it is the source of all concepts. It is the merging of consciousness and prana. Sahasrara is the culmination of yoga, the perfect merging.

Total union and the unfolding of enlightenment

When kundalini shakti reaches sahasrara, that is known as union between Shiva and Shakti, as sahasrara is said to be the abode of higher consciousness or Shiva. Union between Shiva and Shakti marks the beginning of a great experience. When this union takes place, the moment of self-realization or samadhi begins. At this point the individual dies. I do not mean that physical death occurs; it is death of the mundane awareness or individual awareness. It is death of the experience of name and form. At this time you do not remember the 'I', the 'you' or the 'they'. The experience, the experienced and the experiencer are one and the same. The seer, seeing and seen are merged as a unified whole. In other words, there is no multiple or dual awareness remaining. There is only single awareness.

When Shiva and Shakti unite, nothing remains, there is absolute silence. Shakti does not remain Shakti and Shiva is no more Shiva, both are mingled into one and they can no longer be identified as two different forces.

Every mystical and religious system of the world has its own way of describing this experience. Some have called it nirvana, others samadhi, kaivalya, self-realization, enlightenment, communion, heaven and so on. If you read the religious and mystical poems and scriptures of the many cultures and traditions, you will find ample descriptions of sahasrara. However, you have to read them with a different state of consciousness to understand the esoteric symbology and terminology.

Raja yoga, kundalini and samadhi

In the *Yoga Sutras* of Patanjali you will not come across the word kundalini, as this text does not directly deal with kundalini yoga. However, not every saint, rishi or teacher has referred to kundalini by this name. Kundalini is the subject matter of tantra. When Patanjali wrote the *Yoga Sutras* 2,600 years ago, it was during the period of Buddha and about four centuries before the great era of philosophers. At that time, tantra had a very bad reputation in India because the gifts of kundalini, the siddhis, were being misused for petty purposes and people were being exploited. Therefore, tantra and tantric terminology had to be suppressed, and in order to keep the knowledge alive, an entirely different language had to be adopted.

In the raja yoga of Patanjali, emphasis is placed on the development of a state called samadhi. Samadhi actually means supermental awareness. First comes sensual awareness, then mental awareness, and above that is supermental awareness, the awareness of your own self. The awareness of forms, sound, touch, taste and smell is the awareness of the senses. The awareness of time, space and object is mental awareness. Supermental awareness is not a point; it is a process, a range of experience. Just as the term 'childhood' refers to a wide span of time, in the same way, samadhi is not a particular point of experience, but a sequence of experiences which graduate from one stage to another.

Therefore, Patanjali classifies samadhi into three main categories. The first is known as *savikalpa* samadhi, that is, samadhi with fluctuation, and it has four stages: *vitarka*, *vichara*, *ananda* and *asmita*. The second category, *asamprajnata*, is samadhi without awareness, and the third category, *nirvikalpa*, is samadhi without any fluctuation.

These names only indicate the particular state your mind is in during the samadhi experience. After all, the erosion in mental awareness does not take place suddenly; the normal mental awareness does not come to an abrupt end. There is development of one type of awareness and erosion of another. The normal consciousness fades and the higher awareness develops and, therefore, there is a parallel interaction between the two states.

191

Where does meditation end and where does samadhi begin? You cannot pinpoint it because there is an interspersion. Where does youth end and old age begin? The same answer applies, and the same process happens in samadhi as well. Where does savikalpa samadhi end and where does asamprajnata begin? The whole process occurs in continuity, each stage fusing into the next and transforming in a very graduated way. This seems logical when you consider that it is the same consciousness which is undergoing the experience.

In tantra it is said that when kundalini is ascending through the various chakras, the experiences one has may not be transcendental or divine in themselves, but they are indicative of the evolving nature of consciousness. This is the territory of savikalpa samadhi, sometimes illumined and sometimes dark and treacherous.

From mooladhara up to ajna chakra, the awareness is experiencing higher things, but it is not free from ego. You cannot transcend ego at the lower points of awakening. It is only when kundalini reaches ajna chakra that the transcendence begins. This is where the ego is exploded into a million fragments and the ensuing death experience occurs. At this point, savikalpa ends and nirvikalpa begins. From here, the energies fuse and flow together up to sahasrara, where enlightenment unfolds.

In tantra, sahasrara is the highest point of awareness, and in Patanjali's raja yoga, the highest point of awareness is nirvikalpa samadhi. Now, if you compare the descriptions of sahasrara and nirvikalpa samadhi, you will find that they are the same. And if you compare the experiences of samadhi described in raja yoga with the descriptions of kundalini awakening, you will find that they are also the same. It should also be noted that both systems talk about the same types of practices.

Raja yoga is more intellectual in its method of expression and is more in tune with philosophy, and tantra is more emotional in approach and expression. That is the only difference between the two paths. As far as I can understand, kundalini awakening and samadhi are the same thing. And if you can understand the teachings of Lord Buddha and the other great saints and spiritual teachers, you will find that they have also spoken about the same subject but in different languages.

Kundalini Yoga
Practice

25

Rules and Preparation

Introduction

This section includes:

1. Preliminary techniques for individual chakras and kshetrams, and
2. Advanced techniques of kriya yoga.

The aspirant who earnestly wishes to follow the path of kundalini yoga has to approach life with a different attitude. His whole life must become a sadhana and he must be totally devoted to his practices and his goal. He will need to live a life of moderation and higher awareness in the midst of his daily responsibilities. He or she has to be a warrior in life and must seek the guidance of a competent guru who can point the way for the spiritual quest ahead. The kundalini yogi has to be ardent and faithful to his practice and his guru's instructions. He will need to devote more time each morning to perfect the practices given in this book.

Whatever your personal aim in life, and whatever your commitments and responsibilities, kundalini yoga can definitely help you to become more efficient, more peaceful and more aware. Seek the instructions of a sannyasin or a qualified yoga teacher, learn the techniques in this book, and practise them systematically according to the amount of time you are able to spare each day. In this way, your life will be transformed into the most exciting adventure ever – the journey to inner experience and unitive life.

197

The following rules and regulations apply to both the specific chakra practices and to the kriya yoga techniques. They should be followed as closely as possible.

Diet

Most people who are ready for kundalini yoga will be leading a well-regulated life and taking a balanced vegetarian diet. If you are still keeping late hours, drinking alcohol and eating large quantities of meat, we strongly suggest that you slowly reduce these and do some of the hatha yoga shatkarmas, such as *shankhaprakshalana*. In fact, we request you not to start the practices given in this book until you have become a pure vegetarian.

Eat vegetarian food that is fresh, clean and easily digestible, and eat in moderation. Kundalini yoga is a system which purifies the whole body; if there are excessive toxins in your body then there may be a drastic purging process. The consumption of too much food will also make it difficult to do most of the techniques properly, especially pranayama and those which involve uddiyana bandha.You should use your discrimination in choosing the food that you eat. Remember that all kundalini yoga courses given in our ashrams are accompanied by compulsory food restrictions, therefore, you should adopt similar restrictions. But please do not starve yourself or become a food faddist; only try to adopt sensible eating habits.

Illness

If you suffer from any physical illness, we advise you not to start the kundalini techniques given in this book. First of all, you should take steps to cure your illness by any suitable means, possibly hatha yoga. If necessary, write to this ashram, to any of our branch ashrams, or contact any competent yoga teacher for guidance. If you suffer from any serious mental or emotional problems, you should not, at present, start the practices of kundalini yoga. Practise other types of yoga to bring harmony into your life and mind, then start kundalini yoga. The kundalini techniques are very powerful, and if you do not have some degree of mental stability, they may worsen your condition. If in doubt, contact us. Sound health is the basic requirement for kundalini yoga practice.

Yogic preparation

Before commencing the kundalini techniques given in this book, you should have practised other systems of yoga, especially hatha and raja yoga, for at least a few years. In particular, you should be proficient in the following techniques: *pawanmuktasana* (anti-rheumatic and anti-gastric), *shakti bandha asanas, siddhasana* or *siddha yoni asana, surya namaskara,* major asanas such as *vipareeta karani asana, dhanurasana, shalabhasana, bhujangasana, matsyasana, paschimottanasana* and *ardha matsyendrasana,* as well as the shatkarmas, the basic practices of pranayama, such as *nadi shodhana,* and *nasikagra drishti, shambhavi mudra* and *maha bandha.*

All of these techniques are fully described in the Bihar School of Yoga publication *Asana Pranayama Mudra Bandha.* However, to master these techniques you will need to have the regular guidance of a qualified yoga teacher.

Time of practice

The best time of day to do your *sadhana* (practice) is, if possible, early in the morning, within the two hours before dawn. This is known as *brahmamuhurta* in Sanskrit, 'the time divine'. At this time spiritual energy is high and there are likely to be fewer disturbances, both external and internal, than at any other period of the day. However, if you are unable to practise during brahmamuhurta, choose some other time when the stomach is empty. Do the kundalini practices after other sadhana and before meditation practice.

Place of practice

Try to practise in the same place every day. This will gradually build up a positive atmosphere which will be helpful for your sadhana. Your place of practice should be clean, peaceful and well ventilated. It should be dry and neither too hot nor too cold. Do not practise on the bare floor; place a blanket or mat beneath you. If necessary, wrap a blanket or sheet around you. Try to avoid the use of fans, unless absolutely necessary.

Clothing

Clothing will depend on the prevailing climate, but it should be as light, loose and comfortable as possible.

Regularity

Try to practise daily at a fixed time, without fail, following the step-by-step program that we have given in this book. On certain days, the mind may give justification for not practising, or it may be upset, disturbed or restless. Providing there is no illness, you should endeavour to do your practice as normal.

Preliminary practices

Before starting the kundalini yoga practices, try to empty the bowels and take a cold shower. If you live in a cold climate, then at least wash the face with cold water. This is essential in order to remove sleepiness. It is a good idea to do a few asanas before commencing the kundalini practices. If time does not permit, then at least do five to ten rounds of *surya namaskara*, starting slowly and then accelerating the pace. This should be followed by a short period in *shavasana* until the breathing rate returns to normal.

Awareness

If the mind flits here and there like a wild monkey, do not worry. Let thoughts and emotions arise without suppression. Watch them with the attitude of a witness and continue your practice. Gradually the mind will become one-pointed. Whatever happens, your practice should continue. This attitude of witnessing the mind without interfering can be defined as awareness.

26

Posture

Most of the practices for specific chakras and the kundalini kriyas are done in a sitting position, or meditative asana. The best sitting asana is *siddhasana* (for males) and *siddha yoni asana* (for females). Not only do these two asanas apply direct pressure on mooladhara chakra, but this pressure, when applied correctly, brings about an awakening and redirection of nervous energy and blood circulation upwards from the pelvic and abdominal regions to the brain. This extra energy is important in kundalini sadhana, since it keeps the voltage of prana shakti at a high level. The perineal pressure awakens the source of energy and actively distributes prana upward to the higher centres.

Padmasana is also utilized for certain kundalini techniques such as *tadan kriya*. Though siddhasana is generally preferred in most of the other techniques, padmasana can also be used as an alternative. The disadvantage is that padmasana does not apply a direct pressure on mooladhara chakra.

Those who cannot sit comfortably in siddhasana can perform *utthanpadasana*, though it is difficult to maintain for an extended period of time. In the kriya yoga practices of *maha mudra* and *maha bheda mudra*, utthanpadasana can be performed instead of siddhasana, and is by tradition accepted as its equal.

Another asana, *bhadrasana*, also applies a good pressure on mooladhara chakra and can be substituted for siddhasana in

201

many of the practices. It is also the required sitting position for *manduki mudra*, one of the techniques of kriya yoga.

In the descriptions of the kundalini practices, we have stated the best asana for each practice. You should only use one of the alternative asanas if the recommended asana is not suitable.

General practice note

If the hips, knees and ankles are not flexible enough to assume and maintain siddhasana, padmasana, bhadrasana, etc., we suggest that you practise the pawanmuktasana series of exercises daily, especially *goolf naman, chakra* and *ghoornan* (ankle bending, rotation and crank), *janu chakra* (knee crank), *ardha* and *poorna titali asana* (half and full butterfly). *Kawa chalasana* (crow walking) and *utthanasana* (squat and rise pose) should also be practised. To improve the overall health of the body, other asanas can also be done, including surya namaskara.

Pranayama practices, such as *nadi shodhana*, should also be performed to develop control over inhalation, exhalation, and inner and outer retention, so necessary for perfecting many of the kundalini techniques.

These practices can be done daily, side-by-side with the monthly practices that are given for the specific chakras.

Siddhasana (accomplished pose for men)

Sit with the legs extended in front of the body.

Bend the right leg and place the sole of the foot flat against the inner left thigh, with the heel pressing the perineum (the area of mooladhara chakra which is midway between the genitals and anus). This is an important aspect of siddhasana.

Adjust the body until it is comfortable and the pressure of the heel is firmly applied.

Bend the left leg and place the left ankle directly over the right ankle so that the anklebones are touching and the heels are one above the other.

The left heel should press against the pubic bone directly above the genitals. The genitals will, therefore, lie between the two heels.

Push the toes and outer edge of this foot into the space between the right calf and thigh muscles. If necessary, this space may be enlarged slightly by using the hands or temporarily adjusting the position of the right leg.

Grasp the right toes, either from above or below the left calf and pull them upward into the space between the left thigh and calf.

The legs should now be locked with the knees on the ground and the left heel directly above the right heel. Make the spine steady, straight and erect, as though it were planted in the ground.

Contra-indications: Siddhasana should not be practised by persons with sciatica or sacral infections.

Benefits: Siddhasana directs the energy from the lower psychic centres upward through the spine, stimulating the brain and calming the entire nervous system. The position of the lower foot at the perineum presses mooladhara chakra, stimulating moola bandha, and the pressure applied to the pubic bone presses the trigger point for swadhisthana, automatically activating vajroli/sahajoli mudra. These two psycho-muscular locks redirect sexual nervous impulses back up the spinal cord to the brain, establishing control over the reproductive hormones which is necessary in order to maintain brahmacharya for spiritual purposes.

Prolonged periods in siddhasana result in noticeable tingling sensations in the mooladhara region which may last for ten to fifteen minutes. This is caused by a reduction in the blood supply to the area and by a rebalancing of the pranic flow in the lower chakras.

This posture redirects blood circulation to the lower spine and abdominal area.

Practice note: Siddhasana can be practised with either leg uppermost. Other classical asanas such as ardha padmasana and sukhasana can also be used, but not as effectively. Therefore, dedicate yourself initially to the perfection of siddhasana.

In the beginning it is recommended that a folded blanket or small cushion be used to raise the buttocks slightly. This will enable you to rest the knees on the ground and to achieve a balanced posture. However, the blanket or cushion should not be too thick. Three or four centimetres in height should be enough. There must be a sustained but comfortable awareness of pressure on the perineal trigger point.

Siddha Yoni Asana (accomplished pose for women)
Sit with the legs straight in front of the body.
Bend the right leg and place the sole of the foot flat against the inner left thigh.
Place this heel firmly against or inside the entrance of the vagina (labia majora).
Adjust the body position so that it is as comfortable as possible while simultaneously feeling the pressure of the right heel.
Bend the left leg and place the left heel directly on top of the right heel so it presses against the clitoris. Then wedge the left toes down into the space between the right calf and thigh so they touch, or almost touch, the floor.
Pull the right toes up into the space between the left calf and thigh.
Ensure that the knees are firmly on the ground.
Make the spine fully erect and straight as though it were planted solidly in the earth.
Contra-indications: As for siddhasana.
Benefits: As for siddhasana.

Padmasana (lotus pose)

Sit with the legs extended in front of the body.

Bend one leg and place its foot on top of the opposite thigh. The sole of the foot must be upward, with the heel facing or touching the pelvis.

Bend the other leg and place its foot on top of the other thigh.

The spine should be held straight, the neck, head and shoulders should be relaxed and the body should be steady.

Contra-indications: Those who suffer from sciatica, sacral infections or weak or injured knees should not perform this asana. This asana should not be attempted until flexibility of the knees has been developed.

Benefits: Padmasana allows the body to be held completely steady for long periods of time. It holds the trunk and head like a pillar with the legs as the firm foundation. As the body is steadied the mind becomes calm. This steadiness and calmness is the first step towards real meditation. Padmasana directs the flow of prana from mooladhara chakra in the perineum, to sahasrara chakra in the head, heightening the experience of meditation.

206

This posture applies pressure to the lower spine which has a relaxing effect on the nervous system. The breath becomes slow, muscular tension is decreased and blood pressure is reduced.

The coccygeal and sacral nerves are toned as the normally large blood flow to the legs is redirected towards the abdominal region. This activity also stimulates the digestive process.

Utthanpadasana (stretched leg pose)

Sit with both legs extended in front of the body.

Bend the left knee and press the left heel firmly into the perineum or the entrance to the vagina, the location point of mooladhara chakra. The right leg remains outstretched.

Place both hands on the right knee.

Adjust the position so that it is comfortable.

Bend forward just enough to be able to clasp the right big toe with both hands.

Hold the position for a comfortable duration.

Return to the upright position with both hands resting on the right knee.

Bhadrasana (gracious pose)

Sit in vajrasana.

Separate the knees as far as possible, while keeping the toes in contact with the floor.

Separate the feet just enough to allow the buttocks and perineum to rest flat on the floor between the feet.

Try to separate the knees further but do not strain.

Place the hands on the knees, palms down, and make the back straight.

27

Chakra Sadhana Course

Month by month we have given specific practices for the awakening of each chakra, one after the other. These practices must be adopted systematically. For the first month, you should only perform the techniques for ajna chakra. Then in the second month, add those for mooladhara. In the third month, add those for swadhisthana. In the fourth month, do those practices for manipura and selected practices for ajna, mooladhara and swadhisthana chakras. (By this stage, due to the number of practices, it will be necessary to omit some.) In this way, you should continue, adding the practices for each chakra, until you reach bindu during the seventh month.

The first month is concerned with awakening ajna chakra and not the lowest one, mooladhara, which is treated in the second month. It may seem more logical and consistent to start with mooladhara practices, but it is a rule of kundalini yoga that there should be awakening of ajna chakra first. Unless this is achieved, then the awakening of the lower chakras may rock the stability of the practitioner; one may experience physical, mental and emotional shocks which one cannot bear. The awakening of ajna chakra brings a great degree of detachment, which allows one to withstand the lower chakra awakenings without excessive shock. One is able to observe chakra experiences with the attitude of a witness. This is most essential in kundalini yoga.

In the eighth month we have given some practices which influence the chakras as a whole. These should also be done for one month.

Please note that some practices influence more than one chakra, but we have only given each practice once as sadhana for the chakra it is most likely to affect. Also, it should be noted that nothing can be gained by randomly selecting one chakra sadhana program and just practising it for a day or two and then commencing another practice. As each practice is a stepping-stone for another practice, the techniques should be performed systematically. In each chapter, practices are given to locate the position of the *chakra*, and its counterpart, the *kshetram* (which is located in the front of the body). It is important that you can locate these points exactly.

The practices given for each chakra are the building blocks from which the kriya yoga techniques are constructed. As such, you should perfect them before proceeding to the kriyas. Ultimately, you will only need to practise the kriyas, but prior to this you must devote at least one hour a day to the chakra practices for the next eight months.

Kriya yoga

In chapter 38 we have given a full description of the twenty kundalini kriyas, which are widely known as kriya yoga. At this stage, you can leave all the specific practices given in the previous chapters for awakening the chakras individually, or if you wish you can select a few to continue with.

The kundalini kriyas can be learned and practised one after the other, at the rate of one per week. That is, in the first week perfect vipareeta karani mudra; in the second week add chakra anusandhana; then add nada sanchalana in the third week, and so on. At the end of twenty weeks you should be doing the entire series of twenty kriyas daily, with the traditional number of rounds for each kriya, or with a reduced number of rounds as indicated.

Please note that the kundalini kriyas should only be practised under the guidance of a qualified teacher.

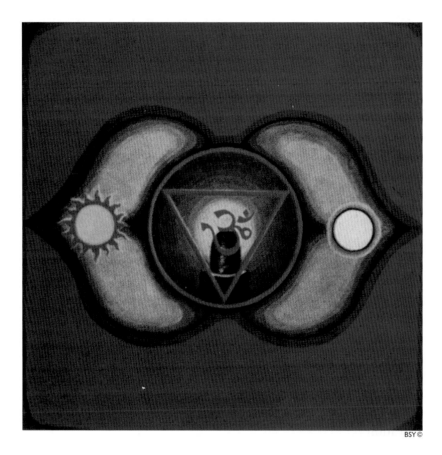

Ajna

28

Practices for Ajna Chakra

MONTH 1

Direct concentration on ajna chakra is very difficult and, for this reason, in tantra and yoga the mid-eyebrow centre (which in fact is the kshetram of ajna) is used to awaken this chakra. This point is called bhrumadhya (*bhru* means eyebrow and *madhya* means centre), and it lies between the two eyebrows in the place where Indian ladies put a red dot, and pandits and brahmins put a mark of sandal paste. This eyebrow centre can be stimulated and awakened by various techniques.

Firstly, there is an important shatkriya (cleansing technique) called *trataka*, which will aid in the awakening of ajna. It is a powerful technique which can be defined as 'fixed gazing at one point'. If practised regularly, it develops the power of concentration and from this concentration, the direct awakening of the latent faculties of ajna chakra is brought about.

Ajna can also be stimulated and awakened by concentration on the nadis directly. The method for this is *anuloma viloma pranayama*, mental or psychic nadi shodhana, also known as 'the coming and going pranayama', and *prana shuddhi*, 'the purifying breath'.

You can also awaken ajna chakra by concentrating on the eyebrow centre, performing such practices as *shambhavi mudra*. Initially, when there is no sensation or awareness at this point, some ointment or oil such as tiger balm can be applied. This facilitates concentration. With practise, the pressure of your concentration at this area increases and the sensations are carried back to the pineal gland. This brings about an awakening in the pineal gland in the form of visions and internal experiences.

Ajna and mooladhara chakras are closely related, and the awakening of one helps to awaken the other. Ideally, ajna should be awakened to some extent before mooladhara, in order to allow an unaffected perception of the energies manifested by mooladhara and the lower chakras. However, the awakening of mooladhara will help to further awaken ajna. In fact, the best way to bring about awakening of ajna is through the practices of *moola bandha* and *ashwini mudra*, which are specific for mooladhara.

Preparatory practices

Jala and *sutra neti* can be practised for a few months to purify the nasal area and the important nerve junction behind it. This will help to sensitize ajna chakra and aid in its awakening. Apart from having a profound effect on the nervous system, neti removes dirt and mucus from the nasal passages, relieving colds and sinusitis, disorders of the eyes, ears, nose and throat, as well as inflammation of the tonsils, adenoids and mucous membranes. It removes drowsiness and gives a general lightness and freshness in the head and throughout the body. At the same time, it profoundly alters psychic awareness, facilitating free flow of breath in both nostrils, so that the meditative state can be attained. It should be practised every morning before you commence your other sadhana. For complete details refer to the Bihar School of Yoga publication *Asana Pranayama Mudra Bandha*.

Practice program

The following sadhana (consisting of practices 1, 2 and 3) for ajna chakra should be continued daily for one month. You may then proceed to the sadhana given for awakening mooladhara chakra.

212

Practice 1: Anuloma Viloma Pranayama with Prana Shuddhi (the coming and going breath and the purifying breath)

Sit in a comfortable meditative posture.

Make sure the spine is erect and the body is relaxed.

The body must become absolutely still.

After some minutes, begin to develop awareness of the breath in the nostrils.

When you breathe in, your whole awareness should flow with the breath from the tip of the nose, up to the eyebrow centre.

When you breathe out, your whole awareness should flow with the breath from the eyebrow centre to the tip of the nose.

Become aware of the triangular form of the breath between the nostrils and the eyebrow centre. The base of the triangle is at the level of the upper lip, its sides are the right and left nasal passages, and its apex is within the eyebrow centre.

Firstly, feel the breath moving in and out of the left nostril, then the right nostril. Then be aware of the breath as it flows in and out through both nostrils together.

Once you are established in this breath awareness, begin to consciously alternate the flow of the breath between the two nostrils in the same way as nadi shodhana, except you practise it psychically or mentally.

Consciously inhale through the left nostril to bhrumadhya and exhale through the right, then inhale through the right to bhrumadhya, and exhale through the left.

This is one round of anuloma viloma or mental nadi shodhana. Complete 4 rounds.

Now practise one round of prana shuddhi, which involves breathing in and out through both nostrils together.

Inhale and exhale through both nostrils simultaneously, visualizing the passage of the breath forming an inverted V-shape.

Continue in this way: four alternate nostril breaths, then one breath through both nostrils.

In the beginning, the rounds can be counted as follows:
1 – inhale left nostril, exhale right nostril; inhale right nostril, exhale left nostril,
2 – repeat, 3 – repeat, 4 – repeat,
5 – inhale both nostrils, exhale both nostrils, and so on.
After some practise, the rounds can be counted from 100 back to zero as follows:
100 – inhale left nostril, exhale right nostril; inhale right nostril, exhale left nostril,
99 – repeat, 98 – repeat, 97 – repeat,
96 – inhale both nostrils, exhale both nostrils, and so on.

Practice note: Accuracy in the counting is absolutely necessary, and if an error is made, the practice must recommence from 100. It is very important to keep count of the breaths, because without keeping count, anuloma viloma is altogether too powerful for many aspirants, swallowing up their awareness in the unconscious sphere.

The aim of the practice is to stimulate ajna chakra on the subconscious, psychic level, and for this, awareness must be maintained.

If you sink into the unconscious sphere, you will only be aware of the vast store of impressions in the unconscious mind, and will completely lose awareness of the practice. This awareness is essential for the development of mind control and also for the awakening of ajna chakra to conscious accessibility.

This practice can also be very well integrated into yoga nidra. (See chapter 35.)

Practice 2: Trataka (concentrated gazing)

Sit in a comfortable meditative asana, in a dark room in which there is no draught or breeze.

Place a lighted candle at eye level, directly in front of the eyebrow centre, at arm's length.

Make sure that the wick is perfectly straight and that the flame is motionless.

Straighten the spine, close the eyes and relax the body.

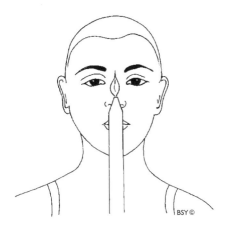

Be aware of the physical body only. Let it become as still as a statue.

From this time on you should try to keep the body absolutely motionless throughout the whole practice. When you are prepared, open your eyes and gaze steadily at the tip of the wick. With practise you should be able to gaze steadily at the flame without blinking or moving the eyeballs. Two to three minutes is sufficient.

The whole of your consciousness must become centred in the flame, to the extent that awareness of the rest of the body and the room is lost. The gaze should be absolutely fixed at the tip of the wick. When the eyes become tired or if they begin to water, close them and relax.

Do not move the body, but be aware of the after-image of the flame in front of the closed eyes.

Everyone has looked into the sun or a bright light, and on closing the eyes for a few minutes, has seen the clear impression of that light on the retina of the eye. Likewise, the after-image of the candle flame will be clearly visible.

You should practise trataka on this image, holding it directly in front or a little above the eyebrow centre. Keep the eyes closed. If the image moves up or down, or from side to side, observe it and try to stabilize it, without straining.

When you are sure the image has appeared and faded for the last time, then open the eyes and continue to concentrate on the external candle flame.

After the last round, gaze into the emptiness for a few seconds then practise palming.

Time of practice: The best times to practise trataka are the dark hours of the very early morning or late at night. At these times, the atmosphere becomes very still and quiet, not only the physical atmosphere, but also the mental and psychic atmospheres. In this stillness, success in trataka is readily attained.

Duration: Trataka can be practised as time permits, but five to fifteen minutes is the usual period in the beginning, building up to thirty minutes gradually over a period of time. Two to three minutes per round is sufficient to spend gazing at the flame.

Contra-indications: Trataka on a flame is not recommended for myopia, astigmatism, cataract or glaucoma.

Benefits: Trataka has many physical, mental and spiritual benefits. Physically, it corrects eye weaknesses and defects such as nearsightedness. Mentally, it increases nervous stability, removes insomnia and relaxes the anxious mind. When the eyes are fixed and unmoving, the mind becomes steady and calm. It helps to develop good concentration and strong willpower. Spiritually it awakens ajna chakra.

Variations: Trataka can be practised on a small dot, the full moon, the rising sun, a shadow, a crystal ball, the nose tip, an image in water, a yantra, darkness, a shivalingam and many other things.

Those who have a personal deity can practise trataka on his or her form and those who have a guru can practise on his or her photograph. Trataka can also be practised on one's own image in the mirror, or the eyes of another person. These should, however, only be done under the guidance of a guru, as there are certain risks involved.

Avoid practising trataka on the sun as the delicate membranes of the eyes may be damaged.

There are two divisions of trataka, *bahiranga* (outer) and *antaranga* (inner). The methods mentioned so far are all part of bahiranga trataka. Inner trataka (antaranga) is internal visualization, perhaps of a chakra, a yantra or your personal deity. The eyes remain closed throughout. One of the best inner objects for concentration is a tiny star or point of light.

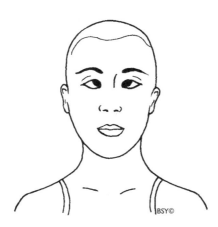

Practice 3: Shambhavi Mudra (eyebrow centre gazing) with Om chanting
Stage 1: External awareness

Sit in any meditative pose with the back straight and hands on the knees.

Look forward at a fixed point, then look upward as high as possible without moving the head.

Focus the eyes and concentrate on the eyebrow centre.

Try to suspend the thought processes and meditate on ajna.

Repeat Om, Om, Om with awareness of the sound vibrations at the eyebrow centre into which you are gazing. Each Om should be produced in a soft clear voice, with awareness of every vibration of the mantra in the eyebrow centre.

217

Each mantra should be one or two seconds in duration, and immediately followed by the next.

Practise for three to five minutes.

Stage 2: Internal awareness

Now the eyes are closed, but the inner gaze remains in the eyebrow centre.

Begin to chant the mantra more slowly, with full awareness of the sound vibration in the eyebrow centre. Imagine that the sound is being emitted from within the eyebrow centre itself. Gradually and effortlessly increase the duration of each Om, making it long and continuous.

The sound should be steady and of an even key, ending on completion of the breath.

Then refill the lungs completely by breathing through the nose, but do not alter the position of the body or head.

Begin the next Om, maintaining awareness of the sound emerging from the eyebrow centre.

Practise for five minutes.

Stage 3: Awareness of sound vibration

Continue to chant the mantra Om, but become aware of the sound reverberating throughout the body.

Try to be aware of the sound only, listening to its vibration emanating from the eyebrow centre and permeating the whole body.

Do not be self-conscious, but allow the sound to manifest itself fully, maintaining awareness of the vibration of the sound only.

Practise for five minutes.

Gradually the duration of the practice can be lengthened. Finish off the practice with palming.

Precautions: Do not strain the eye muscles; when they become tired or slightly strained, release shambhavi mudra and relax the eyes.

Mooladhara

29

Practices for Mooladhara Chakra

MONTH 2

The process of awakening mooladhara chakra is not very difficult. It can be achieved by thousands of different methods, but the easiest of all is the concentration on the tip of the nose. This is because the part of the sensory cortex which represents mooladhara chakra is connected with the nose. At the same time, mooladhara chakra belongs to the earth element, which is directly related to the sense of smell. Therefore, we shall include *nasikagra drishti*, the practice of nose tip gazing, in this section, as well as moola bandha, which directly stimulates mooladhara chakra. Remember that mooladhara chakra does not have a kshetram.

Practice program

This sadhana (practices 1, 2 and 3) for mooladhara chakra should be done for a period of one month. You should also continue the practices for awakening ajna chakra.

Difference between moola bandha, vajroli/sahajoli mudra and ashwini mudra

Often there is confusion between the three practices of moola bandha (used for awakening mooladhara chakra) and vajroli/ sahajoli mudra and ashwini mudra (both used for awakening swadhisthana chakra). The following diagrams for both male and female locations will help to clarify the difference in the points of contraction.

219

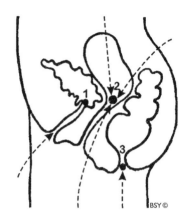

Diagram 1: for the female

Key to location of contraction points: (1) Sahajoli mudra (clitoris, vaginal walls and urethra); (2) Moola bandha (cervix and vaginal muscles); (3) Ashwini mudra (anal muscles/sphincters).

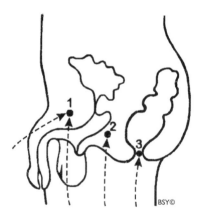

Diagram 2: for the male

Key to location of contraction points: (1) Vajroli mudra (penis); (2) Moola bandha (between anus and scrotum; the perineal body); (3) Ashwini mudra (anal muscles/sphincters).

Practice 1: Mooladhara chakra location

For men: Sit in siddhasana or any asana in which the heel is pressed into the perineum.

Close the eyes, relax completely and become aware of the whole physical body.

Move the awareness to the point of contact between the heel and perineum, midway between the testes and the anus. Become intensely aware of the distinct pressure exerted on the perineal body.

Centre yourself at the pressure point.

Now become aware of the breath.

Feel or imagine that you are breathing in and out of this pressure point.

Feel the breath moving through the perineal body, becoming finer and finer, and finer, so that it pierces the point where mooladhara chakra is located.

You will feel it as a psychophysical contraction.

Say mentally, 'mooladhara, mooladhara, mooladhara'.

Maintain awareness of the perineal body and the breath for up to five minutes.

For women: Sit in siddha yoni asana or a suitable alternative.

Relax the body completely and close the eyes.

Move the awareness to the lower part of the body and focus the attention on the contact point between the heel and the opening of the vagina.

Become intensely aware of the slight but distinct pressure.

Centre yourself at the pressure point.

Now become aware of the natural breath.

Feel or imagine that you are breathing in and out of the pressure point.

Continue for 10 deep breaths.

Now bring your awareness inside the body.

From the point of external pressure, move your awareness in towards the base of the spine.

Follow the natural formation of the vagina, moving up at a slight angle and back towards the spine until you come to the opening of the womb.

You are at the opening of the womb, about two or three centimetres inside the body, just below the base of the spine.

Focus your awareness at this point and begin to breathe in and out from the cervix to the point of outer pressure.

Breathe in and bring your awareness to the opening of the womb.

Breathe out and move again to the outer pressure point, the opening of the vagina.

Somewhere in this area you will find your point for mooladhara chakra.

Feel this point clearly and distinctly and mentally repeat, 'mooladhara, mooladhara, mooladhara'.

Maintain unbroken awareness of this point for up to five minutes.

Alternative practice: Locating mooladhara chakra by touch

For men: Sit in a comfortable position and press one finger onto the perineum, midway between the anus and scrotum, then contract the muscles there. The contraction will be felt. When you can contract those muscles without movement of the anus or penis, the perineal body has been successfully isolated.

For women: Assume a comfortable sitting or lying position and gently insert one finger into the vagina as far as it will go. Then contract the vaginal muscles inwards and upwards so that the walls of the upper vagina contract, and squeeze the finger. If you can do this without contracting the anus or the front part of the perineum (clitoris and urinary opening), the location of mooladhara chakra is correct.

Practice 2: Moola Bandha (perineal contraction)
Stage 1: Contraction with breath retention

Sit in siddhasana/siddha yoni asana or any other posture which will apply a firm pressure in the region of mooladhara chakra.

Close the eyes and relax the whole body.

Inhale deeply. Hold the breath and contract the muscles at the mooladhara chakra region.

Draw the muscles upwards as much as you are able without excessive strain.

Try to contract only the mooladhara chakra trigger point, so that the urinary musculature in front and the anal sphincters behind, remain relaxed.

Keep your attention fixed on the exact point of contraction. Hold this contraction for as long as possible.

Then release moola bandha and breathe normally.

Practise for a few minutes daily.

Practice note: Jalandhara bandha (described in chapter 33 of this section), can also be added to the practice. With breath retention, perform jalandhara bandha, followed by moola bandha. Before exhaling, release moola bandha, then jalandhara bandha.

Stage 2: Physical contraction

Contract and release moola bandha rhythmically.

About one contraction per second is reasonable, or if you wish, you can synchronize the contraction with the heartbeat.

Again, ensure that the contraction is focused at the exact trigger point and at the anus.

Direct all your attention to the point of contraction.

Practise for a few minutes daily.

Stage 3: Mental contraction

Leave all physical contraction.

Try to feel the pulse beat at the trigger point, or try to contract the point mentally.

Direct all your attention to the mooladhara chakra area.

The practice is similar to stage 2, without the physical contraction.

Continue for as long as you have time to spare.

With practise, you will be able to locate the trigger point of mooladhara chakra exactly, merely through thought alone.

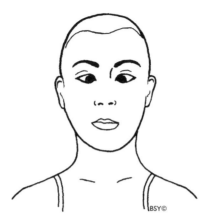

Practice 3: Nasikagra Drishti (nose tip gazing)

Sit in any meditative pose with the spine erect and the head upright.

Close the eyes and relax the whole body for some time.

Then open the eyes and focus them on the nose tip.

Do not strain the eyes, but try to fix the gaze on the tip of the nose.

Respiration should be normal.

When the eyes are correctly focused, a double outline of the nose is seen.

These two lines converge at the tip of the nose, forming an inverted V-image.

Concentrate on the apex of the V.

If you do not see a solid V-shaped outline, then both eyes are not fixed on the nose tip.

It is then necessary to focus the eyes on the finger tip, 25 centimetres in front of the face, and hold the fingertip in focus as you slowly bring it to the nose tip.

Eventually, you can discard this method and easily focus the eyes on the nose tip at will.

At first you may find it difficult to hold your attention on the nose tip for more than a few seconds.

When you feel discomfort, release the position of the eyes for a few seconds and then repeat the practice.

224

Over a period of weeks, as the eyes become accustomed, gradually increase the duration of the practice.

Never strain the eyes.

Once you can comfortably maintain a steady gaze for a minute or more, become aware of your breath as well as the nose tip.

Feel the breath moving in and out through the nose.

At the same time, become aware of the subtle sound the breath makes as it moves through the nasal passages.

Try to become completely absorbed in the practice, to the exclusion of all other thoughts and external distractions.

Be aware of the nose tip, the movement of the breath and the accompanying sound. Continue in this manner for up to five minutes.

End the practice with palming to relax and energize the eyes.

Note: *This practice is also called* agochari mudra *(the gesture of invisibility)*.

30

Practices for
Swadhisthana Chakra

MONTH 3

The sadhana for awakening swadhisthana chakra is solely concerned with the uro-genital systems, the prostate gland and testes in the male, and the genito-ovarian system in the female. Vajroli and sahajoli mudras are two very powerful practices which rechannel sexual energy and help bring about the awakening of swadhisthana. Vajroli is practised by males and sahajoli by females. There are simple forms of vajroli and also more difficult techniques which require the direct guidance of a guru. However, the practices given here can be performed with reasonable ease by anyone who is thoroughly familiar with shalabhasana, dhanurasana and uddiyana bandha. Refer to 'Difference between moola bandha, vajroli and ashwini mudras', given in chapter 29.

Preparatory practices

A large number of asanas have a direct effect on swadhisthana chakra and help to bring about initial purification and sensitization. We suggest that you practise shakti bandha series, bhujangasana, shashankasana, dhanurasana and shashank bhujangasana.

Practice program

The sadhana (practices 1–4) for awakening swadhisthana chakra, should be perfected over a period of one month. It should be kept in mind that swadhisthana is the switch

Swadhisthana

for bindu and, therefore, the sadhana for swadhisthana also brings about a simultaneous effect on and awakening of bindu. You can also continue the sadhana for ajna and mooladhara chakras.

Practice 1: Swadhisthana chakra location

Sit in a comfortable position. Move one finger to the lowest end of the spine and feel the coccyx, the tailbone. Then move the finger up about one inch or 2–3 centimetres, along the sacral portion of the pelvis, and press hard for one minute.

When you take the finger away, you will experience a residual sensation.

About one centimetre deep into that sensation is the location of swadhisthana chakra.

Concentrate on it for two minutes or so repeating mentally, 'swadhisthana, swadhisthana, swadhisthana'.

Practice 2: Swadhisthana kshetram location

If you feel down to the lower end of the abdomen, you will come to a bony portion at the front part of the pelvis. This is called the pubis, and is the anatomical location of swadhisthana kshetram.

Press hard on this area for about one minute.

Then remove the finger and concentrate on the point where your finger was. Repeat mentally, 'swadhisthana, swadhisthana, swadhisthana'.

Practice 3: Ashwini Mudra (horse gesture)

Sit in any meditative posture. Relax the whole body, close the eyes and breathe normally.

Contract the sphincter muscles of the anus for half a second, then relax them for half a second.

Continue this contraction and relaxation for a few minutes. Try to feel the waves spreading up to hit swadhisthana chakra. Focus your whole attention on the lower end of the spine and feel the pressure waves.

Practice 4: Vajroli Mudra (thunderbolt attitude) – for men

Sit comfortably in siddhasana, preferably with a thin cushion or a folded blanket beneath the buttocks.

Close the eyes and relax the body.

Take the awareness to the urethra, the urinary passage within the penis.

Try to draw the urethra upward. This muscular action is similar to that made when trying to control the urge to urinate.

The testes may move slightly due to this contraction.

Try to focus and confine the force of the contraction at the urethra.

Try not to perform moola bandha or ashwini mudra at the same time.

Contract for 10 seconds, release for 10 seconds. Continue this for a few minutes.

Concentrate on the kshetram at the pubis all the time, while repeating mentally, 'swadhisthana, swadhisthana, swadhisthana'.

Practice 4: Sahajoli Mudra (spontaneous psychic attitude) – for women

Sit comfortably in siddha yoni asana, preferably with a thin cushion or folded blanket beneath the buttocks.

Close the eyes and relax the body.

Contract the urethra. This contraction is similar to that made when trying to control the urge to urinate.

The vaginal muscles and the hood of the clitoris may move slightly due to this contraction.

Gradually increase the contraction until it becomes more intense and deep.

Hold the contraction for 10 seconds, release for 10 seconds. Continue for a few minutes, mentally repeating 'swadhisthana, swadhisthana, swadhisthana'.

Manipura

31

Practices for
Manipura Chakra

MONTH 4

There are several methods of awakening manipura chakra. According to hatha yoga, manipura is directly connected with the eyes. Ajna chakra and manipura chakra are very closely related to one another in the same way that vision and wilful action are interdependent processes. Therefore, the practice of trataka brings about manipura and ajna chakra awakening.

Although tantra is not against any particular diet, when manipura chakra is to be awakened, the diet has to be very pure, and at certain stages, fasting may be necessary as well. If manipura is awakened when the diet is faulty, harmful reactions may take place. Because manipura is the centre of the digestive fire, disorders of the gastrointestinal system are corrected by manipura sadhana.

The major constituents of manipura sadhana are uddiyana bandha and nauli kriya. Uddiyana bandha is the contraction of the abdomen and the control of the muscles of the abdominal wall, as well as control over the small and large intestines and the other digestive and visceral organs. The functions of the liver, gallbladder, spleen, pancreas and stomach are brought into harmonious and controlled interaction when uddiyana bandha is perfected. However, agnisar kriya must be mastered before uddiyana is attempted.

Nauli kriya is the control of the rectus abdomini muscles and churning of the whole abdomen. This is a difficult practice which takes some time to perfect. However, with mastery of nauli, it is easy to create a union of prana and apana in the navel, so manipura chakra can be awakened.

Preparatory practices

The following asanas will be found useful in awakening manipura chakra: pawanmuktasana (the anti-gastric series), chakrasana, dhanurasana, marjari-asana, matsyasana, yoga mudra, paschimottanasana and ushtrasana.

Practice program

Practise the techniques for awakening manipura chakra for one month and then proceed to those for anahata chakra. Nauli may be difficult for many people; do not strain or overexert. It is best not to attempt it until you have mastered agnisar kriya and uddiyana bandha.

The practices for awakening ajna, mooladhara and swadhisthana can also be continued.

Practice 1: Manipura chakra and kshetram location
Stand sideways in front of a mirror.
Put one finger of one hand on the navel and one finger of the other hand on the spine, directly behind.
Sit down, press firmly with the finger on the spine for one minute, then remove the finger.
As the pressure sensation continues, concentrate on the area slightly deeper in from that point.
This is the location of manipura chakra.
Whilst feeling the pulse beat at this point, mentally repeat the mantra, 'manipura' for a few minutes.

Practice 2: Manipura purification
Assume a comfortable sitting pose.
Hold the back straight and keep the eyes closed.
Breathe slowly and deeply, feeling the expansion and contraction of the navel as you breathe in and out through the navel.

Feel the breath expanding and contracting in the navel area for a few minutes.

As the navel expands outward, feel that the breath is being pulled in through the navel, straight back to manipura in the spine.

As the navel contracts inward, feel that the breath is flowing from manipura chakra in the spine to the navel and out of the body.

Practise this for a few minutes each day while mentally repeating, 'manipura, manipura, manipura'.

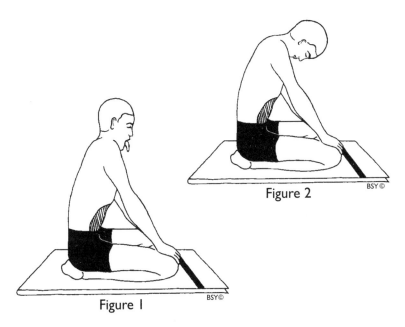

Figure 2

Figure 1

Practice 3: Agnisar Kriya
Preparatory practice: Swana Pranayama (panting breath)

Sit in vajrasana. Keeping the toes together, separate the knees as far as possible (see figure 1).

Keep both hands on the knees, straighten the arms and lean forward slightly.

Open the mouth and extend the tongue outside.

231

Breathe rapidly in and out while simultaneously expanding and contracting the abdomen.

The respiration should be in harmony with the movement of the abdomen and should resemble the panting of a dog. Breathe in and out up to 25 times.

Agnisar Kriya (activating the digestive fire)

Assume the same position (see figure 2).

Exhale as completely as possible.

Perform jalandhara bandha.

Rapidly contract and expand the abdominal muscles repeatedly, for as long as you are able to retain the breath outside.

Release jalandhara bandha and inhale fully.

Perform the practice 4 more times, waiting until the breath has returned to normal between each round.

Contra-indications: People suffering from high blood pressure, heart disease or acute peptic or duodenal ulcers should not practise this kriya, nor should pregnant women or persons who have undergone abdominal surgery in the last six to nine months.

Practice note: Agnisar kriya should be practised on an empty stomach preferably in the early in the morning before breakfast. It should not be attempted until swana pranayama is mastered.

Practice 4: Uddiyana Bandha (abdominal contraction)

Sit in a siddha/siddha yoni asana or padmasana with the spine erect and the knees touching the floor.

If this is not possible, uddiyana bandha can be performed while standing.

Place the hands on the knees, close the eyes and relax the whole body. Exhale completely and hold the breath outside.

Perform jalandhara bandha.

Then contract the abdominal muscles as far as possible inward and upward.

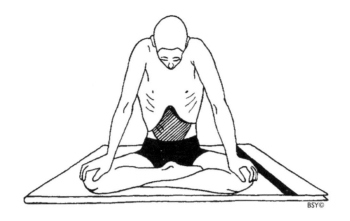

This is a kind of sucking action of the muscles.
Hold this lock for as long as the breath can be retained
outside without straining.
Concentrate on manipura chakra in the spine and repeat
mentally, 'manipura, manipura, manipura'.
Slowly relax the stomach muscles.
Release jalandhara bandha and inhale.
When the respiration has returned to normal, the process
may be repeated.
Practise a few rounds and gradually increase to ten.
Contra-indications: Same as for agnisar kriya.

Practice 5: Nauli (abdominal massaging)
Stage 1: Madhyama Nauli (central abdominal contraction)
Stand with the feet about a metre apart.
Take a deep breath in through the nose and then exhale
through the mouth, emptying the lungs as much as
possible.
Bend the knees slightly and lean forward, placing the
palms on the thighs just above the knees, so that the
knees are supporting the weight of the body. The arms
should remain straight.
Perform jalandhara bandha while retaining the breath
outside.

233

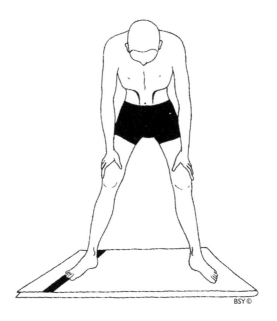

Keep the eyes open and watch the abdomen.

Suck in the lower abdomen.

Contract the rectus abdomini muscles so that they form a central arch running vertically in front of the abdomen.

Hold the contraction for as long as it is comfortable to hold the breath.

Release the contraction, raise the head and return to the upright position. Inhale slowly and deeply, allowing the abdomen to expand. Relax the whole body.

This is one round. Relax in the standing position until the heartbeat returns to normal. Repeat the practice.

Madhyama nauli should be perfected before proceeding to the next stage.

Stage 2: Vama Nauli (left isolation)

Follow the instructions for madhyama nauli to the point where the lower abdomen is contracted and the rectus abdomini muscles form a central, vertical arch down the abdomen.

Isolate the rectus abdomini muscles at the left side.

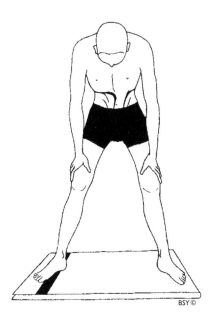

Contract the muscles to the left side as strongly as possible without straining.

Return to madhyama nauli.

Release the abdominal contraction, raise the head and return to the upright position.

Inhale slowly and deeply, allowing the abdomen to expand. This is one round.

Relax in the upright position until the heartbeat returns to normal. Proceed to stage 3.

Stage 3: Dakshina Nauli (right isolation)

After completing vama nauli, practise in the same way but on the right side.

Follow the instructions for madhyama nauli to the point where the lower abdomen is contracted and the rectus abdomini muscles form a central, vertical arch down the abdomen.

Isolate the rectus abdomini muscles at the right side.

Hold the contraction as tightly as possible while retaining the breath.

235

Do not strain. Return to madhyama nauli.

Release the abdominal contraction, raise the head and return to the upright position.

Inhale slowly and deeply, allowing the abdomen to expand.

This is one round.

Relax in the upright position until the heartbeat returns to normal.

Proceed to abdominal rotation or churning only after perfecting this practice.

Stage 4: Abdominal rotation or churning

This practice should not be attempted until the previous three stages have been mastered.

Practise vama nauli, then rotate the muscles to the right, dakshina nauli, and back to the left, vama nauli.

Continue rotating the muscles from side to side. This process is known as churning.

Start by practising 3 consecutive rotations, then release the abdominal contraction.

Next start with dakshina nauli first, this time rotating the muscles from right to left, left to right 3 times consecutively.

Then perform madhyama nauli, isolating the muscles at the centre.

Raise the head and return to the upright position.

Inhale slowly and deeply, allowing the abdomen to expand.

This is one round.

Relax in the upright position until the heartbeat returns to normal.

Practise each round for as long as the breath can be retained.

Do up to six 6 rounds.

Contra-indications: Limitations are the same as for agnisar kriya.

Practice note: Nauli should not be attempted until agnisar kriya and uddiyana bandha have been perfected.

Practice 6: Union of prana and apana

Sit in siddhasana or siddha yoni asana.

Relax the whole body for a few minutes, bringing it to the point of absolute immobility.

Now become aware of the natural abdominal breath.

Centre the awareness on the movement of the navel as you inhale and exhale.

Continue for a few minutes.

Now become aware that there are two forces travelling to the navel – prana and apana.

One force (apana) is ascending from mooladhara to the navel, while the other (prana), is descending to the navel from above. They must both reach the navel at the point of full inhalation. When you feel that the two forces are meeting in the navel, perform kumbhaka, retention of breath, and then develop mental awareness of the single central point of force in the navel.

Do not strain.

Release the breath and continue this practice in your own natural rhythm.

The awareness of the two forces travelling and meeting in the navel centre must be simultaneous.

Now, as the two forces are converging in the navel, gradually allow moola bandha to take place.

Go on contracting moola bandha as you heighten your awareness of the force which is centred in the navel.

Hold your breath for as long as you can, while centralizing the force in the navel and performing moola bandha.

As you release the breath, release moola bandha as well.

Do not strain.

Go on practising for 3 minutes or more.

32

Practices for
Anahata Chakra

MONTH 5

Anahata chakra can be awakened very simply through the practice of ajapa japa. Japa means 'repetition' and ajapa is the repetition of a mantra until it ultimately becomes the spontaneous form of your conscious awareness.

Another important practice in anahata awakening is bhramari pranayama. Although it is called a pranayama, bhramari is actually a meditational practice. It is not directly related to controlling prana, as are other forms of pranayama. In the scriptures, the heart centre is termed 'the centre of unstruck sound' and also 'the cave of bees'. In bhramari, the humming sound of the bees is produced and traced towards its source. This develops deep mental and emotional relaxation and is extremely effective in cardiac disorders.

Anahata chakra is the centre of bhakti or devotion. It is awakened in accordance with the degree of devotion to guru, God, or personal deity, in whatever form or non-form one may visualize or understand the spiritual intelligence of the universe. All practices of yoga, especially when done with the blessings of the guru, will automatically awaken devotion in the spiritual heart (anahata chakra). There are many excellent books on bhakti yoga that will help to inspire the aspirant to follow this path. Any biographies of saints, yogis and bhaktas will also be useful. An excellent description of the process of bhakti yoga is given in our publication entitled, *A Systematic Course in the Ancient Tantric Techniques*

Anahata

of Yoga and Kriya, and in *Bhakti Yoga Sagar*, Volumes 1–5, by Swami Satyananda Saraswati.

Practice program

Practise these techniques for anahata chakra for one month and then begin those for awakening vishuddhi chakra. All the practices given for awakening ajna, mooladhara, swadhisthana and manipura chakras can be done if sufficient time is available. If not, then we suggest that you do a few selected techniques from each chakra sadhana as follows:
1. *Ajna* – trataka and shambhavi mudra
2. *Mooladhara* – moola bandha and nasikagra mudra
3. *Swadhisthana* – chakra and kshetram location, vajroli or sahajoli
4. *Manipura* – chakra and kshetram location, uddiyana bandha and nauli (if possible).

Practice 1: Anahata chakra and kshetram location

Stand sideways in front of a mirror.

Put one finger of one hand on the centre of the chest.

Here you will find anahata kshetram.

Put one finger of the other hand on the spine, directly behind the kshetram; this is anahata chakra.

Sit down, press both fingers firmly for one minute, and then remove the fingers.

The sensation at the chakra and kshetram will continue. Concentrate on the sensation at the chakra and mentally repeat, 'anahata, anahata, anahata', for a few minutes.

Practice 2: Anahata purification

Assume a comfortable sitting posture. Hold the back straight but without strain. Keep the eyes closed.

Breathe slowly and deeply, feeling the expansion and contraction of the chest as you breathe in and out for some minutes.

Then become aware of the breath moving in and out of the anahata region.

239

As the chest expands, feel that the breath flows in through the centre of the chest and back to anahata chakra.

As the chest contracts, feel that the breath flows from anahata chakra in the spine, through the centre of the chest and out of the body.

Practise this for some minutes, mentally repeating, 'anahata, anahata, anahata'.

BSY©

Practice 3: Bhramari Pranayama (humming bee breath)

Sit in a comfortable meditative pose. Adjust your position and relax fully for some minutes. Face forward.

Hold the head and spine as straight as possible.

Close the eyes.

Relax the whole body.

Keep the teeth slightly separated and the mouth closed throughout the entire practice.

This allows the vibration to be experienced more distinctly in the brain.

Plug the ears with the index fingers.

Breathe in slowly and deeply.

Then, while breathing out, produce a humming sound.

The sound should be smooth and continuous for the full duration of exhalation.

The humming need not be loud.
The important thing is that you hear the sound reverberating within your head.
The exhalation should be slow and controlled.
At the end of exhalation, stop the humming sound and breathe in fully.
Keep the eyes closed and the ears plugged.
Again repeat the humming sound with the next exhalation.
Try to relax fully during the practice.
Do not strain in any way.
Continue for 5 or 10 minutes.

Practice 4: Ajapa japa meditation

Sit in siddhasana, siddha yoni asana or any posture which feels completely comfortable.
Close the eyes and relax for a few minutes.
Now become aware of the natural breath as it enters and leaves the body.
Do not try to control the breath, just become a witness of the natural breathing process.
Now become aware that the sound of inhalation is *So* and the sound of exhalation is *ham*. The natural mantra of the breath is *So-ham*. You have only to discover it.
Be simultaneously aware of the natural breath, coupled with the idea of *So-ham-so-ham-so-ham*.
You must be totally relaxed in this practice.
Do not lose awareness of the mantra or your natural breath, even for an instant. Do not be concerned with the thoughts and feelings that arise.
Allow them to come and go as they will. Remain ever aware of the natural breath and the ongoing mantra.
Now become aware of the psychic breath which is flowing in an imaginary or psychic passage in the front of the body between the navel and the throat, and between the throat and the navel.
With inspiration, this psychic breath rises from the navel to throat and its mantra is *So*. With expiration, the psychic

breath descends from the throat back to the navel. Its mantra is *ham*.

Maintain awareness of the breath passing through the psychic passageway and producing the sound *So-ham-so-ham-so-ham*.

Continue this practice for 10 or 15 minutes more, allowing your breathing to be totally relaxed.

Practice note: Ajapa japa can be practised at any time, but it should be done for 5 to 10 minutes per day, either in the morning sadhana session or at night, immediately before sleep. It should be continued for at least one month.

Practice 5: Meditation – entering the heart space
Stage I: Breath awareness

Sit in siddhasana, siddha yoni asana or any other comfortable posture. Close the eyes and relax completely for some time. Concentrate the awareness in the throat region. Now become aware of the breath in the throat.

Only be aware of the sensation of the breath in the throat for some time.

Now add the awareness of the ingoing breath from the throat downwards. You are not concerned with the outgoing breath. Your attention is occupied only with the ingoing breath in the throat.

Become aware of the inflowing breath in the throat passing within the network of the diaphragm.

Be aware of the diaphragm – the rising and falling of the muscular floor separating the chest and lungs above from the abdominal organs below.

With each inspiration, it drops into the abdomen a little, increasing the pressure there and causing the navel to expand.

Simultaneously, the lungs are expanding fully in the chest.

Be aware that with expiration the abdomen contracts, the diaphragm is rising and the lungs are emptying completely.

Develop awareness of the diaphragm for some time.

242

Stage 2: Awareness of the heart space

Now, also become aware of the akasha, the space within which the diaphragm is operating.

With the ingoing breath you feel this space is filling up.

Only be aware of the process of filling up the space.

This process of filling up is only a basis for the awareness of this vast space.

The process of feeling the breath is only the basis for experiencing the heart space.

Become aware of the space in the heart; take your awareness directly there.

Feel the space within the heart centre. It is contracting and expanding with the rhythm of the natural breath.

Breath is only the basis.

The process of filling up is only the basis.

Go on to comprehend the whole space.

Then you are aware of the space alone.

Feel the contraction and expansion of this vast space.

It is taking place on the rhythm of the natural breath.

The breath is natural and spontaneous.

Do not alter it in any way.

Do not make it longer or shorter, deeper or more shallow, faster or slower.

It has to become a spontaneous and voluntary movement of breath.

In this practice, the awareness of the space in the heart is important.

Stage 3: Vision of blue lotus and lake

If the awareness of the expansion and contraction of the heart space is constant and stabilized, after some time, many visions and experiences will manifest there.

You do not have to visualize or imagine anything. The vision will come by itself when the awareness of the heart space is constant.

The image is of a lake and a blue lotus.

If you are able to feel the space of the heart contracting and expanding, then maintain your awareness there.

If that is not possible, then you will have to feel the breath which is filling up the space. That is the first stage of the practice.

The second stage is the direct feeling of the space and its expansion and contraction with the rhythm of the breath.

The third stage is the awareness of the blue lotus and the still lake. It will come by itself.

Keep yourself ready for that experience.

Stage 4: Ending the practice

Now become aware of the natural inflowing and outflowing breath in the throat.

Withdraw your awareness from the heart space and bring it to the natural breath in the throat.

Maintain awareness of the inflowing and outflowing breath in the throat for some time.

Practise for five or ten minutes.

Chant Om three times.

Allow the sound to manifest fully and spontaneously from deep within.

For a few minutes, listen carefully for the inner vibration of the sound.

Release your posture and open your eyes.

Vishuddhi

BSY©

33

Practices for Vishuddhi Chakra

MONTH 6

Vishuddhi chakra can be directly awakened through the practices of jalandhara bandha, vipareeta karani asana and ujjayi pranayama, all of which are essential for eventual mastery of kriya yoga.

A minor chakra which is closely related to vishuddhi is called lalana chakra, which is located at the back of the roof of the mouth, at the soft palate, and it directly helps to awaken vishuddhi. For this reason, one of the kundalini kriyas, called amrit pan, is concerned with its direct stimulation. A simpler practice for awakening lalana is khechari mudra, which is described in this chapter.

Preparatory practices

Many asanas can be utilized for purifying vishuddhi chakra. The most important are: bhujangasana, matsyasana, supta vajrasana and sarvangasana.

Practice program

Perfect these vishuddhi chakra practices over a period of one month and then start the practices for bindu. The sadhana for the other chakras can also be continued with a few selected techniques from each of the other chakras as follows:
1. *Ajna* – trataka and shambhavi mudra
2. *Mooladhara* – moola bandha and nasikagra mudra

3. *Swadhisthana* – chakra and kshetram location, vajroli or sahajoli.
4. *Manipura* – chakra and kshetram location, uddiyana bandha and nauli.
5. *Anahata* – chakra and kshetram location, ajapa japa.

Practice 1: Jalandhara Bandha (throat lock)

Sit in any meditative pose which allows the knees to firmly touch the floor. Those who cannot sit like this can practise jalandhara bandha in a standing position.

Place the palms of the hands on the knees.

Close the eyes and relax the whole body.

Inhale deeply, retain the breath inside and bend the head forward, pressing the chin tightly against the chest (particularly the sternum).

Straighten the arms and lock them into position.

Simultaneously hunch the shoulders upward and forward. This will ensure that the arms remain locked.

The palms should remain on the knees.

Stay in the final pose for as long as the breath can be held comfortably.

Then bend the arms, relax the shoulders, slowly release the lock, raise the head and exhale.

Repeat when the respiration returns to normal.

Practise 5 times.

Contra-indications: Persons with high intracranial or blood pressure, or with heart ailments, should not practise without expert guidance.

Practice note: The whole practice can also be performed with the breath retained outside.

Never inhale or exhale until the chin lock has been released and the head is upright.

Practice 2: Khechari Mudra (tongue lock)

Sit in a comfortable meditative posture.

Close the mouth and roll the tongue upward and backward so that the lower surface touches the upper palate. Stretch the tip of the tongue as far back as possible without strain.

Keep it there for as long as is comfortable.

If there is discomfort, relax the tongue for a few seconds and repeat.

After some practise the tongue may be able to extend beyond the palate and up into the nasopharynx, where it will stimulate many vital nerve centres.

Breathing: Breathe normally during this practice unless ujjayi is used.

Duration: Over a period of months gradually reduce the breathing rate to seven or eight breaths per minute. This may be reduced further under expert guidance.

Practice 3: Ujjayi Pranayama (psychic breath)

Sit in a comfortable meditative posture.

Practise khechari mudra. Feel that the breath is being drawn in and out through the throat, not the nostrils.

Gently contract the glottis in the throat.

When you breathe under these circumstances, a very soft snoring sound should automatically come from the throat region. It is like the breathing of a sleeping baby.

Feel that you are breathing deeply from the abdomen and not the nose.

Try to make the breaths long and relaxed.

Practise for two minutes initially, then gradually extend to ten or twenty minutes.

Practice 4: Vishuddhi chakra and kshetram location and purification

Sit or stand in front of a mirror.

Place a finger of one hand on the glottis (the lump at the throat pit).

This is the location point of vishuddhi kshetram.

Then place a finger of the other hand on the spine, directly behind the kshetram.

This point in the spine is called vishuddhi chakra.

Press the spine for one minute in order to feel a sensation at the chakra area.

Then lower the hands.

Concentrate on the sensation at the chakra and repeat mentally, 'Vishuddhi, vishuddhi, vishuddhi'.

Sit in a comfortable position with the back straight.

Close the eyes and become aware of the breath.

Fold the tongue back into khechari mudra and practise ujjayi pranayama.

For a minute or so, be aware of the sound of the breath at the throat, and let the breathing become slower and deeper.

Then with inhalation, imagine that the breath is being drawn in through vishuddhi kshetram at the front of the throat.

Feel that the breath passes through the kshetram and eventually pierces vishuddhi chakra in the spine.

With exhalation, feel the breath move from vishuddhi chakra, forward through the kshetram and eventually out, in front of the body.

This is one round.

Continue for a few minutes.

Daily practise in this manner will gradually develop sensitivity to vishuddhi chakra and its kshetram.

Practice 5: Vipareeta Karani Asana (inverted pose)

Lie flat on the floor with the feet together, the arms by the sides and the palms flat on the floor.

Relax the whole body.

Raise both legs, keeping them straight and together.

Move the legs over the body towards the head.

Push down on the arms and hands, raising the buttocks.

Roll the spine from the floor, taking the legs over the head.

Turn the palms up, bend the elbows and let the top of the hips rest on the base of the palms near the wrist.

The hands cup the hips and support the weight of the body.

Keep the elbows as close to each other as possible.

Raise both the legs to the vertical position and relax the feet.

In the final position, the weight of the body rests on the shoulders, neck and elbows, the trunk is at a 45 degree angle to the floor and the legs are vertical. Note that the chin does not press against the chest.

Close the eyes and relax in the final pose for as long as is comfortable.

To return to the starting position, slowly lower the spine, vertebra by vertebra, along the floor.

Do not lift the head.

When the buttocks reach the floor, lower the legs, keeping them straight.

Relax in shavasana.

Duration: Advanced practitioners can hold the posture for 15 minutes or even more, Beginners should practise for a few seconds and add a few seconds daily.

Sequence: Shavasana should be done for a few minutes on completion of vipareeta karani asana, followed by a counterpose such as saral matsyasana.

Contra-indications: This asana should not be done by sufferers of thyroid, liver or spleen enlargement, high blood pressure or heart ailments.

Practice note: Vipareeta karani asana is similar to sarvangasana, except that the chin is not pressed against the chest and the trunk is held at a 45 degree angle to the ground instead of at right angles.

Note: *Vipareeta karani asana is widely used in kriya yoga since it helps to redirect the energies of the body from the lower to the higher chakras. It is an integral part of the first of the kundalini kriyas called* vipareeta karani mudra.

Bindu

34

Practices for Bindu

MONTH 7

The bindu trigger point is considered to be a tiny point at the top of the back of the head, but this point cannot be located in the physical body. It can only be found when the nada or sound of bindu has been discovered and traced to its source. Through the practices of *moorchha pranayama* and *vajroli/sahajoli mudra* awareness of the nada can be developed. Then, through practices such as *bhramari pranayama* and *shanmukhi mudra*, the nada can be traced to its source.

It is not intended that you practise all the nada yoga techniques at one time. You should adopt the practice which you can perform without difficulty. It does not matter which practice you commence with, because all the techniques lead to awareness of the same subtle inner sounds.

There is a very close relationship between swadhisthana chakra and bindu. This is because bindu is the point where the primal sound of creation first manifests. It is the point of origin of individuality, and swadhisthana is the source of the impetus towards reproduction and sexual function. This is the material expression of the desire to reunite with the infinite consciousness beyond bindu. Sperm and menses are the material distillates of the drop of ambrosial nectar which emerges from bindu.

It should be noted that there is no kshetram corresponding to bindu.

251

Practice program

Practise the techniques for bindu for one month. Then begin the techniques given in the next chapter for integrated chakra awareness.

The selected techniques for ajna, mooladhara, swadhisthana, manipura and anahata chakras can also be done daily, as given in the 'Practice program' section of the previous chapter. For vishuddhi chakra, jalandhara bandha, vishuddhi chakra purification and vipareeta karani asana can be done. Khechari mudra and ujjayi pranayama need not be done separately, since they are both incorporated into techniques given in this section.

Practice 1: Moorchha Pranayama (swooning or fainting breath)

This practice requires a steady and firm meditation posture, preferably siddhasana or siddha yoni asana. Hold the spine and head upright and relax the whole body.

Perform khechari mudra.

Inhale through the nostrils with ujjayi pranayama while simultaneously bending the head backward and assuming shambhavi mudra.

The inhalation should be slow and deep.

At the end of inhalation, the head should lean backward, but not completely. The position of the head is as shown in the diagram. Retain the breath inside for as long as is comfortable, maintaining shambhavi mudra, but keeping the attention at bindu.

Keep the arms straight by locking the elbows and pressing the knees with the hands.

Fix your whole awareness on bindu.

Then bend the arms and slowly exhale with ujjayi pranayama as you bend the head forward. Slowly lower and close the eyes.

At the end of exhalation the head should face forward and the eyes should be completely closed.

Relax the whole body for a short time, keeping the eyes closed. Release khechari mudra and breathe normally.

Become aware of the lightness and calmness pervading the whole mind.

This is one round. After some time, commence the second round.

Duration: Practise 10 or more rounds, or until a fainting sensation is experienced. Perform each round for as long as possible, but without strain.

Contra-indications: Those who suffer from high blood pressure, vertigo, high intracranial pressure or brain haemorrhage should not practise this technique. Discontinue the practice as soon as the fainting sensation is felt. The aim is to induce a state of semi-fainting, not complete unconsciousness.

Benefits: This practice is very powerful in inducing pratyahara and rendering the mind free from thoughts, especially when kumbhaka is prolonged.

Practice 2: Vajroli/sahajoli mudra with awareness of bindu

Sit in siddhasana or siddha yoni asana, preferably with a thin cushion or a folded blanket beneath the buttocks.

Close the eyes and relax the body.

Take the awareness to the urethra.

Contract the urethra as if it is being drawn upwards and inwards.

This muscular action is similar to that made when trying to control the urge to urinate.

Try to focus and confine the force of the contraction at the urethra.

Try not to perform moola bandha or ashwini mudra at the same time.

Contract for 10 seconds, release for 10 seconds. Continue this for a few minutes.

Each time you attain full contraction of the urinary system, bring your awareness to swadhisthana chakra in the spinal column, at the level of the coccyx. Repeat, 'Swadhisthana, swadhisthana, swadhisthana', mentally.

Then draw your awareness up through sushumna passage to bindu.

Mentally repeat, 'bindu, bindu, bindu'.

Then return to swadhisthana and release vajroli/sahajoli mudra.

This is one round.

Continue this alternately for several minutes, practising up to 25 rounds.

Practice note: This practice should be performed immediately after moorchha pranayama, as both these practices awaken the awareness of bindu.

Practice 3: Perception of subtle inner sound

This practice should be preceded by bhramari pranayama.

In this stage no loud humming sound is produced, you only listen attentively to the inner sound.

Keep the eyes closed and the fingers plugging the ears; this is necessary to block out external disturbances.

Listen for any subtle sounds in the head.

At first you may find this difficult, but keep trying.

As soon as you become aware of a sound, any sound, try to fix your awareness on it to the exclusion of other sounds. Go on listening.

After some days or weeks of practice, you should find that one sound is very distinct, and it will become louder and louder.

Be totally aware of that sound.

This is your vehicle of awareness – let your awareness flow towards this sound, leaving all other sounds and thoughts.

Gradually, through practise, your sensitivity will increase.

Eventually you will hear another sound, a faint sound in the background; it will be almost obliterated by the main, louder sound that you are hearing, but you will hear it nevertheless.

Now listen to the new faint sound.

Leave the other louder sound and continue to listen to the new sound. It will become more and more distinct.

This will become your new, more subtle vehicle of awareness.

Let this sound occupy your whole attention. This will further increase your sensitivity of perception.

Eventually you will hear another faint sound emerging from behind this louder sound.

Fix your awareness on this new sound, discarding the other sound.

Continue in the same manner, allowing the new sound to occupy your whole awareness.

When it becomes loud, try to perceive a more subtle underlying sound and fix your awareness on it.

In this manner your perception will become progressively more sensitive, allowing you to dive deep into your being.

Practice note: It requires practise over a period of weeks and months to perceive these progressively more subtle sounds. For many weeks you may be unable to hear even the first sound.

This is a very simple but powerful technique that will bring results if you persevere. All that is necessary is time and effort. Try to practise for as long as you have time. Begin with 15 minutes or more of bhramari and this practice together.

Practice 4: Shanmukhi Mudra (closing the seven gates)

Sit in siddhasana/siddha yoni asana, if possible. Otherwise take a comfortable meditation asana and place a small cushion beneath the perineum to provide pressure in this area. Hold the head and spine straight.

Close the eyes and place the hands on the knees.

Completely relax the body and mind.

Raise the hands in front of the face, with the elbows pointing sideways.

Close the ears with the thumbs, the eyes with the index fingers, the nostrils with the middle fingers, and the mouth by placing the ring and little fingers above and below the lips.

The fingers should gently but firmly close the seven doors.

Release the pressure of the middle fingers and open the nostrils.

Inhale slowly and deeply, using full yogic breathing.

At the end of inhalation, close the nostrils with the middle fingers.

Retain the breath for as long as is comfortable.

Try to hear any sounds emanating from bindu at the back of the head, from the middle of the head, or perhaps the right ear.

At first you will either hear many sounds or none at all. Just continue listening.

Retain the breath inside for as long as is comfortable.

Then release the pressure of the middle fingers and slowly breathe out. This is one round.

Inhale once more, close the nostrils, and retain the breath. Listen to the inner sounds.

After a comfortable length of time, release the nostrils and breathe out. Continue in this way for the duration of the practice. During the period of breath retention, your full awareness should be directed to the perception of inner nada.

At first there may be a confused jumble of sounds, but gradually you will hear a specific sound. This may take a few days or weeks, but it will be perceived.

When you hear a distinct sound, be totally aware of it.

It will become clearer and clearer. Keep your awareness fixed on the sound. Listen very carefully.

If your sensitivity is sufficiently developed, you will hear another sound in the background. It may be faint, but perceptible.

Leave the first sound and transfer your awareness to the perception of the fainter sound.

In this way, you will transcend the first sound. Eventually this second sound will overwhelm your whole attention.

Again, with practise and enhanced sensitivity, you will hear a further sound start to emerge. It will be faintly perceptible behind the louder second sound.

Direct your awareness to this new sound.

Carry on in this way – perceive a sound and then discard it when you can hear a more subtle sound. The more subtle the sound you perceive, the deeper you will delve into the depth of your being.

Continue this practice for a few minutes.

Breathing: This technique is more effective if you can retain your breath for extended periods of time. Those aspirants who have been practising nadi shodhana pranayama regularly for some months beforehand, will find shanmukhi mudra an easy and effective means of introspection.

Awareness: The point of awareness during the practice should be fixed at the back of the head in the bindu region. However, if you hear a distinct sound in any other area, such as the right ear or the middle of the head, then your awareness should be fixed there.

Some people may find it easier to listen to the nada in the region of the heart space (anahata chakra), especially those of a devotional nature. The important thing is not so much the point of awareness, but that the awareness remains fixed on progressively more subtle sounds. Total absorption on the nada can lead to dhyana or the meditative state of awareness.

Practice note: Do not expect to hear subtle sounds on your first attempt. Practice is necessary. Eventually you will be able to readily transcend the gross external sounds and then the progressively more subtle sounds. Do not dwell on any of the sounds for too long. This is not the purpose of the practice. The aim is to leave behind each sound you discover and to go deeper, to reach the source of all sound. Do not get lost or distracted by the beautiful sounds which will manifest on your journey.

Shanmukhi mudra is a more advanced practice than bhramari. It is slightly more difficult as it is not preceded by a vocalized humming sound, and it is combined with retention of the breath. Shanmukhi mudra is suitable for those who have a reasonably harmonized mind and are not beset by distractions.

Note: Shanmukhi mudra *means 'the closing of the seven gates'. It is so called because the two eyes, two ears, two nostrils and the mouth are closed during the practice. These are the seven doors of outer perception. It is via these doorways that one receives the sense data from the outside world. When these doors are closed, we facilitate the direction of the awareness internally; that is, into the mind.*

35

Practices for Integrated Chakra Awareness

MONTH 8

So far we have given a series of practices for each of the individual chakras. In this chapter we will describe practices which are concerned with the overall awakening of the chakras. Of course, the awakening of one chakra cannot take place in isolation; it has repercussions on all the chakras to a greater or lesser extent. The techniques for specific chakras will also influence all the chakras, but the following techniques systematically help to activate all the chakras together and bring balance into the whole mind-body-chakra axis:

1. Chakra meditation
2. Musical chakra meditation
3. Chaturtha pranayama
4. Chakra yoga nidra
5. Unmani mudra
6. Beeja mantra sanchalana
7. Drawing the chakras

Practice program

You will not have time to do all the practices given in this chapter. Therefore, we suggest that you practise the following for one month: Chakra meditation, chaturtha pranayama, chakra yoga nidra, unmani mudra and beeja mantra sanchalana daily.

Musical chakra meditation and drawing the chakras, can be done if you have the time and the inclination. They can

259

be omitted without any detriment to arousing kundalini. The following practices for each individual chakra can be done:

1. *Ajna* – shambhavi mudra
2. *Mooladhara* – moola bandha and nasikagra mudra
3. *Swadhisthana* – vajroli/sahajoli
4. *Manipura* – uddiyana bandha
5. *Anahata* – ajapa japa
6. *Vishuddhi* – jalandhara bandha and vipareeta karani asana
7. *Bindu* – shanmukhi mudra

After one month you can start to learn kriya yoga, having first of all obtained the advice of an experienced yoga teacher, or by writing to Bihar School of Yoga, Munger 811201, Bihar, India.

Practice 1: Chakra meditation

For the purpose of practising kriya yoga and some of the more advanced forms of meditation, it is essential to develop subtle awareness of the chakras, and to be able to locate them all accurately. In the beginning most people do not actually experience any sensation and initially it is simply a matter of imagination, but as the awareness becomes more subtle, the pulsation will definitely be experienced.

Technique
Stage 1: Preparation

Make yourself comfortable in a meditative asana, preferably siddhasana or siddha yoni asana.

Place both hands on the knees in chin mudra.

Close the eyes and make the whole body still and steady throughout.

The spinal column should be absolutely upright and straight, with the back and shoulders fully relaxed.

The head should be poised comfortably on top of the spinal column.

The whole body is completely relaxed and immobile.

It is motionless like a statue.

Maintain absolute awareness of the physical body for several minutes.

Stage 2: Ajna awareness

Become aware of the spinal column.

Now bring your awareness to ajna chakra.

Ajna chakra is located inside the brain at a point directly behind the eyebrow centre and on top of the spinal column, where the pineal gland is situated.

Try to discover a pulsation within this ajna chakra region. Be absolutely aware of this pulsation.

Now synchronize the mantra *Om* with the pulsation in the ajna chakra region.

Om, Om, Om, Om, Om should be the form of your awareness with the pulsation of ajna chakra.

Count the pulsation 21 times.

Now begin to practise ashwini mudra, contraction and relaxation of the anus.

Do not be concerned with ajna chakra, only practise ashwini mudra. It should be practised at a medium speed, neither too quickly nor too slowly.

After practising like this for a few sessions, you should be able to feel the centre of ajna automatically while performing ashwini.

When that happens you can begin to concentrate directly on ajna.

Until then, practise ashwini mudra for about four minutes.

Stage 3: Mooladhara awareness

Now bring your awareness to the perineal region and the psychic centre of mooladhara chakra.

Discover the precise psychic point of mooladhara chakra.

Try to discover a subtle pulsation there.

Localize the pulsation very precisely in the mooladhara region and count 21 pulsations.

Now open your eyes and adopt nasikagra drishti; gazing at the nose tip.

Do not be concerned with mooladhara chakra, but only with nose tip awareness.

261

The simultaneous awareness of mooladhara chakra will come after some time.

Continue this practice for three minutes.

Stage 4: Swadhisthana awareness

Now bring your awareness to swadhisthana chakra in the region of the tailbone.

Discover the psychic point of swadhisthana chakra.

Try to discover the pulsation in this centre.

Count this pulsation 21 times.

Now perform vajroli/sahajoli mudra – the drawing up and releasing of the urinary system.

Continue vajroli/sahajoli mudra for four minutes.

Stage 5: Manipura awareness

Now bring your awareness to the region of the navel.

Become aware of the psychic breath in the frontal passage from mooladhara to the navel, and from the throat to the navel.

Both these breaths must reach the navel at the point of full inhalation.

When the two forces meet and coincide at the navel, retain the breath there, and develop the mental awareness of the single central point of force in the navel.

Then release the breath and continue this practice in your own natural rhythm.

Continue for four minutes.

Now take your awareness directly back to manipura chakra, within the spinal column, directly behind the navel.

Try to isolate that point and the pulsation there.

Count the pulse 21 times in manipura chakra.

Stage 6: Anahata awareness

Now bring your awareness to the region of anahata chakra in the spinal column, at the level of the centre of the chest.

Isolate that point and try to discover a pulsation within it.

Count the pulsation 21 times.

Now bring your awareness to the space of the heart.

First become aware of the incoming breath in the throat.

262

With the incoming breath, feel the vast heart space expand.
Feel the heart space directly – contracting and expanding
with the rhythm of the spontaneous, natural breath.
Be aware of the vision which will come in the vast heart
space. Allow it to come by itself.
Continue for two minutes.

Stage 7: Vishuddhi awareness

Now bring your awareness to the throat pit and then take it
directly back to vishuddhi chakra in the spinal column.
Repeat mentally, 'Vishuddhi, vishuddhi, vishuddhi'.
Try to discover the pulsation within vishuddhi and witness
it for 21 pulsations.

Stage 8: Chakra awareness in sushumna

Now, as the name of each chakra is given, move your
awareness within the sushumna passage so as to touch
each chakra mentally with a small imaginary flower.
Your awareness of each chakra must be very precise –
mooladhara, swadhisthana, manipura, anahata, vishuddhi,
ajna; ajna, vishuddhi, anahata, manipura, swadhisthana,
mooladhara.
Guide the consciousness through the chakras in
sushumna, ascending and descending four more times.

Stage 9: Ending the practice

Now begin to end the practice.
Bring the awareness back to the body and chant *Om* three
times.

Practice 2: Musical chakra meditation

Sound is a particularly effective and enjoyable means of
developing awareness of the chakras. This is why nada yoga
is so powerful in spiritual awakening. The seven notes of the
musical scale correspond to the vibration of the seven chakras
from mooladhara to sahasrara, and this is the basis for a very
effective musical meditation technique. The best instrument
of all is the human voice, which can be supplemented by
the harmonium. However, other instruments such as the
tampura and tabla can also be used.

Latin scale	Chakra	Sanskrit scale	
Do	Mooladhara	Sa	सा
Re	Swadhisthana	Re	रे
Mi	Manipura	Ga	ग
Fa	Anahata	Ma	म
So	Vishuddhi	Pa	प
La	Ajna	Dha	ध
Ti	Bindu	Ni	नि
Do	Sahasrara	Sa	सा

Technique

Stage 1: At first the musical scale of the harmonium is ascended very slowly while the awareness begins in mooladhara and ascends sushumna from one chakra to the next, feeling each note vibrate in the spinal column in the region of its corresponding chakra.

When sahasrara is attained, descend the awareness with the musical scale down through sushumna to mooladhara. The consciousness ascends and descends sushumna with the scale many times, slowly speeding up as chakra location becomes quick and effortless.

Stage 2: Now the voice is integrated with the notes. The names of the chakras are chanted very precisely. The names themselves are mantras, and if intoned with the correct note and pronunciation, each centre can be set vibrating, and the sushumna passage and the whole body begin to vibrate with energy. This practice is very powerful. It can be continued for ten minutes or more.

Stage 3: In this stage the awareness still ascends and descends through sushumna with the musical scale, but the voice makes a continuous a-a-a-a-a-a sound (as in 'calm') as it ascends and descends through the chakras. In the final stage, the full power of the voice is released and a tremendous energy is generated, provided the pitch is maintained accurately.

264

Practice 3: Chaturtha Pranayama (fourth pranayama)

Chaturtha pranayama combines breathing, mantra and chakra awareness. Although it is not widely taught, it is a powerful technique that is both a pranayama and a meditation. This practice will lead to deeper awareness and knowledge of the chakras. It is also a preparatory technique for kriya yoga as it develops sensitivity to both the psychic spinal passage and the chakras.

Chaturtha pranayama means 'fourth pranayama' or 'pranayama of the fourth state', or a transcendental state where words and definitions fail to reach.

Technique
Stage 1: Breath awareness

Sit in any comfortable meditative posture.
Hold the head and spine erect and close the eyes.
Breathe deeply.
Let the breath become deeper and more subtle.
Fix your awareness on the rhythmical flow of the breath.
Continue for a number of rounds.

Stage 2: Mantra awareness

Mentally synchronize the manta *Om* with the breath.
The sound 'O' should synchronize with inhalation.
The sound 'm-m-m-m-m' should synchronize with exhalation. This sound should only be mental.
Breathe through the nose, keeping the mouth closed.
Continue in this manner with awareness of the flow of the breath and the mantra.

Stage 3: Chakra awareness

Now fix your attention at the eyebrow centre.
Feel you are breathing out through that centre, mentally chanting 'm-m-m-m-m'.
Continue with awareness of the breath, mantra and psychic centre.
Focus your attention on mooladhara.
With inhalation and the sound 'm-m-m-m-m', feel the breath and sound moving down the spine, piercing all the

chakras – sahasrara, ajna, vishuddhi, anahata, manipura, swadhisthana, mooladhara.

Continue for a number of rounds.

Again fix your attention at the eyebrow centre.

Continue the mental repetition of *Om* synchronized with the breath, but do not be aware of the breath. Only be aware of the mantra and the psychic centre.

Feel the 'O' and the 'm-m-m-m-m' sound.

Continue in this manner for as long as possible.

Practice 4: Chakra yoga nidra

Yoga nidra can be used very effectively to develop your awareness of the chakras. Here is an example of a yoga nidra/relaxation session which includes visualization and rotation of awareness through the psychic centres. Teachers can adopt this practice directly for their classes. For personal use, someone can lead you through the practice, or you can put the instructions onto a tape.

Technique
Stage 1: Preparation

Place a folded blanket on the floor and lie on it in shavasana.

Loosen your clothing so you feel perfectly comfortable. If necessary, cover yourself with a blanket to keep warm, or put a sheet over you to keep insects away.

The mouth and eyes should remain closed throughout the practice.

Make sure that the spinal column is straight, in line with the head and neck, and that the hips and shoulders are fully relaxed.

Keep the feet and legs slightly apart.

The arms should be beside your body but not touching, and the palms should be facing up.

Adjust your position so that you feel perfectly comfortable.

Tell yourself firmly that you will not move your body throughout the practice.

266

Stage 2: Sinking of the body

Look at the space in front of your closed eyes.
Imagine that the space surrounds your whole body.
Your body is immersed in that space.
Simultaneously be aware of your body.
It feels very light, as light as a leaf falling from a tree.
Imagine that your body is slowly sinking into the space that you see in front of your closed eyes, like a falling leaf.
Your body is slowly sinking into the infinite space.
Be aware of this feeling.
Continue in this manner for a few minutes.

Stage 3: Rhythmical breath awareness

Become aware of your breathing.
Awareness of the rise and fall of the navel with each breath.
As you breathe in, feel you are sucking in air through the navel.
As you breathe out, imagine that you are pushing air out from the navel.
It is a rhythmical process. Do not alter the natural breath in any way, just become aware of it.

Stage 4: Sankalpa

Repeat your sankalpa in a short positive sentence.
It should be the crystallization of your spiritual aspiration and you should not change it.
Repeat it with feeling, from the heart, not the lips.
Repeat your sankalpa at least three times.

Stage 5: Visualization – body awareness

Now try to visualize your own body.
Imagine that you are viewing it from outside.
Feel that your perception is outside and your body is an object of study.
You may find visualization difficult – do not worry, just do your best.
If you wish, you can imagine that there is a large mirror suspended over your body and that your body is reflected in it.

Look at your own reflection.

See your whole body: feet, knees, thighs, abdomen, chest, both hands, arms, shoulders, neck, head, mouth, nose, ears, eyes, eyebrow centre, your whole face and your whole body.

Combine rotation of awareness of each part with visualization of that part.

Continue in this manner for a few minutes.

Stage 6: Psychic centres – rotation of awareness

Now you have to discover the location of the chakras.

You must develop awareness of each psychic centre .

Start from the base of the spine and move your awareness upward.

First become aware of mooladhara. In the male body it is situated in the perineum, between the anus and genitals, and in the female body it is located at the cervix – the mouth of the womb.

Try to feel the sensation at mooladhara. It is a very specific point which you are trying to isolate.

When you have found it, repeat mentally, 'Mooladhara, mooladhara, mooladhara'.

Now move on to the second chakra, swadhisthana. It is located at the base of the spine, in the coccyx.

Be aware of the sensation at that point and repeat mentally, 'Swadhisthana, swadhisthana, swadhisthana'.

The third chakra is manipura.

It is located in the spine in line with the navel.

Feel this point and mentally repeat, 'Manipura, manipura, manipura".

Then become aware of anahata chakra, located in the spine, directly behind the centre of the chest.

Try to locate that point exactly and mentally repeat, 'Anahata, anahata, anahata'.

Now bring your awareness to vishuddhi chakra, situated in the spine, directly behind the throat pit.

Feel the sensation arising at that point and mentally repeat, 'Vishuddhi, vishuddhi, vishuddhi'.

The next chakra is ajna.

Ajna chakra is located at the very top of the spine in the region of the pineal gland, directly behind the eyebrow centre.

Fix your awareness on that area and mentally repeat, 'Ajna, ajna, ajna'.

Now bring your awareness to bindu, at the top back portion of the head.

Feel that tiny point as precisely as possible, and repeat mentally, 'Bindu, bindu, bindu'.

Finally, become aware of sahasrara, at the crown of the head, and repeat mentally, 'Sahasrara, sahasrara, sahasrara'.

Now repeat this process, slowly descending through the chakras in reverse order: sahasrara, bindu, ajna, vishuddhi, anahata, manipura, swadhisthana and mooladhara.

This is one complete round of chakra rotation.

Now start a second round: mooladhara, swadhisthana, manipura, anahata, vishuddhi, ajna, bindu, sahasrara; sahasrara, bindu, ajna, vishuddhi, anahata, manipura, swadhisthana, mooladhara.

This completes the second round.

Begin a third round, this time a little faster.

As you fix your attention at each point, try to feel a slight vibration there, a tiny pulsation.

If you wish, you can chant *Om* mentally as you locate each point in turn.

Practise at least five rounds and as many more as time permits.

Stage 7: Psychic centres – visualization

Now try to visualize the symbols of each chakra.

You can use your own personal system of psychic symbols or the traditional chakra symbols as follows.

As each chakra is named, try to feel that point being lightly pressed by the thumb, and simultaneously visualize the symbol.

The psychic symbol for mooladhara is a deep red, four-petalled lotus.

Inside there is a smoky lingam around which a snake is coiled three and a half times. The snake's head is facing upward.

Try to visualize this symbol to the best of your ability and associate it with that particular location in the body.

Then proceed to swadhisthana chakra.

The symbol is a six-petalled vermilion lotus, within which is depicted a starry night above the sea. The main focal point is the crescent moon.

Try to visualize this symbol.

Move to manipura chakra.

It is symbolized by a ten-petalled yellow lotus, and in the centre is blazing fire.

Visualize this symbol, imagining that the lotus is actually growing from manipura chakra.

Proceed to anahata chakra, represented by a twelve-petalled blue lotus.

In the centre is a solitary flame burning in the darkness.

Try to visualize this symbol while feeling the exact position in the body.

Move to vishuddhi chakra, symbolized by a sixteen-petalled purple lotus.

In the middle there is a pure white drop of nectar.

Visualize this location in the body.

Then proceed to ajna chakra which is symbolized by a two-petalled silver-grey lotus.

On the left hand petal is the full moon and on the right hand petal, a glowing sun.

In the centre is a black lingam and an *Om* sign.

Create a mental image of this symbol and its exact location.

Move on to bindu. It is symbolized by a tiny white drop of nectar.

Visualize this symbol at the top back of the head.

Finally, move to sahasrara, the fountainhead of all the chakras.

It is represented by a thousand-petalled lotus. In the centre is a white lingam.

Visualize this symbol at the crown of the head.

Now visualize all these symbols in the reverse order: sahasrara, bindu, ajna, vishuddhi, anahata, manipura, swadhisthana and mooladhara.

This is the end of one round.

Spend a few seconds visualizing each centre.

Do a few more rounds according to the amount of time available.

Stage 8: Eyebrow centre awareness

Fix your attention at the eyebrow centre.

Feel your pulse at this point.

Become aware of its continuous rhythmical beat.

Mentally synchronize repetition of the mantra *Om* with this pulse.

Continue for a few minutes.

Stage 9: Sankalpa/Ending the practice

Repeat your sankalpa three times with full emphasis and feeling.

Become aware of your natural breath.

Become aware of your whole physical body.

Become aware of the outer sense perceptions.

Slowly begin to move your body. When you have fully externalized your awareness, slowly sit up and open your eyes.

Practice 5: Unmani mudra (attitude of mindlessness)

Unmani mudra is an excellent practice for developing awareness of the chakras in the spine, from bindu down to mooladhara. It is also an integral part of many of the kriya yoga practices (nada, pawan and shabda sanchalana, maha mudra and maha bheda mudra), and therefore it should be mastered before attempting to learn and practise these techniques.

The word *unmani* means, 'no mind' or 'thoughtlessness', and refers to the state which arises during meditation. Therefore, unmani mudra means, 'the attitude of mindlessness or thoughtlessness'.

Technique

Sit in any comfortable meditation pose, preferably siddhasana/siddha yoni asana or padmasana with the back straight.

Open the eyes fully, without focusing on anything external.

Take a deep breath in and, holding the breath inside, focus the awareness at bindu.

As you breathe out, imagine the breath going down the spine.

Simultaneously, let your awareness descend the spine, passing through all the chakras: ajna, vishuddhi, anahata, manipura, swadhisthana, mooladhara, one after the other.

The eyes should slowly close and be fully closed by the time the awareness reaches mooladhara.

Although the eyes remain open throughout the practice, the attention should be internalized on the chakras and breath; that is, the eyes are open, but you are looking within. Do not try too hard, but allow the process to occur spontaneously.

This is one round.

Inhale deeply and begin the second round.

Do 11 rounds.

Practice note: Physically this practice is very easy to perform. The emphasis, however, should be on the mental process taking place. When the eyes are open they should not register anything outside.

Practice 6: Beeja Mantra Sanchalana (conducting the seed sound)

This practice is one of the techniques of kriya yoga, but is not normally one of the twenty kriyas that we teach. It is concerned with mentally repeating the beeja mantra of each kshetram and chakra, one after the other, whilst simultaneously moving the awareness through each chakra.

The word *beeja* means 'seed', mantra means 'mystic sound' and sanchalana means 'conduction'. Therefore, this practice can be called 'the conduction of the seed sound'.

Psychic passages

In the following kriya, beeja mantra sanchalana, as well as in a number of practices of kriya yoga, you will be required to move your awareness through two psychic passages called *arohan* and *awarohan*. The path of these passages is as follows:

Arohan, the ascending passage, goes from mooladhara chakra, forward to swadhisthana kshetram in the pubic area, then follows the curve of the belly to manipura kshetram, upward to anahata kshetram and vishuddhi kshetram in the front of the throat, then in a straight line to bindu at the top back of the head.

There is also another pathway for the arohan psychic passage that has been taught by tradition throughout the ages. On the ascent from mooladhara, swadhisthana kshetram and onwards, the awareness is taken from vishuddhi kshetram to lalana chakra in the palate, then to the nosetip, to the eyebrow centre, and following the curvature of the skull through sahasrara at the top of the head, to bindu at the back of the crown, where there is a little whorl of hair. In this book we will refer to the arohan passage as connecting vishuddhi kshetram directly to bindu; however, you can experiment with both passages and use whichever one suits you best.

Awarohan is the descending passage which starts at bindu, travels forward to ajna chakra, then down through sushumna in the spine, passing through all the chakras in turn to finally terminate at mooladhara.

In the following practice you will have to familiarize yourself with these two psychic passages, and this will also be useful as a preparation for the kundalini kriyas.

Beeja mantras

The beeja mantras for each kshetram and chakra are as follows:
1. Mooladhara – *Lam*
2. Swadhisthana – *Vam*
3. Manipura – *Ram*

4. Anahata – *Yam*
5. Vishuddhi – *Ham*
6. Ajna – *Om*
7. Bindu – *Om*

Technique

Sit in any comfortable position, preferably siddhasana/ siddha yoni asana.

Keep the head and spine straight and the eyes closed.

Throughout the practice there is no physical movement; the kriya is performed mentally.

Bring your attention to mooladhara chakra.

Repeat the mantra *Lam* mentally, once, and try to feel the vibration at mooladhara chakra.

Then ascend through arohan.

Let your attention jump to swadhisthana kshetram and repeat the mantra *Vam,* feeling the vibration at that point.

Jump to manipura kshetram and repeat the mantra *Ram.*

At anahata kshetram, *Yam.*

At vishuddhi kshetram, *Ham.*

At bindu, *Om.*

Then descend through awarohan.

Repeat *Om* at ajna, in the centre of the head.

Repeat *Ham* at vishuddhi chakra in the spine.

At anahata chakra, *Yam.*

At manipura chakra, *Ram.*

At swadhisthana, *Vam.*

Then return to the starting point, mooladhara, and begin the next round by repeating the mantra *Lam.*

Your awareness should jump from one centre to the next.

Do 9 rounds, or more if you have time.

Practice note: Beeja mantra sanchalana is an excellent preparatory practice for kriya yoga sadhana. You may also practise this by spending some time, for example five minutes, at each kshetram or chakra, chanting the mantra out loud on a low key and feeling it vibrating at the chakra.

Practice 7: Drawing the chakras

Drawing of mandalas, such as the chakras, is an important part of tantra. Many of the practices require that the correct mandalas be constructed first of all. The creation of a chakra diagram should be done with absolute awareness and concentration, and its measurements and dimensions must be exact. You should try to ensure that you will be undisturbed for at least an hour, and approach the exercise as you do meditation. In some Tibetan Buddhist monasteries, mandalas are drawn and painted as part of the daily sadhana, as is the practice in several Greek Orthodox monasteries, where icons are painted in minute detail as daily meditation.

Make sure you have all the necessary materials; pencils, pens, rubbers, ruler, compass, colours or paints, so that you will not have to disturb your concentration once you have started. If you have a sadhana room, then that is the best place to create your mandalas. A good size for drawing the chakras on art paper is about 9" square, as this size is most useful for visual display and concentration practices. Larger and smaller sized chakras can be made for other purposes.

By first using only a black pen, one can plainly see the simple yet subtle lines and formations, and discover the hidden symbology as it becomes visually clearer in the mind. The next step is to colour it, according to the traditional colours described in the text. In this way, mandalas of each of the seven chakras can be completed over seven or more sessions.

This practice is very relaxing and enjoyable. You may like to create more subjective and artistic impressions of the chakras, with your own colours and symbols, as you come to understand them in a personal way. This expands your awareness to the many possibilities of experiencing not only the chakras, but life itself.

The chakras should not be interpreted on just one or two levels, but in many dimensions. After drawing and painting the chakras successfully, you can then take the next step and create the chakras in a three dimensional form. For this you can use any number of materials such as clay, plasticine, wire, fibreglass, copper or stone.

You must remember, however, that the traditional drawings are as subjective as your feelings and experiences of the chakra. Therefore, use your own experiences to express the deeper and inner spiritual aspects, on paper, in clay or stone, etc. Through this, you will find a clarity of vision arising out of what once seemed a confused and blurred picture of life.

36

Your Sadhana Program

The practices of kundalini yoga must be adopted systematically. We suggest that you practise and perfect the sadhana for each chakra for one month or more, before moving on to the next. The sadhana will continue for eight months, as outlined below:

Month   *Page*
1: Practices for ajna chakra   211
   Anuloma viloma pranayama
   Trataka
   Shambhavi mudra with om chanting

2: Practices for mooladhara chakra   219
   Chakra location
   Moola bandha
   Nasikagra drishti

3: Practices for swadhisthana chakra   226
   Chakra and kshetram location
   Ashwini mudra
   Vajroli/sahajoli mudra

4: Practices for manipura chakra   229
   Chakra and kshetram location
   Manipura purification

Agnisar kriya
Uddiyana bandha
Nauli
Union of prana and apana

5: Practices for anahata chakra   238
Chakra and kshetram location
Anahata purification
Bhramari pranayama
Ajapa japa
Meditation – entering the heart space

6: Practices for vishuddhi chakra   245
Jalandhara bandha
Khechari mudra
Ujjayi pranayama
Chakra and kshetram location and purification
Vipareeta karani asana

7: Practices for bindu   251
Moorchha pranayama
Vajroli/sahajoli mudra with bindu awareness
Perception of subtle inner sound
Shanmukhi mudra

8: Practices for integrated chakra awareness   259
Chakra meditation
Musical chakra meditation
Chaturtha pranayama
Chakra yoga nidra
Unmani mudra
Beeja mantra sanchalana
Drawing the chakras

37

Kundalini Kriyas
of Kriya Yoga

The following tantric kriyas provide what is possibly the most efficient method for systematically evolving man's consciousness that has ever been developed. They are said to have been the teachings for the transcendental sadhana which Lord Shiva gave to his disciple and wife, Parvati.

By tradition, kriya yoga was never taught publicly. The kriyas were always communicated verbally from guru to disciple. It is only in recent years that these kriyas have been published in accordance with the needs of this era.

These kriyas are rather advanced and too powerful for the average aspirant. Before an aspirant takes up their practice, he or she should have a thorough familiarity with and practical experience of all the preliminary practices included in the book. Also, it is advisable that he takes up these kriyas only under the guidance of a guru, who can see that the aspirant is fully prepared for them and that any obstacles which arise while the aspirant is practising do not cause any harm in the way of disease, mental imbalance or psychic dislocation.

If possible, try to come to an ashram for one month for full initiation into the higher practices of kriya yoga.

Preparation

One must realize that all the rules and regulations which were enumerated at the beginning of this practice section also apply to all the aspirants who wish to successfully learn and practise kriya yoga.

It is essential that one has developed sensitivity to the positions of the chakras and kshetram by practising the techniques given for the individual chakras (chapters 28 to 34), and also the techniques for integrated chakra awareness (chapter 35). This sensitivity should be such that you can feel them both physically and mentally.

You should also know the position of the two psychic pathways known as *arohan* and *awarohan*. They are explained in the practice called 'Beeja mantra sanchalana' in chapter 35. The following techniques are integral parts of the 20 kriyas:

Name	*Chapter*
Vipareeta karani asana	33
Ujjayi pranayama	33
Siddhasana/Siddha yoni asana	26
Unmani mudra	35
Khechari mudra	33
Ajapa japa	32
Utthanpadasana	26
Shambhavi mudra	28
Moola bandha	29
Nasikagra drishti	29
Uddiyana bandha	31
Jalandhara bandha	33
Bhadrasana	26
Padmasana	26
Shanmukhi mudra	34
Vajroli/Sahajoli mudra	30

These practices are all fully described in the chapters indicated and it is essential that you master them. If you try to learn kriya yoga without first of all perfecting them, then you will find the actual kriya techniques very difficult to follow and you will get very little benefit from them.

Mode of learning the kriyas

It is not possible to learn all the kriyas at once. Therefore, we suggest that you learn each kriya sequentially, spending at least one week mastering each kriya, and progressively adding each new kriya to those already learned. That is, in the first week learn and master kriya 1: vipareeta karani mudra. Then in the second week, learn kriya 2: chakra anusandhana, and do both 1 and 2 daily. In the third week, learn kriya 3: nada sanchalana and do it daily, together with the previous two kriyas. In this way, all the kriyas can be systematically and thoroughly learned in a period of 20 weeks. However, it may take many months of regular practice before the kriyas are perfected and remember kundalini kriyas should be practised under guidance.

Length of practice

As you progressively add more and more kriyas to your practice program, the time required for daily practice will increase. Eventually, after mastering all the kriyas, your daily practice of the 20 kriyas, with the required number of rounds, will take between two and two and a half hours.

If you can spare this amount of time every day, then you will get the maximum benefit. However, most people, no matter how sincere, will not be able to devote this length of time to their practice. Therefore, for those who wish to practise kriya yoga, but have less spare time, we suggest that you reduce the number of rounds per kriya as follows:

Kriya technique	Full	Reduced
1: Vipareeta karani mudra	21	11
2: Chakra anusandhana	9	9
3: Nada sanchalana	13	5
4: Pawan sanchalana	49	11
5: Shabda sanchalana	59	11
6: Maha mudra	12	6
7: Maha bheda mudra	12	6
8: Manduki kriya	1–3 mins	1–3 mins

9: Tadan kriya	7	7
10: Naumukhi mudra	5	5
11: Shakti chalini	5	5
12: Shambhavi	11	5
13: Amrit pan	9	9
14: Chakra bhedan	59	11
15: Sushumna darshan	–	–
16: Prana ahuti	1 min	1 min
17: Utthan	2–3 mins	2–3 mins
18: Swaroopa darshan	2–3 mins	2–3 mins
19: Linga sanchalana	2–3 mins	2–3 mins
20: Dhyana	–	–

This daily program containing all the kriyas, with a reduced number of rounds, will take a total of about one to one and a half hours. The benefits may be slightly less than when you do the complete number of rounds per kriya, but still you will reap much fruit from your practise.

While learning each kriya, you should do the full number of rounds; this can be reduced as you integrate the next kriya.

Hints on practice

The following suggestions will help you to master the kriyas and gain maximum benefit:

1. Do not strain physically or mentally under any circumstances, or you may experience negative side effects. This applies particularly in the case of kriyas such as maha mudra, maha bheda mudra, tadan kriya, naumukhi and shakti chalini. Regular daily practice will gradually bring such changes into the mind and body, so that after some time, you will be able to practise the kriyas almost effortlessly.

2. Do not hold your breath for longer than is comfortable. In many of the kriyas, such as maha mudra and maha bheda mudra, most people will initially find difficulty in completing a full round in one respiration cycle

without strain or suffocation. In the beginning, it may be necessary to break in the middle of each round, or to take a short rest at the end of each round and take a few normal breaths. As you develop the capacity to hold the breath for longer periods, and to control inhalation and exhalation, this concession may be disregarded.

3. After long inner breath retentions, it is best to breathe in slightly before breathing out. In many of the kriyas, such as maha mudra, maha bheda mudra, naumukhi and shakti chalini, where the breath is held inside for prolonged periods, there is a tendency for the lungs to lock. The best way to overcome this problem and release the lungs is to breathe in slightly before breathing out. This will make the kriyas much easier to do.

4. While learning each kriya, check that you are doing all the steps and that they are being done correctly.

38

The Kriya Yoga Practices

By tradition there are a total of 76 kundalini kriyas of kriya yoga. We present the following 20 main practices, which are sufficient for the daily practice of any sincere sadhaka.

These practices are divided into three groups:
1. those which induce pratyahara
2. those which induce dharana
3. those which induce dhyana

It should be noted that these three states are actually a continuity of evolution, that is, the consciousness flows from one to the next without any apparent dividing point – so these practices should be done in an unbroken sequence. Of course, from the first day, the practice of these kriyas will not necessarily lead to such exalted states of awareness, but if they are practised properly with correct guidance, by an aspirant who is ready for them, then most likely, one day they will. It will be at that stage that the constant, unbroken progression of awareness will become essential. Remember, you should learn one kriya per week.

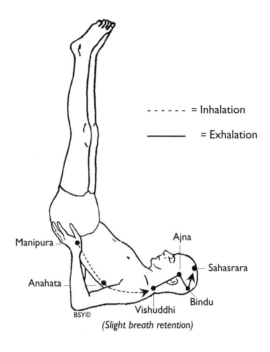

- - - - - - = Inhalation

————— = Exhalation

Ajna

Manipura

Sahasrara

Anahata

Bindu

BSY© Vishuddhi

(Slight breath retention)

1: Vipareeta Karani Mudra (the attitude of inversion)

Assume vipareeta karani asana (described in chapter 33).
The chin should not touch the chest.

Practise subtle ujjayi pranayama Be sure that the legs are
completely vertical. Close the eyes.

Inhale with ujjayi and simultaneously feel a hot stream of
amrit or nectar flowing through the spinal passage from
manipura chakra to vishuddhi in the throat. The nectar
will collect at vishuddhi.

Retain the breath for a few seconds, and be aware of the
nectar remaining at vishuddhi and becoming cool.

Then exhale with ujjayi, sensing the nectar travelling from
vishuddhi through ajna, bindu and to sahasrara.

The sensation is that of the nectar being injected with the
help of the breath.

After exhalation, immediately return your awareness to manipura and repeat the kriya to bring more nectar down to vishuddhi, and finally to sahasrara.

Practise 21 respirations or rounds.

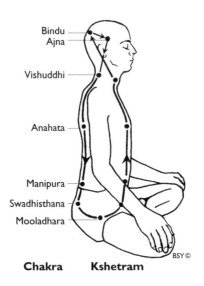

Chakra   Kshetram

2: Chakra Anusandhana (discovery of the chakras)

Assume siddhasana/siddha yoni asana or padmasana.

The eyes remain closed throughout the practice.

Breathe normally.

There is no connection between the breath and the consciousness in this practice.

Bring your awareness to mooladhara chakra.

Your consciousness will slowly ascend the frontal passage of arohan from mooladhara to the frontal point of swadhisthana at the pubic bone, manipura at the navel, anahata at the sternum, the chest centre, vishuddhi at the throat and across to bindu at the top, back of the head.

As you travel upward, mentally repeat, 'mooladhara, swadhisthana, manipura, anahata, vishuddhi, bindu', as you pass through these centres.

Then let your awareness slip down the spinal awarohan passage from bindu to mooladhara, mentally repeating 'ajna, vishuddhi, anahata, manipura, swadhisthana, mooladhara' as you pass through these centres.

From mooladhara, immediately start ascending in the frontal passage as before, mentally reciting the chakra names as you ascend, starting with swadhisthana.

Continue this rotation of awareness through the chakras in a constant flow of rounds.

Do not make a serious, tense effort to locate the chakras as you pass through them. Merely glance at them as you go by, as you would view the scenery from a fast moving train.

If you wish, you can visualize your awareness in this kriya as a thin silver serpent travelling in an ellipse within your body.

Practise 9 rounds.

3: Nada Sanchalana (conducting the sound consciousness)

Sit in siddhasana/siddha yoni asana or padmasana.

Exhale completely.

Open the eyes and bend the head forward, so that it drops downward in a relaxed manner. The chin should not press tightly on the chest.

Bring the awareness to mooladhara chakra.

Repeat mentally, 'mooladhara, mooladhara, mooladhara'. Then, as you inhale, your consciousness should rise up through the frontal passage of arohan to bindu.

Have a clear awareness of swadhisthana, manipura, anahata and vishuddhi, as you pass through them on your way to bindu, and mentally repeat their names.

As your awareness travels from vishuddhi to bindu during the last segment of your inhalation, your head will slowly rise and tilt back slightly into position facing about 20 degrees above the horizontal. With the breath retained inside and the awareness at bindu, mentally repeat, 'bindu, bindu, bindu'.

287

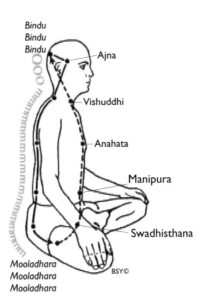

The power of the awareness will build up as you are repeating the word 'bindu' and it will explode into the vocal chant of *Om*, which will carry you down through the spinal passage of awarohan to mooladhara.

The 'O' sound will explode and move downwards, culminating almost in a vibrating m-m-m sound as you approach mooladhara.

As your awareness descends in the spine, your eyes will gradually close into unmani mudra.

As you descend through the awarohan passage with the *Om* sound, you should also be aware of ajna, vishuddhi, anahata, manipura and swadhisthana chakras; no mental repetition. When you have reached mooladhara, open the eyes and drop the head forward.

Mentally repeat, 'mooladhara, mooladhara, mooladhara', with the breath retained outside and start on the ascent as before, with inhalation and repetition of the chakra names as you pass through them.

Practise 13 full rounds or breaths and end after the last 'mooladhara, mooladhara, mooladhara'.

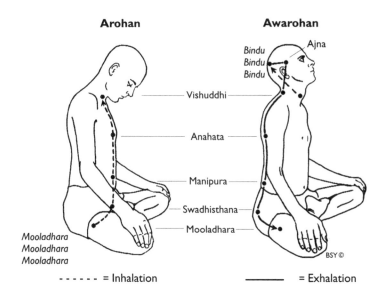

Arohan   **Awarohan**

Bindu
Bindu
Bindu   Ajna

Vishuddhi

Anahata

Manipura

Swadhisthana

Mooladhara

Mooladhara
Mooladhara
Mooladhara

BSY©

- - - - - - = Inhalation   ———— = Exhalation

4: Pawan Sanchalana (conducting the breath consciousness)

Sit in padmasana, siddhasana or siddha yoni asana, with
the eyes closed.

Practise khechari mudra and ujjayi pranayama throughout this kriya.

Exhale completely, open the eyes and bend the head
forward as in nada sanchalana.

Become aware of mooladhara chakra and repeat mentally,
'mooladhara, mooladhara, mooladhara'.

Then mentally say 'arohan' once and begin your ascent
through the frontal passage with a subtle ujjayi inhalation.
As you ascend, be aware of the chakras and as you pass
name them mentally.

As your awareness moves from vishuddhi to bindu,
slowly raise your head until it leans backward as in nada
sanchalana.

At bindu mentally repeat, 'bindu, bindu, bindu'.

Then say 'awarohan' mentally and descend through the
spinal passage with ujjayi exhalation, mentally repeating
the name of each chakra as you pass through it.

As you descend, your eyes will close very gradually into unmani mudra, the attitude of drowsiness.

At mooladhara they will be closed.

Then open your eyes and bend your head forward.

Repeat mentally, 'mooladhara, mooladhara, mooladhara'.

Again begin your ascent with ujjayi inhalation, as before.

Practise 49 rounds or complete breaths.

After the last 'mooladhara, mooladhara, mooladhara', open your eyes and end the practice.

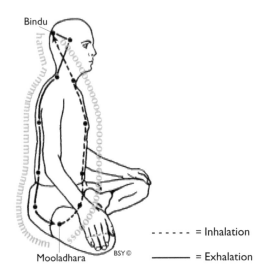

Bindu

Mooladhara   BSY©

- - - - - - = Inhalation

———— = Exhalation

5: Shabda Sanchalana (conducting the word consciousness)

Sit in siddhasana/siddha yoni asana or padmasana. Practise khechari mudra and ujjayi pranayama throughout the kriya.

Exhale completely, open the eyes, bend the head forward and become aware of mooladhara chakra for a few seconds.

Inhale with ujjayi and ascend the frontal passage.

As you ascend, be aware of the sound of the breath which takes the form of the mantra *So*.

Simultaneously, be aware of each kshetram, without mental repetition.

As you travel from vishuddhi to bindu, the head will move upward as in pawan sanchalana and nada sanchalana.

Then, with the breath retained inside, be aware of bindu for a few seconds.

Then descend the spinal passage performing unmani mudra and being simultaneously aware of the natural sound of exhalation and the mantra *Ham*.

Be aware of each chakra without repetition of its name.

After reaching mooladhara, open the eyes and lower your head.

Begin your ujjayi inhalation, rising through the frontal passage with the inhalation mantra of *So*.

Continue in this manner for 59 full rounds or breaths.

6: Maha Mudra (great attitude)

Sit in siddhasana or siddha yoni asana, with the heel of the lower foot pressing firmly in towards mooladhara chakra.

Practise khechari mudra, exhale completely and bend the head forward.

Keep the eyes open in the beginning.

Repeat mentally, 'mooladhara, mooladhara, mooladhara'.

Ascend through the frontal passage with ujjayi inhalation, being aware of each kshetram as you pass through it.

Raise your head as you are crossing from vishuddhi to bindu.

At bindu repeat mentally, 'bindu, bindu, bindu'.

Practise moola bandha and shambhavi mudra with the breath still retained inside.

Say to yourself mentally, 'shambhavi-khechari-mool', while shifting your awareness to the centre of these practices.

When you say 'shambhavi', your awareness should be fixed at the eyebrow centre.

When you say 'khechari', your awareness should be fixed at the tongue and roof of the mouth.

When you say 'mool', your awareness should be fixed at mooladhara chakra.

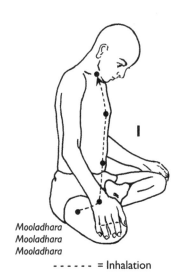

Mooladhara
Mooladhara
Mooladhara

- - - - - - = Inhalation

Bindu
Bindu
Bindu

- - - - - - = Inhalation

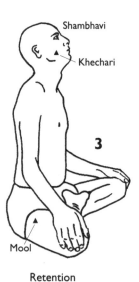

Shambhavi

Khechari

Mool

Retention

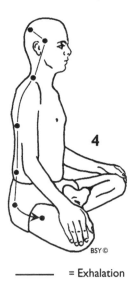

BSY ©

———— = Exhalation

Beginners should repeat this shifting of awareness 3 times. Advanced aspirants can rotate their awareness up to 12 times.

Then, first release shambhavi mudra, then moola bandha.

Bring your awareness back to bindu and travel down your spinal passage to mooladhara, with ujjayi exhalation and unmani mudra, and be aware of the chakras as you pass through them.

On reaching mooladhara, bend the head forward and open the eyes.

Then repeat, 'mooladhara, mooladhara, mooladhara' and ascend the frontal passage with ujjayi inhalation, as before.

Practise 12 full rounds or breaths and end after the last 'mooladhara, mooladhara, mooladhara'.

Alternative practice: This kriya can also be practised in utthanpadasana.

When practising maha mudra in utthanpadasana, a slight change must be made in the technique.

After ascending to bindu, repeat 'bindu, bindu, bindu'.

Lean forward and hold the big toe of the extended foot with the fingers of both hands, to form utthanpadasana. The stretched knee must not bend.

Now practise moola bandha and shambhavi mudra.

Repeat, 'shambhavi-khechari-mool' from 3 to 12 times, passing your awareness to the locations of these practices as you repeat their names.

Release shambhavi, then moola bandha, then utthanpadasana. Sit upright and place the hands back on the knee. Bring your awareness back to bindu, and then descend the spinal passage with ujjayi exhalation and unmani mudra.

Practise 4 rounds with the right leg stretched forward, 4 rounds with the left leg stretched forward, and 4 rounds with both legs stretched forward.

Practice note: This kriya can either be practised in perfect siddhasana/siddha yoni asana or in utthanpadasana. Both alternatives are equally good, as both apply a firm and

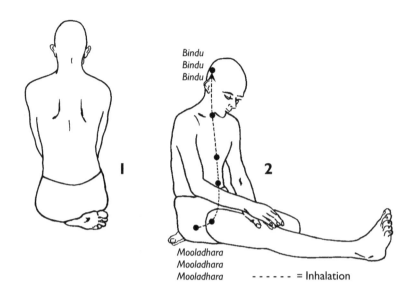

Bindu
Bindu
Bindu

1   2

Mooladhara
Mooladhara
Mooladhara   - - - - - - = Inhalation

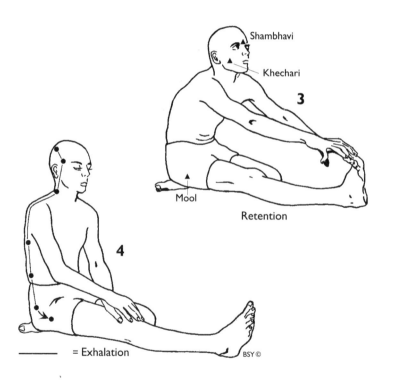

Shambhavi

Khechari

3

Mool

Retention

4

———— = Exhalation

BSY ©

constant pressure at mooladhara. If you can easily sit in siddhasana/siddha yoni asana, then the best method is the first one described. If you cannot sit comfortably in siddhasana/siddha yoni asana, then use the alternative. It is easy to become sleepy while doing kriya yoga and this alternative has an added advantage of helping to remove sleepiness.

The names of the chakras and kshetram can also be repeated mentally as you ascend and descend arohan and awarohan.

7: Maha Bheda Mudra (great piercing attitude)

Sit in siddhasana or siddha yoni asana, with the heel of the lower foot pressing firmly in towards mooladhara chakra.

Practise khechari mudra and exhale completely, with the eyes open. Bend the head forward.

Repeat mentally, 'mooladhara, mooladhara, mooladhara'. Inhale with ujjayi and ascend the frontal passage to bindu. As you ascend from vishuddhi to bindu, raise your head.

Repeat mentally, 'bindu, bindu, bindu', and then descend the spinal passage to mooladhara with ujjayi exhalation and unmani mudra.

Be sure to notice the chakras as you pass through them. Then practise jalandhara bandha with the breath retained outside. Practise nasikagra drishti, uddiyana bandha and moola bandha.

Repeat mentally, 'nasikagra-uddiyana-mool', while simul-taneously placing your awareness at the seats of these practices in turn.

Repeat this cycle of awareness 3 times if you are a beginner, or up to 12 times if you are experienced.

Then release nasikagra drishti, moola bandha, uddiyana bandha and jalandhara bandha, but keep the head down. Bring your awareness back to mooladhara.

Repeat the mantra 'mooladhara, mooladhara, mool-adhara', mentally.

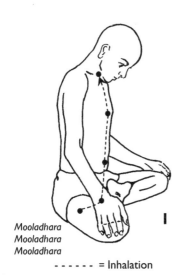

Mooladhara
Mooladhara
Mooladhara

- - - - - - = Inhalation

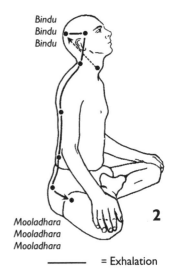

Bindu
Bindu
Bindu

Mooladhara
Mooladhara
Mooladhara

———— = Exhalation

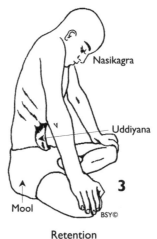

Nasikagra

Uddiyana

Mool

BSY©

Retention

Then with ujjayi inhalation, ascend the frontal passage to bindu for the next round.

Practise 12 full rounds or breaths.

Alternative practice: This kriya can also be practised in utthanpadasana, as with maha mudra.

Place the hands on the bent knee, exhale completely and bend the head forward, keeping the eyes open.

296

Repeat mentally, 'mooladhara, mooladhara, mooladhara'. Inhale with ujjayi through the frontal passage from mooladhara to bindu, raising your head while moving from vishuddhi to bindu.

Repeat, 'bindu, bindu, bindu', and then exhale with ujjayi down the spinal passage, doing unmani mudra and being aware of each chakra en route.

Hold the breath outside and bend forward to grasp the big toe of the extended foot to form utthanpadasana. Press the chin against the chest to form jalandhara bandha.

Practise nasikagra drishti, uddiyana bandha and moola bandha, while still retaining the breath outside.

Repeat mentally, 'nasikagra-uddiyana-mool', while placing the awareness at the locations of these practices in turn.

Repeat this cycle of awareness 3 times if you are a beginner, or up to 12 times if you are experienced.

Release nasikagra drishti, moola bandha and uddiyana bandha.

Bring your hands to your knees and sit up straight. Release jalandhara but keep your head bent down.

Bring your awareness back to mooladhara. Repeat the mantra 'mooladhara, mooladhara, mooladhara', and then ascend the frontal passage with ujjayi inhalation.

Practise in this way for 4 full rounds or breaths with the right leg extended, then practise 4 times with the left leg extended, and finally 4 times with both legs extended.

After the fourth time in each position, ascend once to bindu with ujjayi inhalation. Repeat the bindu mantra, descend to mooladhara and repeat its mantra, relax, then change legs.

The rotation of awareness through nasikagra, uddiyana and mool is done with outside retention of the breath at mooladhara. You are advised to practise only 3 rotations at first, slowly increasing by one rotation per week until you can complete 12 rotations.

Practice note: Make sure that all the bandhas are performed correctly and in the right sequence. At first you will have

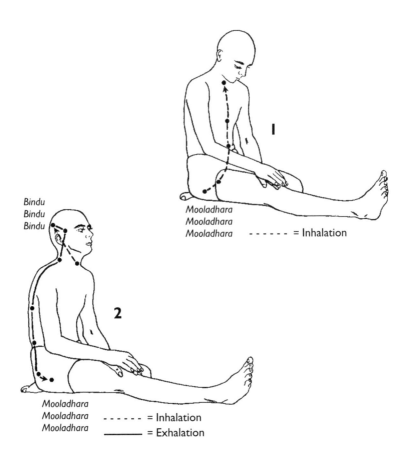

1

Mooladhara
Mooladhara
Mooladhara - - - - - - = Inhalation

Bindu
Bindu
Bindu

2

Mooladhara
Mooladhara - - - - - - = Inhalation
Mooladhara ———————— = Exhalation

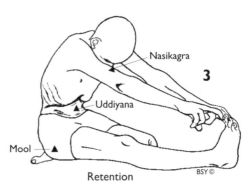

Nasikagra

Uddiyana

3

Mool ▲

Retention

BSY©

to pay special attention to this, but with regular practice the bandhas will lock and tighten automatically, without effort and at the right stage of the kriya.

Nose tip gazing helps to tighten the lock of the bandhas. Make sure that nasikagra drishti and the bandhas are practised simultaneously and that you do not omit any of them while rotating awareness through the centres. Do not strain. If you are feeling pain or discomfort in the eyes, stop nasikagra drishti but continue the bandhas and rotation of awareness. Slowly increase duration of nasikagra as the eye muscles adapt to the practice.

You can repeat the 'mooladhara' mantra 3 times before applying the bandhas as well as repeating 'mooladhara' 3 times at the beginning of a new round.

The names of the chakras and kshetrams can be mentally repeated as you ascend and descend arohan and awarohan passages.

8: Manduki Mudra (frog attitude)

Sit in bhadrasana. The eyes should remain open. The area of the body below mooladhara chakra must touch the floor. If necessary place a cushion under the buttocks to apply firm pressure to this point.

Place the hands on the knees and practise nasikagra drishti.

Become aware of the natural breath flowing in and out of the nostrils.

With inhalation, the breath flows through both nostrils and merges at the eyebrow centre. As you exhale, the two flows diverge from the eyebrow centre and move out through both nostrils.

The breath follows a conical or inverted V-shaped pathway. Feel this.

Simultaneously, be aware of all smells.

The point of this kriya is to smell the aroma of the astral body which has a scent like that of sandalwood. If your eyes become tired, close them for a while and then resume nasikagra drishti.

Practise this kriya until it becomes intoxicating.

Do not carry it so far that you become totally absorbed in it and do not wish to end the practice.

9: Tadan Kriya (beating the kundalini)

Sit in padmasana with the eyes open.

Place the palms on the floor at the sides of the body, next to the hips, with the fingers pointing forward.

Tilt the head slightly backward and practise shambhavi mudra.

Inhale through the mouth in audible ujjayi pranayama.

As you inhale, feel the breath travelling downward through a tube connecting the mouth to mooladhara chakra.

The breath will collect at mooladhara chakra.

Hold the breath in, keep your awareness at mooladhara and practise moola bandha.

Using your hands, lift your body off the ground.

Then drop your body lightly so that mooladhara is gently beaten. Repeat this beating 3 times.

Do not practise this quickly or harshly.

After the third beating, exhale gently through the nose with ujjayi pranayama.

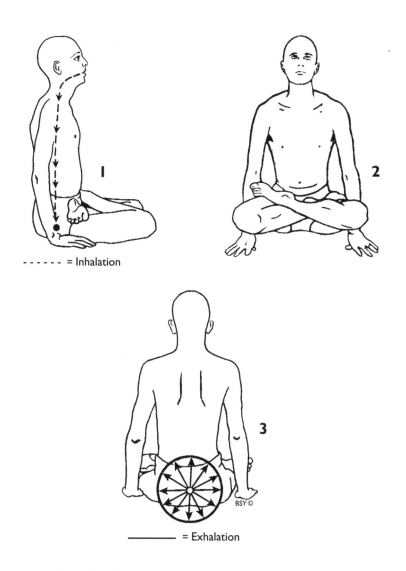

- - - - - - = Inhalation

—————— = Exhalation

The breath will seem to diffuse in all direction from its storehouse at mooladhara.

Practise this kriya a total of 7 times.

The number of beatings practised per round can be gradually increased from 3 to a maximum of 11.

301

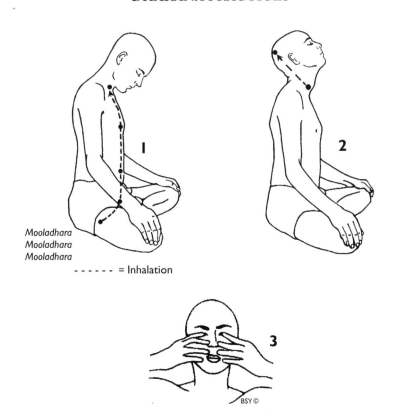

Mooladhara
Mooladhara
Mooladhara

- - - - - - = Inhalation

10: Naumukhi Mudra (closing the nine gates)

Sit in siddhasana/siddha yoni asana or padmasana. The eyes should remain closed throughout. If necessary, use a cushion to ensure mooladhara is compressed.

Perform khechari mudra and bend the head slightly forward (not jalandhara bandha).

Repeat mentally, 'mooladhara, mooladhara, mooladhara'. Then inhale with ujjayi up the frontal passage to bindu. Raise your head as you pass from vishuddhi to bindu. Practise shanmukhi mudra by closing your ears with the thumbs, the eyes with both forefingers, the nostrils with your middle fingers, the upper lip with the ring fingers

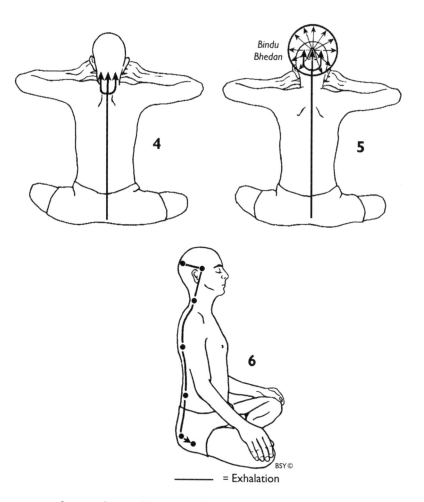

Bindu
Bhedan

4

5

6

BSY©

——————— = Exhalation

and your lower lip with the small fingers (do not apply too much pressure).

Practise moola bandha and vajroli/sahajoli mudra.

The nine gates of the body are now closed (eyes, ears, nostrils, mouth, anus and sexual organ).

Become aware of the spinal passage and bindu.

Now visualize a shining copper trident (trishul), rooted in mooladhara with its stem in the spinal cord and the prongs extending upward from vishuddhi. The prongs are very sharp.

The trishul will slightly rise a number of times of its own accord and it will pierce bindu with its central prong.

As it pierces bindu, repeat the mantra 'bindu bhedan', which means 'bindu piercing'.

After some time, release vajroli/sahajoli mudra and moola bandha. Open the upper gates and bring your hands down to your knees.

Exhale with ujjayi down the spinal passage from bindu to mooladhara. Mentally repeat 'mooladhara' 3 times. Then inhale up the frontal passage to bindu to repeat the kriya. Practise 5 full rounds or breaths, and after the fifth round, end the practice after exhalation.

Practice note: It is extremely important that the back be held perfectly straight throughout this kriya. If not, the sensation that follows the piercing of bindu may not be perceived.

When vajroli/sahajoli mudra is correctly performed it will also heighten the sensation experienced during this practice. When vajroli/sahajoli mudra is perfected, the contraction of vajra nadi can be achieved without contracting the anal sphincter muscles. The sensation can be compared to an electric current running the full length of vajra nadi to the brain. Try to sensitize your awareness to the point where you actually feel the piercing of bindu like an electric shock.

As you ascend and descend arohan and awarohan, you can mentally repeat the names of the chakras and kshetram if you wish.

11: Shakti Chalini (conduction of the thought force)

Sit in siddhasana/siddha yoni asana or padmasana.

The eyes should remain closed throughout.

Practise khechari mudra. Exhale completely, bend the head forward and bring the awareness to mooladhara.

Repeat mentally, 'mooladhara, mooladhara, mooladhara', and then ascend the frontal passage to bindu with ujjayi inhalation, raising your head as you approach bindu.

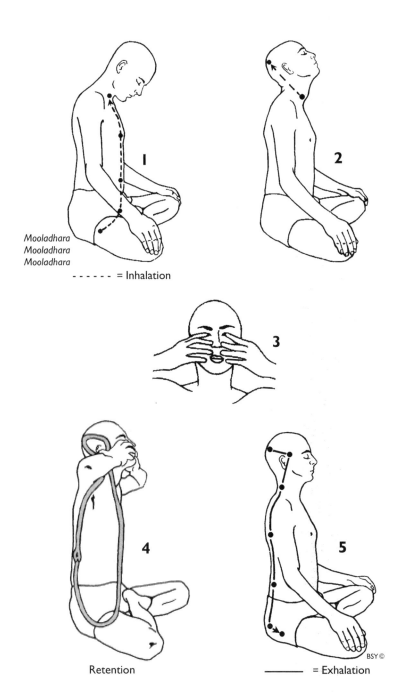

Mooladhara
Mooladhara
Mooladhara

- - - - - = Inhalation

Retention

BSY ©

——— = Exhalation

Retain the breath inside, and then practise shanmukhi mudra, closing the ears, eyes, nostrils and lips with the fingers. Allow your awareness to rotate in a continuous cycle, descending the spinal passage to mooladhara and rising up the frontal passage to bindu in an unbroken loop, while you keep the breath retained inside.

Visualize a thin green snake moving through the psychic passageways.

The tail of this serpent is at bindu, and the body extends down through mooladhara and up the frontal passage.

The head is also at bindu, with the mouth biting the end of the tail.

If you watch this snake, it will start to move in a circle in the psychic passages, or it may even go off this track and follow a new one of its own.

Just watch this snake, whatever it does.

When your retention of breath is becoming exhausted, release shanmukhi mudra, return the hands to the knees and bring your awareness to bindu. Then descend to mooladhara through the spinal passage with ujjayi exhalation. At mooladhara, lower your head, repeat 'mooladhara' 3 times, and ascend the frontal passage.

Practise this kriya 5 times without a break, or for the duration of 5 breaths.

Practice note: Vajroli/sahajoli mudra and moola bandha can also be performed simultaneously with yoni mudra.

12: Shambhavi (Parvati's lotus)

Sit in siddhasana/siddha yoni asana or padmasana.

Close your eyes and practise khechari mudra.

Visualize a lotus flower with a long thin stem extending downward. The roots of the lotus are white or transparent green. They spread out from mooladhara chakra.

The thin green lotus stem is in your spinal passage.

The lotus flower is at sahasrara, and it is closed like a bud.

At the bottom of the bud are a few light green immature petals.

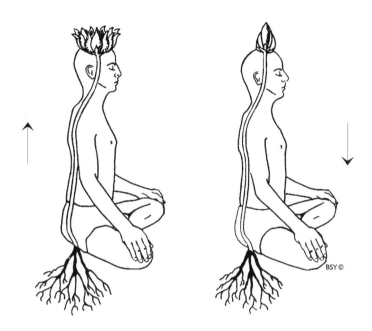

The main petals of the flower are pink with fine red veins.
Try to see this lotus clearly. You visualize it in chidakasha,
but you feel it in your body.
Exhale and take your awareness to the root of the lotus at
mooladhara.
Inhale with ujjayi pranayama and allow your awareness
to rise slowly through the centre of the lotus stem, within
the spinal passage.
At the end of inhalation, you will reach the closed bud at
the top of the stem.
Your ascent will be like that of a caterpillar, climbing up
inside a thin stem.
Hold your awareness at sahasrara with the breath retained
inside. You are inside the lotus, but you can also see it
from outside.
It will begin to open very slowly.
As the bud opens out into a beautiful lotus flower, you will
see the yellow pollen-tipped stamens in its centre.
It will slowly close again, to open again almost immediately.

After the lotus has stopped opening and closing, and it remains sealed, then slowly descend through the stem to mooladhara, drifting down on the wave of your ujjayi exhalation. Remain at mooladhara for a few seconds, visualizing the roots spreading out in all directions.

Then once again, ascend the stem with ujjayi inhalation. Ascend and descend 11 times, and then end this kriya.

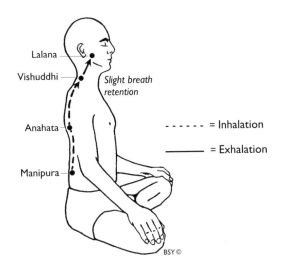

13: Amrit Pan (the quaffing of nectar)

Sit in siddhasana/siddha yoni asana or padmasana.

Keep the eyes closed throughout and practise khechari mudra. Bring your awareness to manipura chakra, where there is a storehouse of a warm, sweet liquid.

Exhale fully with ujjayi. Inhale with ujjayi, drawing a quantity of this liquid up to vishuddhi chakra through the spinal passage with the suction power of your breath.

Remain at vishuddhi for a few seconds.

The nectar that you have raised from manipura will become icy cold at vishuddhi.

Then with ujjayi, exhale up to lalana chakra (at the back of the soft palate), through the nectar passage. Blow the cool nectar up to lalana with the breath. The breath will immediately disperse by itself once you have reached lalana. Immediately return your awareness to manipura chakra.

With another ujjayi inhalation, continue the upward transfer of liquid.

Practise 9 times in all.

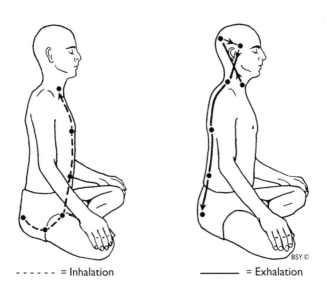

- - - - - - = Inhalation   ———— = Exhalation

14: Chakra Bhedan (piercing the chakras)

Sit in siddhasana/siddha yoni asana or padmasana. Keep your eyes closed throughout.

Practise khechari mudra and ujjayi pranayama.

Breathe without any break between inhalation and exhalation.

Exhale, and bring your awareness down to swadhisthana chakra at the base of the spine.

Inhale and direct your consciousness first to mooladhara and then up the frontal passage.

At about the level of vishuddhi kshetram, the breath will run out and you will immediately start exhalation. Exhale from vishuddhi kshetram to bindu and then down the spine from ajna to swadhisthana chakra to complete one round.

This kriya should actually be practised for 59 rounds, but if introversion starts to occur before you have completed the rounds, discontinue the practice and go on to the next kriya.

Practice note: If desired, mental repetition of the chakra and kshetram can also be performed.

15: Sushumna Darshan (inner visualization of the chakras)

For chakra visualization refer to the diagrams of each chakra.
Sit in siddhasana/siddha yoni asana or padmasana. Close the eyes and breathe normally.

There is no relation between the breath and awareness in this kriya.

Bring the awareness to mooladhara. Imagine a pencil, and with that pencil draw a square at mooladhara.

Draw the largest possible inverted equilateral triangle within that square. Then make a circle touching all the four corners of that square. Prepare four petals, one for each side of the square.

Bring your awareness to swadhisthana. Prepare a circle there with the same radius as the one at mooladhara.

Draw six petals around the edge of the circle, and a crescent moon inside the bottom of the circle.

Now come to manipura. Draw a circle, and then make the biggest possible inverted triangle to fit this circle. In the centre draw a ball of fire. Make ten petals around the circle.

Raise the consciousness to anahata.

Draw two triangles there, one triangle pointed upward and the other inverted. They are interlaced, both crossing each other. Surround them by by a circle with twelve petals.

Then come to vishuddhi. Draw a circle, and place a smaller circle within the circle, like a drop of nectar. Make sixteen petals around that circle.

Move up to ajna. Make a circle and inside it write a big Sanskrit ॐ. Prepare two large petals, one on the right and one on the left side of the circle.

At bindu draw a crescent moon with a very tiny circle above it.

Reach sahasrara. Prepare a circle there, and make the largest possible upward pointing triangle within that circle.

There are 1000 petals all around the circle.

Try to see at one glance all the chakras in their proper places.

If it is very difficult to see them all together, then see only two chakras on the first day and add one more to your visualization each day until all appear together.

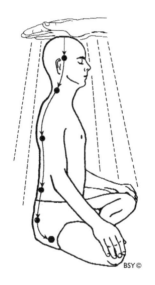

16: Prana Ahuti (infusing the divine prana)

Sit in siddhasana/siddha yoni asana or padmasana.

Close the eyes and breathe normally.

Feel the soft touch of a divine hand lying on your head. The hand is infusing subtle prana into your body and mind and the prana is travelling down from sahasrara through the spinal passage.

You may experience it as a wave of cold, heat energy, electric current, or as a stream of wind or liquid.

Its passage will result in vibrations, shocks, jerks or ticking sensations which course through you.

When the prana has reached mooladhara, then immediately go on to the next kriya without waiting to experience the prana a second time.

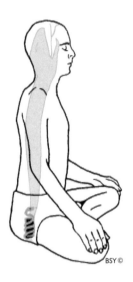

17: Utthan (raising the kundalini)

Sit in siddhasana/siddha yoni asana or padmasana.

Keep the eyes closed throughout and breathe normally.

Bring your awareness to mooladhara chakra.

Try to visualize it clearly and notice all details.

You will see a black shivalingam made of a smoky gaseous substance.

The bottom and top of the lingam are cut off, and circled around it is a red baby snake.

This red baby snake is trying to uncoil itself so it can move upward through sushumna.

As it struggles to release itself and ascends, it makes an angry hissing sound.

The tail of the snake will remain fixed at the bottom of the shivalingam, but the head and body may move upward and come back down again.

Sometimes both the shivalingam and the snake may shift their position in the body, so you may even visualize them for a time at ajna or sahasrara.

The head of the snake is very wide, having the same breadth as your body, but it is not a cobra.

After some time, you may feel your body contract. This will be followed by a sensation of bliss.

When this occurs go on to the next kriya.

18: Swaroopa Darshan (the vision of your Self)

Remain sitting in siddhasana/siddha yoni asana or padmasana and do not open the eyes.

Become aware of the physical body.

Your body is completely motionless, and you maintain total awareness of this fact.

Be sure that you are completely steady, like a rock.

When you are absolutely sure of your bodily steadiness, you should also become aware of your natural breath.

Watch the constant flow of your breath, but be sure your body remains steady.

Your body will start to become stiff.

As it becomes stiffer, your awareness will shift completely to your breathing; however, the body will continue to become stiffer and stiffer of its own accord.

When your body has become as rigid as a stone, and it is beyond your control to move it even if you tried, then go on to the next kriya.

19: Linga Sanchalana (astral conduction)

Remain still in your stiffened asana with the eyes closed.

Due to the stiffness of your body, your breathing will have automatically become ujjayi breathing, and khechari mudra will have been formed.

Be totally aware of your breathing.

313

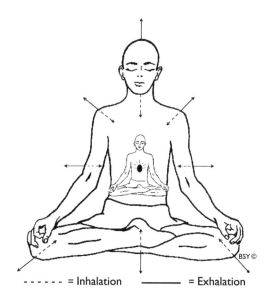

- - - - - - = Inhalation   ——— = Exhalation

You will notice that with each inhalation your body seems to be expanding, and with each exhalation your body appears to be contracting.

It is peculiar though, because your physical body is not moving; it is still and as stiff as a statue.

It is your astral body that you experience expanding and contracting.

As you observe this contraction and expansion process, it will gradually become more and more pronounced.

After some time you will begin to lose awareness of the physical body, and you will only be observing the astral body directly.

However, the degree of contraction will become more pronounced.

Eventually you will reach a stage where, on contraction, the astral body reduces to a single point of light.

When this occurs, discontinue the kriya immediately and go on to the next.

20: Dhyana (meditation)

You have realized your astral body as a single point of light.

Now look closer at that point of light and you will see it take the form of a golden egg.

As you watch this golden egg, it will begin to expand.

The golden egg is luminous and glowing intensely; however, it does not give off any rays of light.

As the golden egg becomes larger, it will begin to take on the same shape as that of your astral and physical bodies.

This form, however, is not a material or even a subtle form.

This form is glowing light.

It is your causal self.

Kundalini Research

Compiled by
Dr Swami Shankardevananda Saraswati MBBS (Syd)

39

Introduction

We have seen time and again that the words and teachings of many of the yogis, saints and sages from all ages have been recently verified by modern science. It has been our function to fit together the bits and pieces of research and to point out:

1. The overlap between modern science and yoga,
2. How the various pieces fit together to give us an expanded concept of man,
3. What directions research can take in order to design and analyze research in the light of yogic psychophysiology.

One of the great traps in attempting to research yoga is to design experiments without a thorough knowledge of yoga itself. This is like looking at only a small part of the whole, just as the six blind 'wise' men, who each examined a different part of an elephant and then pronounced their judgements based on these limitations, could never understand the whole elephant and how it looked. Yogic training requires many years and the skilled guidance of a master to discover its basic principles, its mode of application, and to prepare oneself for the experiences arising from this training.

The totality of man

Perhaps the outstanding feature of yoga is its ability to give us a more total picture of who we are, to put the various elements into a simpler and at the same time more sophisticated and more expanded perspective. Yoga also teaches us that within us all there is a vital power, a basic essence, whose thread can be seen running through life, unmeasurable by even the most sophisticated machines, but palpable and motivating our living, breathing, thinking, body and mind. We can see its effects and measure the forms and changes of this subtle energy as it enters and interacts with the physical domain, in the nerves, in the chemical and intra-cellular processes and in the flows and pressures of the body. However, the energy itself is still undefined scientifically.

Through yogic sadhana we can experience the subtle energy, called prana or kundalini, which underlies all matter. This experience is a transformative one, which makes the subtle more tangible and real than the material and so-called solid, physical universe. It shifts our perspective, broadens our awareness and awakens our consciousness, our higher and greater self. It awakens us to the fact that within us all is an immortal and eternal essence, full of knowledge, bliss and truth.

The very fact that such an experience exists alters our direction and purpose. We see that we are here not only for sensual and mundane satisfaction, but for a higher and greater destiny. This ultimate goal of yoga must always be remembered when we are researching yoga, for we know that yoga can give us relaxation, alter our brain waves and hormonal secretions, endow us with health, induce concentration and better memory, help us to develop better human interrelationships and to enjoy everything we do, to have fun and fulfil ourselves in a balanced, healthy way. However, we must see that these things, though they are all worthy and good in themselves, are not the ultimate goal of yoga, but are side-effects of our pursuit of higher awareness and deeper knowledge of the truth of our existence. To pursue these things in themselves is another trap, a trick of the mind. For they do not exist by themselves but are the outcome of a complete process of living. The yogic process of total development of body, mind and spirit, ida, pingala and sushumna, is the most systematic way to attain these things and more.

Yoga is not a science of healing and does not need to look into the negative side of existence. The teachings tell us to practise and emphasize the good, positive and healthy in us and automatically we will be healthy and happy. There is nothing difficult to understand in this. If we emphasize exercise, moderation, good lifestyle, relaxation, meditation and self-discipline, then we are sure to achieve something worthwhile in life. Research into relaxation, meditation, asana and pranayama continues to demonstrate that yoga exerts real changes in the body and mind, that it can only be a worthwhile addition to our lives if performed under guidance and done correctly. However, we must remember that it is much more than that, and that all our achievements are ultimately, and in the last analysis, useless if we do not transform the quality of our awareness.

Yoga tells us to awaken our minds, to develop the energy within ourselves so that we can attain a much greater, fuller and more total existence. Evidence is piling up to show that there is a psychic side to our lives, that the mental and intangible is far from imaginary, but is powered by an energy, a subtle force which can be tapped and developed and which can totally change and transform the more physical side of our lives. There is also evidence that awareness and consciousness can be independent from the body and this is coming from studies into physics and the nature of energy in our universe.

Purpose of this section

In this section we are more concerned with delineating the research into energy than into consciousness. We are concerned with the research into kundalini rather than with the awareness side of things. We must take it for granted that awareness exists. Research into the energy side of yoga shows us that there is a physically based energy in the body which also has a psychic dimension. This fits the yogic description of prana, whose ultimate and maximum form is that of kundalini.

Many times we have been amazed to hear the stories of yogis and saints and have been awed by reading the ancient and universal teachings of yoga, to realize that they are applicable even today. Often we have wondered how yogis developed this science in the first place. Obviously it has come from a profound and unusual experience, beyond the capacity of the normal person to achieve or even understand without practising yoga.

Swami Satyananda Saraswati is one of those who has reached transcendental heights and come back to tell us about kundalini in scientific terms. He has spoken about the kundalini phenomenon and has laid down the fundamentals of kundalini yoga in a succinct, precise, profound and yet easily understandable and systematic manner, as has been done in this book. He has told us many things about the functions of the body, for example, that the right nostril connects to the left brain, and the left nostril to the right brain, which, in 1983, was verified by researchers at the Salk Institute in America (see chapter 42). Through his own internal experiences he has seen that most of us do not use our potential and that within the brain there are unused areas of potential energy, psychic awareness and total knowledge. It is actually possible to experience the brain from inside. The source is within us, however, we have not connected the various centres and circuits to the main switches and the main generator. The way to do this, Swami Satyananda tells us, is through kundalini yoga.

Often Swami Satyananda has referred to the works of researchers as a means of validating and expressing the kundalini experience in easily understandable scientific terms, and to show that there are many people working on this most important aspect of life. Much of their research is outlined here in simple terms. This research represents pioneering efforts to delineate the broader function of man. No doubt, in the future, new machines and methods will have to be developed, for we are seeing only the bare beginnings of yogic research at this time. However, the efforts of these researchers will be remembered and will set the course for more sophisticated, scientifically acceptable research.

One thing is sure, science and yoga have been running parallel and in the same direction and are now beginning to converge towards a meeting point which promises to transform society. The concept of kundalini and the higher sciences is becoming more widely known and respected and more and more people are taking up its practice. This book and this section are an offering to help you to see kundalini in a more total and easily understood manner, to give researchers guidelines and perspective, and to help you achieve the kundalini experience as a reality in your life.

40

Kundalini, Fact not Fiction

As one opens the door with a key, so the yogi should open the gate to liberation with the kundalini. The great goddess sleeps, closing with her mouth, the opening through which one can ascend to the brahmarandhra . . . to that place where there is neither pain nor suffering. The kundalini sleeps above the kanda . . . she gives liberation to the yogi and bondage to the fool. He who knows kundalini, knows yoga. The kundalini, it is said, is coiled like a serpent. He who can induce her to move is liberated.

—*Hatha Yoga Pradipika* (ch. 3 v. 105–111)

With our present limited state of consciousness, bound by sense experiences which become dull and monotonous through endless repetition, and unable to break out of our tensions, problems and anxieties, modern man is facing both a material and spiritual crisis. This crisis is a two-edged sword. Kundalini both binds and liberates. On the one hand it is 'bad', for it creates anxiety and depression and has precipitated a plague of psychosomatic disease and suffering unparalleled in former times. On the other hand, it is 'good', a blessing in disguise which is forcing us to change and grow, to evolve ourselves at individual and social levels.

We are witnessing a tremendous upsurge of interest in yoga, meditation and spiritual values. There has been a revival of the yogic lifestyle and knowledge. Yoga and related sciences are now recognized as valuable tools within the healing profession and have added tremendous depth and height, a new dimension to psychology and philosophy. Scientists have been inspired to probe deeper into the mysteries of yoga, to investigate the means by which it works and to make the teachings of the ancient rishis and yogis more readily understood and expressed in modern scientific terminology. We are seeing that science is not actually discovering anything new, but is substantiating the ancient knowledge of the yogis.

Scientific investigation into yoga and the allied sciences has made this knowledge more accessible by incorporating it into a whole new set of therapeutic techniques and new methods to develop our potential, for example, biofeedback, autogenic training, mind control techniques, psychic healing, and a myriad of other similar processes. New branches of medicine have come into being, and the recognition of mind, begun by Freud in the early part of the twentieth century, has finally filtered down into common acceptance. Stress medicine and psychosomatic medicine are examples of our deeper understanding of this interaction of energy, mind and body, an understanding developed through our rediscovery of yoga.

In an effort to penetrate the mysteries of prana shakti, the physical side of psychic energy, and chitta, the mental side of psychic energy, a few respected and eminent pioneers, honouring the rigorous demands of the scientific method, have accumulated a solid core of evidence which explains in scientific terms the phenomenon of psychic energy and validates the teachings of yogis. Science has substantiated the yogic knowledge that a subtle energy exists which is body-based and has both physical and psychic properties. This energy, which powers our awareness and transforms and expands our conscious dimensions, is not just a myth or idea; it is not a metaphysical concept, but a fact. Kundalini is defined as the ultimate, most intense form of this energy, which lies dormant within each and every one of us.

Parapsychology

Phenomena such as telepathy, psychic healing, psychokinesis (the moving of matter by mind power), dowsing, telegnosis (psychic reading of history and association of objects), and other paranormal events, are receiving serious attention from the more pioneering members of the international science community as a means of understanding the relationship of energy and consciousness.

Scientists in the USA, UK, Germany, Holland, Scandinavia and Australia have taken the lead from scientists of the Soviet Union, many of whom are financed by their governments. Called bioelectronics or paraphysics in some circles, this field of study is generally known as *parapsychology.*

In Czechoslovakia it is known as *psychotronics,* and one of the leading Czech researchers in this field is Dr Zdenek Rejdak, whose association with Swami Satyananda began in the early 1970s when he stayed at the Bihar School of Yoga. Speaking in Japan at the fifth annual conference of the International Association for Religion and Parapsychology in 1976, Dr Rejdak defined psychotronics, and therefore, the whole field of parapsychology as: "The science which, in an interdisciplinary fashion, studies the distant interactions between living organisms and their environment, internal and external, and the energetic processes underlying these manifestations in order to supplement and widen man's understanding of the laws of nature."

Psychic energy

Psychic energy has been found to affect a whole range of laboratory equipment, from voltmeters to Geiger counters to magnetometers. Yet this does not mean that psychic energy is electrical, magnetic or radioactive. Rather, it seems to both encompass and go beyond these properties. Most researchers agree with the Russians who state that psychic energy may have its origin in electrical activity, but the nature of the energy is entirely different. However, yogis state that prana is the substratum of our material universe, interpenetrating and organizing all matter and being the common ground for all energy. They see prana from a different and higher perspective.

It is also generally accepted by scientists that psychic energy, most widely known as *bioenergy*, is body-based and affects both the physical and mental spheres as indicated by yogis. It has also been measured as a force field surrounding the body up to a distance of twelve feet by Yale neuropsychiatrist, Dr Leonard Ravitz.[1] This seems to support the yogic concept of the subtle pranic body which interpenetrates and is interdependent with the physical structure, motivating it to function.

There is considerable support for this hypothesis, gathered from the monitoring of the physiological changes experienced by psychics during laboratory tests of paranormal events. For instance, as part of his usual experimental procedure, Dr Grenady Sergeyev of the A.A. Utkomskii Physiological Institute (a Leningrad military laboratory), took readings of the brain waves, heartbeat and pulse rates of Neyla Mikhailova during her numerous demonstrations of psychokinesis.[2] He found that while Mikhailova was causing objects to move without touching them, his instruments recorded a tremendous vibration throughout her body and its surrounding force field which pulsed in the direction of her gaze. Her heart and brain waves also pulsed in unison with this energy vibration, indicating that the energy Mikhailova used in her psychic feats is intimately connected with her whole body.

Reports go on to state that: "After doing these tests, Mrs. Mikhailova was utterly exhausted. There was almost no pulse. She'd lost close to four pounds in half an hour. The EEG (brain wave pattern) showed intense emotional excitement. There was high blood sugar and the endocrine system was disturbed. The whole organism was weakened as if from a tremendous stress reaction. She had lost the sensation of taste, had pains in her arms and legs, couldn't coordinate and felt dizzy."[3]

At one time, after making a seven hour film of her abilities, Mikhailova was temporarily blind. Other Soviet investigators have recorded changes in brain wave patterns which coincide with the reception of telepathic signals, and researchers in the USA have shown that the volume of blood in the body alters during telepathic interactions.

This evidence leaves no doubt that psychic energy, or bioenergy, is from the body and is the same energy activating every aspect of metabolism, from functioning of the glands, to the brain and heart. It is the power behind the emotions and senses. At the same time, prana, though based on and affecting the physical structure and function, has a wider range of properties and is associated with clairvoyance, clair-audience and other forms of extrasensory perception. It has a mental or psychic component and is both gross and subtle.

Psychic energy can affect matter without any apparent physical intermediary or medium. There is some undetectable energy at work which we cannot measure though we can see its results. It can even be used in healing. Sister Dr Justa Smith, in America, has demonstrated that psychic energy affects enzymes.[4] She has found that trypsin, a digestive enzyme which is damaged and decreases activity when exposed to ultraviolet light, increases activity when exposed to a high intensity magnetic field. When a water damaged trypsin solution was held in the hands of a recognized psychic healer for 72 minutes, trypsin increased its activity.

R. Yaeger has shown that when a practitioner of kundalini yoga performed certain pranayama techniques and then sat next to an onion for 15 minutes with his hands in a fixed position, about two feet from the experimental plant, cell division, and therefore metabolic energy increased by 108%.[5] A control subject sitting in the same position, but without doing pranayama, had no effects on the plant.

We have clear evidence from these experiments that there is a new kind of psychic physiological energy that fits the description of prana and kundalini as set forth in the yogic texts and verbal traditions.

Summary

Modern science has been able to ascertain that psychic energy is a real and physically-based phenomenon. Though it does not fall into the known categories of modern science, its effects can be experienced and recorded repeatedly. No one really doubts its existence. What it is and how it functions, its relationship to our body and mind and its potential use as an evolutionary tool require further research from scientists who will find guidelines in the perspectives and experiences of dedicated yogis.

Through this, we will be better able to understand the relationship of mind and body and this will have tremendous repercussions on studies into psychosomatic medicine, psychology and other important fields. As we ourselves learn to appreciate that great joy and good health which comes from developing and being sensitive to psychic energy, a large and forgotten area of our being, we will extend our possibilities, develop our innate potential and speed up our spiritual evolution.

41

Defining the Nadis

Yoga and tantra lay down one of the most complete systems for a practical understanding of the human condition. Tantra supplies the philosophy, the theoretical approach. Yoga supplies techniques by which we can validate this philosophy through our own personal experience and thus attain higher knowledge. Tantra is therefore a living philosophy and not just a system of endless intellectual speculation unable to deliver the truth and leaving more questions unanswered than answered. It is also a very potent method by which we can realize ourselves in totality, and attain union, ultimate freedom and fulfilment.

Perhaps the greatest contribution of tantra to the modern world will be its ability not just to define the mind and put it into perspective, but to deliver techniques by which we can experience the mind itself and eventually transcend it through the awakening of kundalini. Modern medicine and psychology, for example, will greatly benefit from tantra's fundamental, basic components of body, mind and spirit – pingala, ida and sushumna. These flows of energy make up our total human personality and are derived from the ultimate polarity of our macrocosmic universe into Shiva and Shakti, consciousness and energy.

In trying to understand the manifestations of these forces in our body, and for research purposes, in trying to prove the reality of the existence of the nadis, we have to understand that they are not physical, measurable, dissectable structures within our physical body, but are the basic energies which underlie and motivate life and consciousness.

It is important to understand exactly what nadis are before we either try to prove their existence or disprove it. When we achieve certain states of consciousness we can see that nadis are, as yogis described them, flows of energy which we can visualize at the psychic level as having distinct channels, light, colour, sound and other characteristics. At the same time, however, these nadis underlie, and can be seen mirrored in, all bodily functions and processes. There is no separation between the nadis, the body and the mind; they are one and the same thing.

The duality of life

In many of the oriental philosophies, the entire universe is seen as a separation into two great, polarized forces, Shiva and Shakti, which are interdependent and opposite, but complementary. The universe hangs as a kind of web of interacting energies, suspended and functioning within the framework of tensions developed by the fundamental polarity. Carl Jung stated, "natural processes are phenomena of energy constantly arising out of a 'less probable' state."[1] This apparent dualism is actually a unified, holistic process from another level of consciousness, but at our own level we see it from a fragmented, limited and partial perspective.

We see polarity everywhere we look, in nature, within ourselves and within our mind. Moving from macrocosmic to microcosmic to atomic, at every level, two great principles or forces can be seen at work motivating our universe; light and dark, positive and negative, male and female. All other forces are seen to be an outcome of these two main forces. It seems amazing to us that things can be so simple and yet so profound; however, to the enlightened mind, the universe and man is just so.

All of life, therefore, has two main aspects upon which all of our perception, activity and experience are based. Our mind and body are the outcome of two main forms or modes of energy interacting and creating endless manifestations in the universe of our body. For example, we have a right and left brain, a parasympathetic and sympathetic nervous system, an anabolic and catabolic metabolism, a conscious and unconscious mind. We are poised between life and death and our whole existence is a struggle to retain balance between these two forces.

Ida and pingala

Yogis realized the existence of these forces and understood their relationship. They said that man has three main flows of energy, which they called the nadis, ida, pingala and sushumna, and which have been roughly translated as mind, body, and spirit. The third flow is the result of the balanced interaction of the first two. They also said that man functions mainly in the first two areas of body and mind, pingala and ida, the third aspect being dormant until it is stimulated by yoga or some other discipline.

Ida and pingala are roughly translated as mind and body. Though this is true at one level, when we are discussing the polarization of the total individual, the body and mind are themselves each polarized. We have to understand, however, that the nadis are not structures but are functional relationships and are really different sides of the same coin. Yogis did not describe the nadis in terms of structures, though structure exists to handle them. They described them in terms of energy, *prana*, vital and life-giving for pingala, and *chitta*, consciousness and knowing for ida. The attributes of the nadis are summarized below:

Pingala can be defined as the dynamic, active, masculine, positive, yang energy within our personality. It has a physical and mental side. Its material qualities are light, heat, solar, energy accumulating, creative, organizing, focused (centripetal) and contractive. The positive, dynamic mental side within Freud's system is Eros, the pleasure principle, and in Jung's system it is the conscious personality, the rational, discriminating side. We can say that pingala is psychosomatic energy, outwardly directed, mind acting on body to motivate the organs of action, the karmendriyas. It is the basic energy of life.

Ida is the energy within the personality which is passive, receptive, feminine, negative, yin. At the physical level it is dark, cold, lunar, energy dissipating, disorganizing, entropic, expansive (centrifugal) and relaxing. At the mental plane Freud called it Thanatos, the death instinct, and Jung called it anima, the unconscious female within, emotional, feeling, intuitive and non-discriminating, the background on which the differences can be seen and which unifies. This is the somopsychic aspect of man, where energy is inwardly direct-ed, and the body acts on the mind. Ida controls the sense organs or jnanendriyas and, therefore, gives us knowledge and awareness of the world we live in.

The third force

Another force exists in nature which is little understood or even appreciated, but which is of vital importance. It is a fact that when two opposing forces are equal and balanced, a third force arises. Strike a match on a matchbox and you create fire, bring positive and negative currents together and you can work machinery, unite body and mind and a third force called sushumna, spiritual energy, arises. This is one of the aims of yoga, because only when sushumna awakens can the super power of kundalini, this maximum force, ascend safely to fuel, power and create cosmic consciousness. Su-shumna is a high tension power line, and ida and pingala carry the domestic lines to power the basic necessities.

Carl Jung outlined the tantric view when he described the driving force of self-realization, which he called 'individua-tion', as a dialectical interaction between the opposites, beginning with conflict and culminating in synthesis and in-tegration. When perfect balance is achieved, stabilized and perfected, a state of dynamic peace is also achieved, which is a paradox, a union of opposites, the synthesis of doing and not doing, a totally new way of perceiving and experiencing life.

Few of us realize this third, spiritualized state and most of us oscillate from one state to another. Every 90 to 180 minutes ida and pingala alternate their dominance and only for a few seconds or minutes does sushumna come into potential being. It is the goal of all yogic techniques to balance and harmonize ida and pingala, life force and conscious awareness, so that they join at ajna chakra to create the inner light of knowledge and bliss and reveal the truth.

In order to balance the flows of energy, yoga prescribes various techniques, asana, pranayama, shatkarma and meditation, which activate either ida, pingala or sushumna. This does not mean we are activating one structure but are, via yoga, able to manipulate the energies underlying the three possible modes of existence.

The functional modes

Nadis are flows of energy which move through each and every part of our body, the subtle counterpart of the physical flows such as nervous energy and blood. All of the thousands of nadis in the body are based on ida and pingala which spiral around the spinal cord. These are the basic two modes of function on which all of our bodily and mental processes work. Sushumna is the royal road which takes us to higher awareness and transforms the function of ida and pingala.

Each and every cell of our body, every organ, the brain and mind, everything is polarized and interconnected at both the physical and subtle levels, and this allows us to think, speak and act in a concerted, balanced, synchronous manner, every part working to help every other part. There are two basic systems in the body that control this, ida and pingala, and if we stimulate any component of one system we turn on the whole system. This is how asana, pranayama, meditation, and the whole armamentum of yogic techniques work, and this is what is meant when we say that yoga affects the nadis.

Arthur Deikman of the Department of Psychiatry, University of Colorado Medical Centre, USA, describes the two main modes of man's being from the perspective of modern psychology. At the same time he describes the nadis ida and pingala using modern psychophysiological jargon. He states, "Let us begin by considering the human being to be an organization of components having biological and psychological dimensions of organization: an 'action' mode and a 'receptive' mode."

"The action mode is a state organized to manipulate the environment. The striated muscle system and the sympathetic nervous system are the dominant physiological agencies. The main psychological manifestations of this stage are focal attention, object-based logic, heightened boundary perception, and the dominance of formal characteristics over the sensory; shapes and meanings have a preference over colours and textures. The action mode is a state of striving, oriented toward achieving personal goals that range from nutrition to defence to obtaining social rewards, plus a variety of symbolic and sensual pleasures, as well as the avoidance of a comparable variety of pain."[2]

Deikman describes ida, the receptive mode as organized around intake of environment rather than its manipulation. The sensory-perceptual system is dominant and parasympathetic function predominates. The EEG tends to alpha waves, muscle tension decreases, attention is diffuse, boundaries become hazy, and so on. It is a state of not doing.

The epitome of the active mode is the state of body and mind a taxi driver would be in while driving through peak hour traffic. The epitome of the receptive mode is the deep relaxation of yoga nidra, or the introverted state of formal meditation. The true meditative state, which few scientific researchers really appreciate but which is the main aim of yoga, is an example of the third mode, or sushumna functioning, in which active and passive are fully balanced. Someone in this state is simultaneously externally and internally focused. For example, we should be driving a taxi and at the same time be in a state of total relaxation or 'not doing'. Or we would be sitting absolutely still and be filled with the dynamic energy of shakti so that we are fully awake and active internally. This is a very difficult state to describe.

We know that our active mode is designed to ensure survival and the passive mode is designed to ensure rest and recuperation of energy in the endless struggle for life and existence. Telepathy and psychic phenomena in general fit into this picture and we can hypothesize that telepathy is also designed to ensure survival. For example, we know that under conditions of extreme stress and in emergencies, people have sent psychic calls for help to close friends or relations, the emergency somehow powering this previously latent faculty. Many 'primitive' peoples also utilize these powers and take them for granted wondering why it is that 'civilized' people make such a fuss about them.

Yogis also tell us that when we practise yoga, purify our nadis and become stronger and more aware, siddhis, powers, must manifest as part of our spiritual development, though these are only side-effects and not the main aim of our practice of yoga. This, it seems, is because we develop a more synchronized functioning of all the components of our body and mind and awaken areas which have been dormant.

The need for balance

Though ida and pingala and their modes of activity are opposite, they are complementary and must be balanced for total health and peace of mind. More than this though, balance can open the door to the transcendental and to a new mode of functioning.

Most of us spend our lives in an unbalanced state. We tend to spend increasingly longer periods in the active mode as we grow out of our childhood and find it difficult to relax into the receptive state. This is probably a major factor in the spiralling incidence of psychosomatic disease today. Deikman's research emphasizes the fact that our imbalance is reflected in every activity as well as in our social, cultural and political organization. He stresses that the often devalued ida, the receptive, feeling and intuitive mode, is far from inferior or regressive and is in fact an essential component in our highest abilities.

Such research suggests that there is a very deep and urgent need for the reintroduction of concepts such as ida and pingala at the grassroots level of society and that the recent explosion of interest in yoga, meditation and esoteric philosophy is the result of deep-rooted pain and tension resulting from imbalance in the nadis. It points to the fact that our whole approach to ourselves, our science, society and culture will require complete review and revision from the more total yogic perspective.

It is time we realized that the subtle and intangible aspects of human existence are as important as the tangible, solid and easily measurable materialistic side. It is because of our reliance purely on technology, the solid facts, and the external, pingala side of our universe that we have not found happiness, real and lasting security or peace of mind, because these things lie within us and are of the mind – ida, and are subtle. Yoga offers the techniques to bring about balance in our lives, to not only realize the subtle, but, through a science of enhanced intelligence, intuition and creativity, to make the subtle side of life a practical reality and experience, a valid and important part of our lives as individuals and within society.

42

Controlling the Nadis and the Brain

The human brain is truly one of the most awesome and amazing of creations. Housed within the skull, it contains some twelve thousand million cells, and each of these cells has an estimated five hundred thousand possible interconnections; there may be even more that we do not know about. When the mathematics are computed there are more possible interconnections in the brain than there are atoms in the universe.

The brain has an almost infinite capacity, and all within the two kilograms or so of amorphous, pinkish grey brain matter with the consistency of jelly or cold oatmeal porridge. How this quivering, pulsating, jellylike substance remembers, thinks, analyzes, feels, discriminates, intuits, decides, creates and directs all the countless functions of the body, integrating the whole so that we synchronize action, speech and thought, is something that each of us should contemplate daily.

Meditation on this miracle of creation, and any attempt to understand how the brain and mind function, can lead to an understanding of the total process of kundalini awakening. Indeed, many theories of how kundalini works are based on the brain, and this research can help us to better understand the basis for kundalini awakening, the nadis and chakras. This is because the brain, housing as it does the master control systems for the body within its unlimited circuitry, must contain the physical circuits for the nadis and chakras.

The brain is also the interface between the body and the mind. All sensory information travels to the brain via the jnanendriyas, the sense organs of knowledge, and is then fed into the mind, and all decisions in the mind are then translated into the body via the karmendriyas, the organs of action, in a continuous, synchronous, dynamic process. Thus within the workings of the brain we can see the workings of the nadis as described by yogis, and research is deepening our understanding of this. Yogic techniques utilize this knowledge to stimulate the body so as to achieve higher and better states of being.

The nadis in the brain

Important research from neuroscience has shown us that the brain fits into the dual nadi model of human personality as handed down to us by yoga. In a radical and last ditch attempt to cure severe, unremitting epilepsy, Roger Sperry and his associates divided the brains of their patients down the midline structure linking the two brain hemispheres, the *corpus callosum*. To their surprise, not only did the epileptics cease seizures, but they came up with startling new findings which are radically altering our neurophysiological understanding of how the brain works and are revolutionizing our whole concept of man.

We have always known the right side of the brain controls the left side of the body, and vice versa. Sperry's findings, though still in the initial stages and requiring more research, show us each side of the brain handles a completely opposite but complementary mode of consciousness. This finding is extremely important as it verifies the yogic viewpoint.

Yogis and scientists, using different terminology and approaches, have come up with the same conclusions, that man is divided into two main modes of functioning. The circuits of the brain are based on ida and pingala nadis, consciousness or knowledge, and action or physical energy. We see ida and pingala at all three major levels of the nervous system.

1. *Sensory-motor nervous system* (SMS): all electrical activity in the body moves in one of two directions, into the brain (afferent), ida, and out of the brain (efferent), pingala. Yogis have called the sensory nerves which are governed by ida, jnanendriyas, and the motor nerves, governed by pingala, karmendriyas. These nerves are concerned with perception of, and activity in, the world.

2. *Autonomic nervous system* (ANS): this is divided into the outward directed, stress handling, energy utilizing, pingala dominant, sympathetic nervous system, and the inwardly directed, rest handling, energy conserving, ida dominant, parasympathetic nervous system. These two systems control and regulate all the autonomic body processes: heart, blood pressure, respiration, digestion, liver and kidneys and so on.

3. *Central nervous system* (CNS): this consists of the brain and spinal cord and contains the controls for the SMS and ANS. The brain contains much more than this though, for it is a huge, ultimately complex computer, which stores and integrates information and puts our decisions into action in a superbly synchronized and orchestrated performance. Its functioning is definitely much more than its parts. Within the infinite circuitry of the brain resides more potential than we can realize in one lifetime; however, with regular practice, the techniques of yoga systematically clear and strengthen these circuits.

This is what the yogis have been telling us, that the circuitry for nadis and chakras exists within the CNS, along the spine and in the brain. If we are able to tap, purify, strengthen and reconnect these circuits via the various yogic techniques, we can totally transform our mind/body complex. The basis for yogic techniques lies in the fact that there is a nadi/chakra system which can be seen, at the physical level, as being the sum total of the input and output of the various sections of the nervous system and the parts of the body which connect to it. This total body/mind complex functions on the power

340

of the three basic types of energy – ida, pingala and sushumna. We can therefore begin to understand why so many yogic techniques are specifically aimed at balancing the ida/pingala flow and increasing our awareness of its fluctuations.

Left versus right

Scientific study of the hemispheres of the brain by Sperry, Myers, Gazzaniga, Bogen and later researchers, has shown us that the left side of the brain is usually concerned with speech, logic, analysis, time and linear function, whereas the right side is silent, dark, intuitive, feeling, spatial, holistic in function, and does not require linear, structured analysis for its knowledge, though how it does know is a mystery. The right side of the brain is the physical side of ida nadi, and the left brain, of pingala. Thomas Hoover, a researcher comparing Zen with neurological discoveries, sums up the situation when he states, "The hemisphere that speaks does not know; the hemisphere that knows does not speak."

A number of word opposites have been used to describe and help us understand this view of brain function. Though the situation is not so simple, and each hemisphere must work in an integrated fashion, there is a definite trend to separate modes of function:

Left Brain (Pingala)	Right Brain (Ida)
analysis	understanding
verbal	spatial
temporal	'here and now'
partial	holistic
explicit	implicit
argument	experience
intellect	intuition
logic	emotion
thinking	feeling
active	passive

We could also add light versus dark, conscious versus sub-conscious, talkative versus silent, solar versus lunar, positive versus negative, mathematics versus poetry, rational versus mystical, objective versus subjective, digital versus analogue, and many others to aid our understanding.

Emotions in the split brain

Research by Marcel Kinsbourne, neurobiologist and neuro-psychologist, director of the Department of Behavioural Neurology at the Eunice Kennedy Shriver Centre for Mental Retardation in Waltham, Massachusetts, throws light on brain functioning which points to the fact that the brain has two main modes of emotional activity.[1] He has found that the two halves of the brain support different emotional states.

Research indicates that the left hemisphere governs happiness and positive feelings and the right brain governs sadness and negative feelings. In the abnormal situation, patients with right brain damage are often cheerful, elated and indifferent to their abnormal state. Left brain damage, on the other hand, can lead to a gloomy outlook on life and unjustified anger, guilt and despair. Most of us fluctuate from one state to another even in the normal situation, though not to the extremes found in brain damaged subjects. Still the experience of fluctuation can be distressing if we are not balanced and healthy.

The fact the left brain is associated with bright, cheerful thoughts and the right with sad and depressing thoughts, Kinsbourne theorizes, points to the conclusion that this dual action of the brain is designed to handle our likes (pingala) and dislikes (ida). The things we like are handled by the left brain, which focuses on and then approaches the object or situation. This fits in with our active mode, the concept of the externally directed pingala nadi. We try to avoid or withdraw from the things we dislike and we tend to be much more concerned with the overall picture in this situation. This is handled by the right brain and fits in with our receptive mode, introversion and ida nadi concept.

342

The necessity of the right brain

The brain has two major modes or systems which must work together and be harmonized if we are not to lose the essentials of our human existence. The nadis must be balanced for optimal functioning, for sushumna to function, and for us to maximize our human elements and potential. Unfortunately, few of us are really balanced and most of us, especially men, tend towards the purely external, materialistic and techno-logical pingala side rather than the subtle, intuitive, feeling ida side. When imbalance between the nadis is minor we may not even notice its effect, though it must manifest in our personality, behaviour, relationships and so forth, in ways that are baffling to us, and which can make our lives miserable. What happens in the normal situation can be better understood when we look at an extreme example.

Howard Gardener and his colleagues studied people with severely damaged right brains (ida) and found that they become robot-like, minus their essential human under-standing.[2] He has found that only when both hemispheres of the brain are working together can we appreciate the moral of a story, the measuring of a metaphor, words describing emotion, or the punch line of a joke.

Without the right brain we lose our understanding and take things very literally. For example, someone might say that he has a broken heart and the right brain damaged person will ask, "How did it break?" They see the explicit, the facts, but cannot understand what has been implied. These people also tell jokes at the wrong moment, their sen-tences become meaningless and they confabulate – make up things. The important points in their sentences are lost and are submerged or flattened, becoming part of the back-ground. There is just a stream of words without meaning or purpose. They also accept the bizarre and argue with what should normally be accepted. It is obvious then that the right brain, which yogis called ida or the receptive mind, is vital in the appreciation of relationships, of seeing how the parts fit together as a whole, in understanding.

There is also evidence to show that the right brain is not only important for normal understanding, but also holds the key for intuition and higher experience. Eugene D'Aquili, Professor of Psychiatry at the University of Pennsylvania Medical School, feels that split brain research indicates that the circuits which underlie higher mental states, from flashes of inspiration to altered states of consciousness, lie within the right brain, ida, and are powered by the emotions.[3] D'Aquili has formulated a neurological description of 'the intuitive perception of God' in which one sees reality as a unified whole, experiencing a feeling of oneness with the world. He feels it is a product of the *parietal-occipital* lobe on the right, 'non-dominant' side of the brain which somehow takes over the brain's functioning. Time is experienced as standing still and a sense of absolute and complete unity of self with the cosmos is felt. Both are features of right brain function and this experience is long lasting and totally transforms people's lives so that they find new motivation and a healthier, more fulfilling perspective of their relationship with life.

This research indicates that unless we begin to take more notice of and develop the right brain, we cannot partake in the experience of higher consciousness. According to yogis, the right and left brain, ida and pingala, must be balanced for such an experience to take place.

The necessity for balance

Most of us fluctuate according to our inner biological rhythms, moving from left to right brain, right to left nostril, active to receptive mode, every 90 to 180 minutes. These biological rhythms are well documented though their actual role and significance is not well understood and understanding of how things fit together is still in its infancy.

From the yogic point of view this rhythmic, or in the case of disease, arrhythmic swing, indicates that we are unbalanced and that one mode, one side of our nature is constantly becoming predominant. We rarely experience the

344

more desirable state in which both sides become equal and balanced. According to yoga, when both the sad and happy hemispheres are balanced for a certain length of time, a new state arises which unites logic and intuition, transforms our emotions and enables us to power a greater range of neurological activity.

We have to understand the necessity for attaining equilibrium and that the resultant state is a better and more pleasant and puissant experience. Einstein is an example of a natural yogi who used both sides of his brain. Meditating on what it would be like to ride on a ray of light, he had a sudden and powerful flash of intuition, a piercing insight into the mysteries of the universe, indicating right brain function, and was able to harness his left brain to construct a theory of energy and matter conversion which totally revolutionized science and replaced the several hundred year old paradigm of Newton. Einstein stated, "The real thing is intuition. A thought comes and I may try to express it in words afterwards." Yogis would say that Einstein had not only experienced the awakening of Shakti in his nadis, but that this initial awakening had also led to activation of a chakra. This powerful experience transformed and enriched not only his life, but many other lives as well.

Perhaps the best known example of non-analytical creative genius is that of Leonardo da Vinci, who in 1490 invented a spring-driven car, a helicopter, as well as many other things which came into common usage centuries after his time. His achievements extend into many more fields, and apparently he used his right brain intuition to create an idea, because most of his work is in the form of drawings and visual images rather than in written words.

Of course, there are times when we only require the left brain, for example, while doing a mathematical equation, working on a factory production line, or implementing man-agement policy. However, these things quickly become boring if the right brain is not being used, and such monotonous repetitive activity can lead to atrophy of our right brain capacities, and even to disease situations, because such a lifestyle lacks creativity and is meaningless for us. It is minus the right brain's capacity to see meaning in the things we do.

There comes a time when we must bring intuition into our lives, though this does not mean that because we use intuition we will become another Einstein. Intuition is as commonplace and necessary as eating and breathing. If our lives are to be happy and creative we must bring it into action more. Most situations, in fact, demand it for their proper outcome even though we do not realize it. Even simple situations require intuition, for example, knowing when to shift gears in a car, knowing when a cake in the oven is baked, knowing when it is the right time to say something nice to a friend, or how much strength is required to turn a screw. We have to feel what is required using our right brain. There is no book and no one who can give us this information. There can be no linear-structured analysis of what must be a non-verbal, intuitive knowledge that springs from within, the intuitive flash has no time dimension and defies logic. Within less than a second a total picture can be presented to our mind, the key to unlocking the mysteries of science is gained and the seeds for hours and years of inspired work and research may be planted.

For many people intuition is an unknown and unknowable commodity. Years of unhealthy living, lack of direction, purpose and meaning, consistent overstimulation of our sensory nerves, leading to dulling of our senses and an inability to find contentment and satisfaction, plus unresolved, ongoing mental tension and anxiety (unhealthy ida), added to lack of exercise, sedentary lifestyle and overeating (unhealthy pingala), all contribute to damaging the intuitive apparatus in the right side of the brain and may even damage the logical, reasoning capacity of the left side. We may find it very difficult if not impossible to repair and reinstitute function by the normal methods of medicine and psychotherapy. Though yoga possesses the techniques by which we can rebalance, reintegrate, regenerate and rejuvenate our body/mind

346

complex by bringing about balance in the nadis, even then it may be too late for some people.

The balanced view

Most of us fluctuate from one side of our brain to the other in well documented 90 minute cycles of rest (ida) and activity (pingala). A study by Raymond Klein and Roseanne Armitage of the Department of Psychology at Dalhousie University in Nova Scotia found that performance of tasks involving left and right brain activity comes in 90 to 100 minute cycles.[4] For 90 minutes, subjects could do well on right brain tasks and then switch over to doing well in left brain related tasks. This also corresponds with the 90 minute fluctuation in nostril dominance and points to agreement with the yogic theory that there is an intimate relationship between the breath and the brain and their cyclical activity.

If we are unhealthy, then our brain cycles may become abnormal in rhythm, duration, quality of function, or in some other way. Our whole life is disturbed and this situation actually occurs much more than any of us, even medical science, has previously realized. Yogis diagnosed dysfunction of brain rhythm by examining the flow of air in the nostrils.

Yogis have repeatedly asserted that there is strong link between not just the nostrils and the brain but between the eyes and ears and all body organs. Of course, today we know from our anatomy and physiology that this is so, however, yogis were saying the same thing thousands of years ago. In meditative experience they could feel the flows of energy in the nerves moving into and out of the brain and the rest of the body. They were able to perceive even more subtle levels of their being because they invented techniques which developed a great deal of sensitivity and strength. These techniques also allowed them to assert control over the nadis, the brain and all bodily processes.

Shambhavi mudra and trataka are two of the most powerful techniques of kundalini yoga, designed to awaken ajna chakra by balancing ida and pingala. If this is so, and if

347

the nadis described by yogis are in the brain then it means that yogic techniques can balance the brain hemispheres. Research from split brains is revealing that this is so. We know that in normal people, pictures appearing on the left side of our viewing field and sound in the left ear, both transmitted to the right brain, are less agreeable than when they are presented to the other side, according to Kinsbourne. Other research shows us that when we are gloomy we tend to gaze to the left, affecting the right hemisphere, whereas happiness causes the opposite to occur.[5]

This research indicates a definite relationship between eye position and hemispheric dominance. It also indicates that shambhavi mudra and trataka balance brain hemisphere activity because the eyes are held steady at the centre of the forehead, crossed in shambhavi and straight ahead in trataka. Even when we practise these techniques we may feel a very powerful stimulation and pressure within the centre of the head, ajna chakra activation, and the subjective experience is that of simultaneous extroversion and introversion. Shambhavi is the more powerful technique and induces an almost immediate effect. Centralized focusing of awareness appears to affect both nadis simultaneously.

Balanced breathing

Even more conclusive evidence of yoga's ability to control the nadis in the brain has emerged in relation to our ability to control the brain via the nostrils. David Shannahoff-Khalsa of the Salk Institute for Biological Sciences in the USA has shown that even a simple breathing exercise can enable us to alter short term brain hemisphere dominance at will.[6] Whereas the previous research has been implied and theoretical, this study shows a definite relationship between brain activity, the nasal cycle and our capacity to control our personality.

Shannahoff-Khalsa found that when one nostril has the dominant air flow the opposite hemisphere of the brain is dominant. Forceful breathing through the more congested nostril awakens the less dominant hemisphere. This is an extremely important finding. The EEG responses consistently showed a relationship between nasal airflow and brain hemisphere dominance for all four types of brain waves, beta, alpha, theta and delta.

Shannahoff-Khalsa states that, "The nose is an instrument for altering cortical activity."[7] He suspects that the nasal cycle is also linked to the basic rest/activity cycle, which includes within the sleep cycle, the rapid eye movement (REM) phase and the non-REM phase, because right nostril/left hemisphere dominance corresponds to phases of increased activity (pingala), and left nostril/right hemisphere dominance corresponds to rest phases (ida). This research verifies what yogis have been telling us and will require more experimentation to repeat the findings and reveal the ramifications in terms of medicine, psychology and our lives in general. It also reveals that buried within the brain are undreamed of capabilities and potentials which can transform our lives if we can tap them.

While scientists search for wonder drugs, external stimuli to probe the deeper aspects of man, yoga provides a concise and precise theoretical framework, within the nadi/chakra system, for a deeper understanding of the total human range of existence and the techniques by which to manipulate our internal environment, to stimulate internal secretions and to maintain balance, optimal health and higher awareness.

43

Evidence for the
Existence of Nadis

O f major importance for scientific acceptance of the whole science of kundalini yoga, is the proof for the existence of the psychic network of energy flows called nadis. The whole process of kundalini yoga rests on the premise that within the human body there exists a system of nadis, flows of energy, which conduct energy, both physical and mental.

There are three main nadis: ida, pingala and sushumna, and there are said to be thousands and thousands of nadis spread throughout the whole body. Though these nadis are body-based they are not physical structures but rather appear to be functional. They are dynamic, alive, moving, powering the body and mind, intimately linked with nerves, blood vessels and all our body organs. While there is no known physical structural support system for them, yogis maintain that they definitely do exist and have even mapped their pathways in the body and their effects on the mind.

Correspondence of yoga and acupuncture

Dr Hiroshi Motoyama, the President of the International Association for Religion and Parapsychology,[1-9] has been working consistently to prove the existence of nadis and acupuncture meridians, as well as the chakras. He is a graduate from the Tokyo University of Education with PhD degrees in philosophy and clinical psychology, and was recognized by UNESCO in 1974 as one of the world's ten foremost parapsychologists. He has even invented his own equipment in order to elucidate the science of yoga and to make this knowledge scientifically clear and acceptable. He states:

"By studying a number of books about the nadis and chakras of yoga over the last two years, I have been able to establish that asana, mudra, pranayama and dharana were ingeniously evolved on the basis of knowledge of the nadi system."

Motoyama states that acupuncture and the yogic concept of nadis have the same foundation and have affected each other for over 2000 years. That is, we are dealing with systems that have been in operation for millennia. This in itself is reason to believe that there must be something firm and solid at their foundations for people to have accepted and followed their theories for so long. Systems which do not give results are usually quickly discarded.

As an example of the correspondence of acupuncture and yoga, Motoyama points out that the concept of the *triple heater meridian* in acupuncture and the five pranas of the body in yogic physiology are almost identical. In acupuncture the lower heater, the area below the navel, corresponds to apana, the middle heater corresponds to samana between the diaphragm and navel and the upper heater corresponds to the prana between the throat and the diaphragm.

Yoga also states that chakras act as transducers, converting psychic energy into physical energy and vice versa. They distribute this energy to the body via nadis. Several acupuncture meridians lie in the areas attributed to the chakras and nadis, for example, the *governor vessel* in the spine corresponds with sushumna nadi and the *conception vessel* running along the front midline of the body is used in kundalini kriyas. Several meridians start or finish in chakra locations.

Proof of nadis

One of the machines Motoyama has developed in order to prove the existence of nadis and meridians is the AMI, or 'Apparatus for Measuring the Functional Conditions of

351

Meridians and their Corresponding Internal Organs'. This is an instrument designed to measure electrical currents in the body. It measures the steady state current that exists all the time, as well as the current in the body in response to an electrical shock from DC voltage. He uses it to measure the charge at special acupuncture points alongside the base of the fingernails and toenails. These are called *sei* (spring, well) points and are said to be the terminals for meridians, where psychic energy either enters or exits from the body.

In an experiment designed to substantiate the existence of acupuncture meridians and nadis, Motoyama placed electrodes on seven acupuncture points lying along the left *triple heater meridian* which runs along the back of the left arm and the front of the body, as well as a random electrode on the right palm, a point far from the area to be electrically stimulated. He then gave the subject a painful 20 volt shock to the 'sei' or beginning point of the *triple heater meridian*, at the tip of the fourth fingernail. A few milliseconds later he recorded an overall and equal physical reaction in all electrodes caused by excitation of the sympathetic nervous system in response to pain.

To prove that nadis do exist he then gave a very mild, painless and sensationless shock to the same point and two to three seconds later recorded an electrical response only in those specific points said, since ancient times, to be connected to the *triple heater meridian*. No response was recorded on the palm electrode or in any other part of the body. It is an interesting fact that the greatest response was found in the electrode at the other end of the meridian, just below the navel. No physiological or neurological connection is known to explain the phenomenon, however, the yogic and acupuncture explanations are validated by this experiment.

It is very important to realize that the effect of stimulating the meridian electrically is not a neurological process because the movement of energy in the nadi and meridian is much slower than we find in nerves. The energy we are dealing with is something else, some other form that we have as yet

352

not understood. This fact is substantiated by the work of Dr Nagahama at the Chiba University Medical School in Japan, who showed that the time it took for the sensation to pass along the meridian was hundreds of times slower (15 to 48 centimetres per second) than nerve conduction (5 to 80 metres per second). Therefore, we have to postulate the existence of some other channel of transmission and nadis fit this description exactly.

In another experiment, Motoyama coated a subject's arm with a paint consisting of liquid crystals which react to changes in temperature by changing colour. When the 'sei' point of an acupuncture meridian was stimulated by heat for from two to five minutes, the liquid crystals in certain subjects changed colour in a band along the meridian being stimulated. This not only further supports the above research but also substantiates another claim of yoga, that one of the characteristics of prana is generating heat in the body.

Motoyama has been able to visually demonstrate and measure subtle changes in the body that point to the fact that there is a flow of some kind of energy in the body which does not fit in with our present day knowledge of body mechanisms, such as in neurophysiology, yet which has a physical counterpart that laboratories can record. The exact nature of this flow of energy, the connections between the subtle and gross physical structures and the method by which prana acts on the body await further clarification.

What we do know is that we are dealing with a new phenomenon, and a very important one which has tremendous relevance to our present day needs in terms of understanding the body and mind and the relationship between energy and consciousness.

The nadis and disease

Motoyama's experiments have also shown that the energy he is measuring is not just a peripheral phenomenon, some by-product of electrical and chemical processes, but of primary importance to our health. He has developed a system by which we can use our measurements of the electrical state of the nadi system to know about our body's state of health and even of each individual organ.

The AMI is supersensitive, able to record minute changes in activity. It measures three different states of the nadi system. The first is the baseline reading or steady state value, that which exists in our body all the time. This tells us about our general long term constitution. Secondly, it measures the body's reaction to a very mild and sensationless electrical stimulation, which tells us how we react to events. And thirdly, it records the after-effects of the stimulus, which gives information on the temporary functions of the body and basic tissue resistance.

Thousands of such readings have been recorded and it has been found that most of us fit into a 'normal' range of values. If the value recorded is more than normal, the meridian is overactive relative to most people, while a low value indicates an underactive nadi. For example, one man whom Motoyama studied at Stanford University in America had lung cancer. Instead of the normal value of 1,000, this man had a value of only 150, showing great depletion of energy in that area, and indeed, he was very sick. A number of hospitals in Japan are using Motoyama's AMI machine to screen patients and the Kanagawa Rehabilitation Centre in Japan is comparing the results of X-ray and biochemistry with it. So far the results have been very favourable.

Motoyama has worked out that by measuring values of electrical skin resistance at acupuncture points in response to a small electric stimulus on both sides of the body, and then comparing the values from the left and right sides, any imbalance in the readings indicates that disease is present in the organ linked to the meridian being measured. He found that any percentage difference greater than 1.21 indicated disease. For example, when the heart meridian value on the left was more that 1.21 times greater than the right, the EGG might show an abnormal rhythm. One patient who was found to have imbalance in the liver, gall bladder and stomach meridians, but who only had symptoms of stomach upset was found on X-ray to have gallstones. One of Motoyama's laboratory assistants showed a large difference between the left and right bladder and kidney values shortly before being diagnosed as having cystitis.

It is interesting to note that yogis are also found to have abnormally high readings, but without disease, and Motoyama states that this indicates a greater range of activity of the nervous system as a result of yogic techniques.

These findings are very important because they indicate that pranic energy, or *ki*, which yogis have experienced as flowing in the nadis, is real. Yogis state that an imbalance in the nadis, especially ida and pingala, will cause disease and that yogic techniques can rectify this situation by acting on the nadis. Motoyama's work substantiates this. It points to the fact that not only is prana real, physical and measurable, but that its balanced activity is vital to our health and that we can use our measurements of pranic activity in the various organs of the body to diagnose impending or existing disease and thereby either prevent or treat the condition before it becomes too far advanced.

Such research is paving the way for new diagnostic techniques in medicine. We are beginning to absorb the subtler aspects of our existence into our modern scientific understanding of the body and are utilizing this knowledge in our armamentum against disease to better our lives and to uplift society.

Imbalance in the nadis

Motoyama's research supports the claim by yogis that within our body are flows of energy with physical and psychic properties. Yogis also tell us that the nadis are intrinsically related to the flows of breath in the nostrils. The breath in the right nostril is related to the function of pingala (left brain), and in the left nostril is related to the function of ida (right brain). This fact is the basis for swara yoga, the science by which we can know about the state of our body and mind in relation to the outer environment by watching the flow of breath in the nostrils.

The fact that the nadis are related to the nostrils is the basis for the science of pranayama, one of the most important and basic ingredients in kundalini yoga. For it is by manipulating the flows of breath that we can learn to control the deeper and more subtle aspects of our body and mind, to release energy and to send it to areas of the body that we wish to energize, heal and awaken. This relationship between the flow of breath and the nostrils has been demonstrated by research from Rumania.

Dr I.N. Riga, an ear, nose and throat specialist from Bucharest, Rumania, studied nearly 400 patients suffering from one-sided nasal obstructions due to distortion and deviation of the nasal septum.[10] He found that 89 percent of cases breathed more through the left nostril and were more prone to certain types of respiratory diseases such as chronic sinusitis, middle and inner ear infections, partial or total loss of the senses of smell, hearing and taste, recurrent pharyngitis, laryngitis and tonsillitis, and chronic bronchitis.

He also found these left nostril (ida) breathers were more likely to suffer from one or more of a wide variety of more distant disorders, such as amnesia, intellectual weakening, headaches, hyperthyroidism, heart failure, gastritis, colitis, peptic ulcer, poor liver function, constipation and reproductive problems, such as a decreased libido and menstrual irregularities.

Patients whose breath flowed predominantly through the right nostril were predisposed to hypertension. Riga found that correction of nasal deformities helped to relieve the disease situation.

Riga's research supports the yogic theory of nadis and indicates that the nostrils and the flow of breath in them are much more important than we previously realized, having many neurological and psychic connections whose function is not known. It supports Motoyama's work which shows that imbalance in the nadis is related to disease states and points to the fact that the nostrils are, as yogis have said, windows into the state of our body and mind, a fact which medical science can use in diagnosing many disease situations.

More than this, the nostrils and the science of pranayama allow us to influence the body and mind by influencing the nervous system and psychic energy at the more subtle levels of our being. The nostrils are switches which can do more than merely alleviate disease. By controlling the speed, rate, rhythm, length and duration of the breath, by altering the ratio of inhalation to exhalation in the nostrils and by stopping the breath, we can activate or tone down neurological and mental processes so as to achieve heightened awareness and altered states of consciousness.

Yoga is a science of self-regulation which is a priceless gem in today's disease and worry-ridden world. It bestows knowledge about internal flows of energy and thereby mastery over the inner processes of our being and autonomy, independence and confidence in our ability to deal with the constant demands and pressures of modern living. In the long run, regular, sincere practice and proper guidance by a competent master balances the nadis and eventually awakens kundalini.

44

Neurophysiology of the Chakras

The chakras can be interpreted from many points of view, for example, physical, psychological, behavioural, psychic, symbolic, mythical, religious, scientific, evolutionary, spiritual and more. They have both a microcosmic aspect within the human framework and, at the same time, a macrocosmic aspect which totally encompasses our perception and experience of life. At whatever level we examine them, they represent a hierarchical, interlocking and interdependent series of mandalas which, when superimposed on one another, make up a total picture of the human personality.

Each of us stands at a certain point of evolution that ascends the chakras and this will determine how we see the world. Someone who lives at swadhisthana sees the world in terms of gratification of his desires, for example, at manipura in terms of gratification of power instincts, at anahata in terms of compassion and love for all humanity. The degree of evolution of the chakras depends to a great extent on the activity within our nervous system and our state of consciousness. Someone at a lower level cannot understand someone at a higher level whereas the person at a higher level has been at the lower level before, has a wider range of experience, and importantly, has more circuits awakened or activated for handling life's experiences, for perceiving at different levels, and for interpreting and acting on the demands of life.

Even within the same chakra there are different levels of evolution, balance and activity, so that someone living at manipura might be more aware than someone else at manipura, their centre being more balanced and awakened, so that, for example, they use their power drives in a constructive and positive manner to help people, rather than in a destructive and negative way for their own personal ego gratification. An adult generally has a more evolved manipura chakra than a child, protecting the child from danger while the child pulls the wings off butterflies or gaily stamps on ants and insects. Of course, this is relative and varies from individual to individual.

Each level in the chakra system is the sum total of various physical, emotional, mental, psychic and spiritual elements. Each chakra has its own neurological plexus and endocrine gland and these link up to various organs and systems in the body. These organs and systems in turn are connected to the controlling mechanisms of the brain, each of which has emotional, mental and psychic components. The chakra is like a transducer, a linking point between the various levels of our being and it converts and channels energy either up or down to the various levels.

Therefore, we can think of each level in the spinal cord as controlling a different segment of the body, and at the same time, representing a level of functioning in the nervous system and mind. Ajna, for example, is a much more complex centre than mooladhara, or any chakra for that matter, controlling as it does the intuitive and higher mental faculties related to the most evolved circuits in the cerebral cortex. Ajna has as its symbol the two-petalled lotus, and we can think of this as representing the two hemispheres of the brain with the pineal gland as its central point. Mooladhara, on the other hand, controls very deep, powerful, primitive, animalistic, unconscious urges and instincts which are related to very simple and primitive neurological circuits at the bottom of the brain common to all animals, reptiles and even birds.

359

The chakras within the brain

Discoveries in neuroscience, precipitated by fantastic advances in technology, measuring capacity, surgical technique and pure pioneering perspicacity, promise to revolutionize our concepts of man and propel us into new and better techniques in medicine, psychology and living in general. Like Einstein's discovery of relativity, the ramifications of these discoveries take time to percolate down into common usage.

The brain is one of the hardest of all areas to research because of the inaccessibility and delicacy of the area to be studied. There is also an inherent and almost insoluble problem in studying the brain. Man is using his brain to study and understand his own brain. This is like trying to understand the mind with the mind, or grasp the hand with the same hand, or see the eye with the same eye. We cannot know ourselves objectively as we can know an external object or person, for we are the knowledge itself. Besides this, very few people are keen to let doctors open up their skulls and look inside.

Neurosurgeons and yogis share common ground because both aim to know the truth and reality about themselves. It is only the approach which differs. While scientific researchers have approached the brain objectively and have attacked and dissected it with knives and scalpels, probed it with electrodes, photographed and X-rayed it, stimulated and drugged it in order to mechanically and externally manipulate its circuits into giving up their secrets, yogis decided to scientifically discover the secrets of the brain by experiencing it directly through meditation. Their findings agree with those of modern science.

Yogis discovered through meditation that within their bodies were circuits and centres with both physical and psychic components, which they called nadis and chakras. Though we take this for granted now, we must remember that these studies were made thousands of years ago without the aid of modern microscopes and equipment. Not only did yogis achieve a wonderfully complete and practical system of techniques, but way back then they also based their techniques on the discovery that there are six major primary centres in the body, the chakras, in a hierarchical, interconnected network within the spinal cord. They also observed that each of these chakras had its own definite physical, psychological and behavioural characteristics, connected to the brain by a network of energy flows, all of which did not necessarily correspond to purely physical structures. They also discovered many secondary centres which were subsidiary to these primary ones.

The chakras in the spinal cord were found to be points manipulated by focusing attention, mental and psychic energy, breath and body postures, so as to derive certain physical and psychic experiences. The techniques allow us to learn to control the most basic and vital instincts and needs of body, emotions, mind, psyche and spirit.

Recent discoveries from neurophysiology and anatomy show that vital nerve plexes and endocrine organs exist within the body, spine and brain and correspond to the levels described by yogis. These findings support the claims of yogis that their system is more than just mere exercises and relaxation. It is a method of supplying the tools to control our body, mind, metabolism and personality.

The triune brain

Dr Paul MacLean, neurophysiologist and head of the Laboratory of Brain Evolution and Behaviour at the National Institute of Mental Health, USA, has demonstrated that the brain of man is functionally divided into three main areas, three interconnected biological computers, each with its own special intelligence, subjectivity, sense of time and space, memory, motor and other functions.[1] Each brain corresponds to a separate evolutionary step and is also distinguished neuro-anatomically and functionally, containing strikingly different distributions of the main neurochemicals in the brain, which are dopamine and serotonin. If we look carefully into these levels and compare descriptions of neuroscientists

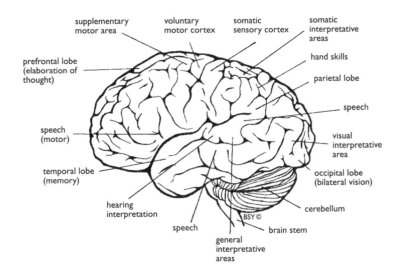

Figure 1: Outer Surface of the Brain

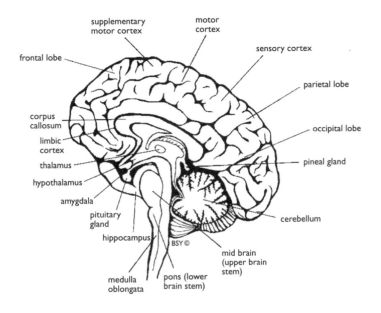

Figure 2: Inner Surface of the Brain

and yogis we see that both were saying the same thing. (See figures 1 and 2)

The three levels are called the reptilian, mammalian and human levels:

1. The reptilian complex includes the very topmost spinal cord and the lower areas of the brain, including the medulla oblongata and part of the reticular activating system, that part responsible for our waking, conscious state. This area contains the basic neural machinery for self-preservation and reproduction, including regulation of the heart, blood circulation and respiration. It controls mating, social hierarchies, insistence on routine, obedience to precedent and ritual, and slavish imitation of fads and fashions.

According to MacLean, the R-complex plays an important role in aggressive behaviour, territoriality, ritual and the establishment of social hierarchies. This area corresponds to the description of the mooladhara and swadhisthana chakras, because yogis have told us these centres maintain our most basic and primitive, animalistic drives and instincts; basic living, eating, sleeping and procreating within a dark and primitive, monotonous and repetitious existence, minus joy, love and self-awareness. They are related to our deepest unconscious and subconscious mind.

MacLean and his co-workers have found that this area dominates the lives of most people, which agrees with the statement by yogis that most people live in mooladhara and swadhisthana, though their function is modified by the higher centres. We spend most of our time controlled by and stimulating the lower chakras within the blinding limitations of our daily rituals.

MacLean has also shown that this is true neurologically. Removing the cerebral cortex from hamsters a day or two after birth and leaving only the R-complex and limbic system, MacLean found that the hamsters grew up normally, gave birth and displayed every form of behaviour normal for hamsters. They could even see without a visual cortex. Leaving only the R-complex in birds, he found that they

363

could function normally and carry on most kinds of communication and day-to-day routines. This research indicates that our day-to-day functions are controlled by these primitive areas and that we do not really need much more of our brain to handle the basic problems and demands of a neatly ordered, socially accepted lifestyle. We rarely stimulate our higher centres, and in fact find it hard to cope with any demands out of the ordinary. This is why yogis tell us to practise yoga so as to develop our inner unused capacity, some nine-tenths of the brain or more, and to stimulate the development of our higher centres.

Psychology also tells us that beneath the sane façade of any human being there lurks a primitive creature, instinctive and irrational, a Mr Hyde composite of all that is animalistic and forbidden. Freud called this the *id*, an unconscious area from which arises our desires, passions and the energy underlying our emotions and sense of who we are. Yogis call this mooladhara and swadhisthana and tell us that the unconscious and subconscious areas have two centres controlling them, one located in the perineum and the other in the spine behind the pubic bone controlling sexuality and all its related behaviour. Both psychologists and yogis tell us that most of us spend most of our time trying to gratify and fulfil these basic urges for food (survival) and pleasure. Much of our time, for example, is organized for making our daily 'bread', a slang term for money, with which we can buy food, shelter, clothing and pleasure. Few of us realize that there is much more to life than this.

By practising yoga we learn to balance and control these centres physically and also at the level of their instincts and drives, freeing their energy from primitive, compulsive ritual and rechannelling it up sushumna to the higher centres for the awakening of higher consciousness.

2. The mammalian structures are under the control of the limbic system, which controls emotion, memory and other behaviour which is less ritualistic and more spontaneous. This system is also thought to control playful behaviour, exhilaration, awe and wonder and the subtler, more human emotions such as love. MacLean has found that damage to areas of this part of the brain results in deficits in maternal behaviour and absence of play.

Within the limbic system are the behavioural centres for rage, fright, fear, feelings of punishment, anxiety, hunger, desire, pleasure, pain, sex, joy and love. This area is thus related to manipura and anahata functioning. If we stimulate the areas of the spinal cord behind the navel and heart associated with the chakras, we will send energy into the brain to turn on the various components at the physical, mental and behavioural levels associated with the chakras.

3. The human side of the brain is the most recently evolved neocortex, the seat of intelligence and many of the characteristic human cognitive functions. It is here that, with amazing speed and precision, the various faculties are integrated and synchronized. The cortex makes possible: thinking, calculation, analysis, discrimination, intuition, creativity, use of symbols, planning, anticipation of the future, artistic and scientific expression, and myriad other highly evolved and purely human faculties.

We know that the frontal lobes of the brain are especially important, being the most recently evolved part of the brain. Some researchers think that this part of the brain, in connection with the other sections, is responsible for the very human capacity of self-awareness and knowledge of this self-awareness; we know that we know, and we know that too.

We know that patients with severe frontal lobe damage or who have had frontal lobotomies, operations which sever the frontal lobes from the rest of the brain, are incapable of planning for the future and lack a continuous sense of self. They cannot see what effect a certain action will have on the future. Such people become dull, slow, cease to care for themselves or others, or about what they say or do. They are friendly, co-operative vegetables with a serious lack of imagination and loss of interest in life. They may be suffering from intense pain and not even care about the fact.

The frontal lobes are, therefore, said to be responsible for planning and discrimination, for anticipation of the future and thus for the purely human emotion of anxiety. This differs from fear which is related to an actual event. Anxiety is a mental event, related to some future occurrence. It is valuable for our survival and evolution as individuals and as a species, caring for the family unit, for society and for compassion. More than this it is the force responsible for motivating the formulation of laws and economic and political systems, for motivating the development of the arts and sciences, religions and systems of ethics, all philosophies, and the development of materially and spiritually secure cultures. As we developed the capacity to plan, the frontal lobes freed our hands for the manipulation of tools, drawing, writing and other bases for human cultural development.

Knowledge of death and the anxiety it engenders spurs us to make the most of life and to develop religious or spiritual systems which help us to cope with the thought of death. It has also led to the yogic sciences which liberate us from death and take us to immortality.

David Loye believes that not only are the frontal lobes involved in anticipation, but are actually involved in seeing into the future.[2] He states that when, for example, a car is rapidly approaching, the frontal brain alerts both right and left hemisphere components to process all the information from the rest of the brain, agreements and disagreements, so that we can discriminate and decide what will most likely happen. He found in two separate studies that people who tended to use both sides of the brain were better able to predict the outcome of events than either right or left-brain dominant people. This supports the yogic view that both sides of our nature must be balanced for proper function, fuller living and the development of our inner potential.

Ajna chakra

All of these intellectual, intuitive, creative and expressive functions are said by yogis to be characteristic of ajna and vishuddhi chakras. We know that yogic techniques are especially aiming at stimulation of ajna chakra, which lies at the pineal gland, midway between the hemispheres.

Yogis state that ajna chakra and the pineal gland as its physical centre, is the master control chakra, the guru chakra. We know from physiology that just in front of the pineal gland lies the thalamus, at the top of the limbic system. The thalamus has been found to be one of the main centres regulating the interaction of our senses and motor activity (ida and pingala), the prefrontal cortex, which includes the right and left sides of the brain (ida and pingala), the hypothalamus, which integrates and expresses emotion and regulates the ANS and the endocrine glands, and the cerebellum, which helps to control movement. It therefore integrates senses, thought, emotion and action. It is also important in the recognition of pain and other sensory modalities, such as variations in the degree of temperature and touch, the size, shape and quality of objects contacting the sense organs. Another interesting fact is that it is involved in the control of movement and especially the degree of squeezing and contracting of muscles and joints.

We see, therefore, that the pineal/thalamic area fits the description for ajna chakra, the area where senses and emotion, both ida functions, and motor and intellect, both pingala functions, meet. Yogis tell us that fusion of ida and pingala at ajna is one of the definitions of yoga. It leads to an explosion within the nervous system which somehow fuels and activates a much larger number of circuits within both hemispheres and the limbic system than would normally occur. It is as though our nervous system suddenly becomes charged with a high tension electric line, which yogis called sushumna.

Yogis also tell us that ajna is involved in intuition and perception of the subtle and psychic. If the thalamic area handles degrees of perception and motor activity, making it possible for us to experience the subtle things of life, then yogic techniques may allow us to develop our sensitivity in

367

this area so as to be able to expand and extend our normal capacities in order to sense the psychic quality of matter, an 'extra' sense or common sense, occurring at the meeting point of all the senses, the thalamus.

The chakras in perspective

Yogis tell us that the chakras lie along the spinal cord, that mooladhara lies in the perineum and the other chakras move upward towards sahasrara at the apex of man's evolution and consciousness. Ajna chakra is the highest centre in which man feels that he exists separate from the universe. Union or cosmic consciousness takes place in sahasrara. Ajna is the controlling chakra, the guru centre where commands are heard.

Neurophysiology points out that there are centres in the brain, stretching upward from the medulla oblongata to the pineal/thalamic area which correspond to the classical description of the chakras as told by yogis. We can say that within the brain all these fall under the control of ajna chakra, that there are layers of evolution within ajna, and as each chakra awakens in the spine, it affects the level of conscious awakening and activity in ajna. The pineal/thalamic area would represent that part of the brain which is most awakened and fully activated by total ajna chakra awakening, while the medulla oblongata area is that part which corresponds to the mooladhara chakra area. This would explain the close link between mooladhara and ajna; that the awakening of one consequentially awakens the other.

In most people, ajna, the thalamic/pineal area, is dormant. Living mostly in mooladhara and swadhisthana would mean that ajna functions mainly from the medulla oblongata, the reptilian brain. When we stimulate and awaken the centres through yoga, we jump levels in our nervous system and consciously awaken the higher pineal/thalamic areas and their concomitant levels of consciousness. When ida and pingala meet in ajna, energy flows from mooladhara to ajna, from the medulla oblongata to the pineal/thalamic area.

There are many techniques which can work on ajna chakra, such as shambhavi mudra, trataka, mantra japa, nadi shodhana and bhramari pranayama, to name a few. When we say these techniques are stimulating ajna chakra we are really stating that somehow they stimulate the integrating and centrally located pineal/thalamic area and thereby awaken our normally dormant, higher intellectual/emotional, logical/intuitive functions. They stimulate the higher elements of ajna and raise our consciousness up out of the lower, reptilian medulla oblongata. The techniques balance the functioning of our total brain/mind complex, ida and pingala, by focusing on the central, stimulating area and set the stage for the awakening of kundalini.

45

Evidence for the Existence of Chakras

Kundalini yoga teaches us techniques to influence our nervous system and mind so as to bring about total balance and reintegration at every level of our being. It is an expanded concept of man, a method of developing creative awareness and, more than this, of putting the knowledge gained to use via a system of experiential techniques. It helps us to develop a new outlook on life and ourselves. The chakras and their interaction within the totality of our personality, stretched between ida and pingala, balanced in sushumna, open up new dimensions for our mind and understanding to explore and develop.

The techniques of kundalini yoga involve kriyas, combinations of asana, pranayama, mudra and bandha, rotation of breath and consciousness through nadis and subtle spaces, repetition of mantra and the piercing of psychic centres. These heat up the psychic and physical energies of man and activate and awaken the chakras to our conscious level of experience and control. The techniques are also designed to bring about balanced purification and activation of all the chakras, with the gentle accentuation of one or two important centres. Techniques, such as ajapa japa, achieve this aim, creating a psychic friction which ignites the spark of higher consciousness.

When conditions for ignition reach the required temperature and pressure, energy is liberated within the body and mind, transforming our total personality. This energy must be real and actual; though perhaps as yet undefined and not qualified. It is measurable at both the physical and psychic levels if we have the correct conditions, equipment and understanding of the phenomena. In this regard, researchers have begun to pioneer exploration into the uncharted depths of the human psyche and are devising techniques and equipment to assess, measure and scientifically prove the existence of the chakras as the primary controlling points for different levels of our being.

Measuring the chakras

Dr Hiroshi Motoyama has helped to pioneer scientific research into yoga and the phenomena of kundalini and chakras. He states: "Fascinated . . . I too began physiological experiments about fifteen years ago to try to determine if chakras actually exist and their relationship to the autonomic nervous system and internal organs . . . through various examinations we have been able to determine that there are significant differences in the physiological function of the organ associated with the chakra that the individual subjects claimed to have awakened. Therefore, this research has led to the conclusion that chakras do, in fact, exist."[1]

In his search for the existence of chakras, Motoyama has developed his own machinery. One of these is the 'chakra instrument' which is designed to detect the electromagnetic field of the body and any changes which take place in it due to chakra stimulation and activation. Looking like a telephone booth and enclosed in a light-proof, lead-shielded room, the machine was designed to detect energy generated in the body and then emitted from it in terms of various physical variables such as electrical, magnetic and optical energy changes. Copper electrodes are positioned at the top and bottom of the cage and a sliding, square panel with electrodes on all four sides (left, right, front, back), is free to traverse up and down the frame structure so as to be positioned at any part of the subject's body. An electromagnetic field is set up between the

371

electrodes and any vital energy ejected from the body affects this very sensitive field.

A copper electrode and a photo-electric cell are positioned 12 and 20 centimetres in front of the subject, level with the classical position for a given chakra. The location is monitored for changes as the individual concentrates his mental energy at the chakra point, and measurements are made for three to five minutes before, during and after concentration on the chakra. Because of its powerful pre-amplifier (impedance near infinity), even the most subtle energy ejection can be picked up and recorded. Information recorded is sent to various amplifiers, computerized analyzers and oscilloscopes and is recorded on a highly sensitive chart recorder. Other equipment is also used to monitor respiration, the autonomic nervous system (galvanic skin resistance), changes in blood flow (plethysmograph), heart (electrocardiograph), subtle vibrations in the skin (microtremor), so as to measure other effects of chakra stimulation on the body and to make comparisons and interpretations.

Motoyama has used his equipment extensively to determine diseases in the body.[2] In one case he measured a woman who was to have a uterine tumour removed a week later. Measurements on his AMI machine (refer to the chapter entitled "Evidence for the Existence of Nadis") showed imbalance in the related meridians. The pattern of energy measured by the 'chakra instrument' in front of the uterus (swadhisthana chakra) was much greater than and quite different from normal. Motoyama's research indicates that there is a definite correspondence between physical disease and disturbance in the energy of the chakra traditionally said by yogis to control that part of the physical body.

Activity in the chakras

Motoyama has also measured chakra activity in normal subjects and recorded and compared readings in subjects practising yoga versus untrained, control subjects.[3] He found that in an untrained subject concentrating on ajna chakra there was no change recorded by the electrodes. The lines on the recording paper remained flat before, during and after concentration.

A subject who had been practising stimulation of swadhisthana chakra for some time showed a great deal of activation of the centre, and much greater than in the control subject who showed none at all. Large amplitude waves were seen before, during and after concentration, indicating activation; however, there was no change during the period for concentration, indicating lack of control over the centre. This compares with another subject who had been practising yoga for five years and who evidenced a marked rise in electrical activity from ajna chakra but only during the time of concentration. The results indicate that he had developed control over his ajna chakra.

'Chakra instrument' studies have been made with several yogis.[4] Dr A.K. Tebecis, a former professor at Canberra University, Australia, who has studied yoga throughout Asia and who claims to have experienced astral projection due to the awakening of kundalini, was tested on the 'chakra instrument'. Dr Tebecis concentrates on anahata chakra during meditation and also has a chronic digestive disorder. The AMI revealed instability in the nadis involved in digestion, in the manipura chakra area, and also in those related to the swadhisthana chakra area. When the 'chakra instrument' was used to measure manipura and anahata, no change was found at manipura. Anahata concentration revealed considerable intensification of energy during the period of concentration.

Two unusual findings have also been reported by Motoyama. In one case, not only did the subject develop a more intense electrical reading during concentration on manipura, but also had the subjective experience that psychic energy was being ejected from manipura. During this time the positive electrical potential vanished, but only during the time of her subjective sensation, and would reappear again as soon as the feeling of emission vanished.

Motoyama states, "One might surmise that the psi energy generated a negative electrical potential which neutralized the positive electrical charge. However, it is also possible to postulate the creation of a new physical energy. In fact, it is my opinion that the psi energy emitted from R.B.'s manipura chakra actually extinguished the surrounding physical energy. I take this stand because the positive potential was precisely neutralized and because there was never any appearance of a negative potential."[5]

The second case involves a subject who concentrated on anahata chakra. As the subject relaxed, the chakra area was seen to be activated. She was then asked to concentrate on the anahata area and it was arranged that any time she had the subjective experience of psi energy emission she was to press a button which caused a mark to be made on the chart. It was found that when this mark appeared the photoelectric cell signalled the presence of a weak light being generated in the light-proof room. Her chakra monitor also detected electrical energy of high potential and frequency.

Motoyama states that these findings imply that psychic energy working in anahata chakra may be able to create energy in the physical dimension (light, electricity, etc.) It appears that whatever energy is being produced in a developed and refined chakra circuit is capable of extinguishing or creating energy in the physical dimension, which supports the yogic view of chakras as transducers, converting psychic energy into physical energy and back. Motoyama feels that if further research substantiated his findings, then the law of Conservation of Energy, as one of the basic foundation stones of modern physics, will have to be revised.

The verification of an energy at the psychic plane which, though of unknown source and substance, can influence matter, has been long claimed by yogis. It is also thought to be the basis of healing and of all sciences in which mind is used to control matter. Yogis even state that the world is a manifestation of mind, a view which is now being supported more and more by physicists, especially those working with the subatomic particles that make up all of matter and which lie midway between matter and pure energy (prana).

Motoyama states, "I feel that the continuation of research into the nature of psi energies, by many others as well as myself, will lead to considerable change in our views of matter, of mind and body, of human beings, and of the world itself."[6]

The psychic level

Objective evidence for the existence of the chakras also appears to have been found by kinesiologist Valerie Hunt and her associates at UCLA in America.[7] Assisted by Rosalyn Bruyere, a psychic 'aura reader', Hunt used a number of measurements in order to study the body's field emission when it is being stimulated by deep muscle massage (Rolfing). This was prompted by an earlier observation that after Rolfing and meditation there was an increase in the electromyographic baseline.

Hunt and associates utilized electromyographic equipment (EMG) which measures the steady, low voltage of muscular activity plus several other instruments. Electrodes were attached to eight sites, including chakra locations such as the crown (sahasrara), eyebrow centre (ajna), throat (vishuddhi), heart (anahata), base of the spine and acupuncture points on the foot and knee. The sites for the electrodes were in places where muscle activity was minimal and, therefore, electrical readings would indicate energy from a different source. The electrodes were placed on the body in consultation with the 'aura reader'.

The individual being experimented on was given Rolfing (deep muscle massage), designed to liberate deeper subconscious tension, and, therefore, theoretically able to effect chakra activity. As the massage progressed the EMG readings were recorded on one track of a two-tracked tape recorder. Simultaneously, while isolated in another room and oblivious to the EMG and subject's reports, Bruyere recorded on the second track her observations of psychic activity in terms of colour change at the various centres. Hunt was able to question the aura reader via a separate audio system so that no clue as to what the subject was experiencing or what was going on at the EMG level could be detected by the psychic. At the same time the subject related his experience which was tape-recorded using a second microphone, and any similarity between his experience, the symptoms of chakra activation and the EMG recording were noted.

It was quickly evident in the central monitoring room where Hunt was sitting, that the EMG changes and the distinctive wave forms being recorded correlated with the colours reported by the psychic person, as did the experience of the subject. Later analysis, whether by wave form, Fourier-frequency analysis or sonogram, produced consistently the same pattern of results.

Hunt acknowledged that the possible interpretations of this data are staggering. The radiations were taken directly from the body surface, quantitatively measured in a natural state and were isolated by scientifically accepted data resolution procedures. The study concluded that there had been direct correspondence in every instance throughout all recordings between the distinctive wave form and the psychic's description of the colour emanating from the chakra. For example, every time a medium-large, sharp deflection with single or double peaks at the top occurred, the psychic reported the colour blue, while red corresponded to large, sharp clumps of regular and irregular spikes of short duration interspersed with plateaux. Yellow was a broad, smooth wave resembling an uneven sine wave.

The relationship between the emotional states and the colours was also accurate. Emotions, imagery, interpersonal relations and the state of resiliency and plasticity of the connective tissue are related to the colour and the state of the aura as seen by the psychic.

It is an interesting fact that in early Rolfing sessions the chakras appeared to be uneven, small, low in frequency and amplitude and with indiscriminate or dark primary colours.

As the technique continued the chakras became large, even in size, and of lighter colour, while the wave forms were of higher amplitude and frequency.

Some chakras which had been closed, opened, producing kaleidoscopic colour effects, e.g. dark blue, yellow, red-orange and olive green. By the fifth hour of Rolfing all subjects had a clear blue aura. By the seventh and eighth hours the colours were predominantly light and blended, for example, peach, pink, ice blue and cream. Higher frequencies were associated with pleasant experiences.

Developing our psyche

Hunt's research is important at several levels. It firstly supports the claims of yogis and psychics that other levels of perception, more subtle and yet intimately connected with the physical body, do in fact exist. Though it has been called extrasensory perception it appears rather to be an extension of the normal range of perception of physical events into the more subtle.

According to yogis, development of ajna chakra and the pineal/thalamic area of the brain, plus relaxed concentration of mind, allows us to see things which most of us miss because of gross physical and mental tensions and a dissipated, distracted state of mind. There is nothing miraculous, abnormal or supernormal about psychic phenomena. Most of us just do not look at things long enough to allow the subtle to register in our brains. We see something and are immediately distracted, thinking that there is nothing else to see or learn from a situation. But if we take our time we can learn much more.

We know that vision is our major information processing system and therefore tied into many other neurological systems. Defects in the visual system are now linked to other problems such as allergies, anxiety, insomnia, postural problems, and a whole range of physical and psychological problems.[8] Connecticut optometrist Albert Shankman is quoted as saying, "The skill of seeing relationships is a principal object of visual training. Visual training is essentially brain training."[9] Shankman and others have observed that visual flow and flexibility are associated with a more flexible, creative thought style.

Yoga follows the same principle, for example in trataka, an essential component of kundalini yoga. Trataka teaches us to gaze at things without preconceptions and to allow the information to impinge on our brains, to allow the connections time to come together and the inner knowledge, the processed information within the brain, time to formulate itself fully and rise up to the conscious plane. This is what yogis mean when they say that yoga balances the external and the internal, the right and left sides of the brain, ida and pingala, and awakens faculties that lie dormant within us all but which we do not know exist and which we do not develop.

Psychic vision, a side-effect of kundalini yoga and part of the awakening of intuition, inner vision and inner knowledge, is one of these capacities. All it means is that we are relaxed and we take our time to look at things without preconception. Hunt's research verifies that this faculty is not a myth and not confined just to yogis practising sadhana for years in isolation in the Himalayas, but is also verifiable within the confines of a laboratory.

Verifying the chakras

The work of Motoyama and Hunt points to the fact that within the physical body there are locations which, though they may not have any obvious physical or structural demarcation, have definite functional characteristics which differentiate them from other parts of the body. It verifies the fact that the yogic descriptions of these points correspond to physical emanations in the case of Motoyama's research and psychic emanations in the case of Hunt's research.

We see then that the chakra locations have both a physical component and a psychic component. This scientific description fits the yogic definition of chakras as vortices of energy, the interacting points of the most powerful psychic and physical forces which control our total human existence. The studies also confirm that the traditional chakra locations, when activated, are related to emanations of light and colour, and to emotions and experiences which are subtle and usually stored in the subconscious mind, beyond our usual conscious capacity. When we concentrate and focus psychic energy, chitta shakti, on the chakra, or if we manipulate the areas of the body under its control, by asana or massage, for example, we can stimulate activity at both the physical and psychic levels of that centre.

What lies at the basis of these energy emanations at the neurological and mental levels, how these forces interact to control our psychophysiology, behaviour and experience, still requires much more research. What we do know is that the concept of chakras has a definite psychophysiological foundation, that they affect our body, emotions and mind, and that they produce both physical and psychic energy which can be measured and quantified. There is something within the body of man, which yogis called chakra, awaiting our discovery and awakening.

46

The Cosmic Trigger

We stand on the shores of a vast universe which continues to amaze us and inspire us with awe and wonder every time a new discovery is made. Despite recent developments in rockets, computers, atomic power and other marvels of science, we are painfully ignorant of the world in which we live. We are even more ignorant of our inner universe which for some reason we have forgotten about and ignore, despite a pressing inner need to uncover the truth of our existence.

Since the concept of kundalini has been introduced in the west, various groups of scientific and yogic minded people have sought to understand and explain this phenomenon which promises to be our rocketship into inner space, to lift us out of the confines and limitations of time and space so as to experience ourselves as we really are. Strangely enough, this inner experience also promises to unveil many of the outer mysteries baffling scientists and researchers in many fields today.

Recent developments in neurophysiology and meditation research have outlined a possible explanation for kundalini which unifies both its physical and psychic aspects. This research outlines a comprehensive approach to understanding how meditation can release energies within our nervous system, unlocking latent capacities and speeding up our evolution at both the physical and consciousness levels. This allows us to perceive the universe from a new and broader perspective, to see things from a more total point of view and to understand more about life and ourselves.

The physio-kundalini syndrome

One researcher who developed an ingenious method to measure bodily change during meditation and the awakening of kundalini is Itzhak Bentov. In his book *Stalking the Wild Pendulum* he has set out an original and also very yogic understanding of consciousness and matter, one which can very neatly explain kundalini from the point of view of physics. He also discusses a model by which we can understand the kundalini experience in physiological terms.

Bentov states that, "the human nervous system has a tremendous latent capacity for evolution. This evolution can be accelerated by meditative techniques, or it can occur spontaneously in an unsuspecting individual. In both cases, a sequence of events is triggered, causing sometimes strong and unusual bodily reactions and unusual psychological states. Some of those people who meditate may suspect that these reactions are somehow connected with meditation. Others, however, who develop these symptoms spontaneously may panic and seek medical advice ... Unfortunately, however, western medicine is presently not equipped to handle these problems. Strangely, in spite of the intensity of the symptoms, little or no physical pathology can be found."[1]

Bentov estimates, on the basis of discussions with psychiatrists, that as many as 25 or 30 percent of all institutionalized schizophrenics belong to this category, a tremendous waste of human potential. There is a vast area of the human psyche which we are totally ignorant of, which we do not experience consciously in our lives, and which we are, therefore, helpless to deal with adequately if something goes wrong. Bentov feels that symptoms do not occur in the healthy, relaxed state, but only when energy reaches tensions in the body. This agrees with the yogic view that we must prepare ourselves for awakening by a long period of preparatory sadhana to avoid unpleasant results.

Bentov states that we urgently need modes that will allow us to understand kundalini in terms which make sense to us. As a result of this need, Bentov has delineated a unique and brilliant model of the meditation/kundalini process so that doctors, psychiatrists and psychotherapists can become aware of this possibility and develop more benign methods of dealing with this situation. More knowledge about the physical basis of spiritual knowledge is required in medical and scientific circles in order to expand our concept of man.

Measuring the waves in the brain

As we start to practise meditation we initially experience its calming, relaxing and stabilizing effects. Prolonged practice, and especially the more vigorous forms of meditative practice, take us far beyond these preliminary changes which many modern researchers have been stressing as the main aim and effect of meditation. After some time, actual psycho-physiological changes take place and amongst these there is a change in the mode of functioning of our nervous system.

In order to measure these psychophysiological changes Bentov used a modified ballistocardiograph, a machine which measures small bodily motions accompanying the motion of blood throughout the circulatory system.[2] He records, "A subject sits on a chair between two metal plates, one above the head and one under the seat, five to ten centimetres away from the body. The two plates of the capacitor are part of a tuned circuit. The movement of the subject will modulate the field between the two plates. The signal is processed and fed into a single channel recorder which registers both the motion of the chest due to respiration and the movement of the body reacting to the motion of the blood in the heart-aorta system."[3]

Bentov states that the spinal cord can be thought of as a spring which, during meditation, reacts to the movement of blood into the heart and circulatory system. The heart pumps blood into the large blood vessel called the aorta. The aorta is curved on top (at the level of the bottom of the neck) and bifurcated at the bottom (in the lower abdomen). Every time blood enters the aorta it moves upward towards the head and this gives a minute upward push to the upper part of the body. The blood then moves downward to strike the bifurcation of the aorta, gently pushing the body downward. This movement is called micromotion and the movement recorded on the ballistocardiograph is only in the order of 0.003 to 0.009 millimetres, a very minute amount.

This gentle upward and downward movement has the tendency to oscillate the whole body, spine and skull up and down. The natural rhythm of this oscillation is 7 cycles/second (7 Hertz, Hz). Of course in the normal situation we do not feel such minute micromotion, however, in the deep stillness of profound meditation even the slightest and most subtle movement of the body or thought creates ripples within the nervous system which, to our introverted consciousness, become magnified and disturb inward progress.

Yogis have always stressed that the most important preliminary ingredient for meditation is to develop a straight and strong spinal cord through asana and to gradually develop stillness of the body, nervous system and mind through pranayama. Through Bentov's model we can now see that this is because immobility of body, breath and mind sets the stage for the production of rhythmic waves within the spine, skull and cerebrospinal fluid (CSF).

When subjects are in a deep meditative state, Bentov's machine measures an almost pure, regular, S-shaped sine wave of large amplitude and moving at approximately 7 cycles/second. This is opposed to an irregular wave in the baseline resting state before and after meditation. Something happens in meditation which does not normally occur in most of our waking, dreaming or sleeping lives. At the same time we enter a hypometabolic state in which our breathing rate slows down and the oxygen need of our tissues lessens. We should note that it is also possible to produce a sine wave on the ballistocardiograph by stopping our breath; however, we quickly develop oxygen deficiency and have to overbreathe to restore balance. In meditation, however, this does not occur; we are balanced at all levels.

The oscillating circuits

The up and down movement of the body produced by the heart during meditation affects the brain which is floating in its protective bony and fluid casing, the cranium and CSF. According to Bentov, this micromotion up and down sets up acoustical and possible electrical plane waves reverberating in the skull. Mechanical stimulation may be converted into electrical vibrations.

The acoustical plane waves are focused within the third and lateral ventricles, small cave-like, CSF filled structures deep within the brain. The plane waves activate and drive standing waves into the ventricles. While the body stays in meditation, the frequency of waves within the ventricles of the brain will remain locked to the heart/aorta pulsation. Bentov felt that these vibrations within the brain are responsible for the sounds yogis hear in meditation. This aspect of meditation is called nada yoga, listening to and following the inner sounds, and is said to herald the coming of kundalini.

The loop circuit

According to Bentov the standing waves in the ventricles are within the audio and superauditory ranges. They stimulate the cerebral cortex mechanically, eventually resulting in a stimulus travelling in a closed loop around each hemisphere. The lateral ventricle lies just under the corpus callosum, the part of the brain connecting the two cerebral hemispheres. The roof of the lateral ventricle acts as the taut skin on a drum which moves rapidly up and down and thereby produces mechanical waves in the ventricles which stimulate the sensory cortex lying just above the corpus callosum.

We can understand the effect of this stimulation by looking at the diagram of the cross section of the brain (see figure 3). Waves would commence at number 1 and travel down to number 22 and back to number 1 again creating a loop circuit. As the current returns to the starting point it stimulates the pleasure centres in the various areas of the brain which surround the lateral ventricle, such as in the cingulate gyrus, lateral hypothalamus, hippocampus and amygdala areas, all part of the limbic system, and this may give rise to the bliss and ecstasy reported by meditators whose shakti awakens. The sensory current travels around the cortex at about 7 cycles per second.

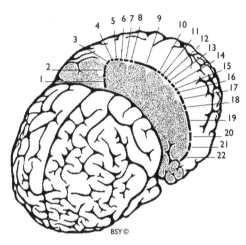

Figure 3: Cross section of the brain revealing the sensory cortex and indicating the body as mapped along the post central gyrus. This is called the sensory homunculus – the symbolic man lying within the brain. After: Pennfield and Rassmussen, The Human Cerebral Cortex, MacMillan, New York, 1950.

1. Toes	9. Hand	17. Eyelid &
2. Ankle	10. Little finger	eyeball
3. Knee	11. Ring finger	18. Face
4. Hip	12. Middle finger	19. Lips
5. Trunk	13. Index finger	20. Jaw
6. Shoulder	14. Thumb	21. Tongue
7. Elbow	15. Neck	22. Larynx
8. Wrist	16. Brow	

Bentov theorizes that stimulation of the corpus callosum will in turn stimulate the sensory cortex to produce the sensations of something moving in the body from the feet, up the spine, up over the head and then down the abdomen and pelvis. It is this experience which many people associate with the awakening of kundalini.

The experience of movement in the spine and body has been reported in many cases of the awakening of shakti or energy within the nervous and nadi systems. From areas as far apart as India, China, Africa and America, the symptoms are often similar if not the same. Energy is felt to rise upward and these sensations must be handled in progressive sequence in the sensory cortex. We can also theorize that if we sit in padmasana (lotus pose) or siddhasana/siddha yoni asana (accomplished pose for men and women) that we may short-circuit the sensations in the legs so that we subjectively experience the movement as commencing in or near mooladhara.

In normal situations, motor and sensory impulses usually travel in straight lines, either into or out of the brain and via the thalamus. However, in meditation we introvert and cut ourselves off from outside stimulation (pratyahara). This also tends to develop a loop circuit.

We should note that sensory signals come to the cortex through the thalamus, the area of the brain in front of the pineal gland that we can associate with the highest functioning of ajna chakra. And it is said that ajna chakra must be stimulated if kundalini is rising because of its direct connection to mooladhara.

Bentov felt that the movement of waves through the cortex is responsible for the effects of the awakened kundalini and for internal experience. From our point of view this may not be the actual kundalini experience, which transcends all bodily sensations, but would correspond to the awakening of prana shakti which ultimately leads to the kundalini experience. The gradual development of the brain may take many years before the loop circuit and the various connections develop, and enough energy can be generated to actually stimulate all the circuits involved and required.

Psychic circuits

As a result of the circular currents in the brain, Bentov states that a pulsating magnetic field is produced in each hemisphere of the order of 10^{-9} gauss. On the right side of the brain the field is from front to back, north to south, and on the left side, south to north. This would correspond to ida and pingala at this level of body energy. Bentov feels that the interaction of these waves with the environment may be responsible for the psychic experiences which are often felt as a by-product of systematic and deep yogic sadhana. He states his findings as follows: "This magnetic field – radiated by the head acting as an antenna – interacts with the electric and magnetic fields already in the environment. We may consider the head as simultaneously a transmitting and receiving antenna, tuned to a particular one of the several resonant frequencies of the brain. Environmental fields may thus be fed back to the brain, thus modulating that resonant frequency. The brain will interpret this modulation as useful information".[4]

It is interesting to note that the rhythmic magnetic pulsation of the brain which is set up in meditation at 7 cycles/second is almost the same as Earth's magnetic pulsation whose doughnut-shaped field has a strength of 0.5 gauss. These extra low frequency (ELF) waves have a predominant frequency of about 7.5 cycles per second, and this is called the Schumann resonance. Another interesting point is that the brain wave frequency of 7 cycles/second is the region between alpha waves and theta waves. This is the borderline between waking and sleeping, where we are most relaxed, and if we can stay awake in meditation, it sets the brain up for creativity and intuition. It is the time we are most psychically receptive. Professor Michael Persinger of the Laurentian University Psychophysiology Laboratory hypothesizes that ELF waves may serve as the carriers for information connected with psychic phenomena.[5] This fits in with Bentov's theory that our brain's magnetic pulse of 7 cycles/second resonates with the environment to either transmit or receive information.

The five oscillating systems

Up to this point Bentov tells us there are five oscillating systems tuned to each other:

1. *The heart-aorta system,* producing an oscillation in the spine and skull of 7 cycles/second which accelerates:
2. *the skull and brain up and down,* producing acoustical plane waves (KHz frequencies) which create:
3. *standing waves within* the ventricles of the brain in the audio and above ranges which stimulate:
4. *a loop circuit in the sensory cortex* at 7 cycles/second which result in:
5. *a magnetic field* of opposite polarity, pulsating at 7 cycles/second, and interacting with the environmental fields, especially the ELF field which is resonating at about 7.5 cycles/second.

As we meditate over a prolonged period, we begin to progress and lock in more and more of these systems so that eventually all the systems of the brain begin to harmonize and resonate at around the same frequency. We can speculate that this ultimately unifies the whole brain and results in unlocking of our dormant potential, a quantum leap to a new field of experience that yogis tell us is powered by the explosive release of kundalini. Yogis state that if we can sit still for three hours, completely immobile and aware, we will awaken our internal energies and enter into samadhi. Bentov's model explains this.

Another interesting point is that Bentov feels that these changes in the brain most probably start in the right hemisphere, because many meditative practices develop the non-verbal, feeling, intuitive, spatial right brain, balancing out the almost constant dominance of the logical, reasoning, rational, linearly-thinking left brain in our day-to-day extrovert, tension-filled, energy-demanding existence. He came to this conclusion because many meditators he talked to felt their experiences started on the left side of their bodies which is governed by the right brain.[6] This agrees with the work of D'Aquili who posits that inner experience is governed by activity in the right brain.[7]

Kindling the kundalini

We know that a log on a low flame is likely to blaze up suddenly on its own, even after the original fire goes out. A threshold point is reached and internal reactions take over spontaneously. The same mechanisms are thought to occur in the nervous system to lead up to a series of events analogous to the kindling of wood. Scientists are using this model to explain such diverse phenomena as everyday learning memory, epilepsy, the radical mood swings of manic depression and kundalini.

The kindling phenomenon was first identified by C.V. Goddard and his associates at Waterloo University in Canada in 1969.[8] They observed that repeated, periodic, low-intensity electrical stimulation of animal brains leads to stronger brain activity, particularly in the limbic system, the part of the brain that handles emotions. For example, stimulating the amygdala (part of the limbic system) once daily, for half a second, has no effect at first, but after two or three weeks, produces convulsions. Goddard also observed that kindling can cause relatively permanent changes in brain excitability. Animals can have seizures for as long as a year after the initial kindling period.

According to John Gaito of York University, over a period of time the bursts of electrical activity kindle similar patterns in adjacent brain regions.[9] Also the threshold is progressively lowered so that smaller doses of electricity trigger convulsions.

It should be understood that mild continuous electrical stimulation does not cause kindling, rather it causes adaptation and tolerance. The stimulation must be intermittent, preferably every twenty-four hours, to be effective.

Robert Post found that kindling can also be induced by drugs such as cocaine or other anaesthetics which stimulate the limbic system.[10] He found that using these stimulants led to changes of behaviour such as increased aggression.

Apart from providing a model for epilepsy, which we know is sometimes associated with mystical insight, and psychosis, which can be thought of as prematurely awakened kundalini activity in one of the chakras, kindling can explain how meditation exerts its effects on our brain and psyche. According to Marilyn Ferguson, "Analogies of the kindling effect and meditation effects – especially of the dramatic kundalini phenomena – are interesting. Obviously, most human subjects don't perceive their experiences as pathological, although they may be somewhat unnerving. The effects typically occur after a history of regular meditation and in an unthreatening setting. There is no onset of seizures in the classic sense, and the nervous system effects appear to be positive over the long run."[11]

Bernard Gluek of the Hartford Institute of Living speculates that mantra meditation might set off a resonance effect in the limbic brain.[12] Mantra repetition is the most obvious form of meditation to be analogous to kindling; however, if we look at Bentov's model, any form which involves sitting absolutely motionless and developing introspection will do the same.

According to Bentov, the loop circuit in the sensory cortex set up by sitting immobile in meditation may stimulate the pleasure centres in the amygdala, the part of the brain most amenable to kindling. This would, over a period of time, lead to permanent changes within the nervous system in an ongoing and progressive manner. This is the aim of meditation and all masters of yoga and the inner arts and sciences tell us that for success, the most important ingredient is regularity of practise and persistence. Whether our experiences in meditation are good or bad is of no consequence. They are all just steps on the way to higher experience, part of the process of preparation for kundalini awakening.

Two important points should be noted about kindling. The first is that it induces relatively permanent changes and the second is that it increases activity in the brain. It steps up the energy processes. This fits in with the theory that meditation can energize the nadis so as to send energy to various centres to awaken higher functions within those centres in order to take them to a higher octave of activity by supplying them with a better energy source.

Meditation and the brain

When studying kundalini we must remember that there are as many methods to awaken it as there are people practising, in fact there may be more methods than people. The four basic methods studied by modern research are raja yoga, kriya yoga, zazen and transcendental meditation. Basically these techniques involve one or more of the following: sitting, breath awareness, and mantra. Yogis normally divide meditation into either the relaxation type or concentration type of practice. However, we also know that whichever technique we choose we will have to first develop relaxation and then allow the internal process to unfold.

Most of the brain research into meditation has focused on brain waves, which are divided into four main groups and which can be generalized as follows:
1. *Beta*: extroversion, concentration, logic-orientated thought, worry and tension.
2. *Alpha*: relaxation, drowsiness.
3. *Theta*: dreaming, creativity.
4. *Delta*: deep sleep.

Most meditation techniques show that meditators, however, usually develop relaxation in meditation, with alpha waves being predominant and occasional theta waves, which are different to those seen in sleep, occurring in more advanced meditators.[13–15] This result, the basis of meditation's use in such psychosomatic diseases as high blood pressure and in anxiety, has probably resulted from either relaxation techniques or because the meditators were mainly novices.

Occasionally, in the laboratory, a researcher stumbles on findings which seem to run contrary to the claims of meditation as a relaxation method. In this situation the meditator moves through the usual relaxation process, sinking into alpha and theta, but at this point something startling happens. He again develops beta waves, despite the fact that he is introverted, and these are usually big, rhythmic, synchronized high amplitude waves, unlike the normal small amplitude found in the random chaotic brain waves of normal subjects.

This occurrence was first seen in 1955 by Das and Gastant who studied kriya yoga.[16] It was later seen and confirmed by Banquet, who studied transcendental meditation and found that after the theta waves, rhythmic beta waves were produced, present over the whole scalp and "the most striking topographical alteration was the synchronization of anterior and posterior channels."[17] The whole brain was pulsating synchronously, rhythmically and in an integrated fashion. This was subjectively experienced as deep meditation or transcendence.

Banquet states that, "We must deduce, therefore, that the EEG changes of meditation are independent of the interaction between the subject and the outer world but produced by the specific mental activity of the practice. The initiation of the loop between cortex, thalamo-cortical co-ordinating system and subcortical generator . . . could account for the different alterations."[18] This agrees with Bentov's theory of a loop circuit being responsible for the kundalini experience.

Levine, studying transcendental meditation, confirmed Banquet's findings of coherence and synchronization of brain waves, both within each cerebral hemisphere from front to back and between both hemispheres.[19] Corby and his associates found that using tantric meditation there was arousal of the nervous system rather than relaxation.[20] The episode of sudden autonomic nervous system activation was characterized by the meditator as approaching the yogic ecstatic state of intense concentration. Corby's subjects experienced: rushes of energy; chills, laughter, changing and varied emotions; early life flashes; total energy absorption; yearning to be one with the object of ideation; a great sense of merger and understanding of experience and its meaning.[21] Corby's meditators meditated, on the average, for more than three hours per day and used more advanced techniques than usually studied in the laboratory.

Kundalini in the laboratory

Though it may be difficult, if not impossible, to record the actual kundalini experience in the laboratory (either because such advanced meditators do not usually talk about their own experiences, or because the laboratory setting and environment is not correct, or because our machinery might interfere with or explode under the force of the actual experience), the research findings do tend to support Bentov's and the kindling model for kundalini.

In the studies of meditation in which activation of the nervous system was found, there was generalized coherence and integration of the brain and/or blissful, ecstatic experiences. The experiences of awakening of shakti recorded within the laboratory setting and their physiological correlates agree with the yogic theory that awakening takes place in mooladhara chakra and travels up to ajna chakra, affecting the deep, primitive, animalistic and energizing circuits within the R-complex and limbic system of the brain, near the medulla oblongata. Energy flows from here to the thalamus to stimulate all the areas of the cerebral cortex simultaneously and thereby creates a loop circuit which gradually awakens latent and unused activity within other areas of the brain. The whole brain begins to pulse as a single unit as energy pours into the central controlling area of ajna chakra.

We can understand that as we progress in meditation, we set the stage for the eventual awakening of shakti within the nadis, chakras and brain. An explosion occurs as we reach the threshold required for kindling to take place. Once we reach this concentrated, integrated state, neurological circuits take over and spontaneously begin to stimulate themselves, so that the energy liberated awakens new centres in the brain, creating a transformed state of awareness and being at a new and higher level of energy. The process of awakening of shakti has begun.

From this point on as long as we continue our practise, the process of unfoldment continues because once kindling has taken place the effects are relatively permanent. We develop more and more purity and strength, so that we can handle the internal experiences as they arise for longer and longer periods of time, until final awakening of kundalini takes place.

47

Cross-Cultural Evidence

Kundalini is a transcendental phenomena, one which lies outside the realms of time and space. We cannot understand how powerful the experience of kundalini awakening really is, however, we can see its effects on our lives and the effect that awakening has had in terms of changes in the functioning of society and in various cultures. For example, the effect of kundalini awakening is said by many researchers and yogis to be at the basis of the experiences had by Christ, Buddha, Krishna, Rama, Mohammed, Mahavir and various other great religious and spiritual figures from history.

While researchers continue to scientifically probe the phenomena itself, its components, its related events and ramifications, and its ability to affect machines, another type of researcher is examining the phenomena both in its social setting and anthropologically. As a universal phenomena we can see kundalini everywhere, in every culture and at all times. John White states: "Although the word kundalini comes from the yogic tradition nearly all the world's major religions, spiritual paths and genuine occult traditions see something akin to the kundalini experience as having significance in divinizing a person. The word itself may not appear in the traditions, but the concept is there nevertheless, wearing a different name yet recognizable as a key to attaining a God-like stature."[1]

Altered states

Kundalini induces an altered state of consciousness (ASC), that is, it takes us to realms of inner experience beyond those normally accessible. Arnold M. Ludwig writes, "Beneath man's thin veneer of consciousness lies a relatively uncharted realm of mental activity, the nature and function of which have been neither systematically explored or adequately conceptualized."[2]

Ludwig and other ASC researchers cite daydreaming, sleep and dreams, hypnosis, sensory deprivation, psychosis, hysterical states of dissociation and depersonalization, pharmacologically induced mental aberrations, sleeplessness, fasting and meditation as examples of ASCs. Anything can induce an ASC, any place or event can trigger a change in consciousness, however, usually we have to manoeuvre ourselves or use some agent to bypass the so-called 'normal' functioning of the brain. We can say that our normal state of consciousness is the one in which we spend most of our waking lives.

There are many people, however, who believe that the state of consciousness most people exist in is very limited and fixed, itself a retarded, degenerate and unhealthy state which induces fear of change, neurosis and disease. In terms of our inner experiences we are like retarded dwarfs, like the flea kept under a glass who, after hitting its head on the glass a number of times, ceases to jump hundreds of times its own height but rather, even when the glass is removed, continues to hop at a reduced capacity far below its innate potential. Yogis claim that we are like the flea, pathetic shadows of our former selves and far less than our potential, confined by vague fears and illusions, ghosts and memories in the mind. We are much more than we think we are.

The kundalini experience is at the peak of human evolution. It is the absolute and final state attainable by man, the experience in which he realizes and merges with his pristine glory; the ultimate ASC. All other experiences fall short of this and are mere steppingstones on the way, making up the repertoire of our lesser human lives. The real yogi or swami is the master of all realms of consciousness and can move into and out of any state he wants at will, depending on the degree of his skill and mastery. Various cultures have developed ways and means to attain these different realms of consciousness, each varying in its capacity to do so.

According to Erica Bourguignon, an anthropologist at Ohio State University, 90 percent of human societies practise some kind of institutionalized ritual to achieve altered states of consciousness.[3] For example, there is the solitary-vision quest of Sioux warriors, the hallucinogen-powered flights of South American shaman, the dream oracles of the Senoi people of Malaysia, the tribal dances of the Samo people of New Guinea, and the whirling dances of the Sufi dervish, to name but a few of the better known societies.

In the West we use alcohol and drugs, revival meetings, rock concerts and discotheques with their mind and logic-numbing, trance-inducing, megadecible music and 'tribal' dance. Are we so far from 'primitive' societies? Bourguignon wonders, "The fact that they are nearly universal must mean that such states are very important to human beings." The need for attaining higher states of consciousness seems to be as basic as the need for eating or sleeping.

Somehow we have forgotten at our conscious, normal level of consciousness, that we have immense potential and that we can achieve bliss, knowledge and inner experiences which are more satisfying than the monotonous, humdrum existence we lead at present. Somewhere in our subconscious minds, at another level of consciousness, we know that something is missing and this knowledge nags at us. We want to get away from it all, to have a holiday (from the root for Holy day). From this there arises an instinctive and irrepressible urge and drive to fulfil ourselves and to attain higher and better states and experiences, though we may often fail to achieve them or real inner satisfaction. The alcohol ritual is one example of a self-defeating and destruc-tive attempt to achieve true joy and inner bliss.

It appears that our methods are incorrect for attaining inner fulfilment, satisfaction and security. We have lost the keys and can no longer gain access to the higher and transcendental. We have been thrown out of the Garden of Eden. It is for this reason that so many people have turned to yoga, meditation and the transcendental sciences for the means and techniques to enlarge their repertoire of experience and to attain insight into themselves and reality.

Kundalini, a universal phenomenon

Reports have come from all over the world indicating that there is a psychophysiological phenomenon existing outside the barriers of social, cultural, religious, geographical and temporal boundaries, and which resembles the phenomenon called kundalini by the yogis and sages of India.

In Northwest Botswana, Africa, the *!Kung* people of the Kalahari Desert dance for many hours to heat up the *n/um* so that the *!kia* state can be obtained. This state of transcendence resembles that in many yogic texts on kundalini in which states of consciousness beyond the ordinary, and participation in eternity, are described. One tribesman reports: "You dance, dance, dance. Then the *n/um* lifts you in your belly and lifts you in your back, and then you start to shiver . . . it's hot. Your eyes are open but you don't look around; you hold your eyes still and look straight ahead. But when you get into *!kia* you're looking around because you see everything."[4]

Judith Cooper writes about the *!Kung*: "In one of the darker corners of the Dark Continent the *!Kung* people of the Kalahari keep in touch with the gods. Two or three nights a week the men dance around a fire, graceful as leopards, to the sonorous drone of the women's chants. Soon the mood turns solemn, and the night air swells with unseen presences. Sweat rolls down the dancers' bodies like sweet rain, as the *n/um*, the healing power, starts to boil. The moment of transcendence is painful. When the inner fire shoots from their bellies up their spines, the dancers shiver and tremble, fall to the ground or go rigid as stone. Some of them dance into the fire and out again, perfect as gods, their feet unburned. They can see into the essence of things now, even into the insides of other people, where malignant ghosts feed on diseased livers or prevent the conception of sons. Laying their healing hands on the sick, they bid the *n/um* to drive out the forces of darkness."[5]

In the Chinese Taoist tradition it is said that when prana or *chi*, the vital principle, has accumulated in the lower belly, it bursts out and begins to flow in the main psychic channels causing involuntary movements and sensations such as pain, itching, coldness, warmth, weightlessness, heaviness, roughness, smoothness, internal lights and sound and the feeling of inner movement. It may cause the physical body to brighten and even illuminate a dark room. Yin Shih Tsu reported that he felt heat travel from the base of the spine to the top of the head and then down over his face and throat to his stomach.[6]

These kinds of reports tally exactly with the experiences of yogis who describe kundalini as travelling up the spine with heat and light or with the surging energy of a snake preparing to strike. A classical description of kundalini from the yogic tradition comes from Swami Narayananda: "There is a burning up the back and over the whole body. Kundalini's entrance into sushumna occurs with pain in the back . . . One feels a creeping sensation from the toes and sometimes it shakes the whole body. The rising is felt like that of an ant creeping up slowly over the body towards the head. Its ascent is felt like the wiggling of a snake or a bird hopping from place to place."[7] This also sounds very much like the description of the so-called 'primitive' people of the *!Kung* tribe in the Kalahari desert in Africa.

In medieval Spain, St. Theresa of Avila described her experience, which yogis call the awakening of nada, the manifestation of transcendental consciousness as sound: "The noises in my head are so loud that I am beginning to wonder what is going on in it . . . My head sounds just as if it were full of brimming rivers . . . and a host of little birds seem to be whistling, not in the ears, but in the upper part of the head, where the higher part of the soul is said to be; I have held this view for a long time, for the spirit seems to move upward with great velocity."[8]

Conclusion

The above are classical kundalini type experiences, but they have occurred in different geographical locations and at different times in history, because kundalini is not dependent on time and space. However, few cultures have documented the kundalini experience so well or consistently as the sages in India. The Indian culture seems to have been ripe to allow the yogic sciences to be preserved, cultivated and revered. As a result, a sublime philosophy has emerged and has been recorded in many books, a few of which have come down to us through the ravages of time and history. Books such as the *Bhagavad Gita*, the yogic texts such as *Yoga Vashishta* and *Hatha Yoga Pradipika*, and the sublime beauty of the books of the Upanishads and Vedanta, which have inspired many of the great men and women of history from all over the world, are testaments to the existence of this great culture. Sophisticated maps of consciousness, charts to allow us to enter the sublime bliss of altered states of consciousness and meditative experience, myriad techniques and processes, and untold works and books for guidance have emerged and have been handed down over thousands of years. Nowhere else has the kundalini experience been so well, richly or scientifically recorded in all its sublimity and variation.

Swami Vivekananda sums up the whole question of kundalini as a universal phenomena when he states: "When by the power of long internal meditation, the vast mass of energy stored up travels along the sushumna and strikes the chakras, the reaction is immensely more intense than any reaction of sense perception. Wherever there was any manifestation of what is ordinarily called supernatural power or wisdom, a little current of kundalini must have found its way into the sushumna."

We see then that an experience exists which is one but which has had a vast impact on society and culture wherever it has occurred. The experience is one but the names are many. Yogis call this the awakening of shakti or kundalini and have developed a vast, intricate, systematic and progressive science by which they can awaken this power which lies dormant in each of us and one which can evolve ourselves and society to new and undreamed of heights of experience and achievement.

48

Analysis of the Chakras from a Psychophysiological Viewpoint*

PSYCHOPHYSIOLOGY

Swami Shankardevananda: What are the psychodynamics of the chakras?

Swami Vivekananda: From a physiological viewpoint there are aspects of the chakras that deal with mood, with the mind, aspects dealing with experiences on the psychic plane and also aspects concerned with the energy turnover of the body and mind.

The brain, which is divided up in terms of its emotions and cognition, can also be divided into the aspects of the different chakras. It seems to me that from the physiological and anatomical point of view, the chakras are the sum total of the input and output of the different segments of the body. The throat (vishuddhi) section deals with perception, especially the voice. Many of the psychic aspects of this chakra are actually telepathic communication. The chest (anahata) deals mainly with the love aspect. The upper abdomen (manipura) deals with the assertiveness and drive aspect. The lower abdominal or upper pelvic area (swadhisthana) deals with the pleasure aspect. The lowest segment (mooladhara), according to Freud and many yogis before him, deals with security, possessions and material objects.

---

*A discussion with the swamis of Bihar School of Yoga, Munger, 1980

Consider manipura chakra. It deals with hunger and it is directly connected with hunger centres in the hypothalamus. It is closely related to the next chakra down, swadhisthana, which deals with pleasure. The hunger and pleasure centres are adjacent in the posterior part of the hypothalamus. They are so close to each other that some of the cells actually intertwine and it is hard to separate which is which. It is interesting to note that when people are sexually tense and sexually dissatisfied, they start reaching for sweet things – they get hungry, start putting on weight and all that. This indicates the close interconnection of these two chakras.

There are also what we can call energy circuits involved in these interconnections. These energies can be directed up or down. If the instincts or desires related to specific areas are not actually satisfied, then there is a tendency for the energy to build up. We see it especially in relation to the sexual impulse, which is connected mainly to swadhisthana, and also partly to mooladhara and manipura. An unfulfilled sexual life at swadhisthana level tends to redirect energy either into the desire for power and dominance at manipura or the neurotic craving for possessions at mooladhara.

Energy is built into this chakra system and all of its connections with the hypothalamus and the limbic system. The limbic system, amongst other things, generates a continuity of emotions, and emotions of course motivate action. If there is, for example, competition, then anger is stirred up within the solar plexus, stomach areas and related organs, including the adrenal glands. The adrenals, of course, activate a person to fight if it is over territory or food. Also, adrenaline increases the sugar content in the blood by breaking down glycogen in the liver, so it keeps the animal going even though it is hungry and short of food. If necessary, adrenaline will supply the bloodstream with sugar, so it can win the fight and get food.

It seems to me that a lot of the physiological energy that is inherent in all these chakra circuits is this sort of energy. I do not really believe it is energy per se, but I think it is

403

nerve impulses, for instance in the case of manipura chakra, stimulated by a block in blood glucose which then activates the stomach and the hunger centres in the hypothalamus, which then activates these mechanisms.

Swami Shankardevananda: So you do not believe in a specific localized energy, but a total body functioning within that circuit. And one circuit becomes dominant if it is neglected or overactivated.

Swami Vivekananda: Yes. It can be constitutionally dominant in a person too. You see people who are all manipura chakra, a lot of drive, ambitions and right in there. They are not sexual people (swadhisthana motivated) and they might not even have a security drive (mooladhara motivated). I have known many business people and lawyers who dabble here and there and do it only for the fun of the game. They are just very competitive people. Everyone says to the wives, "Well, it must be great to be married to a guy like that," and they say, "Ugh, he has little swadhisthana (sex) or anahata chakra (love) working. He is a bad husband, but makes a very good provider (manipura)."

Swami Shankardevananda: In a study of sociopaths and those people who are fearless, it was found that there is in fact very little difference between them. People who are testing jet planes and rocketships and climbing mountains without ropes etc. have fundamentally the same character as sociopaths.

Swami Vivekananda: If a person's behaviour is accepted by society, then he is a hero. If it is unacceptable he is a psychopath. It reminds me of the old joke that you can murder someone if the government approves of it. This is interesting because these people have that same kind of drive. They are driven by an overactive manipura chakra.

Mooladhara chakra deals principally in security, swadhisthana principally with pleasure, manipura principally with assertiveness, courage and personal power, anahata with love, vishuddhi with communication out and also the ability, mainly because of the perception of our external environment, to feel at home virtually anywhere. It is a state of consciousness that is inherent in vishuddhi chakra. When it develops to a certain point you can be sitting on a pile of garbage and still everything is just right. Ajna chakra, of course, deals with intellect, intuition and the psychic power (siddhis) such as telepathy.

As well as these qualities within the different chakras there is another parameter, which is the degree of evolution. Each one of us has these circuits constitutionally energized to different degrees. One person may have a lot of energization of swadhisthana chakra; that person is very much pleasure bent, and has perhaps less development at manipura or anahata.

Swami Shankardevananda: That would be very much a hormonal thing depending mainly on the drive from the hypothalamus.

Swami Vivekananda: That is right. I have not thought very much about what governs the constitutional factors of it. Each one of us is proportionately energized differently in different chakra circuits. Each one of us strikes a different chord. There is a different frequency of energization of the chakras. There are individual differences between each one of us, because each one of us has different degrees of evolution of the quality of the manifestation of each of the chakras. A sociopath who goes round beating up old ladies to steal their handbags, and an astronaut, may have the same chord. They may be identical in the level of activity of each of the chakras, but the guy who is an astronaut, hopefully, has a higher degree of evolution in most of his chakras. So these are two important parameters which define the qualities of the chakras – percentage of activity and degree of evolution. These define the character of each person.

Swami Shankardevananda: You mentioned that there are chakras which express energy and certain chakras which take in energy.

Swami Vivekananda: No, what I was saying is that we know these circuits exist in anatomical form, that there are whole areas down there in the body which do not only trigger off something up here (in the brain), but are also triggered by something up here. And we know that there are, for instance, the hunger and the sensual centres in the hypothalamus. We know that they are directly connected with the relevant organs in the body. As the hunger builds up, more neuronal activity builds up within those circuits. And if an emotional component comes into it, it's very likely that other parts of the limbic system will start generating energy too. You will go rushing around to get something to eat as quickly as possible. This implies that there is an increased neuronal activity within that circuit.

People talk about energy within those circuits, and they are certain it is an energy. They say these circuits are energized because when they start getting activated, you can feel throbbing, shaking, etc. But is it energy like electricity running through a wire, or is it in actual fact only a message like the electricity running through a telephone wire? The mere fact that a person shakes can mean that it is a message that is being transmitted to the muscles and the muscles do all the shaking.

I tend to prefer the physiological point of view which says that it is neuronal activity; that is, the nerves and circuits conduct impulses and the muscles create the shaking and energy.

Swami Shankardevananda: But there is energy even in neuronal activity.

Swami Vivekananda: Well, there is, but the energy is produced secondarily to the neuronal activity. The primary object of the circuit is to convey an impulse. The message is carried and it uses energy as a carrier in the same way as a telephone uses energy. You would not get a telephone wire and try to light a 100 watt bulb, because there is just not enough energy there. Telephone wires run only on about 2 volts; it is not primarily an energy transmission, but primarily a message transmission; the energy is a secondary issue and comes from another source.

406

Some people, by their nature, have some of these circuits much more activated and 'energized' than others. There are some people who are very much more into the whole manipura thing. They eat a lot and have big muscles; they are all manipura chakra. You get anahata people who are very paternal and loving and always sensing other people's feelings, everywhere they go. The same applies to the other chakras.

Chakra types can be easily seen at a party where there are a whole lot of people around and you do not know anybody. Then you will see the person who's very much into feelings will start picking up all over the place who is kind and who is not kind. That is what he perceives in the environment. He is predominantly an anahata type. A person who's into the intellectual trip will listen to all the conversations going on and if there is good intellectual tone, he will fit into that circle. If a group is talking about football or something like that, he will go straight past. He will be the vishuddhi/ ajna type. Then you will get the manipura chap who will notice first of all who's in the power scene and he will start associating with that. If there is no obvious power position, it usually develops towards the end of the night. Sometimes you will go into a place and say "That is it." It is a special chair and a special place. Now if you are on a power trip you go and sit there.

The emotional person, when he perceives the scene, is perceiving the feelings all around the place, the swadhisthana chap will be seeing other things such as food, sexual encounters and so on. Each one of us has a preference in these things, and that preference seems to me to be driven by energization or activation of those particular circuits which may be predominating. And some people are balanced and versatile and will fit into any situation. These people are the yogic types.

I think there is an inbuilt rhythm and activation of these particular circuits within the body. I somehow suspect that we go along on a number of different levels of consciousness at the same time. Sometimes we have dreams of total experiences of something that is going to occur in three or four months' time. That means time, instead of being a longitudinal thing, is a vertical thing. How do we explain that in our neurophysiological framework? There are a lot of experiences that are difficult to explain scientifically. I don't think that necessarily means that a physiological explanation is invalid.

These days it is possible to measure certain physical manifestations of chakras and the dissociated chakras. Maybe you could get a personality break of a person who was obviously into a certain chakra and test the activation of that chakra. I think the energy around the chakra is easily explainable in that it is the energy that would be given off by the activated field.

Swami Shankardevananda: In terms of circuits, some of the chakras have more receptive properties, especially in mooladhara and ajna, whilst certain chakras seem to be more expressive, such as swadhisthana and manipura.

Swami Vivekananda: Probably it is associated with the jnan-endriyas and karmendriyas (sensory and motor nerves).

Swami Shankardevananda: All the chakras must have a dual purpose: there must be a receptive and active side to them. For example, ajna is receptive to psychic and intuitive energy, but it also transmits at the subtle, telepathic level. Vishuddhi, which expresses and communicates that intuition at the verbal level, simultaneously expresses compassion felt through anahata, and also expresses the experiences felt through manipura and swadhisthana. All chakras have a two-way channel and that is because of ida and pingala.

Swami Vivekananda: I think that vishuddhi expresses the qualities of the other chakras only as an agent of their quality, because the other chakras will express energy in a different way. If you are with a person who is loving, especially if you get close, you can feel the love pouring out. Therefore, anahata is expressing in that way, but I think that anahata would use vishuddhi chakra to say the words that go with it.

408

Swami Shankardevananda: Yes, the energy flows through the other chakras, so the activation of one chakra affects them all and modifies them according to its major harmonic, but in its own way. Manipura and swadhisthana chakras would then become love dominant if anahata becomes active. All the other chakras would then line themselves up with anahata.

Swami Vivekananda: Manipura chakra is an expressive chakra and if you feel high in manipura, then it would tend to flow out love more than feel the experience of love, which is anahata.

Swami Shankardevananda: There is a definite connection between mooladhara and ajna. Also, there appears to be a connection between swadhisthana, vishuddhi and bindu, a very direct connection, and lalana, which is a sub-chakra of vishuddhi. Then it seems that manipura and anahata are also related. This intimate connection between the chakras is symbolized by the seven candles on the Hebrew candlestand (menorah). This is a representation of how chakras are interacting, but actually it is a much more complicated diagram in which all chakras interact with each other. We can regard mooladhara and swadhisthana as being tamasic chakras, manipura and anahata as being predominantly rajasic, and vishuddhi and ajna as being sattwic. These pairs function together. Vishuddhi and ajna, for example, are connected on a receptive, expressive merger, one being active and the other being receptive.

Swami Vivekananda: But I see rajasic and tamasic qualities being in each of the chakras and I see the chakras as being horizontal rather than a vertical ladder form. They all have qualities from rajasic, right through to sattwic.

Swami Shankardevananda: That is also true. Some people think the word tamasic carries moralistic connotations.

Swami Vivekananda: In the context of evolution, is the bliss that the yogi experiences any different to the bliss of orgasm? It might be at a more highly evolved level. Is the selfish love of a mother for her child, to the exclusion of all other

409

children, anything more than just a lower level of transcendental love?

Swami Shankardevananda: In his article on kundalini, Carl Jung says that from above manipura chakra you leave the whole sphere of the earth behind, the individuality – and the diaphragm which lies at the manipura level could be an important anatomical separating component as far as the chakras are concerned. The movement away from individual love towards universal love takes place at that point just above the diaphragm – anahata chakra.

Swami Vivekananda: It is very likely that these different opinions are all right. The mountain looks different from different angles, but from above you see all the people looking at the same mountain. The problem comes when you go back down to earth and talk to all the individual people. It is very difficult to describe what you experienced when you saw the whole mountain. This is why we get so many different opinions, philosophies and religions.

MOOLADHARA AND SWADHISTHANA CHAKRAS

Swami Shankardevananda: Can you discuss the nerve complexes associated with mooladhara and swadhisthana chakras?

Swami Vivekananda: Well, for all of these segments there are somatic nerves, which deal with the sensory input and the voluntary motor output, and also there are the autonomic nerves, divided into sympathetic and parasympathetic. And usually there is an appropriate endocrine gland for each segment, like the pineal, pituitary and thyroid. The exception is mooladhara, and to date, medical science has not found an endocrine gland associated with it. This of course does not mean that one will not be discovered in the future.

Let us try to work out the psychophysiological aspects of mooladhara. In the male it is actually associated with the base of the penis and with the female, the cervix. So it has a very deep-rooted sexual link.

If you repeat a mooladhara chakra mantra and you concentrate in that area somewhere, you will feel a certain vibration occurring. Now what is the mantra doing? Is it stimulating some physiological organ, or is it some sort of occult stimulation? Is it stimulating a physical organ or is it activating a lot of energy which seems to appear in a certain place which we call a chakra? I think it is perhaps the last one of these.

Swami Shankardevananda: I believe that the mooladhara trigger point and the place of actual experience may be different, but the general location of mooladhara chakra is certainly in the perineum; it is clearly felt in that area. If it is felt higher, then it is not mooladhara chakra, it is swadhisthana. Either the mantra is wrong or the vibration is stimulating something else which is more receptive and reactive.

Swami Vivekananda: Is there a physiological basis for this? It is quite possible that the repetition of a mantra is stimulating the spinal cord. You can certainly feel it in the area being stimulated and it is not only there, because all the fibres that are coming out from the body are stimulated. Therefore, no matter at what level you stimulate your spinal cord, no matter what chakra is stimulated, you are going to collect the fibres from so called mooladhara chakra. At swadhisthana chakra you will also get the mooladhara chakra fibres; at manipura you get the mooladhara fibres back to swadhisthana and manipura as well – and all the way up. Mooladhara chakra is always there in the act because its fibres come from the lowest part.

Swami Shankardevananda: Could we consider the sexual energy of mooladhara and its possible transmutations?

Swami Vivekananda: This basic sexual energy that Gopi Krishna has written about is actually the sattwic or subtle essence which can be perceived when the consciousness becomes very sensitive. This is the essence of the kundalini experience, the sublimation of sexual energy, the basic life force which is the source of all generation, regeneration and reproduction. Gopi Krishna felt what he was seeing was semen being converted into energy and distributing itself throughout the body. I feel that what he was perceiving was a clairvoyant view of energy given off by the simple nerve fibres in those organs he was talking about. However, he identified it as semen because that is what is written in the scriptures. I do not know what women are supposed to have, he did not mention that and I do not think the scriptures do either.

Swami Nischalananda: The *Hatha Yoga Pradipika* and certain tantric texts do talk about women; however, generally that side has been neglected. According to yoga the sexual energy in men and women is sublimated and transmuted into the ascent of the kundalini. The starting point is mooladhara. For some reason, the Buddhists say that the ascent commences at manipura, not mooladhara. How is it that the enlightened Buddha completely bypassed the two lower chakras? Actually the whole concept of where kundalini lies is a matter of experience. I don't think that Buddha actually said that kundalini starts in manipura; more likely he stated that real spiritual evolution starts from manipura. Swami Satyananda has said many times that only when the kundalini reaches manipura is it stabilized. It starts in mooladhara but stabilizes in manipura.

I think this apparent discrepancy comes because of the philosophy of Buddha who was a jnani, and he didn't get much into kundalini yoga. Vajrayana, on the other hand, which was an offshoot of Buddhism at a later date, is very much concerned with mooladhara. But let us get back to the functioning of mooladhara.

Swami Shankardevananda: Mooladhara chakra has two basic modes of function, one is energy depleted and the other is energy activated. Within that system there is a sick and a healthy mooladhara. What are the symptoms of these different states of mooladhara chakra? It is simple – you are either sick or healthy, balanced or unbalanced. If you are unbalanced you are going to have ida over or under active or pingala over or under active. You are going to have physical and mental symptoms, fear, insecurity and all those things. Freud said that everyone who denies mooladhara becomes constipated and hoards money. Every miser is constipated. These symptoms may be mild or very extreme. In the fully awakened state they are either going to rip you to pieces or take you to a higher awareness. So what is the basic quality of a well functioning mooladhara chakra?

Swami Vivekananda: Renunciation.

Swami Shankardevananda: We can say that security and renunciation are interchangeable in the mooladhara system. We can say that in this chakra basic security is the key. Renunciation obviously implies security and if you are secure within yourself, you don't need any external security.

Swami Satyadharma: When awakening of mooladhara takes place then there is no such problem as insecurity.

Swami Vivekananda: Of course, this is the state of consciousness of an awakened mooladhara. A low energized mooladhara chakra generally means low vitality, emotional insecurity, fear of the future. I also think low self-esteem is involved in this. It almost forms the syndrome of depression, although you don't necessarily have to get the joylessness of the low energized swadhisthana chakra. If there is low evolution and high drive in mooladhara, then you get the ambitious person out to collect as much as he can. He can be a multimillionaire and still accumulate all sorts of things because he still feels insecure. The security is a state of consciousness, not a physical reality. As mooladhara chakra starts to evolve the person attains security, which is totally unrelated to circumstances.

You can see varying degrees of renunciation not only between sannyasins and the community, but within the community of sannyasins as well.

Swami Satyadharma: When energies pool at mooladhara chakra, do they stimulate or aggravate the chakras? What is the difference between stagnation of energy and activation of the chakra?

413

Swami Vivekananda: Well, I just see that the mooladhara circuit in some people is sometimes poorly energized; the whole circuit itself has low energization. This varies between people and varies within people, depending upon cosmic events, the position of planets, the weather and all sorts of things, including psychological factors such as disappointments, hurts and threats to one's security. It varies with each of us. Some people are very much in mooladhara; hooked on the basic sexual aspect of mooladhara in which case they are very much involved in money and possessions. If they are low energized, they will still think about these things, but they will not do anything about it.

I think you need a certain amount of energization to produce the drive that is inherent in each chakra; the basic sexual hunting drive in swadhisthana chakra, the territorial and dominance drive in manipura and the nurturing drive in anahata chakra. Remember, there are two parameters, the amount of energization of each chakra and the degree of evolution.

It seems that yoga practices balance the energy inherent within each of the chakra circuits, and by virtue of eliminating the blockages (samskaras), evolve the quality of the chakras at the same time. And of course, if you have the grace of the guru you are on the express line.

Swami Satyadharma: So does pooled energy act to block or can it be used to activate the chakra? For example, if a person has a lot of pooled energy in mooladhara, would that be an energy block or could that pooled energy be utilized to activate and awaken a chakra?

Swami Vivekananda: It can be used to activate it if the psychological blockages are eliminated.

Swami Shankardevananda: I think there is a difference between storage and blockage. The ability to hold or store energy takes place consciously, whilst having an unconscious or subconscious blockage leads to repression.

Swami Vivekananda: And repression of a highly energized chakra can produce all sorts of physical symptoms, such as

414

muscle tension, malfunctioning of internal organs, etc., as well as emotional problems.

Swami Shankardevananda: What are the psychological effects of mooladhara awakening?

Swami Vivekananda: As I have already said, renunciation.

Swami Shankardevananda: The feeling of separation, the beginning of your individual awareness, awakening to the fact that you are separate from something else.

Swami Nischalananda: Primal alienation or something like that.

Swami Shankardevananda: Do you think that the basic energy at mooladhara is anxiety, fear, or is it insecurity?

Swami Vivekananda: The basic emotion? Well, it depends on the energization of the circuit. If there is not much energy, it will tend to be depression and hopelessness. But if there is a lot of energy, it will then depend upon the evolution of the chakra. If it is little evolved, then there will be intense insecurity, which is anxiety. If it is highly evolved there will be a sense of oneness and complete security. Generally mooladhara is blocked to some extent in most people and blockages may manifest as muscle tension.

Muscle tensions are manifestations of the circuits of mental blockages, samskaras. It is the samskaras that keep down the evolution of the quality of consciousness that is within these chakra circuits. I think that low evolution, muscle spasms and the maladjustments of the organisms that are supplied by that part of the autonomic nervous system are due to psychic tensions.

Swami Shankardevananda: These psychic and personality tensions are due to various events in the environment.

Swami Vivekananda: That is right. The inner unconscious conflicts coming into conflict with certain events in the environment. For example, if a person feels very insecure and someone steals a valuable possession from him, he may go into an absolute frenzy. This is opposed to the reaction of someone else who does not have the same sort of conflicts and insecurities.

415

If a person cannot express the feeling that is involved at mooladhara, that feeling can express itself in somatic problems like spasms of the muscles, in autonomic problems, blood pressure, constipation, and who knows what else, maybe functional urethritis, cystitis, colitis, rectitis, dysmenorrhea and so on.

PSYCHOSIS

Swami Shankardevananda: Would you associate a highly energized, low evolved mooladhara problem as the cause of manic depression?

Swami Vivekananda: I think manic depression is an ida/pingala thing. We are in another dimension there, because a manic person will undergo all the manifestations of a very highly energized and controlled chakra. He will be rushing around gambling all his money away, trying to get more, getting into all sorts of sexual exploits, going round pushing other people around, the rajasic aspect.

Swami Sambuddhananda: Would you say that schizophrenia and paranoia are related with ida and pingala imbalance?

Swami Vivekananda: Yes, there are people who are stuck in ida. Ida is very much overactive. It is interesting that research shows that the taking in of negative aspects of the environment through the right hemisphere (ida) is paranoia. This is what paranoia is all about. A lot of people, some of them quite highly evolved people, who have specialized much in ida are a bit paranoid. Ida seems to have a negative aspect about it. Even if you come into it at a high level of consciousness, it seems to have a bit of a negative pull. If you are going to activate your chakras, you have to make sure your ida and pingala are balanced.

Swami Shankardevananda: But manic depression, psychosis and other mental problems relate to either mooladhara or ajna because it is only at these two points that you have the fusion of ida and pingala. Therefore, psychosis, manic depression and all these things would seem to relate very much to the mooladhara/ajna circuit. If ida and pingala are coming out of mooladhara chakra, then what would be the mechanism dealing with psychosis?

Swami Vivekananda: I think that ida and pingala are only related to the activities of the cerebral hemispheres.

Swami Shankardevananda: But the whole body is controlled by the hemispheres. The whole body gets the energy. Arteries and veins, sensory and motor nerves, right and left hemispheres are all reflections of the ida and pingala process.

Swami Vivekananda: I see ida and pingala anatomically up here in the brain, not crossing down the spine. I believe that ida and pingala crossing each other is a concept and a symbol of experience.

Swami Satyadharma: I think that awakening of mooladhara is the beginning of psychic awareness. That is why with mooladhara awakening, people often become disturbed.

Swami Vivekananda: Yes. They can get caught in the psychic consciousness, which is the consciousness in which you have hallucinations, etc.

Swami Shankardevananda: It is much more powerful than anything they have ever experienced before.

Swami Vivekananda: We slide in and out of it twice a day anyway, even if we are not doing any formal closed eye meditation techniques. I think if you hold the awareness at the psychic level, and you can do it with yoga nidra, you will experience a state in which there is thought blocking – what is called thought disorder – where one thought leads on to another one that is unrelated to it and it just goes off into the distance. Paradoxical thinking – where two paradoxical things can exist together, hallucinations, voices talking to you, you see things and so forth.

Swami Shankardevananda: So, therefore we assume that pingala is blocked and ida is flowing. All that stuff is coming out through ida from mooladhara; basic subconscious material.

Swami Vivekananda: At the same time there is psychic withdrawal.

Swami Shankardevananda: Yes, so what does that imply?

Swami Vivekananda: If there is a psychic withdrawal, then even though we appear to be in communication with the outside, in actual fact we are still inside from the psychic point of view. Paradoxical thinking, suspicious feelings, voices and all these things, and not being able to keep your thoughts together on one topic for any more than a couple of seconds; all these come from a psychic, inner plane.

PHYSICAL DISEASES

Swami Shankardevananda: What about physical disease associated with mooladhara chakra problems? We have already talked about constipation; this of course brings about things like haemorrhoids.

Swami Vivekananda: There are many types of constipation involved too – of energy, emotions, information – all inherent in mooladhara chakra as hoarding of any type.

Swami Gaurishankar: What about disease?

Swami Vivekananda: Statistics involved in diseases in this area tend to relate to the manipura and anahata areas, and the diseases of hypertension, heart problems, peptic ulcers etc. I assume many diseases of the lower excretory and reproductive organs are associated with a malfunctioning mooladhara.

Swami Shankardevananda: Cancer?

Swami Vivekananda: Yes, of the rectum and bladder.

Swami Shankardevananda: The helplessness associated with it too?

Swami Vivekananda: I don't know if it is all cancers we are talking about now. I don't know if they would be segmental or not. Hypertension, for instance, appears to be a generalized condition. It is mainly related to the manipura chakra circuits. Cancer may well be a generalized condition that is related to one of the chakras, perhaps mooladhara.

Swami Paramananda: How far can you take the relationship between the chakras and the physical organs like the heart?

If the heart is not functioning well and it affects the anahata chakra which is love, can that also mean that there is a lack of love going through that person and physically it comes out in anahata chakra and the heart as disease?

Swami Vivekananda: Yes, it can be in both. If a person has a need to receive love and it is not coming, and/or that person has imbalanced constructions of love, then anahata problems can arise in the form of cardiac problems such as angina, palpitations, etc.

Swami Paramananda: Do you think that applies to all the chakras? If you find a particular organ not functioning in a sick person, does it mean there is a deficiency of the qualities of the chakra related to that part of the body?

Swami Vivekananda: As a general rule, yes, but you can get other problems as well. For instance, you can get an activation of manipura chakra, which activates the sympathetic nervous system which produces restriction of the coronary artery.

There is interaction between the different chakras, and this is the beauty of a well-taught yoga class – it balances all these qualities, and balance is the key to the whole thing. Rather than trying to work on one area, which is a more specific medical style, yoga therapy works on the whole human structure.

Swami Muktibodhananda: How do the physical organs relate to the chakras and spiritual evolution?

Swami Vivekananda: Consider hysterectomy. Let us assume the wrong woman is wheeled into the operating theatre and she has a hysterectomy. This will then cut off the end organ for a lot of nerve fibres and the atrophy will run up the nerves and eliminate the brain centres involved in that. This is an example of a deficiency in the organ producing changes in the centres involved, the circuit. Does that make it any more difficult for her to realize higher aspects of swadhisthana chakra?

Swami Shankardevananda: It depends how much of the centre is lost. If she just loses the uterus and not the ovaries, for example, all the hormonal secretions will be maintained.

As women reach menopause they will undergo a natural hysterectomy.

Swami Vivekananda: Yes, but they don't lose the nerve endings. When the uterus is removed, because the nerve endings are useless, they atrophy. Does this affect the associated chakras?

Swami Nischalananda: Swami Satyananda says it does not make any difference if there is a vasectomy, because it is only the physical body. I think, as regards swadhisthana for example, that if they are already on the spiritual path and have developed some psychic awareness, then that operation would definitely not affect them much, if at all. If they had no background of yogic practise, then probably the destruction of that organ would slightly hamper progress, because initially you depend upon those organs to stimulate something, especially in the practices of hatha and kriya yoga. If you follow the path of bhakti or jnana yoga, of course, it makes no difference.

Swami Shankardevananda: If you lose one centre or two centres, physically I think it does not hinder you because a lot of other centres are left. There are tons of potential left within the brain.

Swami Vivekananda: To sum up, we function on physical, emotional, mental, psychic and spiritual levels. The chakras span all these levels. The purpose of yoga and tantra is to stimulate the chakras at all these levels. Then, and only then, can we become healthy human beings.

MENTAL PROBLEMS

Swami Sambuddhananda: What is the cause of depression?

Swami Vivekananda: I think low activation of the swadhisthana circuit is the prime cause of depression.

Swami Shankardevananda: I thought it was due to low activation in mooladhara.

Swami Vivekananda: Well, the qualities in both these chakras are very close.

Swami Shankardevananda: So what is the difference between mooladhara and swadhisthana?

Swami Vivekananda: You can see the different qualities in the various types of anxiety you see in different people. In psychiatry, the various forms of anxiety all come under the name of anxiety, yet they are all different syndromes, and they are also related to different chakra circuits. People with a low energized mooladhara chakra are not just apprehensive about the future, they also feel insecure about the present. They simply don't feel that this is a secure world, and the state of consciousness they have at any time is that things are dangerous.

There is another type of depression which I perceived in a woman who was forty-five years of age. Her husband had left her when she was about thirty-five, and she led a very quiet life. But she was still pretty energized in swadhisthana chakra. She was describing the anxiety that she had. Through empathy I started to experience what she was describing. It was a sort of quivering vibration going on in the pelvis. It was a quivering all around the area of swadhisthana chakra, not specifically genital, but all around the upper part of the pelvis. It really was a type of anxiety.

I gave her the general swadhisthana practices such as shalabhasana, etc. She improved a lot. The yogic practices seemed to deactivate her pent-up emotion. I think it was just sexual tension that she had in that area and she was perceiving it as anxiety. She also had a fear of it because she did not know what it was.

There is another case of depression which is a well-known one – butterflies in the stomach, accompanied by palpitations, which is just activation of the sympathetic nervous system. One case I saw was a taxi driver who had a minor accident in his cab. He got this phobia and he couldn't get in his taxi without experiencing butterflies. In Aruba (South America), where he lived, taxi fares are minimal so that the taxi drivers are really hard up. This man had to employ someone else to drive his cab for him and he was losing money. He had been off work for six weeks. Every time he went up to his cab he would get this terrible churning in the stomach and he developed hypertension. He was a very dynamic Aries.

So I thought, "What to do?" I taught him kunjal in order to get all that energy out of manipura chakra. He did it once in the ashram and then immediately went out and got in his cab. This type of anxiety and depression is obviously manipura overactivity.

There is another type of anxiety which arises through too much thinking: "Wouldn't it be terrible if such and such happened, and if that happens maybe something else will happen, and if that happens maybe . . .?" People with this problem just think and think and think, until that preoccupation produces a fear within them which is not necessarily contained in the symptoms. That is dealt with by practising bhramari pranayama. So within the diagnosis of anxiety there seems to be these four types. There may be others related to the other chakras, but I have not yet noticed them.

Swami Nischalananda: Maybe stuttering, loss of voice and things like that, related to vishuddhi, can be cured by simhasana.

Swami Vivekananda: Exactly, tightening up of the throat. It seems to be more related to a lack of self-confidence rather than the feeling of anxiety. Simhasana works wonders.

When I was in general practice, I used to do a lot of spinal adjustments and manipulation, and after a while I specialized in spinal problems. I did a lot of backs at that stage. I found that patients came in clusters. I would get a lot of people with an upper cervical lesion, migraine headaches, tightness in the neck region, with all the symptoms of chronic sinusitis and all the other things related to upper cervical tension.

I found that all the people with upper cervical problems were coming in when the moon was full, all the people with lumbar/sacral problems were coming in when the moon was new, and in between all the others were spread out. This is interesting because it is related to chakra activation. Almost before the patient told me, I could pinpoint the exact spinal segment in which he would be having problems. I knew according to the moon phase. This relationship became obvious, especially towards the end of the time I was manipulating, because I took on the symptoms of my patients.

Swami Shankardevananda: This means that we need a whole set of asanas working on all the segments of the spine.

Swami Vivekananda: Yes, we have them, for example, surya namaskara. In Australia we used to use the leg lock posture for mooladhara chakra; shalabhasana and bhujangasana for swadhisthana chakra. These asanas are actually supposed to be for manipura chakra, but so many people have such stiff backs that they activate swadhisthana chakra instead. Then paschimottanasana and dhanurasana for manipura; for anahata, supta vajrasana and matsyasana; for vishuddhi, sarvangasana; and for ajna chakra, sirshasana and ashwa sanchalanasana. Halasana also activates vishuddhi because the inflection is brought right up to the upper cervical area. However, people who have a stiff upper cervical spine should not do any of those upper spine flexion practices, because the discs are very tiny at that part and these asanas can be too much.

Swami Nischalananda: Khandharasana is good for this area. It's not so strong because a lot of the body weight is taken by the feet.

Swami Gaurishankar: Let us get back to the subject of depression.

Swami Vivekananda: I think there are different qualities in the thing that we call depression. The dread of the future is one of the symptoms of depression and I think it is a mooladhara chakra problem. But the dejection, lack of joy and loss of sense of humour that you find in many people is due to a low energized swadhisthana. With a low energized manipura comes loss of appetite and low emotional activity.

In depression there is a vicious circle; the whole mechanism, the whole noradrenalin/dopamine mechanism seems to slow down. It involves hormones. Most of the anti-depressants act upon this noradrenalin/dopamine system.

Swami Shankardevananda: I would also imagine that depletion of testosterone, excessive sexual activity, depletion of adrenaline, excessive fear and anxiety, etc., all lead to a depressed state.

Swami Vivekananda: That is right. I have often suspected too, that when the moon is new for instance, then people tend to function to some extent on the energy of the lower chakras. The other ones are functioning too, but it is the lower chakras that are carrying a lot of the energy. Actually, the normal person experiences a depressed feeling lasting a couple of days during that phase. Then the moon starts activating the other chakras and the person comes out of it.

Swami Nischalananda: This relationship is also indicated by the fact that some people go crazy at the time of full moon. It means that energy comes up to and accumulates at ajna chakra. The high energy affects the mind.

Swami Vivekananda: It is strange that the medical profession denies that the full moon has any effect on the mental state of people, and there are comprehensive statistics from psychiatric hospitals to show that the admission rate is no higher at the time of the full moon than it is at the time of new moon. To this I say that there are different conditions for which people are being admitted at the time of the full moon and at the time of the new moon; this can be seen most clearly.

Swami Shankardevananda: In hospitals, all the nursing staff knows that when the full moon comes there are going to be problems. There will be more road accidents, more crazy people coming in and people going off their heads, etc.

Swami Muktibodhananda: What is the difference between fear, anxiety and phobia?

Swami Vivekananda: Fear is a normal response to a threatening situation. If a tiger came into this room, nine people would be frightened and that would be a natural response. Anxiety, on the other hand, is really a collection of symptoms which go on for a long time, usually not provoked by an external situation. Phobias are immediate responses, just like fear, except that the responses are to a non-threatening situation. A mouse a hundred yards down the corridor, for instance, would not affect any of us, but someone with a phobia about mice would panic.

Swami Shankardevananda: Phobias are actually a displacement from an original object on to a different situation.

Swami Vivekananda: That is the ego-defence mechanism that Freud used to talk about. Freud used to talk about anxiety, psychic complexes and so on, but the man in the taxi who had butterflies in the stomach did have an accident which may have activated some old samskara somewhere, which turned into a full fear of getting into his taxi. But the whole thing was cleared so quickly; it was not deep-seated. Sometimes I believe these things just build up in a susceptible moment rather than in a susceptible person. They build up from a small bit of anxiety to a bigger anxiety on the basis of a vicious circle. You break that vicious circle anywhere and the whole thing just dissolves.

Swami Shankardevananda: The longer it is sustained the more difficult it is to break.

Swami Vivekananda: Each chakra has its own work to perform and if one centre is blocked or diseased, then another centre takes over its work. Because this work or function is being done by another centre, it becomes perverted. This happens a lot if a person is inhibited in swadhisthana chakra. Manipura will take over the work and then the sexual activities will be just a power play, competition and that sort of stuff – completely perverted.

This perversion also occurs if manipura chakra takes over the job of anahata. It is seen in do-gooders, those people who come and force you, almost by threats of violence, to let them help you.

Swami Shankardevananda: Another example is of those persons who get involved in a sexual encounter to fulfil the anahata centre, and of course they don't get that fulfilment.

This can lead to problems in marriage and all the things you were saying about perversion of normal function.

Swami Vivekananda: So the purpose of yoga is to balance the functioning of the chakras and at the same time to awaken the associated energies. Only then can we function as joyful, spontaneous human beings, without depression, psychosis or physical problems. Only when we balance and awaken all the chakras can life become meaningful.

Appendix

Table I

Chakra	Nature	No. of Petals	Colour	Physical Location	Kshetram	Physiological Relationship	Endocrine Relationship	Dhatu
Mooladhara	root lotus	four	deep red	perineum cervix	perineum cervix	sacro-coccygeal plexus	perineal body	bone
Swadhisthana	one's own abode	six	orange-red	coccyx	pubic bone	pelvic plexus	testes, ovaries	fat
Manipura	city of jewels	ten	yellow	behind navel	navel	solar plexus	adrenal glands	flesh
Anahata	source of unbroken sound	twelve	blue	behind heart	centre of chest	cardiac plexus	thymus gland	blood
Vishuddhi	centre of nectar	sixteen	purple	behind throat	pit of throat	pharyngeal & laryngeal plexus	thyroid gland	skin
Ajna	centre of command	two	clear or grey	centre of head	eyebrow centre	cavernous plexus	pineal gland	marrow
Sahasrara	thousand petalled lotus	thousand (infinite)	red or multi-coloured	crown of head	crown of head	hypothalamic pituitary axis	pituitary gland	semen (the essence of all others)

Table 2

Chakra	Prana Vayu	Kosha	Tattwa	Yantra	Tanmatra	Jnanendriya	Karmendriya
Mooladhara	apana	annamaya	prithvi (earth)	yellow square	smell	nose	anus
Swadhisthana	vyana	pranamaya	apas (water)	silver or white crescent moon	taste	tongue	sex organs, kidneys, urinary system
Manipura	samana	pranamaya	agni (fire)	red inverted triangle	sight	eyes	feet
Anahata	prana	manomaya	vayu (air)	smoky six-pointed star	touch	skin	hands
Vishuddhi	udana	vijnanamaya	akasha (ether)	white circle	hearing	ears	vocal chords
Ajna	all five	vijnanamaya	manas (mind)	clear or grey circle	mind	mind	mind
Sahasrara	beyond	anandamaya	beyond	beyond	beyond	beyond	beyond

Table 3

Chakra	Beeja	Loka	Devi	Deva	Animal	Yoni	Lingam	Granthi
Mooladhara	lam	bhu	Savitri or Dakini	Ganesha	elephant (airavata)	tripura	swayambhu	brahma
Swadhisthana	vam	bhuvah	Saraswati or Rakini	Vishnu	crocodile (makara)		dhumra	
Manipura	ram	swaha	Lakshmi or Lakini	Rudra	ram			
Anahata	yam	maha	Kali or Kakini	Isha	antelope	trikona	bana	vishnu
Vishuddhi	ham	janaha	Sakini	Sadashiva	white elephant			
Ajna	om	tapaha	Hakini	Paramshiva		trikona	itarakhya	rudra
Sahasrara		satyam	Shakti	Shiva				jyotir

Table 4

Chakra	Psychic Experience	Associated Powers
Mooladhara	Inverted red triangle with coiled serpent	Full knowledge of kundalini and the power to awaken it. Levitation, control of body, breath and mind; ability to produce any smell for one self or others; ever free from disease, cheerful and full of gladness.
Swadhisthana	Total darkness, unconsciousness	No fear of water, intuitional knowledge, knowledge of astral entities, power of tasting anything desired for oneself and others.
Manipura	Bright yellow lotus	Acquisition of hidden treasure, no fear of fire, knowledge of one's own body, freedom from disease, withdrawal of energy to sahasrara.
Anahata	Blue lotus upon a lake of stillness; golden flame in a dark cave	Control of prana and ability to heal others, cosmic love, inspired speech, gift of poetry, words bear fruit, intense concentration and complete control of the senses.
Vishuddhi	Feeling of cold and drops of nectar	Imperishability; full knowledge of the Vedas; knowledge of past, present, future; ability to exist without eating; power to read others' thoughts.
Ajna	Golden egg and spontaneous trance (unmani)	Able to enter another's body at will; becomes all-knowing and all-seeing; acquisition of all siddhis; realization of unity with Brahman (supreme consciousness).
Sahasrara	Luminous lingam surrounded by bright red or multicoloured lotus of infinite petals	Samadhi, total awakening, self-realization.

Glossary

Adwaita – non-dual; the concept of oneness.

Agni – fire.

Ajapa japa – meditational practice in which mantra is repeated in coordination with the ingoing and outgoing breath.

Ajna chakra – the psychic command centre situated in the midbrain.

Akasha – ethereal space, e.g. the inner space before the forehead known as chidakasha, the heart space known as hridayakasha, and the ether of outer space known as mahakasha.

Amaroli – yogic tantric practice in which the urine is used either internally or externally for mental and physical health.

Amrit – psychic nectar which is secreted in bindu and drops from lalana chakra to vishuddhi chakra, causing a feeling of blissful intoxication.

Amygdala – small area of grey matter in the temporal lobe, part of the limbic system.

Anahata chakra – the psychic centre related to the region of the heart.

Anandamaya kosha – blissful transcendental dimension; personal and collective unconscious.

Annamaya kosha – the physical body or level of existence; the conscious aspect.

Aorta – largest artery of the body, which takes oxygenated blood from the heart for distribution throughout the body.

Apana – vital energy in the lower part of the body, below the navel.

Asana – a steady and comfortable position of the body.

Ashram – yogic community where the inmates live and work under the guidance of a guru.

Astral body – the subtle, psychic body; finer than the physical body.

Atman – the pure self, beyond body and mind.

Atma shakti – spiritual force.

Aushadhi – awakening of spiritual power through the use of herbs or plant preparations.

Autogenic training – psychotherapy that works with the body and mind simultaneously; learning to manipulate the bodily functions through the mind.

Avatara – divine incarnation.

Avidya – ignorance.

Awareness – the faculty of conscious knowing.

Ballistocardiograph – machine which measures small body motions accompanying the movement of blood through the circulatory system.

Bandha – psychomuscular energy lock which redirects the flow of psychic energy in the body.

Beeja mantra – seed sound; a basic mantra or vibration which has its origin in trance consciousness.

Bhajan – devotional song.

Bhakta – one who follows the path of bhakti yoga.

Bhakti yoga – the yoga of devotion.

Bhrumadhya – the eyebrow centre; kshetram or contact point for ajna chakra.

Bindu – the psychic centre situated at the top back of the head; a point or drop which is the substratum of the whole cosmos, the seat of total creation.

Brahma – the divine spirit, Hindu god; creator of the universe.

Brahmacharya – control and redirection of sexual energy towards spiritual awakening.

Brahma granthi – knot of creation. Psychomuscular knot in the perineum which must be released for kundalini to enter and ascend through sushumna nadi. It symbolizes the blockage posed by material and sensual attachment.

Brahmamuhurta – the time between 4 and 6 a.m. This is the sattwic time of day, best suited to yogic sadhana.

Brahma nadi – the most subtle pranic flow within the sushumna nadi.

Brahmin – a member of the priestly caste.

Buddhi – the higher intelligence, concerned with real wisdom; the faculty of valuing things for the advancement of life and conscious awareness.

Causal body – the body you experience in deep sleep and in certain types of samadhi.

Central canal – the hollow passage within the spinal cord. In the subtle body, this is the path of sushumna nadi.

Cerebral cortex – grey matter on the surface of the brain responsible for higher mental function.

Cerebrospinal fluid – (CSF) cushion of fluid protecting the brain and spinal cord.

Cervical plexus – autonomic nerve plexus in the neck associated with vishuddhi chakra.

Cervix – the circular opening leading into the womb; seat of mooladhara chakra in the female body.

Chakra – literally 'wheel' or 'vortex'; major psychic centre in the subtle body, responsible for specific physiological and psychic functions.

Chela – disciple.

Chitta – mind; conscious, subconscious and unconscious levels of the brain.

Cingulate gyrus – a convolution of the brain, part of the limbic system.

Coccygeal plexus – small nerve plexus at the base of the spine behind the pelvic cavity, related to swadhisthana chakra.

Consciousness – the medium of universal and individual awareness.

Corpus callosum – fibres connecting the two hemispheres of the brain.

Deity – a form of divinity, a divine being having subordinate functions.

Devata – divine power.

Devi – a goddess; a manifestation of Shakti.

Dharana – concentration; continuity of mental process on one object or idea without leaving it.

Dharma – duty; code of harmonious living; spiritual path.

Dhumra lingam – smoky (obscured) lingam; the symbol of Shiva as manifest in mooladhara chakra.

Dhyana – meditation, in the sense of intense meditation for an extended period of time.

Diksha – initiation into spiritual life by a guru.

Dopamine – chemical involved in the excitatory systems of the brain.

Durga – Hindu goddess; a personification of Shakti, pictured riding upon a tiger, to whom personal ambition is rendered.

Dwaita – the philosophy of dualism in which man and God are considered to be separated.

ECG – electrocardiogram. Tracing of electric current produced by the heart.

EEG – electroencephalogram. Recording of electric current produced by nerve cells in the brain.

EMG – electromyography. Recording of electrical properties of muscles.

Epiglottis – flap of cartilage at the back of the throat which integrates the swallowing and breathing processes.

Frontal lobe – anterior portion of the brain containing the motor area.

Ganga – the river Ganges, the longest and most sacred river in India.

Gauss – measurement of intensity of a magnetic field.

Granthis – the three psychic knots on the sushumna nadi

436

which hinder the upward passage of kundalini – brahma granthi, vishnu granthi and rudra granthi.

Gunas – the three qualities or matter of prakriti – tamas, rajas and sattwa.

Guru – literally, 'dispeller of darkness', the spiritual master or teacher.

Guru chakra – another name for ajna chakra, the eye of intuition; through which the inner guru's guidance manifests.

Hatha yoga – a system of yoga which specially deals with practices for bodily purification.

Hippocampus – an elevation on the floor of the lateral ventricle, part of the limbic system.

Hiranyagarbha – the golden egg; womb of consciousness, the seat of supreme awareness in the crown of the head; known as sahasrara chakra.

Hridayakasha – the etheric space visualized within the heart; the heart space.

Hypometabolic state – state of lowered metabolism, for example, decrease in respiratory, circulatory and secretory rates.

Hypothalamus – portion of the brain that integrates temperature, sleep, food intake, development of sexual characteristics and endocrine activity.

Ida – major psychic channel which conducts manas shakti, mental energy, located on the left side of the psychic body; the 'tha' of hatha yoga.

Indriyas – sense organs.

Ishta devata – one's personal symbol, form or vision of God.

Itarakhya lingam – symbol of Shiva in ajna chakra.

Jalandhara bandha – chin lock. It compresses the prana in the trunk of the body and thereby helps to control psychic energy.

Japa – repetition of a mantra until it becomes the spontaneous form of your conscious awareness.

Jivanmukta – liberated soul, one who has attained self-realization or moksha.

437

Jivatma – the individual soul

Jnana yoga – path of yoga concerned directly with knowledge, self-awareness.

Jnanendriyas – the organs of knowledge or sensory organs such eyes, ears, skin, etc.

Jyotir lingam – the symbol of Shiva in sahasrara chakra. This lingam is of pure white light, symbolizing illumined astral consciousness.

Kabbalah – text dealing with the esoteric mysticism of the Judaic religion.

Kali – form of Shakti who arouses terror and fear, destroyer of ignorance in her devotees.

Karma – actions, work, the inherent subconscious imprints which make a person act.

Karma yoga – action performed unselfishly, for the welfare of others and the fulfilment of dharma.

Karmendriyas – organs of action, e.g. feet, hands, vocal chords, anus, sexual organs, etc.

Kevala kumbhaka – spontaneous breath retention.

Khechari mudra – mudra of hatha yoga and tantra, in which the tongue passes back into the pharynx to stimulate the flow of amrit from lalana chakra, activating vishuddhi.

Kirtan – repetition of mantras set to music.

Koshas – sheaths or bodies.

Kshetram – contact centres or trigger points for the chakras, located in the front of the body.

Kumbhaka – breath retention.

Kurma nadi – (tortoise nadi) associated with vishuddhi chakra. Its control brings the ability to live without physical sustenance.

Lalana chakra – minor chakra in the region of the back wall of the pharynx, where amrit is stored from bindu and released to vishuddhi.

Limbic system – group of structures in the brain associated with certain aspects of emotion and behaviour.

Lingam – symbol representing Lord Shiva; the male aspect of creation; symbol of the astral body.

Loka – world, dimension or plane of existence or consciousness.

Lord Shiva – archetypal renunciate and yogi who dwells in meditation high in the Himalayas; Hindu god; destroyer of the universe.

Madya – wine; also refers to spiritual intoxication resulting from drinking the nectar of immortality, amrit.

Mahakala – great or endless time.

Mahatma – great soul.

Maithuna – literally 'sacrifice', sexual union with a spiritual purpose.

Mala – a rosary-like string of beads used in meditational practices.

Manas – one aspect of mind; the mental faculty of comparing, classifying and reasoning.

Manas shakti – mental force.

Mandala – tantric diagram used for meditation.

Manic depression – psychosis marked by severe mood swings.

Manomaya kosha – mental dimension; conscious and subconscious aspects.

Mantra – a sound or a series of sounds having physical, psychic or spiritual potency when recited in a certain prescribed manner.

Marga – path.

Matra – unit of measurement.

Maya – principle of illusion.

Moksha – liberation from the cycle of births and deaths.

Moola bandha – practice of stimulating mooladhara chakra for the awakening of kundalini. It is practised by contracting the perineum in males, or the cervix in females.

Mudra – a psychic attitude often expressed by a physical gesture, movement or posture, which affects the flow of psychic energy in the body.

Nada – sound, especially inner sound.

Nada yoga – the yoga of subtle sound.

Nadis – psychic channels for the distribution of prana in the astral body.

439

Neti – cleansing technique in which warm saline water is passed through the nasal passages; one of the shatkarmas.

Nirvana – enlightenment, samadhi; harmony between the individual consciousness and the universal consciousness.

Nivritti marga – the path leading back in towards the source from which we have first come.

Nuclear fission – the process of extracting energy from matter by splitting the atom.

Om – the underlying sound of creation; the mantra from which all others have originated.

Paranoia – chronic mental disorder characterized by delusions or hallucinations.

Parasympathetic nervous system – division of the autonomic (involuntary) nervous system concerned with restorative processes and relaxation of the body and mind.

Pashu – the instinctual or animal aspect of man's nature.

Pineal gland – small pinecone shaped endocrine gland in the midbrain directly behind the eyebrow centre; the physical correlate of ajna chakra.

Pingala – the conductor and channel of prana shakti or vital force, located on the right side of the psychic body; the 'ha' of hatha yoga.

Prakriti – the basic substance or principle of the entire phenomenal or manifest world, composed of the three gunas (triguna) or attributes.

Prana – the life force in the body; bioenergy in general; the vital energy which operates in the region of the heart and lungs; the psychic equivalent of the physical breath.

Pranamaya kosha – energy dimension; conscious aspect.

Prana shakti – pranic or vital force.

Pranayama – yogic practice of manipulating and controlling the flow of prana in the subtle body by controlling the respiratory process.

Pranotthana – the impulses which pass up sushumna nadi to the higher centres of the brain when a chakra is transiently aroused. These impulses purify the sushumna passage in preparation for sustained kundalini awakening.

Pravritti marga – the path of expansion outwards into greater and greater manifestation, further away from the source of our origin.

Psi – psychic phenomena.

Psyche – the total mental aspect of man.

Psychosis – major mental disorder characterized by loss of contact with reality.

Purusha – consciousness; the spirit or pure self.

Raja yoga – eightfold path of yoga formulated by Patanjali. It begins with mental stability and proceeds to the highest state of samadhi.

Rajo guna – the guna of prakriti characterized by restlessness, activity and ambition.

Rakshasa – demon; negative or self-defeating force.

Reticular activating system (RAS) – that part of the brainstem especially concerned with arousal from sleep and maintenance of the alert, waking state of consciousness.

Rishi – seer or sage; who realizes the truth directly.

Rolfing – structural integration. Deep massage to rebalance the body structures.

Rudra granthi – (also known as Shiva granthi) the knot of Shiva. This is the psychic knot within ajna chakra, which symbolizes attachment to siddhis or higher mental attributes which must be transcended before full awakening of kundalini can occur.

Sacral plexus – nerve plexus in the back wall of the pelvis associated with swadhisthana and mooladhara chakras, and responsible for the functioning of the urinary and reproductive systems.

Sadhaka – a student of spiritual practices.

Sadhana – spiritual discipline or practice.

Sahajoli – the form of vajroli mudra practised by women; contraction of the urethra sphincter muscle.

Sahasrara – the thousand-petalled lotus or chakra manifesting at the top of the head; the highest psychic centre; the threshold between psychic and spiritual realms which contains all the chakras below it.

441

Samadhi – state of being above mortal existence; all-knowing and all-pervading state of being; the fulfilment of meditation; state of union with the object of meditation and the universal consciousness.

Samana – vital energy operating in the region of the navel.

Samkhya – the ancient scientific philosophy of India which classifies all that is known without reference to an external power (God).

Samskara – past mental impression; archetype.

Sandhya – ritual worship conducted at dawn, at noon and evening.

Sangha – associations, company, acquaintances.

Sankalpa – spiritual resolve.

Sankalpa shakti – the power of will.

Sannyasa – total renunciation, perfect dedication.

Satsang – spiritual instruction, discussion and guidance from an illumined being or guru.

Sattwa – one of the three gunas of prakriti; the pure or equilibrated state of mind or nature.

Saundarya Lahari – tantric prayer of Adi Shankaracharya.

Schizophrenia – a severe mental/emotional disturbance characterized by hallucinations and disconnection between thought, feelings and actions.

Schumann resonance – magnetic resonance of the earth – 7 cycles/second.

Shabda – sound or word; the materially creative principle.

Shaivism – philosophy of Shiva worship, perhaps the most ancient faith in the world.

Shakti – power, energy; the feminine aspect of creation; the force expressed through all manifested phenomena.

Shambhavi mudra – mudra named after Shambhu (Shiva); focusing the eyes on bhrumadhya.

Shankhaprakshalana – a method of cleansing the entire alimentary canal.

Shanti – peace.

Shastras – scriptures.

Shatkarmas – the six cleansing techniques of hatha yoga.

Shivalingam – oval-shaped stone which is the symbol of Shiva, consciousness or the astral body.

Shoonya, shoonyata – the state of absolute nothingness or void; mental vacuum.

Shuddhi – purification.

Siddha – adept, yogi; one who has control over nature, matter and the mind.

Siddhi – perfection; one of the eight occult powers; a psychic power associated with awakening of chakra functions.

Solar plexus – intersection of a group of nerves in the abdominal region; the physical manifestation of manipura.

Soma – amrit; a plant used by the rishis of ancient India for the purpose of spiritual awakening and immortality.

Sushumna nadi – the most important psychic passageway. It flows in the central canal within the spinal cord.

Swadhisthana chakra – the psychic centre corresponding to the coccyx or pubic region.

Swami – literally 'one who is master of his own mind'; sannyasin disciple initiated into sannyasa by a guru; one who has renounced mundane experiences as goals in life.

Swara yoga – the science of the breath cycle.

Swayambhu – self-created.

Sympathetic nervous system – the division of the autonomic (involuntary) nervous system responsible for maintaining physical activity of the organs and expenditure of energy.

Tamas – darkness; inertia; one of the three gunas of prakriti.

Tanmatra – the sense activities – sight, hearing, taste, touch, smell, and also inner intuitive perception via the subtle organ of mind, which is the sixth sense.

Tantra – the ancient science which uses specific techniques to expand and liberate the consciousness from its limitations.

Tantra shastra – scriptures of the tantric tradition devoted to spiritual techniques, in the form of a dialogue between Shiva and Shakti. These texts outline a code of living which includes ritual, worship, discipline, meditation and the attainment of powers.

443

Tapasya – the practice of austerity; conditioning of the body for the removal of impurities and for overcoming the deficiencies and weaknesses of the body, mind and senses.

Tattwa – elemental nature or quality, e.g., fire, water, air, earth, ether.

Thalamus – area in the brain which receives most sensory stimuli and integrates most incoming and outgoing information. Also the centre for appreciation of pain, touch and temperature.

Trataka – the meditational or hatha yoga technique which involves steadily gazing at an object.

Trishula – trident; three pronged implement held by Lord Shiva and carried by many holy men and renunciates. The three prongs symbolize the three main nadis.

Udana – the vital energy operating above the throat.

Uddiyana bandha – literally 'flying upward'; a yogic practice of pranic manipulation utilizing the abdominal muscles and organs.

Vairagya – non-attachment; state where one is calm and tranquil in the midst of the tumultuous events of the world.

Vajra nadi – the nadi which connects the expression of sexual energy with the brain and is concerned with the flow of ojas, the highest form of energy in the human body which is concentrated in the semen.

Vajroli mudra – contraction of vajra nadi; contraction of urethra sphincter muscle in men.

Vasana – the desires that are the driving force behind every thought and action in life.

Vayu – air.

Vedanta – the ultimate philosophy of the Vedas.

Vedas – the oldest known religious texts of the Aryans, written more than 5000 years ago.

Ventricles – cavities in the brain where the CSF is formed.

Vijnanamaya kosha – intuitive or astral dimension; subconscious and unconscious aspects.

Vishnu – Hindu god; preserver of the universe.

Vishuddhi chakra – the psychic centre located in the throat region.

Vritti – a modification arising in consciousness, likened to the circular wave pattern emanating when a stone is dropped into a still pool of water.

Vyana – vital energy which pervades the whole body.

Yantra – a symbolic design used for concentration and meditation; the visual form of a mantra.

Yoga – union; the methods and practices leading to union of individual human consciousness with the divine principle or cosmic consciousness.

Yoga nidra – psychic sleep; a yogic practice in which one can raise oneself from the mundane state of body consciousness.

Yoga Sutras – text written by Patanjali, delineating the eightfold path of raja yoga, the systematic path of meditation which culminates in the samadhi experience.

References

Chapter 40: Kundalini, Fact not Fiction

[1] Ostrander, S. & Schroeder, L., *PSI – Psychic Discoveries Behind the Iron Curtain*, Abacus, London, 1977, pp. 88–89.

[2] Ibid, pp. 88–99.

[3] Ibid, p. 398.

[4] Ibid, p. 237.

[5] Yaeger, R., 'The Effect of Kundalini Yoga on Onion Root Cells Mitosis', Unpublished paper, California State College, 1979. Quoted in *Kundalini, Evolution and Enlightenment*, White, J. (Ed.), Anchor-Doubleday, New York, 1979, pp. 266–267.

Chapter 41: Defining the Nadis

[1] Jung, G.G., 'Mysterium Coniunctionis', *Collected Works*, Bollingen Series, Princeton University Press, 14: xvi–xvii.

[2] Deikman, A.J., 'Bimodal Consciousness', *Archives of Gen. Psychiat.*, 25: 481–9, Dec. 1971.

Chapter 42: Controlling the Nadis and the Brain

[1] Kinsbourne, M., 'Sad Hemisphere, Happy Hemisphere', *Psychology Today*, May 1981.

[2] Gardener, H., 'How the Split Brain Gets a Joke', *Psychology Today*, Feb. 1981.

[3] Black, M., 'Brain Flash: The Physiology of Inspiration', *Science Digest*, August, 1982.

[4] Ingber, D., 'Brain Breathing', *Science Digest*, June 1981.

[5] Kinsbourne, op. cit.

[6] Breathing Cycles Linked to Hemisphere Dominance', *Brain Mind Bulletin*, 8 (3), Jan. 3, 1983.

[7] Ibid.

Chapter 43: Evidence for the Existence of Nadis

[1] Motoyama, H., 'Chakra, Nadi of Yoga and Meridians, Points of Acupuncture', *Instit. of Religious Psych.*, Oct. 1972.

[2] Motoyama, H., 'The Mechanism Through Which Paranormal Phenomena Take Place', *Religion & Parapsych.*, 1975, 2.

[3] Motoyama, H., 'Do Meridians Exist, and What are They Like', *Research for Religion & Parapsych.*, 1 (1), Feb. 1975.

[4] Motoyama, H., 'A Psychophysiological Study of Yoga', *Institute for Rel. Psych.*, 1976, 6.

[5] Motoyama, H., 'An Electrophysiological Study of Prana (ki)', *Res. for Rel. & Parapsych.*, 4 (1), Nov. 1978.

[6] Motoyama, H., 'Yoga and Oriental Medicine', *Res. for Rel. & Parapsych.* 5 (1), March, 1979.

[7] Motoyama, H., 'Electrophysiological and Preliminary Biochemical Studies of Skin Properties in Relation to the Acupuncture Meridian', *Res. for Rel. & Parapsych.*, 6 (2), June, 1980.

[8] Motoyama, H., 'A Biophysical Elucidation of the Meridian and Ki-Energy', *Res. for Rel. & Parapsych.*, 7 (1), August, 1981.

[9] Motoyama, H., 'The Meridian Exercises', *Res. for Rel. & Parapsych.*, 8 (1), Oct. 1982.

[10] Riga, I.N., 'Neuro-Reflex Syndrome of Unilateral Nasal Obstruction', *Revue D'Oto-Neuro-Ophthalmologic*, 29 (6): 1–11, 1957.

Chapter 44: Neurophysiology of the Chakras

[1] MacLean, P., *A Triune Concept of the Brain and Behaviour*, Toronto Press, Toronto, 1973.

[2] Loye, D., 'Foresight Saga', *Omni*, Sept. 1982.

Chapter 45: Evidence for the Existence of Chakras

[1] Motoyama, H., 'A Psychophysiological Study of Yoga', *Instit. for Religious Psychol.*, Tokyo, 1976, 6.

[2] Motoyama, H., 'The Mechanism through Which Paranormal Phenomena Take Place', *Instit. for Religion & Parapsych.*, Tokyo, 1975, 2.

[3] Motoyama, H., 'An Electrophysiological Study of Prana (Ki)', *Res. Religion & Parapsych.*, 4 (1), 1978.

[4] Motoyama, H., *Theories of the Chakras: Bridge to Higher Consciousness*, Quest, Illinois, 1981, pp. 271–279.

[5] Ibid, p. 275.

[6] Ibid, p. 275.

[7] Electronic Evidence of Auras, Chakras in UCLA Study,' *Brain Mind Bulletin*, 3 (9), March 20, 1978.

[8] Vision Training Provides Window to Brain Changes', *Brain Mind Bulletin*, 7 (13), Oct. 25, 1982.

[9] Ibid.

Chapter 46: The Cosmic Trigger

[1] Bentov, I., *Stalking the Wild Pendulum*, Fontana, Great Britain, 1979, p. 174.

[2] Bentov, I., 'Micromotion of the Body as a Factor in the Development of the Nervous System', Appendix A in *Kundalini – Psychosis or Transcendence?* by Lee Sannella, San Francisco, 1976, pp. 71–92.

[3] Ibid, p. 73.

[4] Ibid, p. 73.

[5] Satyamurti, S., 'Pranic Mind Field', *Yoga*, 15(6); 29–37, June, 1977.

[6] Bentov, I., op. cit., p. 180.

[7] Black, M., 'Brain Flash: The Physiology of Inspiration', *Science Digest*, August, 1982.

[8] Post, R.M., 'Kindling: A Useful Analogy for Brain Reaction', *Psychology Today*, August, 1980, p. 92.

[9] Gaito, J., *Psychological Bulletin*, 83: 1097–1109.

[10] Post, op. cit.

[11] Ferguson, M., 'Kindling and Kundalini Effects', *Brain Mind Bulletin*, 2 (7), Feb, 21, 1977.

[12] Ibid.

[13] Wallace, R.K. and Benson, H., 'The Physiology of Meditation', *Scient. Am.* 226 (2): 84–90, Feb, 1972.

[14] Anand, B.K., Chhina, G.S., Singh, B. 'Some Aspects of EEG Studies in Yoga', *EEG & Clin, Neurophys.*, 13: 452–456, 1961.

[15] Kasamatsu, A. & Hirai, T., 'An EEG Study of the Zen Meditation', *Folia Psychiat. Et Neurologica Japonica*, 20 (4): 315–336, 1966.

[16] Das, N. & Gastaut, H., 'Variations de l'activite electrique du cerveau, du coeur, et des muscles squelettiques au course de la meditation et de l'extase yoguie.' *EEG & Clin, Neurophys.* Sup. 6, 211–219, 1955.

[17] Banquet, J.P., 'Spectral Analysis of the EEG in Meditation', *EEG & Clin Neurophys.*, 35: 143–151, 1973.

[18] Ibid, p. 150.

[19] Levine, H., Herbert, J.R., Haynes, C.T., Strobel, U., 'EEG Coherence during the TM Technique'. In *Sci. Res. on the T.M. Program, Collected Papers*, Vol. I, (Ed) D. W. Orme-Johnson & J.T. Farrow. Pp. 187–207, Meru Press: Germany.

[20] Corby, J.C., Roth, W.T., Zarcone, V.P., Kopell, B.S., 'Psychophysiological Correlates of the Practice of Tantric Yoga Meditation', *Arch. Gen. Psychiatry*, 35: 571–577, May, 1978.

[21] Corby, J.C., 'Reply to Dr Elson', *Arch. Gen. Psychiatry*, 36: 606. 1979.

Chapter 47: Cross-Cultural Evidence

[1] White, J. (ed.), Kundalini, *Evolution and Enlightenment*, Archer, New York, 1979, p. 17.

[2] Ludwig, A.M., 'Altered States of Consciousness', in *Altered States of Consciousness*, Tart, C.T. (ed), Doubleday Anchor, New York, 1972, pp. 11–22.

[3] Hooper, J., 'Mind Tripping', *Omni*, Oct. 1982.

[4] Katz, R., 'Education for Transcendence: Lessons from the !Kung Zhu Jwasi', *F Transp. Psychol.*, Nov. 2, 1973.

[5] Hooper, op. cit.

[6] Luk, C., *The Secrets of Chinese Meditation*, Samuel Weiser Inc., New York, 1972.

[7] Narayananda, Swami, *The Primal Power in Man*, Prasad & Co., Rishikesh, India, 1960.

[8] *Interior Castle*, (tr. & ed.) E. Allison Peers, Doubleday & Co., New York, 1961, pp. 77–78.

Index of Practices

A Agnisar Kriya (activating the digestive fire) 232
Agochari Mudra (Nasikagra Drishti) 225
Ajapa Japa meditation 241
Ajna chakra practices 211
Amrit Pan (the quaffing of nectar) 308
Anahata chakra practices 238
Anahata chakra and kshetram location 239
Anahata purification 239
Anuloma Viloma Pranayama
(the coming and going breath) 213
Ashwini Mudra (horse gesture) 227

B Beeja Mantra Sanchalana
(conducting the seed sound) 272
Bhadrasana (gracious pose) 208
Bhramari Pranayama (humming bee breath) 240
Bindu practices 251

C Chakra Anusandhana (discovery of the chakras) 286
Chakra Bhedan (piercing the chakras) 309
Chakra meditation 260
Chakra meditation with musical scale 263
Chakra Yoga Nidra 266
Chaturtha Pranayama (fourth pranayama) 265

451

D   Dhyana (meditation) 315
Drawing the chakras 275

J   Jalandhara Bandha (throat lock) 246

K   Khechari Mudra (tongue lock) 247
Kriya Yoga practices 284

L   Linga Sanchalana (astral conduction) 313

M   Maha Bheda Mudra (great piercing attitude) 295
Maha Mudra (great attitude) 291
Manduki Mudra (frog attitude) 299
Manipura chakra practices 229
Manipura chakra and kshetram location 230
Manipura purification 230
Meditation – entering the heart space 242
Moola Bandha (perineal contraction) 222
Mooladhara chakra location 221
Mooladhara chakra practices 219
Moorchha Pranayama (swooning or fainting breath) 252
Musical chakra meditation 263

N   Nada Sanchalana
(conducting the sound consciousness) 287
Nasikagra Drishti (nose tip gazing) 224
Nauli (abdominal massaging) 233
Naumukhi Mudra (closing the nine gates) 302

P   Padmasana (lotus pose) 206
Pawan Sanchalana
(conducting the breath consciousness) 289
Perception of subtle inner sound 254
Prana Ahuti (infusing the divine prana) 311
Prana Shuddhi (purifying breath) 213

S Sahajoli Mudra (spontaneous psychic attitude)...............228
Shabda Sanchalana
(conducting the word consciousness) 290
Shakti Chalini (conduction of the thought force).............304
Shambhavi (Parvati's lotus)...306
Shambhavi Mudra with Om chanting 217
Shanmukhi Mudra (closing the seven gates)...................256
Siddha Yoni Asana (accomplished pose for women)........205
Siddhasana (accomplished pose for men).......................203
Sushumna Darshan
(inner visualization of the chakras) 310
Swadhisthana chakra location 227
Swadhisthana chakra practices 226
Swadhisthana kshetram location 227
Swana Pranayama (panting breath)................................231
Swaroopa Darshan (the vision of your Self)....................313

T Tadan Kriya (beating the kundalini)...............................300
Trataka (concentrated gazing)..214

U Uddiyana Bandha (abdominal contraction)....................232
Ujjayi Pranayama (psychic breath) 247
Union of prana and apana 237
Unmani mudra (attitude of mindlessness) 271
Utthan (raising the kundalini)...312
Utthanpadasana (stretched leg pose) 207

V Vajroli Mudra (thunderbolt attitude)..............................228
Vajroli/sahajoli mudra with bindu awareness..................253
Vipareeta Karani Asana (inverted pose) 249
Vipareeta Karani Mudra (attitude of inversion)...............285
Vishuddhi chakra practices...245
Vishuddhi chakra and kshetram location
and purification 248

Notes

Praise for Deon Meyer

"Mr. Meyer, the leading thriller writer in his native country, traffics in crime-novel situations familiar the world over: drunken cops, charming robbers, dangerous murderers, sudden violence—and sometimes, issues of race. Mr. Meyer's South Africa, however, is unique. His books, translated from Afrikaans, are usually set in the Cape Town region, where mountains spectacularly meet the sea on the Horn of Africa. Amid these vistas his detective confronts his own—and his country's—tortured past and the legacy of Apartheid."   —*Wall Street Journal*

"Meyer has a fine eye for people and places . . . Meyer is a serious writer who richly deserves the international reputation he has built."
—*Washington Post*

"Meyer's thrillers . . . well understand the need to maintain momentum: mixing and matching multiple viewpoints, switching off between characters and portraying his native country as one in a perpetual state of flux and angst."   —*Los Angeles Times*

"Deon Meyer deserves his international reputation."
—Thomas Perry

"With Deon Meyer you can't go wrong. He's a writer whose work I admire, wait for and then devour."   —Michael Connelly

"I love Meyer . . . The problem with having Meyer on your nightstand is that you don't get any sleep. So if I look like hell, it's Meyer's fault. The guy owes me."   —Don Winslow

"Meyer has few equals when it comes to combining biting social critique and riveting action scenes."   —*Booklist*

"A writer not to be missed."   —*Publishers Weekly*

COBRA

Also by Deon Meyer

Dead Before Dying
Dead at Daybreak
Heart of the Hunter
Devil's Peak
Blood Safari
Thirteen Hours
Trackers
Seven Days
Icarus

DEON
MEYER

COBRA

Translated from Afrikaans
by K. L. Seegers

Grove Press
New York

First published in Great Britain in 2014 by Hodder & Stoughton
An Hachette UK Company
Originally published in Afrikaans in 2013 as *Kobra* by
Human & Rousseau

Printed in the United States of America

ISBN 978-0-8021-2422-7
eISBN 978-0-8021-9191-5

Grove Press
an imprint of Grove Atlantic
154 West 14th Street
New York, NY 10011

Distributed by Publishers Group West

groveatlantic.com

15 16 17 18 19   10 9 8 7 6 5 4 3 2 1

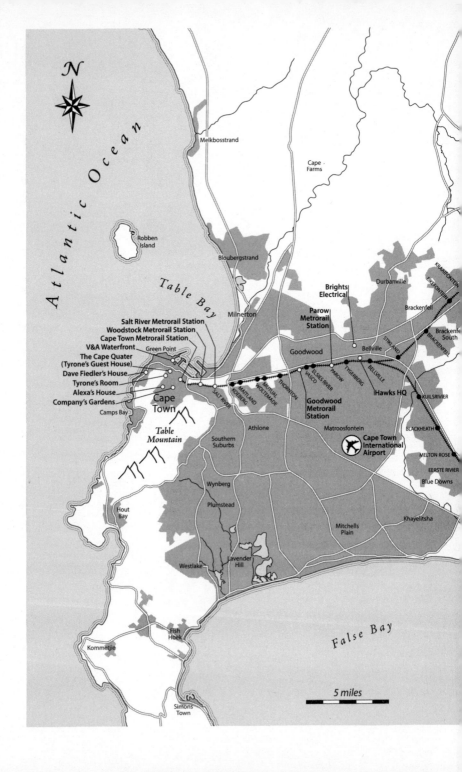

I

The rain drummed down on the corrugated iron roof. Ten past eight in the morning. Captain Benny Griessel clicked open his homicide briefcase on the wall of the wide, high veranda, removed the shoe protectors first, then the thin, transparent latex gloves. He pulled them on, vaguely aware of respectful eyes on him, the uniforms and two station detectives who sheltered in the open garage beyond the curtain of rain. His anxiety and fatigue faded, his focus was on what awaited him here in this big old house.

The heavy front door stood open. He approached the threshold. The grey morning cast the entry hall into deep dusk, the second victim appeared as a dark, shapeless mass. He stood still for a moment, holding his breath. Considering the advice of Doc Barkhuizen: *Don't internalise. Distance yourself.*

What did that mean, now?

He looked for a light switch, found it inside, just beside the door jamb. He clicked it on. High up against the baroque ceiling a chandelier shone white and bright. It did nothing to dispel the chill. The man lay outstretched on the gleaming oak floor, four metres from the door. Black shoes, black trousers, white shirt, light grey tie, top button undone. Arms outstretched, a pistol gripped in the right hand. Mid-thirties. Lean.

Griessel warily stepped closer. He saw the bullet wound in the forehead, diagonally above the left eye. A thin streak of blood, now almost black, ran down to the right. Under the head, which was turned to the left, a puddle, thicker, saucer-sized. Exit wound.

He felt relief at the simplicity of this death, the swiftness of it.

He sighed, long and slow, trying to rid his body of this tension.

It didn't work.

He surveyed the hallway. On an antique table to the right was a light blue vase filled with a green and white mass of fresh arum lilies. On the opposite side, against the left-hand wall, was a hat stand beside an umbrella rack. Six old-fashioned portraits hung on the wall in heavy oval frames. Dignified men and women stared out of each one.

And at the back, deeper in, a sitting room opened out between the two pillars.

He made his calculations from the position of the body, the probable trajectory of the shot, so he could walk where it would least disturb the invisible blood spray and spatter. He stepped around and crouched down beside the pistol, saw the Glock emblem on the barrel, and after it *17 Gen Austria 9x19*.

Griessel sniffed the barrel. It hadn't been fired. He stood up.

Most likely the shooter had stood in the doorway, the victim more or less in the centre of the hallway. If the murder weapon was a pistol, the casing would have been ejected to the right. He searched for it, didn't find it. Perhaps he had used a revolver. Perhaps it had bounced off the wall, lay under the victim. Perhaps the shooter had picked it up.

The exit wound meant the bullet would have hit the wall somewhere. He drew an imaginary line that led him to the sitting room.

He trod carefully, making a wide detour around the corpse, past the pillars, where he picked up the faint scent of burnt wood. The hall chandelier illuminated only a small track in the spacious room and it cast a long Griessel shadow, sending him in search of another light switch. He found three in a row, just behind the pillar, pressed them one by one, and turned around. Soft lighting. Thick wooden beams in the ceiling. Shelves against the walls, filled with leather-bound books. A huge Persian carpet, silver and blue, giant sofas and easy chairs arranged in two separate seating areas. Coffee tables, gleaming, golden wood. Too many lamps and vases, combined with the fussy wallpaper, all intended to create an impression of old-world elegance. In the centre, stately and impressive, was the great hearth, the embers cold. And to the right, just visible behind a dark blue chair – the shoes and trouser legs of the third victim. In the background, on the stark white passage wall, he saw a bright fan of blood spray, like a cheerful, surreal artwork.

Griessel noted the similarities, and unease settled on his heart.

The body in the passage had the same military haircut, the same build – broad-shouldered, with a lean fitness – as the one in the hallway. Also the same black shoes, black trousers, and white shirt. Another bloodied Glock beside a ruined hand. Only the tie was missing this time.

Another head wound, between the temple and the right eye. But the first bullet must have hit the hand – two joints of the finger lay rolled against the white-painted skirting board.

And then he spotted the two shells shining dully on the edge of the carpet in the sitting room. The shooter's, had to be, lying there within ten centimetres of each other. His mind started to play its old tricks; he heard and smelled exactly how it had all happened. The murderer was a shadow slipping through this space, pistol stretched in front of him, he saw the man in the passage, two shots, the hand was a small scarlet explosion. The intense agony, short-lived, before death, no time for fear, just the short silent scream into eternity.

Griessel let out an exclamation, deliberate and loud over the drumming rain, to suppress it all. He hadn't had enough sleep. The fucking stress of the past weeks. He must pull himself together now.

He walked carefully around the body, crouched down beside the pistol. Exactly the same as the other one. *Glock 17 Gen 4*. He sniffed. No smell of cordite.

He stood up, eyes scanning around him, and further down the passage he found the two holes in the right-hand wall.

He had to tread carefully, because the body, the finger, the pistol, and the blood covered the full width of the passage. He hopped from one foot to the other until he was over it. Bent down at the holes. Both bullets were there, buried deep in the plaster. That would help.

Then he went in search of the fourth victim.

The first room, up the passage to the left, had the door open, curtains drawn. He switched on the light. There was a suitcase on the double bed, open. A blue-grey tie, and an empty black shoulder holster lay on the dressing table. In the en-suite bathroom, shaving material and a toothbrush were neatly arranged. Apart from that, nothing.

He walked to the second bedroom. Tidy. Two single beds. A small travelling case at the foot of one. A jacket on a hanger, hooked into the handle of the dark brown wardrobe. A toilet bag hung from a rail in the adjoining bathroom.

He walked out into the passage again, opened a door to the right. It was a big bathroom, gleaming white, with a bath on ball-and-claw feet, a washbasin on a marble slab, bidet, and a toilet.

The next two bedrooms were empty, with no sign of occupation. The last one was right at the end, on the left. The door was open, the room inside almost in darkness. He switched on the light.

Outside the rain stopped abruptly, leaving an eerie silence.

It was a large room. In chaos. The loose carpet lay rucked up. The double bed was askew, the mattress and bedding thrown off. The chair in front of a beautiful antique desk lay on its back, the standard lamp on the desktop was overturned, all the drawers were pulled open. And the doors of the massive wardrobe stood wide too, a pile of clothes on the ground. A large suitcase in the corner, upside down.

'Benna!' A sharp interruption to the softly dripping silence, from the front door, startling him.

Captain Vaughn Cupido had arrived.

'I'm coming,' he shouted back. His voice echoed hoarsely through the huge empty house.

Cupido stood on the threshold in his long black coat, a new piece he confessed he had picked up 'at a factory shop in Salt River, for a song, pappie; classic detective style, the Hawk in Winter, I'm telling you'.

And as Griessel carefully negotiated the hall, he was suddenly conscious of his own crumpled trousers. The thick blue jersey and jacket hid his shirt at least. Yesterday's clothes. And Cupido wouldn't miss that.

'Howzit, Benna. How many are there?'

Griessel walked out onto the veranda, began taking off the gloves. The dark mass of clouds was gone; the sun was trying to break through, making him blink. The view was suddenly breathtaking, the Franschhoek valley unveiled in front of him.

'One of the farm workers is lying in the vineyard. There's been too much rain; I haven't been able to get there. And there are two inside.'

'*Jissis* . . .' Then Cupido looked sharply at him. 'You OK, Benna?'

He knew his eyes were bloodshot, and he hadn't shaved. He nodded. 'Just slept badly,' Benny Griessel lied. 'Let's go and look at the one out there.'

★ ★ ★

The first victim lay on his back, between two rows of vines – a coloured man, dressed in what looked like a dark red uniform with a silver trim. Cupido and Griessel stood on the edge of the lawn, just four metres from the body. They could see the large exit wound between the eyes.

'He was shot from behind. And dragged over there.' Griessel pointed at the two faint, washed-out furrows that ended at the man's heels. 'And these are the footprints of the labourer who found him lying here this morning.'

'It's a brother,' said Cupido, and then, accusingly, 'In a slave outfit.'

'He works at the guesthouse. According to the—'

'This is a guesthouse? I thought it was a wine farm.'

'It's a wine farm with a guesthouse—'

'As if they don't make enough money. You're sure you're all right?'

'I'm fine, Vaughn.'

'Did you go home last night?'

'No. According to the—'

'Was there a case I don't know about?'

'Vaughn, I worked late. You know how the admin piles up. And then I fell asleep.' He hoped Cupido would just let it go.

'In your office?' Sceptical.

'Yes. The station—'

'So that's how you got the call so early?'

'That's right. According to the station detectives, around about nine last night this worker was supposed to come to top up the firewood and check that all the guests were happy. When he didn't come home, his wife thought he must have gone out on the town . . . Then the morning shift found him here. Then they saw the other one in the hallway. The trouble is, they say there were three.'

'Now you're losing me, man. I thought there were three?'

'There were three guests. Inside.'

'So there shoulda been four victims?'

'Yes . . .'

'So where's number four?'

'That's the big question. The thing is . . . We have three head shots, Vaughn. The other one in there was shot through his pistol hand *and* in the head, the two shells are lying this close together . . .'

It took a second for Cupido to grasp. '*Jissis*, Benna. Double tap.'

'On a moving target . . .'

Cupido merely shook his head in awe. 'That's sharp shooting, pappie . . .'

'What bothers me most: the last bedroom shows signs of a fight. Now why would a man who can shoot like that wrestle with a person?'

Cupido looked at Griessel anxiously. 'You thinking what I'm thinking?'

Benny didn't want to say it, the implications were serious. He merely nodded.

'There's a newspaper photographer at the gate, Benna.'

'Fuck,' said Griessel.

'Kidnapping. When last did we see *that*?'

'There's more trouble. Both the men inside look like . . . If I think of their build, hair, the clothes, both carrying Glock Seventeens. I think they are law enforcement. Or military, or Spooks . . .'

'You're kidding me.'

'And a man who shoots like that, faultless . . . He's had training. Task force, Special Forces, Intelligence . . . Something like that. A pro.'

Cupido turned around and stared at the house. 'Shit. Trouble, Benna. Big trouble.'

Griessel sighed. 'That's right.'

'We'll have to get moving, pappie.'

'I'll have to call the Giraffe. They'll have to manage the press.'

They didn't move. They stood side by side, heads bowed – Cupido a head taller than the stocky Griessel – mulling over all the implications, hesitating before the chaos that they knew would ensue.

Until Cupido, with the tails of his Hawk in Winter coat flapping in the icy wind, put his hand protectively on Benny's shoulder.

'Benna, at least there's one silver lining.'

'What do you mean?'

'The way you look this morning, I thought you must've gone on a bender again. But a *dronkgat* couldn't do it; you couldn't have figured all that out if you'd been pissed . . .'

He turned and began to walk towards the guesthouse.

2

Tyrone Kleinbooi saw the aunty climb up into the third-class carriage, here where the Metrorail train 3411 stood at Platform 4 of Bellville Station, just before 8.50 on the Monday morning. She was clearly in her best outfit, wearing a sober headscarf, clutching her large handbag with both hands. He shifted up a little to make the empty seat beside him seem more alluring.

She looked at the seat, and at him, and then she headed towards him, as he knew she would. Because he looked respectable. *Even features*, as Uncle Solly used to say. *You've got even features, Ty. It's a boon in this industry.*

Industry. As if they worked for a company.

She sat down with a sigh, balancing the handbag on her lap.

'Morning, aunty,' he said.

'Morning.' She looked him up and down, taking in his tall, skinny frame, and asked: 'Now where do you come from?'

'From the city, aunty,' he said.

'And where are you going to?'

'Stellenbosch, aunty.'

'You swotting there?'

'No, aunty.'

'Then what you doing there?'

'Going to see my sister, aunty.'

'So what's she doing there?'

'She's swotting, aunty. B.Sc. Human Life. First year.'

'That's a grand course, *nè*? What do you *do* with that?'

The train lurched, and pulled out of the station.

'There's lots you can do, but she wants to become a doctor. She didn't make the selection last year, now she's trying to get in like this.'

'A medical doctor?'

'*Ja*, aunty. She's a *slim kind*, very clever.'

'I would say so. Medical doctor *nogal*. And you? What do you do?'

'I'm a pickpocket, aunty.'

She gripped her handbag more tightly for a moment, but then she laughed. '*Ag*, you,' she said, and bumped her elbow in his ribs. 'What do you do, really?'

'I'm a painter. But not pictures. Houses.'

'I didn't take you for a manual labourer, but that's good honest work,' she said, 'for a young *lat* like you.'

'So where is aunty going to?'

'Also to Stellenbosch. Also to my sister. She struggles with gout. It's so bad she has to go and lie down . . .' And Tyrone Kleinbooi, dark as full-roast coffee beans, and even-featured, nodded politely and listened attentively, because he really did enjoy it. He was only vaguely aware that the rain had stopped. And that was good. Rain was bad for his industry. Pickings had been slim this month.

The modern farmyard of La Petite Margaux was higher up the mountain, minimalist, stacked glass squares held in almost invisible frames of concrete and steel.

The German owner met Griessel and Cupido at the front door, clearly disturbed. A large, bald man with the neck and shoulders of a weightlifter, he introduced himself as Marcus Frank. 'It is a great tragedy,' he said, with just a hint of a Teutonic accent, as he led them to the sitting room. The ceiling was two storeys high. On both sides was a wide, impressive view over mountain and valley.

Two women stood up when they came in: one, young and attractive, the other, older – with an unusual, eccentric air about her.

'Captain Cupido, Captain Griessel, this is Christel de Haan, our hospitality manager,' said Frank, and touched the younger woman's arm sympathetically. Her eyes were red-rimmed behind the trendy dark-framed glasses. She gripped a tissue in her left hand and just nodded, as if she couldn't trust her voice.

'And this is Ms Jeanette Louw,' he said with an inflection that was just a tad too neutral, making Griessel focus more sharply, noticing the body language. There was something in the atmosphere here that didn't quite fit.

Louw stepped forward and put out her hand. She was possibly

around fifty, with big bottle-blonde hair, a chunky frame and a strong jaw. No make-up, and she wore a man's black designer suit, with a white shirt and red-and-white striped tie. 'Hello,' she said sombrely in a deep smoker's voice, her handshake firm as she greeted the detectives.

'Christel and I will leave you now, at Ms Louw's request,' said Frank. 'We will be in my office, when you need us.'

'No,' said Cupido, 'we need to talk to you now.'

'I want to talk with you alone first,' said the blonde woman with an air of authority.

'Please. My office is just here.' Frank pointed down the passage.

'No. We don't have time for this,' said Cupido.

'Those were my people in the guesthouse,' said Louw.

'What do you mean "your people"?'

'Vaughn, let's hear what she has to say.' Griessel didn't have the energy for a confrontation as well. And he had picked up the atmosphere between these people. Along with the loss, there was friction, a certain tension. De Haan began to cry.

Cupido nodded reluctantly. With murmured words of consolation, Marcus Frank sent his hospitality manager down the passage.

'Sit down, please,' said Jeanette Louw, and took a seat herself on one of the angular couches.

Griessel sat down, but Cupido remained standing with his arms folded over his chest. 'What's going on here?' he asked, clearly not happy with the state of affairs.

'I am the managing director of Body Armour, a private security company in the Cape. We rented the guesthouse, and our contract with La Petite Margaux includes an NDA. They have no—'

'A what?' asked Cupido.

'A non-disclosure agreement,' she said as though maintaining her reasonable tone with some difficulty.

'What for?' asked Cupido.

'If you give me a chance, I will explain—'

'We are working against the clock, ma'am.'

'I realise that but—'

'We are the Hawks. We don't have time for small talk and monkey business.'

'Small talk?' Griessel could see her control beginning to dissolve, and her expression altered to a mixture of anger and grief. She leaned forwards, thrust an accusing finger at Cupido. 'You think I want to make small talk while some of my men are lying dead in that guest-house? Drop your act, and sit down, so I can give you the information that you need. Or I will walk out of here, and you can come and find me if you like.'

'I don't take orders from a—'

'Please,' said Griessel curtly.

Louw sank back slowly into the couch. It took a while before Cupido reluctantly said, 'OK,' but he remained on his feet with his arms crossed.

It took Louw a minute to control her emotions, then she addressed herself to Griessel. 'First of all, may I ask: how many bodies are there in the house?'

'Two,' said Griessel.

'Only two?'

'Yes.'

She nodded as though that's what she had expected. 'Can you describe them please?'

'Mid-to late-thirties, short hair, lean, clean shaven, both were appar-ently carrying Glocks . . .'

Louw held up her hand, she had heard enough. Her eyes closed, then opened again. 'They are both my men. B. J. Fikter and Barry Minnaar.'

'I'm sorry,' said Griessel. And then: 'You mean they worked for you?'

'Yes.'

'What sort of work, exactly?' asked Cupido.

'They were bodyguards.'

'Who was the third person in the house?' asked Griessel.

'My client. Paul Anthony Morris.'

'Who's he, that he needs bodyguards?' asked Cupido.

'I . . . he's a British citizen. That's all . . .'

'Shit,' said Cupido, because he could see the complications already.

Louw misread his reaction. 'Captain, that is all the information that he was willing to provide.'

'Ma'am,' said Griessel, 'at this stage we suspect that he . . . is missing. And he is a foreigner. That means . . .' he searched for the right word.

'Big trouble,' said Cupido.

'That's right,' said Griessel. 'We need all the information we can get, as soon as possible.'

'That's why I am here,' said Louw. 'I will give you everything I have.'

'But not in front of the farm people. Why?' asked Cupido.

'Because of the confidentiality clause, La Petite Margaux had no knowledge of who was in the guesthouse. And I have a discretionary duty towards my client. That is why I must talk to you alone.'

Cupido shrugged.

'Tell us what you know,' said Griessel.

She nodded, and took a deep breath, as if to gather her strength.

3

'Last Wednesday, just before sixteen hundred hours, Morris contacted me by phone, and enquired about the nature of our services and the background of our personnel. With a . . . I suppose what they call an Oxford accent. I referred him to our website, but he said he had already studied it, and wanted to make sure it was not merely marketing. I assured him that everything was factually correct. He had a few questions about the training background of our personnel, which I answered—'

'How are they trained?' asked Cupido.

'Most of my people are former SAPS bodyguards, Captain.'

'OK. Proceed.'

'Morris then said that he had, and I quote as well as I can recall, "a need to get out of circulation for a while, and enjoy the benefit of very vigilant, discreet and professional bodyguard services". And he needed this from last Friday. I said yes, we can accommodate him, and asked whether I could work through the standard procedure to determine our service according to his needs. He wanted to know what that procedure entailed. I said it was a series of questions about his occupation, circumstances, next of kin who could be contacted in case of emergency, possible threats, time period, and budget limitations. His reaction was that there were no budget limits, and that he wished to use the services for a couple of weeks, but he would prefer not to supply any further information. I said I would prepare a plan and quote, and email it to him. He preferred to phone back, which he did an hour later.'

Griessel listened to the official tone, the precise word choice. As if she sought refuge in the familiar territory of the official statement. There was a military air about her. He wondered if she had also been in the Service.

'My recommendation was this guesthouse, and a team of—'

'Why this one?' Cupido asked.

'We use it on a regular basis. It complies with our requirements. It is less than an hour from the airport, but outside the city. It is remote, with good access control, an open, manageable perimeter, and staff that understand our needs and requirements.'

'OK. Proceed.'

'My recommendation to Morris included a team of two armed bodyguards per day and night shift. He accepted immediately, and asked what the next step would be to close the deal. I asked him to deposit one week's daily tariffs. He—'

'How much?' Cupido asked, uncrossed his arms and sat down in a chair beside Griessel's. 'How much was the deposit?'

'Just over five thousand two hundred pounds. About seventy thousand rand.'

'For a week?' In disbelief.

'That's right.'

'And he paid it?'

'Within half an hour. And the next day, the Thursday, he sent a scan of the photo page of his passport via email, which I had requested for identification and registration purposes. It showed that he was a fifty-six-year-old British citizen. He also called that Thursday with details of his arrival. During that call I notified him of procedures at the airport, and gave him a description of my people who would meet him. That was the sum total of my communication with him. Fikter and Minnaar went to meet him at the airport on Friday afternoon – he was on flight SA337 from Johannesburg which landed at fifteen ten. They—'

'Johannesburg?' asked Cupido. 'So he didn't fly out of England?'

'It's possible that he flew from the UK to Johannesburg, and caught a connection to Cape Town. I can't confirm that.'

'OK. Proceed.'

'Fikter sent me a SMS on Friday afternoon at fifteen hundred seventeen to confirm that Morris had arrived safely, and another at sixteen hundred and fifty-two that they were at La Petite Margaux guesthouse and that everything was in order. They took the night shift that Friday night, and Stiaan Conradie and Allistair Barnes the day shift. Every team reported via SMS at the beginning and end of each

shift. There were no problems. On Sunday morning, at the end of the
night shift, I had a telephone conversation with Fikter to check on how
things were going. He said Morris was a very courteous and refined
man, and that he appeared relaxed and jovial. Conradie and Barnes
are here at the moment, down at the gate. They are ready to talk to you
as soon as the SAPS allow them entry to the farm.'

'So let me get this straight,' said Cupido. 'All that you know, is that
this *ou* is a Brit with a fancy accent and seventy thousand to burn.
No address, no job description, *nada*. For all we know he could be a
serial killer.'

'That's correct.'

'But you are happy to sell bodyguard services to such a person?'

'Captain, if you have cash and you want to buy a new car, the dealer
doesn't ask you if you have a criminal record.'

'A cop with cash for a car? Fat chance. And it's not the same.'

'Oh?'

'Bodyguard services are sort of personal, don't you think?'

Louw began to lean forward again, and Griessel asked: 'When you
spoke to him on the telephone – did he sound scared? Anxious?'

She shook her head. 'No. During the conversation I drew only two
conclusions. The first was that he had not used this sort of service
before, and the second was that he wanted to reveal as little about
himself as possible.' She looked at Cupido. 'And that's not unusual.
Personal security services are by their very nature discreet. The
majority of our clients are businessmen who don't want it trumpeted
about—'

'Why not?'

'A need to maintain a low profile. And I think that's also because
they don't want to offend their hosts. They come to do business with
local companies, and the very public display of security gives the
impression that they believe South Africa is a dangerous place.'

'Then why do they use the service? There's just about no crime
against tourists.'

'It's a general misconception among foreigners—'

'Which you are happy to indulge. Could you see from the email
address where he works? What was the domain name?'

'It was a Gmail address. And the name was Paul underscore Morris fifteen or something.'

'And the payment of the deposit? EFT?'

'Yes. From a Swiss bank, Adler, if I remember correctly. I will confirm that.'

'Ma'am . . .' began Griessel.

'Please. I am not a ma'am. Call me Jeanette.'

'The two bodyguards in there . . .'

'B. J. Fikter and Barry Minnaar.'

'Yes. How long ago did they leave the SAPS?'

'About seven, eight years . . .'

'How long have they worked for you?'

'For the same time period. I can assure you the attack had nothing to do with—'

'No, that is not what I'm getting at. How . . . good were they?'

She grasped his meaning. 'I only appoint the best. And for the sort of work they do, there is annual refresher training and testing, and the standards of fitness, weapon handling, and self-defence is high. We even do six-monthly drug tests. I can assure you Fikter and Minnaar were outstanding operators.'

'And yet . . .' said Cupido sceptically.

Jeanette finally lost her control. She planted her feet apart, leaned forward, put her elbows on her knees. 'Let me tell you, if you weren't a policeman, I would *bliksem* you right now.'

The young woman, not much older than Tyrone Kleinbooi, looked at the pile of notes, and then at the computer screen. 'You still owe seven thousand rand,' she said, each English syllable precise.

'Why do you *gooi* English at me – I thought this was supposed to be an Afrikaans university here,' said Tyrone. 'This is all I can pay now. One thousand two hundred and fifty.'

She bristled a little. 'It doesn't matter what language a person says it in, mister, *die rekening is agterstallig.* You are in arrears. Results are only released when it is paid in full.'

It was frustration that made him tease her. 'You can *gooi* in as many fancy white Afrikaans words as you like, but I can tell you're actually a Cape Flats girl.'

'*Ek kom van die Pniel af*, I'm not from the Flats. And I can see you have more money in your wallet. Does your pa know what you're up to?'

'*Jirre*,' said Tyrone Kleinbooi. 'What name is there on your computer, dollie?'

'"Nadia Kleinbooi". And I'm not your "dollie".'

'Do I look like a Nadia?'

'How should I know? There are some funny names on this computer.'

'Nadia is my sister, dolly. We don't have a ma, and we don't have a pa. This is money that I earned with my own two hands, *versta' jy*? And what is left in my wallet, I have to go and give to her to pay her rent on her flat. So don't you sit there and judge me. Have a heart, we pay as we can, she worked flippen hard, those results belong to her, not you lot – so why can't she see them?'

'I don't make the rules.'

'But you can bend them, *net 'n bietjie*. For a brother.'

'And lose my job? Not today.'

He sighed, and pointed at the screen in front of her. 'Can you see them there?'

'The results?'

'*Ja*.'

'I can.'

'Did she pass?'

Her face revealed nothing.

'*Ag*, please, sister,' he said.

She glanced around first. Then said softly and quickly: 'She passed well.' She took the money and began counting.

'*Dankie*, sister,' he said, and turned to go.

'*Jy kannie net loep nie*, you must wait for your receipt.'

'*Sien jy*, I knew you could *gooi* Flats.'

4

They felt the pressure, the urgency of time slipping away.

'Cyril was a friend to me,' said Marcus Frank, the German owner. 'A valued employee.'

Benny Griessel knew there was a risk that Cupido would say something like, 'So why did you make him wear a slave uniform?' and so he interjected quickly: 'You have our condolences, Mr Frank. Now, one of the—'

'Our reputation is in tatters,' said Frank. 'The media is waiting at the gate.'

'I understand. But one of the guests is missing, and we have to move as fast as possible. Can you tell us what Mr January was doing at the guesthouse last night?'

Frank made a helpless gesture in the direction of the still weepy Christel de Haan.

The woman put on her glasses and said: 'He cleared the dinner table, and lit the fire.'

'What time?' asked Cupido.

'At exactly nine o'clock.'

'How do you know that?'

'That was our agreement with them.'

'The bodyguards?'

'Yes. Breakfast at exactly eight o'clock, house cleaning at nine, lunch at one, dinner at eight p.m. Final clearing, and hospitality at nine. They are very strict, they have a lot of rules.'

'Like what?'

'They screened all our people. Only six were cleared to work when they rented the guesthouse, two for breakfast, two for house cleaning in the morning, and two for dinner and evening hospitality. It made things very difficult . . .'

'Why?'

'Because sometimes members of our staff are ill, or they want to take a vacation . . .'

'So why did you rent the house to these people?'

'They pay almost double the going rate.'

Cupido shook his head again in amazement. 'OK. So Cyril January was one of the cleared people?'

'Yes.'

'How did it work? Did he have keys?'

'No, no, if they wanted to enter, they had to call one of the guards when they were at the door.'

'How?'

'With a cellphone. They had to say a code word. They had to say "breakfast in the green room" if it was safe, or "breakfast in the red room" if they thought there was danger.'

'*Jissis*. And then the guard unlocked the door?'

'Yes.'

'But you said there were two people serving dinner?'

'Yes. Cyril's daughter . . .' De Haan's eyes filled, and her voice became hoarse. 'I'm sorry. His daughter, she's only eighteen . . . She served dinner with him, and they cleared the table, and then she left with the trolley. Cyril was doing hospitality . . .'

'What does that mean?'

'Chocolates on the pillows, check the bathroom supplies, like soap and shampoo and shower gel and hand cream, and light the fire . . .'

'Do you know what time he usually finished?'

'Between nine and half past.'

'And his wife thought he went to town last night?'

'He did do that sometimes.'

'Where would he go?'

'To friends.'

'And he would stay out all night?'

'Sometimes.'

'What was the procedure when he left the house?' asked Griessel.

'He just left, and they locked the door behind them.'

'And this morning?'

'One of our agricultural workers saw Cyril's body. At about

six-thirty, on his way to report for work. And then he saw the front
door of the guesthouse was open . . .'

'OK,' said Cupido, 'we'll have to speak to the daughter . . . We have
to speak to all the staff, in about . . .' he looked at his watch, 'in about
an hour's time. Can you assemble them for us?'

Cupido began to rant as they walked towards the car, just as Griessel
knew he would.

'"They pay almost double the going rate." That's the trouble with
this country, Benna. It's just naked greed, no fucking ethics.
Everybody just wants to score, it's just *skep, pappie, skep*, before
doomsday comes. Seventy thousand bucks for a week's personal
security? We're in the wrong business, I'm telling you. And that
lesbetarian wants to *bliksem* me? What for? Because I tell it like it is?
She can't do that, I mean, what do you say? There's just no appropriate response to a lezzy, you're *gefok* if you say come try me, you're
gefok if you zip your lip. There should be a law against that sort of
thing. Wants to *bliksem me*? With seventy thousand in her back pocket
and her Calvin Klein suit and that hair . . . And what is this here?
German owner of a Boer farm with a French name where a Brit is
kidnapped. Fucking United Nations of Crime, that's where we're
heading. And why? 'Cause they bring their troubles here. Like those
French at Sutherland, and the Dewani thing, and who gets the rap?
South-*fokken*-Africa.'

They got into the car.

'I'm telling you now, the perpetrator will be a foreign citizen, but
d'you think the TV will mention it? Not on your life, it'll be like "crime-
ridden society" all over again, all that *kak*. It's not right, Benna. Wants
to *bliksem* me. But they screen the little *volkies* in slave uniforms and
let them clean up after their whitey backsides until ten o'clock at night.
Chocolates on the pillows . . .'

'Forensics are here,' said Griessel when he spotted the white minibus
parked at the guesthouse, beside the SAPS photographer's Corolla,
and the two ambulances.

'They'll have to get a move on – we have to search the Brit's room.'

'And the Giraffe.' Beside the big Ford Territory of the Directorate
of Priority Crime Investigations – DPCI, or the Hawks – stood tall,

thin Colonel Zola Nyathi, commanding officer of the Violent Crimes Group.

As the first Hawk on the scene, Griessel reported as succinctly as he could. He was aware of the colonel's sharp eyes on him, with that unreadable, unchanging poker face of his.

When he had finished, the Giraffe said: 'I see,' and stood with his head bowed, deep in thought.

Eventually: 'You're JOC on this one, Benny.'

'Yes, sir.' His heart sank, because the last thing he needed in his current situation, was the responsibility of the so-called Joint Operations Command.

'You already have Vaughn. How many more people do you need?'

He knew the Hawks liked big teams who could hit hard and fast, but he was still sceptical about this approach. Too many people falling over each other, especially on an investigational level. And he knew command didn't always mean control over the direction of the investigation. 'Four detectives, sir.'

'You sure?'

'Yes, sir.'

'I'll get Cloete out. And start oiling the consulatory wheels.'

Captain John Cloete was the Hawks' media liaison officer. And Griessel knew they were going to need all the help they could get with the British Consulate. For though the Brits weren't as bad as the Canadians, and the Canadians were not as difficult as the Chinese – embassies were not keen to share their citizens' information, especially when there was crime involved. And in any case, they were bureaucratic dead-ends. So all he said was: 'Thank you, sir.'

He noticed Nyathi's gaze dwell on him a moment before the colonel nodded, turned, and walked back to his vehicle. He knew it was because he looked so terrible. He cursed himself again. Last night he should have . . .

'Come, Benna,' said Cupido, 'let's check how far Forensics are.'

In Dorp Street in Stellenbosch, a tour bus was parked in front of Oom Samie se Winkel, the now-legendary old-time store and tourist magnet.

Tyrone Kleinbooi eyed up the tourists on the pavement. Europeans, he recognised them by their pale legs, their get-up. He had given up wondering why European and American visitors were the only people in Africa who bought and wore safari outfits – the hunting jackets (with pockets for ammunition), the Livingstone helmets or wide-brimmed hats, the boots.

His senses sharpened. He focused on the group lining up at the door to get on the bus. At the back stood a middle-aged woman with a big raffia shoulder bag. Easy target. She would be expecting contact with other tour members. Her purse would be in the bag, right at the bottom, in the centre, big and fat, loaded with rands and euros and credit and cash cards, ripe for the picking. All he had to do was to take the hair clip with the little yellow sunflower that he had in his pocket, hide it in his hand, bend down in front of her, and pretend to pick it up.

Uncle Solly: *I had an appie who tried that trick with money, a ten-rand note. He flashed it at the mark, and the mark's attention went immediately to his wallet. Now that's just stupid. You use something that is colourful and pretty. But not money.*

'I think you dropped this, ma'am,' he would say quietly, intimately, confidentially, with his big innocent look-how-honest-our-locals-are smile. And his even features. With his right shoulder nearly touching her.

With her eyes and all her attention focused in surprise on the hair clip, he would slide his right hand into the bag, get a sure grip on the purse.

She would beam with grateful goodwill, because these white people from the north are black people pleasers, probably feeling guilty about their own colonial escapades. She would reach out her hand to the clip, and then shake her head. 'Oh, thank you, but it's not mine.' He would bump her lightly with his right shoulder as he withdrew his hand from the bag, and put the purse in his pocket.

The withdrawal is the key. Smooth and fast. Keep the wallet upright, don't let it hook on anything – the last thing you want at that crucial moment is a snag. And remember, there are other people who might be watching, so you want everyone's attention on the dropped object, you hold it high and handsome. And then you get the wallet out of sight, and your hand out of your pocket. Show it to the people, here is my innocent hand.

'My apology, ma'am,' he would say.

She would reply in a Dutch or German accent: 'No, please, don't apologise.' Except the Austrian woman, two years ago, who said 'thank you' and took the clip out of his hand. He had the last laugh though. The profit from her purse was nearly two thousand rand.

He would smile, turn, and walk away, look back and wave at her. *Don't rush it. Saunter, Ty. But be aware,* want jy wiet nooit ... *You never know,* the words echoed in his head.

He was in between the tourists, next to the woman, ready, every nerve ending tingling, the adrenaline flowing, just enough.

And then his brain said, Don't.

If it feels wrong, walk away.

He saw the pair of security guards just beyond the shop, their eyes on him.

He walked past, to Market Street, and his sister's flat.

5

From the front door, Griessel and Cupido could see the two men from Forensics at work under the bright spotlights in the sitting room. And hear their heated rugby conversation .

'I'm telling you, Bismarck is not a man, he's a machine,' said Arnold, the short fat one, vehemently.

'You shoot your own argument in the foot,' said Jimmy, the tall thin one. They knelt side by side, in the spacious lounge.

'What makes you say that?'

As a team they were known as Thick and Thin, a relic of the tired old quip from the days when they first began to work together: 'Forensics will stand by you through thick and thin', which in turn had been inspired by fat Arnold's previous Forensics partner, a freckled, cheeky and pretty redhead woman, who had self-deprecatingly referred to their partnership as 'Speckled & Egg'. There was a fair bit of murmuring when she left in search of greener pastures, and Jimmy – male, and far less attractive – was appointed.

'Bismarck is a machine? How does a machine get injured? Anyway, this year we will win the Cup, because your Sharks machine is going to seize up when the chips are down. Just like last year . . .'

'May we come in?' Griessel called.

'Thank the Lord, the Hawks are here,' said Arnold.

'I feel so safe now,' said Jimmy.

'Are you wearing shoe covers?' Arnold asked.

'Haven't you finished up front here yet?' Cupido retorted. 'Maybe you should stop talking rugby *kak* and get your arses into second gear.'

'Rugby *kak*? What sort of Cape coloured are you?'

'The sort who will kick your whitey arses if you don't pull finger.'

'If you're a kicker, the Stormers need you,' said Arnold. 'All fifteen fly-halves are injured again.'

'*Fokkof,*' said Jimmy. 'Come in if you have shoe covers on. There's something very weird here you should see.'

The 'something very weird' was a cartridge case.

'It's a Cor-Bon .45 ACP +P,' said thin Jimmy as he held it up for display with a pair of silver pliers.

'Not all forty-fives can shoot the Plus P,' said Arnold.

'Only the more recent models.'

'Your Plus P has a higher maximum internal pressure.'

'And higher velocity.'

'We can explain that in layman's terms if you don't understand.'

'We know easy words too.'

'So now you are ballistics *and* language experts?' asked Cupido.

'Your modern Forensic's scientific knowledge is vast,' said Jimmy. 'Bordering on genius . . .'

'In contrast with your average Hawk,' said Arnold.

'AKA the bird brains,' said Jimmy.

'*Fokkof,*' said Griessel. He knew it wouldn't help to try to be witty, because they always had the last word.

'Benny, you look particularly appealing this morning.'

'Or is that "appalling"?' The Forensics duo grinned at each other.

'Not so very bright-eyed and bushy-tailed, eh? And not too sharp-eyed for a Hawk either,' said Arnold.

'Don't you see it?' asked Jimmy.

'See what?' asked Cupido.

'The engraving.' He held the cartridge closer and rotated it.

'What is it?' asked Griessel.

'Take this,' said Arnold, and he held out a magnifying glass. Griessel took it, and studied the copper tube.

'It looks like a snake. Ready to strike.'

'Amazing,' said Jimmy. 'That he can see anything at all through those bloodshot eyes.'

'And what's under the rearing snake?' Arnold asked.

'Are those letters?' The engraving was tiny.

'Praise the Lord. The Hawks can read.'

'We can *bliksem* you too,' said Cupido. 'What do the letters say?'

'"N", dot, "m", dot,' said Arnold.

'So what does that mean? "Never mind"?'

'Where do you dig that up?'

'NM. Never mind. Don't you understand texting language? I thought you were so clever?'

'Sophisticated people don't use texting abbreviations. Capital N, small letter m stands for "newton-metre". If both were small letter it would stand for "nanometre". But in both cases without the dot,' said Arnold.

'So what do the two capital letters with two dots stand for?'

'I thought *you* were the detectives.'

'Because you rocket scientists don't know?' said Cupido in triumph.

'We can't do *all* your work for you.'

'Or, at least we can't do all your work for you *all* the time.'

'*Fokkof,*' said Griessel. 'We have to search the last room. Are you finished there?'

'Haven't even started.'

'*Jissis,*' said Cupido.

They went to interview Scarlett January, daughter of the murdered worker, Cyril.

Cupido sat beside her on the comfortable couch in the sitting room. He held her hand, his voice gentle and sympathetic. Griessel and Christel de Haan each sat in a chair.

'I'm so sorry for your loss, little sister.'

The pretty, petite girl nodded through her tears.

'If I could, I would not have bothered you. But we want to catch these evil people. They must pay for what they have done to your daddy.'

Another nod.

'Are you OK to answer a few little questions?'

She sniffed, blew her nose, and said: 'Yes, uncle.'

'You are very brave, *sistertjie,* your daddy would be very proud of you. Did you work with him every day in the guesthouse?'

'Yes.'

'The night shift, *nè*?'

Nod.

'Did you see the Englishman?'

'*Ja.*'

'What can you tell us about him?'

'He was very friendly.'

'Did he talk to you?'

'*Ja.*'

'What did he say?'

'My table looked nice. And the food was good.'

'Is that all?'

'And it's so lovely here. On the farm. If he looks out the window. That's all.'

'OK, *sistertjie*, that's very good. Now the bodyguards. Did you talk to them too?'

'Not really.'

'Were they nice to you?'

'*Ja*, uncle. But they didn't talk much.'

'Now, last night, what time did you leave there?'

The memory of the previous evening caused Scarlett's shoulders to shake. It took her a time to say: 'I don't know.'

'It's OK, *sistertjie*. So more or less nine o'clock?'

Nod.

'And everything was OK. There in the guesthouse?'

Nod.

'The same as the other nights?'

'*Ja.*'

'The bodyguards weren't different?'

'No, uncle.'

'Can you tell us how you left? Did one of them walk with you?'

'*Ja.* The one they call B. J.'

'OK, tell me nicely.'

'I told B. J. I was finished. He went and unlocked the front door. He went out first and looked, and then he came back in and said everything is fine. Then I called Daddy, because he had to help me with the trolley down the steps. Then—'

'What trolley?'

'The trolley with the leftovers and the dishes.'

'OK, and then?'

'Then we went out, Daddy helped me down the steps, and I pushed it back to the restaurant.'

'And then they locked up again?'

'I don't know.'

'That's OK. And you didn't see anything, while you were pushing it back to the restaurant?'

'I just . . .' And Scarlett January began to weep again. Christel de Haan stood up, gave her a couple of tissues and sat down again.

When she had regained some control, she said: 'Uncle, I . . . I'm a bit shy, uncle . . .'

Cupido leaned closer and whispered in her ear. 'So just tell me, I won't tell a soul.'

She nodded, blew her nose, and turned her mouth to his ear. 'Daddy says I was born with the *helm* . . .'

'OK.'

'Because I get these *gevoelentes*; premonitions.'

'I understand.'

'When I was walking there, I got this feeling, uncle.'

'What sort of feeling, *sistertjie*?' he whispered, barely audible.

'Evil, uncle. A terrible evil. Over there by the bougainvillea.'

6

Tyrone told his sister about her results. He sat on the only easy chair in Nadia's one-bedroom flat – the one with the broken leg that he had found thrown out in front of a house in the Bo-Kaap. He had mended it. Not good workmanship, because he didn't know much about woodwork. But it was sturdy, and it was comfortable.

'So, I'm very proud of you,' he said.

She sat at the big work table with her long black hair, and delicate, almost fragile beauty. He had swapped it for a stolen iPhone at the second-hand shop in Woodstock's Albert Street.

'Thanks, *boetie*.'

'Don't worry, I'll have the money by the end of the month,' he said. He took out his wallet. 'Here's the rent for the flat.'

'No, I only need a thousand, I got *lekker* big tips.'

'That's what I want to talk about. Tips or not, you're here to study.'

'But I like the work, *boetie*.'

'I understand, but *nou's dit* crunch time.'

'I can't just sit and swot all day.'

'So go for a walk. Or socialise a bit.'

'No. We eat for free, at the end of the shift, it saves me good money. And where will you get more than five thousand rand by the end of the month?'

'Big paint job in Rose Street, a whole block of flats. I'm one of the subcontractors for Donnie Fish. And it's interiors too, so it can *ma'* rain. And in any case, the Cape economy is booming again, tourism is up seventeen per cent. *Ek sê jou*, by December there will be enough for half of next year's class fees as well. You just swot, so that you make the selection. I don't want you wasting your time with waitressing.'

'It's not wasting time.' She had that stubborn look around her mouth that he had known since they were little. 'And I *will* make the selection.'

He knew he wasn't going to convince her. 'That's what I want to hear.'

The four extra Hawks detectives arrived – Lieutenant Vusumuzi Ndabeni, small of stature, with a manicured goatee and wide-awake eyes; Lieutenant Cedric 'Ulinda' Radebe, the ex-boxer, whose nickname in Zulu meant 'honey badger'; Captain Mooiwillem Liebenberg, the DPCI's best-looking detective and most respected skirt-chaser; and Captain Frankie Fillander, the veteran with a long scar from his ear to his crown from a knife wound.

Standing on the lawn of the guesthouse, Griessel brought them up to date with the details. He had to concentrate, because the weariness was a burden growing steadily heavier. And he was increasingly self-conscious about his appearance, and the looks that he was getting from his colleagues. He asked Ndabeni and Fillander, the gentlest of the officers, to question the farm workers, and told Radebe and Liebenberg to talk to the bodyguards.

Then he and Cupido walked to the veranda to hear whether Forensics were finished yet. The wind blew suddenly chill again.

'Global warming?' said Cupido as he looked up at the dark clouds once more looming in the east. 'Seems to me every winter is colder and wetter.'

Griessel's cellphone made a cheerful sound in his trouser pocket. He knew who and what it was.

His colleague looked keenly at him. 'But that's an iPhone you got there.'

'Yes,' said Griessel.

'Since when?'

'Friday.'

Cupido's eyebrows remained raised.

'Alexa gave it to me,' said Griessel.

Alexa Barnard. The new love in his life, the once famous singer, now a rehabilitated alcoholic, one hundred and fifty days sober now, and slowly rebuilding her career.

'The iPhone 5?'

'I don't know.'

'*Jy wietie?*' Cupido chortled at his ignorance.

Griessel took the phone out of his pocket and showed it to him.

'Yip, iPhone 5C. It's not an Android, but Benny, *broe'*, *dai's kwaai*. Welcome to the twenty-first century. You have graduated from appie to pro.'

Over the last few months Cupido had been one of Griessel's technology mentors. He had been nagging Benny for a long time to get an Android smartphone. 'An HTC, Benna. Just don't go and get a Samsung. Those guys are the new Illuminati, taking over the world, gimmick by gimmick. Never trust a phone company that makes fridges, pappie.'

At the front door of the guesthouse Cupido called inside: 'Jimmy, are you done?'

Griessel quickly read the SMS on his screen. *Missed you. Good luck. Can't wait for tonight. Have a surprise for you. Xxx*

From inside the house came the reply: 'Close enough. Just put shoe covers and gloves on again.'

They obeyed in silence, and picked their way through the hall, sitting room, and down the passage. They found Thick and Thin in the last bedroom, busy packing away fingerprint paraphernalia.

'Found a couple of weird things,' said Arnold.

'So did we,' said Cupido. '*You* two.'

'Sticks and stones,' said Jimmy.

'Water off a duck's back,' said Arnold. 'Firstly, there is blood spray on the front door, which doesn't make sense with the way the bodies are lying.'

'Inside or outside?' asked Griessel.

'On the outside of the door.'

'The door was open when I got here. The blood could have come from inside.'

'We considered that,' said Jimmy, 'but it still doesn't make sense.'

'Secondly,' said Arnold, 'we found another cartridge in the hallway. In amongst the arum lilies. The same calibre, the same cobra engraving.'

'One shooter for both victims,' said Jimmy.

'Thirdly, all the man's clothes are new,' said Arnold. 'As in brand new. And I mean everything. Even the underpants.'

'The suitcase too,' said Jimmy. 'Practically out of the box.'

'*And* his passport.'

'Where's the passport?' asked Griessel.

'Top drawer, on the right, in a little leather cover, new, fancy,' said Arnold.

Griessel stepped carefully over the rucked-up carpet and the bed linen on the floor, and pulled open the drawer of the bedside table. Inside was a shiny leather pouch. He picked it up, unzipped it. There were boarding pass stubs for Air France and SAA inside. They showed that Paul Anthony Morris had taken Flight AF0990 from Charles de Gaulle airport in Paris to Johannesburg on Thursday at 23.20, and on Friday, Flight SA337 from Johannesburg to Cape Town. Business class, both times.

The passport was tucked into a compartment of the pouch. Griessel pulled it out. It seemed very new still, the red cover with its gold lettering and national coat of arms was smooth and without creases or marks.

He opened it, paged to the photo ID. It showed a man in his fifties with a long, symmetrical face, no hint of a smile. His hair covered his ears, but neatly trimmed, dark, with grey wings at the temples. He looked slightly downwards at the camera, which made Griessel wonder whether he was tall.

To the right of the photo was his date of birth – 11 September 1956 – and the date the passport was issued. Barely a week ago.

Cupido came and stood beside Griessel as he paged over to the immigration stamps. There were only two: France, last Thursday, and South Africa, Friday.

'Brand new,' said Cupido.

'That's what we were trying to explain to you,' said Jimmy with an exaggerated long-suffering sigh.

'Did you see a wallet anywhere?' Griessel asked.

'No,' Arnold said. 'If he has one, it went along. Or it's somewhere else in the house.'

'Anything else?'

Jimmy put his hand in his briefcase and took out a transparent evidence bag. 'A cable tie,' he said, and held the bag up. 'It was here, half under the bed.'

Griessel took the bag and inspected it closely. The cable had been tied, and then cut.

'Just the one?'
'That's right.'

Griessel let the police photographer take pictures of the passport first
– the outside page, stamp page, and information pages. He asked
Cupido to travel with the photographer, wait for prints, and take them
to the British Consulate. 'Be diplomatic, Vaughn, please . . .'

'Aren't I always?'

'And phone the Giraffe first, find out if he's greased the wheels yet.'

'Sure, Benna.'

He would rather have gone himself, so he could think. About the
case. About his sins. And also because Cupido was the least diplomatic of all the Hawks. But he was JOC leader. For now he would have
to stay here.

He jogged through the drizzle to the garage where Radebe and
Liebenberg were questioning the two Body Armour employees.

The four men stood in a tight circle, which they opened up to include
Griessel. Liebenberg introduced him to the two bodyguards, Stiaan
Conradie and Allistair Barnes. The same short haircut, broad shoulders,
black suits, and white shirts as the victims. Their faces were grim.

'I'm sorry about your colleagues,' said Griessel.

They nodded.

There was an uncomfortable silence, eventually broken by Captain
Willem Liebenberg who spoke while referring to his notebook: 'They
relieved the night shift every morning at seven-thirty, and worked
twelve hours, till nineteen-thirty. The procedure for handing over was
a cellphone call from outside, with "green" and "red" as code words
for safe or unsafe. Then the front door would be unlocked from inside,
and locked again. They said the British guy . . . Morris, was friendly,
but not very talkative—'

'You do understand, we don't encourage conversation,' said Barnes.

'It distracts us from our work,' said Conradie.

'So they actually know very little about the man,' said Liebenberg.
'He's about one point eight metres tall, more or less ninety kilograms,
black hair, brown eyes. He speaks with a distinct British accent. Every
morning after breakfast, and every afternoon after four, he went for an
escorted walk of about forty minutes here on the farm, and every—'

'Did he request that? The walk?' asked Griessel.

Conradie replied: 'We give the clients a portfolio of choices. That was one that he chose.'

A portfolio of choices. If Cupido had been here, he would be going on about that: *An ex-policeman talking fancy.*

'And that's safe?'

'Safety is relative,' said Barnes. 'Unless the client divulges the nature of the threat. Which Mr Morris did not do.'

Radebe shook his head. 'Did you ask him?'

'Miss Louw does that. The background research. She said the client chose not to divulge. Our responsibility is to convey the portfolio of choices to the client, and to accommodate them. If he believes the threat is of such a nature that it's safe to go for a walk, we must accept that,' said Conradie.

'He asked us if we were sure no one had followed them from the airport,' said Barnes.

'Were you?'

'If there were any signs, Fikter and Minnaar would have reported it.'

'OK,' said Griessel.

7

The bodyguards said Morris sat in the dining room during the day with his computer and iPad, and in the evening, by the fire with a book that he had found on the sitting-room bookshelves. Sometimes he just stood at the window in the dining room, looking out over the Franschhoek Valley. 'I never knew this country was so beautiful,' he had apparently once said.

Griessel asked them where he kept the computer and iPad.

'He didn't. Every time that we left, they were still on the dining-room table,' said Conradie.

'And at mealtimes?'

'Morris ate in the dining room; we ate in the kitchen.'

Conradie saw Griessel frown. 'It's protocol,' he said.

'Did he have a cellphone?'

'He must have. We never saw him with it,' said Conradie.

'But he could have used it in his room at night when you weren't with him.'

'It's possible.'

'He never asked you to phone anyone?'

'No.'

'Is there Wi-Fi in the guesthouse?' asked Radebe.

'Yes.'

Radebe made a note.

'This place . . .' Griessel indicated the wine farm. 'I still don't understand why you brought him here. It's not hard to get in, if you really want to.'

Barnes frowned, sighed softly, and said: 'Personal security is as good as the client's briefing. We have safe houses and safe apartments that a full SWAT team would not get into, if there were enough PSOs that knew what they—'

'PSOs?'

'Personal Security Operatives.'

'OK.'

'But this guy said nothing about the nature of the threat. We can't force him. The protocol is, if they don't tell us anything specific, the boss describes all the options, and then he has to decide for himself.'

'This place is fine if no one knows you're here,' said Conradie.

'But someone *did* know he was here,' said Griessel.

The bodyguards nodded, uneasily.

'How? What are the possibilities?'

'He might have told someone,' said Barnes.

'Before he came,' said Conradie. 'Or while he was here. He could have sent someone an email . . .'

'What else? The men who abducted him are professionals.'

The silence stretched out longer, before Conradie said: 'If the pros follow you . . . It's not always possible to spot. If they're very good. If they use two or three cars. If they attach a GPS tracker to your car.'

'That's it,' said Barnes. 'The only possibilities.'

Griessel nodded. 'And he never seemed afraid or concerned?'

'No. He was relaxed. And a nice guy. One of the easier clients we've had in the past few years.'

'Anything else?' asked Radebe. 'Anything that he wanted?'

'Yesterday Morris asked for South African financial magazines and newspapers. I bought them yesterday evening at the CNA at the Waterfront, and brought them along this morning.'

They took down both bodyguards' details, and let them leave.

'I will follow up the Wi-Fi, Benny,' said Radebe. 'Find out who the service provider is for this place. Philip and his guys can get the logs.'

Over the past months Griessel had worked hard at his limited technological knowledge. Cupido and Captain Philip van Wyk of IMC, the Hawks' information management centre, were good, enthusiastic teachers. He didn't know very much yet, but he did know it was possible to track someone's Internet footprints in that way.

'Thanks, Ulinda. IMC will have to look at cellphone calls as well. Morris must have had one. Any foreign numbers . . . and if we can identify his phone . . .'

'. . . we can trace him. These bodyguards would have phoned to be let in the door; if we can get the phone numbers of the two victims, it will make it easier to track Morris. Same cellphone tower, if you get my drift.'

Griessel nodded. He should have thought of that. 'Vaughn is in the city – I will ask him to get that from Body Armour. Thanks, Ulinda.'

'No problem.'

The rain whispered softly on the roof.

Griessel and Liebenberg searched the big guesthouse from top to bottom. Griessel was in Morris's bedroom carefully going through everything again when Fillander and Ndabeni returned from questioning the farm workers. They came and stood in the doorway, their heads and shoulders shiny and wet with rain.

'Nothing,' said Fillander. 'The ones who were here didn't hear or see anything unusual. There are four labourers who left on Saturday for Robertson for the weekend. Family funeral apparently, they will only be returning today. Maybe too much of a coincidence, Benny. I asked that they phone us when the people are back.'

'Thanks,' said Griessel.

'What's next, Benny?' Ndabeni asked.

'I need you to walk the farm perimeter,' he said. 'The perpetrators did not enter at the main gate, so there might be signs somewhere . . .'

'OK, Benny.'

'I'm really sorry, but I don't trust the station uniforms to do a thorough job in this weather. And if we wait until the rain stops, there might be nothing left. Ask Christel de Haan, the hospitality manager if you can borrow umbrellas.'

'OK, Benny, no problem.'

And then he was alone again, and he picked up the overturned desk chair and sat down so that he could think and get the weight off his feet.

Jissis, he was getting old. Two, three years ago he wouldn't have been so *poegaai* after an exhausting night of . . .

Better stick to the matter at hand.

He tried to visualise it, the entire event: Last night. Just after nine. The suspects hiding here somewhere, watching Scarlett January and her father, Cyril, carry the trolley down the steps, Scarlett wheeling it away.

One gunman for both victims, Thick and Thin had said. But to abduct a man would be hard for just one person.

One gunman, with helpers?

They hide until the bodyguards open the door, survey the area, and let Cyril out.

They wait until the door is closed again. They close in on Cyril. Pistol to the head. They take him back to the front veranda. *Phone them inside. Tell them you forgot something.*

Cyril calls.

They shoot him from behind. Blood spray on the outside of the front door. With a silencer? Probably, as no one on the farm heard anything, and the sound of a shot would have alerted the bodyguards inside.

Why hadn't Cyril used the alarm code over the phone?

If they don't open, if anything goes wrong, you're dead.

Shoot Cyril before the door opens. Ram the door so the bodyguard staggers backwards. Shoot the bodyguard. He falls back, in the hallway.

The second bodyguard is in his room, deep inside the house. He hears something, grabs his pistol, comes running down the passage. The suspects are already in the sitting room. The executioner shoots the second bodyguard, first through the hand, then in the head.

The executioner gets Morris. Pistol to the head, but it doesn't help, he puts up a fight. Wrestles him to the ground. Makes him lie down. Handcuffs his wrists with cable ties.

Why snip off one cable tie? Was it too tight?

Morris's wallet is missing. Morris's computer and iPad are missing. Probably a cellphone too, though the bodyguards have never seen it. The clothes were strewn about, the cupboard moved.

At first they tie Morris to the bed with a spare cable tie – or something else – while they search for something? And cut it loose when they take him away from the house?

Why take the wallet, computer and iPad?

What else is missing?

What were they looking for?

Why not shoot Morris too, why kidnap him?

There was only one person who could answer those questions: Paul Anthony Morris. And they didn't have the faintest idea who he was.

Suddenly Griessel's cellphone rang in his pocket, the old-fashioned ringtone that Alexa had chosen. He took it out.

'Vaughn?'

'Benna, the photos of the passport are now in the hands of the Deputy Consul General of the British Empire, Madam Carlisle. She says it will take a day or two.'

'I'll phone the Giraffe, Vaughn. Maybe he can do something.'

'Where do you want me?'

He hesitated before asking: 'Can you go see Louw again?'

'Of course. I'm not scared of a bit of lesbetarian,' he said with glee.

Griessel wondered if it wasn't a big mistake. 'Vaughn, we must work nicely with her. She's lost some of her men.'

'Sure, Benna, I'm cool.'

'Get Morris's email address and all the documents that he filled in. And we want his cellphone number, Vaughn. Ask whether she kept records of all the calls last week. And the cellphone numbers of the two deceased as well.'

'I'm all over it. Like a rash.'

8

On the train back to Cape Town, Tyrone Kleinbooi switched off, leaned back, swaying with the motion of the carriage. He liked riding the train. It was an escape from his industry, here in third class. Everyone poor, but there was a hint of hope, as though you were on your way to something better. When he was down, if he had had a hard day at the office, he would often take the train and go somewhere. Lentegeur, Bellville, Simon's Town, he had twice gone all the way to Worcester by Metrorail, and then he dreamed of Europe by rail, one day. To Barcelona, *the Holy Grail of pickpocketing,* Uncle Solly always called it.

He knew why his thoughts kept turning to Uncle Solly today. It was the pressure. He had lied to his sister – OK, he had been lying about his job for years now, but he had added an extra untruth today, *by December there will be enough for half of next year's fees as well,* which naturally was a blatant lie. That tourism was up seventeen per cent, that the economy of Cape Town was booming, was all true. But it was *fokkol* help to a pickpocket.

Why? The cameras, that's why.

When Uncle Solly began coaching him nine years ago, everything was different. Here and there there was a CCTV camera in a shop, but he was not a shoplifter, *shoplifting is for amateurs and teenagers, Ty, too easy to get caught, da's just one exit, and you always want more than one, always.* Never mind that nine years ago, he, Tyrone, was only twelve years old, not yet a teenager, but that's Uncle Solly for you.

Take the postcard trick – those days you could still do it. Saunter in between the outside tables of Café Mozart, there in the Church Street Mall, go up to the tourist with your twelve-year-old even features and your charming smile, and the postcards, all hand-picked by Uncle Solly, pretty ones, Table Mountain, Table Bay, cute Boulders Beach penguins, and a couple with Madiba on. New and shiny.

'Madam, have you sent your loved ones a Cape Town postcard yet?' you ask in your sweetest little kid voice.

'Oh, aren't you just the cutest. That's a great idea. George, we should send Shirley a postcard . . . Oh, aren't the penguins adorable . . .'

And he would put the postcards down on top of the wallet or the cellphone or the passports that lay there on the table, his fingers fanning them out, swift and trained like a card sharp, while he took the wallet and gripped it under the postcards. And the husband asks: 'How much?' and he would say: 'Just five rand, it's for my school fees,' and the aunty would say: 'We'll take two,' and she would reach out with her fat, beringed fingers for the postcards, and the husband would begin looking for his wallet. 'I'm sure I had it . . .'

You hadn't been able to try that trick for a long time, there were too many cameras around every corner of the city, and somewhere a *blou-baadjie* officer sitting watching the screens and telling the Metro cops over the radio that you were stealing the tourists blind. Now you had to go back to your little room in the Bo-Kaap about four times a day to change into a different colour shirt and put on another cap or beanie or hat, so that the cop in front of the screens wouldn't start noticing you.

So what's a guy to do?

In *this* industry you went where the marks were, the marks with money. And that meant foreign tourists, because your locals didn't carry cash – except for the Gautengers and the Free Staters over December, easy pickings if you get them away from a camera, Clifton beach and Camps Bay. And the Biscuit Mill on a Saturday morning, now *there's* a paradise, all those milling people, but you could only get two or three wallets before word went around.

Foreign tourists hang out at the Waterfront and in the city and that's CCTV country, so you have to steal sharp, always in the crowd, you have to move on foot between the V&A and Long Street, between the Castle and the cable car, because the weird routes of the minibus taxis take too long, and the common taxis rip you off . . .

Before November he had to get twelve thousand rand, for this year's university fees. Before the end of January, another nine thousand for next year's first payment.

Twenty-one K. How do you do that, Uncle Solly? In this grim winter, with this rain that will keep on till September? With the fences who squeezed you with 'recession' and 'tough times'?

How do you do that and stay out of jail?

Benny Griessel and Mooiwillem Liebenberg found nothing.

They searched the big old house carefully and thoroughly. Morris's computer, iPad and possible cellphone were not there.

Captain John Cloete, media man for the Hawks, arrived. They went and sat at the dining-room table in the guesthouse to confer.

'The Giraffe says it's your call, Benny.' Cloete had nicotine stains on his fingers, and permanent shadows under his eyes. Griessel suspected that that was the price that the liaison officer paid for his apparent unshakeable calm and patience, despite the inhuman pressure that his job brought with it.

'It's a foreigner, John.'

'So I hear.'

'We will have to contact next of kin first. That could take a while.'

'Shall I say "presumably a British citizen"?'

That was not what Griessel wanted. Kidnapping was a delicate, complicated, dangerous mess. If a demand for ransom were received, today or tomorrow, with instructions for no media, the cat would already be out of the bag. And there was no way to put it back in. On top of that, it would be like blood in the water for the media sharks. The fact that it was a foreigner would make them crazy. And they would ruin everything.

'We don't know enough yet. I don't want to say anything about the Brit.'

'An unknown third party?'

'No. Absolutely nothing about a third party.'

'You know it'll come out, Benny.'

He nodded. There were too many people on the farm who already knew. Colonel Nyathi would have the final approval of the press release anyway, but for now Griessel must try to do what he believed was best for the investigation.

'I'll ask the owner to talk to his people, but I think we should just say that one farm worker and two guests were shot. Nothing more.'

'The moment we identify the two bodyguards, the media will want to know who they were guarding.'

'Then we must withhold their identities.'

'Hell, Benny . . .'

'I know, John, but if the Brit is still alive, we must do the right thing. Imagine if we fuck this one up, what the UK newspapers will write about us.'

'You'll have to talk to the bodyguard people. They will have to cooperate.'

'I agree.'

Cloete sighed. 'I will say the investigation is in a sensitive stage, we will release more information when we're sure it will not hinder the process. That should cover us, but they'll know we're hiding something.'

'Thank you, John.'

'Wait until the Giraffe approves it.'

Just after one, Christel de Haan and two restaurant workers brought them food – steaming plates of *waterblommetjie* stew. Griessel thanked her, and phoned Vusi Ndabeni and Frankie Fillander to tell them to come and eat.

Then he explained the dilemma over the kidnapping and the media to de Haan.

'Can you request that no one talks to the press?'

'We would have asked them anyway. Marcus is very concerned about our brand and reputation. All our wine goes to Europe.'

He thanked her, and called Cupido.

'I have the Gmail address, Benna. Paul underscore Morris, one five. Helps us *fokkol*. And there's nothing in the contract that says who Morris is, no next of kin. I don't understand how these people do business. And you should see that Body Armour office. Grand, pappie, big bucks.'

'Where are you now?'

'N1, at Century City, I'm on my way to you. Found anything?'

'Nothing. We're nearly done, Vaughn, you can go straight to the office. Give IMC the cellphone numbers of the two bodyguards, so they can identify the cell tower and begin checking all the calls from Friday.'

'That's smart, Benna . . .'

'It was Ulinda's idea.'

'That darkie, hey. Nobody's fool, despite the battering.' Radebe was a light heavyweight who had lost all four of his professional fights on points before he left the sport. It was his capacity to absorb blows that earned him his nickname of '*Ulinda*', the hardy honey badger.

'See you at the office,' said Griessel, and rang off.

Just after dinner, he, Liebenberg, Ndabeni, Radebe, and Fillander went walking along the remainder of the farm boundary, but they found nothing. If there were tracks, the rain had washed them all away in the interim.

Just after three, when the state pathologist had come and gone, and the last ambulance had driven away, they sealed the crime scene. His colleagues went back to the office, and Griessel drove into the city to go and negotiate with Jeanette Louw of Body Armour.

He turned on the heater in the car to banish the cold and damp. The pressure of being JOC leader made him uncomfortable, so that he thought through it all, slowly and with extreme concentration. Because his head was not clear. He didn't want to make a fool of himself. Not after all the odd looks his appearance had drawn.

He swore out loud over the stupidity of last night. Because JOC leader was an opportunity to be relevant again. He had worked so hard over the last six months to catch up, to fit in with the Hawks, to accept the whole team thing and become an efficient cog in the Hawks' wheel. Despite the fact that he was the oldest detective in the Violent Crimes group, steeped in the traditional way of doing things.

And now he looked like *this*.

He would have to keep his head.

He focused on the case, ran through everything that he had seen and heard that morning. He came to the same conclusion: first they must know who Morris was.

Fuck knew, tonight he would *have* to get some sleep, he couldn't look and feel like this tomorrow as well.

What worried him most, was that he had begun lying again. This time to Alexa, to Nyathi, to his colleagues. And the déjà vu that brought back all the old, bad memories of ten, eleven years ago. Anna, at that time still his wife: 'Where have you been, Benny?'

'At work.' Breath reeking of alcohol, drunken eyes, swaying on his feet.

'You're lying, Benny,' she would say, with fear in her voice. That is what he remembered – the fear. What was going to happen to her husband, what was going to happen to her and the children?

It had been so easy to lie to Alexa this weekend, and to Cupido this morning. The old, slippery habit was like a comfortable garment, you just slipped back into it.

In those days he could justify it. Rationalise. The stress, the trauma of inhuman violence and what that did to his head, the impossible hours, the sleeplessness, dreams, and his own phobias, that something like that could happen to his loved ones.

But no more.

He didn't want to lie any more.

9

When he emerged from the lift on the sixteenth floor of the office building in Riebeeck Street, he saw what Vaughn meant by 'grand, pappie, big bucks'. Bold masculine letters on the double glass doors announced *BODY ARMOUR*. Below that, in slim sans serif: *Personal Executive Security.*

He pushed open the door. The walls and luxury carpets were grey, the minimalist furniture was of blackwood, only here and there a splash of verdant green and chrome. Behind a black desk, with only a silver Apple laptop computer, a slim green telephone, and a small aluminium name-plate that said *Jolene Freylinck*, sat a beautiful woman – long dark hair, deep red lipstick, black blouse and skirt, elegant legs ending in black high heels.

'You must be one of the detectives,' she said, her voice serious, muted.

He was all too aware of how she might know this.

He nodded. 'Benny Griessel.'

She reached out a manicured hand for the telephone, pressed a button, waited a second. 'Detective Benny Griessel is here.'

She listened, glancing at him with a slight frown. 'You may go in,' she said and pointed at the black doors with the chrome handles.

He could see how upset she was. 'Thank you.'

Jeanette Louw sat behind her blackwood desk. The jacket hung from a stand in the corner, her striped tie was loosened. She seemed older and more weary than this morning.

'Captain,' she greeted him. 'Come inside. Please take a seat.'

He could hear the suppressed antagonism. He sat down in a black leather chair.

'I understand from your colleague that you still have no leads.'

'That's correct.'

'You know he's an arsehole. And that has nothing to do with race.'

Griessel sighed. 'He's a very good detective.'

Louw just stared at him. He was unsure how to address her. 'Were you in the Service?' he asked.

'The police?'

'Yes.'

'No.' With distaste.

He was too tired to react.

'I was the Regimental Sergeant Major of the Women's Army College in George,' said Louw.

He merely nodded. It would have been easier if she were a former officer. 'It seems as though Morris has been kidnapped,' he said.

'So I understand.'

'It makes things awkward with the media.'

'Oh?'

'The trouble is . . . We assume he's a rich man . . .'

She grasped the point instantly. 'Because he can afford my services.'

'That's right. It may be that they want ransom . . . And we don't know whether his next of kin have been contacted by the kidnappers yet. Usually they demand that nothing appears in the press, and the police may not be contacted, or they will kill their victim.'

'I understand.'

'If we tell the media that there were two bodyguards, they'll want to know who was being guarded.'

'And who they were working for?'

'Yes.'

'You don't want to reveal anything for now.'

She was smart. 'Is it possible to . . . Would the families of your men understand? If we keep the names out of the media? For now?'

Louw leaned back in her chair. She rubbed a hand over her strong jaw, then said: 'As much as it will be best for the reputation of my company not to have publicity, I would have to leave that up to the families. I owe them that at least.'

'Of course.'

'B. J. Fikter has a wife and child . . .'

Griessel said nothing.

'I'll try,' she said.

At the Hawks' offices on the corner of Landrost and Market Street in Bellville, he knocked on the frame of Zola Nyathi's open office door.

The colonel waved him in, motioned him to sit.

With Nyathi's eyes glued on him, he reported back precisely and fully.

'Thank you Benny. Good work. But we have a media problem.'

'Yes, sir.'

'I've approved your strategy, but Cloete says they're going nuts. The radio stations are already throwing around words like "massacre" and "bloodbath", and are speculating about drugs and gang violence. I don't know how long we can keep this under wraps.'

'I'll move as fast as I can, sir. The Consulate . . . If we can get hold of Morris's family . . .'

'The brigadier has spoken to our Deputy National Commissioner, who has asked Foreign Affairs to get involved. So we should soon see results.'

'Thank you, sir.'

Griessel stood up.

'Benny, just a moment,' said Nyathi, very seriously.

He sat down again. He knew what was coming.

'Benny, I don't want to pry. But you understand that your personal well-being is very important to me.'

'Yes, sir.'

'Can I ask you a favour?'

'Yes, sir.'

'You have a mentor, at the AA—'

'A sponsor, sir. But I can assure you—'

He stopped talking when Nyathi lifted his hand. 'You don't have to assure me of anything, Benny. We have a few hours before the cellular data and consular information comes in. I want to ask you to go home, take a shower, and speak to your sponsor. Would you do that for me, Benny?'

'Yes, sir. But I want to—'

'Please, Benny, just do that for me.'

He didn't want to go home. As he drove, he phoned Alexa.

'You must be totally exhausted,' she answered with a voice full of sympathy.

'I'm just coming for a quick shower and change,' he said.

'Ay, Benny, I understand. Is it the Franschhoek murders?'

'It is.'

'I heard about it over the radio. Do you want something quick to eat?'

'Thanks, Alexa, but there won't be time. See you in half an hour . . .'

And then he phoned Doc Barkhuizen, his sponsor at Alcoholics Anonymous.

'Doc, I want to come and talk to you.'

'Now?'

'Around six o'clock, Doc.'

'Come to my consulting rooms. I'll wait for you.'

Doc, who never reproached him. Was just always available.

But he would have to lie to him too.

The garden gate of Alexa's large Victorian house in Brownlow Street, Tamboerskloof, didn't squeak any more. Nearly seven months' worth of restoration work completed, and the garden had been redone. Now it looked like the home of a veteran pop star.

She must have been waiting at the window, because she opened the door for him and hugged him.

'I don't smell good,' he said.

'I don't care.' She squeezed him tightly. 'I'm just so glad you're safe.'

'Alexa . . .'

'I know, I know . . .' she let go of him, pulled him by the hand. 'But that's the way it is if you love a master detective. I made a sandwich, come and eat quickly.'

He didn't like being called a 'master detective'. He had at least persuaded her to stop introducing him that way to her friends.

'Thank you very much,' he said.

'Pleasure. I will keep the surprise for later, after you've showered.'

The pickpocketing week has a very specific pattern. Fridays and Saturdays are prime time, people take to the streets, their thoughts are *los* and casual, Uncle Solly used to say, *and they are flush, cash in pocket.*

Tuesday, Wednesday, and Thursdays are OK, no great shakes, but you can work. Especially now that the clubs are pumping way into the night, lots of young people with lots of money, and you might argue you are helping, taking the money that would have been spent on cocaine.

The seventh day is for rest, Tyrone, because Lord knows da' ga' niks aan nie, *nothing at all, not even in the malls, except before Christmas, that was another story.*

And Mondays were also basically *kak*, thank you.

So he made a loop through Greenmarket Square, just to check whether there might be a lost tour bus full of Europeans ooh-ing and aah-ing over the cheap merchandise with 'African flavours' that actually came all the way from China.

There wasn't.

He bought a meat pie on the corner of Long and Wale. Walked up Longmarket, past the home-made Frederick Street sign, probably not smart and grand enough a neighbourhood for the DA government to hang an official street sign. As bad as the ANC, they were *ammal* useless. The northwester was blowing *kwaai*, it was a long steep hike to his little outside room, in Ella Street, up in Schotsche Kloof, which he rented in the back yard of the rich Muslims' grand house for four-fifty a month. One wall was kitchen counter and sink. One wall was built-in cupboards. He had a single bed and a bedside table. Tiny bathroom. At the outer door hung the intercom, a reminder that this was once the servants' quarters. And now and then the eldest twenty-something daughter of the rich Muslims would buzz him. Nag him about the garbage, or because he hadn't closed the front security gate properly. She hung around the house all day. She was a little fat, and lonely.

Shame.

He would listen to his 32GB iPod touch, the one he had stolen from a German backpacker in December, half the music was death metal, but the rest was OK.

Time to ponder.

10

Doc Barkhuizen was seventy-one years old. He had thick glasses, wild eyebrows, and long grey hair that he tied back in a cheeky ponytail, usually with a light blue ribbon. He had a mischievous face that reminded Benny of one of the seven dwarves in *Snow White*, and a surgery in Boston where he – after a short-lived retirement to Witsand at the age of sixty-five – still saw patients every weekday as a general practitioner.

And he was an alcoholic.

'I am four hundred and twenty-two days sober, Doc,' said Griessel promptly.

'Do you want to drink?'

'Yes, Doc. But not more than usual.'

'So why are you keeping me away from *Hot in Cleveland*?'

'*Hot in Cleveland*?'

'It's a sitcom, Benny. It's the sort of thing that normal, elderly, rehabilitating men watch in the evening with their wives, to keep them from boredom and the lure of the bottle.'

'Sorry, Doc,' he said, though he knew Barkhuizen was only teasing him.

'How are the children?'

He would have to get through this first, it didn't help to try to hurry Doc. His sponsor searched far and wide for danger signs, and he always wanted all the details. 'Well, in general. Fritz has now decided that he wants to go to film school next year. Just because he has shot a few music videos with Jack Parow. Now he wants to "make movies" with a passion. And the AFDA tuition fees, Doc . . . I'll have to take a bond on a house that I don't have. But it's probably better than no education. Or joining the police.'

'And Carla? Is she still going out with that rugby player?'

'Yes, Doc, I'm afraid so.'

'I can hear you still don't like the boy.'

It was the boyfriend Etzebeth's tattoos that bothered Griessel most – that stuff was for prison gangs – but he knew Doc would say he was prejudiced. 'He was kicked off the team for fighting, Doc.'

'I saw that in the newspapers. But you must admit, it's not bad to be already playing for the Vodacom team at the age of twenty.'

'He's aggressive, Doc.'

'With Carla?'

'I'll lock the fucker up if he ever tries *that*.'

'You mean on the field?'

'Yes.'

'It's his job, Benny.'

Griessel just shook his head.

'Why are you here?' asked Doc.

'Because my colleagues think I'm drinking again.'

'What gives them that idea?'

'Last night I slept in my office. Not for very long either. So I looked really bad today.'

'That's all?'

'Last week there were two nights I slept in the office.'

'From pressure of work?'

'No, Doc.'

'Are you going to tell me what's wrong, or must I drag it out of you?'

Griessel sighed.

'It's Alexa,' said Doc Barkhuizen with certainty. He had advised strongly against Griessel's relationship with her – he said two dodgy alcoholics together spelled trouble, 'and if one is an artiste as well, then you have the recipe for a big mess'.

'Alexa is one hundred and fifty days sober, Doc.'

'But?'

'I've moved in.'

'With her?'

'Yes, Doc.'

'Christ, Benny. When?'

'Three weeks ago.'

'And?'

'And it's difficult, Doc. Not to do with drink, I swear. We . . . it's easier, she understands the craving, Doc, we help each other.'

'You know I think that's a crock of shit. But go on.'

All the way here he had considered *how* he would lie; at the beginning of his rehabilitation Barkhuizen had caught him out every time – he knew all the sly evasions of an alcoholic so well. Griessel decided on half-truths, that was the safest. And now he couldn't find the right words. '*Jissis*, Doc . . .'

'Do you have trouble with commitment, Benny? Or are you still missing Anna?'

'No, Doc. It's just . . . I suppose it's the commitment, sort of . . .'

'Sort of?'

'Doc, I got used to being on my own. For two years. Coming and going as I chose. If I wanted to drink orange juice out of the bottle in the morning, if I wanted to play bass guitar in the evening, if I just wanted to do *fokkol* . . .'

'So what possessed you to go and move in with her? Wait, don't tell me. It was *her* idea.'

'Yes, Doc.'

'And you felt too bad to say no.'

'No, Doc, I wanted to.'

'And now you're sleeping at the office so you can be alone for a while?'

'That's more or less . . .'

'*Jissis*, Griessel, you're a moron.'

'Yes, Doc.'

'Did you give up your flat?'

'Yes, Doc.'

'A moronic ape.'

'Yes, Doc.'

'You know what the right thing to do is.'

'No, Doc.'

'You know, but you don't *want* to know. You have to sit down and talk to her. Tell her you need your space. And then she's going to feel threatened and insecure, because she is an artiste. And she will wonder whether you really love her. And she is going to cry, and resort to drink, and you will feel responsible. That's the problem. You don't want to face up to all those things. You've never been very good with conflict.'

'*Fok*, Doc.'

'So tell me, how long did you think you could continue sleeping at the office before it caused complications?'

Griessel stared at the floor.

'You didn't think, did you?'

'No, Doc.'

'Why are you here, Benny? You knew exactly what I would say.'

'My CO told me to come.'

'Did you tell him you haven't been drinking?'

'I tried, but . . .'

'What are you going to do?'

'I don't know, Doc.'

'You will have to do *something*.'

'Alexa is going to Johannesburg tomorrow, until Thursday. I'll think about it, Doc. When she comes back . . .'

Doc Barkhuizen looked at Benny from under his bushy eyebrows. Then he said: 'You know that we are personally responsible for ninety-five per cent of the trouble in our lives.'

'Yes, Doc.'

'Do you want me to phone your CO?'

'Please, Doc.'

'OK. And don't worry, I'll be discreet.'

His cellphone rang as he walked outside with Barkhuizen. An unknown number. He answered while Doc locked up the surgery. The wind was icy.

'Captain, it's Jeanette Louw.'

'Hello,' said Griessel, still unsure of how to address her.

'I have spoken to the next of kin about your request. It's going to be difficult. They have already notified family members, and some of them are already on their way to the Cape to support them, and for the funerals.'

'I understand completely,' he said.

'They say they'll try, but they can't guarantee it won't reach the media.'

'It'll give us a bit of time,' he said. 'Thank you very much.'

'Captain, they are doing it because they want to help catch the murderers.'

He didn't react.

'You are going to catch them, Captain?'

'I will do my absolute best.'

She remained silent for a long time, before she said: 'If there is anything that I can do. Anything . . .'

II

Griessel drove away, looking back in the rear-view mirror at the skinny, slightly bowed shape of Doc Barkhuizen standing under the street light. He felt a huge compassion for the man, for the generous heart hidden behind the strict, inflexible facade.

His sins weighed heavily on him.

Doc was the one person he did not want to lie to. It was a sacred relationship, the one with your AA sponsor, if you truly wanted to quit drinking. It was the cornerstone of rehabilitation, in the end, it was your only lifebuoy in the stormy sea of alcoholic thirst. If you couldn't trust one another, you were basically fucked. For the past few years, Doc had been the one constant in his life, the one he shared everything with.

Until today.

That's why unease stirred down in his gut: once you began telling half-truths and concealing the Big Problem, you quickly slid down the slippery slope of relapse. He knew. He had *been* there.

If he couldn't speak about the actual problem, why wasn't he at least honest about the other things that haunted him?

Because Doc would say: 'You know what to do.'

And Doc would be right.

He would say to Doc: 'I'm afraid Alexa will catch me out, I'm afraid that she will see through me some time or other. And then she will drop me. And though I'm looking for some room, I don't want *that*. Because I love her, she's actually all that I have. So, it worries me a lot, Doc.'

He would at least be able to explain where the problem began, where the origin was. It was back when he met Alexa. He had been involved in the investigation into the murder of her husband. He was the one who recognised her as the former singing sensation, it filled him with nostalgia and admiration and a bittersweet longing. And then he was sympathetic about her drinking and he told her he was also an alcoholic. He was the one who believed from the beginning that she was innocent, he was the one who unravelled the whole mess, and the one who took her flowers afterwards in hospital and talked with her about music.

And then she thought he was brilliant.

He tried to tell her, several times, in different ways, that she was wrong. But he hadn't made a very good job of it, half blinded as he was by who she was, her musical talent and her Story, and her determination to get back on her feet again. And her sensuality – *fok weet,* despite the damage, despite the years, she was a sexy, beautiful woman. And then he went and fell in love with her. And when you are in love, you put your best foot forward, you hide who you really are. And she only heard what she wanted to hear.

And then, in the months since, something had developed: 'a dynamic' Doc Barkhuizen would call it. Alexa treated him as though he was a good, solid man. A hero. Confidant, advisor. Introduced him as her 'master detective', and to his dismay even once or twice as her 'rock'.

He, Benny Griessel, someone's rock? Solid? A hero?

He was an idiot and an ape, because despite his discomfort, despite his awareness of fraud, he loved it. That Xandra, the former star who could still bring people to a standstill in the street, thought he was OK. It was the first time in more than ten years that anyone except his daughter Carla thought and said he was OK, in any way. And he was weak, he didn't want it to end.

And now?

Now he had been drawn in, and his sins had caught up with him.

It wasn't that he could no longer play the bass guitar in the evenings. It was that he was ashamed of what he *wanted* to play when he *was* practising.

Last week, on the way home, he heard Neil Diamond's 'Song Sung Blue' over the radio – the *Hot August Night* recording that began with just acoustic guitar, and where the bass guitar only kicked in halfway through the first verse, suddenly giving the song rhythm and depth and familiarity – and he thought he would like to play it as soon as he was home. Only to remember he lived with Alexa now, maybe she would think Neil Diamond wasn't sophisticated enough, that he should rather practise something else, that he had an image to maintain . . .

He had to be what he was not.

And that was just the beginning, the tip of the iceberg.

There was the money thing as well. Alexa had inherited well from her late husband – including his record company Afrisound, which brought in a constant stream of royalties. The firm was not in good shape, but she was rebuilding it with a natural, instinctive business acumen. Alexa's own comeback album, *Bittersoet*, was doing better than expected, her concerts were fully booked again.

She was a rich woman. And he was a policeman.

She had bought him the iPhone. And a new amplifier for his bass guitar. And clothes – a jacket, and expensive shirts that he didn't want to wear to work, because he knew that colleagues like Vaughn Cupido would tease him mercilessly. Not to mention the new winter pyjamas. They were an embarrassment to him – he felt like a baboon in fancy dress. What was wrong with an old pair of tracksuit pants and a T-shirt? But when he put on the new pyjamas and stood there in front of Alexa like a moron, she said, with a big, appreciative smile, 'Come here, Benny,' and she held him tightly and kissed him until his knees buckled . . .

What would it help to share it all with Doc?

That's why he avoided all mention of the Big Problem. He could never tell Barkhuizen about that. Or anyone else, that was the big fuck-up. He would have to sort it out himself, but he couldn't, not at all – he didn't even know where to begin.

And as if that wasn't enough to complicate his life, Alexa added another dilemma this afternoon.

When he had showered and was putting on fresh clothes in their bedroom, Alexa had come to sit on the bed, excited, as though she couldn't keep the 'surprise' to herself any more. She said bass guitar player Schalk Joubert was going to perform with Lize Beekman at *Die Boer* in Durbanville next Friday night. 'But Schalk has to rush to New York for a gig, and I said to Lize, what about Benny? He knows all your music off by heart and he's not only a master detective, he's grown amazingly as a musician. And then she said that's a brilliant idea. Benny, you're going to play with Lize Beekman – I'm so proud of you . . .'

At first he felt relief that it was not the surprise he had suspected.

And then the knowledge dawned on him: he was not in that league, no matter how hard he practised with Rust, his foursome of amateur-veterans. They did covers of time-worn hits, played every now and then at golden and silver wedding anniversaries in front of middle-aged audiences. But this was Lize Beekman, the singer who, the one or two times he'd been in her presence, had left him tongue-tied and dumbstruck by her immense talent and her quiet beauty and her aura.

What was he to do? Alexa sat there in joy and expectation, waiting for his response to the great gift. He had forced a smile and said '*Sjoe*,' an innocuous exclamation that he *fokken* never used. He said: 'Thank you, Alexa, but I don't know if I'm good enough,' and knew exactly what her reaction would be.

'Of course you are good enough. I didn't start singing in bands yesterday, Benny. You've grown so much in your music the past year.' One of her typical artistic expressions that he struggled to handle. 'Lize is emailing me the repertoire, and you have to go and rehearse a few times, but that's only next week, you'll be able to arrange that with work . . . Put on your new blue shirt, you look so good in it.'

So he put the blue shirt on.

He was fucked. In at least two ways.

He found his team members at IMC, the Hawks' Information Management Centre.

'You look a bit better, Benna,' said Cupido when he looked up from the computer screen he was staring at, along with the other Violent Crimes detectives. 'Nice shirt, partner . . .'

The whole room gawped at him.

'We got the two-oh-five subpoena quickly,' said Captain Philip van Wyk, IMC commanding officer, referring to the Hawks' responsibilities according to article 205 of the Criminal Procedure Act when obtaining cellphone records. 'Seems like this has really caught the attention higher up . . .'

''Cause why, it's a foreigner,' said Cupido reproachfully.

'. . . But it's the data from three cellphone towers that's relevant,' said van Wyk. 'And weekends are prime time in Franschhoek. It'll take time to analyse everything.'

'And I can tell you now, there are going to be lots of international calls,' said Cupido. 'Half of those wine farms are in the hands of foreigners.'

'The logs of the Internet service provider to La Petite Margaux show there were seven computers and three iPads on that IP address since Friday. We'll have to identify and isolate the computers and traffic belonging to the farm personnel before we know what Morris's activities were.'

Griessel tried to remember what van Wyk had taught him. 'That means we'll have to go and collect their computers.'

'Please.'

'They're not going to like that.'

'I can send Lithpel to them. It may be less disruptive, and it shouldn't take too long.'

'Maybe Ulinda as well; those foreigners won't understand a word Lithpel says,' said Cupido.

'I'm right here,' said Reginald 'Lithpel' Davids, the lisping computer whizz van Wyk had recently poached from Forensics. Davids was small and frail, with the face of a schoolboy. He shook his big Afro hairstyle indignantly. 'It'th sometimeth like I don't exthitht to you.'

'I rest my case,' said Cupido.

'I'll phone Franschhoek so long,' said Radebe and reached for a phone. 'This is new, it's the first time I've been an English interpreter for a coloured *outjie*.'

'*Jithith*,' Lithpel said, but he grabbed his worn old rucksack of computer equipment and stood up.

'Anything on Paul Anthony Morris?' Griessel asked.

One of van Wyk's researchers said: 'We started with Google, Captain. It's a relatively common combination of names, and there are quite a lot of references that don't have photos with them. But we're working on it.'

'And the snake on the cartridges?'

'That's a difficult one to isolate in the database records,' said van Wyk. 'The query is still running, we might have to refine it. But nothing so far.'

Nyathi walked in and the room fell silent. 'Benny, the British Consul General's office just called. She has news about the passport, we can go and see her now.'

Eyebrows were raised. Cupido looked at his watch. 'Twenty past seven at night? Maybe this Morris is royalty or something.'

In the car Nyathi said, 'I spoke to your sponsor. Thanks, Benny. I hope you understand.'

'Of course, sir,' he said, because he did understand. The Hawks were a team environment. The weakest link determined their success. And at the moment that was what he was. The weakest link.

'Everything else OK? Your health? The family?'

'Yes, thank you, sir.'

The Colonel nodded his bald head slowly and thoughtfully, like a man who has come one step closer to insight and truth.

They drove in silence until they reached the N1. 'Cloete has his hands full with the media,' said Nyathi. 'We need a break. Quickly.' And then, 'Do you think it's about ransom, Benny?'

'Yes, sir.'

'Have you investigated a kidnapping involving a ransom before?'

'Three or four times, sir. But not where there's a foreigner involved.'

'I've never had one,' said Nyathi.

'They're all bad news, sir.'

They parked in Riebeeck Street and first had to search for the entrance to Norton Rose House, a tower block that was deserted at this time of the night.

The British Consulate, with bullet-proof glass doors and a comprehensive security system, was on the fifteenth floor – Griessel and Nyathi had to identify themselves before a woman came to fetch them and escort them to the Consul General's office.

The dignified middle-aged woman introduced herself as Doreen Brennan. She was not alone. With her was a younger woman with dark hair cut short, black-rimmed glasses, and a pretty mouth. 'This is one of our vice consuls, Emma Graber. Please, gentlemen, sit down.'

When the courtesies were dispensed with, Brennan pushed the police photographer's photo of the passport across the desk. 'I'm afraid this is a forgery,' she said apologetically.

Griessel's heart sank into his shoes. That meant they still did not know who Morris or his next of kin were.

'Are you sure?' asked Nyathi.

'Yes. The passport number belongs to a seventy-six-year-old woman from Bexhill-on-Sea who passed away thirteen days ago. It might be her passport that was modified, but we'll need to analyse the original to be sure.'

'No, the passport is very new,' said Griessel as he wrestled with disappointment.

'Would it be possible for us to take a look at the document itself?' asked Graber. 'We have a comprehensive database of forgeries, which might help us trace its origin.'

'Of course,' said Nyathi. 'I'm sure that can be arranged eventually . . .'

'I see,' said Graber thoughtfully. Then, 'Of course, we only want to aid your investigation. As I understand it, the first seventy-two hours are usually crucial.'

'Indeed. And your offer is much appreciated,' said Nyathi.

'We actually know very little about the crime that this person was involved in,' said Graber. 'Unfortunately, the detective who brought the photographs spoke to one of the clerks. Could you tell us more?'

Nyathi hesitated, then smiled politely. 'I'm really sorry, but the investigation is at a very sensitive stage. And now it seems as if Morris may not be a British citizen . . . I do hope you understand. . . .'

'Of course,' said Graber, and she smiled sympathetically. 'We're just trying to help. And I'm curious. Was it a robbery or something?'

'I'm not at liberty to say.'

Griessel wasn't concentrating, and only became aware of the uncomfortable silence when Nyathi gave him a swift but meaningful glance. He finally grasped that there was something on the go here, a verbal chess game – Graber wanted very much to get her hands on the passport and to know more about the crime. Nyathi was most unwilling to share it with her. And he remembered Cupido's reaction: *Twenty past seven at night? Maybe this Morris is royalty or something.*

All at once he was alert, as if the fatigue had just rolled off him.

There was a snake in the grass here. And the Colonel wanted him to help catch it.

He knew he must now ask his questions right. 'Do you monitor missing persons?'

He noticed that the Consul General waited for Graber to answer.

'Well, only if they're reported missing, and are presumed to be travelling, of course. There is a process . . .'

'Was a Paul Anthony Morris reported missing?'

'Not that we know of,' said Graber.

'Someone of his age and description?'

'It's hard to say. The info you have provided is rather sketchy. If we could analyse the original document?'

'Do you have any idea who this Paul Anthony Morris might be?'

'Well, it's quite a common name. As you can imagine, it is going to take some time to scour the Home Office database, which might turn up nothing.'

It was almost as though she was encouraging him to ask the right question, but he didn't know what that was. 'But do you . . . have you got any idea?'

'What we *do* know, is that no person by that name has been reported missing in the United Kingdom in the past fortnight.'

Griessel tried to understand the game. She wasn't giving him a direct 'no'. Why not?

'Are there any other persons who were reported missing that you think he might be?' Not entirely correctly phrased, she was clever, he would have to think carefully.

Without hesitation Graber said, 'The Metropolitan Police in the UK run a database called Merlin, which, in addition to other information, also logs missing persons reports. We have to assume that the age indicated on the passport is more or less correct, because it has to correspond to the photograph. And of course the photograph must bear a close enough resemblance to the man who entered this country last week in order to fool customs. Now, I can tell you that Merlin provided absolutely no data on persons generally resembling this photograph, and in this broad age bracket, that have been reported to UK authorities over the past fortnight as missing.'

Why was she going on about 'fortnight'?

'And in the past six to twelve months?'

'In the previous fiscal year, Merlin logged more than forty thousand records of missing persons. That type of enquiry might take several days before I could answer with confidence.'

'Ladies, with all due respect,' said the ever-dignified Zola Nyathi quietly and courteously, 'there is a man's life at stake here.'

'I can assure you, Colonel, we're doing everything in our power to help,' said the Consul General.

'Is Morris's life at stake?' asked Graber. 'Or is he a suspect in a criminal case?'

'You know who he is,' said Griessel, because now he was sure.

They looked him in the eye, calm and direct.

'Captain,' said Doreen Brennan, measured and diplomatic, 'I receive Foreign Office bulletins about persons of interest on an almost daily basis. To be absolutely honest, this Paul Anthony Morris could be one of at least twenty British subjects of concern to our government. But at this stage – with no certainty as to his real identity, and with you not being very forthcoming about the details of the criminal incident – speculation will do more harm than good.'

From a thousand interrogations of suspects Griessel knew that when people began to use phrases such as 'to be absolutely honest', they were lying through their teeth. He suspected the two Brits had conferred at length before he and Nyathi arrived, and they knew exactly what they would say.

But before he could respond, Nyathi said, 'I'm reading between the lines that you are willing to trade information, should we be willing to divulge details about the case.'

The Consul General got up from her chair. 'If you'll excuse me, I need to call my family to tell them I'll be home soon . . . No, please sit down, gentlemen . . .' She walked slowly to the door, and closed it behind her.

Maybe he should hold his tongue and let Nyathi talk, since he had missed the subtle message entirely.

'I have to tell you that the Consulate cannot officially comment on an identity based on a fake passport, unless we've had time to thoroughly examine the document in question,' said Graber.

'And unofficially?' asked Nyathi.

'I've been known to speculate, should a conversation catch my interest . . .'

'And how do we obtain your interest?'

'That would depend.'

'We'd consider lending you the passport, in a day or two . . .' said Nyathi.

'I'd surely appreciate that, but . . .'

'You want it sooner?'

'That isn't my strongest need.'

'You want details of the case?'

'Now *that* would be immensely helpful.'

'We could provide them, if we were properly motivated,' said Nyathi with a faint smile, and Griessel realised the colonel was good at this sort of thing. The rumour was that he had been in the intelligence wing of Umkhonto we Sizwe, in the old days. Perhaps it was true.

'I'm a firm believer in motivation,' said Graber, 'but as you know, speculation is not fact. And the idea of speculative information reaching our friends in the media is too ghastly to contemplate.'

'I absolutely share that fear,' said Nyathi. 'That is why, despite tremendous pressure, the media is still very much in the dark about the details of this case.'

'How do we ensure that it stays that way?'

'By giving you our word that Captain Griessel and I will not divulge any speculative information, unless third parties are mutually agreed upon.'

'Does that include your colleagues at the Directorate of Priority Crime Investigation?'

'It does.'

Graber gave a slight nod. 'Has this "Morris" committed a crime?'

'No.'

'Has he been the victim of a crime?'

'Do you know who he is?'

'We have a very strong suspicion.'

'How?'

'The photograph.'

'He resembles someone your government is looking for?'

'He does indeed. Is he the victim of a crime?'

'He is.'

'A serious crime?'

'Yes.'

'Has he been killed?'

'Who?' Nyathi smiled again, as if he were really enjoying this.

'Paul Anthony Morris.'

'Is that his real name?'

'No.'

'Who do you think he is?'

'Has he been killed?'

'No.'

'Is he in your custody?'

'No.'

That silenced her. Her face was expressionless, but Griessel could see the gears turning.

'Who do you think he is?' asked Nyathi.

'Do you know where he is at this moment?'

Nyathi did not reply.

'Has he been kidnapped?' asked Graber.

'Who is he?' asked Nyathi.

'Colonel, I really need to know whether he has been kidnapped.'

'We really need to know who he is.'

She looked at the photo of Queen Elizabeth on the wall, then back at Nyathi. 'We think he is David Patrick Adair.'

Griessel took out his notebook and began to write.

'Why are you so concerned about Mr Adair?' asked Nyathi.

'Has he been kidnapped?'

'Yes,' said Nyathi. 'All evidence points in that direction.'

'Shit,' said Emma Graber with that mouth which Griessel found so lovely.

She asked them to excuse her for just a minute.

They stood up when she left the room, and sat down again when she closed the door behind her.

Griessel looked at Nyathi. The colonel waved an index finger at the ceiling, then in a circular motion, in the end placing it in front of his mouth.

Griessel nodded. He understood. They were probably being listened to.

Odd world this. He wondered what Nyathi's role in Umkhonto had been. And what Emma Graber's job at the Consulate was. He suspected her interest was not criminal by nature, but political. He wondered who David Patrick Adair was, and why Graber was so careful – yet keen at the same time. And what she had gone to do now. Consult with the Consul General? Or with someone else who might have been eavesdropping on their conversation in an adjoining office? Or was she sitting there herself listening, in the hope that he and Nyathi would start talking?

As if this case needed further complications.

Seven minutes passed before she returned. 'I *do* apologise,' she said, and sat down. 'Now, gentlemen, if you Google the name "David Patrick Adair" you will eventually establish that a man by that name is a King's Fellow in Computer Sciences at Cambridge University, and Professor at DAMTP, the Department of Applied Mathematics and Theoretical Physics, at the same institution. The DAMTP website will furthermore show a photograph of Adair which is almost identical to the one in the counterfeit passport.'

There was a subtle shift in her attitude, businesslike, a greater urgency.

'Last week Tuesday, Professor Adair failed to deliver his usual lecture at the Department. Because of his varied commitments and hectic schedule, this in itself isn't unusual. But he has never failed to let his personal assistant know about such an absence before. She reported this to one of his senior colleagues. Upon investigation by this colleague, it was finally established that there had been a burglary at Adair's house in Glisson Road in central Cambridge. A back door was forced and the interior left in complete disarray. Adair was nowhere to be found. Given the sensitive nature of his work, this colleague had the good sense to notify the right authorities, thereby keeping the matter contained . . .'

'So it was never logged on Merlin,' said Nyathi.

'That is correct,' she answered, without a hint of remorse.

'What is the nature of his work?' asked Nyathi.

'Therein, Colonel, lies the rub.'

13

'For starters, you should know that Adair has been divorced for nine years. He is completely estranged from his ex-wife. The marriage was childless. His next of kin is his younger sister Sarah, lecturer at the School of Mathematics at the University of Birmingham. By all accounts she is an extremely competent academic, but alas, not quite the genius her brother is. We have made highly discreet inquiries as to her knowledge of her brother's whereabouts, and it is clear that she has not heard from him since his disappearance. In other words, there is no need for you to contact her.'

'Ah,' said Nyathi. 'I'm assuming that you have also been . . . monitoring her communication channels since last Tuesday?'

'We are positive that no attempt has been made to communicate with her about her brother since that time.'

'May I ask to which "we" you are referring?'

'I beg your pardon?'

'You said "we are sure" . . .' said Nyathi patiently.

'The British authorities,' she said, with an ironic smile herself now.

'And the nature of Professor Adair's work?'

She nodded. 'Now please bear with me, because this gets a little complicated. But I want to get it right, not least so that you will also understand the great need for circumspection in this matter.'

'Please,' said Nyathi.

Griessel said nothing, just listened.

'An Internet search of his name will eventually lead you to the good professor's responsibility for the so-called Adair Algorithm. To save time, and to enunciate the necessity for discretion, I would like to explain what that is. Have you heard of the Society for Worldwide Interbank Financial Telecommunication, or SWIFT?'

'Vaguely.'

'Very well. Please allow me to elaborate: SWIFT is based in Belgium.

It is a network that enables financial institutions across the globe to send and receive information about monetary transactions. Your bank, for instance, would have a SWIFT code, which is part of this system. Should you receive money from abroad, this code is used, and the information about the transaction is registered on SWIFT's computers. Simple stuff, is it not?'

They nodded in unison.

'Now, shortly after 9/11, the CIA and the US State Department set up the top secret and pretty controversial Terrorist Finance Tracking Programme, also known as TFTP. In a nutshell, this programme provides US authorities with access to the SWIFT database, in order to trace financial transactions that might identify potential terrorist activities. You might have heard of it . . .'

'Yes,' said Nyathi.

'In June of 2006, the *New York Times* ran the first media exposé on TFTP, but the project survived, due to the public sentiment at the time, perhaps, but also because TFTP proved extremely useful right off the bat. However, being a US-only initiative, it was lacking in reach and scope. To be truly effective, it needed to go global. So, the USA invited the European Union to come on board. Of course, Europe was equally concerned about the terrorist threat, and keen to cooperate. But initially the European Parliament rejected an interim EU–US TFTP agreement, because they felt it did not offer EU citizens enough privacy protection. Are we still on the same page?'

'Yes,' said Nyathi.

'Good. This is where David Adair enters our story. He was invited to become a member of the EU evaluation team of the TFTP agreement, because of his expertise in database search algorithms. Adair took a long, hard look at the US system, and came to the conclusion that it could be vastly improved – not only in terms of privacy safeguards, but also in effectiveness. He then proceeded, as geniuses do, to write a vastly superior algorithm on a whim, and offer it to the authorities. Of course, they gratefully accepted, and in 2010 the EU announced their resumption of the TFTP. The so-called Adair Algorithm then became the standard methodology to sniff out terrorists in the international banking system. It has been responsible for the identification and subsequent termination of at least seven terrorist cells, and an impressively large number of senior al-Qaeda leaders and operatives.'

Emma Graber leaned back in her chair, spreading her hands, palms open, as if she had nothing more to hide.

'Gentlemen, the Adair Algorithm is one of the best-kept and most vital international security secrets in history. If it falls into the wrong hands . . .'

She let the thought hang in the air for a minute, then she said, 'Now please tell me about the nature of the kidnapping.'

Griessel listened to Nyathi skipping over certain details of the investigation.

With carefully chosen words and in perfect English, the Giraffe told Emma Graber about Adair's initial contact with Body Armour, his arrival and stay on La Petite Margaux, the death of the farm worker and two bodyguards, and the signs of struggle in the master bedroom. He described the security measures, and how they thought the crime had happened.

Graber asked Nyathi for the email address of the Paul Anthony Morris alias.

He said he would have to consult their notes, but he would send it on. Griessel remembered the address well, but kept quiet.

Nyathi said not a word about the cartridges with the snake and the letters NM engraved on them. Nor of the missing laptop, iPad, and possible cellphone – the Hawks' only clues.

Griessel suspected it was deliberate, but he wasn't sure.

When the colonel had finished, they negotiated a joint press release to quell the hunger of the media, and relieve the pressure on the families of the bodyguard victims and the wine-farm personnel.

It would state that an unidentified man, presumably a European tourist, was missing after a guesthouse employee and two security officials were shot dead during a break-in. Missing and possible incorrect passport details had made the identification of the missing person difficult at this stage, but he was thought to be male and a British citizen. The Directorate of Priority Crimes Investigation was grateful for the willingness and cooperation of the British Consulate regarding this matter. As soon as a positive identification could be made with certainty, and the sensitivity of the investigation allowed it, the media would be fully informed. In the meantime, no stone would be left unturned to bring the perpetrators to book and to track down the missing person. Various leads were being followed.

Nyathi told Graber they would have to inform one more Hawks' colleague of the identity of David Adair: Major Benedict Boshigo, member of the Statutory Crimes Group of the Hawks' Commercial Crimes in the Cape – their expert in financial affairs. But he could give her the assurance that Boshigo, just like them, would handle the information in confidence. 'Until such time as we agree otherwise.'

'Very well,' she said amiably.

They solemnly agreed to inform each other of relevant develop-ments, as often as circumstances allowed.

Graber walked them to the lift, where they said goodbye.

Only once they turned into Buitengracht, in the direction of Bellville, did Nyathi speak.

'I want you to call the Body Armour boss, Benny, and inform her that the British authorities might contact her. I want you to tell her that divulging any information to anyone other than the SAPS would constitute a crime . . .'

'Sir, I think we should . . . She's a tough one, it would be better not to . . .'

'Threaten her?'

'Yes.'

'See what you can do. But above all, ask her not to share Morris's email address.'

He rang. She answered promptly.

He told her that the Hawks would issue a press release later that night that would relieve the pressure on the families of the two murdered bodyguards. He agreed to send it to her as well.

'I appreciate that,' she said.

'There's a possibility that someone from the British Consulate might contact you. We ask whether it would be possible to refer all their queries to us.'

She remained silent for so long that Griessel thought the connec-tion had been lost.

'Hello?' he said.

'I'm here.'

He waited.

'Here's the deal,' she said. 'I won't tell them a thing. But you tell me everything.'

'That is not possible at the moment.'

'You are going to tell me everything when it *is* possible. I don't want to read anything in the press that I don't know, or I'll phone the Consulate.'

'All right,' said Griessel, and rang off.

'Mission accomplished?' Nyathi asked.

'Yes, sir.'

'Well done. You're pretty good with people, Benny . . .'

He didn't know what to say to that.

'The first thing you have to understand about the intelligence community is that they only tell the truth if it serves a purpose. Their purpose, mostly.'

'Yes, sir.'

'Graber is most likely MI6. Also known as the Secret Intelligence Service, or SIS. She is probably working closely with MI5, the British national security service, which hunts terrorists inside the UK, amongst other duties.'

'Sir . . .' He couldn't sit on it any more. 'You seem to know a lot about all this?'

Nyathi laughed, and Griessel wondered whether it was the first time that he had seen the colonel do that.

'Twenty-six years ago I was recruited for MK Intelligence, Benny. Because I was a schoolteacher, they thought I was intelligent. And I worked in London for a while . . . What I'm trying to say is that lying is part of that profession. And I think she is lying to us. Or at least not telling the whole truth.'

'Why, sir?'

'Two things, Benny. The first one is that she tried very hard to have us believe that this is about terrorism, but she never actually said it. Her problem is that she is working in a foreign country, and she has to tread very carefully not to lie directly. Very bad for diplomacy, should things get out of hand later. She has to keep the back door open, the one that allows her to say: "Oh, you must have misunderstood, would you like to listen to the recording again?"'

'I understand.'

'The second is the channel she's chosen. If this were purely about a potential terrorist act, their High Commissioner in Pretoria would have approached our Minister of Security. Musad and I would have been called by him, not by them.'

Burly Brigadier Musad Manie was the commanding officer of the Hawks in the Cape.

'You think this is about something else, sir?'

'All I know is that Adair probably is who she says he is. As for the rest, we'll have to see.'

Griessel began to understand. 'Is that why you did not just send me and Vaughn when they called, sir? You knew, when they called this late on a Monday evening . . .'

'I suspected something might be brewing.'

'And that's why you did not tell her everything, sir?'

'Yes, Benny. When you're working with intelligence people, you should always have an ace up your sleeve. Always. We have a few, and I want to keep it that way. So, the first thing you do, is send her the wrong email address for Paul Anthony Morris. Just a small typo . . .'

He wondered whether he detected a note of nostalgia in Nyathi's voice.

Griessel had always experienced him as a fair, thoughtful man, but quiet and modest, largely unreadable and enigmatic. Tonight he had also discovered a keen intelligence, a feel for this strategic game that Benny would have trouble matching.

The colonel had enjoyed himself in the Consul General's office, that was clear to see. And now, here in the car, there was enthusiasm, a sparkle that he had not previously detected in the Giraffe. How had it felt after the adrenaline and excitement of spying in London, to fill a senior command – really mainly personnel management, administration, and strife from the higher-ups – in the SAPS?

Did he enjoy his job?

When they had gone past Canal Walk, Nyathi asked him to call Cloete, the liaison officer, and ask him to come in. And also Major

Benedict 'Bones' Boshigo. 'Tell Bones to come directly to my office, and not to talk to anyone.'

When that was done – and Bones had responded with a 'that's never a good sign, hey' – he and the colonel decided what they would say to their colleagues.

14

'Wait a minute,' said Cupido in the big IMC room. 'They let you ride all the way, this time of a Monday night, jus' to tune you the passport is a fake? They could have told you that over the phone.'

'It's called diplomacy, Vaughn,' said the much older and more experienced Frankie Fillander. 'You should try it some time.'

'Show me some love, Uncle Frankie. I smell a rat.'

'What kind of rat?' asked Griessel.

'This was a professional hit, pappie, and *jy wiet* who sanctions professional hits. Gangstas and governments.'

'That's true . . .'

'Any news?' asked Griessel, to change the subject.

'Nothing yet,' said van Wyk. 'And we're still waiting for Ulinda and Lithpel. It's going to be a late night.'

'Then you'd better go home so long,' said Griessel to the Violent Crimes detectives. 'I'll call if there's anything.'

They murmured their thanks. Only Cupido stood a while and looked at Griessel. Then he nodded and left.

'*Ja*, I know about the Adair Algorithm. *Maar dit maak nie sense nie, nè*, it just doesn't add up,' said Bones Boshigo in his characteristic mix of languages, after they had told him everything. He owed his nickname to the fact that he was mere skin and bone, thanks to his murderous marathon-training programme. He was also one of the most intelligent detectives that Griessel knew, a man with a degree in economics that he had earned at the University of Boston's Metropolitan College.

Behind his desk, Nyathi just raised his eyebrows.

'Kidnap him, Colonel? Why?' asked Bones. 'Everyone knows what the algorithm does, even the terrorists, and there's nothing anyone can do to stop it. Al-Qaeda must have figured out long ago that moving money through conventional banking channels is pretty stupid. Last I heard about TFTP is that it helps to nail a few small operators. I think this is really about the Adair Protocol, *nè*?'

He noticed his two colleagues hadn't the faintest idea what he was talking about.

'They didn't tell you about the Adair Protocol?'

'No,' said Griessel.

'*Nogal* funny. This *ou*, David Adair, he wrote a paper on the use of his algorithm, about two years ago . . . early 2011, just after the EU joined TFTP. He basically said the scope of the programme was too small, and that his algorithm had the capability to do much more – the authorities had a moral obligation to employ it. He published the paper in a scientific magazine, and it became known as the Adair Protocol.'

'The capacity to do much more what?' Nyathi wanted to know.

'Tracing other dubious financial transactions. His main argument was that the black market is worth about two thousand billion dollars per annum internationally, and tracking that money can have a huge impact on the containment and prosecution of organised crime.'

'OK,' said Griessel, struggling increasingly to keep up. The day was growing very long.

'So they're doing that now?' asked Nyathi.

'No, sir.'

'Why not?'

'The banks didn't like it, *nè*. And you can understand – they're making big bucks from black market money and the whole laundering process. If TFTP starts looking at their organised crime clients, they will lose them all, quickly, to obscure little off-line banks in the Cayman Islands. So they pleaded invasion of privacy concerns, and the EU Parliament and the British government sang the same song.'

'Bones, I don't understand, if TFTP isn't being used against organised crime, why can this kidnapping be about the Adair Protocol?' asked Nyathi.

'Adair is an agitator, *nè*. *Baie* liberal, *baie* vocal. *Hy bly nie stil nie*, he makes a lot of noise. Two months ago, he was saying in *The Economist* that the British Conservative Party is in cahoots with the banks and basically assisting organised crime. He's canvassing, Colonel, all the time. I think the gangstas would maybe really like to get rid of him, before he gets public opinion on his side.'

'So you think they killed him?'

'*Yebo*, yes.'

Jy wiet, *who sanctions professional hits. Gangstas and governments*, Cupido had said. But Griessel also knew that Bones was in essence a numbers guy, not a homicide detective. 'No,' he said.

They waited for Griessel to explain. He took a moment to gather his thoughts. 'Organised crime . . . Bones, when they order a hit, they want to make a statement. They would have left him dead at the guesthouse.'

'No, Benny, not in the current political climate. Then the British press will say Adair was right, there will be big pressure on government to institute the Protocol. The way I understand this whole thing, nobody knows for sure that Adair came to South Africa. If they can make him disappear, *nè*, no names, no pack drill . . . Problem solved. And maybe they want him to suffer first, Benny. You know how the gangstas are.'

'Maybe,' said Griessel, because aspects of the argument did make sense. 'But for that reason they could have murdered him here, and then the media would have said: Look how dangerous South Africa is . . .'

Nyathi's phone rang. The colonel answered, listened, said a few times: 'Yes, sir', and then: 'I'll wait for him.'

After putting the phone down, he looked at Benny. 'That was our Hawks commissioner, in Pretoria,' he said. 'He asked me to receive a representative of our very own State Security Agency. To share the details of the case.'

'But how did they know . . . ?' asked Griessel.

'They monitor the Consulate, of course,' said Nyathi. 'Probably their telephones too.'

'All cloak and dagger, *nè. Dis 'n lekker een dié*, what fun,' said Bones. 'Colonel, thanks for including me. Much more exciting than investigating pyramid schemes. Let me go do a little digging on Adair . . .'

When Cloete came in, Griessel went straight to his office to send Emma Graber the incorrect email address for Paul Anthony Morris/

David Patrick Adair. The one that Cupido had confirmed was Paul_
Morris15@gmail.com. He thought for quite a while before deciding
on a false address. Nyathi had asked for a typing error, something
that could be explained as a simple error, should Graber realise the
address was false. One possibility was to swap letters around, but
that was too easy. The one he eventually sent to the British embassy
was Paul_Morris151@gmail.com – making him feel ever so slightly
like a spy.

Then he walked back to IMC.

Captain Philip van Wyk said they had searched the national data-
bases and there were no references to bullet cartridges with snake
engravings or the letters NM on them. And all the other processes
were still running.

At twenty-two minutes past ten, Griessel sat down in his office, bolt
upright, so that the fatigue and despondency would not overcome him
too quickly.

In truth, they had nothing.

If you thought about it.

Now that they knew who Morris truly was, the cellphone and
computer records wouldn't really help.

And if Bones was right, that meant Adair was already dead, and the
murderers would likely feed his remains to the sharks, or bury them.

Once again foreign mischief brought over here. Just what this
country needed.

Seven detectives, Forensics, IMC, and Nyathi's whole day dedicated to something that would come to nought, he knew it already.

Maybe the Spooks of the SSA should take over the whole thing.

He should rather just go to sleep.

But he didn't want to. That *fokken* snake on the cartridge, that was
the thing that had snagged his attention, that would not let go.

What sort of fool made a stamp of a spitting cobra, and then marked
his ammunition, every round? Which would take a hell of a lot of time.
For what?

Leaving them on the crime scene like a visiting card . . .

With the letters. NM. Initials? Nols Malan or Natie Meiring or
Norman Matthews, like the pretentious number plates of the rich that
said 'look how *fokken* common but cute I am'.

Then he made the international connection, and he got up and he walked back to IMC, his brain back in gear again.

'We will have to do an Interpol enquiry,' said Griessel to van Wyk. 'About the cobra and the letters.'

'Good idea.' Van Wyk halted. 'You know they also have a database of stolen and lost travel documents. Shall I look up Paul Anthony Morris on that?'

Griessel knew it wouldn't help, but he kept up appearances. 'Please.'

He turned and walked back to his office. While he waited for Nyathi and the SSA agent to finish talking, he wanted to bring his admin up to date. The file would have to be created. He must write an email to his team, remind them to forward him their interview reports and witness statements for Section A. Then he must write out his own interviews and notes, and in Section C, he must fill in the investigation journal on the SAPS5 form, a detailed, chronological history of the case.

It made him wonder: should he leave out the discussion with the Consulate entirely? Or just not mention the full content?

Nyathi called him within fifteen minutes.

'They want to be kept in the loop,' said the colonel. 'So now I have to liaise with an SSA agent as often as I deem necessary.'

'Sir, if we ask the SSA to look in their database for a hit man who engraves his shell casings . . .'

'I did not tell him about the engravings, Benny. I had to tell them about Adair, because I don't know what they might have eavesdropped on. But I told them no more than we told Graber.'

'OK.'

'Anything new?'

'No, sir.'

'Go and get some sleep, Benny. Tell Philip's people to alert you only if they find something big.'

15

He drove home.

Alexa would still be awake.

She was a true creature of the night, staying up till all hours. In the evenings she answered emails and talked on the phone when he wasn't there. She went over the figures from the record company while she listened to demo CDs of hopeful artists ('One never knows . . .'), and she talked with him about his day when he eventually arrived home.

And she cooked for them. He suspected it was her method of suppressing the urge to drink, an attempt at a degree of normality, to create a homely atmosphere after the chaos of her first marriage, and the bohemian nature of her world. He also suspected that she thought that he expected it of her, even though he had denied it.

But Alexa was no chef. She had no natural aptitude for cooking, and she was easily distracted if a text or a call came in, so that she couldn't remember which of the ingredients she had already added to the pot. And her sense of taste was decidedly suspect. She would carefully taste the pasta sauce, declare it perfect, but when she dished it up and began to eat, she would frown and say: 'Something is not right. Can you taste it too?'

He would lie.

But these were insignificant untruths. White lies.

The big lie, the unmentionable, unshareable and increasingly unbearable lie, the fraud that assailed him now on the dark, silent N1 on the way to Alexa, was the one about sex.

He swore out loud in the car.

Life just never gave him a break.

If you drank as he used to drink, seven days a week, sex was not a big priority. When lust sometimes overcame him, his alcohol-soaked equipment wouldn't cooperate anyway.

But then you dried out, and that had consequences. The biggest problem of being on the wagon was the desire for the healing powers of the bottle. Close on those heels was the return of the libido, at a time when you have way too much mileage on your middle-aged clock, and desirable women were not necessarily queuing up to accommodate you.

Which was what was so damn ironic. Six months ago he was head over heels in love with Alexa, and a big chunk of that was his desire to make love to her, good and proper. Look, he was a sucker for a beautiful mouth, and she certainly had one, broad and generous and soft. And like most guys, surely, he appreciated a royal pair of jugs – as Cupido, faced with an impressive bust measurement, would longingly, admiringly describe them.

And there was Alexa's voice, and her attitude, and that look in her eyes, as if she knew what you were thinking, and she wanted you to keep on thinking just that. He had always had a thing for her, from way back, when she first hit the limelight and he was just one more nameless fan staring at the sexy singer on the TV screen, harbouring his unseemly secret thoughts.

He was crazy for her.

But then, after the chaos of the Sloet case, six months ago, it happened for the first time, and it was everything that Benny Griessel had dreamed of. Lord, that woman could kiss, and her body was just the right combination of soft and firm, even though she was closer to fifty than he was. She was so instantly responsive, her hands all over his body. Her eagerness, her spontaneity, she didn't mind showing her pleasure, shouting, in her jubilant velvet voice: 'Oh yes, Benny, yes. Good, Benny, so good, more, more, more,' along with a few other things that you wouldn't ever mention to anyone, but that were thrilling all the same.

Afterwards, he would lie beside her, spent and wet with perspiration, in love, lost, and so immensely pleased with himself and with her, and with them. He thought, fuck, finally life had given him a break, this sexy creature, this fabulous woman.

And from there on it only got better.

Between her busy scheduleand his unpredictable work, at least once a week – now and again two heavenly times – they would repeat the miracle in her big double bed. A couple of times in the sitting room, and once in the shower, soaking wet and slippery with soap. They learned more of each other's tastes and bodies and pleasures, grew relaxed and easy, and Griessel was happy for the first time in he didn't know how long.

And then he went and moved in.

'It would be so nice to have just a little more of you, Benny. Even if it is a half an hour in the morning, or evening.' That's how Alexa brought it up.

He thought that, if it was so amazing when he saw her so seldom, it could only be better when he saw her more. Logical argument. In addition, it made economic and practical sense. She was alone in that rambling house, he was cooped up with his cheap furniture in his cramped bachelor flat.

And they loved each other.

So he gave up his flat, and took the furniture back to Mohammed 'Love Lips' Faizal's pawn shop, and with the proceeds he took Alexa to her favourite restaurant, Bizerca, where he, SAPS Detective Captain, sat eating oysters in the knowledge that his constant struggle was over, life was good. That first moving-in night they fucked like teenagers, and he knew it had been the right decision.

The second night, when he came to bed, Alexa slipped her hand under the elastic of his pyjama bottoms and she stroked and teased and kissed him, and he *njapsed* her again.

The third night, the same thing. His soldier struggled to stand quite to attention, and his performance was not what you'd call first rate, but he pressed through.

And by night four he knew he was in trouble.

In his twenties, when he and his ex, Anna, were young and horny and newly married, he could do the deed two, three times a day.

But that was in the old days. A quarter century and a thousand litres of Jack Daniel's ago.

Now it was altogether a different matter.

So, what did you do?

He couldn't say to Alexa 'no, *fok weet*, this is a bit much'. Not when she looked at you with those eyes full of love and compassion and sexual need, not when you had been *njapsing* her with such abandon for the past six months. Not if she had bought you clothes and an iPhone, and treated you like this big hero.

There was no way he could sit in front of a doctor and say 'I want a prescription for Viagra'. His sexual prowess had nothing to do with anyone, he didn't have that sort of courage, and he couldn't swallow those pills every day. Then he would be addicted all over again to something new, walking around with a permanent Jakob Regop – a constant boner was trouble that he really didn't need.

All he could do, was to sleep over at work. To get the lead back in his pencil.

Which meant he looked rough in the morning, and lied to all and sundry, and his boss and his colleagues thought he was drinking again.

He knew it couldn't go on like this.

But what was he to do?

He was fucked. He knew it.

She met him at the door, kissed him, clucked over him, led him to the kitchen 'for lasagne, it didn't come out exactly as I hoped, Benny, but you must be terribly hungry'. She sat with him in the kitchen. He ate, and told little white lies about the taste of the food. She asked about his day. He told her everything, except the part about Adair. She listened so attentively, was so impressed. Then she said: 'My master detective. You'll catch them.'

He asked about her day. She told him about the negotiations and recordings, about the battle to get publicity and time on air for her artists. 'The market is getting a bit overcrowded.'

They went to the bedroom.

He brushed his teeth, put on his new pyjamas. She sat in front of the mirror chatting, taking off her make-up, told him she had left Woollies food in the fridge for while she was away in Johannesburg from tomorrow. She said she would miss him. And he must keep safe. And phone when he could, she had a horde of meetings and one appearance at Carnival City, but by Thursday she would be back again.

He made the calculations. Two nights to recover, to reload his pistol.

She undressed, rubbed her body with creams and oils. She put on her nightclothes, switched off the light. She lay down close to him, held him tightly, her mouth against his neck.

'I love you, Benny.'

'And I love you too.'

Her hand moved to his belly, slipped under the pyjama bottoms.

'Where's that rascal?' she asked playfully.

The ringing of his cellphone woke him.

He saw it was the DPCI number. It was 2.12 in the morning. He picked it up and walked out so as not to disturb Alexa any more. It was cold in the passage without the pyjamas that still lay bundled up somewhere under the sheets.

'Griessel,' he answered.

'Benny, this is Philip. I'm sorry to wake you . . .'

'No problem,' he said, and tried to keep the sleepiness out of his voice.

'I thought you should know: we have just received a call from Senior Superintendent Jean-Luc Bonfils from Interpol in Lyon. It's about the snake on the cartridges.'

He went into the sitting room. There had been a heater on when he came in earlier.

'Do they know something?'

'Yes, "something" is probably the best description. He received our query, and he's sending us everything they have within the next hour, but in the meantime he wanted to tell me: this is the sixteenth international murder that they know of with that "snake trademark", as he calls it . . .'

'*Jissis*,' said Griessel. The heater in the sitting room was off, but the room was not as chilly as the passage. He turned it on, up to maximum while he listened and stood wide-legged over it.

'I made a few quick notes,' said van Wyk. 'The details are not quite right, but here is what I have: the first crime scene where such a marked cartridge was found, was seven years ago in Portugal. I'll come back to that just now. Most of the consecutive murders were in Europe – Germany, France, Spain, Holland, Poland, Belgium, and Italy. One was in Britain, one in New York, and one in Reykjavik, Iceland. He says there may be one or two in Russia, but these have never been officially handed over to Interpol. This one in Franschhoek is the first in the southern hemisphere.'

'Each time the cartridges had the snake on them?'

'That's right.'

'And the targets?'

'That's the funny thing. He says they have no doubt it is a hired assassin, but there is no specific pattern, except for the engraving, of course. In Poland, Spain, and France, the victims were definitely organised crime. The one in New York was a woman of eighty-two, a multimillionaire and an art collector. In Germany it was a young dotcom entrepreneur, and the other a very pretty teacher in her thirties. They were not connected in any way, and the murders were fourteen months apart. I could go on. Bonfils said their theory was that he works for anyone who is prepared to pay. And apparently he charges a lot. A hundred thousand euro per victim, at least.'

'Do they know who he is?'

'They have a few interesting theories, really just based on a single informant who doesn't know the whole story either. Bonfils says the snake on the cartridges is most probably the Mozambican Spitting Cobra, and the letters NM stand for *Naja mossambica*, the Latin name for the snake. Apparently very poisonous, and deadly accurate . . .'

He struggled to link a European hit man with an African snake. 'Mozambique? That's . . . odd?'

'Indeed. And that's where the story gets interesting. The hit man is known as the Cobra, and Interpol think he is Mozambican. Bonfils says the reasons for that are all in the report, but it starts with the first murder, in Portugal.'

'He's sending it now?'

'That's what he promised.'

'I'm coming in . . . You should get some sleep, Phil.'

'I will, as soon as I have read the report.'

Griessel rang off and stood there, cellphone in hand.

A Mozambican. A British professor. On a Cape wine farm belonging to a German.

Where were the days when this land was the polecat of the world, when no one came here? When at least you knew the suspect would be a local *fokker*?

Then he grew aware of the musky scent of sex rising along with the warm air from the heater. He looked down at his penis, now small and shrivelled.

Rascal.

In the big dark room he laughed quietly, mockingly at himself.

16

Just past three in the morning, in the perfect silence of his cramped office beside the IMC hall, van Wyk gave Griessel the print-out of the email and said: 'Read this first . . .'

He took the page and read.

Jean-Luc Bonfils <j-lbonfils@interpol.int>
To:philip.vanwyk@saps.gov.za
Re:Cobra (Cobra/B79C1/04/03/2007)
Dear Captain van Wyk

It was a pleasure talking to a fellow law enforcement officer on the graveyard shift, albeit a continent and hemisphere away, and under these circumstances.

Allow me to start with the most important:

1. I am not the Interpol officer assigned to the Cobra dossier. This is Supt. Marie-Caroline Aubert, and she will be very anxious to assist you in any way. I will share all our communications with her later today.

2. May I respectfully request a copy of your investigation records for our database as soon as your schedule allows? If you could please also keep me informed, should you make positive progress (or, of course, an arrest). Interpol is keenly interested in this subject, especially given the fact that this is the first reported homicide committed by the Cobra in the southern hemisphere.

3. Please find attached twenty-one (21) documents, which is the full complement of available material at Interpol, and includes notes on all the known Cobra dossiers.

4. Please allow me one clarification: you will notice that the Légion étrangère (L.E. or French Foreign Legion) photograph is of very low resolution, and that the information supplied by the L.E. is limited. This is not an omission on the part of Interpol. Usually the L.E. does not release any information on their enlistments to law enforcement (not even French authorities). However, they do screen all applicants for serious crimes through an agreement with Interpol before acceptance. It was this connection we leveraged for the little information on Curado that was released (unofficially, as a favour).

Please let me know if we can be of assistance in any way, and best of luck with your investigation.

Jean-Luc Bonfils (Superintendent)
INTERPOL
200, quai Charles de Gaulle
69006 Lyon
France

'OK,' said Griessel.

Van Wyk pressed his finger on a bundle of documents. 'This pile contains summaries of all the relevant murder investigations in the northern hemisphere,' he said. 'There isn't anything new, but the cartridges are there every time. The only interesting thing is that the Cobra began using a new Heckler & Koch MK23 in 2009 and 2011. But it seems as though he acquires the latest model every two years . . .'

Van Wyk pushed more print-outs across to Benny. 'Read *these* first. That's how they put two and two together.'

Griessel picked up the top page.

INTERPOL
General Secretariat
200, quai Charles de Gaulle
69006 Lyon
France
Intelligence report: Cobra/B79C1/04/03/2007/19/03/2009
Report date: 2 May 2010
Report submitted by: Stefano Masini, Procura della Repubblica presso il Tribunale di Milano
Interview by: Stefano Masini, Procura della Repubblica presso il Tribunale di Milano
Interview with: (Name withheld, paid informant, Bari.)
Interview venue: Bari, Italy
(Edited Transcription, translated by M.P. Ross, Interpol, 19 May 2010)

SM: The shell casings found on the scene of the Carnevale killing are engraved with a snake, and the letters N and M. Do you …

X: (Expletive.) That's bad, man.

SM: Have you ever heard of such markings?

X: Yes, yes, I've heard the rumours, lots of rumours. It's the Cobra. Very dangerous guy.

SM: Does he work for 'ndrangheta?

X: No, (expletive) no, he's a freelancer, he works for anybody, he's a gun for hire. Very expensive, hundred thousand euros for a hit, but they say he never misses, he always delivers. If the Cobra takes a contract on you, you're (expletive) dead, man. For sure.

SM: Do you know who he is?

X: Nobody knows this guy. He's a ghost. Just bullshit stories …

SM: What stories?

X: Bullshit, man. Some say he was in the French Foreign Legion, and he lives in Amsterdam, or Madrid, or Marseilles, but they don't know. Nobody knows. Lots of stories, lots of rumours. The wannabes, they talk about him, they want to be him, man. If you want a clean hit, no comebacks, you get the Cobra. (Expletive) psychopath, man, they say he has the eyes of a snake, you know? He never blinks, cold eyes … That type of shit, people make it up. They even say he killed his own father, I mean, you know, there's a new … how do they say? A new … twist every time …

SM: How did he kill his father?

X: It's crap, man.

SM: I'm sure. But let's not waste a good story.

X: (Expletive.) Don't write in that report that this came from me. I need the money, man …

SM: Of course …

X: OK. So … They say, he killed his father, because he needed a reference, you know? To get business. Three, four years ago, in Portugal. His father was this retired Russian Army colonel, worked in Africa most of his life teaching those baboons to shoot each other with an AK, you know? What do they call them? Military advisor? So this Russian colonel (expletive) some black woman in one of those hell-hole countries, got her pregnant. And then he just left, never cared for the kid or the woman. Big suffering. But she knew his name and everything. So this kid grew up and he joined the French Foreign Legion, became a real killer, you know?

A badass soldier. No fear. Nobody (expletive) with him. And then he left, and became The (expletive) Cobra, man, they say it was his first hit. He traced his father, the guy had retired to Portugal with all his stolen African money, and that was the Cobra's first hit with the snake on the bullets. That's where it all started.

SM: So he's a mulatto?

X: That's what they say.

SM: Who?

X: You know. The rumours. Just guys talking shit.

SM: Guys in the trade?

X: Yes.

SM: Has anybody actually seen him?

X: Maybe the bosses.

SM: Capos?

X: Yes. They say, two of them have met the Cobra. But in the beginning, few years ago, when he was selling.

SM: Selling what?

X: His service. You know. He had to market himself, in the beginning. As an assassin.

SM: Anything else?

X: Not really. OK maybe … But you know this is really all (expletive) crap. Because of the snake on the bullets, they make up new things.

SM: Tell me anyway.

X: They say there's this tattoo he has. Bird and a snake. On his arm. Right here. Guy must love snakes.

SM: That's it?

X: There's nothing else to tell. Oh, they say, if you want to contact him, you place an ad on … what's it called ….? Loot. That's it.

SM: Loot?

X: Yes. It's a website in England where you can sell anything. So you place an ad and you use the word snake, like 'snake for sale' or something, some special code. And then he will contact you. (Expletive) snakes. I mean, you have to be a psycho man, to be that into snakes.

Griessel looked up at van Wyk. 'There's a lot of speculation.'

Van Wyk nodded. 'It gets better. Read the next one.'

He picked it up and read.

INTERPOL

General Secretariat

200, quai Charles de Gaulle

69006 Lyon

France

Intelligence report: Cobra/B79C1/04/03/2007/27/6/2010

Report date: 27 June 2010

Report submitted by: Superintendent Marie-Caroline Aubert,
InterpolGeneral Secretariat, Lyon

Investigation: Murder of Zakhar Perminov, Vila Praia da Ancora,
Portugal on 13 September 2006

Source: Dossier of the Polícia de Segurança Pública, and personal inter-
view with Superintendent Christóvã Formigo, Polícia de Segurança
Pública, Lisbon, Portugal

(Translated by P.A. Shilling, Interpol, 28 June 2010)

At 07.55 on the morning of 13 September 2006, the body of Zakhar
Ivanovich Perminov was found (by a Portuguese cleaning woman) in the
living room of a villa on the outskirts of Vila Praia de Âncora, a coastal
holiday resort in northern Portugal, about five kilometres south of the
Spanish border.

Perminov had been shot twice – once in the forehead, and once through
the heart. Bullets recovered from the crime scene indicated a Heckler &
Koch MK23 (a weapon popular with American Special Forces) and Cor
Bon ammunition (45 ACP +P 230 grain).

Two shell casings that were found on the scene match this firearm and
ammunition. The casings were engraved with the likeness of a snake with
a flared head, and the initials/letters NM (capitalised, no full stops).

The villa had no security measures, and no sign of forced entry was
found. According to a statement by the cleaning woman the villa's glass
sliding doors leading to the pool were never locked when Perminov was
in residence.

No forensic evidence of the intruder, other than the shell casings and
bullets, was found on the scene. No arrests were made, and the dossier is
still open.

Perminov, the deceased, was a Russian citizen. The Russian Embassy
in Lisbon supplied limited details about the deceased's career, but it was
confirmed that he was a retired former Russian paratroop colonel.

Perminov served as reconnaissance squad leader for the 103rd Guards Airborne Division in Vitebsk in Belarus, and was deployed to Mozambique as military advisor to the Mozambique Liberation Front (FRELIMO) from 1978–1980. He also served in Angola as a member of the staff of the Soviet chief military advisor, Lieutenant-General Leonid Kusmenko, in 1986.

Re. Intelligence Report Cobra/B79C104/03/2007/19/03/2009:

After a written submission to the Mozambican Embassy in Paris, it was confirmed that Zakhar Ivanovich Perminov was registered as the father of Joaquim Curado. Joaquim Curado was born on 27 January 1979 in Cuamba, Mozambique, to Dores Branca Curado (herself born of a Makua mother and Portuguese father).

The Mozambican authorities also confirmed that the same Joaquim Curado is still a citizen of that country. A passport was issued to him (in the name of Joaquim Curado) in 1999, and was replaced by a new passport in 2003. (Note: It is common practice for the Légion étrangère [L.E. or French Foreign Legion] to confiscate enlistees' passports, which might explain the replacement.)

This 2003 passport was used for a return journey from France to Mozambique in 2006, but no further legal entries/exits were logged.

It was further established that a Joaquim Curado, a Mozambican citizen (passport number corresponded with first issued Mozambican travel document), served in the Légion étrangère from 2000 to 2005 as Legionnaire 1e Classe (Lance Corporal/1st Class Legionnaire) in the 1st Foreign Regiment (1° RE).

(Note MCA: The insignia of the L.E.'s 1st Foreign Regiment [1° RE] is a framed bird of prey [black] and a snake [green]. See Intelligence Report: Cobra/B79C1/04/03/2007/19/03/2009, page 2: 'There's this tattoo he has. Bird and a snake. On his arm. Right here. Guy must love snakes.')

According to his partially and unofficially released L.E. records, Curado received special forces training, and showed no exceptional leadership skills. However, he was regarded as a proficient soldier and excellent marksman, and served with distinction in several African operations.

He is 1.89 metres (6 ft 2 inches) tall, and weighed 95 kg (209 lbs) at induction into the L.E.

Curado was honourably discharged from the Légion étrangère at his own request in 2005, having served his compulsory five-year term. In the

*same year, on the strength of his L.E. service, he was granted French citi-
zenship, and thus now holds dual citizenship of Mozambique and France.
A French passport was issued to him on 19 January 2006. The passport
has not since been used for travel outside the European Union.*

No current address was found for Joaquim Curado.

*(Note MCA: A theory might be formulated that Joaquim Curado is
the assassin known as 'the Cobra'.)*

*★ A photograph of Curado was supplied by the L.E. and is herewith
attached. It was taken during his L.E. induction in 2000.*

17

INTERPOL

General Secretariat

200, quai Charles de Gaulle

69006 Lyon

France

Intelligence Report Addendum: Cobra/B79C1/04/03/2007/04/07/2010

Report date: 14 September 2010

Report submitted by: Superintendent Marie-Caroline Aubert, Interpol General Secretariat, Lyon

Investigation: Series of murders in the European Union connected to 'The Cobra' (Original dossier Cobra/B79C1/04/03/2007)

(Translated by P.A. Shilling, Interpol, 15 September 2010)

With reference to the series of nine murders in the European Union (2006–2010) where bullets recovered from the various crime scenes indicated a Heckler & Koch MK23 and Cor-Bon ammunition (45 ACP +P 230 grain), and shell casings were engraved with the likeness of a snake with flared head and the initials/letters NM (capitalised, no full stops):

A theory might be formulated that the snake engraving represents the Mozambique Spitting Cobra:

1. The engraving shows a high likeness for Mozambique Spitting Cobra – also the scale and the size of the hood.

2. The genus name of Naja mossambica corresponds with the initials NM.

3. Interpol Intelligence Reports Cobra/B79C1/04/03/2007/19/03/2009 and Cobra/B79C1/04/03/2007/27/06/2010 indicate a credible link between the suspected hired assassin 'The Cobra', and Joaquim Curado, a Mozambican and French national.

4. It is believed that 'The Cobra' is mulatto in complexion. In every homicide where his involvement is suspected, the victims suffered at least

one shot between, near, or through the eyes. Note the behaviour (accuracy, eyes as target) and the colouring (tawny brown) of the Mozambique Spitting Cobra:

(Source, quoted verbatim: http://www.africanreptiles-venom.co.za/ mozambique_spitting_cobra.html)

The colour varies between olive-grey, tawny brown or grey, with the scales in-between a black colour. The distribution includes Natal, Lowveld, south-eastern Tanzania and Pemba Island, and west to southern Angola and northern Namibia.

Behaviour:

This snake is a nervous and highly strung snake (sic). When confronted at close quarters it can rear up to as much as two-thirds of its length, spread its long narrow hood and will readily 'spit' in defence, usually from a reared-up position. By doing this the venom can be ejected at a distance of 2–3 metres (5½–8¼ feet), with remarkable accuracy. The spitting cobra does not often actually bite despite its aggressive behaviour, and also displays the habit of feigning death to avoid further molestation.

Venom:

This is probably the most dangerous snake, second only to the Mamba.

Its bite causes severe local tissue destruction (similar to that of the Puff Adder). Like the Rinkhals, it can spit its venom. The venom is ejected from two small holes near the tip of the teeth, usually aimed at the eyes. The effect is instantaneous causing intense smarting and inflammation and if not washed out with milk or water will cause permanent blindness.

The photograph of Joaquim Curado was small, scarcely two by three centimetres. It was printed in colour, but faded.

The face that stared out at Griessel was somewhere between boy and man. His hair was cropped very short, the features almost feminine in their refinement – high forehead, even, strong jawline, big dark eyes, straight nose, full lips, in the photo completely neutral. It reminded Griessel of a police drawing. There was no emotion – it was a face waiting to be filled in by life. But by no means the 'cold eyes' the Italian informant had speculatively described.

And there was something about the width and musculature of the neck that created the impression of an athlete.

Nearly 1.9 metres. Just under 100 kilograms. And that was before he started training with the French Foreign Legion. He would be a handful to arrest now.

'Can we make a bigger photo?' he asked van Wyk.

'Not without losing resolution. Maybe a centimetre or two . . . It's thirteen years old, Benny.'

'I know . . .'

He had that light-headed feeling that came with only three hours of sleep, his thoughts erratic, flitting and floundering.

He wanted to read all the Interpol documents carefully. Then he wanted to compile a time line of Adair's last week. He wanted to consider how the photo of the Cobra could help them.

He wanted more sleep.

He looked up at van Wyk, now pale, his bloodshot eyes weary. 'Phil, I want to work through this stuff carefully first. You should go home now.'

'OK, just two more things. Lithpel and the guys came back just after twelve. We managed to isolate Morris's computers from the other farm people by the IP address . . .'

'Computers?'

'Technically speaking. It's an Apple computer, and an iPad. Lithpel said Morris visited a lot of financial news websites. *The Economist, Financial Times, Bloomberg* . . . And then he was on his Google mail at least five times. Lithpel says you must talk to him when he gets back; he might be able to get into the emails.'

He nearly said 'Adair's email?' Stopped himself in time and said 'Morris's email?'

'That's right. Lithpel says there is a way.'

'But not through the channels?'

'No.'

He sat in his office and started with the documents, right from the beginning.

He read the summary of each of the Cobra assassinations – sixteen since 2006 – concise descriptions of the victims and murder scenes. Some reports contained notes by 'MCA', whom he subsequently realised must be Marie-Caroline Aubert.

She sometimes speculated about the possible motive behind the murder, made comments about the quality of the investigations, and carefully suggested theories.

Slowly, he gained respect for the way her head worked. Griessel picked up his pen and circled two of her notes. The first was an insert, in brackets, to the murder of the American billionaire in New York in 2011: *(Note MCA: One possible consideration is that the Cobra does not brand all his hits with the marked shell casings. If one takes into account the fact that he has averaged only two assassinations per annum since 2006, for an assumed (relatively modest for his skills and talents) yearly income of €200,000, there is the distinct possibility that he has completed other contracts on a more anonymous basis. An Interpol database search on H&K MK23 murders in Europe since 2006 shows eleven unconfirmed and forensically unmatched possibilities. For further investigation.)*

The second was in the murder of an Iranian engineer in Warsaw in 2012: *(Note MCA: During a telephone interview with the investigating officer, it became apparent that the victim, Omid Rostami, was involved with the Iranian uranium enrichment project. It is suspected that Rostami was in Warsaw to seek a black market uranium or nuclear equipment contract. It is further suspected that this was a Mossad hit, subcontracted to the Cobra.)*

It reminded him of Cupido's words: *This was a professional hit, pappie, and* jy wiet wie *sanctions professional hits. Gangstas and governments.*

Mossad. Intelligence Services. They knew about this hired assassin. And they were prepared to contract him.

What about other intelligence people? Such as Emma Graber of MI6?

Griessel pulled an A4 pad from his top drawer and paged past the rough notes of his previous dossiers, till he had a clean page.

At the top he wrote *Morris/Adair.*

He consulted his notebook, then the calendar on his iPhone. He wrote:

Monday 24 June: Break in at Adair, Cambridge.
Tuesday 25 June: Adair reported missing.

Wednesday 26 June: Adair phones Body Armour (as Morris).
Thursday 27 June: Adair sends passport scan and flight number to Body
Armour.
Friday 28 June: Adair arrives in Cape Town.
Sunday 30 June: Adair abducted/murdered, Franschhoek.

He sat staring at his timeline, trying to make sense of it.

So many things, such a short time. And his head wasn't clear.

The break-in at Adair's flat was just over a week ago. *A back door was forced, and the interior left in complete disarray,* Graber had said.

That meant someone had been looking for something.

The room in La Petite Margaux guesthouse was in the same condition. As if there had been a search.

He made a note: *Who is looking for what?* Bones Boshigo said *everyone knows what the algorithm does, even the terrorists, and there's nothing anybody can do to stop it.* Why then were people searching through Adair's flat and guesthouse room?

Last Monday Adair had got away just in time before the burglary at his home. Or perhaps he hadn't been there at the time, maybe he came home after the incident, saw the chaos and fled? Where to? And why?

He wrote: *False passport?* The question was: Did Adair already have one at his disposal? Or did he acquire one in haste between Monday and Thursday last week? Both possibilities had interesting implications. A Professor of Mathematics who kept a false passport handy? Or knew where to get one at short notice?

Didn't sound right.

And then the big question: How did the Cobra – or the people who hired the Cobra – know that Adair was in a guesthouse on a wine farm in Franschhoek?

If they knew where Adair was before his flight to South Africa, surely they would have kidnapped or murdered him there?

But somewhere between last Monday and yesterday they found out where he was, and sent the Cobra from Europe to do his job.

If Adair was lying low, with his false name, false passport, and false email address, how did they know?

He put the pen down, opened his steel cabinet, and took out the rolled-up camp bed. He put it together, set his iPhone for seven, turned off the light, lay down on his back, and closed his eyes.

He only wanted a few hours of sleep so that he could think this through with a clear head, do what he needed to do. Such as, that he must get a bulletin out to all stations to let them know, should the body of a white man in his fifties be found somewhere. Such as, the fact that someone must sit down and compare all the video material from Oliver Tambo and Cape Town International Airport since Friday with the old photo of Joaquim Curado.

Perhaps luck would be on their side.

18

Tyrone Kleinbooi's Casio G-Shock wristwatch woke him at 6.45.

He had stolen it one Sunday morning last year on the common in Green Point, from a mountain biker whose attention was distracted by his sexy cycling partner.

Tyrone tuned the radio to Kfm, because he wanted to hear the weather forecast. Isolated showers, clearing towards midday.

That was a relief. For his industry.

He made instant coffee. He ate Weet-Bix with milk and sugar. Brushed his teeth, showered, shaved, and dressed. Black, slightly faded Edgars chinos with deep open pockets. Old black T-shirt, reasonably new black polo-necked jersey. *Black is beautiful, Tyrone. Smart. And invisible. You can be anything in black.*

He pushed up the sleeves of his jersey to just below the elbows, he could work better that way. He put the silver Zippo and the hairpin with the small yellow sunflower in his left trouser pocket. He picked up the light blue Nokia Lumia 820, put it in the small neat rucksack that he had bought, because the size and the material and look were important. It mustn't rustle, mustn't look cheap, and it mustn't interfere with his hand movements. But it must be able to hold the loot, cellphone, and his rain jacket.

He had taken the Lumia out of a businessman's pocket up in Kloof Street – the man had been occupied with his coffee and croissant at Knead, reading the sports pages of the *Cape Times,* did not look like the Windows phone type. And no self-respecting fence was going to pay for a Windows phone, zero second-hand value, so Tyrone just kept it for himself. So he could at least phone Nadia, and she him.

He locked his room and walked around the Slamse's triple garage, along the wall to the gate. He typed in the security code. The gate clicked open. He walked out, to the city.

Weather looking OK.

He walked briskly. Tuesdays were not your best days of the pickpocket week, but the early bird catches the worm if you keep your eyes
open between the suits in Strand, Waterkant, Riebeeck, Long and
Bree, and you blend in with the office workers hurrying along in
groups, late for work, take-away coffee in one hand, as you squeeze in
through the doors with them, up the escalators or in the lifts.

He was a man on a mission. Twenty-one thousand bucks by the end
of Jan.

Tall order.

But every journey starts with one small step.

That wasn't one of Uncle Solly's. He'd heard that one time in St
George's Mall, this pretty whitey girl trying to motivate her hangdog
loser boyfriend.

And he liked it. So he didn't steal anything from her, except the
quote.

Out of habit he looked north, across Table Bay. He saw the cruise
ship, beyond Robben Island. He smiled. Tin can full of marks, that
boat would be here in an hour or two.

Rich pickings.

Griessel dreamed a giant snake was chasing him, the mouth agape,
spitting, so that it dripped off the back of his head and he felt the sour
venom burning down the back of his neck. The alarm was a sudden
reprieve, catapulting him to the silent safety of his office.

He folded up the camp bed and stowed it away, took the toilet bag
and a worn old towel from the filing cabinet, and went to shower in the
bathroom on the third floor.

While he shaved, he realised he felt rested. Fresh. Just over two
extra hours of deep sleep, and the cobwebs were gone.

Perhaps because he knew he was alone for at least two nights. He
and his rascal, solo.

A little less pressure.

He stood looking at himself in the mirror, and he felt the urge come
over him. The urge to catch the Cobra.

Something inside him revolted against the concept of a hit man
with a trademark. It was sociopathic, arrogant, it represented everything that was wrong with this world. Everyone was obsessed with

money and status and fame. More than ever, it seemed, it was the root
of evil, the source of more and more crime.

The murdered bodyguards, B.J. Fikter and Barry Minnaar, were
former members of the Force, and not one of the highly advanced,
First World detective services had been able to apprehend the Cobra
so far. After all the mess of the past few months, with the SAPS derided
as never before, it would be good to show the world . . .

And catching men was what he did. At least, all that he did well.
There was no denying that he often struggled, made mistakes, but
that moment when you clicked the handcuffs around the fucker's
wrists and said 'You're under arrest', there were few things that
measured up to that, it was when the universe balanced out, just for
a moment.

He wiped off his face, packed his toiletries in the bag, checked
himself in the mirror. One of his new shirts, only slightly creased, with
the blue jacket.

This morning no one would think he was drinking again.

Just before seven he knocked on Nyathi's door jamb.

The Giraffe waved him in and said, 'Benny, I think we should tell
the team everything.'

'Yes, sir,' he said in relief. He had been feeling guilty since yesterday
about lying to IMC.

Nyathi gathered up his papers. 'I have to go and chair the morning
parade. You get your guys into your office. Just your team, Bones, and
Philip van Wyk. Make it very clear: we trust them completely, but they
have to be utterly and completely circumspect. We cannot afford a
single leak.'

'Yes, sir. But we are going to need more people.'

'Something happened?'

'Interpol has a lot on the assassin. He's called the Cobra.'

Nyathi checked his watch. 'Walk with me, please.'

On the way to the morning parade, Griessel told him in broad
strokes about the new information, the thirteen-year-old photograph,
and what he planned to do.

'Good,' said the colonel. 'Go ahead, and keep me posted.'

'Just one more thing, sir. Philip says Sergeant Lithpel Davids can get into Adair's email . . .' And he left that hanging there so that the colonel could draw his own conclusions.

Nyathi stopped and looked at Griessel. 'Do it,' he said, barely audibly.

First he thanked the detectives who had worked very late. Then he told the team everything.

They joked about the Cobra's nickname.

'The bastard probably has a Twitter account too,' said a surly Cupido, his reproachful eyes on Griessel.

They studied the photograph. Griessel explained his strategy. He asked Ndabeni and Radebe to liaise with the SAPS office at O. R. Tambo Airport in Johannesburg, and to fly up as soon as possible to study the video material of the Arrivals Hall. Liebenberg and Fillander must do the same at Cape Town International.

'It's a long shot,' said Radebe.

'It's one of the few shots we have,' said Fillander.

'We are only looking at international flights since Thursday,' said Griessel. 'We know he's coloured, we know he will probably be wearing a hat or glasses, he will be aware of cameras, so he will look away or keep his head down. What we really want, is a name, because then we can link it to a passport, and the way he paid for the flight. Maybe a credit card number . . . That's more than Interpol has now.'

'If he killed Adair, he's long gone,' said Bones.

'Maybe,' said Griessel, 'but someone searched Adair's house in England, and his room in Franschhoek. I don't think they found what they were looking for. I think that is why Adair could still be alive.'

'That's how a Violent Crimes cop thinks, Bones. Live and learn,' said Fillander.

'Touché,' said Bones.

'Don't talk of my girl like *that*,' said Mooiwillem Liebenberg.

They laughed.

'Bones, have you anything new on Adair?'

'Now learn how the genius department thinks, *nè*. I looked at everything, and here's the thing: *daars niks nuut nie*, absolutely nothing new. Now, for you hot-headed blood-lust cops that would mean *nada*. But look at the bigger picture: until about four weeks ago Adair was blogging and writing lots of letters to the press, and gave interviews, all about the Adair Protocol. And then he went quiet.'

'So?' asked Cupido.

'Why, Vaughn? Why did he stop agitating?'

Cupido shrugged.

'Something happened, *nè*,' said Bones.

'You don't know what,' said Cupido.

'Not yet,' said Bones. 'Not yet.'

When they were finished and walked out, Cupido approached Griessel. 'I thought we were partners, Benna.'

'Vaughn, I was under orders.'

'But still,' said Cupido, deeply wounded, 'where's the trust?'

Tyrone was early enough, so he walked into the Parkade Mall in Strand Street, opposite the Cape Sun.

Seven storeys of parking. A lot of cars, a lot of people. And they all had to go down in those lifts, to the street. And there were no cameras in the lifts.

He rode them, up and down.

Lots of coloureds. He didn't steal from coloureds.

Darkies and whiteys were fair game.

He chatted up a sexy, slinky dolly on his second trip down in the lift, but she wouldn't divulge her cell number.

He talked to an aunty on the fifth descent. He made her laugh. He enjoyed that.

He stole two cellphones and two wallets. He rode down to the first storey, and checked his loot in privacy behind a black BMW X5.

A new BlackBerry. Worth three-fifty from the fence. An iPhone 4S. Eight hundred bucks. Three credit cards, fifty each. One driver's licence, fifty bucks. Seven hundred in cash.

Total of about two K. Not bad for an hour's work.

He dumped the empty wallets under the X5.

Time to rob a shipload of tourists.

19

Griessel concentrated hard on understanding Sergeant Lithpel Davids. Cupido sat there too, arms folded, his mouth a straight, sulky line, saying nothing.

'Cappie, you know it's illegal. Fun, but illegal,' said Lithpel. Just one 's' in the entire sentence, easy to follow.

'I know,' said Griessel, 'but Morris is not a suspect. We won't have to explain it in court.'

'Cool. Now to hack a Gmail account, that's easy. You can phish, or you can download an app, or you can use your own Gmail account,' was more or less the translated version, once Griessel had filtered out all the lisps.

'OK,' said Griessel.

'Phishing does not apply, since the dude has been kidnapped, right?'

'OK.'

'And we don't want comebacks, we don't want to leave tracks, so I'm not going to use my own Gmail account.'

'OK.'

'Which leaves us with the app. And it just so happens *lat ek een hier het*, right here on my system. Keeping up with the dark side, Cappie, if you know what I mean.'

'OK.'

'You haven't a clue what I'm on about, Cappie.'

'That's right.'

'No worries. Just sit back, relax, and watch me work.'

Body language, Tyrone. Be a student of body language.

That was how he spotted the woman. She came walking past the Cape Union Mart, in the direction of the V&A shopping centre on the Waterfront. She was somewhat lightly dressed for this weather, jeans, and a thin, blood red sweater. She gripped the handbag tightly under her arm as though it contained a fortune. She looked scared. She walked quickly, looking around as though she didn't know where to go. In the crush of tourists from the ship.

And she was pretty, Mediterranean dark. His age.

What's not to like?

He kept behind her, two, three metres.

She looked around once. He looked away.

He would have to strike before she got too close to the shopping centre. There were cameras.

He pushed his hand into this left pocket, grasped the hairpin. Increased his pace, caught up.

Four women approached from the left, cutting between them, so that he fell behind again.

She was only five metres from the amphitheatre.

He must turn back, it was too near the cameras.

She held the handbag, with its easy clasp, so anxiously. He knew that attitude. It usually meant there was something valuable inside. Cash? Jewellery? Carried by someone who was not accustomed to it.

A real challenge.

He jogged faster.

Just before the steps to the rows of seats in the amphitheatre. There were a lot of people.

He took a chance, tapped her on the shoulder, the hair clip held up in his fingers.

She was startled, looked around at him in confusion. Scared.

He smiled his most charming smile, relaxed and helpful. 'I think you dropped this, ma'am.' His shoulder against hers, his right hand at the handbag.

She looked at the clip, then at him, frowning, not understanding.

She was *very* pretty, he registered. 'The hairpin. You dropped it.'

His hand was at the flap of the handbag, while he twirled the pin in his fingers and kept on smiling.

'Oh,' she said. 'No . . .'

His right hand was under the flap. He felt the leather of a purse.

'You sure it's not yours? Take a good look.'

At that instant, when she gave her full attention to the hairpin, he bumped her with his right shoulder, just lightly, as though someone had pushed him from behind, as though he had lost his balance for a second, and he slipped the wallet out and pushed it, lightning fast, into his trouser pocket.

'No,' she said, looking left and right, worried.

'Sorry, then,' he said, and lowered the pin. He turned around and walked, away from the shopping centre.

Only six paces away, the security man grabbed him from behind, a steely grip on his wrist.

He jerked. His arm came free.

He ran.

Then the second security guard tackled him to the ground.

'And we're in,' said Lithpel Davids.

Griessel leaned forward to see.

'Only one mail in his in-box,' said Lithpel.

On the screen, beside a yellow arrow, he read **Lillian Alvarez** *(No Subject) Arrived in CT. Phone on and working.* And to the far right: *8:12 a.m.*

'That bold means he hasn't opened the mail yet,' said Lithpel. 'But no worries, we can open it and then mark it as unread again.'

'OK.'

Lithpel clicked on the message.

'That's it,' he said. Because there was nothing more than *Arrived in CT. Phone on and working.* 'Sent about an hour ago. Do you want to look at his other mail, Cappie?'

'Please.'

On the navigation bar on the left, Davids clicked on 'More', and then 'All Mail'.

Only the single post from Lillian Alvarez appeared.

'Talk about good housekeeping,' said Davids.

'What does that mean?'

'It means he's cleaned up everything. There is no other mail. Everything he sent or received, is gone.'

'*Fok,*' said Griessel.

'Shall I try to find out who Lillian Alvareth ith?' asked Lithpel Davids.

★ ★ ★

The security guard with the pimples held onto his left arm and the one with muscles pulled his right arm painfully up against his back.

'Let me go!' said Tyrone, his voice shrill and frightened.

'We've got him, control, we're bringing him in,' said Pimples, white and young, into his radio. Then to Tyrone: 'Not as clever as you thought, hey?'

They pushed and dragged him towards the shopping centre.

'What are you talking about?' Tyrone tried to bring his fear under control, tried to sound indignant, but his heart beat in his throat. *Deny, deny, deny, Tyrone. And when that won't help any more, then you lie.*

'*Maaifoedie, fokken* pickpocket,' said Muscles, the coloured one. 'We've been after you for a long time.'

Bystanders made way for them, staring.

'Pickpocket?' said Tyrone. 'Where you come with that?'

'No. It's where *you* are *going*,' said Muscles, and he pressed Tyrone's arm even higher 'Now shut up.'

Through the pain he thought: They don't have anything, the cameras were too far away. They must have been following him, he hadn't spotted them in the crowd of tourists, he was too focused on the woman and the handbag. He must get her wallet out of his trouser pocket. It was the only evidence they had. But he wouldn't be able to get his arm free.

He was stuffed – that knowledge came down suddenly like a black curtain.

Christ, what would Nadia say?

Who would pay for her studies?

A good thing Uncle Solly was dead. All that training, and he let himself get caught like an amateur. A total disgrace.

Fear gnawed at his guts.

They took him into the shopping centre via a service door, and down the stairs. Their radios crackled and rasped, excited voices echoing down the wide corridor. Two sharp turns, then he saw the sign: Security: Control Room. A security man came out, stood waiting. He had stars on his shoulders. A general probably. He was white. He smiled, but not in a good way. 'Little shit,' he said, 'we've got you.'

The general stood aside so they could bundle him through the door.

Two more men sat inside, both coloured. They looked up. '*Ja*, that's him,' one of them said.

Big room, one wall was just TV monitors, a number of radios were recharging on long workbenches down the walls. A double door right at the back, and a single door just here, beside the map of the V&A against the wall. Photos of people, low resolution, as if they were print-outs of TV screen shots, on a noticeboard beside a handwritten notice saying NO TIME SHEETS, NO PAY!!!! Tyrone saw his picture there. Maybe four months old, he was in just black chinos and a black T-shirt. Summer time.

He was fucked. More adrenaline, more fear shot through his body.

Muscles let go of his arm and the relief was instant. His rucksack was pulled off, and Pimples shoved him into a chair. The general took the rucksack, came to stand in front of him, feet planted wide. Pimples and Muscles covered the door like two soldiers on guard.

'Check this,' one of the coloureds in front of the TV monitors said to him. Sneering.

There was Tyrone standing beside the Mediterranean beauty, the hairpin in front of her, frozen and beautifully zoomed in on the screen.

From a camera that he had never seen.

'Call the SAPS,' said the general.

'So I wanted to give her back her hairpin,' Tyrone spoke in desperation.

'And now her wallet is in your trouser pocket,' said the general. 'And we're going to leave it right there, until the police come. So they can get your fingerprints nicely. Call them, Freddie. And tell Vannie to bring the girl in, she probably still doesn't know she's been robbed.'

'She dropped the wallet, look there on your cameras,' said Tyrone. If only he could gain some time . . .

Freddie was one of the guards who were sitting at the monitors. He picked up a phone. They listened in silence as he reported the whole thing.

'Police on their way,' said Freddie, his eyes searching the screens. 'But the girl . . . I don't see her . . .'

Two minutes later it was not the police who came.

20

It was an odd noise that came from the direction of the door, almost like an asthmatic cough, then a low, sick sound. Pimples dropped like a sack of potatoes. Tyrone felt a spattering on his face.

A cartridge clinked on the bare floor.

Blood ran out of Pimples's head.

That sound again, and Muscles went down, right beside him. The same story.

Tyrone saw the man appear in the doorway. The pistol, the long black silencer. The general looked around, indignant that his authority was being undermined. Another quiet shot. The general collapsed. The delicate metallic sound of a bullet cartridge against the wall, then the floor.

It was surreal. Tyrone felt he wasn't really there, he was paralysed, a mingling of fear and shock and relief. '*Jirre*,' he said, and looked at the shooter, who now stood directly in front of him. A coloured man under a faded grey baseball cap, eyes like an eagle, all-seeing, looking through you. A fleeting thought: Who is this guy? Had he come to rescue him? Why was he shooting everyone?

The pistol swung towards Tyrone.

The security men at the TVs screamed.

The firearm was aimed at Tyrone, between his eyes.

Freddie jumped up, rushed towards the shooter.

Pistol swung away, to Freddie.

Tyrone did not think, it was just a sudden knowing: One chance.

He dived blindly, under and past the gunman, grabbing the rucksack beside the general. It snagged, he looked back, a strap was looped around the general's arm. Everything happened in a weird slow motion, like someone was holding back time. Freddie screamed, then the scream was cut off sharply. Freddie fell. Tyrone let go of the rucksack, because the shooter was turning towards him. He leaped at the door, adrenaline giving him strength and speed. The pistol was pointed at him again. He was at the door. The pistol coughed as he kicked off to the left, and out, he felt the burning pain across his shoulder blades. He was shot. He screamed, and ran the way they had brought him in. *Jirre*, Thank God for the sharp turns in the passage. One, two, and then the steps were ahead.

Up the stairs, yelling in terror. The second to last step hooked his foot, he fell forwards, reached out his hands to fend off the closed door. He banged his head hard, a thundering, against the wood, just above his right eye. Scurried to his feet, half dizzy, grabbed the door, jerked it open. He heard the footsteps behind him, ducked instinctively and suddenly as he went out, a bullet smacked against the door jamb. He was outside, he ran to the people, the tourists, he ran as he had never run before. He didn't look back, he sidestepped suddenly left, then right, he ran till he was in the midst of the crowd, he kept running, weaving between them. He felt blood run down his face, and down his back. Through the wide esplanade, into Mitchell's Waterfront Brewery, right through to the kitchen, people standing dumbfounded. He ran out of the back door, turned right, up the steps to Dock Road.

He wiped his hand over the blood, to get it out of his eyes.

He felt his back was soaking wet. The gunshot wound was bleeding.

He ran right in front of a car on Dock Road, tyres screeching. hooter blaring, it only just missed him. He ran over the central island, down to the Granger Bay car park, running right through, between parked cars, then took the stairs to the Coast Road level.

Outside. Turn right, his chest was on fire. He looked back. Saw no one.

Ran across the street, through the gate at Somerset Hospital, then through the big wooden doors.

Someone at the reception desk shouted after him.

He ran past, down the long cold corridors, past frowning nurses, and out of the back.

Hospital grounds.

He kept directly south, ran around buildings, past cars. Looked back again.

Nobody.

He saw the ruins, a building half demolished. Abandoned. He aimed for it, into it.

He found a dark room with no windows. He staggered against the wall, his breathing like a bullet train, sweat pouring off him. Loose bricks, broken planks in the worn floor. The stink of cat piss.

He picked up a length of wood, like a truncheon.

He turned to face the door-less opening, raising the wood high, and stood there waiting, gasping.

On Facebook Lithpel Davids found eighty-seven people with the surname of Alvarez, of whom only one had the first name Lillian.

'At least we know it's most likely a woman,' he said drily.

Cupido was still sitting back, not participating, while Benny Griessel and Lithpel went down the list. To number twenty-two. Beside the small photo and an icon of a house it said *Cambridge*.

'That one,' said Griessel.

David clicked.

A Facebook page opened up. A big photograph on top showed a kitten sleeping on the keyboard of a laptop. A smaller photo beside her name showed a young woman in her twenties, with long black hair and a sultry dark beauty.

'Looks like a Spanish dolly,' said Lithpel.

Griessel did not hear him, his eyes scanned further down: below 'Work and Education' it stated *Research Fellow at Applied and Computational Analysis (ACA) at DAMTP.* He said, 'That's her.'

For the first time Cupido sat up straight. He looked at the screen. 'I don't like this.'

Griessel waited for him to explain. It took a while.

'Is this Adair married?' Cupido asked at last.

'The Consulate said he's divorced.' And then he remembered Emma Graber's little games, and how positively she had passed on that information. As though she didn't want them making further enquiries.

'I'm calling Bones,' said Griessel.

* * *

Tyrone Kleinbooi stood with the piece of wood in the air for a long time.

But nobody came.

His hands and knees began to shake uncontrollably.

He lowered the plank slowly. He felt his face. The blood had begun to clot. He put the wood down without making a sound, and stretched an arm around his back. His jersey was torn across his back. Wet. Sore, but not unbearably so.

He sat down, his ears still pricked. His heart hammered and his body trembled slightly.

Shock. He was in shock. So this is what it feels like. He let his head drop, tried to slow his breathing down. He would survive, for now. I survived, Uncle Solly. Escaped. And then he thought of his rucksack, and the blows began to hit home. His cellphone. All the cash from this morning's work. The video. The radios that had crackled . . .

They were going to find the cellphone, the police. They would see there was only one name and number in the address book. Nadia's. If the police phoned with it, she would say: 'Hello, Tyrone.'

Then they would have him.

He had to go back. He had to get the rucksack before they came.

It was too late. His face was bloody, and his back, and his clothes.

He was large as life on that TV screen, the image frozen. His photo on that noticeboard.

When the police walked in, they would see it. They would play the whole video back, of how he stole the wallet.

There were other security guards at the V&A who would have heard over the radios that they had caught the pickpocket. That they had taken him to Security.

Everyone would think that he had done the shooting. They would put his face on national TV, and in the papers. *Crazy pickpocket killer on the loose*. Police all over the country would be hunting him.

Nadia would see all of that.

Jirre.

He would have to phone her. He would have to tell her some story. A story she would believe.

He had to steal a phone. Quickly. He would have to lie low. Quickly.

But first he had to get to his room, and wash, and put on clean clothes, and get his cash stash.

He better get going.

Bones let them carry on while he searched for information. He found it. 'No, Adair is not married. That's what Wikipedia says, *nè*. A bachelor.'

Griessel relayed the information.

'OK, so maybe she isn't his *skelmpie*,' said Cupido. 'But still. Check out that chick, pappie. She's *fokken* prime, she works with the *donner*, and she arrives here in the Cape saying: "Come into my arms, you bundle of charms." Doesn't that make you wonder?'

'About what?'

'About the whole thing, Benna.'

'I don't understand.'

'There's a lot that doesn't make sense in this thing. I mean, nothing quite fits. So I think it's time that we consider a few alternative theories. Let's say he's the one who did the shooting. I mean, Benna, we really don't know what went down there on the slave plantation.'

Griessel wondered if Cupido was being deliberately obtuse because he was still unhappy that they hadn't taken him into their confidence. 'Why would he shoot them?' he asked. 'The people looking after him?'

'It's not as wild as you think, Benna. This guy has his hands on the whole financial system. Now that's a very big temptation, doesn't matter who you are. And he's an expert, he knows how the whole system works. How difficult can it be to skim off the top. Just tell the system, just pay me two cents off every transaction, and I'm telling you, within months you're a millionaire. Huh, Lithpel, that's possible?'

'Pothible, but they will catch you, thooner rather than later.'

'And that's my whole point,' said Cupido.

Griessel tried to object, but Cupido held his hand up in the air. 'Just hear me out, Benna. With an open mind. Let's say it's something like this. Let's say the professor had a big scheme, and he planned it a long time ago. And he knew, sooner or later, someone would realise it. You have to leave tracks, I mean, everyone knows you're the guy who wrote this software. They know you've got your fingers in the pie, you'll be suspect, eventually. So you build an exit strategy . . .'

'Hell, Vaughn, I think that's . . .'

'No, Benna. Here we have an academic who suddenly has a false passport? How? I don't buy it. Here's this innocent professor who has a whole other Morris identity, and he makes his Gmail cleaner than a virgin's conscience? I mean, come on. Here's a man who for months protests about terrorists and organised crime, and then he goes suspiciously quiet? Here's a middle-aged *bok* with a pretty young thing, but what can he offer her? A university salary? I don't think so. And I ask you, where's the soft spot in the whole bodyguards and safe house set-up? Inside, pappie. You'd never see it coming . . .'

'But what about the cobra on the . . .'

Griessel's cellphone rang. He took it out of his jacket pocket.

UNKNOWN.

He answered. 'Griessel.'

'I have information for you about David Patrick Adair. I will call you back in two minutes. Make sure you are alone.'

In the lecture hall Nadia felt the vibration of her phone. She peeped, saw it was Tyrone phoning. Three times.

She waited for nine minutes, until the lecture was over. Then she walked out and phoned him.

'Hello?' an unfamiliar voice.

'Who is this?' she asked.

'I'm the guy who picked up this phone on the street. I called you, because your number is the only one on here.' It was an accent she could not place, but the man sounded polite.

'Oh,' she said. 'It's my brother's phone. Where did you pick it up?'

'Here in the city. He must have dropped it – it was just lying there. Where can I contact him?'

'You are a good person,' she said. 'I . . . His phone is the only way . . .'

'Sorry, what is your name?'

'Nadia.'

'OK, Nadia, I can take the phone to him. Where does he work?'

'I . . . He's on a painting contract, somewhere in the Bo-Kaap. I'm not sure . . .'

'I'm flying out today, so I would really like to get it to him.'

'That is very nice of you. Uh, let me . . . Can I give you his home address? He has a ... There might be people at home, at the place where he has a room. Or you can drop it in the mailbox or something?'

'Of course. What is your brother's name?'

21

Griessel walked out into the corridor. The voice over the phone was a woman's, full of self-confidence and authority. Speaking in Afrikaans. About something to which only the Hawks and the British Consulate were privy. It made no sense.

His cellphone rang again. He answered quickly. 'Griessel.'

'Are you alone?' The same voice.

'*Ja.*'

'Let me just tell you up front, you can try to track these calls, but it won't work.'

'Oh?'

'Your name is Benny Griessel. You're a captain in the Directorate of Priority Crimes Investigation in Bellville. You have an eighty-three per cent crime solving rate, but you have a serious drinking problem. Your ex-wife's name is Anna Maria, your children are Carla and Fritz. In 2006 and in 2009 you were involved in disciplinary hearings with the SAPS. Every time you were acquitted. You have three outstanding traffic fines against your name.'

He said nothing, felt deeply uneasy.

'The point is, I have access to information. That is all you have to know. If you doubt my trustworthiness, ask me a question.'

'Who are you?'

'Call me Joni.'

'Joni who?'

'Joni Mitchell.'

'The singer?'

'Yes.'

He had never been crazy about Joni Mitchell, she hardly ever used decent bass guitar. But he just said 'OK', because he smelled Intelligence Services. Spooks.

'Your only problem is, you can't talk about these calls. Not to anybody. If I hear you blabbing, they will stop. Do you understand?'

'Yes.'

'You should also know, this is not one-way traffic. *I* give a little, *you* give a little. Understand?'

'It will depend on what you give.'

'Naturally. I will give what I can, when I can . . .'

'Why?'

'Good question. Because I want to. That is all I am going to say.'

'OK.'

'Here is an example so long: last night at 20.42, the British High Commissioner in Pretoria asked via the Department of International Relations and Cooperation for a talk with the Minister of State Security. This meeting took place at ten o'clock at the minister's house. The rumour is that you are going to receive an order not to proceed with the investigation.'

'Someone will have to investigate it . . .'

'SSA. The State Security Agency is going to take it over.'

'That is . . . It doesn't work like that.' But his guts started to contract, nobody was going to take *this* case away from him.

'We'll see,' said Joni. 'I don't have much time. Emma Graber told you about the Adair Algorithm.' It was a statement, not a question.

Now he was sure that Joni was a Spook. 'Yes.'

'It's an old trick. Divulge part of the information to create a false trail. There is more, Captain. According to my information, Adair loaded a new version of the algorithm into the international banking system some time in the past six weeks, without permission.'

He waited, but she said nothing more. 'Why?' he asked. 'What is different about the algorithm?'

'I don't know yet.'

He thought of Cupido's theory, and he wondered suddenly whether he had something there. 'Would Adair have . . . Could he channel money out of the system?'

She was silent for a moment. 'It's an interesting theory,' she said with a measure of respect. 'And surely a possibility . . . Now you must give me something. The correct email address that Adair used as Morris.'

The question surprised him, because he had only sent the incorrect email address to Emma Graber of MI6. By email. That meant that Joni had intercepted it. And she was a Spook who spoke Afrikaans. That meant SSA. Who didn't trust Zola Nyathi to reveal all the information. And if he gave her the correct Morris address, the SSA would know about Lillian Alvarez. And *that* he did not want.

But he also didn't want to spoil this new information channel. You never knew . . .

He gave her the correct address.

The line went dead.

Griessel ran back to Lithpel Davids.

The stolen wallet in Tyrone's trouser pocket yielded four hundred British pounds in notes, and just over two thousand five hundred South African rand. The urgency made him use some of the rand for a taxi home – from the stop in Portswood Street.

The driver looked at his injuries and asked: 'Now who *bliksemsed* you, my brother?'

'You charge me two hundred rand for a trip of four kilos and then you want to get personal with me too?'

'*Ek vra ma net.* Just asking.'

'*Fokken* rip-off.'

'So why don't you take the bus?' And a few seconds later, 'No wonder you look like you do.'

He almost lost his temper, the anger welling up, a surge of jumbled emotions. He suppressed it with difficulty, knowing with a deep certainty that he had to stay calm. He had to plan his way ahead, the next step, the urgent things.

He made the taxi drop him off at the corner of Longmarket and Ella Street, in case this *doos* went to the cops when the paw-paw hit the fan, he didn't want a specific address to be available.

'No tip?'

Tyrone just shook his head. He waited for the taxi to disappear over the curve of Longmarket. Then he jogged home. He hoped that the rich Muslim's oldest daughter, who hung around the house during the day, wouldn't see him come in now, not with all this damage.

In his room he undressed. He saw that the bullet had made a long tear across his sweater. It was caked with dried blood. He tossed it in

the corner and turned around so he could see the damage to his back
in the mirror.

He gave a moan to the heavens: there was a lot of blood. But no
fresh bleeding. The wound was a thick stripe across his shoulder
blades. Trouble was he wouldn't be able to reach it. He would have to
rinse off in the shower and hope for the best.

He quickly checked his face. He had to get out of here. He had to
call Nadia, the clock was ticking. Thank God for a dark skin. Because
once he had washed thoroughly, he would look OK.

He hurried to the tiny bathroom.

At 9.27 the SAPS sergeant at the V&A shopping centre radioed the
charge office at the Sea Point Station, breathlessly and somewhat
disjointedly, to report 'a bad shooting'.

The constable on radio duty had the good sense to run down the
passage to tell his station commander the news.

The station commander was a captain with twenty-two years' service.
He pushed the pen he had been using into his pocket, stood up quickly,
asked precisely what had been reported, and ordered the constable to
tell his two most experienced detectives to meet him at his official SAPS
car. 'As in *now.*'

While he hurried to the car park, he thought of the style of the
meetings he had had with the provincial commissioner over the past
months. And the bulletins that had been issued in that time with
monotonous regularity, all in support of the same basic message: the
president, the minister and the national commissioner were deeply
concerned about the fact that the SAPS' reputation stank. In the last
year there had been the Marikana massacre, the Oscar Pistorius case,
and the video of a police van dragging the Mozambican Emidio Macia
to death. Trumpeted out from here to *Time* magazine and the *New
York Times.* It had to end now. Keep our individual and collective butts
out of the media and out of trouble. Maintain discipline in your people.
Don't let raw *blougatte*, still wet behind the ears, mess up your crime
scenes. Don't let inexperienced people be placed in a position where
they need to take important decisions. Take them yourself. With
wisdom and balance.

Or bear the consequences.

The Sea Point commander had three children at school, a bond on his house of over a million, and a wife who thought he worked too much and earned too little. He didn't want her to bear the consequences. He frowned, feeling the tension in his body. And the urge to go to the V&A Waterfront himself. Along with his two best detectives. Because the Waterfront was a key area, an international tourism jewel. It was the sort of place where 'a bad shooting' would bring down the media vultures in hordes. Including those of *Time* magazine and the *New York Times*. It was the sort of place where you could very quickly land very deep in the soup if you didn't make the right decisions – with wisdom and balance.

The two detectives approached, their jackets flapping in the cold wind. 'Bad shooting at the Waterfront,' said the station commander. They quickly got into the car. The captain switched on the sirens and the lights, and they drove away.

At the main entrance to the V&A Waterfront in Breakwater Lane, the station commander parked on the pavement. A SAPS sergeant had heard the sirens and came running up. This was the one sent out after the original call from the Waterfront security about the pickpocket. The one who had discovered the scene of the homicides.

'This way, Captain,' he said, eyes wild.

'How many?' asked the station commander as he and the detectives jumped out and ran after the sergeant.

'At least five, Captain.'

Christ. He didn't say it though, just thought it. 'Where did it happen?'

'At the security centre. It's a bloodbath.'

And it was. Standing in the doorway of the *Security: Control Room*, the station commander saw five people crumpled into the characteristic helpless awkwardness of death. As he stared at the blood and brain spatter, the pools of blood, the spray and the footprints, he knew it was going to be impossible to keep anyone's collective butt out of the media, thank you. The best he could hope for was to keep everyone's butts out of trouble.

So he turned around and led the whole team of two detectives and the uniformed sergeant, and the seven black-clad security men who stood in stupefied curiosity in the corridor, to the door that opened into the shopping centre (where he spotted a bullet hole in the door frame). He walked out, closed the door, and said: 'Nobody goes in here.'

And then he phoned the Hawks.

Brigadier Musad Manie was the commander of the Directorate of Priority Crimes Investigation, the 'Head Hawk Honcho', as Cupido sometimes referred to his coloured brother with a measure of pride. Manie's nickname in the DPCI was 'the Camel', because 'Musad', one of the Hawks detectives had learned from a Muslim friend, meant 'camel set free' in Arabic. And the Hawks, like most SAPS units, liked to give each other – and especially senior officers – nicknames. But Manie didn't look like a camel. He had the looks of a leader. He was a powerful man, broad of breast and shoulder, with a granite face of strong lines and a determined jaw.

It was this jaw that entered Nyathi's office first. In his deep but always muted and calm voice he said, 'Zola, there has been a shooting at the Waterfront. Five security guards dead, as far as we know. Sea Point has requested our assistance.' Only the final word was coloured with a light shade of irony.

'What sort of assistance?'

'Full crime scene and investigative assistance.'

They exchanged a look that said: 'Can you believe it . . .'

'I can send Mbali.'

'That would be perfect.'

'And I'd better get Cloete out there too.'

22

Griessel hurried back to Cupido and Davids. He had asked Davids to make a copy of Lillian Alvarez's email to Adair urgently, and then delete it. 'Quickly, Lithpel. Please,' he said, with Cupido's suspicious gaze on him.

When it was done, he asked that the Facebook photo of Lillian Alvarez be sent out as a bulletin to all SAPS stations. And as he walked out of Lithpel Davids's kingdom, he said to Cupido, 'I want to show you something.'

Cupido followed him with a half-spoken 'What?' forming.

Griessel held a finger to his mouth and trotted down the stairs, to the basement, with Cupido in pursuit.

Right at the back, beside the 'clubhouse' door, he stopped.

'I don't see anything,' said Cupido.

'I didn't want to talk in there. I think the SSA is eavesdropping on us.'

'The SSA?'

'Yes.'

'*Jissis*,' said Cupido. 'Benna, are you serious?'

'I had a call from a Spook. And she didn't mind me knowing that she had intercepted my email.'

'*Now*? That call that you took just now?'

'Yes. And she said she would know if I told anyone about the call.'

'How do you know she's a Spook?'

'Put two and two together. She knows about Emma Graber, the MI6 agent at the British Consulate. The thing is, I think they tap our cellphones, and I wouldn't be at all surprised if there were microphones in some of our offices too.'

'She could be CI also,' said Cupido, now muted and wary, as if they were being listened to here as well.

Griessel considered the possibility. It wasn't far-fetched. 'CI', as the

SAPS Criminal Intelligence unit was known, had become a sinister place in recent years. First there was the fiasco with Lieutenant-General Richard Mdluli, the former station commander for Vosloorus, who had been appointed as head of Criminal Intelligence – and who was subsequently sacked due to alleged involvement in fraud, corruption, attempted murder, and conspiracy. Now rumours were flying about his successor, the new acting chief of Criminal Intelligence, especially about his close ties with the highest authority of the state. In the halls it was whispered that this unit concerned itself more with the dirty laundry of the president's enemies, than with collecting evidence to fight crime.

'I don't think so. CI wouldn't bug the Consulate. It's SSA . . .'

'Crazy country, Benna,' said Cupido. 'Crazy world . . . OK. So what did the bitch say?'

Griessel told him everything.

'Why now, Benna?'

'I don't know.'

'No, I mean, why trust me now?'

'Vaughn, it was a mistake. I didn't have a choice.'

'Apology accepted. And you believe me now about Adair and the great digital bank robbery?'

'Hell, Vaughn, anything is possible, but that would mean that Adair or an accomplice knew enough about the Cobra to use the same pistol and engravings. So that it looked like the Cobra had done the shooting . . .'

'No, Benna, I've been thinking . . . Adair might have hired the Cobra. Remember, he's for sale to anybody. And if Adair had been skimming off dough, then money is no problem.'

Sometimes he battled to keep up with Cupido's wild mental leaps. The problem was, his colleague was right at least sixty per cent of the time.

Tyrone put an old T-shirt on first. In case his shoulder started bleeding again. Another T-shirt, then the grey Nike sweatshirt. His raincoat was in the rucksack. He would have to buy a new one. And a new rucksack. Because he would have to run now. To Johannesburg? Durban? He didn't know any of those places. He only knew the Cape.

Where would he go?

He put his black beanie on. *You never wear a beanie, Tyrone. Makes you look like a criminal. Baseball caps too. Hats are better if you want to change your profile, but in the Cape wind* daai's *difficult.*

It's a crisis, Uncle Solly. Camouflage.

In the bathroom he climbed onto the toilet, pushed up the trapdoor in the ceiling, reached for the hot-water cylinder, and loosened the pack of notes that he kept there. Two thousand rand. His emergency stash. He put the trapdoor back neatly.

He jumped in fright when the intercom at the door sudden growled.

The cops were here.

So soon?

He was shaking now, but he grabbed the stolen wallet and the iPod on his bed. The intercom made that irritating sound again. He stuffed the wallet, the stash, and the iPod in his trouser pockets, and pressed the button.

'What?'

'There's a guy at the gate asking for you,' said the rich Muslim's daughter. She always spoke English.

'A guy? What kind of a guy?' The cops were here. His heart jumped.

'I don't know.' Irritation. 'Just a guy.'

'What does he look like?'

'Coloured guy, grey baseball cap.'

And then Tyrone had a horrible suspicion, as dread descended on him. 'Black windcheater?'

'Yes. I'll buzz him in.'

'No! Tell him I'm not here.'

He knew his voice would convey his panic, and he waited in suspense for her to answer. *Jirre*, please, don't let her *gooi* that fat rich girl mentality, he thought.

'What have you done?' she asked. She was *mos* always suspicious.

'Please. Just tell him I'm not here. Please!' Then he grabbed the doorknob, opened it quietly, and slipped out, grateful that the gunman could not see him here in the backyard. He jumped up against the back wall.

That man was going to shoot her.

He jumped down again, ran back to his room, pressed the intercom.

'Be careful, lock your door, the guy is dangerous. He'll kill you. Call the cops. Now!'

He ran out, jumped up against the wall and clambered over.

On the other side a *moerse* big dog came for him.

Nyathi found Griessel and Cupido in the passage. 'I was looking for you. Can I see you in my office?'

As usual, the Giraffe displayed no emotion.

Nyathi closed the door behind them. 'Sit, please.'

They did so.

'The brigadier had a call from our commissioner. We have to hand over all case material to officers of the Department of State Security.' He put 'officers' in quotation marks with his fingers. 'And stop the investigation.'

Griessel saw Cupido trying to make meaningful eye contact. He was too afraid that Nyathi would ask what was going on. He was afraid of microphones.

'Yes, sir,' he said quickly.

Tyrone screamed, the sound slipping involuntarily over his lips. The dog, huge and growling, teeth bared, rushed at him.

One hot summer night, hanging out with some mates on a Mitchell's Plain street corner, one of them said if a dog attacked you, you should do two things. You rush at him with your arm like this, hanging out. Because they train dogs to go for the arm. And then, just before he grabs your arm, you hit him on the nose.

That's the first thing that came into Tyrone's head.

He didn't think, just rushed at the dog holding out his skinny arm. *Jirre*, wasn't his body hurting enough already?

The dog skidded to a halt in cloud of dust and Tyrone could swear he had a look of 'what the fuck?' in his eyes. The beast stood still as Tyrone ran past, alongside the house. He didn't know if there was anyone home.

And then the dog came for him again.

For all his failings Vaughn Cupido was always quick on the uptake.

When Griessel took out his notebook and pen and put them on the desk to make a note, his colleague realised the Giraffe was going to say something about it.

'State Security? That's bullshit,' said Cupido indignantly.

Griessel hoped Cupido would not overdo it, it sounded melodramatic, and he had never talked to Nyathi like *that* before. He scribbled hastily: *Office bugged? Talk outside*, and slid it over to the colonel, while Cupido said, 'With all due respect, of course, sir. But what does State Security know about investigating a criminal case?'

Nyathi read and nodded.

'I'm sorry, gentlemen, but that's the way it is. If you could bring me all relevant documentation, please.'

And he wrote in Benny's little book: *5 mins.*

Griessel replied with: *Clubhouse.*

He was almost at the high railing fence at the front of the neighbour's house. But the dog was too close, Tyrone had to spin around to confront the creature.

This time the animal didn't stop. He came at him, jumping at Tyrone's midriff, his crotch, which in that moment seemed so unfair to Tyrone, so totally unacceptable – what sort of person taught his dog to bite a guy's dick? – that rage drove away fear, and he hit out blindly, connecting with the dog's muzzle. A sudden sharp pain in his fist. The dog yelped.

'Hey!' A voice came from one of the windows. A man.

It made the dog turn away, and Tyrone ran and leaped. Adrenaline made him agile, and suddenly he was over and on the pavement, he wasn't sure how.

He just ran.

23

Captain Mbali Kaleni was the only woman in the DPCI's Violent Crimes team. For six long months now. She was short and very fat. She was never to be seen without her SAPS identity card on a ribbon around her neck, and her service pistol on her plump hip. When she left her office, there was always a huge handbag of shiny black leather over her shoulder. Her expression was usually grim, as though she was constantly angry at someone. It was a defence mechanism, but only two of her colleagues understood that.

She had an honours degree in Police Science, and an IQ of 138. Her name meant 'flower' in Zulu. Behind her back she was called 'the Heavy Hawk', 'the Flower', 'Cactus Flower', and sometimes, when she had once again antagonised certain male colleagues with her unbending rigidity, 'That *fokken* Mbali'.

Nyathi knew Mbali Kaleni and Vaughn Cupido did not necessarily see eye to eye.

The Flower could recite every article in the Criminal Procedure Act, and every ordinance of the Hawks. She always acted strictly according to these regulations. While Cupido saw everything as a vague, voluntary guideline. Nyathi knew that these divergent philosophies were frequently a recipe for conflict. Which he had to manage.

That was why he had not included his female detective in Griessel's Franschhoek team, so she was now free to be sent to the bloodbath at the shopping centre.

The Sea Point Station commander stood at the door of the Waterfront Shopping Centre. He saw Captain Kaleni waddling towards him, filled with fire and purpose. His heart sank; her legendary reputation preceded her. He knew she was clever, but she was difficult.

He greeted her politely. He stretched out his hand for the door.

'No,' said Mbali, 'you are not wearing gloves.' All he wanted was to keep his station's collective butt, and his own individual one, out of trouble. He didn't say that many hands had already touched that handle. He merely nodded and watched as she dug a pair of gloves out of her handbag and put them on.

'Don't you have gloves?' she asked.

'In the car,' he said.

'Go and fetch them.'

He nodded, and asked one of his detectives to fetch them.

'Do you have shoe covers?' she asked.

He called to the detective to bring them too.

Mbali shook her head in disbelief. 'You wait until you are properly attired. And then you come in. Only you.'

'But the sergeant was first on the scene . . .'

'I will question him when I come out.' She pointed at the other detective, and the uniform sergeant. 'You guard this door.'

Then she walked in.

'What makes you think they've bugged our offices?' Nyathi asked.

They were standing in the underground car park, beside the club-house door, where no one could see or hear them: the Giraffe, Griessel and Cupido.

'It was something she said, sir,' said Griessel. 'When she warned me not to tell anybody. "If I hear you speaking out, the phone calls will stop." She didn't say "if I heard", but "if I hear". Maybe I'm wrong, but it made me very uneasy.'

Nyathi stood there for a long time, his head tilted. He sighed. 'They are already monitoring our email and our phone calls. The sad thing is, you might be right. And we have to assume that you are.'

'Yes, sir.'

'You go back, and you make copies, just the two of you. Don't talk to anybody about it. Just do it. Bring me all the original material and I'll hand it over when the agent comes.'

'Does that mean we continue the investigation, sir?' asked Cupido.

'Damn right it does,' said Nyathi.

Mbali Kaleni wanted to cry.

It was her greatest secret, greater than the secret packets of crisps or KFC or chocolate that she ate alone in her office. Greater than the fantasies about the actor Djimon Hounsou that she sometimes allowed herself in bed at night. At a murder scene she wanted to cry. It was all about the loss, the senselessness, tragedy, but above all the human capacity for evil. *That* broke her heart, and she often mused on this with great solemnity and concern. Why did people do it? What was it that, especially in this country, drove people to rape and maim and murder? The heavy burden of the past? Or was it something that came from the bedrock of South Africa, a demonic energy field that unsettled people's minds?

She was purposefully strict with the SC back in the passage, because she really wanted to come in here alone. That way she would not have to work so hard to hide the tears. She knew, just one sign of weakness, and her male colleagues would be crowing. But now, at least, she could let her shoulders sag and allow the silent tears to well up. She dug in her handbag and took out a bunch of tissues, gripping them in her fist as she looked at the five lifeless bodies. This afternoon their loved ones, fathers and mothers, wives, children, would be torn apart by grief. A few days only in the headlines, but this deed would last so much longer, would ripple outwards creating single breadwinners and greater poverty and misery, far into the future, when a son or daughter of one of these men would say to a social worker or a magistrate: 'My father died when I was four . . .'

She wiped away the tears, pushed the tissues back into her handbag. She straightened her shoulders, and began to study the crime scene.

Tyrone Kleinbooi ran across August Street, over the empty plot, and jumped up against the high concrete wall of the school. He wanted to be among people, that was his only defence up here in Schotsche Kloof, where the houses were too few and the streets too wide.

He clambered over the wall. The school grounds were quiet.

Holidays, he had forgotten it was the holidays.

He ran past the school buildings, down to the main gate, next to the netball court. An ageing security guard with a military cap set on askew, struggled across a concrete area, shouting and waving a knobkierie stick at him.

Tyrone kept on running.

The main gate was high and locked, but the chain was long, so that he could force it open a crack and squeeze his skinny body through.

He looked back.

He didn't see anyone, except for the old uncle with the cap, gesticulating wildly and shouting inexplicable things.

He was through. He ran past the Schotsche Kloof flats, the ugly housing projects where washing flapped from windows. An aunty shouted from up there: 'Hey, look at him run now.'

He was grateful it was downhill. He swerved left, through backyards, into the upper end of Church Street.

He looked back again.

Nobody.

They made hurried copies of everything. Griessel passed the documents on, and the more technologically skilled Cupido copied them.

Griessel's phone rang. He took it out, annoyed by the interruption while they were under so much pressure. MBALI on his screen.

He answered.

'Benny, I'm at the Waterfront. There's been a shooting. Five security people dead . . .'

Griessel suppressed the '*Jissis*', because Mbali didn't like expletives or swearing.

'I think you'd better come,' she said.

'Mbali, we're very busy . . .'

'I know. But the colonel briefed us on the Franschhoek shooting at morning parade, and he said there were shell casings with the etchings of a snake . . .'

'Yes?'

'There are a lot of them here, Benny. And I mean a *lot*.'

Fok, thought Griessel, he should not have been so impatient and hasty – his cellphone was being tapped, now the whole SSA knew it too.

'I'm on my way,' he said.

'Can you bring Sergeant Davids too? There's a lot of technology we'll have to figure out.'

'OK,' said Griessel, and rang off.

* * *

Nadia Kleinbooi sat at the bottom of the Neelsie, the student centre of the University of Stellenbosch, at a long wooden table with some of her classmates. Her cellphone rang. She barely heard it, because it was a noisy environment, the voices of students, music playing.

TYRONE, she read. The guy must have delivered the phone.

She covered one ear and put the phone to the other. 'Hello?'

'I'm really sorry to bug you, but there's nobody home.' The Good Samaritan's voice again.

'No, please, you're not bugging me. My brother works in the city, he'll only be back tonight. I . . . Can you maybe put the phone in the mailbox? I will try to . . .' Tyrone lived in the back room, and she didn't know if the Muslims would realise that it was his phone. She didn't know what to do.

'I'll bring the phone to you,' said the man.

'No, I'm in Stellenbosch, it's far away . . .'

'Stellenbosch . . .' His voice became clearer. 'I have to go there, before I fly out.'

'Really?'

'Yes. My hotel is there.'

'Oh. That is . . . You are a very kind person.'

'No, no, I know about losing a phone. It is a . . . *grand dérangement.*'

'You are French?'

'*Mais oui.*'

'That's so cool.'

'So where do I find you?'

'Oh, yes. I have class until one o'clock. Where is your hotel?'

'Right there in Stellenbosch. I will call you when I get there?'

'OK, just after one. Call me just after one.'

24

Further down the corridor, in the belly of the Victoria and Alfred Waterfront shopping centre, was the office of the head of security. At two minutes past twelve, Mbali sat on one of the visitors' chairs. A coloured security official sat opposite her. The Sea Point Station commander stood against the wall.

'I was on duty at the Red Shed when I heard them on the radio,' said the security man. He was shocked and nervous.

'What time was this?' asked Mbali.

'I can't say exactly.'

'More or less?'

'I'd say about nine. Maybe . . . maybe quarter to, ten to nine . . . I'm not sure.'

'OK, what did you hear on the radio?'

'That they've caught Knippies.'

'Who is Knippies?'

'He's the pickpocket. We've been trying to catch him for a long time now.'

'Is that his name? Knippies?'

'That was what we called him. He's . . .'

'What is his real name?'

'I don't know.'

'Did your colleagues know?'

'No. Nobody knows.'

'What do you know about him?'

'We . . . He . . . We've had complaints, for a long time, two years, maybe longer. People who report they've been robbed. By a pickpocket. Every time, it's the same thing, this guy, Knippies, he would come up to them and ask if they dropped this hair *knippie*, what do you call it, a hairpin, you know, the thing women put in their hair, with a butterfly or a flower on it. Sometimes he would use a lighter, like a

Zippo, when it's a guy he wants to rob. And they all said it's a black guy, slim, about one point eight metres tall, wears black, sometimes blue denim. So, for a year ... maybe more, we were looking for him, all the security officials, we would look for a skinny black guy. And the control room would scan for him, and tell us there's a suspect ...'

Mbali put her hand in the air. The security official stopped talking.

'The control room is where the CCTV is?'

'Yes.'

'This Knippies, how often did he rob people?' she asked.

'Once a month. Maybe ... It ... I don't know, sometimes it would be two on one day, and then nothing for weeks.'

'But about once a month?'

'About.'

'OK.'

He said nothing.

'Go on,' she said.

'Oh. OK. I ... Yes, once a month. But he was clever, he knew where the cameras were, so he always robbed people where there weren't any cameras. And then about a year ago, maybe less, maybe August ... I'm not sure ...'

'That's OK.'

'OK. Thank you. So, maybe August, they put in extra cameras, the small ones. And in March – yes, it must have been March – they caught him on camera, just by the pier, at the charter signs. They caught him on video stealing from a guy, a photographer, he stole a lens from his bag with the lighter trick. But they didn't see it live, he is very slick, very quick. When the guy came in to report it, they played the video back, and they saw him. And then we had a shot ... a photograph of Knippies. Turns out he's coloured, but dark, you know? So they showed all of us the photograph, and the video ...'

'That's the same photograph that is on the wall? In the control room? The one that looks like the guy on the TV screen?'

'Yes, that's Knippies.'

'OK. And this morning?'

'I heard it on the radio.'

'Exactly what did you hear on the radio?'

'I heard Control call Gertjie and Louw. They patrol the

amphitheatre. Control said they had spotted Knippies, and Gertjie and Louw must look for him. There were a lot of civilians, we had the cruise ship in this morning, so Control was directing them, you know. Go left, go right. And then I heard Louw call it in, they caught him.'

'Is that what he said?'

'Yes, but in Afrikaans. "*Ons het hom, Control, ons bring hom in.*"'

'And then?'

'Then everybody called in to say well done. And Control said: "His ass is grass, he's on video."'

'And then?'

'Then I heard Jerome call on the radio about the shooting.'

'Who is Jerome?'

'He's an official.'

'A security official?'

'Yes.'

'Like you?'

'Yes.'

'What time was this?'

'I don't know. After nine. Some time after nine.'

'How did Jerome know about the shooting?'

'He had his tea break, and he said he wanted to take a look at Knippies, so he went to the control room, and he saw everybody was dead.'

'Where is Jerome now?'

'He's in the bathroom. He's throwing up. A lot.'

Tyrone stole a Samsung S3 in St George's Mall, from a man's windcheater.

He hated Samsung S3s, because they have seven sorts of screen lock. Most people used the pattern, the nine dots that had to be connected in a certain order.

He tried the three most popular patterns.

Nothing. The thing stayed locked.

He didn't have time. He tossed it in a rubbish bin and looked for his next victim.

★ ★ ★

They threaded their way through the traffic on the N1, blue lights on, but sirens off. Griessel drove. Cupido blew off some steam about Mbali.

'Last week she tells me, a man's worth is no greater than his ambition. Just because I was taking a break with Angry Birds. I mean, can't a man take a break now and then . . .'

'Who is Angry Birds?'

Lithpel Davids laughed from the back seat.

'Not "who", Benna, "what",' said Cupido patiently. 'It's a game. On my phone. You should try it, there's an iOS version too. Great stress reliever. Anyway, so then I want to say to her: "Mbali, if I had as much ambition as you have, I would also be a *doos*," but *fok weet*, then you would never get her to shut up about your swearing, and how that's also a sure sign of weakness, she's always got a *fokken* quote. What's wrong with swearing? I mean, it's just another word. What really pisses me off is people that want to say "*fokken*", but then they *gooi* "*flippen*" instead, and that's OK. It's not *fokken* OK, they mean the same thing. And intent is nine-tenths of the law, pappie. But you can *ma'* say "*flippen*" in front of Mbali, *daai's* cool. I mean, Benna, there's no justice when it comes to that woman.'

'Possession.'

'Huh?'

'Possession is nine-tenths of the law.'

'OK. True. But what is possession without intent?'

'Also true.'

'*Fokken* Mbali . . .'

Cupido was quiet for a while, and Griessel thought of a conversation he had had in the Wimpy at the Winelands Engen service station on the N1, one morning on the way back from a case in Paarl. Over coffee, Mbali had hauled a textbook out of her massive handbag. *The Law of Contract in South Africa*.

'I'm sorry, Benny, I have an exam tonight.'

He hadn't known she was studying again. She, who already had an honours degree in Police Science. So he asked.

'I'm doing a B Iuris at UNISA.'

'Do you want to leave the Service?'

'No, Benny.' She had hesitated and looked at him in a measured way, then decided she could trust him. 'I want to be the commissioner. One day.' There was no arrogance in the statement, just a quiet determination.

He had accepted that she meant the national commissioner, and he had sat thinking in amazement. About people. About himself. His trouble was that he had never wanted to be *something*. He had just wanted to *be*.

A man's worth is no greater than his ambition.

Perhaps that was why he had become a boozer and fuck-up. Perhaps you should have three- and five- and ten-year plans for yourself, higher aspirations. But how do you get there if you are still struggling with all the trouble that life throws at you?

What was he to do about this trouble between him and Alexa?

His only 'ambition' was to avoid a *njaps*.

What did that say of his worth?

Maybe it said everything.

Where did you get an agenda for this sort of trouble, a three-day plan. Or was he the only one who battled with this kind of shit?

25

Pickpocketing is a lucky dip, Tyrone. You take what you can get. That's why you need more than one fence. 'Cause everything's got value for someone.

But what do you do, Uncle Solly, if you don't have time for the lucky dip, if you need to steal a phone *specifically*, and opportunity doesn't exactly come knocking? And you've never really thought about this before, and you don't have the time or inclination to ponder on it? 'Cause the clock is ticking like crazy, and you can't phone your sister from a public phone, 'cause that's exactly the problem, right, they are public, especially the row of coin and card phones up in St George's Mall. You can't just go stand there and say: 'Nadia, I'm in deep trouble, if the cops phone you, say you don't know who the call is from.' It's noisy there by the phones, it's not like you can stand there and whisper. Or you waltz into a restaurant and say here's a hundred bucks, please let me use the phone, it's an emergency. And the maître d' hangs around suspiciously to check that you're not phoning Beijing. And Uncle Solly, Nadia is going to *skrik*, she'll be so scared, and she'll ask: 'Now what's going on?' and if I don't say, she'll worry. 'Cause I'm all she has. I've always been all she has.

And in his urgency, his haste, eyes flitting from one pedestrian to the next, it hit him suddenly, out of nowhere: How had the gunman known where he lived?

The thought made Tyrone stop in his tracks, and shiver.

When the fat Muslim chick buzzed him, he thought it was the cops. But it wasn't, and he hadn't had the time to work that one out.

How the fuck?

Did the shooter tail him?

Must have. He didn't want to shoot Tyrone in public. He wanted no eyewitnesses. So he tailed him, all the way behind the taxi. He's good, never saw it coming.

He looked around, slowly, carefully, his eyes scanning for the man in the grey baseball cap. Or a reasonable facsimile thereof.

He saw nothing. He moved on, searching for possibilities.

The time, time was running out.

Why did that bro' want to shoot him?

Because he was a witness.

Why had that bro' come in there with a silenced gun like a secret agent and blown all those mall cops away?

Maybe a big heist in the mall?

Probably drugs, and the mall cops were all dealers who were skimming. That's the only thing that would have brought a coloured bro' out of the woodwork with a silenced gun.

Tyrone searched for a mark, to steal a phone.

And then he thought, what a *blerrie* fool he is, that's what stress will do for you. Don't steal a phone. Buy one.

The Sea Point Station commander was still leaning against the wall of the security chief's office. He listened to Captain Mbali questioning Jerome, the official who was first on the scene. All stuff he would have asked, he thought, it wasn't as though she was *that* clever.

Jerome was clearly still in shock. He was as white as a sheet, his voice muted, and he hesitated before each answer, as though he didn't want to recall the events. He said the roster was such that only one official was off duty at a time. His break was from 'oh nine hundred hours', but he was on duty at the Clock Tower car park, and he first had a chat with a friend on his way back to the tea room. And then he wanted to see what Knippies looked like in real life, and so he went to the control room. He wasn't even sure the super would allow him to look at the pickpocket, but he thought he would take a chance, as they had looked for the *ou* for so long.

'So you came in?'

'Yes.'

'And the door was open?'

'Which door?'

'The one to the corridor.'

'No. It was closed.'

'Did you see anything out of the ordinary?'

'Jeez, lady, I saw all of them dead . . .'

'That's not what I mean. Before you got to the control room. Did you see anybody or anything that did not belong there?'

'No. It was just very quiet.'

'Did you touch anything?'

The Sea Point Station commander's cellphone rang. He saw Captain Kaleni give him a dirty look. He wondered: How does she think I can help it? He recognised his station's number and walked out of the office as he answered it.

It was his charge office, and the constable's voice was weighted with drama. 'Captain, we have another shooting. Up in Schotsche Kloof.'

'Yes?' His heart sank, but he mustn't show it.

'A woman phoned at eleven thirty-three, Ella Street number eighteen, and reported an intruder at her gate, he was busy climbing over the fence. So I asked her, are the doors locked and she said yes. So I sent a van, they were there at eleven forty-four. The gate was still locked. They rang the bell, but no one answered . . .'

The SC's patience ran out. 'Is she the one who was shot?'

'Yes, Captain. They found her there inside. One of the windows is broken . . .'

'I'm coming.'

It was not his day.

Tyrone bought a phone from the Somalians in Adderley. First they tried to palm an LG E900 Optimus 7 off on him for R900.

'Nine hundred for a hot Windows phone. Do you think I'm stupid?'

'It's a good phone. Not hot. Cool.'

'I don't care if it's a good phone. I'm not paying nine hundred for a hot phone. And I don't want a Windows phone. Nobody wants a Windows phone. What else do you have? For under two hundred?'

'No. Two hundred? Nothing for two hundred. We only sell good phones. Not hot phones.'

He didn't have time to tell the Somalian with his soft eyes and big smile that he was talking shit. He shook his head, turned, and walked off.

'Wait,' said the Somalian, as Tyrone knew he would.

'Two hundred.'

'For that? It's a relic. One hundred.'

'One seventy-five. It has a SIM card. It works.' The man switched the phone on.

'Let me test it.'

'No. I will show you. I will call my friend.' He typed in a number and held it out so that Tyrone could listen. It rang. Someone answered.

'You see. It works. Pay as you go, you can top up. Not a hot phone.' He switched it off.

'How much time on the card?'

'Ten hours' talk time.'

'OK.' He didn't believe the man. Probably closer to an hour or two. But that was all he needed. He took out the stolen wallet.

'So, did you touch anything?' Mbali asked again.

'No,' said Jerome, the security official.

'What about the outside door handle?'

'Yes, I touched that.'

'And inside?'

'No, nothing. Wait. I touched the inside door handle too. And the toilet door, and the basin and . . .'

'I'm talking about the crime scene.'

'No, I never touched anything in there.'

'OK. Did you look at the TV screen when you were in there?'

'Yes. But just for a moment. I mean, all my friends . . .'

'I understand. Is that Knippies on the screen?'

'I think so.'

'So there is a video of Knippies that was taken today?'

'Yes, they watched him, and all the cameras are recording.'

'OK. Thank you.'

Tyrone ran up to the Company Gardens so that he could phone Nadia without a hundred ears listening.

She didn't answer. He got her voicemail, drew a breath to leave a message, then reconsidered and rang off. What could he say that wouldn't frighten her?

Her phone was on silent. She was in class. It was twelve minutes to one. She would probably come out just after one.

By that time the cops would have got hold of the rucksack, and probably the phone too.

He would *have* to leave Nadia a message. He would just say that this was his new number . . . No, he would say it was a temporary new number, he had lost his old phone, and please phone him, there was something urgent . . . no, there's something important he wanted to tell her. Phone as soon as she can.

He took a deep breath so that she wouldn't hear the tension in his voice, and pressed the numbers.

For the first time Mbali saw the bullet hole in the door that led into the mall. She studied it carefully, and then she tried to understand the meaning of it, in the context of the whole crime scene.

She opened the door and walked into the corridor of the shopping centre. She still had her gloves and her shoe covers on. Her eyes searched for a camera that could have covered the door to the control room.

She found one, ten metres away, high up on the wall.

She measured the angle from where it was. Perhaps it hadn't covered the door, but it would at least have caught a great deal of the wide corridor in front of it.

'Mbali?' She heard a familiar voice and turned. Benny Griessel. He, Vaughn Cupido, and Lithpel had arrived. She steeled herself. Griessel was her favourite colleague. Sergeant Davids' apparel and grooming were a bit of a scandal, but he did his job well, and he knew his place. Cupido she could not stand. But she was a professional woman. She must be able to handle everything.

She greeted all three, then went and stood in front of the door that led out of the mall's walkway. 'The crime scene starts here. You'll have to put on protection.'

26

Nadia Kleinbooi walked out of class.

In the corridor a guy behind her said, 'Do those jeans come with the cute bum, or is that an optional extra?'

She looked and laughed at him, a passing flirtation. She enjoyed the attention. She wasn't as skinny as her brother. 'You got the calves that they forgot to give me,' Tyrone always said.

Then she would reply, 'And you got the looks.'

'There's nothing wrong with your looks. *Jy's* beautiful.' But she knew he was the good-looking one. All her girlfriends used to hang around Uncle Solly's house in the hope that Tyrone would be there. But Tyrone wasn't there much. Though he was always there when she needed him.

Only once she was outside, in the weak winter sun, did she take out her cellphone.

Two SMSs beeped immediately.

You have two missed calls.

You have two voicemail messages.

At that very moment it rang, and she saw it was Tyrone's phone. She answered.

'Hi,' said the guy with the sexy French voice. 'I'm in Ryneveld Street.'

But he pronounced it 'Rinerval', which made her smile. 'There's a building here, I think it says Geology.'

'I know where that is. I'll be there in two minutes.'

'*Très bien,*' he said. 'I am at the entrance to the parking. With a silver Nissan X-Trail.'

'OK,' she said, and rang off.

She wondered what the Frenchman looked like. It was such a sexy, sexy accent, and his voice was nice – there was a hint of laughter in it, as though he found the whole situation very amusing.

★ ★ ★

Griessel held the cartridge in his glove-protected fingers.

'It's the same snake. And the same initials.'

'OK,' said Mbali, and gave them a short, bullet-point summary of what had happened, according to the security men.

'The Cobra is a pickpocket now?' Cupido asked, shaking his head scornfully.

Mbali ignored him.

'That's not the Cobra.' Cupido pointed at the screen, and then at the photo on the noticeboard. 'This guy is too dark. And that's not racist, Mbali. That's just a fact.'

She didn't look at him. She told Griessel the hardest decision they had to take now, was at what stage Lithpel could sit down in front of the video console so that they could look at the material. Because the console was in the middle of the crime scene, and there was the risk that they would disturb forensic evidence if they were all standing around, among the dead. But Thick and Thin were on their way, and their procedures, the video and photography department's recording, the pathologist's *in-loco* examination, and the removal of the bodies could take hours. The longer they waited, the more likely it was that any possible video evidence would prove useless. While the culprit fled further afield.

'Easy decision,' said Cupido. 'There's no big mystery here. He came, he shot, he left. And we're already in. Let's do it.'

Mbali looked only at Griessel.

'He's right,' said Griessel, 'but we still have to be very careful not to disturb the scene.'

'OK,' said Mbali. 'There's one other problem. Because the shooting was localised, and the Sea Point SC managed everything appropriately, it has not attracted much attention yet. But when Forensics and the pathologist and the ambulances arrive, that will change. Someone needs to go and tell the shopping centre management. They will want to manage the public and media attention.'

'Don't look at me,' said Cupido.

'Where's the SC?' asked Griessel.

'He had to leave. He has another shooting somewhere to attend to.'

'What shooting?' asked Griessel, heart sinking, because he didn't believe in coincidences.

★ ★ ★

Nadia saw him standing beside the silver X-Trail. A blond man in old denims and a white T-shirt with a cellphone in his hand. Looking around, as though he was searching for someone. Brush cut, narrow hips, broad shoulders, white skin, but tanned, like a surfer. Maybe he was a surfer.

A pity he was on his way back to France . . .

But as she approached, while he looked enquiringly at her and she waved and nodded, she realised he was probably in his mid-thirties. Too old for her. Although . . .

He held the phone up and asked: 'Nadia?'

'Yes.'

He smiled broadly. White, even teeth.

'How can I thank you?' Out of the corner of her eye she saw two other men in the X-Trail.

'It is only a pleasure.' He held out the phone to her.

She reached him and put out her hand to take the phone from him. Then he grabbed her arm.

Two male students in a Volkswagen Citi Golf drove out of the car park beside the R.W. Wilcocks building. The passenger was busy on his cellphone. It was the driver who saw it – the white man grabbing the coloured girl. The rear door of the Nissan X-Trail opened, and he half carried, half dragged her into the vehicle.

'What the fuck?' he said and wound down his window.

'What?' asked the passenger.

'That *ou* . . .' He saw the X-Trail pull away calmly. He pressed the hooter of his car three times, short and urgent.

'What is it, bro?' asked the passenger.

The X-Trail drove on.

The driver bellowed out of the window. 'Hey!'

'Cool it, bro,' said the passenger.

'Those guys in the Nissan kidnapped that girl right now . . .' He accelerated, and set off in pursuit of the X-Trail.

'What girl?'

'The one in the car.'

'You're not serious.'

'I *am*. Call the police.' The X-Trail turned right into Crozier.

'There's no girl in that car . . .'

The driver hooted again, reduced his following distance so that he was on the tail of the X-Trail. 'They're pushing her down. I'm telling you, call the police. I *saw* it.'

The passenger wasn't convinced. 'Bro, we can't just call the police. I mean . . .'

The driver swore, a staccato of reproach. He took his cellphone out of his shirt pocket. 'I will *fokken* phone them myself . . .'

The X-Trail turned right into Andringa. They followed, the driver had to look up from the cellphone, then down again, to type in the number.

'Watch it!' said the passenger.

The driver looked up quickly. The X-Trail had stopped suddenly. The doors opened and two men came running back, each with a pistol in hand.

'*Fok*, bro, reverse!' screamed the passenger. But the driver hadn't even stopped yet, and when he did, with a short shrill screech of tyres, it was too late. The men were right there, moving impossibly swiftly. And surely. One aimed a weapon at the front wheel. A soft explosion, then the hiss of the tyre going flat, and then they were at the doors of the Golf, jerking them open, grabbing the cellphones from their hands. Then they slammed the doors, ran back to the X-Trail, jumped in.

The X-Trail drove off.

The students sat there.

'*Jissis*,' said the passenger.

The driver let out a sound that was just like a tyre deflating.

Benny Griessel didn't use his cellphone. He phoned the Sea Point SC from a telephone beside the video console in the control centre.

The first thing that the station commander said to him was: 'There's a cartridge here with a snake on it.'

'How do you know about that?'

'I was present at Captain Kaleni's interrogation at the V&A. She phoned someone and talked about "shell casings with the etchings of a snake" . . .'

'OK, who is the deceased?'

'She hasn't been identified yet. Young coloured woman, she seems to have been alone at home. Intruder gained access via a broken window in the sitting room. He forced open the woman's bedroom door, the lock is broken. And he shot her once, in the forehead.'

Jissis, thought Griessel. What the fuck was going on? 'OK,' he said, and tried to keep the vexation out of his voice. 'It's definitely linked to two other murder cases. I'm sending Captain Vaughn Cupido, if you can just seal the scene so long.'

'Already done,' said the SC.

'Thank you, Captain,' said Griessel, with relief. And satisfaction, because the SSA didn't know about *this* one yet. 'What's the address?'

'Ella Street number eighteen, up in Schotsche Kloof'

Griessel rang off. And then everything happened at once.

'Vaughn, I'll have to send you to the Bo-Kaap,' said Griessel.

'It's that girl.' Lithpel Davids pointed a finger at the TV console where a video was being played back.

'*My fok*,' said Cupido.

'That is very unprofessional language,' said Mbali.

Griessel's cellphone began to ring.

'What girl?' asked Mbali.

'The Facebook girl. Alvarez,' said Lithpel.

They climbed slowly and carefully over the bodies of the security men to reach the TV screen.

'What Facebook girl?' asked Mbali.

'It's her,' said Cupido.

Griessel's cellphone kept ringing, but his eyes were glued to the screen. Lillian Alvarez stood with her face to the camera. She stared at a hairpin in the hands of the pickpocket. Knippies's face was turned to her, his hand touching her handbag.

'What Facebook girl?' asked Mbali again.

From outside came the voice of Arnold, the short, fat Forensics guy: 'Hallooo? Anybody home?'

Griessel answered his phone: 'Hello?'

'You had better hurry,' said the woman's voice, the one who called herself Joni Mitchell. 'SSA are on the way. They are going to take over the scene.'

'The Waterfront scene?'

'Yes.'

Then she rang off.

'He stole something from Alvarez,' said Cupido.

'*Liewe ffff* . . .' said Jimmy, the skinny Forensics detective, when he saw the five lifeless bodies. But he never completed the word because Captain Kaleni shot him a withering look.

27

'Out,' said Benny Griessel to Thick and Thin.

'Don't you think it's you who should leave?' said Jimmy. 'You are occupying the whole—'

'Out!' said Griessel more sharply.

This was very unlike the Griessel they knew. They just stood there.

'Jimmy, please, go and wait out in the corridor. And hurry up.'

They heard the urgency in Griessel's voice, and responded.

'Is somebody going to tell me about this Alvarez girl?' asked Mbali.

'Later, Mbali,' said Griessel. 'We have very little time. The SSA are on their way . . .'

'Shit,' said Cupido.

'The SSA?' asked Mbali in disbelief. 'The State Security Agency?'

'Please, everybody. We'll talk later. Right now we need to look at that footage. Quickly, Lithpel, play it back.'

Tyrone walked up and down the Company Gardens path. Once again Nadia had forgotten to turn her phone back on. Not for the first time.

He phoned again.

It rang. For a long time.

His heart sank more. He was going to get voicemail again.

Then she answered. 'Hello?' and he could hear in that single word that something was wrong. The cops had already phoned her.

'Nadia, it's me. I can explain, doesn't matter what they told you, it's not true . . .' He heard something on the line, a hiss, as if Nadia were in a car.

'They've got me, *boetie* . . .' There was fear in her voice, fear as he had never heard it, and his gut contracted.

'The cops?'

'Is this Tyrone?' A man's voice. But it wasn't a cop accent.

'Who's this?'

'Tyrone, I have Nadia, and you have something I want. If you give it to me, we will let her go. If you don't, I will shoot her, right between the eyes. Do you understand this?'

Tyrone began to shake uncontrollably. 'I don't have anything . . .'

'You stole a wallet at the Waterfront this morning.'

He said nothing.

'Do you have the wallet on you now?'

'Maybe.'

'Why are you being funny, Tyrone. Do you want me to hurt your sister?'

'No.'

'Do you have the wallet on you now?'

'Yes.'

'I want you to look in the wallet. There should be a memory card in there.'

His heart leaped. A memory card? There was no memory card there. 'There's just cash and credit cards . . .' he said.

'I want you to look very carefully, Tyrone. Take your time.'

'You will stay on the line?'

'I will stay on the line.'

He sat down on a garden bench, put his cellphone down beside him, took out the wallet. Trembling, his fingers riffled through the cash. There was nothing slipped between the notes.

The wallet had three flaps for bank cards. He went through each one.

He found it in the back flap, when he pushed his fingers into a sleeve that seemed empty from the outside at first. He pulled it out.

A blue card, light and thin. *Verbatim SDXC. 64GB.*

He grabbed the phone. 'I have it.'

'I want you to look at the card, Tyrone.'

'I'm looking.'

'That card is your sister's life. If you lose it, she dies. If you break it, she dies. If you damage it in any way, and I can't read the data, I will kill your sister. I will shoot her right between the eyes . . .'

'Please!' screamed Tyrone, and squeezed the memory card tightly in his hand. 'I will give it to you.'

'That's good. Where are you now?'

'I'm in the Gardens.'

'Where is that?'

'In Cape Town.'

'That's good. Did you call your sister from a mobile?'

'A cellphone. Yes.'

'And you will keep this phone with you?'

'Yes.'

'And you will keep it on?'

'Yes.'

'That is good, Tyrone. I will call you.'

'When?' he asked with fear in his voice.

But the line was already dead.

Mbali, Griessel, and Cupido watched Sergeant Lithpel Davids play the video back for them. They saw Knippies, the pickpocket, catch up with Lillian and attract her attention. He held the hair clip up in front of her while his right hand fiddled with her handbag.

Smooth as silk, and fast. They observed the thief's skill, the woman's nervousness.

'Lithpel, stop. What did he steal out of the handbag?'

Davids rewound the video. They watched again, but the pickpocket's hand was too fast. The item could not be identified.

'Try slow motion,' said Cupido.

'Won't help,' said Lithpel, but he did it.

The stolen item was still only a light brown, fast-moving blur behind the thief's hand.

'It's a package of some sort,' said Mbali.

'Play it further,' said Griessel.

The camera turned slowly to follow Knippies when he walked away, showing how the two security guards grabbed him and escorted him to the shopping centre door, until they disappeared out of the image.

'That bro is a pro,' said Cupido. 'But they all get caught in the end.'

'You see that screen there?' asked Mbali, and pointed at one of the smaller CCTV screens.

'Yes,' said Lithpel.

'Can you get the video to play back to the time of the crime?'

'Of course.'

'We'll have to hurry,' said Griessel.

Lithpel operated the mouse, moved the cursor on the computer screen. A new image appeared on the main screen – the scene in the corridor of the shopping centre outside the control room – and then became a comical fast-moving blur of people hurrying backwards when he rewound it at high speed. In the bottom corner a time indicator ran back just as fast.

'Around nine o'clock,' said Mbali.

Lithpel rewound past the two officials bringing Knippies in. He stopped the video, fast forwarded, missed it again. 'Dammit,' he said, then found the right moment and played it back.

The time code said 08:49:09:01. The guards pushed and pulled Knippies, the pickpocket's arm pressed up high against his back.

'Now just let it roll.'

'We don't have time,' said Griessel. 'Can you speed it up a bit?'

'OK.'

The speed doubled. The three people disappeared, camera left.

Shoppers hurried past. Everyone on a linear path to the inside or outside.

Only one man walked diagonally across the walkway, in the direction of the door. Disappeared.

'Stop,' said Mbali. 'That guy.'

Lithpel manipulated the video, wound it back, played it at normal speed.

The man was athletic, tall, light brown complexion. Black windcheater, his right hand in his pocket. The head in the baseball cap was subtly but unmistakably bowed, as though he was aware of the cameras. At 08:49:31:17.

'That's him,' said Cupido.

'I don't know . . .' said Griessel.

'That's him, pappie,' said Cupido.

'Who?' asked Mbali.

'The Cobra.'

She drew a sharp breath to ask something, but Griessel pre-empted her.

'I'll tell you everything later,' he said, and looked at his watch. 'Lithpel, speed it up. I want to see who comes out.'

Fast forward. Just over five minutes later, and a dark figure sped diagonally across the walkway. 'There he is,' said Lithpel. He worked the console, found the right point. 08:55:02:51. Normal speed. Knippies ran, long skinny legs stretched, arms pumping.

'Stop,' said Griessel, and leaned closer. 'Can you make it sharper.'

'No,' said Lithpel. 'Motion blur, nothing you can do.'

'OK,' said Griessel.

'Play it, Sergeant,' said Mbali.

Lithpel let the video run. Knippies disappeared from camera range. And then the man in the baseball cap ran across the image. With a rucksack in his hand.

'Look,' said Mbali.

'Wait,' said Griessel. He raised his hands, as though to make everything stand still for a moment. He closed his eyes for a moment, thinking over what they had here, and what lay ahead.

His colleagues looked at him expectantly.

Griessel opened his eyes. 'Vaughn, the passage door out there. See if it locks from inside. If the SSA come, delay them for as long as possible.'

Cupido smiled happily and left in a hurry.

'Lithpel, can you hide the videos? Or put them on a system where only you can find them?'

'The files are too big, Cappie, we don't have time. All I can do now is delete them.'

'Do it.'

'Benny, that's tampering with evidence,' said Mbali, deeply concerned.

'Mbali, we've already seen the evidence. The SSA are not criminal investigators.'

'You will be in trouble.'

'Yes,' he said. 'Lithpel, erase the videos.'

'Roger, Cappie.'

They heard someone hammering on the door.

Griessel moved fast. He took his iPhone out of his pocket. 'Does your phone have a camera?' he asked Mbali.

'Yes.'

Griessel aimed his cellphone at the notice board and took a picture of Knippies. 'If you could take the same photo? Just in case . . .'

'OK,' she said, and dug in her handbag.

Bellowing, indignant voices out in the corridor.

Suddenly the doorway darkened. 'Everybody out,' said the herd leader of the State Security Agency. 'Right now.'

28

Tyrone sat curled up on the bench in the Company Gardens, cell-phone and wallet in one hand, memory card clutched in the other. He scarcely heard the footsteps that shuffled up to him, and only properly registered when the shadow fell across him.

'Brother,' came the voice abruptly, making Tyrone jump.

'What?'

'*Askies*, brother, I didn't know you were meditating.'

It was a *bergie*, a little, crumpled man, bent right over. The tramp's apologetic grin was nearly toothless.

Tyrone was back in reality. He stood up, pushed the wallet and cell-phone instinctively and hastily into his pocket as he walked away.

'Now where you going, brother? No offence, five rand for a loaf of bread, children didn't eat last night, you've got it good, I saw.' The whining words came ever faster as Tyrone walked away. The beggar pursued him. '*Moenie soe wies nie*, brother, hey man, don't be like that. Show some solidarity, show some charity, just five rand . . .'

Charity. Tyrone stopped.

The *bergie* was startled by this turn of events. He took a step backwards.

Never forget charity, Tyrone. To ease another's heartache is to forget one's own.

Tyrone took out the wallet. He carefully put the memory card away in its original place. He remembered an Uncle Solly quote: *But you don't just give when you have. A bone to the dog, that's not charity. Charity is the bone shared with the dog when you are just as hungry as the dog.*

He took out a fifty-rand note from the stolen wallet and gave it to the man.

'God bless you, brother.' The little grubby hands made the note disappear like a stage magician, and then he, too, melted away, as though he were afraid Tyrone would regret his lavishness.

Tyrone began walking towards Queen Victoria Street.

Keep moving.

He could think while he walked.

A pickpocket can't afford to hang around. Keep moving.

He could handle the dreadful tension inside better if he was moving.

OK, so this is what happened. He stole the wrong wallet, on the wrong day.

It wasn't a drug deal gone south.

The mall cops were dead because he stole the wrong wallet, at the wrong time.

And now they had Nadia. For the same reasons.

Keep moving.

It didn't help to beat himself up over this mess. He had to get Nadia out of there. Then he would worry about himself.

It was easy. He would just swap the card for his sister.

Then why are you so afraid?

He walked along Perth and Vredenburg, towards Long Street.

He was afraid, because that *guy* with those eyes, a guy who strolled in so calm and collected and shot mall cops, like one, two, three, four, five, fish in a barrel, no emotions . . . That guy wasn't going to stand there and say: 'Thanks, my brother, pleasure doing business with you'. He was going to take his memory card, and he was going to shoot him and his sister just like that.

He shivered, because he had got Nadia involved in all this. If they laid a finger on his sister . . . His heart beat in his throat. He turned left into Long Street and walked south, towards the mountain.

Keep moving.

Get those pictures out of your head. Think.

Tyrone Kleinbooi slowly suppressed his fears, and he walked, and he thought. He went through the whole thing from the beginning. He must forget about what happened to him, he must get into the mind of the man with the cool eyes, he must get a bird's-eye view, that's what he needed.

He walked over the Buitesingel crossing and up Kloof Street, through the hubbub of students, business people, tourists, slim models, and *bergies* trying to guide motorists into parking places. He walked to the front of Hudsons The Burger Joint Est. 2009. Then he stopped, his hand resting a moment on the back of his head, deep in thought.

Tyrone turned around and began running in the opposite direction.

Griessel drove with Mbali to Schotsche Kloof so that he could tell her everything. He left nothing out.

It wasn't easy. She was a painfully law-abiding and over-cautious driver. And she was upset. She interrupted him, shaking her head, over the interference of the State Security Agency, over the 'colonial tendencies' of MI6, over the fact that she was an accessory to the destruction of evidence in a robbery and five murders.

Griessel pressed on. He only finished when they had been parked in front of the house at 18 Ella Street for five minutes, beside the ambulance and the six SAPS patrol vehicles.

'This is completely unacceptable,' said Mbali.

'I understand. But it is what we have,' said Griessel.

'This is a democracy,' she said.

'You think so?' said Cupido.

'*Hhayi!*' said Mbali as if he was committing blasphemy.

'That's why I asked you to switch off your cellphones at the Waterfront,' said Griessel. 'Because I am now absolutely sure they are eavesdropping on our calls, and they can track us. We don't want them to know we are here. We must remember they have access to exactly the same technology as us, but they don't need subpoenas. And there's a good chance our offices are bugged . . .'

Mbali shook her head.

'We have to assume,' said Griessel.

She merely nodded.

'I'll ask the Green Point SC to suppress the info of the cobra markings on the shell casings. If this shooting,' Benny pointed at the big house, '. . . leads us anywhere, we'll stay ahead of them.'

'Now, let's talk about what happened at the Waterfront. With the pickpocket, I mean. Mbali how did you see it?' He hoped Cupido would understand what he was trying to do, and shut up now.

Mbali was quiet for a long time, her hands on the steering wheel.

From the back seat Cupido sighed impatiently.

'I think that this Cobra person kidnapped David Adair, and he is still alive.'

Griessel heard a detached note in her voice. Her usual self-confident matter-of-fact manner was missing.

'OK,' he said.

'I think Adair contacted Lillian Alvarez, because she had to bring something from Cambridge to Cape Town. Something this Cobra person wants. I think she was going to hand it over to him at the Waterfront, but then the pickpocket stole it.'

'I'm not sure that makes sense,' said Cupido.

'Why?' asked Mbali.

'Because that pickpocket is quick. We couldn't see what he stole, and I saw nobody in that video of the theft itself that looked like the Cobra. So, if he didn't see, he couldn't have known.'

'Maybe he spoke to Alvarez just after the wallet was stolen, and she told him what happened. Maybe he saw it happen, from a distance. Maybe he wasn't sure what was stolen. We could have seen all that on the other cameras, if we hadn't destroyed the evidence. And then this Cobra person followed the security officials, he was only about twenty seconds behind them on the video. And he shot everybody. The pickpocket escaped.'

'Maybe . . .' said Cupido, but he wasn't convinced.

Mbali shifted in her seat, eventually, turned to them. 'The backpack is important,' she said.

'Why?' asked Cupido.

'The pickpocket had it on his back when he was arrested. But when he ran out, it was not there. The man who might be this Cobra person was carrying it in his left hand.'

'So?'

Mbali shrugged.

Griessel nodded. 'Vaughn? You sound as if you have another theory.'

'There's no evidence that the Cobra thought Knippies still had the stolen item. Maybe he found what he was looking for, and just ran away from the crime scene . . .'

'He would not have run if he had what he wanted. He's a professional,' said Mbali.

'Maybe. But my theory still stands: Adair skimmed money on TFTP. And the Cobra is after the money. Alvarez brought something that said where the money is, or how you can get it. Swiss Bank account number . . .'

'She could have emailed that,' said Mbali.

'Maybe,' said Cupido.

Griessel nodded, and opened the door. 'Let's go and see how this fits in with the rest.'

From the sitting room of the big house, where he sat with the grieving owner, the Green Point SC saw the three detectives approach. In front walked the stout, short Mbali with her big handbag swinging from her shoulder, then the taller Vaughn Cupido in a black coat that made him look a bit like Batman, and then Benny Griessel, in height just nicely in the middle between the Zulu and the coloured man. His tousled hair needed a trim, and he had strange Slavic eyes. Everyone who had been in the Service for more than ten years knew about Griessel, the former Murder and Robbery detective who had once arrived at a murder scene so drunk that they had to load him in the ambulance along with the victim's corpse.

These were the Hawks, thought the SC. The crème de la crème. A *vetgat*, *windgat* and a *dronkgat*. The fat, the vain, and the drunk.

What was going to become of this country?

Woodstock lies only two kilometres from the heart of Cape Town's business district.

Two hundred years ago it was a farm, and an outstretched white beach where the wintry northwester spat up the wrecks of sailing ships like driftwood. A hundred and thirty years ago it was the third biggest town in the Cape Colony. And fifty years ago it was one of the very few suburbs in South Africa where brown, black, and white could live undisturbed side by side under apartheid, before it decayed ever faster into poverty, with all the social evils that brought with it.

The minibus taxi dropped Tyrone off in Victoria Road, where the neighbourhood was going through a systematic revival – new boutiques, décor, and old-fashioned furniture shops existed comfortably beside old businesses selling hardware and motor vehicle spares. Office buildings, warehouses, and old bakeries were being restored, and to the south more and more yuppies were buying the pretty old houses.

But when Tyrone jogged north up Sussex Street, this sense of resurgence evaporated rapidly. The little houses here were dilapidated, squat and poor, despite the lovely old Cape architecture. Like the one on the corner of Wright Street, a corrugated-iron building bearing a weathered, insignificant sign, red letters on a blue background, indicating that it was the home of PC Technologies.

The veranda was secured with heavy-duty, white-painted burglar bars, and the door to the street was protected by a security gate. Apparently to keep thieves out. But also to allow for time, should the SAPS appear with a search warrant. Because PC Technologies belonged to Vincent Carolus, a specialist in the handling, cleaning, and fixing of new, second-hand *and* stolen computer and related equipment.

Carolus grew up in Begonia Street, Mitchells Plain, only three houses from where Tyrone and Nadia lodged with Uncle Solly. Nobody knew how he acquired his first personal computer, but everyone knew that at fourteen he was already a technology wizard. He had been called 'PC' ever since.

He was one of only five people at this present moment who knew what Tyrone's true occupation was. The other four were also dealers in stolen goods.

Tyrone stood gasping for breath at the steel door. He pressed the button under the video camera, hurriedly and perhaps a touch too hard.

It took fourteen seconds before the electronic lock opened.

29

The owner of the big house in Ella Street wept unashamedly, uncontrollably. Mbali sat beside him. She held the man's hand tightly, her face twisted with sympathy.

'How am I going to tell my wife?' the man kept asking.

'I'm so sorry,' said Mbali every time.

They waited for him to calm down a little, then asked him the usual questions.

In Cape English he told them that his daughter had been studying fashion design. She had so many plans. She was only twenty-four years old. 'And now she's gone.'

Mbali comforted him again.

They asked him whether anything was missing from the house. He said nothing that he had noticed.

They asked whether his daughter had been to the Waterfront today.

'No, she was home. She would have called if she . . . She did not go out much.'

Griessel took out his cellphone, retrieved the photo of Knippies, and showed it to the man.

'Do you know this person?'

'Was it him?' he asked, shock and horror in his voice.

'No, sir, we don't think it was him. Do you know him?'

'Yes, he is my tenant. Why are you showing me his photograph if it wasn't him?'

'We think the person who came into your house might have been looking for him. He rents a property from you?'

'No. Yes . . . He lives out in the back. In the servants' quarters. What has he done?'

'Right here? At the house?'

'Yes, behind the garage.'

Cupido moved towards the door. 'I'll go and look.'

Griessel nodded. 'Does he work for you?'

'No, we are renting it as a flat . . . What has he done? What is he mixed up in?'

'Sir, please,' said Griessel, 'at this stage we know very little. And we are hoping you can help us.'

'I'm sorry. It's just . . . I always thought . . . I never believed him.'

'We want to know everything, but right now, can you please tell us his name?'

'Tyrone Kleinbooi.'

'Do you know where we can find him?'

'I don't know. He is . . . He says he's a painter. He does contract work, all over. We . . . I hardly see him.'

'OK. How long has he been renting from you?'

'From the beginning of the year.'

'Do you have a prior address for him?'

'He used to live somewhere in Mitchells Plain. I don't have the address.'

'Do you have any information about his family?'

'I don't know if he . . . I . . . I don't know. We advertised the flat, last year in November. And he came to see us. He was very well mannered, looked like a good boy. He told us this story, about him being an orphan. Him and his sister, they were . . . they lived in Mitchells Plain, with old people who brought them up, and then they died. And he said his sister was going to university to become a doctor, and he was a painter, and most of the work was in and around the city, so he wanted to rent. He had the deposit, he paid on time, every month. My wife . . .' He began to sob again, they could see him struggling to bring himself under control. 'My wife really liked him. He would come and talk to her. Just talk. Like he wanted . . . like he would to a mother . . .'

'Sir, do you know at which university the sister is studying?'

'Stellenbosch. That's what he said. But I . . . I thought it was a little too sad to be true, being orphans, you know. And her studying medicine. I thought he just told us all that to get the flat, because there were other people who wanted it too. But my wife said we must help the less fortunate, and that he's a good boy . . .'

He began to cry again, then said, 'How am I going to tell my wife?'

★ ★ ★

'That's heavy encryption, my bru,' said PC Carolus. He was two years older than Tyrone, but short and swish – always decked out in modern labels. Even the big black-rimmed glasses were fashionable.

'How heavy?' asked Tyrone in the dusky room. They were both staring at the computer screen where PC had opened the memory card.

'AES heavy. 128-bit heavy.'

'What's that supposed to mean?'

'AES is Advanced Encryption Standard. That's way heavy.'

'But you can do anything.'

'No, not that. Maybe if I had months.'

'So what is it?'

'It's an encrypted ZIP file, Tyrone.'

'Like I know what that means.'

'It's like . . . a ZIP file is like a box. Something is stuffed into the box, but you don't know what the contents are until you open the box. And this box can't be opened because there's a lock on it. A heavy lock, that's the 128-bit encryption. And you can only open it if you have the key. And I'm assuming you don't have the key?'

'I don't.'

'I rest my case.'

'So what do you think is in there?'

'Tyrone, *wiet jy* what's in a box if you just *look* at the box?'

'Well, if it says fragile on it, then you know . . .'

'But here's *fokkol* written on the box. It can be anything – a few porn movies, a shit-house full of documents, pirated software . . . anything digital. You understand?'

'OK. But you can copy it?'

'Now let me get this straight. You come in here, it looks like you've been beaten up real good, you walking funny, and with all due respect, you look *kwaai* jumpy to me. But you say nothing and you know I won't ask. Now I scheme you want to pull a digital scam. You, who don't even know what a ZIP file is?'

'It's not a scam, PC, it's an ace in the hole.'

PC shook his head. '*Wiet jy wat jy doen?* Do you really know what you're doing?'

'*Ek wiet, ja.*'

'And you're not going to tell me?'

'Not now.'

'OK, cool, my bru', a man's got to do what a man's got to do. *Ja*, you can copy it. Anybody can copy a ZIP file. You just can't open it if you don't have the decryption key.'

'OK, and you can substitute it, so no one can see the difference?'

'If you decrypt it, yes, you will *mos* see it's not the same stuff in the box.'

'I understand that, but *sê nou* you make a box that looks just like this box. And when the guy looks he just sees a box, but he doesn't know there's other stuff in the box. Can you do that?'

'Of course. If you make the file the same size, and you make the file name the same, and you push it through 7-ZIP for AES encryption, nobody will know the difference. But if they try to decrypt it, then you're in your *moer*.'

Tyrone thought for a moment.

'Maybe if you tell me what you want to do, I can help you,' said PC Carolus.

Tyrone hesitated, weighed up the possibilities. He said, 'Here's the deal. There's a guy who wants this card with a sore heart. But he owes me. And if I give him the card, he can take it and run. And I don't get what I want.'

'So you want insurance.'

'Just so.'

'Why didn't you say so?'

In the little room where Tyrone Kleinbooi lived, the cupboard doors and drawers were pulled open. The floor was strewn with clothing, most of it black, dark grey, or dark blue. Cleaning products and cloths, a few bits of cutlery, and some documents were spread in front of the sink.

'Even if the pickpocket was in a big hurry, I don't think it was him who did this. It was the Cobra. And he was looking for something,' said Cupido. 'But look at this first.' He led Griessel to the bathroom.

In the corner of the small room lay a thin black sweater. Cupido picked it up with his rubber gloves and held it up for Griessel to see. It had a long, blood-clotted tear across the back. 'That's a lot of blood,' said Cupido, 'looks like he was badly cut. And look there by the shower and the basin. Blood washed off. The pickpocket was here. In the last hour or two.'

'Shooter followed him?'

'Must be. And no fresh blood. The pickpocket escaped, I think. Maybe he saw the Cobra coming.'

'His sister is a student, Vaughn, we must . . .'

'Look, there on the floor, in there. Those invoices from Stellenbosch. For a Nadia Kleinbooi.'

They walked back out to the room. Cupido had to pick up the documents, because Griessel was not wearing gloves.

'There's an address. West Side 21, Market Street, Stellenbosch 7613.'

Griessel looked up from the document in concern. 'Vaughn, the shooter could have seen this too.'

'*Fok*,' said Cupido.

And right on cue, Mbali appeared in the doorway, like their conscience.

Tyrone sat at one of the little tables in Shireen's Kitchen. The aroma of the peri-peri chips Gatsby made him realise suddenly how terribly hungry he was. He gobbled his food in a hurry, washing it down with Coke. Before he was finished, his mouth still stuffed with bread and chips, the Nokia rang, an ancient tune as ringtone. It was the first call that he had received on it, and he didn't immediately realise it was his phone. He gulped the food down, took the phone out of his pocket.

Nadia's number.

'Hello,' he said as he rose to his feet, not wanting the man behind the counter to overhear. He walked out into the cacophony of Victoria Street where the hooters of the minibus taxis shrilled and bellowed back and forth like migrating herds.

'Nadia tells me you don't have a car.' The same accented voice.

'Yes.'

'But you have the wallet you stole?'

'Yes.'

'So you have money.'

'Yes.'

'I want you to take a taxi. Do you know the Fisantekraal Airfield?'

The pronunciation was so odd that he couldn't decipher the words.

'The what?'

'Fisantekraal Airfield.'

'No, I'm not going.'

'What did you say?'

'I'm not going there. If you want the card, I will tell you where we will meet.'

'You want me to kill your sister?'

'No, I want my sister alive. But you want the card. Let me tell you where I will meet you,' he said, and he wondered whether the man could hear how wildly his heart was beating.

30

It was while he was walking away from the Company Gardens an hour ago that Tyrone had begun to understand the whole thing.

He realised that there was something on the memory card that this guy wanted so badly that he, cool like a swimming pool, strolled in at the V&A and blew away five mall cops, in cold blood, with not even a blink of those chilly eyes. The man had shadowed him all the way to Schotsche Kloof, then had gone and kidnapped Nadia in Stellenbosch. Broad daylight. Capital crimes. Serious, serious stuff.

You didn't do that for a memory card with your holiday snaps on it. You did that for something with more value than Tyrone could imagine. And you wanted it back with a vengeance.

He realised it was a fact he could use. Leverage. And that was what he needed. Because he had to get Nadia out of this mess, clean and quick.

And that was when he grew angry. What sort of cunt involved innocent women? If you want the card, motherfucker, you come after *me*. But nobody messes with my sister. He had never tolerated that, not since he was five years old. And he was going to keep it that way.

Tyrone wanted to hurt the bastard. He wanted to punish him. Get revenge.

Then he thought, steady now, don't get ahead of yourself. Just get Nadia back first, keep her safe.

But how was he going to do that?

You ask yourself, Ty, what is your exit strategy? Doesn't matter where you steal, you've got to have an exit strategy. Just in case.

And slowly he put together a rough plan, and with PC Carolus, he added the finishing touches. And now Tyrone stood on the pavement in Victoria Street, with buses and lorries, cars and taxis rushing and rumbling by, the tension gnawing at him, cellphone to his ear, as he waited for the man to answer. It took some time, and it sounded as though the man was holding his hand over the phone.

Then the voice was back suddenly. 'Where?'

'Be in Bellville at ten to three. And then you call me on this phone.'

'No. You will meet me next to the Fisantekraal Airfield at that time.'

'No.'

With as much firmness as he could muster.

'I am now going to hurt your sister. I am going to shoot her through the left knee, and then the right one. She will be . . . *un infirme* . . . a cripple. Then I will shoot her in the elbows . . .'

Tyrone's body twitched, but he knew there was only one way to get himself and Nadia out of this alive.

'If you touch my sister, if you hurt her in any way, I will burn this card. I am not stupid. I saw you kill five guys. I know you will kill us anyway when you get the card, so don't try to fool me. But I swear I will give it to you if Nadia is there and she is not hurt. I will give it to you when you have let her go. But if you touch her, I will destroy this card.'

Again the phone was muffled. Then, 'You think you are very clever. It is a bad mistake. I warn you: if you are not alone, I will shoot your sister, and I will shoot you. If you don't show up, I will kill her, and I will hunt you down, and I will kill you slowly. If the card is not there, or if it is damaged, I will kill you.'

'OK.'

Fear made his voice hoarse.

'Where in Bellville?'

'At the corner of Durban and Voortrekker Roads. Ten to three. Then call me. And bring a laptop or something. I want you to check the card. I don't want any misunderstandings.'

Griessel and Cupido switched their cellphones on when they were on the N1.

The instruments beeped in a duet of text messages. Benny saw he had five voicemails, four from the same number: the Hawks' Bellville office.

He called, and listened. Nyathi's voice: 'Benny, I need you to contact me very urgently. I need you to terminate the investigation of the Cobra case immediately and return to the office. You, Vaughn, and Mbali. Immediately.'

He deleted the message and listened to the next three. All from the Giraffe, all to the same effect, but his voice growing increasingly urgent and impatient.

The last one was from Alexa: 'Benny, I left you some meals in the fridge – there's something for every evening. Miss you already. I will phone tonight, when the function is over. Love you. Bye.'

He felt guilt at the relief that washed over him. He could sleep at home. And his little rascal was safe, for the next few nights at least.

He put the phone down. Cupido had also finished listening.

'Nyathi?' he asked.

'*Ja*,' said Cupido. 'We have to go to the Kremlin. Mbali as well.'

'Call her.'

'Do you think The Flower is going to answer her cellphone while she's driving?'

Griessel slowed down and moved to the left lane. They would have to wait for her to pass and then try and get the message to her through the window. All a waste of time. They had to get to Stellenbosch. He was deeply concerned about Nadia Kleinbooi.

The Metro train station at Woodstock had recently been refurbished. The concrete and steel building was painted the green and blue of the sea, but it was already looking shabby.

Tyrone barely saw it. He waited on the platform for the train to Bellville, and thought about his scheme. He knew he could not make it work on his own. He needed an assistant.

A pickpocket has no friends, Tyrone. You can't trust anyone, that's why. Nobody. So, if you want to be the life of the party, if you want to make friends and influence people, go and sell insurance.

He would have to buy a friend. And that never comes cheap.

He would have to exchange the four hundred British pounds for rands. And that was always a losing deal, because the Nigerian money-changers ripped you off. The exchange rate was thirteen rand to a pound. If you got eight, you were lucky.

Three point two K was a lot of money if you wanted to buy friends.

But he must spend the minimum, because if it all worked, he *and* Nadia would be on the run. And that was going to be expensive.

In his mind, he worked through the plan, and he thought, *jirre*, there are a lot of holes in this scheme.

But it was the only thing that could work.

They sat around Brigadier Musad Manie's round conference table. Colonel Zola Nyathi twirled a pen thoughtfully in his hand. Griessel and Cupido looked like guilty schoolboys. Mbali looked angry.

'Benny, did you remove or destroy evidence from the Waterfront scene?' The Camel's voice was heavy and solemn.

'No, Brigadier.'

'You did not delete the video material?'

'No, Brigadier.'

Manie looked at Mbali. 'Is this true?'

'Yes, sir. Benny did not touch any evidence whatsoever.' She said it carefully, as if choosing her words like steps in a minefield. Griessel felt a rush of gratitude towards her. He knew how painfully honest she was, how this technical skirting of the truth would conflict with her principles.

'I want you to understand that this is a very serious matter. The national commissioner phoned. From the office of our minister. According to the Department of State Security you deliberately wiped out video material, and hindered a task team from SSA in their investigation of a matter of international importance. International security Mbali. There's a lot at stake here. Not only the reputation of this unit and the SAPS, but of our country. Is that understood?'

'Yes, sir.'

'So I want to ask all three of you again: did you or did you not destroy evidence at the Waterfront?'

'Brigadier, why would we do such a thing?' asked Cupido.

'Answer my question.'

'No, Brigadier, not one of us did,' said Griessel, following Mbali's strategy. Because Lithpel Davids had deleted the evidence. And the brigadier hadn't mentioned the sergeant's name.

Manie looked at them, one after the other. 'If I find out that you have lied to me, I will suspend all three of you. Is that clear?'

They confirmed their understanding with grave nods.

'And do you understand that you are officially off this case?'

'Which case, sir?' asked Mbali.

'Excuse me?'

'There seems to be more than one case, sir. There is the Franschhoek case, and the Waterfront case . . .'

Griessel didn't want her to say anything about the Schotsche Kloof case. Not now, not *here*. For various reasons, of which one was that all hell would break loose. And the other one was that Zola Nyathi had perhaps told Manie about possible bugging devices. And that Manie was playing along.

'Both, Mbali,' said Manie. 'You are to hand over anything and everything that you think might aid our colleagues at the SSA, on both these cases. Am I making myself very clear?'

It was the emphasis on 'both' that gave Griessel hope.

'Yes, sir,' said Mbali.

'Benny? Vaughn?'

'Yes, Brigadier,' they said.

'Very well. You are excused.'

Nyathi gestured to Griessel, an index finger pointing downwards. Griessel understood.

Griessel led the way down the long corridor of the DPCI building. He was in a hurry, his mind on Nadia Kleinbooi. She was the same age as Carla, his daughter. Still a child, though students considered themselves adults. They would have to go and look for Nadia, and they would have to watch over her. They would have to use her as bait, because that was all they had. And time was running out, and there was so much uncertainty, because he didn't even know if they really should drop it. Apparently, Musad Manie's tirade had been for the benefit of the possible bugging devices. He hoped. Because if Manie was serious, they had a major problem.

And there was another thing gnawing at him, a profound sense of unease, a hunch, but he hadn't had time to formulate it yet.

They walked down the stairs, and out into the basement. Griessel stood beside the clubhouse and waited for them all to form a circle.

'Colonel, we need to tell you . . .' began Griessel, but Nyathi stopped him with a 'No' and a shake of the head.

'We'll really have to let it go, Benny. The pressure on the brigadier is immense. Just let the whole thing go.'

Griessel wanted to tell him about Nadia Kleinbooi, but it was Mbali who said, 'No, sir, we can't let it go.' Not in her usual decisive tone, the one that Cupido confused with arrogance. Her voice was strange now, almost despairing.

Nyathi looked at her with a frown. 'I don't think you understand, Captain. It's a direct order.'

'I am sorry, sir, but I am not going to stop investigating this case.'

All three men stared at her in disbelief. Nyathi was the first to come to his senses. 'You're not serious.'

'I am very serious, sir.'

'Mbali, do you want to be suspended? Do you want to get the whole lot of us fired?'

'Let them try.'

There was still no confrontation in Mbali's voice. It confused Nyathi. 'Captain, you are very, very close to insubordination. What the hell has got into you?'

'Sir, I am wondering the same thing about you and the brigadier . . .'

'Captain, I am now officially warning you that you are going too far. One more word, and you are suspended.'

'Sir, you can suspend me or you can fire me, I don't care . . .'

Nyathi's eyes narrowed and he drew a breath to respond, but Captain Mbali spoke with a passion and conviction that none of them had heard before. 'My father used to tell me stories of how he did not dare use his phone, because the security police were always listening. He was part of the Struggle, Colonel. Back when the secret services conducted all the important criminal cases, when they told the police what to do. When everybody was spying on each other. And everything was hushed up by the media. And the public knew nothing. Today it is happening again. Now Parliament is passing this Security Bill. Why? Because they want to hide things. Now this. State Security eavesdropping on us, and taking over a criminal case. Just like in the apartheid times. We are destroying our democracy, and I will not stand by and let it happen. And it will, if we let it. I owe it to my parents' struggle, and I owe it to my country. You and the brigadier too. You owe it to all the comrades who gave their lives for the cause. So, no, I will not stop. And if you try to stop me, I will go to the press and I will tell them everything.'

31

Zola Nyathi, the inscrutable, stood there, his intense gaze fixed on the fat captain. For perhaps the first time Griessel saw emotion on the colonel's face, rage that was gradually replaced with something else. Regret? Shame?

The Giraffe suddenly turned his back on them and raised his eyes to the stretch of Market Street that was visible between the rear wall and the vehicle entrance. He clasped his hands strangely in front of his chest, almost as if in prayer.

Silence, just far off the sound of traffic on Voortrekker Road, and an ambulance siren on the way to Tygerberg Hospital. Seconds passed while Nyathi stood stock still.

He turned back to them. 'What do you think, Vaughn?'

'I never thought I'd say this, Colonel, but I'm with Mbali.'

Griessel thought he actually had no right to ally himself politically with his colleagues. He had been a law enforcer under the former regime, and he couldn't pretend he'd been something he wasn't. But Nyathi did not spare him, he looked him in the eyes and asked, 'And you, Benny?'

'Sir, I don't think we have a choice. There is a young woman in Stellenbosch who might be in real danger, and we are the only ones who know . . .'

'What young woman?'

Griessel told him.

'Jesus,' said Nyathi. Another first, as far as Griessel could remember.

The colonel raised his hands in frustration, and dropped them again. He looked at the three of them, then in the general direction of the entrance to the building. 'Oh, what a tangled web we weave . . .'

'Amen,' said Mbali.

'And have you thought how you would approach this?' Nyathi asked Griessel.

He hadn't.

'Sir, I . . .' His thoughts raced as he spoke. 'I want Mbali and Vaughn on the team, sir.' Then his discomfort and suspicions found words and he said, 'And Bones. Because we need to try and find out why State Security wants control. It's about Adair, that's what this case is really about, and Bones is the only one . . . Just the four of us. We'll report to you. Here, where no one can listen. But we need to get to Stellenbosch fast, and we need to get clean cellphones.'

'I can get the cellphones,' said Cupido.

'Where from?'

'You don't want to know, sir.'

Nyathi was quiet. He shook his head as if he was about to do some-thing crazy, like jump off a cliff. Then the expressionless mask was back, control restored. 'This is not just about losing our jobs. If they find out, they will prosecute us. Aggressively. At worst, they'll send us to prison. Or permanently ostracise us, at best. We will never work for the government again. Do you understand?'

'Yes, sir.'

'I have children. So do you, Benny.'

'Yes, sir.'

'I'm going to try and keep the brigadier out of this. For as long as I can. I don't want to destroy his career as well. So you'd better get it right. Do you understand?'

'Yes, sir.'

'Switch off your phones. Check your cars for tracking devices. Get moving.'

Griessel told Cupido to go and buy the five cellphones, and bring one each for Nyathi, Bones and Mbali. 'I'm going to drive to Stellenbosch so long, meet me at the girl's flat. Vaughn, we don't know if they're following us. Just keep an eye on your rear-view mirror . . .'

'Vigilant, pappie, that's my second name.'

He asked Mbali to bring Bones to the underground car park and brief him fully. 'You have to tell him everything, and you'll have to give him a choice. He has a family too. Bones said he'd do more digging on Adair. Ask him if he's found anything, and let me know on the new number. And I want you and Bones to start calling every hotel and guesthouse in the city. Use your land lines in the meantime. It's a risk, but I'm sure they'll be monitoring our cellphones, and there are simply too many Telkom lines going out.' He hoped he was correct. 'Check at the hotels if a Lillian Alvarez has booked in. She must be staying somewhere. Start with the City Lodges, that kind of place – she's a student, she won't be staying at the Cape Grace . . .' He saw the misgiving on Mbali's face, and then: 'I know it's a needle in a haystack, but if we find her it could help a lot. Our biggest problem is that we don't know who we are chasing.'

'OK,' she said solemnly before she began to walk away.

'Mbali,' Griessel called after her.

She turned around.

'Thank you for not saying anything. About the video. I know it must have been difficult.'

'No, Benny. My father said he had to lie many times, under apartheid. He believed, most of the time, that the truth will set you free. But under certain circumstances, a lie can do the same thing. I often pray for the wisdom to know what circumstances those are.'

'You've always been a wise woman.'

'I know,' she said in all seriousness.

He lay under his Hawks' vehicle, the BMW 1 Series. He was looking for tracking devices. His cellphone rang and he nearly bumped his head on the undercarriage. He should have switched the damned thing off. Griessel wriggled out from under the car. On the screen he read *UNKNOWN*.

He had a suspicion who it might be.

'Griessel,' he said, as he straightened up.

'There are bugging devices in Musad Manie and in Werner du Preez's offices,' said the woman's voice. Joni Mitchell.

Colonel Werner du Preez was group head of the Hawks' CATS unit, an abbreviation for Crimes Against the State. It made sense that the SSA would monitor him too, but Griessel was infuriated. Why was she still bothering him? She was part of the organisation that had taken over the case now.

'And you people are listening to our cellphones,' he said angrily.

'We are?' she asked, as if it were a light-hearted game.

'You work for the SSA,' he said.

'Interesting conclusion. How did you arrive at it?' Still playful and teasing.

'My phone is bugged by the SSA, but you phone me on it. That means you know when it's safe to call.'

'I did hear that you're not stupid.'

'What do you want?' He saw no point in this conversation, and time was short.

'Information. I gave you something, now I want something in return. That was the agreement.'

'And now we're off the case. Your information is no use to me.'

'I had hoped you wouldn't be so easily discouraged . . .'

'What do you mean?'

'Exactly what I said. I hoped you would go on with the investigation discreetly.'

It made no sense. 'Why would you . . . ?' He'd had it with these games. 'I can't talk now, I've got work to do.' He got into the BMW.

'What work?'

He switched on the engine. 'I have other cases too. Goodbye.'

He rang off. And he drove.

His cellphone rang again immediately.

UNKNOWN.

She had warned him, at the Waterfront, that the SSA were on their way. And now: *I hoped you would go on with the investigation discreetly.*

He stopped at the exit to Market Street, and answered.

'Please,' she said seriously, 'we *must* help each other.'

'What for?'

'I know you found something at the Waterfront. On the video you deleted. I know all three of you turned your cellphones off after that, and you went somewhere where you were busy for more than forty minutes. I think it also had something to do with the investigation. Something tells me that you don't so easily drop a matter just because another state department wants to take over.'

'I really have nothing more to say to you.'

'You don't have to say anything to me. Just don't drop the investigation.' For the first time she sounded desperate.

He couldn't understand what game she was playing.

'Are you there?' she asked.

'Wait,' he said, and dug the iPhone's earphones out of his pocket, plugged them in, before he drove again.

'I will lose my job if I investigate the case.'

'They won't know.'

'Now who is "they"?'

'I work for them. But I don't share their agenda. Please.'

'I don't trust you.'

'That I can understand. Ask me anything.'

'What are you doing at SSA?'

She hesitated. 'You drive a hard bargain.'

He didn't answer.

'I am head of the monitoring programme.'

'And eavesdropping on us.'

'Yes.'

That was why she could phone. 'What is your name?'

Again a silence. Then: 'Janina.'

'And your surname?'

'Mentz.' With a sigh of resignation.

Janina Mentz. Joni Mitchell. The same initials. Not very original. 'Why does the SSA want us off the case?' he asked.

'I can't put my head on a block, you must understand that. I am senior management, but not part of the top management, I don't have access to all the information. But I have a theory, based on a strong rumour doing the rounds. That Adair wanted to embarrass the British government. Two years ago he published a memorandum on the Internet in which he said a new version of his algorithm could expose a whole string of dodgy bank transactions, and that Britain and the USA had a moral obligation to implement it . . .'

'The Adair Protocol,' said Griessel.

She remained quiet for a moment. 'I underestimated you. I won't make that mistake again.'

'Go on,' he said.

'We suspect that he deployed this new algorithm on the SWIFT system without sanction. We suspect he gained access to information in this way about corrupt activities of British parliamentarians, of much greater scope than that which was already known. Bribe money from media interests, from weapons manufacturers, from interest and pressure groups. Large amounts in Swiss bank accounts. And it goes up to very high levels. Up to the cabinet. Then he tried to blackmail the British government. Something like "use the Protocol to fight organised crime, or I'll make this public".'

'It still doesn't explain why the SSA wants to take over the investigation.'

'If we can get Adair, Captain, we can get all that information. And in the diplomatic sphere, that has incalculable value. You know that the British Department of International Development wants to halt their financial support to South Africa in 2015?'

'No.'

'Our government is very unhappy about that. And that sort of information could definitely make the Brits reconsider.'

He mulled over this for a moment.

'OK. But what is your agenda?'

'Are you familiar with the Spider-Man-principle?'

'The what?'

'The Spider-Man-principle. With great power comes great responsibility. That sort of information would give our government great power, Captain. I don't think our government can be trusted with such great responsibility.'

32

Under normal circumstances Tyrone Kleinbooi liked Bellville Station. It reminded him of Uncle Solly's stories about District Six – the *mengelmoes* of people and colours, the hustle and bustle, the music blaring out, competing from every point of the compass, the aromas of food stalls and takeaway cafés wafting at you as you walked by. His favourite clothing store just around the corner, in Durban Road: H. Schneider Outfitters. A *continental* name. And *Outfitters*. The sound of sophistication, just like their pinstriped suits and shoes and colourful waistcoats. And there, on the square at Kruskal Avenue and among the informal traders' stalls in the alleyways and malls, you found more characters and shysters per square metre than any other place in the Cape. Look any which way and there's counterfeit brand clothing and accessories from China, so much of it, such a racket, that you couldn't even take a picture. If you took out your phone to snap something, the stall owners were on to you at once, 'No, brother, please, no photos.' They asked nicely, but there was a vague, veiled threat behind it.

It was no place for his industry – mostly poor and lower-middle-class moving through here – for him it was a place to relax, to check things out, to shoot the breeze. Because the other great feature of the station was that you almost never saw a policeman here. He had already worked it out for himself: law enforcement turned a blind eye to all the counterfeit, and probably also the stolen goods, because there's no serious crime here. Maybe because everyone was in transit, and there weren't *kwaai* valuables to steal. Perhaps because all the shysters and counterfeit traders looked out for each other, did their own policing.

So the cops don't scratch where it doesn't itch, and they don't bother you here.

Which was a good thing right now.

Logic told him the cops were already looking for him. A nationwide manhunt, for the fugitive from the Waterfront killings. Tomorrow morning his face would be on all the front pages, but now his CCTV star appearance was probably a Kodak moment in every policeman's breast pocket.

Here he didn't need to worry about it. He could just look for helpers. And that was where his trouble lay. It wasn't going to be easy. There were a few coloured businessmen, mainly in the Bellstar Junction in front of the station. Rich cats, they weren't going to do any monkey-business for a brother for just a few hundred rand. The Nigerian money-changers and drug dealers were also a no-go area. They had the good taste to make themselves invisible in small apartments on the second and third floors of the buildings in the area. And they didn't come cheap either.

But mostly, on the ground, it was all Little Somalia here.

And your trouble with Somalians is that they're cat-footed. They tread warily. Because of the xenophobic attacks. And the fact that so many of them are illegal aliens. They don't trust anybody except fellow former countrymen. You see it in their sceptical Somalian eyes. If you didn't buy anything at his stall, if you loitered, or you came to *gooi* a scheme, then they checked you out doubtfully, talk about *under suspicion*. And the shake of the head came early on, no, no thanks, not interested.

But he had better get an assistant quickly. Because his time was running out. It was twenty past two.

Griessel told Janina Mentz to text her number to him. He would think everything over and phone her back. Then he rang off, and he switched off his phone, and drove to Stellenbosch by the Bottelary Road, because it was easier to spot a tail on that route.

And when he crossed the R300, his eyes constantly checking the rear-view mirror, the whole situation crashed down on him. Not gradually, but with a sudden, crushing weight.

And with it, as always, like a whirlwind, the thirst for booze descended on him: he instantly felt the smooth, cool weight of a glass in his hand. Short. Neat. No ice. No mixer, just the raw, rich taste of Jack Daniel's on his tongue, and the heat down his throat. He shivered and gripped the steering wheel; his body craved the tingle of alcohol, *now*. '*Jissis*,' he murmured. His mind told him there were places he could go, here in Kraaifontein, shebeens and a few bars, and nobody would even know.

But what about Nadia Kleinbooi?

Just a quick stop. Five minutes. Brackenfell or Kuils River, it was just a little detour, two lightning doubles, line them up, barman. Christ, the bliss that would flow, slip, slide through his veins and fibres to the deepest reaches of his body. Only two, they would heal him, of everything, they would last him till tomorrow, and tomorrow everything would be better again.

Saliva gushed into his mouth, his hands shook. It had been months since he had last had this uncontrollable thirst. Part of him was aware of what was happening. He knew the trigger. The 'secondary one' was what Doc Barkhuizen called it. When he realised how rubbish and useless and irrelevant he was. And he needed the drink to confirm it, and he needed the drink to heal it.

Phone Doc.

Fok Doc. Doc didn't understand. Doc's life worked; his did not. He was hopeless, useless, bad. His work was increasingly becoming a joke. He had drunk away his life, lost his wife, the respect of his children. He could hear it in Fritz's voice when he talked to his son. Fritz just kept him informed, but he *talked* to his mother. His colleagues gave him one look on a bad morning, and immediately jumped to the conclusion that he had hit the bottle. They were merely tolerating him, that uneasy sympathy you have for the handicapped. And Alexa Barnard, she would drop him as soon as she had her alcoholism and her life under control again, as soon as she saw through him once more and realised how shit he really was. He, who lied and ducked and dived from her because his *fokken* rascal couldn't keep up. And why couldn't it keep up? Because he had poured his libido, along with the rest of his life, down his throat.

He put his indicator on to turn left in Brackenfell Boulevard. There were drinking holes down near the hypermarket, his old, old hangouts when he used to pour one last *dop* before going home. Warm places in this wintry weather. Welcoming.

At the back of his mind there was a voice asking: What about Nadia Kleinbooi? She was Carla's age, Christ, would he go drinking if it were *his* daughter?

He turned the indicator off again. It was faster to make a quick stop in Stellenbosch. Buy a little bottle. For the afternoon and the evening. That's what he would do. He settled on that.

Only once he drove past the entrance to the Devonvale golfing estate, did he focus on the true origin of his self-hatred and the urge to drink.

Mbali Kaleni had spoken with so much feeling about the devastation of democracy. And then Janina Mentz said this government could not be trusted with such a great responsibility. The fuck-up was that they were both right. And therein lay two big problems. First and foremost was déjà vu. Because he still remembered what it was like under apartheid. It didn't matter how hard he used to believe he was only fighting the good fight against crime, that he was on the side of the good guys, there was always the niggling little voice in the back of his head. You couldn't avoid the hatred in the others' eyes, or the rage of the media, and the grubby association with colleagues who were doing evil things – even a few senior men in what was then the Murder and Robbery Squad. It wore you down slowly, because when you worked with death and violence and everything that was sick in a community, impossible hours for a ridiculous salary, then you wanted to, no you *had* to, believe you had good and right on your side. Otherwise you lost your self-respect, your faith in the whole business, and you began to ask yourself: What was it all for?

That had been one of the reasons for his drinking. That pressure. They all needed to soften the sharp edges of reality.

And then came the New South Africa and the great relief: now he could do his job in the bright, clear daylight of justice and respect.

It was what carried the SAPS through the first decade after apartheid, through the massive transformation, and the mess of national commissioners who were fired under one dark cloud after another. But now it felt like it was back to the bad old days again. A government that was slowly rotting. And it was catching. More and more policemen were doing stupid things, and there was more and more mismanagement, corruption and greed, sinking the Service deeper and deeper into the quicksand of inefficiency and public distrust. Despite the new national commissioner, who tried so hard, despite the work of thousands of honest and dedicated policemen, despite senior officers like Musad Manie and Zola Nyathi, whose integrity was entirely above suspicion.

Just as in the old days, he was increasingly reluctant to tell people he was a policeman.

Where did that leave him? A rat on a sinking ship. Once again. He couldn't leap off, he had one child at university and another that wanted to go to a *fokken* hellish expensive film school. At forty-five he was just a stupid career policeman who could do nothing else.

Which brought him to the second problem that Mbali and Mentz's words had revealed: his inability to think about stuff like the powers of the government, information laws, and Struggle history. What was wrong with him that he was stuck at ground level, always wrestling with such basic, mundane things? So that he was embarrassed when Mbali pointed out the bigger picture, the deeper principle, with so much passion and integrity.

What was wrong with him? He had become irrelevant in a vocation that demanded deeper thought and insight and intelligence. In a country and a world that was changing far faster than he could adapt to it.

What was *wrong* with him?

Just about everything.

But nothing that drink would not put right.

The irony did not escape Tyrone Kleinbooi.

Beggars can't be choosers, he thought, but to go and choose a beggar?

He had no choice: time was running out, and fast. He was hurriedly scanning the stall in front of Bellstar Junction for a helper, a sidekick, and then this *ou* appeared beside him, as abrupt and unexpected and embarrassingly silent as a wet dream. Filthy, and with many hard years on the clock. But under the brown layers of sunburn and lack of personal hygiene, he saw to his surprise that the guy was a whitey. In a faded blue overall jacket, ragged orange jersey underneath, eyes bright blue in a red-brown face, he said, 'Brother, I haven't eaten today.'

At first Tyrone wanted to say, 'Brother? *Watse* brother, nowadays you're a brother of everyone that lives and breathes, what's up with that?' But he thought better of it and looked more closely at him. This *ou* would pass for a coloured.

He'd never thought to ask a whitey. Because the ones you could trust wouldn't help with a coloured man's troubles. And the rest . . .

'Show me your hands . . .'

'Excuse me?' said the man.

'Show me your hands.'

The man slowly lifted his hands, palms up. Tyrone looked. He saw no tremor.

'You're not on *tik*?' Tyrone asked.

'That's not my drug.'

'What is your drug?'

'*Boom*,' he said with a measure of pride.

'When last did you smoke weed?'

'Day before yesterday. But I'm hungry now, brother.'

'What's your name?'

'Bobby.'

'Bobby who?'

'Bobby van der Walt.'

It was such an unlikely name for a bum that he felt like laughing. 'OK, Bobby, so you're looking for a bit of money?'

'Please.'

'You can earn it, Bobby.'

He could see the man lose interest instantly. 'Just a small, easy job,' said Tyrone quickly.

The blue eyes were suspicious. 'What kind of job?'

'A legal job. Easy money. A hundred bucks for ten minute's work.'

'What must I do?'

'Do you see that flyover?' Tyrone pointed at the M11 flyover that ran past the station building on concrete pillars, high in the air.

'I'm a smoker, but I'm not stupid,' said Bobby van der Walt. 'I see it. It's the Tienie Meyer Bypass.'

'Fair enough, brother,' said Tyrone. 'Now let me tell you what you must do.'

When Benny Griessel drove into Stellenbosch, and his eyes began searching Bird Street for an off-licence, he thought: four hundred and twenty-three days clean. Four hundred and twenty-three long difficult days. He didn't have a political struggle, he had a drink struggle, a life struggle. His whole being said, Fuck it all, but somewhere in his head there was an objection: You will have to tell Doc why you threw away four hundred and twenty-three days. You will have to tell Alexa as well.

At the Adam Tas traffic light he stopped.

Phone Doc.

He couldn't. His cellphone had to stay off.

Phone Doc. The SSA would not be able to draw any sensible conclusion from the fact that he was in Stellenbosch.

He sighed and turned on his phone.

33

At 14.40 Tyrone stood in front of the Sport Station in the Bellstar Junction shopping centre. The shop's name was on a big sign on the wall behind him. When he had first walked up to it he thought for a fleeting second that they were *lekker* stupid when they made that logo because there was one giant S that had to serve for both words. But it didn't really work – at first glance it looked like *Sport Tation*.

But his mind was focused elsewhere now. He had the cellphone in his hands, he kept an eye on the time. He was shaking, his heart pounding in his chest, too fast, too hard. He wondered about Nadia, how scared she must be. What had they done to her? Tied her up? Hurt her? He didn't want to think of it . . . He *must* believe she was OK, and afterwards she was going to be heavy the *moer in* with him, that fury that transformed her into a spitting, hissing feline creature. If she was heavy angry, her eyes went a funny colour, and words streamed out of her mouth fast and furious, like a waterfall. *What were you thinking, Ty? Are you mad? I thought I knew you.*

But that was all OK, as long as she was *orraait*.

He had begun to work out a story that he would spin to her, but he didn't know if she would fall for it. And if the cops put the CCTV footage on the TV, he was going to have his work cut out for him.

Jirre, he hoped she was OK.

If they so much as touch her . . .

14.43.

He had a view from here, all down the broad corridor from the shopping centre, between steelwork curved into triumphal arches, to the entrance of Bellstar Junction. Happily he could see across Charl Malan Street, under the M11 freeway. Not a perfect view, because there were always people in the way, people coming and going, everybody always moving, moving.

He could see Bobby van der Walt, a forlorn figure up there beside the concrete barrier of the flyover. Bobby's eyes were on him. He could hear the hiss and hum of the traffic racing past behind Bobby.

He kept still, made no gestures, in case Bobby thought it was The Sign. With dagga smokers you had to be careful, the brain cells weren't always firing in sequence.

That *blerrie* whitey better do his part today, bum or not.

14.46.

When he'd recruited Bobby and explained carefully what he would have to do, he'd asked Tyrone, 'Is that all?'

'That's all. But you have to wait for my sign.'

The narrowed eyes were still suspicious. 'For a hundred bucks?'

'I told you it was easy money.'

Bobby's expression showed it might be *too* easy. There had to be a catch, somewhere.

'It's an important job, Bobby. That's why I'm paying you properly.'

'OK.'

Tyrone could see how his head was working. Bobby liked it that he had been sought out for an 'important job'.

Then he took Bobby along and went to talk to the Somalian at the clothes and backpack stall. Bobby stood and listened attentively, keen to know how payday was going to work.

That Somalian was called Hassan Ikar.

'Hassan, I want to buy this backpack.' Tyrone pointed at a compact black rucksack.

'I'll give you good price.'

'No, Hassan, I don't want to pay a good price. I want to pay full price, and a little more, but I need a favour.'

And he quickly explained to Hassan Ikar: he was going to pay him a hundred and twenty rand too much for the rucksack. Out of the change he must give Bobby van der Walt a hundred. The rest he could keep. But only when Tyrone phoned Hassan and said Bobby had done his work correctly and well.

'Do we have a deal?'

Ikar thought it over. He couldn't see any risk. Then he nodded. 'OK.'

'So give me your phone number.'

Tyrone phoned Hassan Ikar's number to make sure it was working. Bobby stood listening to everything, and eventually agreed with a nod.

The plan was made.

But was it going to work?

14.47.

Tyrone checked the cellphone's battery. More than enough juice, one of the few advantages of the Nokia 2700. Yesterday's tech, but there weren't a thousand apps sucking up the power.

A group of coloured labourers walked from the direction of the platform.

'Are the trains running on time?' asked Tyrone.

'Just about,' one called back. 'Few minutes late.'

That was OK. A few minutes late. 'Cause he was cutting it fine. If everything went according to plan, if he and Nadia got away, he wanted to catch Metrorail 3526, at 15.08 on platform 9, to Cape Town. And he could use 'a few minutes', just in case.

Tyrone breathed deeply. Get a grip, you had to be cool and calm and collected. He looked up again at Bobby van der Walt – the figure was still standing there, solitary. Keep looking at me, Bobby, don't let your concentration lapse . . .

14.49.

The security guard came walking towards him, a young black guy in a red beret with a fancy metal badge on it. 'Can I help you?'

'No, thanks, I'm waiting for my sister.'

'OK.'

Then the cellphone in his hand rang and his whole body jumped and the security guard gave him a keen look.

'That must be her now,' he said, his voice hoarse.

The security man didn't move.

Tyrone looked at the screen. Nadia's number. It was them. He answered. 'Hello.'

'I am at the corner of Durban and Voortrekker Roads.'

Same voice, same accent.

'Is my sister with you?'

'Yes.'

He wanted to ask to hear her voice, but the security man was still standing right beside him, keeping an eye on him. He said, 'I need you to come down to Bellville Station. There's lots of parking . . .'

'I don't know where the station is.'

'OK. You carry on straight down Durban Road. When you cross Church Street, you start looking for parking. There are always a few spots available. And then you call me again.'

The man didn't answer him. He waited, heart hammering in his chest. The man broke the silence, 'OK.'

Tyrone cut the connection. The security man gave him one last look, turned, and walked away. Tyrone looked up at the M11 bridge.

Bobby had disappeared.

Griessel battled to find the entrance to West Side in Stellenbosch's Market Street where Nadia Kleinbooi lived. The apartment blocks were hidden behind an old Victorian house, the sliding gates had to be opened electronically with an access system. And when he parked outside and walked to the entrance, he saw there was no reference to a caretaker on the small keyboard beside the gate.

It was good news, he thought. If they wanted to harm her, they would have had trouble getting in.

He pressed twenty-one on the keyboard. Nadia's flat number. There was no answer.

He pressed twenty in the hope of finding a neighbour home.

Silence.

He worked from twenty-two up.

Eventually, at twenty-six, a man's rough voice rasped over the intercom: 'Yes?'

'Captain Benny Griessel of the SAPS. I am looking for Nadia Kleinbooi from number twenty-one.'

'I don't know her.'

'Can you open up, please.'

'How do I know you are from the police?'

'You can come to the gate and see.'

Ten seconds later the gate began to roll open.

Panic scorched like a veld fire through Tyrone. His eyes were glued to the concrete rail of the M11, visible just above the Shoprite banner that screamed *U Save* in red and yellow letters. Bobby's silhouette was gone.

Never trust a whitey. Now Uncle Solly's warning thundered through him. *Never trust a whitey, you steal from them, but never do business there, because when the chips are down, we coloureds are the first ones they sell out.*

But he didn't have a choice, he hadn't had time. He looked at the clock on the cellphone. 14.51.

It would only take that guy four or five minutes to find parking in Durban Road. Another three minutes to walk to the end of Kruskal.

He had seven minutes to track down Bobby van der Walt. And the memory card. Because it was in the pocket of Bobby's faded, dirty blue overall jacket.

34

Don't panic, don't panic, don't panic.

But he panicked anyway, because he didn't know what else to do. If he ran, it was nearly three hundred metres from here to where the Tienie Meyer Bypass dropped down to Modderdam and you got access to the M11. It was the shortcut route that he had made Bobby take – but you had to also climb over two high wire fences. Not difficult, but it took time. Which he did not have. It would take him at least four minutes to the Modderdam crossing, where he would have a view over the highway. If he didn't see Bobby then, he was fucked, six ways till Sunday. Because then he would not have enough time to get back and stand here again.

And the memory card was in Bobby's pocket.

Jirre.

He dithered, this way and that, he tried to control his breathing and the lameness in his knees, he knew he must keep the panic off his face, because that damned security guard with the red beret was lurking around, getting kickbacks from every counterfeit-selling stall owner to keep the suspicious and the overly curious away.

He had got Nadia into this mess. Now he had better get her out.

14.54.

He would just have to stand here and wait, there was no other choice.

If the guy phoned, he would have to play for time.

But that's going to wreck the schedule, because the next train to Cape Town from Bellville D was only at 15.35, platform 11, and the trains were running late, and that meant twenty to, or quarter to four, and that gave that guy twenty minutes to find him and Nadia at the station and take them out with that silenced gun. If he could walk in at the Waterfront and shoot people left, right and centre, he wouldn't be scared of Bellville Station.

The blur of a lorry raced over the flyover, but Bobby was missing in action. Had the idiot stood too close to the road, and got run over, the memory card now in its glory?

14.55.

The cellphone in his hand rang.

Deep breath.

'Yes?'

'I have parked.'

'OK. Find Wilshammer Street, you should be close to it. Then walk down Wilshammer Street . . .' He had to think hard about compass directions, the sun came up on that side: '. . . towards the east, to the corner with Kruskal.'

'The corner of what?'

'Kruskal.' He spelled it in English, slowly and clearly.

'OK.'

Again he wanted to ask if Nadia was there, if she was safe, but he didn't. He wanted the guy to think he could see them.

'Call me when you get there. But not from Nadia's phone. You give her phone back to her, and you use your own phone from now on.'

And he rang off.

After two flights of stairs Griessel knocked on the door of 21 West Side. There was glass set into the apartment door. He kept an eye on it, but saw no movement, heard no sound from inside.

Perhaps she was on campus. Safe.

He knocked again, but he knew there was no one home.

He turned away, looked out over Stellenbosch. The place that Vaughn Cupido called 'Volvoville'. With the usual tirade: 'Volvos, Benna? Why Volvos? *Daai is* the most boring cars in automotive history. And ugly. But the rich whiteys of Stellenbosch all drive Volvos. Explain that to me. Just goes to show, money can't buy you style.'

That Cupido, really. He didn't drink – instead he spewed out insults. That was his safety valve. Maybe Griessel should try it too.

He heard footsteps on the stairs to his right. A young man appeared, walking up. Big and athletic, broad shoulders in a fashionably weathered leather jacket. Griessel's hand dropped to his service pistol. The young man looked at him, curious.

'*Middag*,' said Griessel.

'*Goeie middag.*' The Afrikaans greeting made Griessel relax. Black hair, dark brown, smiling eyes. Carla's age. Must be a student.

'Do you live on this floor?'

'Twenty-three,' he said and walked past Griessel.

'I'm looking for Nadia Kleinbooi.' Griessel nodded towards the door of number twenty-one.

The student stopped. 'Oh.' He looked at the flat, then back at Griessel. A frown appeared.

'I'm from the police,' said Griessel. 'Do you know her?'

'The police?' It was as though something fell into place. 'Why are you looking for Nadia?'

'Do you know her?'

The student came closer. The frown had disappeared, but now there was a different anxiety on his face. 'Is it about the kidnapping?'

'What kidnapping?'

'On campus. The whole varsity knows about it.' His voice became anxious. '*Was* it Nadia?'

'I'm not aware of any kidnapping,' said Griessel.

The man's eyes narrowed. 'Are you genuinely from the police?'

Just wing it, thought Tyrone, there was no other choice now. His eyes were glued to the M11 bridge, in the dwindling hope that Bobby van der Walt would appear. Just wing it. It makes no sense. Didn't the bum know he was throwing away a hundred bucks? That's what you get when you do business with *dagga* smokers.

Tyrone stood on tiptoe to see if he could spot the Waterfront shooter and Nadia on over by the stalls.

Nothing.

Out of the corner of his eye a movement, someone rushing up to him from his right. He leaped in alarm.

It was Bobby, he realised – eyes wide, gasping for breath, mouth agape. 'Sorry, brother, sorry. *Fokken* traffic cop stopping there . . .' a grubby finger pointed in the direction of the flyover '. . . and asked me if I was planning to jump. And I said: "Do I look like a jumper?" and the *doos* said: "Yes" . . .' Bobby stood bent over with his hands on his knees, wheezing long breaths back into his lungs. 'Can you believe it?'

Tyrone wanted to laugh and cry at the same time. 'Where's the memory card?' he asked.

Bobby slapped the pocket of his overall jacket. 'Right here.'

'OK,' said Tyrone, and he stood thinking.

'Can you believe it?' asked Bobby, starting to catch his breath. 'That cop stood there and he says to me: "You look a lot like a jumper to me." And I say: "*Nooit*, I'm just admiring the view." And he says he doesn't want to argue with me, and he doesn't want a traffic jam. If I want to jump, I'd better jump, just don't fall anyone *moer toe* down below. So I just ran. Sorry brother, what do we do now?'

Tyrone didn't hear him. His brain was working overtime. His plan had been that Bobby would wait on the flyover for his signal, and when the guy let Nadia go, then he would throw down the memory card. And the guy would have caught it. He might have believed that it was Tyrone up on the highway, he would have known he couldn't get at him up there. His attention split between the flyover and Nadia. Bobby would have been out of harm's way. Nadia would be free, he would have grabbed her arm just before the Sport Station, they would have run for the train . . .

What the hell was he to do now?

His cellphone rang.

Bobby stood waiting, his eyes wide and impossibly blue.

Tyrone looked at the phone. It wasn't Nadia's number, but it was a familiar one. His own. His phone that had been in the rucksack, at the Waterfront.

He answered.

'What makes you think it was Nadia?' Griessel asked the young man in the leather jacket.

'They said on Twitter it was a coloured girl,' he said, but his attitude had changed. He was suspicious now.

'The girl who was abducted?'

'*Ja*. If you're from the police, how come you don't know about this?'

Griessel barely heard him. 'Do you have a cellphone?'

'Of course I have a cellphone.'

'Could you please make a call for me?'

'Don't you have your own phones?' He took a step back.

Griessel took his wallet out of his jacket pocket, and showed him his SAPS identity card. '*Meneer*, please, will you make a phone call. My phone is out of order.'

The student's body language was antagonistic now. He studied the identity card, then said, 'Sorry, but it looks fake to me.' He started to move away, towards the stairs.

Griessel sighed, opened his wallet and put it away. 'I am going to ask you one more time to make a call.'

'Now you're getting weird.'

Griessel unclipped his service pistol from the holster, and pointed it at the young man.

'What is your name?'

The student froze, raised his hands. Waxen. 'Johan.'

'Take out your phone, Johan.'

The student stood there with his hands in the air.

'Drop your hands, take out your phone and call the police station.'

The mouth opened and shut twice, then he realised what Griessel had said. 'You want me to phone the police?'

'That's right. Stellenbosch Station.'

With visible relief he said, 'I don't know the number. Can I google it?'

'I'm at the corner of Wilshammer and Kruskal,' said the man over the phone.

Tyrone stared down the long passage, over Charl Malan Street and the alley between the stalls, but there were too many people, he couldn't see Nadia or the man. And first he had to give Bobby new instructions, a new plan, cobbled together with a slim chance of success, but he was out of time, he had no more choices.

'Wait there,' he said. 'Stand in the middle, between the stalls, so that I can see you. So that I can see that Nadia is OK.'

Silence.

'We are standing in the middle.'

'OK,' said Tyrone. 'I will call you back.'

'*Merde*,' said the man.

Tyrone didn't know what that meant. He rang off and told Bobby, 'Listen carefully.'

35

The student phoned the number of the Stellenbosch SAPS.

'Tell them you want to talk to Brigadier Piet Mentoor,' Griessel said. The student followed instructions with a voice of new-found authority.

'Now tell him to hold for Captain Benny Griessel of the Hawks.'

The student looked at Griessel with apologetic respect and whispered a low '*Fokkit*'. Then the brigadier must have come on the line, because he said his piece and passed the phone to Griessel.

'Brigadier?' said Griessel.

'Benny, to what do I owe this privilege?'

'I hear there was an alleged abduction this morning, Brigadier, on campus.'

'You *okes* are wide-awake, *nè*. It's a strange one, Benny.'

'How so, Brigadier?'

'Only one eyewitness who swears high and low that a coloured girl was forced into a car in Ryneveld Street, a Nissan X-Trail. Then he followed the vehicle. In Andringa Street the Nissan stopped, two white men jumped out, shot up the tyres of the car pursuing them, grabbed their cellphones, and raced away. There were five witnesses who saw that happen. But not one of them saw the girl in the Nissan. So we are at least sure of cellphone robbery.'

Griessel tried to make sense out of it. 'What time did this happen, Brigadier?'

'Must have been just after one, when the classes stopped for lunch. What's your guys' interest in the case, Benny?'

He hesitated. 'Brigadier, it might be connected to the thing in Franschhoek. Sunday.'

'*Bliksem*. Any idea who the girl might be?'

He would have to lie. 'No, Brigadier. I gather there was more than one person in the car that was following the X-Trail?'

'Yes, the one who saw the kidnapping, and his friend. Students, both of them. Trouble is, the friend didn't see anything. They only got a part of the registration. We are following up on that. And there's one other thing. The bloody students picked up both of the bullet casings in the road. That's after the tyres were shot out . . .'

Griessel knew what was to come. 'Forty-five calibre?'

'That's right . . .'

'With a snake engraved on them.'

'Hell, Benny . . .' The brigadier didn't complete his sentence. Griessel guessed he was putting two and two together.

'Brigadier, are the eyewitnesses absolutely certain there were two gunmen?'

'Yes, Benny. And probably another chap who stayed behind the steering wheel.'

'Three in total?' He couldn't believe it.

'That's what most of them say.'

'And both the gunmen fired off shots?'

'Each one blew one of the front tyres.'

'The snake engraving – was it on both the casings?'

'Both of them. They are here with the detectives, totally contaminated, of course. You can come and have a look.'

'*Fok*,' said Griessel.

'OK,' said Tyrone over the cellphone. 'Look towards the south. There is a big banner that says *Shoprite, U Save*. Do you see it?'

'Yes,' said the Waterfront murderer.

'I want you to walk towards it. Slowly.'

'*D'accord.*'

'Please speak English.'

'OK.'

'And stay on the line.'

Tyrone moved to his right, just in front of A. Gul Cash & Carry, so that he could use the corner of the opposite side of the shopping centre as cover. The guy knew exactly what he looked like, and he didn't want to be spotted now. But his greater concern was that Nadia would see him, and run to him. Or do something else that could spook the gunman.

There were people blocking his view. He had to twist from side to side to see. He focused on Charl Malan Street, just in front of the flamboyant entrance to Bellstar Junction.

Still nothing.

At least Bobby van der Walt was still standing, ten metres away, right in front of the Hello Mobile cellphone shop, his eyes on Tyrone, his forehead furrowed in concentration.

Then he saw Nadia, and it was like a sudden pain in his chest. Her head hung low and she looked scared and forlorn – she was looking at the ground like someone who had lost all hope. The big bag she always carried over her shoulder to class seemed too heavy for her now. Then the stream of people opened up for a second, and Tyrone saw the man beside her. He had a hoodie over his head now, and he held her right arm tightly, his other hand hidden under his grey hoodie jacket. But from the angle of the elbow and forearm, it looked as if he was holding a firearm.

Must be a hands-free kit, thought Tyrone. That's why he's not holding a phone.

'Stop!' said Tyrone over the phone.

Hoodie and Nadia halted.

Hoodie turned his head slowly. He was checking out everything.

He looked like a whitey. He didn't look exactly like the guy from this morning. Maybe it was just the hoodie. But Tyrone's unease deepened.

'Now cross the road. Slowly.'

He lost them again in the press of the crowd. He zigzagged, he stooped, he stretched up to see over shoulders, careful not to show too much of himself, and also not to make Bobby think it was some kind of sign.

He caught sight of them again. 'Keep walking until you are exactly below the Shoprite sign.'

And he gave Bobby the signal: his index finger, held up in the air, to show Bobby he must get ready, the hand-over was near. 'But after that don't look at me again, Bobby,' he had explained urgently earlier. 'That's crucial, understand?'

To his annoyance, Bobby now gave a thumbs-up, acknowledging the signal.

Tyrone nodded vehemently.

Bobby turned away.

The bum had remembered.

Maybe this would work after all.

Hoodie and Nadia had crossed the road. He steered her past the steel railing, to right under the Shoprite sign.

'OK. Stop, I can see you clearly. Did you bring a laptop?'

'Yes.'

'Where is it?'

'On my back.'

For a moment they were out of sight again, behind a knot of people. When there was a gap again, he saw Hoodie had turned sideways. He could see the rucksack now.

Tyrone breathed deeply. Everything depended on the next few minutes. 'Now listen very carefully. You know there is a ZIP file on the memory card? Fifty-six gigabytes in size.'

'Yes.'

'And you know that the ZIP file has a password?'

'Yes.'

'OK. I had the ZIP file encrypted again. With a new password. Do you understand that?'

'*Va te faire foutre, connard!*'

'Excuse me?'

'You are playing games, *connard*. I will shoot your sister. I have a gun, right here.'

'I know you have a gun. I'm telling you, if you don't follow my instructions, you will never get the password. If you hurt Nadia, if you don't do what I say, I will not give you the password.' Tyrone shot a lightning prayer heavenwards that he would get the words right that PC Carolus had so patiently taught him. 'The encryption is AES 128 bit. It will take you thousands of years to decrypt it without the password. Do you understand?'

There was tangible fury in the silence, before Hoodie answered, 'Yes.'

'Right. You must also know I haven't written the password down. It is in my head. So if you kill me, you won't have the password.'

Hoodie did not reply.

'The password is sixteen letters. Remember that. First, I will give you the disk. Then you can test it on your laptop. OK?'

'Yes.'

'When you see that the file is there, we will start to open it with the decryption key. But then you have to tell Nadia to start walking, slowly, straight ahead, and around the corner, past the hairdresser. As long as she walks, I will give you a letter of the key. Do you understand?'

'Yes.' Impatient now.

'Now, I want you to look up the passage, between the shops. Straight ahead,' said Tyrone.

Hoodie stood still, his features shadowed by the hood, but he was facing in the right direction.

'Do you see the shop with the big green sign that says Hello Mobile?'

'Yes.'

'Do you see the guy with the blue jacket standing next to the door?'

'Yes.'

'He has the card, and he will give it to you when you reach him. If you hurt him, I will not give you the password.'

'OK,' said Hoodie.

'Walk towards the guy now. Slowly.'

36

Griessel gazed out at the Stellenbosch mountains, the student beside him momentarily forgotten.

At La Petite Margaux he had had a vague suspicion that it could have been more than one assailant, but the cobra on the bullet casings had muddled his thinking. The same engraving, the same shooter. That was the logical assumption, though instinct had argued against it. He had made the same mistake as Interpol. And their report had reinforced his error.

He should have known. Two highly trained bodyguards, a reasonably good security system, the abduction of a man who did not want to be caught at all costs – naturally there would have been more than one operator. Now it made absolute sense.

Cobra was not one killer for hire. It was a group.

That explained superintendent Marie-Caroline Aubert's speculation over the different pistols used. And that there were hits that did not carry the Cobra trademark.

It changed a whole lot of things.

Also the fact that a single operator would always be harder to catch. But three men working together, who had to stay together, travel together, move around together, were perhaps slightly more obvious.

Griessel looked back at Nadia Kleinbooi's door, saw the student waiting there eagerly. He would have to temper that enthusiasm.

'Johan, I want you to understand one thing very clearly,' he said strictly. 'You can't repeat anything of my conversation with the brigadier. It's very sensitive information. If it leaks out, I'll have to arrest you for obstructing the law.'

'Never, Captain.' But Griessel could see his disappointment.

He took his wallet out of his jacket pocket and took out a twenty-rand note.

'We need to make one more call,' said Griessel, and held out the money.

'That's OK, Captain, keep it,' said the student.

'You're going to hear more things that you would love to tell your friends, but if I hear you've repeated a single word, I will lock you up. You stay off Twitter, and off Facebook and What's Up . . .'

'WhatsApp.'

'That's right. Understand me?'

'Yes, Captain.' Solemnly.

'Thank you.' Griessel looked at the phone in his hand. It was a BlackBerry Z10. The screen had locked.

'Can you show me how to phone from this thing?'

The student tapped in his code, brought up the dialling panel and passed it to Griessel. He phoned the DPCI's land-line number, and asked to speak to Mbali Kaleni.

The first thing she said was: 'Benny, Ulinda Radebe called from O. R. Tambo. He thinks he has identified the Cobra.'

Tyrone watched Hoodie and Nadia slowly climb the steps under the Shoprite banner and walk towards Bobby.

Don't look at me, Bobby – whatever you do, don't look at me.

Bobby stood still. He looked worried. He looked around, but he didn't look at Tyrone.

'When the guy has given you the card, tell him he can go.'

Hoodie did not answer.

Nadia still looked as though she was in a daze. She kept looking down, as if she didn't know what was going on.

Had they drugged her?

Four metres from Bobby. Three. Two.

Bobby noticed them.

Don't look at me, Bobby. Please.

Hoodie and Nadia reached Bobby.

'You have the card?' Tyrone heard Hoodie say.

A fat couple obscured his view for a second. When he could see again, Bobby was taking his hand out of his pocket. Too far away to see if the memory card was in it, but Hoodie put out his hand, it looked as if he took something.

'You can go,' Tyrone heard Hoodie say.

Bobby's head turned in Tyrone's direction.

Don't look at me, you idiot.

But Bobby looked at Tyrone, as if he wanted to know if he had earned his money, if he could really go now.

Tyrone ducked behind the corner of the shop. He didn't know if Hoodie had seen him. He counted one, two, three, four, five. He peered around the corner of the shop. He saw Bobby was walking away towards Kruskal. He would be heading for Hassan Ikar, the Somalian, for his pay. That's for sure.

Well done, whitey, even though you did look when you shouldn't have.

'Your sister not here yet?' The voice took Tyrone by surprise, because all his attention was on Hoodie.

It was the security man with the red beret. He came and stood right in front of him, too close, no respect for personal space, this guy, so that he couldn't see Nadia.

Tyrone shook his head. He couldn't talk now, it would confuse Hoodie, it would make him look around. And identify Tyrone, if he hadn't already.

'I can't let you stand here for so long,' said Red Beret. 'You must go wait on the platform.'

Probably a complaint from a shop owner: What's that guy doing there so long?

Tyrone nodded. Go away, please, he thought.

Red Beret stared at Tyrone in disapproval.

'OK,' said Tyrone. He covered the phone as much as he could. 'Just a few more minutes, please. She says she's almost here,' and he pointed at the phone.

For what felt like an eternity, Red Beret did not move. Then he walked away, to the left, with a smug swagger.

Tyrone looked anxiously at where Hoodie was standing.

Hoodie made Nadia hold the small laptop, right up against the row of bright yellow MTN logos of Hello Mobile's display window. The man's fingers were busy on the keyboard.

'Can you see that the memory card is in working order?'

'Wait,' said Hoodie.

Tyrone saw Red Beret standing on the other side of the passage, arms crossed, watching him with a dissatisfied scowl.

I'm running out of time, the trains are coming. How long would it take to check the memory card?

He quickly looked at the cellphone's clock: 15:04. Could it be? It felt like the whole thing had taken an eternity. He had nine minutes, maybe ten, before the Metrorail 3526 left for Cape Town. If the train was five minutes late. Please.

'The card is good,' said Hoodie at last over the phone.

'OK,' said Tyrone. 'The first letter of the password is "Y". Now tell Nadia to start walking towards the sports shop straight ahead. Sport Station. You can see it from where you are. And when she gets there, she must turn left, towards the station entrance. I can see her, and I will give you a letter for every step she takes, until she turns the corner. But you don't move. You stay exactly where you are. Or I will stop giving you the code.'

'OK.'

'Tell her.'

Five schoolchildren in rust brown jerseys and blazers walked between them. Then he saw Hoodie had the laptop in his left hand, and he was talking into Nadia's ear.

Nadia began to walk.

'The next letter is the number zero.'

Griessel had forgotten about Radebe and Ndabeni, who'd been sent to O. R. Tambo Airport. In the mix-up of the Waterfront shooting no one had thought to recall them.

'Ulinda sent a photo,' said Mbali to him over the student's phone, her voice excited. 'Taken at the airport's scanner. And it might be him, Benny. He arrived on Saturday morning, on a flight from Paris. He is wearing a grey baseball cap and dark glasses. A coloured man, very athletic. They matched the guy to the passport control records, and he is travelling under the name of Hector Malot, a French citizen. Vusi checked all the flights to Cape Town, and the same guy was on an SAA flight that arrived just after two on Saturday.'

'That's very good, Mbali,' said Griessel. 'Are Ulinda and Vusi still at O. R. Tambo?'

'Yes, Benny. We had to recall them, of course. They're waiting for their flight back.'

'Tell them to cancel the flight. Tell them Cobra isn't just one guy. There are at least three of them. We are going to need all their names.'

Tyrone gave Hoodie a letter for every step that Nadia took towards him.

'U.'

'M.'

'Zero.'

Hoodie wasn't writing anything down – the laptop was folded shut under his arm. It didn't make sense, but it wasn't Tyrone's problem.

'T.'

'H.'

'The number three.'

'R.'

Nadia was now in front of the door of Hair International, just five metres from the corner, only eight metres from him. She didn't look up, not to the left or the right. Just walked, slowly.

'F.'

'U.'

'C.'

That was when he saw Red Beret look at Nadia. Intently. And then he began to walk towards her.

37

Mbali asked him how he knew that the Cobra was not a single individual, and he said he was talking on a borrowed cellphone, he couldn't say right now.

'Oh. OK, Bennie, I will tell them.'

'Get them to call you from a pay phone first.'

'Of course.'

'What did Bones say? Is he in?'

'Yes, he's in.'

'Has Vaughn brought the phones yet?'

'No, we're still waiting.'

'Please tell him I'll be at Nadia Kleinbooi's flat. I'm going to try and find a caretaker to unlock the door, and then search it.' Griessel saw the student beside him shake his head. He gave the young man a querying look.

'You don't know Oom Stoffel,' said the student.

Red Beret walked right up to Nadia.

Tyrone knew why. She was moving like a sleepwalker, it looked as if there was something wrong with her.

'What is the next letter?' Hoodie asked over the phone.

Red Beret was next to Nadia. He said something to her, aggressively. She looked at him in a daze.

'What is the next letter?' Hoodie sounded threatening.

Tyrone could not remember where he had been. 'Wait,' he said. C. He had given the C last.

'K,' he said.

Red Beret gripped Nadia's arm.

She was startled, pulled away and looked around her, confusion on her face.

Tyrone knew he could no longer just stand there.

'The number three.' And he began to walk towards Nadia. Hoodie was going to see him, but he had no choice. 'There's one more letter. I will give it to you when Nadia is safe.'

He was close enough to hear Red Beret say to Nadia, 'Are you drunk?'

He reached them. 'Leave her alone,' said Tyrone. 'She's my sister. She's sick.'

Nadia looked at him. That's when he knew for sure they had drugged his sister. That was when his fear and anxiety gave way to fury.

'*Boetie*,' she said with a crooked smile.

'*Sussie*.' He felt like crying.

'She looks drunk to me,' said Red Beret.

Tyrone put his arm around Nadia. 'Come,' he said. 'We must hurry.' He pulled her along, they needed to get away. He knew Hoodie's eyes were on them now, the train was already at the platform, they would have to run for it. But Nadia didn't look like she could.

'Hey, I'm talking to you,' said Red Beret, and pulled his baton out of a ring on his wide black belt.

He wanted to tell the man to 'Fuck off', but he didn't.

'What is the last letter?' asked Hoodie over the phone.

They were around the corner, out of sight.

'R.' said Tyrone and cut the connection. Then he reached his arm around Nadia's back, took a firm grip of her shoulder, and pushed her carefully forwards so they could begin running.

Red Beret was next to them, the baton threatening. 'Stop,' he said.

And right in front of Tyrone stood the gunman from this morning, the guy from the Waterfront, the coloured one with the baseball cap and the eyes that made you shiver. He blocked the way to the station entrance. He had the same silenced pistol in his hand, and it was pointed straight at Tyrone's forehead.

Weird, was the word that stuck in his mind at that moment. How did he get here?

He ducked, instinctively jerking Nadia to get her out of danger. But she stumbled and a knee gave, weakened by drugs and the heavy bag of textbooks and stationery and who knew what. She fell, pulling him down with her.

The pistol's aim followed them. There was a shot, a muffled, almost apologetic noise, and his sister's body twitched as she fell back onto him.

Griessel and the young man walked down the stairs.

'Oom Stoffel is a *drol*,' said the student. 'Difficult arsehole. He'll never unlock for you. Unless you have ten documents saying you have permission from Nadia, her grandma, and the state president.'

'We shall see,' said Griessel.

'You can always threaten to shoot him too,' the student urged him on with relish.

Tyrone grabbed Nadia in his arms and screamed, all the fear, all the tension, all the despair released in a single, raging bellow.

People turned to look.

The gunman stood patiently, the pistol stretched out in front of him, waiting for Tyrone to keep still so that he had a clean shot.

Red Beret, hidden behind Tyrone and Nadia, stepped around them, his baton raised. He moved surprisingly fast for the somewhat plump body. He shouted a reprimanding *'Hhayi!'* The shooter's response was smooth and skilful. He aimed the pistol at the guard. He fired, just a fraction of a second before the baton hit his right wrist. Tyrone felt the blood spray over his face, saw Red Beret sink down, and the pistol clatter on the brick paving. The gunman swore, bent down to the ground, trying to pick up the pistol with his left hand; his right hand hung limply.

Tyrone kicked him with so much desperate violence that he lost his balance, because of the growing weight of Nadia in his arms. He knew that it was their only chance of survival. He hit the man against the side of his face, across his jawbone and cheekbone and temple, with the full length of the bridge of his foot. He felt the pain in his foot, and it gave him a moment of satisfaction. The gunman dropped like an ox.

Tyrone wanted to pick Nadia up and run.

The pistol lay right there in front of him.

He steadied his sister with his left arm, bent and picked up the firearm, quickly shoved it into the deep pocket of his trousers, then swept Nadia up, cradling her in his arms. He saw the blood on her left breast. *'Sussie.'*

It was a whisper, a sob. He had to get her to a hospital. The train was no longer an option. He ran to the right, to the eastern exit of Bellstar Junction, staggering under Nadia's now-unconscious weight.

He saw the delivery van in Charl Malan Street, a white Kia. Two brothers unpacking cartons at the back. Ossie's Halaal Meats on the side. He staggered up to them and cried out, 'My sister, please, she's been shot, I have to get her to a hospital.'

He knew his voice was high and shrill, he felt the wet blood spatter on the left side of his contorted face, Nadia's blood glistening on his hand.

The two men stopped what they were doing and stared at Tyrone, mouths open.

He ran up to them.

'Please, my brother,' he begged. 'She's all I have.'

The older one reacted first. 'Get in,' he said. He looked at his colleague, and pointed at the boxes on the pavement. 'Look after the goods, nè.'

Oom Stoffel, the caretaker, was a sour old man, somewhere in his sixties. His flat was opposite, in Block One. He opened the door, without a word, didn't even look at them. Just pointed at the sign on the wall. *Caretaker. Hours: 09:00 to 12:00. 13:00 to 15:00.* He made a big show of looking at his watch. Then he began closing the door again.

Griessel put a foot between the door and the frame. 'SAPS,' he said. 'And if you do that again, you're in trouble.'

Now Oom Stoffel looked at him under heavy raised brows. 'SAPS?'

'That's right. I am Benny Griessel . . .' He took out his wallet and identity card.

'He's from the Hawks, Oom,' said the student helpfully.

'The what?'

'The Directorate of Priority Crimes Investigation,' said Griessel, and displayed his card. 'Will you please come and unlock number twenty-one. It's a crime scene now.'

Oom Stoffel took his reading glasses from his breast pocket, put them on and studied the identity card.

'He's *mos* genuine from the Hawks, Oom,' said the student.

'Where are your papers?' the caretaker asked Griessel.

'Here.' He waved the identity card.

'No, where is your warrant?'

'Are you certain you want to be difficult, *meneer*?'

'I know the law,' he said stubbornly.

'Then you should be acquainted with Articles Twenty-Five to Twenty-Seven of the Criminal Procedure Act.'

'All I know is, you can't just go in there.'

'Now listen to me, *meneer* . . .'

'He's got a gun,' said Johan, the student.

'Shut up,' said Griessel. He looked at Oom Stoffel again. 'If you want to sleep in your own bed tonight, you had better listen. Article Twenty-Five, Three B says I may enter the premises if I believe the obtaining of a warrant will subvert the purpose of it. Article Twenty-Seven says I can lawfully search any person or any premises, I can use such force as may be reasonably necessary to overcome any resistance against such search or against entry of the premises, including the breaking of any door or window of such premises, provided that I first audibly demand admission to the premises and notify the purpose for which I seek to enter such premises. I'm telling you now, in the presence of a civilian witness, the legal resident of number twenty-one is the victim of an alleged crime. Unlock it, or I will lock you up, and break down that door.'

'He's not joking, Oom Stoffel,' said the student, enjoying every moment.

Tyrone held Nadia tightly.

'Gangstas?' asked the guy at the steering wheel.

'Something like that,' said Tyrone, his eyes on Nadia's face.

'To Tygerberg?'

'No, uncle. There's a private hospital just on the other side here, near the police.'

'Louis Leipoldt. It's a Mediclinic. Those people are expensive.'

'I know, uncle. But she's my sister.'

'OK.'

And just before they turned off in Broadway, Tyrone remembered Bobby. He dug his cellphone out of his pocket, and phoned Hassan Ikar.

38

Tyrone knew the Mediclinic people would phone the cops. It was the law, if a gunshot wound came in. That's why he was anxious about how long it was taking.

They had put Nadia on a stretcher in Emergency. He also told them someone had drugged her, they ought to know.

An administrative aunty approached and asked, 'What drugs?'

He said he didn't know.

'What drugs does she use, sir?' In white Afrikaans, adamant and strict.

It made him angry. 'She doesn't *use* drugs. They forced her to take them. She's studying to be a doctor, she's not some *hierjy*. Get her to the doctors now, please.'

'Calm down, sir. First we need the details of her medical aid,' said the admin aunty.

He pulled out his wallet, took out three thousand rand in cash, and gave it to her. 'There is no medical aid, aunty. This should cover it for today. If you need more, let me know, but please, get her in there to the doctors.'

Her heart softened a bit and she said to the nurses, 'Take her in.' She turned back to Tyrone. 'It's a gunshot wound, we have to notify the *polieste*.' This time speaking naturally, *Kaaps*.

'Tell them, aunty, she has nothing to hide. She's pure class.'

'Your girlfriend?'

'No, aunty. She's my sister. I'm rubbish, but she isn't.'

'*Nee, wat*, a man who looks after his sister like that, he's also pure class.'

'Thanks, aunty.'

'Where did they shoot her?'

He hesitated.

'I have to ask, because the police will want to know.'

'Down by the station, aunty.'

'Bellville?'

'Yes, aunty.'

She shook her head in horror. 'Gangstas . . .' She looked at him. '*Ai,*
do you know how you look, with all that blood all over you?'

'No, aunty.'

'Here's her bag, you'll have to keep it with you, or let us book it in
for safekeeping. Come, let's get you cleaned up, then you will give me
all her details for admission.'

He told her he had to go to the toilet first. He wanted to move the
pistol from his trouser pocket to the backpack he had bought from
Hassan Ikar. Then he came back and sat with the admin aunty to give
her the admission details. And also so he could know when she phoned
the cops.

Oom Stoffel muttered, all the way down the stairs of Block One, across
the car park, and up the stairs of Block Two. Under his breath, but
Griessel picked up a phrase here and there. 'Can't recite the numbers
of the laws, but I know my rights . . .' was more or less the drift.

He knew people like the caretaker, wielding a little bit of power that
they obstinately abused, after a lifetime of being victimised in the same
way. There was only one way to deal with them: give them a dose of
their own medicine. Then they crumbled.

Griessel let the man go ahead while he fetched his homicide case
from the boot of the BMW. The student trotted enthusiastically after
him.

They rejoined Oom Stoffel at Nadia's door, where he was searching
through a big bunch of keys for the right one. He found it, unlocked,
stood back, and waved his arm theatrically.

'There you go,' he said.

Griessel took a pair of gloves out of his case. 'Please wait for me
here.'

'I have things to do,' said the caretaker.

'Like what?' asked the student.

'You've got no business here,' said Oom Stoffel.

'I'm supporting the Hawks,' said the student.

The old man snorted.

Griessel picked up the case, opened the door, and went in. He closed the door behind him again, with a measure of relief.

The flat was tidy. A small kitchenette to the right, a sitting room ahead, and the bedroom behind that, to the left.

He was in a hurry, gave it only a cursory going over. He saw no sign that anyone had searched the place yet. It looked as if she had been the last one here.

A porridge bowl, spoon, and coffee mug were on the drying rack, washed. A few photos were stuck on the fridge. Group photos of four or five students. In one he recognised Tyrone Kleinbooi, from this morning's video clips. He was with a girl he assumed to be Nadia; Tyrone's arm was draped protectively around his sister's shoulder.

Griessel opened his case, took out a plastic evidence bag. He took the photo off the fridge and put it in the bag.

In the sitting room there was a beige couch, covered in corduroy, old and a bit frayed, but clean. And a pine wood coffee table. Two books on it. The uppermost one showed an attractive woman eating pasta from a bowl. *Nigellissima: Instant Italian Inspiration.*

He went into the bedroom.

A single bed, made up. A teddy bear propped against the cushion stared at him with all-knowing glass eyes. An old easy chair covered in faded red material. One of the wooden legs was mended, soundly, but not very skilfully. Against the wall was a long table of Oregon pine. There was a mouse and a power cable, but no laptop. Textbooks in a row against the wall. More books on a small bookshelf below the window.

Griessel opened the built-in wardrobe.

The subtle scent of a pleasant perfume. A young girl's clothing filled half the space. Jeans, blouses, a few dresses, a denim jacket. Below, six pairs of shoes. To the left, on different shelves, neatly piled and arranged, were her underwear, jerseys, T-shirts, and a shelf with perfume, a jewellery case. And a cellphone box for an iPhone 4. He picked up the box and slid it open.

Inside was a Vodacom information card for a pre-paid account. With the IMEI and phone number on it.

He held it between his fingers and walked to the front door. He went outside. Oom Stoffel stood there, arms folded, face thunderous. Beside him, the student looked very pleased with himself.

'Can you please phone this number?' asked Griessel and showed him the Vodacom card.

'And now? Don't the police have their own phones?' asked Oom Stoffel.

'His one is broken. So I'm helping him,' said the student.

'Typical.' A disparaging snort. 'God save our country.'

'Please pass it to me as soon as it rings,' said Griessel.

The student phoned, listened for a moment, and gave Griessel the phone.

He stood listening to it ring, without much hope.

They sat in front of a computer at Admissions, Tyrone opposite the admin aunty.

'Is that your phone?' she asked when the ringtone sounded.

He was very tired. The terrible day weighed down on him, a veil over his thoughts. And he was worried about his sister – his thoughts were inside with her. 'No,' he said.

Then he realised the sound came from Nadia's bag. Hoodie must have pushed it in there. He leaned over, took it out, looked at the screen. A number on the display. If it was one of Nadia's contacts there would have been a name.

'You'd better answer,' said the aunty.

'Hello,' he said.

'Who's this?' The voice of a white man.

'Who do you *want* to talk to?'

'To Nadia Kleinbooi.' There was authority in the voice.

'She isn't available.' Adrenaline flowed again and the fatigue was gone. 'Who am I talking to now?'

Tyrone smelled police. He knew the aunty was listening, but he had to get off this line. They could do a lot to trace the call; they would know where he was.

'Hello?' said the voice. 'Who am I talking to?'

'OK,' said Tyrone for the benefit of the aunty. 'OK, I'll give her the message. OK, bye.'

He ended the call and put the phone back in Nadia's book bag.

'One of her classmates,' he said. 'Where were we?'

★ ★ ★

Griessel stood with the phone in his hand and he thought: that was Tyrone. It had to be. He didn't know how it worked, he didn't know how it all fitted together, but his instinct told him that was the pickpocket. The man had a shade of Cape Flats in that accent, and something else: a caution, a suspicion, a wariness.

And he was somewhere with people that he could not speak in front of.

The Cobras had Tyrone too.

That was the only explanation.

He took out his wallet again, fished out thirty rand in notes and pushed them into the pocket of the student's leather jacket.

'No, Captain, really it's not . . .'

Griessel was tired of struggling with other people's phones, with the whole bloody situation. 'Take it,' he said. Then he realised how it sounded. 'Please. I have to make one more call.'

'Any time. It's our duty to help the police,' said Johan, looking pointedly at Oom Stoffel.

The old man snorted again.

Griessel phoned Mbali.

When she answered, he said: 'We need to track a number, Mbali. Very urgently.'

'*Ingels*,' said Oom Stoffel. 'There's your problem, right there, when our police have to start talking English . . .'

39

He had to get away from here, Tyrone thought.

He must phone PC Carolus and ask how long it would take someone to check where a phone was, but he thought it would be quick, the cops just checked on their computers. He might have ten minutes or so, then they would be here.

'Aunty, please, I have to get back to work, they gonna fire me, but first I must know if my sister is OK.'

'I've *mos* got your number here on the system. I'll let you know.'

He thought. The cops would swarm all over this place. And they would find out everything. That Nadia was here in the hospital, and that she had been shot. They would interview her when she recovered. And they would tell her her brother was a pickpocket, and that he had shot people at the Waterfront, and she was going to get a shock, in her state. And there was sweet blow-all he could do about it, 'cause she needed serious medical attention, he couldn't get her out of here now.

But at least she'd be safe. And he would phone her, and he would tell her nothing was like it seemed, first she must recuperate, then he would tell her everything.

Now he had to get out of here. Get rid of this new phone, 'cause the number was on Nadia's phone, from when he talked to Hoodie. He was traceable.

He must become invisible again. So he could do what had to be done.

It was payback time.

'Are you OK?' asked the aunty.

'Can I have your number, aunty, please; I'm not allowed to take calls at work.'

'Now what kind of work is that? Surely they will understand if your sister is in the hospital.'

'Paint contractors, those people are *kwaai*, aunty.'

She shook her head over the unfairness of it. Then she grew serious. 'The police will want to talk to you. About what happened.'

He thought about that. 'OK, give them my number. But I have to go. If aunty could just quickly go and see if she is *orraait*. Please.'

'Sign here so long,' she said, and pointed at a document she had printed out. 'Then I'll see what I can do.'

Griessel had told Mbali to keep Vaughn Cupido at the DPCI head office when he returned with the cellphones. He stretched yellow crime-scene tape across the door of number twenty-one and threatened dire consequences if the caretaker allowed anyone access.

'Except if they also throw article sixty B around here,' the old man muttered

Griessel ignored the sarcasm.

He thanked the student again.

'Any time, Captain, any time.'

'And not a word from you.'

'My lips are zipped.'

For how long, Griessel wondered, and ran down the stairs to the BMW. He put the siren on, stuck the blue light on the dashboard, and drove off as fast as he could.

On the N1, just beyond the Winelands Engen, he switched his cellphone back on. It beeped, and he saw that he had four voice messages.

They would have to wait, he didn't want to waste time putting on his earphones now.

Tyrone grew anxious, as the minutes ticked away, the cops must be on their way already. His ears were pricked for sirens, but he heard nothing.

Maybe it takes a while to trace a phone. And if he just ran out of here, the aunty would know he was not innocent.

To his immense relief she returned with a smile. 'Your sister is going to be OK, they say she was very lucky, that bullet must have hit something in front of her, because she only has broken ribs over here.' She indicated the side of her upper torso. 'There's no internal damage or bleeding there, just external. And it's very sore, the ribs. She's stable so you can stop worrying.'

Stop worrying. Not for a while.

'Thank you very much, aunty,' he said while he tried to think what the bullet could have hit. He recalled that moment, Nadia stumbling and falling in front of him, the pistol making its dull bark. And then he had a hunch and picked up her bag, and began unpacking it on the admin desk. He held up the thick textbook: *Chemistry & Chemical Reactivity.* Kotz, Treichel & Weaver. At the top end was a mark, a piece of the thick hard cover and a chunk of pages were shot away.

'Saved by chemistry,' said the aunty. 'Can you believe it.'

'I'm going to leave the bag here, aunty. So she can get it when she wants her stuff.'

'That's fine.'

'How long is she going to be here?'

'I can't say myself, but I guess four or five days.'

'How much money must I still bring, aunty?'

'For safety sake, another three thousand, then we can just settle at the release.'

He didn't think he would be here at the release, he was a wanted man. And a hunted man. But he said 'OK', thanked her, said goodbye, and left.

On the N1, at a hundred and forty-five kilometres per hour, disgust overcame Benny Griessel. At himself, and at the SSA. It was their fault that he couldn't use his phone. That he had to make calls in front of two idiots. With a *fokken* borrowed phone.

He should have phoned Nadia's number again. He should have talked to Tyrone. If it was Tyrone. But who else could it be? A straight line of reasoning ran to Tyrone. The bullet casings at the abduction scene showed it was the Cobras. The eyewitness said it was a coloured girl who was kidnapped. The Cobras had been in Tyrone's rented room in the Bo-Kaap, and they knew Nadia was studying at Stellenbosch. They were looking for her. And they found her. To get at Tyrone, because he had something they wanted. The Cobras were foreigners. They didn't speak Afrikaans. It had to be Tyrone.

Somehow or other he had got hold of his sister's phone.

Borrowed maybe?

Didn't make sense. He should have phoned again. He should have said: 'Come in. We won't arrest you for anything, just come in, and tell us everything. We aren't after you, we want the Cobras. And your sister.'

But it was the one number rule that he could not call from his own phone. Because it would give the SSA a short cut.

He swore and turned off the N1, onto Durban Road, the sirens still wailing. The traffic opened up for him. He just hoped Cupido was already there with the new cellphones.

'*Jissis*,' said PC Carolus. 'What have you got yourself into?'

Tyrone walked up Duminy Street, on the way to catch a taxi on Frans Conradie Drive, cellphone to his ear.

'Nothing I can't handle. Tell me now, what info can they get from a cellular number?'

'Everything, Tyrone. Where you are, where you've been. Who you phoned, who phoned you. SMSs, the works. They can even read your SMSs, brother, so I hope you kept it clean.'

'OK, how long will it take?'

'Depends. Who are the people who want to trace your phone?'

'I don't know them.'

'Now you're lying to me. Is it private individuals or the cops?'

'What's the difference?'

'The cops have to get a warrant first. That takes time. Private individuals can do what they like, if they have the right equipment. Within half an hour, then they find you.'

He wanted to ditch the phone. Now. Because these guys, Hoodie and the Waterfront shooter, you didn't know what they could do. They got Nadia so fast, they knew where his room was, they stalked him there at the station. They were sly bastards. And they wanted him dead.

'OK, thanks, PC . . .'

'Don't thank me. Just stop all the monkey business. You're not a player, you're a pickpocket, for fuck's sake.'

Griessel found Cupido in Mbali's office busy putting SIM cards into cellphones.

Mbali was talking on the land line. 'Alvarez,' she said into the receiver. 'With a "z" at the end. No, I'm not going to hold. This is a serious police matter. You stay on the line, and give me the information . . . You know I'm a police officer because I am telling you I am. And I don't need a room number, I just want to know if you have a booking . . .' She looked up at Griessel and shook her head in frustration.

'Vaughn, I need to use a phone.' Griessel pointed at the cellphones on the desk.

'This one is ready. Take it for yourself.' He passed one to Benny. 'Battery's not completely charged yet. ZTE F Nine Hundred, sorry, Benna, it's all I could get. Earphones are still in the plastic.'

Griessel had never heard of a ZTE. It was a simple phone with a keyboard. At least he would know how to use it.

'Thanks,' he said as he took Nadia's Vodacom information card out of his pocket.

He phoned the number.

It rang for a long time.

'Thank you,' said Mbali over the land line. 'That wasn't so hard,' and she put the receiver down.

'Hello?' said a woman's voice over Griessel's ZTE.

'Nadia?' he said in surprise.

'No, this is Sister Abigail Malgas of the Louis Leipoldt Mediclinic. Who's speaking?'

Mbali's office door flew open and Bones's face appeared. 'I've found Lillian Alvarez,' he said in triumph. 'Protea Hotel Fire & Ice!, New Church Street.'

'Hello?' said Sister Malgas. 'Are you there?'

40

You're not a player, you're a pickpocket for fuck's sake.

Not a player?

Tyrone stood in front of Brights Electrical in Frans Conradie Drive and he thought, sure, he was a pickpocket. And usually he lived according to Uncle Solly's code. *Steal from the rich. Never use violence. Be kind to the less fortunate.*

Yes, he had never been a player. Until today. Until these guys changed the game. Till they introduced a whole new set of rules. Until they shot him and chased him. Until they messed with his sister, kidnapping and drugging her, and he didn't want to think what else. And then they shot her too.

Enough is enough. Code or no code, you don't do that. Not to the Kleinboois of Mitchells Plain.

Now he was a player. Now they would pay. Because now Nadia was safely in hospital, the police would be on the scene there soon, and he was beyond fear. Now he was the hell-in.

He called his old phone number, and he hoped they still had it, and that it was on. The phone rang and rang, until at last Hoodie answered it.

'Yes.' All formal and semi pissed off, like a man taking a call from his mother-in-law. And Tyrone liked that, because he knew Hoodie would not be pleased to hear from him. Because he had kicked Baseball Cap a *snotskoot* that he hoped gave the cunt a migraine for a week.

'Listen, motherfucker, did you think I'm stupid?'

'What do you want?'

'It's what you want. I have a small surprise for you.'

'Yes?'

'I'm not stupid. I knew that a guy who just walks in and shoots people is a crazy motherfucker. So I got myself a little insurance.'

'What insurance?'

'That ZIP file on the card is bullshit. You used the password I gave you?'

'Yes.'

'And you saw another ZIP file?'

'Yes.'

'If you use the same password I gave you, it will open, sesame. And you will see a hundred and two high-res, full-colour photographs of the beauty of Cape Town, for your viewing pleasure. You want to do that now, to see if I'm pulling your chain?'

Silence over the line.

And Tyrone thought, Take that, MoFo, put that in your pipe and smoke it.

It was a while before the man asked: 'Where is the original file?' But cool and calm.

'I have it right here, in the famous stolen wallet, motherfucker. Do you want it?'

'You are a dead man.'

It was just a statement, no emotion, and Tyrone shivered, but he said, 'Fuck you. Do you want the original file?"

A heartbeat of silence, then, 'Yes.'

'Then you are going to pay.'

'How much?'

It was a question he had thought deeply about, all the way from the Mediclinic. His gut feel was one million, but then he thought, these guys are not local, that accent is continental, they work in euros and dollars, one million is chump change.

'Two hundred thousand euros. That's about two point four million rand. And that's how I want it. Local currency.'

No hesitation. 'That is not possible.'

'Tough shit, motherfucker. Then you can kiss the ZIP file goodbye. Hang on to my phone. I will call you again later tonight, in case you change your mind.'

And he took the phone he had bought from the Somali, still switched on, and he dropped it in the dustbin in front of Brights Electrical. Let the cops or the Hoodie gang trace it now.

Fuck them all.

He ran for a taxi.

* * *

In Mbali's office he held his hand up in the air for silence. He said to Sister Abigail that he was Captain Benny Griessel of the SAPS Directorate of Priority Crimes Investigations, and they were urgently looking for Nadia Kleinbooi.

'Yes, the phone belongs to Nadia. You are very lucky, Captain, I was on the way to take her personal effects to storage when you phoned. She was admitted about an hour ago for a gunshot wound. We have already reported it to the Bellville Station. They said they would come as soon as—'

'Is it serious?' asked Griessel, while his colleagues stared at him in silence.

'No, thank goodness, it's not critical. They are busy treating her wound now, but she is conscious.'

'Sister, thank you very much. We're on our way.' He ended the call and told his colleagues the news. Mbali said something in Zulu that sounded like a prayer of thanks.

'Bones, is Lillian Alvarez at the hotel?'

'I didn't ask, Benny. But she has definitely checked in.'

'Vaughn, can you and Bones go and find out?'

'Of course we can,' said Bones enthusiastically. He was a member of the Statutory Crimes group of the Hawks' Commercial Crimes branch. For the most part his daily routine involved wrestling with financial statements, but like most Hawks detectives he would never pass up a chance to be part of a violent crimes investigation.

Cupido laughed. 'There's a phone and a charger for everybody. Watch the batteries, plug them in whenever you can. I'll drop off the Giraffe's on the way out. And I'll SMS the numbers to everybody.'

Griessel thanked him and said to Mbali, 'Let's go talk to Nadia.'

The taxi stopped in front of Parow's small, grey Metrorail station, Tyrone got out and walked straight to Station Street, nowadays a lively pedestrian market with a host of colourful stalls. It was different from Bellville, here it was mostly South Africans doing business – in cheap Chinese bric-a-brac, vegetables, fruit, sweets, cigarettes. But between the butchers, fast food, clothing and furniture shops that flanked the street, there were at least seven cellphone shops. And one of them was Moosa Mobile.

That was where he went, as fast as he could, even though he felt the fatigue in every fibre of his body, and the pain across his back, even though he wished he could just lie down on a soft bed somewhere and go to sleep.

Eat your veggies first, Ty. Work, then play.

That's what I'm doing, Uncle Solly.

He had come to Moosa Mobile because, in his industry he had heard that if you want to peddle a hot phone in the northern suburbs, Moosa was the fence to see. Tyrone didn't do business in this area, so Moosa didn't know him. But he was looking for three second-hand phones that were not traceable.

He walked in and said straight out what he wanted. And the little man gave him that look, and he knew he looked awful, but at least no one was going to take him for an undercover cop. The man took out three phones from the back, no boxes, no trimmings, just the instruments and their chargers. Cheap stuff, that the little man put in a Pick 'n' Pay plastic bag. Then Tyrone bought three prepaid SIM cards: Vodacom. MTN. Cell C. He put sixty rands of airtime on each one.

Then he walked to the stalls and bought a small, cheap travel case, two shirts, white and blue. A smart pair of black trousers, a grey pullover, a purple windcheater – because that was the only colour they had in his size – six pairs of underpants, four pairs of black socks, and a dark grey tweed jacket. Because a jacket, Uncle Solly used to say, is the ticket.

And then he walked back to the station. He would have liked to be near Nadia. But it wouldn't help him; he couldn't afford to go near there, that's what the cops would expect. But still, the urge to be close to her was strong. To protect her. But he must do the smart thing. The northern suburbs were a foreign country. He must get back to the city. That was his hunting ground. That was where he was at home.

Sister Malgas told Griessel and Mbali what she knew. Someone had drugged Nadia Kleinbooi, and then she had been shot, at Bellville Station. Her brother Tyrone had brought her in.

Griessel took out the photo of Tyrone and Nadia from his jacket pocket, and showed it to her.

'Yes, that's the brother.'

He asked if Tyrone was still around, but he already knew what the answer would be.

Had he left a contact number?

Sister Malgas said the number was on the system – she looked it up and gave it to him. 'But he can't take calls.' She explained about a strict boss at a paint contractor.

Griessel nodded as if he believed it, and asked if they could see Nadia.

No, they would have to wait. Perhaps in the next hour.

She had spoken of Nadia's personal possessions. Could they look through them?

She would ask the superintendent. She made the call, got the OK, and went to fetch them.

While he waited, Griessel phoned the SC of Bellville police station to get the details of the shooting. He heard that a security guard had been fatally wounded, and a girl had been admitted to Louis Leipoldt. That was all the station commander could say for sure now, because his detectives were still at the scene, busy questioning witnesses. But he thought it was gang-related, most likely drugs.

'Colonel, at what time did this take place?'

'Just after three.'

While he had been in Stellenbosch, the Cobras had shot people, less than a kilometre from the Hawks' headquarters.

'We are at Louis Leipoldt now to interview the wounded girl. If you retrieve any bullet casings, let me know. And when the detectives are finished, ask them to phone me. We suspect the case is related to an urgent matter that we are investigating.'

'I'll do that.'

Sister Malgas approached with a bulging shoulder bag, which she put down on the desk in front of them. Mbali took out rubber gloves from her equally large handbag, pulled them on, and began to unpack Nadia's belongings: textbooks on biology, chemistry, physics, and maths.

'Look here, the bullet hit the book,' the sister pointed out.

Two notebooks. A bright yellow zipper bag for pens and pencils. A transparent lunchbox with a sandwich and two sticks of dried fruit. A charger for an iPhone, and the phone itself. A small toilet bag with a comb, make-up, and women's things. A purse, of denim fabric, with Nadia's student card, a cash card from FNB, a few cash slips for groceries from Checkers, prepaid airtime from Vodacom, and just over a hundred and fifty rand in cash. Two packs of chewing gum, one half empty. A single condom. And last, a key ring with the black and white yin and yang symbol on it, with a round chip for an electronic gate, and a key that would probably fit her apartment's front door.

Griessel took the phone and began to look at the call register. TYRONE was listed for all the calls from ten o'clock this morning and just after one. Her brother had been phoning her continuously. Or she him. After that, numbers that were not identified in her contacts. The last call, before his own, new phone number appeared, was just before five.

He saw that there was not much charge left in the battery, but he used Nadia's phone in any case to call Tyrone's number

Perhaps he would answer.

It rang for a long time, and then went over to voicemail.

'Hi, this is Ty. You're looking for me. Why?'

The same voice that had answered Nadia's phone a while back.

With the leaden feeling of frustration and disappointment he rang off, without leaving a message.

This whole thing had played out at Bellville Station. And David Patrick Adair's death warrant had been signed there.

'Cool,' said Vaughn Cupido as they walked into the Protea Hotel Fire & Ice! and he spotted all the neon lights, the slick fittings in glass and wood.

'Funky,' said Bones.

They walked to reception, Cupido's long coat tails flapping.

Bones showed his SAPS identity card to the woman behind the desk. 'Major Benedict Boshigo, Priority Crimes Directorate of the SAPS.'

Cupido could hear how his colleague relished saying it. He knew Commercial Crimes were mostly desk jockeys; they didn't get the chance to flash plastic every day.

'How may I help you, sir?'

'We called earlier about a Miss Lillian Alvarez. You told us she has checked in.'

'That must be our reservation desk, sir.'

'Could you please give us her room number?'

The woman was uncertain. 'I . . . Our policy . . . I'll have to check with my manager, sir.'

'Could you call him for us?'

'Her. Just a minute . . .'

Cupido looked at an iPad that stood on the counter. Photos of the hotel's rooms flashed up and dissolved on a constant loop, and below that, Today's tariff: R899.00 per night (Room Only).

'Can't be doing too badly as a research fellow to be able to afford that,' said Cupido. 'Unless the rich, digital bank robber of a sugar daddy is paying.'

'That's nothing if you're from England, nè,' said Bones. 'Less than sixty pounds.'

Cupido only nodded, unwilling to discard his financial fraud and mistress theory.

A woman came walking up on black high heels, accompanied by the receptionist. Late thirties, black skirt and jacket, white blouse, thin smile. She knew the SAPS were not good news.

'Gentleman, how may I help?'

Cupido knew Bones was eager to speak. He stood back.

Bones explained the situation to the manageress. She asked for their identification cards, and studied them carefully.

She looked up. 'Is there some sort of trouble?'

'No, she was the victim of a pickpocket this morning. We would just like to talk to her.'

'A pickpocket? That does not seem like a priority crime.'

'Uh . . .' Bones was taken by surprise.

Cupido stepped forward. 'Ma'am, please, we don't want to do this the hard way.' His expression was stern, but he kept his voice low and courteous.

The manageress's smile disappeared entirely She looked at Cupido, thought for a moment, then nodded to the receptionist. 'You can give them the room number.' While the younger woman consulted the computer, the manager said, 'If there is something I should know . . .'

'We'll tell you, of course,' said Cupido. 'Thank you.'

Griessel and Mbali had to wait in the hospital restaurant until they could question Nadia Kleinbooi.

They walked from Emergency in Voortrekker Road to the new wing of the hospital on Fairway Road. He walked half a step behind his colleague, still trying to process and express his disappointment. At least the girl was safe, he thought.

And he hadn't had a drink today, though it had been close, so fucking close. He shivered as if someone had walked over his grave. It was always a danger, when there was so much chaos in an investigation, so much crazy rush and pressure. And trouble. He just mustn't let the lost battle with the Cobras mess with his head as well. Let him first test his theory on Mbali.

He looked at her, saw how she turned up the collar of the blue SAPS windcheater to keep out the cold late afternoon wind. There was a quiet strength in her walk. On the way to the hospital she had been very quiet, and in the interview with the nurse she was as solemn as ever. But he knew she had been like that from this morning, since the conversation in the car outside the house of the Schotsche Kloof murder. The disapproving frown, the determined, almost arrogant attitude had given way to something else – dismay.

He thought he knew what it was. And he understood.

He had walked that path himself, when he had been appointed by Murder and Robbery – and before he started drinking. Christ, it was a lifetime ago. He had been so full of fire and full of himself and his status, and his responsibility as a Servant of Justice. As Detective. Because when you worked at Murder and Robbery, your role was spelled with a capital letter. What you did *mattered*.

Part of his smugness was because he had started to run with the big dogs then. The living legends, the guys whose investigations, break-throughs, interrogation techniques, and witticisms were passed on in seminars, tearooms and bars, with an awed shake of the head. They were his role models and his heroes long before he joined them – in the beginning he was wide-eyed with respect and awe.

But the longer he worked with them – through intense days and nights, weeks and months where he learned to know them as they really were – the more he realised they had feet of clay. Each and every one of them. Everyone had weaknesses, deficiencies, demons, complexes, and syndromes that were laid bare by the inhuman pressure, the violence, the homicides, the powder keg of politics.

It was a depressing process. He had tried to fight against it, rationalise and suppress it. Later he realised that it was partly out of fear of the greater, inevitable disillusionment: if they were fallible, so was he.

And so was the system.

He remembered having a moment of insight, after a few years with Murder and Robbery, when his drinking was still under control and he still spent time pondering such things: life is one long process of disillusionment, to cure you of the myths and fictions of your youth.

Mbali was going through that now, and there was not much he could do.

But she would handle it better than he did. Women were stronger. That was another lesson he had learned over the years. And Mbali was one of the strongest of them all.

* * *

Cupido knocked on the door of Room 303 of the Protea Hotel Fire & Ice! Not loudly, not urgently; he wanted it to sound like room service. In case Lillian Alvarez was there. Which he very much doubted.

They stood and waited in silence. He kept an eye on the peephole for a movement, a shadow.

Nothing.

Cupido raised his hand to knock again, perhaps a little harder. Then something moved in front of the peephole, and it went dark. A voice, female and frightened, said, 'Who is it?'

'Miss Alvarez?' asked Cupido.

'Yes?'

'I'm Captain Vaughn Cupido of the Hawks. We would like to talk to you, please.'

'Of the who?'

'The Hawks. The elite investigative unit of the South African Police Service.'

The peephole went light again. Bones and Cupido looked at each other. Cupido thought, it's the third floor, and the way he pictured it, there were no balconies or places to climb down, surely she wouldn't . . .

The door opened.

There she was, the woman from the Facebook photo and the Waterfront video. She was in her late twenties, sultry and beautiful, far more striking face to face.

She looked at them with big, dark eyes, from the lean marathon athlete to the tall, broad-shouldered Cupido. Emotion marred the beauty – her generous mouth twisted, her eyes red and tearful.

'Please tell me you really are from the police.'

'We are,' said Bones.

'Why are you here?'

'Because of David Adair, and what happened at the Waterfront this morning.'

'Is he OK? Please tell me he is OK.'

'We are trying to find him, ma'am. That's why we're here. We hope you can help us.'

'Oh God,' she said. And then her face crumpled and she began to cry. When Bones put his hand out to touch her shoulder in sympathy, she moved instinctively forward so he could hold her.

'I'm sorry,' she said.

'Don't be sorry. It must have been a rough day,' Bones comforted her and gave Cupido a meaningful look.

'I'm so glad you came,' she said, and began to sob.

Cupido thought, fuck, why wasn't he the one who'd put his hand on her shoulder?

The Sunwind restaurant was small. Griessel didn't know what the name had to do with a hospital, or with food. It was probably meant to refer to the Cape. But not this sunless winter.

They studied the menu at the self-service counter. Decided on the Grilled Beef or Chicken Burger, for only thirty rand. He chose the beef, Mbali asked for the chicken, 'But no rocket, please, and the chips must be hot.' But with less authority than usual.

While they waited for the food, he said, 'I want to test my theory on you.'

'Please, Benny.'

He said he thought she was correct: Lillian Alvarez had brought something from England that the Cobras wanted from David Adair. She would have handed it over to them at the Waterfront, but Tyrone Kleinbooi stole it. They knew the Cobras had been at the Schotsche Kloof house. Perhaps they had followed the pickpocket there, but then he managed to get away, with the stolen article still in his possession.

Mbali nodded. She was still in agreement.

He said there was a university account in Tyrone's room with Nadia's address on it. But the Cobras did not kidnap her at her flat, it had happened on campus. That didn't make sense. The only thing he could think of was that the Waterfront gunman left with Tyrone's rucksack. Something in that rucksack allowed them to identify Nadia, and to track her down on campus.

'It's possible,' said Mbali.

'And once they had Nadia, they knew how to contact Tyrone. To set up a meeting and an exchange: the article for his sister. That happened at the Bellville train station. And in the process, she was shot.'

'Yes.'

'It means they now have what they want, Mbali. They have no further need of Adair.'

Again she nodded, despondent. Then she said, 'We have the name on the passport for one of them. If he keeps travelling with that passport, we might be able to apprehend him at an airport.'

'Perhaps we should let the SSA know. They probably have better systems for tracking travellers.'

'No, Benny, don't do that,' said Mbali quietly, as their burgers arrived.

Cupido asked Lillian Alvarez to accompany them to the hotel lounge, knowing that an average hotel room was not designed to seat three people comfortably.

She asked them to excuse her for a moment, disappeared into the bathroom and closed the door.

They waited patiently.

'She's very beautiful,' whispered Bones.

'Yes,' said Cupido. 'But you're a married man.'

'And she smells nice.' Teasing, because he was the one she had embraced, and he had seen what an impression that had made on his colleague.

'You paid a big *lobola* to your wife's parents, pappie. Don't make me phone her,' said Cupido.

'But I'm allowed to look, *nè*. And allow myself to be hugged.'

'Strange accent,' said Bones. 'She's not English.'

'She looks like a South American.'

'Latin American,' Bones corrected him in his schoolteacher voice. 'When I was studying in the States . . .'

'Here we go again,' said Cupido, teasing, because Bones was known for being eager to talk about his time there – he was very proud of the B degree in Economics from Boston University's Metropolitan College.

Bones grinned. '*Ja, ja*. But seriously, in Boston there were lots of Latin American chicks. They were all stunning. And I wasn't married then . . .'

The bathroom door opened. Alvarez appeared. Her hair was brushed, her make-up and her self-confidence were restored. She was even more breathtaking now.

'Let me just get my bag. And my phone,' she said with a small, self-conscious smile when she became aware of their undisguised admiration.

'In case Professor Adair calls,' she said when she returned, putting her phone away in the brown leather handbag.

In the lift she asked, 'How did you find me? I mean . . .'

'We'll explain everything in a minute.'

'God, it's nice to get out of that room.' Her earlier emotions had subsided, and her relief was palpable.

'You've been in your room all day?' asked Cupido sympathetically.

'Yes. I didn't know if David – Professor Adair – would call . . .'

'Shame,' said Cupido, resting his hand gently on her shoulder.

She just smiled gratefully at him.

While Mbali ate, Griessel's burger and chips grew cold. Because his sense of duty made him call Nyathi – he knew he could not postpone it any longer.

He brought the colonel up to speed with the afternoon's events. The Giraffe clicked his tongue when he heard about Nadia Kleinbooi, and he said he would personally phone the commanding officers of the Stellenbosch and Bellville stations to ask them to keep the engravings on the cartridges quiet.

'I think they now have what they want, sir,' said Griessel. 'All we can do is to try and apprehend them if they attempt to leave the country through a major border post. If we can get a bulletin to Customs Admin. We have at least one possible passport we can track.'

'I'll do it myself, Benny.' A brief silence, and then a deep sigh. 'The question is, will they now kill Adair?'

'Yes, sir.' He knew they were thinking the same thing: if Adair's body was found somewhere in the Cape, there'd be hell to pay with the media. And if they started digging, and found out about the SSA's bullying tactics, and the Hawks' attempts to suppress evidence, everyone's name would be stinking mud, at home and abroad, all over again. And it always came out, because when there were slip-ups, there were always scapegoats and blame, to save other arses and reputations and careers.

'Thanks, Benny. I'll be here when you get back.'

They looked for a quiet corner in the lounge, on the modern sofas and chairs, and asked Lillian if she would like something to drink.

'Oh God, yes, a whisky, please.'

Cupido beckoned a waiter nearer, and ordered the drink for her, and coffee for them.

'We know you've been through a lot, Miss Alvarez,' Cupido said sympathetically, as he took his notebook and pen out of his inside pocket. 'We know what happened this morning at the Waterfront. We know you work for David Adair, at the university. And we know he has gone missing. But we would like you to tell us . . .'

'He's gone missing? I mean, I know something's not right, but I thought . . .'

She appeared agitated and looked to Cupido for an explanation.

'If we can hear your side of the story, we might be able to explain,' he said. 'Could you tell us, please?'

'You don't know where he is?'

'Not at this time. But perhaps you can help us find him. Please. Tell us what happened.'

'Well,' she said. 'I . . . Professor Adair called me on Monday morning, very early . . .'

'Ma'am, sorry, could you start with your . . . you work for him, is that right?'

'Yes. I'm his assistant.'

'Like a secretary?'

'No, no, I'm his research assistant. I'm doing my Masters Degree in Applied and Computational Analysis. I'm a research fellow at the Department of Applied Mathematics and Theoretical Physics, where Professor Adair teaches. He's my supervisor. But I also do research for him on some of his projects.'

Cupido noticed her leaning forward, focused and serious. And a little bit tense. And he thought, she keeps referring to the man as 'Professor Adair' in such a pointed way, every time the inflection just a little bit over-emphasised and forced. Or was that his imagination?

'You don't sound British at all,' said Bones.

'Oh, no, I'm from the United States.'

'Where in the US?'

'Kingsville in Texas. Small town, nobody's ever heard of it. It's near San Antonio.'

'I ran the Rock 'n' Roll Marathon in San Antonio,' said Bones. 'Pretty place. But the heat . . .'

'You know it?'

Cupido knew Bones was going to use the opportunity to bring up his studies again. He pre-empted him, 'If we can get back to Professor Adair?'

'Sure. Where were we?'

'How long have you worked for him?'

'Since the beginning of the Lent term.'

'When was that?'

'This past January.'

'And you see him every day?'

'Well, not every day. He is a very busy man. Maybe two or three times a week, at the department.'

'When did you last see him?'

'On the Thursday of the week before last.'

'Where?'

'At DAMTP.'

'On campus?'

'Well . . . yes, at his office.'

In his eleven years as a detective, Vaughn Cupido had questioned hundreds of people – first at the Mitchells Plain police station, later with the Organised Crime Task Force in Bellville South, and over the last few years with the Hawks. Thanks to this experience, and the many lectures and courses with the SAPS Forensic Psychology section, he had learned a great deal about the art of lying. He knew the ability to tell an untruth varied radically from person to person. Some did it so naturally, skilfully, and smoothly that you couldn't help but admire them, even after you had arrested them. Others telegraphed all the predictable signs of lying with an astounding clarity and awkwardness, but so totally oblivious to what they were doing, that they were still highly indignant if you confronted them about it. And then there were those who fell somewhere on the sliding scale between the two extremes. Lillian Alvarez was not an accomplished liar, but for an amateur she wasn't doing badly. It was not her eyes, her body language, or gestures that betrayed her, but the timing and tone of her words. That over-eagerness to be helpful, to please, that touch too much obvious sincerity: 'Look, see how honest I am.'

The way to handle people like this was to pretend you believed them, give them more rein, let them paint themselves into a corner.

'And he was . . . Did you notice anything different?'

'Not at all. He was his usual witty self. He can be very funny – he's always making mathematical puns . . .'

'I see,' said Cupido, as if he understood. 'And he didn't mention that he was going to travel?'

'No.'

'So, the next thing you hear from him, is the call yesterday morning?'

'No, Monday . . . Yes, yesterday! It seems longer . . . Well, I had an appointment with him last week, Tuesday, for a progress report, but he wasn't at the office, and nobody seemed to know where he was. But it's not all that unusual. Because of all the work he does for the financial industry, and the fight against terrorism, you know . . .'

'You mean his algorithm.'

'Exactly. Usually he'll send me a text or an email to cancel. But still, I didn't worry too much.'

The waiter brought the whisky and coffee. Bones reached for his wallet, but Cupido was faster. 'Keep the change,' he said.

When the man had gone, Cupido said, 'OK. And before his call yesterday morning, nobody contacted you about him?'

'No.'

'OK. Now, yesterday morning . . . You said it was very early. Can you remember the time?'

'It was around three o'clock in the morning. Maybe that's why it feels so long ago . . .'

'UK time?' Bones asked.

'Yes.'

'About five o'clock South African time?' said Bones.

'I suppose . . .'

'The call, was it from his own phone?' asked Cupido.

'How do you . . . ? Oh, you mean, did it show on my phone that it was him?'

'Yes.'

'That's a good . . . I can't remember. I don't think I looked. It was . . . He woke me up, so I was a bit sleepy.'

'Could you take a look now? On your phone?'

'Sure, I should have thought of that.' She opened her handbag and took out the phone. Her deft fingertips managed the screen with practised finesse, till she found what she was looking for.

'No,' she said in surprise. 'It's from a different number . . . And it was at seven minutes past three in the morning.'

'Could you read the number to me?'

She read out the number, which began with a +44. Cupido scribbled in his notebook.

'Do you recognise the number?'

'Not at all.'

'OK. So what did he say?'

'He apologised for the time of the call, and I said it's not a problem. Then he asked me if I could do him a big favour . . .'

'How did he sound?'

'Apologetic.'

'Not stressed?'

'No, I wouldn't say he was stressed out . . . He's very calm, always, so I . . . No, not stressed out.'

'OK. And then?'

'Well, I said of course I would do him a favour. And he said he's in a bit of a bind, it's very embarrassing, so it's a really big favour, and it's going to mean I have to travel halfway around the world, but he's asking me because I've said more than once that I would love to visit Africa, and if I don't feel comfortable, I should just say so, he would fully understand. So I said, wow, that sounds exciting, when did I have to go? And he said he's booked a flight for me . . . Well, you know, in that very polite British way, he actually said he really hopes I don't mind, but he's taken the liberty of booking a flight for me, and it leaves at seven thirty on Monday night, from Heathrow, for Cape Town in South Africa.'

43

Griessel was still eating, without enjoyment. Mbali pushed her empty plate away, wiped her fingers with the paper serviette, and said, 'Bones has found something interesting about David Adair.'

'Yes?'

'It might not . . . I'm trying to figure out what it means. Adair apparently belongs to a group of British scientists who are starting a protest group against government secrecy, and invasion of public privacy.'

Griessel raised his eyebrows, and Mbali continued, 'Bones and I thought it was strange too. Because Adair's algorithm does exactly that. It infringes on the privacy of anyone who uses banks.'

'They are *planning* to start a protest group?'

'Well, Bones says he only found one reference, and that is perhaps significant too. He says there was so much on the Internet about Adair and his protocol, and his algorithm, and his other academic work, that he almost missed it. He came across a small item in a weekly scientific newspaper, in the USA. It reported that a group of British scientists attended a conference on the Association . . . no, the . . . Project for Government Secrecy. It was held by an association or a federation of American scientists at the end of last year in St Louis. The leader of the British delegation was a political scientist, who told the newspaper that they were planning to start a similar project in the UK. And that they were very worried about their government's suppression of information, but also the hijacking of new technologies to infringe the privacy of citizens. The newspaper listed one of the British team members as a Professor D. P. Adair.'

Griessel tried to fit this information in with what they knew, but it would not make sense.

'I've been thinking, Benny, we know the UK ambassador has been talking to our minister of state security. And then MI6 and the SSA got involved very quickly, and we were taken off the case. So, now I wonder if this whole thing about Adair is maybe not about his banking software. I think it might be about government secrets. And with our government now passing legislation to be even more secretive . . . That's maybe why they are cooperating so enthusiastically with the British.'

Lillian Alvarez took a gulp of her whisky, and she said, 'That really woke me up, so I said, wow, that's a real surprise, it would be incredible, but don't I need a visa or something? And he said no, US citizens don't need a visa, and he will email me the ticket a little later. So, I asked him how long would I be staying, you know, I had to know what and how much to pack. But right then, he didn't answer me, he just said there's something else he needs me to do. So I said, sure, and he said, I should go to his office, and find a book. He told me where the book was on his shelf, and he told me where to look in the book, because there is a memory card, and I should take the card . . .'

'What kind of book?' asked Bones Boshigo.

'*On Numbers and Games*. It's the classic by John Horton Conway . . .' She saw that they didn't have the faintest idea what she was talking about. 'The famous British mathematician? He's one of David's – Professor Adair's – heroes, it's about game theory. The book, I mean. The memory card was stuck to the first page of the First Part, which is really the second part . . . Look, it's one of those mathematical inside jokes that he loves.'

'OK. So he said you must go fetch the card . . .'

'Yes. He asked me to go early, before anyone else arrived at the office. And that I shouldn't tell anybody about his call, or the memory card, he'll explain later, but it was about his security work, and discretion is the better part of valour. He apologised again, and thanked me, and said he would call again later that morning. And then he rang off.'

'Did he call you again?'

'Yes, at . . .' She suddenly remembered she could give the exact time, took out her phone again, and consulted the call register. 'At seven minutes past ten.'

'Yesterday morning?'

'Yes.'

'UK time?'

'Yes.'

'From the same number?'

'Yes.'

'OK, so after that first call, what happened?'

'I set the alarm for six o'clock, and tried to go to sleep again, which wasn't easy. I was pretty excited . . .'

'And not worried?'

'No, not at all. I mean, you know . . . I was getting this trip for free to a cool place, and it was helping this man I respect so very much with something very important and . . . well, interesting, you know? It was only later that I thought it was a little bit strange that he didn't say anything about where I was going to stay, or how long the trip would be . . . He's such an organised man, so very methodical . . .'

'And then you went to his office?'

'At seven sharp.'

'How did you get in?'

'I have a key.'

'And you found the book?'

'Yes.'

'And the memory card?'

'Yes. It was right where he said it would be.'

'Could you describe the card?'

'Well, you know, it was one of those SD cards, sixty-four gigabytes. Verbatim, blue and purple. Not the micro-SD. The regular size.'

'What was on the card?'

'I have no idea.'

'You didn't look?'

'No!'

'And what did you do with it?'

'I put it in my purse.'

'And you kept it there all the time?'

'Yes. Until this morning. The purse was in this bag . . .' She pointed at the handbag that lay between her thigh and the armrest of the chair. 'I thought it would be safe. I always keep the bag with me. Always. And then the asshole stole it this morning.'

He smiled at the word. 'Did anybody see you at Adair's office?'

'Not that I know of. Seven is early for the department.'

'And you went home?'

'Yes.'

'And he called again, just after ten?'

'Yes. But before that, I received an email with the electronic ticket for the flight.'

'From his usual email?'

'No, it was from a Morris guy, which was kind of strange, but then I asked him and he said, don't worry, it was just his security name.'

'Paul Morris Fifteen at Gmail?'

'Something like that. I can check . . .'

'No, that's fine. So you asked him this on the second call?'

'Yes.'

'How did he sound?'

'More together, I think.'

'What else did you talk about?'

'He said he would make a deposit for me, to pay for my accommodation in Cape Town, and asked me if I could do the hotel booking myself. And he said, if I wanted to, I could stay for the week, he'll deposit one thousand five hundred pounds into my account, which should cover a good hotel, and some spending money. Then he said my flight would arrive in Cape Town just before eight o'clock in the morning, and that when I got off the plane, I had to switch on my phone and check that it was working on the local networks, and send an email to the address from which the ticket was sent, the Gmail address. Just to say that I had arrived. He said this was very important, and that I should then take a cab to the V&A Waterfront directly, not go to the hotel first. And when I got to the Waterfront, I should put on something bright red, like a jacket or something, and find the amphitheatre, and he described it to me, he said there was a stage, and I should go and wait at the foot of the stairs leading up to the stage. And I shouldn't talk to anybody, just wait, a guy will come and meet me, and ask me for the memory card, and I should give it to him. But only if he specifically asks for the card. And then I could go to the hotel and have a nice little holiday.'

'And that's all?'

'No. I . . . I asked him . . . how I would know if it is the right guy, and he said I shouldn't worry, only a few people know I'm coming, so as long as the guy specifically asks for the card, I should give it to him. And then he again said, remember to test your phone, send the email, and go straight to the Waterfront, and wear something bright red. He thanked me again, and then he rang off.'

'Did he transfer the money for the hotel?'

'Yes.'

'From his usual account?' asked Cupido.

'Actually, no. It was from his security name. Morris. And a bank in Zurich.'

'I see,' said Cupido, and he knew he had her.

'Do you know which bank?' asked Bones.

'Well . . . I can check . . .'

'Perhaps later,' said Cupido. 'OK. So what did you do? After the last call?'

'I went shopping. For the trip. And then I took the Tube to Heathrow. And the flight was delayed. So I started worrying, will the guy still be there if I was late? But the delay was only twenty minutes, so I thought it would be OK. And when I arrived, I sent the email, and I changed two hundred pounds into rands in order to pay the cab, and then I took the cab, and I got to the Waterfront. And then I realised, I had to do something with my suitcase, I had no idea how far it was to this amphitheatre, and I didn't want to lug the suitcase with me. So I spoke to the cab driver, and he said he'll take it to the hotel for a hundred rand, which is like ten dollars, so I said OK. And after that, everything just went haywire.'

44

'Could you tell us exactly what happened at the Waterfront?' asked Cupido.

'It happened so fast,' she said, and shifted to the edge of her chair. 'I asked the cab driver where the amphitheatre was, and he didn't know, so there was this security guy, and I asked him, and he directed me. So I was walking, there were lots of people, which was a real surprise, so many white people, I mean, you know, you expect . . . No offence, but you know, when you come to Africa . . . Anyway, so I saw the amphitheatre, and I was almost there, when this asshole started bugging me about a hairpin, and I was in a hurry, I was a little worried, because there had been no contact from Professor Adair, and I was about half an hour late because of the flight delay, and getting off the plane, I wasn't thinking—'

'Did you expect the professor to contact you?' Cupido interrupted her deliberately. He could hear her anxiety from the quickening pace of her narrative, her rising tone. He thought this part was probably the truth, but she was providing unnecessary detail – he suspected that since yesterday she had been replaying the incident over and over in her mind, to try to make sense of it, to rationalise.

'No, no, I mean, yeah, I suppose, sort of. Here I was, having flown halfway around the world, I thought, maybe, if he got the email, he would call . . .'

'And he didn't contact you again?'

'No.'

'No email, nothing?'

'No.'

'Even after the Waterfront? This afternoon?'

'No.'

'But you are hoping he'll call?' Cupido pointed at her cellphone.

'Well, you know, I got worried, after what happened . . .' She flipped her hand palm upwards to emphasise that it was a natural response.

'OK. Please continue.'

'Right. So this guy is bugging me, and for a minute there, I thought he might be the guy, you know, for the card, and then he wasn't. And I was thinking: David said, don't talk to other people, it sort of . . . I think anybody, under the circumstances, would have felt . . . Look, I'm not stupid, but maybe I did get a little carried away with the whole clandestine thing, sort of cloak and dagger, you know, and I thought this guy might be, like, the enemy, a terrorist, you know? So I got a little panicky, and I tried to get rid of him, and the bastard stole my purse, and I didn't even know it. So, the thief walks off, and I start jogging, I'm late, I can see the amphitheatre, I'm looking for the steps to the stage, but I'm still ten yards away, and the next thing I know, there's this guy with a baseball cap and shades, and he's really in my face, he says, "Do you have the card?" I mean, I'm not even near the steps yet, it's right after the hairpin guy, I'm still a bit disoriented, I suppose, but he says, "Do you have the card?" and I'm sort of anxious, and I say, "But this is not where I'm supposed to give it to you." I was . . . You have to understand, I was on the plane all night, thinking about what Da— Professor Adair had said I should do, I was all geared up, and I was expecting a . . . I'm really not racist, my granddaddy on my father's side came from Mexico, so please, don't take this the wrong way, but it's just that I expected, you know, an English guy, a white guy—'

'Miss Alvarez,' Cupido interrupted her.

'Yes?'

'I want you to take a deep breath.'

She stared at him, not understanding. Then she took a deep breath, and said: 'I was going a little fast, wasn't I?'

'That's OK.'

'And you don't have to worry about expecting a white guy,' said Bones. 'We understand.'

'Thank you.' She sipped some more whisky, gave a small, self-conscious smile, and took another deep breath. 'It's just that, right then, it got really weird. I mean, this guy is all over me, he's in my face, and he has this strange accent, and when I say, "But this is not where I'm supposed to give you the card," the guy in the cap takes a gun from his pocket, with this black silencer, and he sticks it in my ribs, and there's this commotion behind us, people giving little yelps, and I want to look, and . . .'

She realised she was talking too fast and too anxiously again, and she reined herself in. 'Sorry,' she said, taking another gulp of whisky. When she did continue, she was more measured. '. . . And I was completely freaked out and scared. And he says, "That man stole something from you, do you have the card? Look. Now." And he looks over my shoulder at the commotion, and when I want to look, he jams the gun into my side again, and he says, "Look at me." So I froze, I just completely froze. He grabbed my arm and he shook me, and he asked for the card again, and I stuck my hand in my handbag, and the purse was gone, and I thought I was going to faint I was so scared, and he said, "Do you have it?" and I said, "My purse is gone," and then he said, "It was in the purse?" and I say, "Yes," and he says, "Are you sure?" and I was busy looking in my bag, and I nodded, and I started to cry like a damned baby, and then he ran, and the next thing I know I'm just standing there, amongst all these people, and nobody knew what had just happened . . .'

Tyrone lied.

He had got his story right on the train, thought through everything he must say, just to be on the safe side.

He walked into the Cape Calm B & B in De Waterkant, wearing his new jacket, with his new little suitcase. He looked legit, he had checked that in the mirror of the men's room at Cape Town Station. He had washed his face, combed his hair. OK, maybe he didn't smell like a rose garden, but he was a traveller, after all.

He said to the Cape Calm B & B aunty, a kindly lady, of the type with the exaggerated friendliness that comes from white guilt: 'Hi. My name is Jeremy Apollis,' in his best white English. 'I'd love to have a room for the night, OK, if I pay cash in advance?'

And Uncle Solly was right, the jacket was the ticket, and the cash in advance did not hurt, she came back *daatlik* with: 'Of course, of course, where you from?' He had that worked out too. 'Johannesburg, but I'm from here originally. I lived up in Schotsche Kloof.' He pronounced it 'Scots kloef', the way he heard English people say it.

She asked, 'Here on business?'

He'd anticipated this and wanted to contain the lie – too much detail is a dangerous thing – so he said, 'No, just came to spend some time with my sister. I'm flying back tomorrow night.'

He signed the register and he paid the six hundred and fifty rand and thought that the bed *and* the breakfast better be *blerrie lekker*, it's a lot of money. She took him to his room, and after she had left, he locked the door and put the case on the bed. Then he took out the gun and silencer, and the three cellphones. Put them on the bed, neatly in a row. He took off the jacket, hung it up in the wardrobe. Stood in front of the bed, looking at the cellphones. And he thought, he must concentrate. Use one at a time. And remember which one he was using. Where and when.

He got undressed, went into the bathroom and turned the shower on full, a blast of hot, soothing, beautiful water, and he stood like that for a very long time, so that it would wash away all the day's troubles, would soothe the pain across his back.

It didn't really work.

Griessel felt he should encourage Mbali. He wanted to tell her that at least one good thing had happened – she and Vaughn Cupido had found each other in some way, the antagonism between them was gone. He wanted to tell her that life and the world worked in cycles. Things would come right again, the wheel would turn. It always did.

He wanted to tell her the downturn of the wheel was more frequent than the up, but you had to ride it all the same.

But he didn't, because he thought, why on earth should she believe a middle-aged white drunkard from the apartheid era?

He had no credibility.

And he thought he should phone Radebe at O. R. Tambo Airport to hear if they had found anything more, because the more names they had, the easier it would be to arrest the Cobras at a border post. But he couldn't phone Ulinda, because the SSA were monitoring Radebe's cellphone too, and he thought: Fuck cellphones. *Jissis*, they managed without them for so many years, and they arrested just as many criminals. If not more. Using the old methodology. They investigated. Built dossiers bit by bit, with thorough footwork. They used their heads, thought and pondered and argued amongst each other, and debated, tested theories, outmanoeuvred suspects with clever tricks and snares in the interrogation rooms. They learned to spot a lie a mile off, just by watching and observing.

And now? Now technology had to do everything. And when it failed, then so many of the young detectives sat there saying, no, this case can't be solved.

He didn't like to be reachable everywhere, all the time. He didn't like trying to type a text on a tiny keyboard with his out-sized fingers. People sent messages for any shit that came into their heads, in a language that took you half an hour to decipher, and if you didn't answer, then they wanted to know why.

And the SSA could eavesdrop on you, track you, follow you, because the technology worked both ways – if you could catch a criminal, then someone else could find *you*.

He sighed, and tried to think of something else, but all that popped into his head, was his Alexa dilemma.

And it was not something that he could discuss with Mbali or anyone else, no matter how oppressive the silence was, here at the table.

When he saw Sister Abigail Malgas approaching, he felt relieved.

The nurse had Nadia's big book bag over her shoulder. 'The girl is in a ward now,' she said. 'The doctor said she will be able to talk to you. But only for a half an hour, and the child must give permission first.'

He didn't tell her that Nadia had no choice. They followed her, into the hospital. In the lift, Sister Malgas said, 'They still don't know what those people drugged her with, but it doesn't seem to be something serious.'

She made them wait outside the door to the ward, and disappeared behind the cream-coloured curtains that were drawn around the bed.

45

'So what did you do then?' asked Cupido.

'I tried to call Professor Adair, but he didn't answer. So I left a message, and I sent a text—'

'What was the message?'

'I just said . . . things didn't work out like I expected, I'm sorry . . .'

'Can I take a look at the text message?'

'I . . . uh, sorry, I've deleted it.'

'What did you do then?'

'I started walking. I mean, what could I do? I couldn't go to the police. This was about the professor's security work, he said I shouldn't talk to anybody, I mean, I couldn't just go to the police and say, look, this is . . . You know, I couldn't tell them everything, so what's the use of telling them anything?'

'You're telling us now.'

'Sure, but you guys know, right. About Professor Adair, and the pickpocket. I mean, this morning, I was . . . confused. And scared. And it all happened so fast, and the guy who wanted the card just ran off, and I did not have the card any more, and I thought, the professor will call, eventually, and I could tell him.'

'OK. Where did you go?'

'I walked to the hotel. This guy had stolen my purse, and all my cash. Thank God my bank cards were in my suitcase, with my passport. But I had no money for a cab, so I asked directions, and I walked to the hotel, and it rained a little, and I was damn cold, and my jacket was in my suitcase because I had to wear something red. And it was much further than I thought, I got very tired. And all the time I was so very worried that I had fucked the whole thing up, if you'll pardon my French.'

'Wasn't your fault,' said Bones.

'I know, right?'

'I just want to make sure, when you talk about "his security work", you mean the algorithm – for finding terrorists?' asked Cupido.

'That's right.'

'You said you work with him on some of his projects. The algorithm project too?'

'Oh, no, nobody worked with him on *that*.'

'How many research assistants work with him?'

'Four.'

'So why did he choose you?' asked Cupido.

'Excuse me?'

'Why did David Adair choose you to bring the card to Cape Town?'

'Because . . . I suppose he thought he could trust me? Or he knew I love travelling, and I wanted to come to Africa . . .'

'When he transferred money to your account, why did he not ask for your account details?'

'I . . . He . . . I didn't say that.'

'Did he ask for your details? During that second call, yesterday at ten. Did he ask for your account details to transfer the money?'

'Well, I . . . Yes, I think so.'

'But you specifically said it wasn't from his usual account. It was from a bank in Zurich.'

'Yes, but I . . .' she realised she had talked herself into a corner.

'Do you get paid for your work at the university?'

'Yes.'

'By David Adair?'

'No.'

'So how did you know it wasn't from his usual account?'

She didn't reply.

'You're not telling us the whole truth, are you?'

With fearful eyes, Nadia Kleinbooi looked from Griessel to Mbali, and back at him again.

They stood beside her bed, both on one side.

'You don't have to be scared,' said Mbali.

'We're here to help,' said Griessel.

'Do you know where my brother is?' She was pale and tired, her voice was hoarse.

'No. But we know that he brought you here.'

'Is he OK?'

'How do you feel?' asked Mbali.

'It hurts,' said Nadia, and touched her side.

'Is it OK if we ask you a few questions?'

'Yes. I don't . . . They injected me, in my arm. With something. I was very sleepy, so I can't remember everything that happened . . .'

'You can just tell us what you remember,' said Griessel.

'And if you get tired, just tell us.'

'OK.'

'We would love to hear everything. About the . . .' And then Griessel stopped, because a cellphone was ringing. He thought it was his, because it had the same ringtone, but he touched his pocket, and realised his iPhone was off.

'It's my phone,' said Nadia, and looked at her bag on the chair beside Griessel.

He bent, opened the bag, saw the light from the screen of the ringing phone. He took it out. 'Do you know this number?' he asked as he passed the phone to her.

'No.' She took the phone, answered it. 'Hello?'

She listened for a moment, then they saw her face brighten as she said, '*Boetie*! Are you OK?'

Tyrone had showered and changed into clean clothes. He pushed the pistol into the back of his belt, under the jacket. He put the stolen wallet, where the original memory card was still stored, in the inside pocket of his jacket. After that he took cellphones One and Two, put them in the side pockets, and walked to the Cape Quarter Lifestyle Village on Somerset Road.

He shouldn't have pondered everything that happened that morning, because that's what caused him to make the mistake. But he couldn't help it, it was so close to the Waterfront, and the Schotsche Kloof, and he recalled everything so vividly – how he had been shot, how he had run for his life, the dog that nearly bit him. He relived the fear, and that moment at Bellville Station, when he realised they had drugged his sister. And the heart-wrenching moment when they shot her. It all made him so angry, a fierce anger coiled in his brain, the thirst for revenge overpowering everything.

His mind was still full of it when he switched on the cellphone at the entrance to the Food Spar and phoned Nadia's number.

Nadia's number? What was he thinking, he thought later, get a grip you fool, because he'd actually meant to phone the hospital's number and ask for Sister Abigail, but his head was filled with vengeance, and he was tired, finished, done in, *klaar*. A *kwaai* crazy day, big lapse of concentration. The phone rang and rang, and suddenly his sister answered, startling him. His heart thumped and he wondered, was she alone?

'I'm fine, *sussie*. Are you OK?'

'Where are you? Why aren't you here?'

'*Sussie*, are you OK? What do the doctors say?'

'They say I was lucky. Two broken ribs, and I bled a bit . . .'

'What did those bastards give you?'

'I don't know. Something that made me very *dof*. I got so sleepy. They injected me in my arm . . . Where are you, *boetie*?' He heard fear in her voice.

'I am busy sorting things out. I'll come and get you, as soon as I'm done.'

'What things? Done with what? Didn't you give them what they wanted? I can't remember that well, *boetie* . . . The *polieste* are here now. You must come and talk.'

He had thought as much, that's why he had phoned from here. Thought he was smart and clever and alert. He must finish this call, but he didn't want to leave her like this. 'Don't you worry, *versta' jy*? Everything is going to be all right. You must just get better now. Just tell me, how many of those *ouens* were there that kidnapped you?'

'What things must you sort out, Tyrone?'

She only said Tyrone when she was angry. It was a good sign, that she could be angry at him. 'Don't worry. How many were there?'

'I think four. But you can't say I mustn't worry. What card were they looking for? How did you get mixed up with such people, Tyrone?'

'I will explain everything, *sussie*. I just tried to help someone, then there was this massive misunderstanding . . .' He stopped talking, it wasn't the time for explanation, he didn't even know what she knew.

The cops were sitting there, maybe listening. He must finish up. 'Just get better. Do you need anything?'

'What I need is to know what you mean by "As soon as I'm done".' And he could hear, there wasn't too much wrong with her, she would be OK after all.

Then he made his second mistake, out of sheer relief, and because the anger and revenge still clung to every fibre of his being: 'Nobody touches my sister. I've got something they want. Now I'm a player. And they're going to pay.' It just came out, and he was immediately sorry that he'd said it.

'No! *Boetie*, no! Those are *annerlike* people. Let the *polieste* deal with it.'

'Keep that phone with you. I have to go. And remember one thing: I love you very much.'

He pressed the button to kill the call before he could hear her reaction, then he switched the phone off completely. 'Shit,' he said out loud. He began walking immediately, purposefully, out of the shopping centre.

Fifty metres on, he said quietly to himself: '*Jirre*, Tyrone, you didn't handle that well. Get a grip.'

46

Lillian Alvarez wept.

Bones sat and glared at Cupido.

Cupido knew that his colleague clearly did not understand the very first defence mechanism of a woman caught out in a lie. 'I know you're trying to protect him,' he said with great compassion. 'But if you want us to find him, you will have to tell us the truth.'

Bones stood up, took a snow-white handkerchief out of his pocket, and held it out to her.

'There really isn't anything to tell.' She took the handkerchief, dabbed beneath her eyes, then at her nose, and looked at Cupido, pleading.

Bones sat down again.

'It's not like we're going to call the university and tell them the good professor was having an affair with his beautiful young student.'

She stared at the carpet.

'Maybe that's not the case, Vaughn,' said Bones.

'Maybe,' said Cupido, but the word was loaded with irony.

'I know what you're doing,' said Lillian Alvarez.

'We're trying to save your lover.'

'I watch TV. You're playing good cop, bad . . . Save him? What do you mean, save him?'

'David Adair was kidnapped, Miss Alvarez. By the people who wanted to get their hands on that memory card. So the sooner you start telling us everything, the sooner we can try and save him.'

Her mouth was half open, her tearful eyes expressed shock and reproach. She fought against emotions, and eventually she said, 'I knew it.'

Then she began weeping again.

'My brother,' said Nadia Kleinbooi to Griessel, distress in her voice.

'He's mixed up in something ugly.' She pressed call-back on the number that Tyrone had phoned her from, but a recorded message said: 'The subscriber you have dialled is not available. Please try again later.'

'What do you mean?' asked Griessel.

'Tyrone said they are going to pay, because he has something they want. And he wanted to know how many they were. Those people are going to kill him.'

'Your brother has something they want? A card?'

'Yes. He says he's a player now.'

'A player?' asked Mbali.

'Whatever that means,' said Nadia. 'I don't like it.'

'The people who are looking for the card are the same ones who kidnapped you?'

'Yes.'

'He still has something that they want?'

She nodded anxiously.

'Do you know what it is?' asked Griessel.

'I thought . . . I don't know. It must be the card. But I thought . . . I was very confused . . .'

'What kind of card? A credit card, a bank card?'

'The one Frenchman, he phoned Tyrone after they grabbed me. And he said Tyrone had stolen a wallet, and there was a memory card in the wallet, and he would exchange the card for me . . .'

'A memory card? What memory card?'

'I don't know.'

'But . . . Hang on . . .' Griessel struggled to understand the new angle. 'We thought that was what happened at Bellville Station. Tyrone gave them something, and he got you back.'

'I was very confused. I also thought . . .'

'Nadia, this is very important: What can you remember from the station?'

She closed her eyes, shook her head. 'I don't know . . . The guy held me so tight, we first went to a man in a blue jacket. He handed over something. I couldn't see exactly, something small . . .'

'Wait, slowly. What guy held you?'

Nadia opened her eyes. 'I'm not even sure that things really happened this way.'

'Just tell us exactly what *you think* happened,' said Mbali.

'OK,' she said, with conviction.

'When did you start having an affair with Adair?' asked Cupido.

Lillian Alvarez looked towards the entrance of the hotel, wiped away tears, and blew her nose. She kept looking out ahead of her as though they weren't there.

'Bones, if she doesn't want to save him, perhaps we should just abandon the search. He's not a South African citizen. Let the British Consulate look for him.'

Bones realised what he was doing. 'But they don't have the resources, Vaughn. And his life is in real danger,' he said.

Cupido stood up. 'If she doesn't care, why should we?'

Bones hesitated before he got up. 'Good day, Miss Alvarez,' he said.

'Happy holiday,' said Cupido, and began walking towards the door, and Bones followed suit.

'Wait,' said Lillian Alvarez, before they had taken four paces.

Nadia Kleinbooi told them everything, as she remembered it. They had shoved her down in the Nissan X-Trail, two of them. Frenchmen, she thought. That was the language they spoke to each other. One was white and blond. He looked like a surfer. The other one was bald. Also white. Of the driver, she could only see the back of a head in a cap. The blond one phoned Tyrone and right after that one of them injected her in the arm with something. Then she became very drowsy, and everything was as vague as a dream.

She could remember driving down Durban Road later, the effect of the drug was not so strong then. But then there was another man in the car. Left front. Coloured she thought.

Four, then?

Yes, four.

One was on the phone all the time. He talked about the card. They stopped. Blondie made her get out. Her knees buckled. He swore at her and dragged her with him. To the station, she could remember the stalls, the colours of the stalls. Then they stopped for a while. It was like she was slowly waking up. Then they walked up to a scruffy man in a blue jacket, a workman's jacket, 'with a zip'.

She wasn't sure if the man in the blue jacket had handed over the card. He did give Blondie something. She had to hold a laptop. But then Blondie said she must walk until she saw Tyrone. She walked a long way, it felt very long, then Tyrone was there with her. Then she got very confused. There was a black man who said she was drunk. She wanted to protest, but the words wouldn't come out, it frustrated her so much. She remembered the other coloured one who shot her. It was the other man, who hadn't been in Stellenbosch in the Nissan.

Perhaps, she said, he shot her because Tyrone hadn't given him the card. But that was all she could remember. Except for Tyrone's arms around her in a lorry, on the way to hospital.

'Your brother definitely said he has something they want?' asked Griessel.

'Yes.'

'And that they are going to pay?'

'Yes.'

'Nadia, if you show me the number, we can see if we can trace him.'

She held the phone against her breast. She asked, 'Do you know who these people are?'

'We think so.'

'Do you know how Tyrone got mixed up in this?'

'What does your brother do for a living?' Mbali asked before Griessel could say anything.

'He's a painter. A house painter. He works so hard . . .'

'We think he got into this by accident,' said Mbali. 'That is why we want to help him.'

Griessel knew why Mbali told this white lie. To upset Nadia now with the truth about her brother the pickpocket might cost them her cooperation.

'Yes, that's what I thought. He's a very gentle person. They will kill him.'

'We can help him. If you just show me the number.'

'But he turned the phone off.'

'If we have the number, we can find out where he phoned from.'

'He lives in Schotsche Kloof. I can give you his address.'

'He's not there any more. We went to look.'

She thought for a moment, then nodded and held out the phone to him.

Cupido and Bones sat down again.

The lovely Lillian Alvarez put her feet on the stool and pulled her knees up under her chin. She wrapped her arms around her legs, as if she was embracing herself, and didn't look at them. She said something, but so quietly that they could not hear.

'I'm sorry, but we can't hear you.'

'We didn't have an affair.'

They said nothing.

'An affair is when one person is married. An affair is something . . . fleeting. It's not like that.'

'What is it like?' asked Cupido.

'You will do a lot of damage,' she said.

'We don't need to tell anybody,' said Bones, and he shot a pleading look at Cupido.

'That's right,' said Cupido. 'All we want to do is to find him.' He got up, shifted his chair closer to her, and sat down again. Bones followed his example.

She waited until they were settled, looked from one to the other. 'Do you promise?'

'Yes,' they said almost in unison.

47

Lillian Alvarez did not start talking again immediately. She sat there as though gathering her strength. And when she told the story, the subtle signs of lying were gone for the first time.

She said the last thing she expected was a love affair with her supervisor. She was so grateful and happy when she was accepted by DAMTP for her Masters degree, she looked forward to Britain, to the whole English experience. She wasn't well travelled. Not then. No one in her family was well travelled. Her father had been to Washington, DC. She did graduate studies at the University of California, Los Angeles campus. She had been to Vegas and San Francisco with her student friends, but no one in her middle-class family had even been in New York or Chicago. Never. Not to mention crossing the Atlantic Ocean.

And then she was accepted at Cambridge. Cambridge! One of the best universities on the planet. Another country, another culture, with a history that stretched back thousands of years. The world of the Beatles and Princess Di and the Queen and Prince William and Kate. On the edge of the European continent, with the opportunity of weekends in Paris or Milan or Madrid.

Cupido began to listen. He knew the art of being father confessor. As people started spilling all, you had to shut up, and let them talk, let them free themselves. Sometimes they needed to take long detours.

The university was everything she had dreamed of. The first time she saw King's College Chapel – nearly six hundred years old – it had taken her breath away. To study mathematics at the same institution that produced Newton and Lord Kelvin and Lord Rayleigh. And Charles Babbage, the father of computers . . .

And then, as she knew she could not put it off any longer: 'A week after I arrived, I walked into David Adair's office and I fell in love. Just like that,' with a soft snap of her thumb and middle finger. There was still a sense of amazement to how she said it. It was such a shocking joy, that moment. It was a first. She had waited so long to fall head over heels in love that she had begun to suspect it would never happen to her. She had had relationships before – a school romance, and two friendships of more than a year each at UCLA. She loved them, for sure, but was never intensely in love. And then she said pensively, and without any arrogance, that perhaps it was because neither of them was her intellectual equal.

And then David Adair happened.

She only realised much later that he was actually twenty-five years older than she was. He could have been her father (said with the easy irony and self-mockery of someone who had verbalised it before). But it was never relevant, because their souls were equally old. She said that twice.

They couldn't stop talking. About mathematics, about the world, about life. About people and their ways. About food. Did they know he was a foodie? He was a good cook too, at weekends he prepared them the most delicious meals, just the two of them, Chopin on the hi-fi, the Sunday papers, a good bottle of French wine, and David busy over the cooking pots.

But that was later. She guarded her love for him closely. Thought it was one-sided. It took him nearly two months to confess that he had 'feelings' for her.

She relived it all with a strong voice, with the self-confidence that it was good and right, clearly also trying to portray him as a true gentleman: he had asked her to drive with him, please. He took her to a restaurant in Huntingdon, he didn't want to do this in his office where the power balance of lecturer and student reigned. He bought her lunch. They finished eating. His face grew suddenly serious. He said he had thought over the matter for a long time, but he could no longer remain silent. He had feelings for her. She wanted to respond in jubilation, she said his name, and he stopped her with a hand on hers. He said, please, let him finish. He was sincerely sorry. He would absolutely understand if she wanted to change supervisor. He would help her to make the change, he would take responsibility, he would explain that his schedule had become too full. There would be no embarrassment for her. But his feelings were so strong that sooner or later he was going to do something stupid. That was why he was telling her now, before he humiliated himself and put her in an impossible situation.

'And when he was done, I said, "David, I love you very much".'

While Mbali tried to get the best possible descriptions of the four 'Frenchmen' out of Nadia Kleinbooi, Griessel walked out into the hospital corridor and phoned the colonel. He explained what had happened. That there was a chance that the Cobras were still in the Cape, and that they still hadn't got what they were looking for. And that David Adair might still be alive.

Nyathi was businesslike, and Griessel wondered if someone was there with him. 'Let's meet as soon as you're back, Benny.'

'Yes, sir.'

He stood in the corridor and tried to process that odd feeling – half an hour ago he was resigned to the fact that the Cobras were going to get away. Now there was a chance.

Tyrone Kleinbooi had bought them time. How much, he didn't know.

And the chances were slim. To track someone down quickly in this city, someone with false passports, who took professional precautions, who did not want to be found, was well-nigh impossible.

But there was another possibility. The chances were marginally better.

It depended on what Nadia could remember.

He took a deep breath and walked back into the ward to go and ask his questions.

Cupido thought she was a *kwaai* smart girl, so pretty, but emotionally so immature. Still he said nothing, let her tell the whole story. Alvarez said she and David Adair agreed to keep their affair secret until she attained her degree. Because, although they were both adults, morally unencumbered and not involved with third parties, a relationship between a middle-aged lecturer and a much younger student remained a serious and thorny problem in the corridors of academia. In addition, he was the DAMTP study leader who could best support her with her specific thesis. The most logical alternative was a transfer to another university, but neither of them wanted that. He insisted on the appointment of a fourth external examiner for her degree, and got one from the Massachusetts Institute of Technology. So that no fingers could be pointed when she graduated in a year and a half, and their relationship became public.

And then there were serious problems from what she described as 'his position': on the one hand, his work with highly secret anti-terrorism algorithms, and on the other hand, his protests against the British and European authorities and the banking industry. The 'position' meant that for security reasons he was watched like a hawk, but also that different factions would very much like to shut him up, muzzle and control him, should they get the right sort of ammunition.

'What factions?' Bones interrupted her for the first time.

She answered quickly. Her haste, the tone of her voice betrayed something again. 'Well, politicians, to start with. He had been fairly vocal in his opposition of privacy intrusion, and had been publicly criticising the government for not going far enough in fighting organised crime, for instance. Then there's organised crime itself. You should see the threats he received . . .'

'What threats?' asked Cupido.

'Death threats.'

'From whom?'

'They didn't exactly sign their names, but he knew it was from people in organised crime. He just laughed it off as scare tactics, and posturing. He said they would not dare, because if they killed him, the government would be forced to act. So it wasn't in the Mafia's interest to carry it out.'

'Anybody else? The factions, I mean.'

'Just every terrorist organisation in the world, of course . . . You know . . . You can imagine, I'm sure. Anyway, a lot of factions, so we had to be very careful with our relationship.'

'I don't think you're telling us everything,' said Cupido.

'I swear I'm telling you everything.'

He let it go for now.

'So you had to be very secretive in your relationship.'

'Very.'

'How did you know which bank he usually used?'

'David would transfer money for a plane or train ticket to Brussels or Paris or Zurich, for me to spend a weekend with him.'

'OK, getting back to the past week, could you now tell us the whole truth?'

'There really isn't all that much to say that will make a difference. I lied about last seeing him at the department Thursday a week ago. We actually spent that following Sunday in Ipswich, and much of the Monday night in my apartment. David left just after twelve o'clock that night . . .'

'Where did he go?'

'To his place. That's why I was so surprised when I went to see him at the office the next morning – we had an official appointment – and he wasn't there. I mean, he always told me if he had to travel. But he did mention that it might happen, you know, with all his responsibilities, that he might be called away at short notice. So I wasn't really worried then. But when there was no contact for four days . . . We've never been apart for that long . . .'

'But you had no idea where he was?'

'No.'

'And the call on Monday morning?'

'OK, that wasn't the first call. David called me last Friday night, at about eleven. It was a very short, hurried call. He just said he was fine, he had to rush off on security business, and he might be away for a while. And he said I mustn't tell anybody that he had called.'

'That's it?'

'He did say he loved me. That's it.'

'And the Monday morning call, the early one?'

'It happened almost like I told you. I did ask him where he was, and said that I had been worried, and he replied that he understood, but it's his anti-terror work, he can't talk about it, and everything is fine. But he said that he needed my help. And then he told me about coming to Cape Town.'

'Nothing else?'

'Before he rang off, I told him that I loved him. And he said he loved me too. But . . .' She shook her head slightly, as if she was unsure.

'But?'

'I don't know. He said he loved me, but there was something . . . As if he was the tiniest bit embarrassed. As if . . . I don't know, as if someone was listening?'

'Maybe you're right. And the second call?'

'I asked him where he was staying, because usually he booked us into a hotel, you know, in Paris . . . And he said he has official accommodation. So I asked when I would see him, here in Cape Town. And he said perhaps on Tuesday, if he could conclude his work. Oh, and when I was on the plane, I . . . I know I shouldn't have, but I thought nobody would know, and I was just so damn curious. I mean, I . . . Look, if you're really into what I'm studying, the Adair Algorithm is like the Holy Grail. It's bleeding edge, and it must be brilliant, because David is just so . . . Anyway, I thought, maybe if I can just look at the code, what harm could there be? So I popped the memory card into my Air. And there was a ZIP file. Password protected. So I took it out again. I really don't know what's on the card.'

'Anything else?'

'That's about it, really.'

'You didn't think it was a little strange that he wasn't going to be able to see you in Cape Town?'

'Of course I did. But this was the first time that David had involved me in his other work. I thought, maybe that's just how it was . . . How he was, when he was busy with the security stuff.'

'Who kidnapped him?' asked Cupido.

'I don't know,' she said, too vehemently.

'I think you suspect a specific . . . faction.' Cupido put the last word in quotation marks with his fingers.

'No, I don't—'

'Yes, you do.'

'No.'

'This is life and death, Miss Alvarez,' said Bones. They could see her internal struggle. Her fists were balled, her lovely mouth pinched, her eyes darted.

'The life and death of the man you love,' said Cupido.

'I . . . can't tell you.'

'Even if it means David Adair gets killed?'

'Oh God . . .'

'We're on your side, Miss Alvarez. We are the good guys.'

'I'm really not sure I can share this with you. It's ... very, very delicate.'

'Do you think this *delicate* group is behind his kidnapping?'

'I ... maybe.'

'Do you want to save him?'

'Of course,' she said emphatically. 'But he trusted me with some very secret information, and I ... I just don't know ... I mean, this is the sort of thing that could ... It has very big implications. Internationally.'

'Do you want to save him?' asked Cupido, slow and measured.

She began to cry. 'I don't know what to do.'

'Just do what you think is right,' said Bones.

'Oh God ...' Her head drooped so that the thick black hair hid her face.

Cupido knew there was nothing he could do. They would just have to wait.

She lifted her head. Her eyes were still filled with tears.

48

Tyrone bought a packet of Panados, two chicken-mayo sandwiches, and a half-litre of Coke at the BP service station's Pick n Pay Express on the other side of Somerset Road. Then he walked in the strong, chilly northwester, to the front of the Rockwell All Suite Hotel. He sat down on the low wall between the hotel and the service station, beside the big green recycling bin, where the wall of a storeroom provided shelter from the wind.

The pistol pressed against the small of his back and he had to shift it so it didn't chafe him. He liked the feel of the gun there. Very *empowering*, he thought, and he grinned in the half-dark.

Pickpocket with a pistol. Uncle Solly would turn in his grave.

He swallowed two Panados with a mouthful of Coke. The wound across his shoulders throbbed with a dull, growing pain.

From here he could see the entrance to the Cape Quarter Lifestyle Village. So he could see how long it was going to take before the cops arrived.

He ate and drank. And he thought.

How was he going to get the money? Conclude the transaction without getting shot in the head.

The easy way would have been an electronic transaction, but Uncle Solly taught him long ago: *Stay away from banks, Ty. They have tentacles that pull you in, you don't want to leave tracks, you don't want to be connected with a paper trail if a fence is prosecuted, you don't want the tax man to come asking questions. Cash is King.*

There would be a lot of questions if a coloured *outjie*, formerly of Mitchells Plain, suddenly got two point four million in his bank account.

The exchange would have to be manual. Hard cash, the hard way. But how? He couldn't involve anyone else, because these guys were bent on murder. Look what they did at Bellville Station, even after he gave them the card. And how stupid was that? If he had been lying dead now, all they would have would be a card full of Cape tourist pics.

'Cause they underestimated him, thought he was just a local yokel, too stupid to be a player. Surprise, surprise, motherfucker, *ma' nou weet hulle.* They wouldn't make the same mistake twice.

But the fact remained: he would have to be extremely clever if he was going to get out the other end alive. He had made one big mistake himself. He thought the guy with the eyes was a lone operator. Now he knew there might be four of them.

Four. Against one.

Bad odds.

He would have to be smart.

He thought for an hour, while the wind blew stronger, and fatigue crept up on him again. Slowly he began to formulate a plan. Until the wind became too cold and miserable, and he knew the cops were not too fast when it came to cellular tracking. He stood up, walked west on Somerset, to the corner of Ebenezer. He walked into the Victoria Junction Hotel, past reception as if he belonged there, into the bar and lounge.

He enjoyed the warm interior for a moment. There were only a few guests – three businessmen at the bar, a group of four men and women in a square of couches and chairs in the middle of the big room.

He sat down at one of the small tables against the wall, where he knew no one could hear him. He took out Cellphone Number Two.

A waiter approached, brisk and friendly. Tyrone shook his head to show he didn't want anything.

He watched until the waiter was far enough away, then he turned the phone on and waited for a signal.

He called his old cellphone number.

The guy answered a little faster this time.

'Yes.'

'Hello, motherfucker, how are you?' asked Tyrone.

'I am good, because I have a future. But not you.'

'Do you want the original card?'

'Yes.'

'Do you have the money?'

'Not yet.'

'When will you have it?'

'Tomorrow morning. Maybe nine o'clock.'

'OK, motherfucker, here is what you are going to do: tomorrow morning you are going to stack that money on a table, and you are going to take a photograph. And then you are going to take a bag, and put the money in the bag. Then you take another photograph, of the bag with the money in it. And then you are going to get your buddy to take a photograph of you and the bag. Full length, so I can see exactly what you look like and what you are wearing. Do you understand?'

'Yes.'

'Then you are going to MMS me those photographs to this number. And when I receive them, I will call you with instructions.'

'You will not call on this number again. We will break this phone now.'

'No.'

'Yes. I will not negotiate on that.'

'So how do I contact you tomorrow?'

'On the number we send the photos from.'

Tyrone thought. That should be all right.

'OK.'

'We know your sister is in hospital,' said the guy.

'If you go near my sister again, I will destroy the card,' he said, but he had to concentrate to keep the panic out of his voice.

'We know which hospital. If you don't deliver the card, or if there is something wrong with the card, we will go in there and kill her.'

'The police are protecting her.'

The guy laughed quietly. 'You think so? You think they will stop us?'

Tyrone's hand began to shake.

Then the guy said, 'I will send you the photos tomorrow morning,' and he rang off.

They sat in the Hawks' clubroom, the legendary, hidden bar room where only members of the unit were allowed in: Nyathi, Griessel, Mbali, Cupido, and Bones Boshigo. The only door was locked.

Griessel did not come in here often, but sometimes on a Friday afternoon he stood with the guys outside at the braai. Now he thought,

it could be the first line of a joke: 'An alky is locked inside a police
bar . . .'

He realised everyone was waiting for him to say something. 'Vaughn,
do you want to report first?' He saw his colleague was burning to
share something with them.

'The CIA, pappie,' said Cupido. 'Lillian Alvarez says it is the CIA
who abducted Adair.'

After the stunned silence, Zola Nyathi asked, 'And she knows that
how?' Very sceptical.

'It's a long story, Colonel.' Cupido gave them the main points of
Alvarez's experiences over the past week. 'But I'll let Bones tell you
about the bank stuff.'

'It seems,' said Bones, 'that the good professor unleashed a new
version of his algorithm about six weeks ago, *nè*. New, improved,
expanded. All in the name of hunting terrorists. Now, the way this
algorithm works, is to use SWIFT data to track the source of the
money – the country, the bank, and the account – and unique transaction patterns, because terrorists receive and withdraw and use money
in a very specific way, aimed at avoiding attention. So the algorithm
generates patterns, and Adair's data-mining software then identifies
possible suspects, and looks at the names and nationalities of all the
account holders and money movers, and spits out the most likely
suspects to the intelligence people, who follow it up. But the terrorists
are not complete idiots. They know about the algorithm, and they
have started to change their financial behaviour and the paths through
which the money flows. That's why Adair wrote the new software: to
adapt to the new behaviour. And apparently he is the first one who
gets the results every day, 'cause he has to study them to see if the
whole system is working properly, *nè?*'

The last '*nè*' was a question, and everyone nodded. They were still
following.

'So what happened was, Adair started to identify a new category of
suspects that had the right financial profile – or the wrong one,
depending on your side of the fence – but did not fit in with any of the
software's parameters for nationality, origins of names, and other stuff
that would indicate terrorists. So he started digging, without telling
anybody, because he was very worried that the software was screwed

up. And then he realised that this new group of suspects were probably spies. Clandestine operatives, working for intelligence agencies. Alvarez says what gave him the big clue was the fact that if you tracked the money all the way to the original source, a hell of a lot of it came from very obscure Chinese and Russian accounts. The kind of stuff governments bury deep in red tape and dummy corporations and funny names. And there were as many payments going the other way – coming from the Americans and the British, going to people and little companies in the Middle East, Russia and China—'

Cupido could not keep it in any longer. 'So basically he was building a list of all the undercover spies and sleepers and even double agents of the world's major intelligence agencies. And he was the only one who knew, the only one with all this data.'

'Why did he tell Alvarez?' asked Nyathi. 'She's a student, isn't she?'

'Long story, Colonel. Let's just say they are having a red-hot affair, and he was very troubled by this spy thing, and she kept asking him what was wrong, why was he so glum, had she done something to upset him, nagging all the time, until he told her. Poor guy must have wanted to share it with someone, all that pressure . . .'

'How did the CIA find out?'

'That's the thing. About three weeks ago, Adair got very crafty. He went to MI6, and told them what he had. They wanted it all, of course, but he said he'll horse trade. If the British and American governments agreed to take on the banks about their money laundering, to make a real effort to use all the financial data to cripple organised crime, he'd release the spy data to them. But it had to be done with legislation, and real results. And he had some demands about public privacy too, and the limits of government snooping. MI6 was furious, and threatened him with all sorts of legal action, but he didn't budge, *nè*. Then they blocked his access to the SWIFT system and his software, brought in their own people, and tried to find the data themselves. But it turns out Adair suspected they might do just that. So before he went to MI6, he deleted his new software, and loaded the old version again. The spy data was just gone.'

'That's what's on the memory card,' said Griessel.

'Exactly,' said Cupido. 'The girl says she doesn't think MI6 would kidnap their own citizen. If it all goes wrong, they want deniability.

Clean hands. But she says of course MI6 is very good friends with the CIA. And the CIA has no scruples, everyone knows about Guantánamo Bay and drone attacks and all that monkey business. So, if the CIA kidnapped Adair, everything is sweet.'

Mbali shook her head in revulsion.

'It will explain why our very own SSA is so keen to get hold of Adair,' said Bones.

'That's right, pappie,' said Cupido. 'Just think how they could play puppet master with all those spies' names. Talk about horse trading . . .'

Zola Nyathi clasped his hands together, slowly and formally. Griessel knew it was not a good sign.

'I think the girl is wrong,' said the Giraffe. 'Or she's lying.'

They waited for him to explain. Nyathi looked down at his hands. 'When Benny and I spoke to Emma Graber, the woman from MI6 at the British Consulate, the overwhelming impression was that they did not know that Adair was kidnapped, let alone by whom. If it was the CIA and they knew about it, they would not even have bothered to involve us, or the State Security Agency. They would have responded very differently to our passport enquiries.'

They digested the logic in quiet disappointment. Cupido said hopefully, 'So maybe it's the Russians. Or the Chinese . . .'

Nyathi shook his head. 'Sadly, I don't think so. Unfortunately you're not the only members of this unit that have had a busy afternoon. But my news is bad, and perhaps less . . . shall we say, about international intrigue. I have to tell you, if we decide to continue to pursue our investigation . . .' and the colonel looked straight at Mbali '. . . it will lead to further disappointment in our government, and it will be a considerably higher risk to our careers. And it will probably lead nowhere else but into deep trouble, because we have nothing to go on. So I'd like to give you all the opportunity to walk away, right now. I will understand, absolutely and completely.'

49

The northwester was up to gale force when Tyrone walked up Somerset Street, and then south, up the hill along Dixon and Loader. He wanted to shelter in the warmth of the guesthouse, take his tired body to bed and sleep, because tomorrow he must have his mind clear and sharp.

But there were still two things he had to do. Of the one, the last call that he had to make, he didn't want to think now. He was focusing on the other task, getting that last bit of insurance in place.

He walked to the top of the rise, where Strand Street ran around the belly of Signal Hill. There was no shelter from the wind here, it screamed in his ears, it shoved and plucked at his body. He waited for a gap in the traffic, and jogged across the street. Then, on the other side, he ducked into the bushes.

When he was sure that no one could see him, he took the pistol out. In the faint glow of the city lights he worked the safety catch clumsily, aimed at a tree's broad trunk about eight metres away, and pulled the trigger.

The pistol made a muffled retort, and bucked in his hand.

He walked to the tree.

Missed completely.

Jirre.

He hoped it was just the strong wind.

In the Hawks' bar, no one moved.

'Are you sure?' asked Zola Nyathi.

They nodded, one by one.

'OK,' said the colonel. 'Let me tell you about my afternoon. The brigadier and I had a telephone conference with both the National and the DPCI commissioners. We were asked if we had terminated our investigation. Several times. The brigadier told what he thought was the truth. I lied. Several times. I am ashamed of that, because Musad Manie is a good man, and he trusts me. I'm not sure the commissioners believed us. Then they asked us if we had destroyed any evidence, because there is a strong indication that we did. Both the brigadier and I told them what we thought was the truth. I am not going to ask you about that again, but if they can disprove it, our careers are over, and we will drag down the brigadier as well. But be that as it may, the point is that both commissioners were clearly under extreme pressure from above. And we all know what that means. About forty minutes later, the brigadier had a call from the acting head of Crime Intelligence. The general told him that CI is sending in a team to, and I quote, "oversee the conclusion of our investigation, and to inspect our systems for compliance". They are flying in from Pretoria tonight. I'm expecting them any time now.'

'*Hhayi*,' said Mbali under her breath.

'Yes, Mbali,' said Nyathi in sympathy.

Vaughn Cupido hissed through his teeth, a fricative that sounded very much like the suppression of a swearword.

'Then it's probably not about spies and the CIA,' said Bones.

'No, it's probably not,' said Nyathi.

Mbali was correct, thought Griessel, when she said in the hospital that this was about South African government secrets. But as Criminal Intelligence was involved that high up, most probably it meant very specific secrets. Because it was common knowledge that the head of that unit frequently received calls from the highest office in the land.

'I must tell you,' said Nyathi, still sombre and deliberate, 'that I had no choice. After the calls, I told the brigadier everything. I offered him my resignation. He did not accept. He did, however, demand an apology for the fact that I did not trust him to support us. He then asked me what I was going to do. I told him that I was going to have a meeting with you all and tell you the truth. And the truth is that, as noble as the cause may be, we have nothing. We are being investigated, watched, listened to. We have no room to manoeuvre. We are not going to discover what is on that memory card, and we are not going to save David Adair. So you have to ask yourself: why do you want to endanger your lives and your careers by chasing quixotic windmills?'

Nobody moved. The atmosphere was heavy, heads were hung low. Everyone's except Griessel's.

Tyrone fetched the third cellphone from the guesthouse.

This time he walked towards the city. Despite the wind that propelled him with an invisible hand, and the cold that penetrated his jacket, he concentrated on the call he had to make. He had considered phoning the hospital, but he didn't know if that would help. He would have to talk directly to the cops. And he would have to be convincing.

How had Hoodie and his henchmen known she was in the hospital?

Who were these men?

What was on the *fokken* memory card?

They shot her, and they must have known what he would do – take his sister to the nearest hospital. They knew her name, and his. Doesn't take a genius.

The cops would have to look after Nadia. Lots of them. Because these guys were afraid of nothing.

If something happened to her ... For a moment he considered dropping the whole thing. Just telling the guy tomorrow, I'll leave your card somewhere, take the thing and go away, leave us alone.

It's not worth the trouble.

But of course, it wasn't that simple.

Even if you took the anger away, at what they had done, to him and Nadia. He couldn't carry on like this. Every day it got harder to work in his industry. The cameras everywhere. The cops, the patrols in the city, the security, wherever you found affluent marks, there was law enforcement. And he had targets to meet so that Nadia could study and he could survive. And he was getting further and further behind, and the pressure was growing. And the more pressure, the more he had to take risks. And taking risks was trouble, no matter how you looked at it.

Two point four million.

A lot of money.

It could take away all his troubles. All the pressure. All the risk.

Long-term security.

It was Nadia's bursary. And maybe even he could better himself – finish school, and go and study to run a business. Something small, a hat shop for men, an exclusive clothing shop. Tyrone's Outfitters. He would like that.

And maybe that train trip across Europe.

But only if he could get the cops to protect Nadia.

He sheltered on the threshold of a big closed door, just a few metres from the Zanzibar restaurant in Castle Street. It was deserted in this weather.

He called Vodacom directory enquiries and got the number of the Bellville cop shop.

In the oppressive silence of the Hawks' bar Griessel said, 'It doesn't matter what is on the card.'

They looked at him, caught unaware by the positive note in his voice. While disappointment and disillusionment had wafted through the room, he had had a sudden moment of clarity and insight: he was the only one here who knew how it felt to work in a broken system. He had been through it all before. Even if he was a drunk and a fuck-up. Maybe *because* he was drunk and a fuck-up. In those days, in the darkest years of the old system, he had to find a reason to get up in the morning and do his work, despite everything. It was the only thing that stood between him and total devastation and despair.

It made Benny Griessel here, now, suddenly feel useful again. Relevant. For the first time in months. Or years, he didn't think he could remember. It was almost a euphoric experience: he could think of more important things than life's meaningless little frustrations. He could make a contribution. A difference. That was why there was excitement in his voice.

And now he had to find the right words to explain it. Without making a total fool of himself.

'It doesn't matter why the SSA is involved, or CI, or MI6,' said Griessel. 'It doesn't matter where the pressure is coming from, or if we are disappointed in our government, or our commanders . . .'

He saw Mbali looking at him, hurt and disappointed. 'We don't work for the president, or the minister or the commissioner,' he said. 'We work for the people who were killed in Franschhoek and in the

Waterfront, and for their families. We are all they have. We are the police. We enforce the law, the law that says if you kill someone, you have to pay. That is what I want to do: catch them, and make them pay. It is the only thing I can do. It is the only difference I can make. And I just think . . .' and he wondered, where all this shit was coming from that he was going to say now, but he said it anyway, in the full expectation that Cupido would laugh out loud '. . . if we all . . . if everybody in this country can just try to make a difference, then everything will be OK.' In the silence, only the humming of the big beer fridge in the corner could be heard.

Then Mbali said, 'Benny, that was beautiful.'

And Bones nodded in agreement, and Zola Nyathi had a little smile on his usually unreadable face.

Vaughn Cupido, however, was never one for hallowed moments. 'But how do we catch them, Benna, if we don't know what is on that card?' he asked.

'Like you taught me,' said Griessel. 'With technology. Cellphones.'

'Benny, with CI coming, there is no chance we can use IMC. They will be sifting through everything. I've already terminated all the existing cellphone tracking.'

'Sir, we can use an outside operator,' said Griessel. 'An independent.'

He knew they weren't going to like this. The biggest problem was that the SAPS, according to the Criminal Procedure Act, was not allowed to use independent cellphone tracking operators. Any evidence or testimony that was acquired in that manner would be angrily rejected by the court, and they would be crucified in the media. In addition, the private digital detectives were not popular with the police, because they frequently worked in the shadows and on the margins of the law, and sometimes paid key people at cellular companies a little something under the table.

But they were fast and frequently effective.

When no one responded, Griessel said, 'We're not looking for evidence. All we want to do is find the pickpocket.'

'And those guys don't need subpoenas,' said Cupido with rising enthusiasm. 'They're off the grid, sir.'

'But we're going to have to pay them,' said Griessel.

Nyathi didn't look as though he liked the idea.

Griessel wondered if he was worried it would get out. 'Sir, the private operators have to be discreet. It's the only way they can stay in business.'

The colonel stared at his hands.

'Do we have phones to track?' asked Bones Boshigo.

'Yes,' said Griessel. 'One to start with. But we are going to need a bit of luck.'

'How much money are we talking about?' asked Nyathi.

50

Griessel turned his iPhone on when they were standing in the parking area. Seven voice messages.

He sighed, not in the mood for this now, they had a plan, they had little time, and he wanted to get going. He wanted to catch the fuckers.

He phoned his voicemail number. The first message was from Janina Mentz of the SSA.

'I have information that can help you. Call me.'

Fuck you, he thought and deleted it.

The second was from Alexa. 'Hello, Benny, I just wanted to tell you I'm safely here. Remember the food in the fridge. I'm going to miss you so much tonight, not having you beside me in bed. I love you very much, don't work too hard. Bye.'

He deleted it.

The third was from Emma Graber of the British Consulate.

'Captain, I would really appreciate it if you could give me a call.' She provided her personal cell number, and concluded: 'It's really urgent.'

Fuck you, he thought, and deleted it.

The fourth was from Janina Mentz again. 'We're reasonably sure now why the Brits got our government's cooperation so easily. This could help you. Call me.'

He deleted it, not without a measure of satisfaction. Because all of them – along with the arrival of Criminal Intelligence, and the calls from the national and the DPCI commissioners, meant only one thing: the bastards of the SSA had made no progress with the investigation. They were all desperate now.

The fifth voicemail was from Bellville SAPS commander. 'Benny, *hier's nou 'n ding*. Something's come up. Call me, please.'

He called.

'We had a strange phone call at the charge office, Benny,' the colonel said. 'A guy who said the shooting at the train station was Flats gangsters. And the girl in the hospital is a target, she knows the big guns, she has information that could be very damaging to them. And there's a contract out on her: now I want to know, does that match with the thing you are investigating?'

It took Griessel a while to realise what was going on. 'Yes, Colonel.'

'So there is a real risk?'

'Yes, Colonel. Will you be able to allocate people for protection?'

'I have already sent two uniforms.'

Griessel shook his head. Two uniforms, against the Cobras. 'They might not be enough, Colonel. These guys are dangerous.'

The colonel sighed. 'I don't really have more people, Benny. And my overtime budget . . . You know how it is.'

Griessel pondered the dilemma. There was no one at the Hawks who could help. Not with CI on the way, not with SSA eavesdropping, not with the danger that each of them that they coopted could lose their job and career. But he knew what would convince the colonel.

'I understand, Colonel. It's just . . . if the media finds out you knew about the risk . . .'

The station commander sighed deeply. 'Yes, I know. Let me see if I can spare two more.'

Griessel suspected that even four constables would not be enough.

They had to hope that things would work out so that more comprehensive protection of Nadia Kleinbooi would not be necessary.

The sixth message was from Jeanette Louw of Body Armour. 'Captain, I would love to know how the investigation is going. Remember your promise.'

What could he tell her now?

And technically speaking, it was SSA's problem now.

He deleted her message.

The seventh message was from Ulinda Radebe. 'Benny, we're back. Where are you? We have five photographs and names. Five potentials. Call me.'

He ran back to Nyathi's office to discuss this development.

'We can't involve them too, Benny,' said the Giraffe. 'Ulinda has four kids. Vusi takes care of his mother. Given the choice, I'm sure they'll both insist on taking the risk, but I'm not going to do that. Let me handle it. I'll get the names and the photographs, I'll tell them we've been taken off the case.'

'Yes, sir.'

'I'll call you.'

'Thank you, sir.'

Then he ran to the car park, where the others were waiting for him.

They drove to Sea Point – Mbali, Cupido, Bones, and Griessel – to Dave Fiedler, the most respected freelance operator in the business.

On the way, Benny tested his theory on his colleagues. He said the key to the hunt lay in the rucksack that Tyrone Kleinbooi had with him this morning at the Waterfront. The deleted video showed Tyrone had it on his back when he was apprehended by the security men. But when he ran away after the shooting, he was without it. The Cobra team member had a similar rucksack in his hand when he followed Tyrone.

And he was sure Tyrone's phone was in that rucksack, and that cellphone was their only way to catch the murderers.

Cupido asked him why he was so certain the cellphone was in the rucksack.

Because the Cobras, said Griessel, did not track down Nadia in Stellenbosch through her address details on the university account in Tyrone's room in Schotsche Kloof. That account showed her flat address. But Nadia had told him and Mbali how she had been in class the whole morning. And then someone had called from Tyrone's phone, and said he had picked it up on the pavement in the city, and made an appointment to meet her on campus. That was where they had kidnapped her.

'I still don't get it,' said Bones. 'How are we going to catch them based on that information?'

'Because Nadia says as far as she can remember, the Cobras used Tyrone's phone to talk to him. All afternoon.'

'So Tyrone has another phone as well.'

'I think Tyrone has two other phones. Three in total. Or at least one other phone and two SIM cards.'

'How do you figure that out, Benna?' asked Cupido, his technology mentor, who was frequently sceptical of his apprentice's ability to grasp all the nuances.

'There is the phone that was in the rucksack. Let us call it Phone One. That is the one the Cobras have now.'

'Check.'

'There is the phone that he used around one o'clock to call Nadia on her iPhone. The number was on Nadia's register. Phone Two.'

'Check.'

'But tonight, while we were with Nadia at the hospital, he called her again, from another number, but definitely a cell number. Phone Three.'

'Check. That pickpocket is a canny coloured.'

'But now we know Tyrone wants to continue to negotiate with the Cobras. And how is he going to contact them?'

'By calling the phone that was in his backpack,' said Mbali. 'Phone One. Because the Cobras still have it.'

'We hope,' said Griessel.

'So we try and plot Tyrone's phone?' asked Bones.

'We try and plot all three phones,' said Griessel. 'So we can find him and the Cobras.'

Cupido was driving, but he took a moment to look at Griessel with amused pride. 'Who said you can't teach an old dog new tricks?'

'I'm trying,' said Griessel, pleased with himself.

'Then we and Dave Fiedler will have to get a move on. Before the pickpocket completes his payback.'

Tyrone put the three phones in a row on the guest room dressing table. He made doubly sure they were all off. He propped Number Three in his recharger, because tomorrow it was the one that had to be fully loaded.

He hung up his jacket, trousers, and shirt in the cupboard. He laid out clean underwear for the next morning. He placed the pistol beside the bed.

He gulped down another two Panados, pulled the duvet back, and slid into the bed.

Jirre, that was good.

One day, when all these troubles were over, he would like to ask the aunty here what kind of mattress this was.

He would surely be able to afford one, with two point four million stashed away.

Then he thought about Nadia, and he prayed that the cops would take his call seriously. He had used his best Flats Afrikaans, had used all the slang of the gangs, he had dropped a few names of known mob bosses, he had said there was a contract out for any gang member who walked into the hospital and shot her.

It wasn't easy, because when you said it, then you saw it, here in your head.

And that's the last thing he wanted to see. Because it was his fault.

But he mustn't think about that now. Let him go over his plan. Bit by bit, step by step. He had picked the turf that he knew.

Work the places you know, Ty.

And everything was geared so that, when all was said and done, he could get to his sister quickly.

Just in case. Because he wasn't going to crook anyone, he would keep his part of the bargain.

But you never knew. And he was a pickpocket with a pistol now.

Outside the rain suddenly slashed against the window, rattling and raging.

And he thought, at least his plan was reasonably weatherproof. Unless it rained so much that the trains stopped running.

When they turned out of Buitengracht into Helen Suzman Boulevard, Griessel's ZTE phone rang.

He answered.

'Benny,' said Zola Nyathi. 'I think we can be fairly sure there are five Cobras. The photographs don't show much of their faces, probably because they were aware of the cameras, had their heads down and were all wearing some sort of disguise – hats, caps, glasses, bandanas, or scarves. But they are all mid-thirties, probably. Military types. Which isn't conclusive, of course. But then there are the names. I'm not sure about the pronunciation: Hector Malot, Raoul de Soissons, Jean-Baptiste Chassignet, Xavier Forneret, and Sacha Guitry. I'll SMS them all to you. But Vusi had an idea, while they were waiting for their flight back. He googled the names. And that's why I'm sure they are all part of a team. All the names belong to famous French authors. Famous deceased French authors.'

51

Dave Fiedler handed Griessel's SAPS identity card back to him. 'You've gotta be kidding me, china,' he said in a rich baritone.

He was chunky and hairy – short beard and moustache, hair growing out of his ears, hair out of his nose, hair that pushed out from under the collar of his grey pullover, like plants reaching for light.

They were standing at the door of 2A Worcester Street in Sea Point, the double-storey where Fiedler lived and worked. The four of them only just fitted in under the small porch, with the rain falling in a thick, hissing curtain behind them.

'We're not kidding. Just get us out of the weather,' said Cupido.

Fiedler stood aside and waved them inside, his luxuriant eyebrows raised in disbelief.

'I hope you have a warrant,' he said when Griessel walked past him.

'We don't need a warrant, we need your help.'

'No wonder it's fucking raining,' said Fiedler, and shut the door behind Bones.

'I will not tolerate such language,' said Mbali. 'Have some respect. I'm a lady.'

'Oh, Jesus Christ,' said Fiedler, but so quietly that only Bones, right at the back, could hear him. He walked ahead, to a large room – probably once a sitting room before he had converted it into work space. To the left against the wall was a table with a coffee machine, mugs, sugar, and milk, beside a conference table with eight chairs. To the right was a long, low table with a couple of computers. There were film posters on the walls.

The story was that Fiedler had emigrated here seven years ago from Israel, a former senior member of the Israeli army's legendary Unit 8200. This unit not only produced, according to the rumours, the most sought-after technology alumni in the world, but had also developed much of the programming and apparatus that Fiedler now used to do digital detective work for private investigators, the security industry, and the public.

Nobody knew why he addressed everyone that lived and breathed as 'china'.

'Please, sit down,' he said, and he pointed at the table. 'There's a fresh pot of coffee, so help yourselves. I hope you brought the doughnuts . . .'

They didn't get the joke. He shook his head.

'What's with the posters?' asked Cupido.

'Have you seen the movies?'

Cupido read the titles: *American Pie, Blue Thunder, EDtv, Enemy of the State, The Bourne Supremacy, Minority Report, Cape Fear, 1984, The Osterman Weekend, La Zona.*

'Some of them.'

'What do they have in common?'

Cupido shook his head.

'Surveillance flicks,' said Fiedler. 'And they all get it wrong . . . So the first thing I tell a new customer, if he wants movie tech, he should go watch a movie.' He stood beside the table, clearly still not at ease. 'This is very weird, but I'll play along. What can I do for you?'

Griessel took out his notebook, and tore the page out. 'We want you to plot these three numbers.' He slid the page across the conference table. 'We want to know where the phones are, and we want to know which numbers called them today.'

'For starters,' said Cupido.

Fiedler stared at Griessel with an expression that said he was waiting for the punch line of the joke.

When it was not forthcoming, he said, 'You're from the Hawks, it said on your ID.'

'You'd better believe it,' said Cupido.

'And you want me to plot three numbers for you?'

'Yes,' said Griessel.

'And you can't ever tell anybody that this happened,' said Cupido. 'If we hear even a whisper that you mentioned this, ever, we will make your life a misery.'

Fiedler laughed, a short, deep guffaw. They didn't react. 'It's the end of the world,' he said. 'God's truth.'

Mbali made a disapproving sound.

'You're gonna pay me?' asked Fiedler.

'You talk money, you talk to me,' said Bones. 'What is your rate?'

'This is real. This is actually real,' said Fiedler, pulling up a chair and sitting down. He looked at the numbers. 'Where are the IMEIs?' He pronounced it in the trade lingo, *eye-me-eyes*.

'We don't have them.'

'I should have known. Then it's going to take a while, china.'

At ten thirty-five, Dave Fiedler spoke out, from behind one of his computers: 'That second number has been static in Bellville since four o'clock.'

They sat around the conference table. They were familiar with the art of waiting. Each was busy with his own thoughts.

'Where in Bellville?' asked Griessel.

'Boston. Frans Conradie Drive, about halfway between Duminy and Washington. Google Earth shows a place called Brights Electrical.'

'He's still there now?' asked Cupido.

'Yep.'

Griessel stood up. 'Static. Completely static at the same place?'

'Yep. Phone's on, but no calls or texts. Last call was made at fifteen fifty-two.'

Griessel walked to the computer screen. 'How accurate is the plotting, the position of the phone?'

'About fifteen metres. But because it's been static, I'd say closer to ten.'

Cupido also came close. They looked at the screen, where Fiedler had Google Streetview open.

'Those are flats there beside Brights,' said Cupido. 'On both sides.'

'Could it be in those flats?' Griessel asked Fiedler, and pointed at the screen.

'Yes. Probably the one on the right.'

'And it's near the hospital,' said Griessel. 'Let's go.'

They walked quickly to the door. Griessel stopped. 'And the other phones?'

'I'll tell you in ten . . .'

'Call me on this number,' said Griessel and scribbled it down hurriedly on a page in his notebook, tore it out and passed it across to Fiedler.

They drove up the N1 with the siren on and the blue light balanced on the dashboard, from where it frequently slid off into Griessel's lap.

Just beyond the N7, Fiedler phoned. 'What you call Phone One has been off for the past two and a half hours, china. Plotting says it was all over the place today. Smack in the city, then the Waterfront, then all the way to Stellenbosch, then Bellville . . .'

'What was the last location?'

'The R304.'

'Where's that?'

'It's the road that runs from Stellenbosch all the way to Malmesbury. Before it was switched off, the phone was about three kilometres from the R312 crossing. That's the one running from Wellington to Durbanville.'

Griessel knew the area. 'But there's nothing there.'

'That's right, china.'

'Do you have the call registry yet?'

'Nope. But it's coming.'

'And Phone Three?'

'Phone Three was on for just eleven minutes, about three hours ago. It made one call. From Somerset Road in the vicinity of the Cape Quarter mall.'

That was when Tyrone phoned Nadia in the hospital.

'That's it? Just the one call?'

'Just the one. And then it was switched off.'

Cupido switched the siren and light off when they turned out of Mike Pienaar Drive into Frans Conradie.

Griessel said they would have to use the old trick to get into the flats without a warrant: tell the residents there was a very dangerous, heavily armed murderer in the area. He might be hiding in one of the flats at that very moment, they just wanted to secure everything.

'Then we focus on the flats that don't want to let us in.'

Bones grinned. 'You old salts,' he said, but with respect.

They paired off and went to knock softly on all the doors of the

Darina apartment block in 12th Avenue, Boston. White and brown faces opened doors warily. The team displayed their identity cards, apologised for the inconvenience, and spun their tale.

Everyone allowed them in, wide-eyed, standing frightened at the door while their humble one- and two-bedroom spaces were searched, for Tyrone Kleinbooi.

Less than a quarter of an hour later they were back on the pavement in front of the building.

'Maybe it's that block over there.' Mbali pointed at the flats on the other side of the big, red Brights facade.

There too, and in the rooms above the Boston Superette, they found nothing except shocked and anxious residents.

They called Dave Fiedler, who went through his computers again and said the phone was still there, right where they were.

It was Cupido, ever bold and impulsive, who looked at the long row of rubbish bins in front of the Brights steel gate and said: 'He dumped the phone.'

None of them was keen to brave the minimal shelter of the facade's narrow overhang, where the cold rain splashed down, to rummage in the contents of the filthy rubbish bins.

At 23.52 Mbali pulled the phone from the rubbish.

It was a Nokia 2700.

52

Griessel took his colleagues back to the DPCI headquarters, because Dave Fiedler said there was one call to Tyrone Kleinbooi's Phone One – the device that the Cobras most likely had in their possession now. The number had been active for sixteen minutes in Castle Street, and after that had disappeared off the air.

'Go get some sleep, china. I'll call you if there's any action.'

They met Nyathi down in the basement and informed him of the latest developments.

The Giraffe gave them the photos of the five possible Cobras that were taken at O. R. Tambo Airport – not very useful, but better than nothing. 'These are our five famous French authors. Take them with you. Maybe it will help.'

Griessel agreed with Bones, Cupido and Mbali that they would phone as soon as there was news. It was better to get some sleep. He was going home, his house was only five or ten minutes away from Fiedler, and he would let them know if there was any activity on the numbers.

Then he drove alone to Alexa's house, mulling over the events of the past hour or two.

The pickpocket had deliberately left Phone Two, according to Cupido a 'prepaid special' that you could buy at any backstreet cell-phone shop for a couple of hundred rand, in a rubbish bin at Brights. Still switched on. As if he knew someone was going to trace the number and try to determine the location of the phone.

It made sense. Tyrone knew they would find Nadia's iPhone in the hospital and start analysing it.

So Tyrone was nobody's fool. He knew what could be done with technology. And he wanted to make some kind of statement. 'I'm in Bellville,' perhaps?

Only to make the next call from De Waterkant?

Which was not too far from where Tyrone rented the room in Schotsche Kloof.

Did he go back to the city, to Bo-Kaap, because he felt at home there? Safe?

That's what fugitives from the law often did when the heat was on, when the chase became too intense, and their flight chaotic.

And shortly after Tyrone had called Nadia, a new, unknown number had called Phone One, now with the Cobras.

Jissis, thought Benny Griessel. How many phones did the fucker have?

But then he realised the man was a pickpocket. He had as many phones as he needed.

And if you were negotiating with a team that walked into the Waterfront in broad daylight and shot dead five security guards in cold blood, you'd want to make doubly sure that they can't track you down via cellular technology.

He felt a great sense of determination rising in him. He would have to keep his head, with all the phones, all the technological possibilities. He would have to show he had learned to be a modern-day detective. Even if Cupido called him an 'old dog', and Bones joked about the 'old salts'.

When he got home, he phoned Dave Fiedler and said he also wanted a complete analysis and monitoring of the number that had called Phone One from Castle Street.

'Sure, china, but the meter is running.'

'Just let me know as soon as there is any activity on any of those phones.'

He walked through the cold, empty house to the kitchen. The rain drummed fiercely on the roof.

And suddenly he missed Alexa, her presence, her happiness when she saw him, her embrace, her chatter, every evening so intense and enthusiastic, as if he really mattered. As if she really loved him.

All this he saw and felt, now that she wasn't here.

He took the Woolworths food out of the fridge – chicken and broccoli, his favourite, which she'd bought specially for him – with a pang of guilt about his relief earlier in the day, at the thought of having the house to himself.

He put the container in the microwave, pinged it on. Two minutes, thirty seconds.

What was he going to do, between the devil of his self-doubt and his inadequate rascal, and the deep blue sea of his attraction to her? And the pleasure of being with her. She was so . . . full. Full of everything. He sometimes wished her *joie de vivre*, her intensity, her naivety would infect him.

She was his perfect polar opposite. He didn't want to, he dared not, he could not lose her. Despite, everything, he had begun to love her very much. And tonight, after he had regained a measure of relevance as a policeman, as a team member of the Hawks – for the first time in his career – he felt optimism. He *wanted* this thing with Alexa to work.

If he could just find a solution to his dilemma.

Griessel ate his supper.

When he had finished, rinsed his dishes and put them on the drying rack, he phoned the Louis Leipoldt Hospital. He asked to be put through to the ward where Nadia Kleinbooi lay, identified himself to the night sister, and asked how the patient was.

'We gave her a sleeping pill, Captain. She's sleeping peacefully.'

He thanked her and said she must see that the four constables got coffee regularly so that they were awake and alert.

The night sister said yes, she'd see to that.

He rang off.

At least he knew now that there were four uniforms on guard.

He went to shower, put on his pyjamas, which still smelled faintly of sex. He made sure both his cellphones were on. He set the alarm on the iPhone for seven o'clock, but he suspected Dave Fiedler would call him long before then.

Then he slept.

53

Twenty to six.

Tyrone woke suddenly from sleep, released from a dream where a man in a grey cap was shooting Nadia, one shot after the other. He felt his sister's body jerk in his arms, and he tried to shield her with his hands, but it didn't help, the bullets went right through, leaving big holes in his palms, but there was no blood, only Nadia bled, and then he was awake and a huge wave of relief washed over him.

Just a dream.

Had he screamed out loud in his sleep, the way he had heard his own voice in the dream?

Moments of disorientation, the strange room, sounds of water dripping off a roof outside the window.

And then, the full onslaught of reality returning. He was here. This was the day he had been preparing for. His body was stiff, his back was sore.

Was Nadia OK?

He wanted to phone the hospital straight away.

But he couldn't phone from here.

He got up and walked through to the bathroom.

Tyrone sat on the end of the bed. He was washed, dressed, packed. He'd taken two Panados already, but the pain still throbbed across his back. The cellphones on the dressing table lay neatly in a row, the pistol next to them.

Phone the hospital. Hear if Nadia is OK.

Switch on the phone the guys are going to send the money photo to.

Twenty past six in the morning? You're too anxious, Tyrone. Get a grip. Take a deep breath. Don't fuck this up.

Turn on the TV. If there was an attack at the hospital, it would be on the news.

He switched it on. The high, exuberant voices of a children's programme were suddenly too loud and shrill for the morning silence. He stabbed at the remote's volume button over and over again until it could barely be heard. Navigated to SABC2 and *Morning Live*. An interview with a darkie dude that he didn't know. The news would probably come on at half past.

Breathe. Go through the schedule.

He wanted to know if Nadia was OK. Watch the news. If there was nothing, phone later, once he was out of here.

He must have breakfast, 'cause it was going to be a hectic day.

He must buy chewing gum, to stick the memory card to.

He must double-check the train times.

He must wait for the photos of the money, the suitcase, and the guy.

And then it was lights, camera, action.

He looked at the TV screen.

Twenty-four past six.

Time stands still when you're not having fun.

The iPhone alarm woke Griessel at seven.

When he switched it off and lay back for a second, holding the phone, he was grateful for the six hours of unbroken sleep. And then he realised that it meant there had been no action on any of the numbers, and he wondered if his plan was going to work.

Perhaps none of the cellphones was still in use.

Wouldn't that be typical: just when he started getting his head around all the technology, it turns out to be useless.

He got up, in one restless, uneasy movement, walked to the toilet, lifted the seat, pulled his pyjamas down, aimed, and urinated.

He suppressed the urge to call Dave Fiedler now.

If there was news, he would have known.

He flushed, put the seat down again, and walked to the hand basin. He must finish up and drive over to Fiedler's.

News item, four minutes past seven, *Morning Live*: 'Western Cape police spokesperson Wilson Bala denied that the SAPS was investigating a shooting that allegedly occurred at Cape Town's Victoria and Alfred Waterfront yesterday. This, despite claims by family members of Waterfront security personnel, and eyewitness reports of extensive medical and law enforcement presence at the shopping centre yesterday morning. Both the centre management and the Blue Shield security company declined to comment on the matter. The alleged shooting even drew attention in parliament today . . .'

What the fuck? wondered Tyrone.

And then a moment of huge relief. His face was not on TV.

But why not?

He watched the news until it was over, his thoughts occupied with possible reasons, his heart fearful of news of a hospital shooting.

It didn't come.

But now he wasn't sure if that meant anything. If the cops were denying that they were investigating a Waterfront shooting? A shooting he had seen with his own eyes.

What was going on?

The urge to move, to get going, to gain momentum, overwhelmed him. He must get out of here. He must phone Nadia.

And then get breakfast, even though he felt queasy now.

07.27

Griessel had a coffee mug in his hand and a mouth full of toast with Marmite, when his ZTE phone rang.

'Hello,' he answered, swallowing quickly.

'China, we've just had action. Phone Number Three came alive four minutes ago and called the same number as yesterday afternoon. Call lasted just thirty-seven seconds.'

'Hang on . . .' Benny plonked down the half full coffee mug and ran to the bedroom to get his jacket.

He grabbed his notebook out of his jacket pocket, riffled through the pages until he found what he was looking for. 'This number?' He read it out to Fiedler.

'That's the one.'

Nadia's iPhone. It was Tyrone phoning her again.

'Where's the phone now? Phone Three.'

'It's gone off air, the call was too short for a good fix, but it was made in the vicinity of the Waterkant and Loop Street crossing, give or take five hundred metres.'

'I'm on my way.'

He rang off, and began calling his colleagues as he jogged to the front door.

Tyrone sat on the planter box of black marble in front of Atterbury House in Lower Burg.

Nadia was OK.

In a manner of speaking.

She was cross with him. 'Tyrone, come in, and leave those things, the *polieste* say you're not in trouble, please, *boetie*.'

'Everything is fine, *moenie worry nie*. Are there cops guarding you?'

'*Ja*, Tyrone, and it's because you won't let this thing go.'

'Everything is going to be just fine, *sussie*.' Then he'd ended the call and walked over here.

Time to check in for the money shot.

He switched the second cellphone on.

On the way, Griessel phoned Nadia.

She said, yes, her brother had phoned, he wanted to know how she was.

Then he heard another call coming in, said goodbye, and took it.

Dave Fiedler: 'Funny thing, china. That fourth number you asked me to keep an eye on, the one that called Phone One from Castle Street last night . . .'

'Yes.'

'It just came alive. I'm trying to get a fix on it now . . . hang on . . . Damn!'

'What?'

'Went off again. All I can tell you is it's in the city.'

Old dogs don't believe in coincidences, thought Benny Griessel. Two phones calling shortly after each other from the city?

Phone Four was also Tyrone's.

07.51.

Tyrone ordered a Big Breakfast at McDonald's in the Golden Acre. And Premium Roast coffee.

He carried everything carefully on a tray in one hand, dragging the suitcase with the other. He sat down so that he could watch the door, although he couldn't quite say why.

Three sugars in the coffee.

He ate and drank. The coffee was OK, the food was basically tasteless.

He would have to dump the suitcase, he couldn't drag it around with him all day, he had to travel light. Be highly mobile. Time to rock 'n' roll, and yes, some running would be involved.

He had only needed it to look legit for the guesthouse. He would leave it here, just put the underpants, socks, and shirts in the rucksack.

When he had finished eating, he switched the cellphone on again. Only long enough to see there were no pictures of the money, the bag, or the guy yet.

54

08.12.

Rush hour, the city traffic was crazy, even though it wasn't raining – the sun broke through dramatic clouds, the sunbeams blindingly bright on the wet road.

That's how the Cape is, thought Griessel when he eventually parked in front of Fiedler's house and office. When rain looked likely, every *fokker* in the Peninsula drove his own car to work, although it then took everybody twice as long.

He got out. His ZTE rang. It was Fiedler. He answered and said, 'I'm at your door.'

'Phone Four was alive for three minutes. I'll open up for you.'

And when Fiedler opened the door, 'Three minutes, and then it went dead again. Still in the city centre. I can't get a close fix.'

'So that's twice?'

'Yes, china. Twice, three minutes every time, then off again, for about five.'

'He's checking in for something. A call . . . ? And he's worried that he will be tracked.'

'If you check in like that, you're waiting for an email, or a text,' said Fiedler. 'Not a call.'

'Yes,' said Griessel. 'Will we be able to see a text?'

'I was afraid that you'd ask that.'

'Why?'

'Because accessing the server is against the law.'

'Can you do it?'

'For a Hawk? Are you crazy?'

'Can you do it?'

'Of course I can do it, china. But it's going to cost a little extra. And you'll have to sign something. I'm not going to incriminate myself.'

'How much extra?'

08.17.

Griessel phoned Nadia Kleinbooi again. He apologised for bothering her.

Anxiously, she asked if there was any news.

No, he said. But he would love to know: did Tyrone have an email address?

She said no without hesitation.

'Are you absolutely sure?'

'Why?'

'We just want to make sure.'

This time she thought a bit before she answered. 'No, he's not into those things.'

'Does he have a car?' Something he should have asked a long time ago.

'No.'

'Does he have access to someone else's car?'

'No. I . . . No, I don't think so.'

Griessel thanked her and rang off. And he thought, Tyrone knew enough about technology to be careful with cellphones, and to hoodwink the Cobras with a memory card. He wasn't so sure she was right.

If the pickpocket had an email address, and that was how he was communicating with the Cobras, they were fucked. Completely.

Metrorail train 2561 on platform 10 of Cape Town Station was full.

At 08.26 Tyrone slipped through the door of the middle third-class carriage and stood in the aisle.

He waited till just after 08.30, when the train jerked and pulled away, before he switched the cellphone in his hand on again.

He held it so that the people pressing against him couldn't see the screen.

He watched it search for a signal, and find it.

It always took a while for an MMS to come through.

At least he was on the move. And he was going to stay on the move, until this thing was finished.

He watched the time passing on the screen.

One minute.

The train picked up speed.

Two minutes.

The train began to lose momentum.

Three minutes.

He felt the action of the brakes as the train slowed to a stop at Woodstock Station.

He waited until it came to a complete standstill.

The doors opened. More people got on.

He switched the phone off.

Still no photos.

Jirre.

08.49.

Mbali arrived first.

'Turn around and drive to Bellville Station,' said Griessel to Cupido over the phone. 'We think he's on a train – we picked him up in Woodstock, and again in Maitland, he was on for about three minutes . . . Hold on, Mbali is here . . .'

Griessel pointed to where Dave Fiedler was busy at the computers. 'We think Tyrone is taking a train. See if you can look at the Metrorail schedule. We need to know which train.'

He turned his attention back to Cupido and the phone again. 'Vaughn, are you there?'

'I'm here. I turned around at the N7, but the traffic is hectic, pappie, it's going to take a while to get back to Bellville.'

'OK. We're trying to find out which train it could be.'

'How sure are you it's a train?'

'He doesn't have a car, and he can't move this fast in a bus or taxi during rush hour. Dave said three minutes is not long enough to get a precise fix, but every time it was within a kilometre of the stations, and the phone is moving, it looks like it's moving.'

'OK, Benna, keep me posted.'

'I'm looking at the Metrorail schedule,' Mbali called.

The front doorbell rang.

'Jesus,' said Dave Fiedler. 'It's like a bloody beehive here.'

Mbali clicked her tongue at him.

Griessel said, 'It must be Bones, I'll open up for him.'

09.01.

At Parow Station Tyrone got off and walked quickly over to the train schedules on the wall in the station building, just to be sure.

Train 3412 ran back to Cape Town, from platform 11. In five minutes, at 09.06.

He jogged around to the platform. Stopped. Switched the phone on. Stood and stared at the screen.

It found a signal.

He waited.

He couldn't go on like this for the whole day, *fok weet*, when were those guys going to send the photo?

Or were they trying to track him?

Good luck with that, motherfuckers.

Train 3412 pulled into the station.

Still no photos, no message.

Shit.

He got on the train, heading back to Cape Town.

'I think it is train 2561. It was at Woodstock at 08.33, and in Maitland at 08.42 . . .'

'He's back on-line,' called Dave Fiedler. 'Hang on, the fix is coming . . .'

Griessel looked at his notes. 'Mbali, I think you're right.'

'He should be in Parow now,' said Mbali.

'Yes, Parow it is,' said Fiedler.

'What time does that train reach Bellville?' asked Griessel.

'Six minutes past nine,' said Mbali.

'*Fok*,' said Griessel, because it was too soon. Cupido would never make it.

'This once, I forgive you,' said Mbali, also dismayed.

55

At 09.14, Tyrone got off at Goodwood Station.

He switched the cellphone on again.

The first MMS came through.

On the small screen he saw the photo. The money, stacked on a table: hundred- and two hundred-rand notes, tied in bundles with rubber bands.

His heart leaped. Could that be two point four million? It seemed so little?

The next photo came through.

A black rucksack, with the money visible through the open zipper. The bag was pleasingly full. That looked better.

The third photo. A man in a blue windcheater and black beanie. High cheekbones, stubble. The rucksack on his back.

Tyrone felt his heart beating. This was a face he had never seen before. It wasn't Hoodie, it wasn't the Waterfront shooter. But this one looked so . . . terrifyingly ruthless.

He felt the phone in his hand tremble.

Stick with the plan, Tyrone.

He steadied himself, tapped the phone to call the number,

It rang.

The guy answered immediately. 'No, don't call me. Send me text messages.'

'Why?' asked Tyrone.

But the line was already dead.

Griessel, Mbali, and Bones Boshigo stood and stared at the photo on Dave Fiedler's computer screen.

'That's a lot of money,' said Fiedler.

'I'm guessing at least a million, million point five,' said Bones.

'Track the number it was sent from,' said Griessel.

'I'm busy . . . He's just called it.'

'Who called what?'

'The train guy . . .'

'Tyrone. Call him Tyrone.'

'OK, Tyrone's just called the number from which the photographs were sent. He's still in Goodwood. I'm getting a better fix, hang on. Yes, definitely at or very near the station.'

'He's clever,' said Mbali. 'He got them to send him a picture of the money. He's selling them the memory card . . .'

'There's another photo,' said Fiedler. 'And another . . .' His hand moved quickly, adeptly with the mouse.

The new photos appeared on the screen, one beside the other.

'*Hhayi*,' said Mbali, because the last one was the one of the man with the rucksack. 'That's a Cobra.'

'A Cobra?' asked Fiedler, but Mbali waddled hastily away to the conference table, where the O. R. Tambo photos of the five suspected Cobras lay. She flipped through them, and found the one that looked like the man in the photo that was sent to Tyrone's phone. She trotted back.

'It's this one.' She held the photo up beside the screen. The resemblance was clear.

'Print that photo, Dave,' said Griessel. 'And send one to Captain Cupido's number.'

'Give me his number,' said Fiedler.

Griessel looked it up on his phone, and held it out so that Fiedler could see.

'Tyrone is very clever,' said Mbali.

Griessel wasn't listening, his brain was too busy now. Tyrone on the train. Tyrone deliberately took the train from Cape Town Station. He could have taken a taxi. He could have taken the bus, but he didn't.

Why?

Tyrone, who travelled to Parow, and was now on the way back towards Cape Town.

'We have a new text,' said Fiedler. He read: '"Why must I only SMS?" That's from Tyrone's phone, to the other guys.'

'The Cobras,' said Griessel, because he wanted their communication to be very clear. What lay ahead was going to be messy enough.

'Who the f— Who are the Cobras?'

'The bad guys.' Griessel read the SMS over Fiedler's shoulder.
Why must I only SMS?

'They must have told him not to call,' said Griessel.

'But why?' asked Bones. 'They can still be traced and tracked, can't they?'

'I think I know, but you'll have to tell me what the hell is going down here,' said Fiedler.

Griessel knew it was the right thing to do now. 'Tyrone is selling a very valuable item to some very dangerous people. We call them Cobras, it's a long story . . . Tyrone is trying to set up the exchange of the item, for the money in the photo.'

'Is it a gang? How many Cobras are there?'

'Five, at least.'

'OK. I think they want him to text so that they can share the message quickly. Doing that on a voice call is tricky in peak time – our cellular network is just too up to shit if you're on the move and you're not using the same service provider.'

They all read the new message from the Cobras to Tyrone on the screen: *Because I say so.*

There was silence in Dave Fiedler's big room. Everyone trying to make sense of the text messages.

'They are setting a trap for him,' said Mbali.

'Yes,' said Griessel. 'They are.'

Fiedler was busy at another computer, while the detectives stood and looked at the screen where the money photos and text messages appeared. Time dragged.

Go to Bellville Station.

'That's Tyrone to the Cobras,' said Bones.

'I have a fix on the Cobra phone,' said Fiedler.

New text: *No.*

'The Cobras are saying "no"?' asked Bones.

'Where is the Cobra phone?' asked Griessel.

'It's moving along the R304, going south, towards the N1.'

Do you want the card?

Nobody said a word, waiting for the Cobras to answer.

Bellville Station too dangerous after yesterday. Choose another place.

'Fair enough,' said Bones.

Nothing on the screen.

Fiedler, at the other monitor, said, 'The Cobras are now on the N1, heading towards the city.'

Griessel wished he could call in the SAPS helicopter, or that he had the time and manpower for a roadblock.

His phone rang. It was Cupido.

'Vaughn, we still don't have anything, I'll phone you back.'

'Roger, Benna.'

'Why isn't Tyrone answering?' Bones asked.

'Because they have messed up his plan,' said Mbali.

Go to Parow Station.

'Trains,' said Griessel suddenly.

They looked at him questioningly, but he picked up his ZTE and phoned Nadia again.

It rang for longer this time. She answered with a scared 'Hello?'

'Nadia, does Tyrone ride the trains often?'

'*Ja*, he comes to me a lot, in Stellenbosch. He's always saying he likes the trains. Loves riding them.'

'First class or third?'

'I think third class.'

'Thank you, Nadia. We still don't have news, but I'll let you know as soon as there is.'

'Thank you.'

He killed the call. He heard Fiedler talking, and Mbali answering, but he wasn't listening. He wanted to make sure his reasoning was correct, that he understood Tyrone. He tried to put himself inside the pickpocket's head. He didn't have a car. Taxis and buses were subject to the flow of traffic. Unpredictable, at best. And also not private if you want to make calls or receive photos of money. The Metro trains were reasonably predictable. In the morning they ran at regular intervals. They were public, but if you wanted to make a call, you could get off and put distance between yourself and your fellow passengers.

It was familiar territory, as well.

And now The Great Transaction. The trains gave Tyrone a moving exchange location – there were not the same dangers of a specific street corner or abandoned building, where the Cobras could hide or stalk him.

Tyrone was clever, as Mbali had pointed out. He knew the trains, apparently he knew the stations. They must be good places to steal from people's pockets. And there would be some small comfort in the crowds of other people, possible eyewitnesses. The Cobras were rightly wary about going back to Bellville. On the rail system, Tyrone could keep moving, in two directions, keep them guessing. Every station offered its own escape routes, within minutes from each other . . .

He phoned Cupido.

'Where are you?'

'Just past Karl Bremer, on the N1. Traffic is a bit better this side.'

'Tyrone is on his way back to Cape Town.'

'*Jissis*, Benna, he's fucking us around.'

'*Ja*. I think you must still go to the station. Take the first train to Cape Town.'

'Then I'll be without a car.'

'I know, but I think he's going to do the whole thing on the trains. He knows the system, and it gives him a lot of options.'

'It's taking a big chance, Benna.'

'It's all we've got.'

56

'Bones, you're going to stay here and you're going to be our controller,' said Griessel.

'Me?' In disbelief.

'Yes. Mbali and I need to get to the city station. I think Tyrone is going to make the handover somewhere along this railway line. At a station or on a train. And the quickest way to get from station to station is by using the train.'

Griessel searched through his pockets, until he found the earphones for the ZTE. He plugged it into his phone, pushed them in his ears.

'Dave, you're going to have to help. You'll have to call Captain Cupido and give him instructions, but wait until I tell Bones what to do.'

'Sweet, china.'

'Bones, call me on this phone. Tell me everything that is happening.'

'I'll do my best,' said Bones nervously.

'You'll be OK,' said Mbali, and adjusted the pistol on her hip.

'You'll have to hide the weapon,' said Griessel. 'And the ID card. We're going undercover.'

Tyrone was on train 3414, from Goodwood to Cape Town.

He stood with bated breath and waited for Black Beanie's answer.

He hadn't expected them to refuse to go to Bellville. He should have thought of that, it was common sense, he didn't want to show his face there either for a while.

But it had made his timetable a bit weird. Because Metrorail's trains ran less frequently until late afternoon.

But it was still OK, if he kept his head.

The phone vibrated in his hand.

OK.

That was their answer.

He let out a sharp, explosive breath.

It was on.

Griessel and Mbali, in the BMW, with the siren and blue light on.

The ZTE rang. Griessel answered, 'Bones?'

'Tyrone is moving again, train 3414 to Cape Town.'

'OK.' He thought for a moment and then spoke loudly, so that Bones on the phone as well as Mbali beside him could both hear him clearly, 'He's moving between the city and Parow. Bones, look at the schedule, is that where the most trains are running?'

'Hang on . . . Tyrone has just replied to the Cobras' text, he said "Tell me when you are at Parow Station".'

'Has Dave called Vaughn yet?'

'Yes. Vaughn is on train 3214, it left Bellville at ten, direction Cape Town. It's the one right behind Tyrone's.'

'OK, tell him we're undercover. No ID, no firearm visible.'

'Roger . . . Benny, you're right. The bulk of the trains will be running between Eerste River and Cape Town from now until about four. Just about twenty per cent go to the Strand.'

'OK, Bones. I think it is going to happen between the city and Parow, maybe Bellville. When is Vaughn going to reach Parow?'

'He's already past Parow, according to the schedule. He should be at Thornton now.'

'Tell him to get off at Maitland. Unless you can see Tyrone leaving his train somewhere.'

'Tyrone still seems to be moving.'

'Hang on.' Griessel wove though the traffic in Strand Street. He had to concentrate on the road for now. Mbali sat staring with wide eyes, clutching the big black handbag on her lap.

Then they were across Adderley, alongside the station. He saw a loading zone, switched off the siren, and parked. Mbali's door was already open, as though she was relieved to be getting out of the car.

'Mbali!' he shouted as they ran to the station. 'We are going to take two separate trains, just to cover more bases.'

'Yes,' she said, already puffing.

★ ★ ★

Tyrone got off at Woodstock.

Where was Black Beanie? Why was it taking so long to get to Parow Station?

They were going to fuck everything up.

He went over to the schedules again. He would have to wait.

Time to begin chewing the gum. He dug in his pocket, took out the pack, put six strips in his mouth, began to chew.

His cellphone vibrated.

We are at Parow.

He shivered. Was his plan going to work?

His fingers trembled as he typed *OK. I know u are 4. Money guy . . .* and he looked closely at the time tables . . . *goes on train 3520, leaving Parow at 10.36, Plfrm 9. Must be alone, or u won't get card. I will hide card on train 3515, reaching Parow at 10.50. when I have money, will tell u where on train card is hidden.*

And then he waited for them to answer.

Bones's voice was high and almost panicky when he passed on the news to Griessel.

'OK, Bones, Mbali has just left the station on that exact train, so we are covered. I am going to call her now, and I'm going to warn her. Now you and Dave must try to get Vaughn on the same train, Mbali will need backup.'

'Roger, out.'

'No, wait. Where is Tyrone?'

'Woodstock.'

'OK, that's where I'm going.'

If card is not on train, we WILL kill your sister. Just 4 guards at hospital.

How did they know that? wondered Tyrone. Had they been there?

Of course they had been there, you ape.

He would have to get the money, and then take the pistol and go to his sister, these guys just wanted to kill.

Take a deep breath, Tyrone.

He typed on the phone: *If money is right, card is there.*

Train 3515 pulled into Woodstock Station.

Tyrone ran for the train.

Time to put the card under a seat.

Mbali Kaleni saw the pickpocket running towards the train. Her cellphone against her ear, she told Griessel, cool as a cucumber, 'I see him.'

'Good,' said Griessel.

'He's getting on the train . . .'

'OK.'

'He's in the next carriage, I can see him . . . He's taking off his backpack. He's sitting down . . . He's opening his backpack, he has taken something out. I can't see what it is. He has it on his lap. Wait . . . Now he's taken something from his mouth. He's looking around . . . Sorry, Benny, I had to look away . . .'

'OK.'

'He . . . Benny, I think he has stuck the card under the seat. Now he's getting up, the train is going to stop at . . . Salt River Station. I think he's going to get off.'

'Mbali, go and see if the card is there.'

She waited until Tyrone had left the train. She watched Tyrone go and stand on the platform. She felt sorry for him, in that instant, he looked so scared and bewildered.

Still she remained seated. Till the doors closed, and the train jerked, and began to move.

Then she got up and walked to the seat he had vacated. She saw Tyrone standing on the platform staring at the departing train.

A young black man sat down on Tyrone's seat. He had earphones on and his head moved in time to the music he was listening to.

Mbali stopped in front of him and said: 'I want you to move.'

He didn't hear her.

She tapped him on the knee and he looked up, irritated by the intrusion. She gestured that he should move up.

He stared at her, challenging. '*Ungachopha apho,*' he said. You can sit there.

She smacked him against the ear, like a naughty child.

That shocked him, he ducked to avoid another possible smack, and said in agitation, '*Yintoni eyebayo?*' What is *wrong* with you?

But he took in her severe expression, the fearless attitude, and he shifted up, three seats further away. He shook his head in disbelief, trying to regain a little dignity.

Mbali ignored him, sat down, put her handbag beside her, and leaned over. She felt underneath the seat, until she found the wodge of chewing gum. She pulled it loose, and held it up.

She said to Benny Griessel, 'I have the card.'

57

Griessel was still waiting at Cape Town Station for train 2319.

On his cellphone, Bones said, 'Tyrone has just sent the Cobras a message. It says: "Card hidden on train now. Let me know when money is at Maitland Station." And the Cobra said: "OK." But there's a problem. I could not reach Vaughn in time, he says there was no signal. So he missed Mbali's train.'

'Shit.'

'What do you want me to do?'

'Can you tell me where Tyrone is now?'

'He is still at Salt River Station.'

'Tell Vaughn to get off there.'

'OK, Benny.' He rang off.

On platform 7, Griessel saw his train's doors open at last. He jogged up and got in.

He stood, holding on to the metal rail near the roof.

Mbali was going to have to confront one of the Cobras all on her own – the one who would go to find the memory card under the seat as soon as he got on, probably at Parow. There was no time, no one else to help. He would have to warn her now.

Vaughn Cupido got off the train at Salt River Station, and within seconds he spotted Tyrone Kleinbooi sitting on a bench beside the platform.

The pickpocket had a phone in his hand, and all his attention was focused on it.

Cupido walked calmly down the platform, called Dave Fiedler, and told him.

'Hang on, china,' said Fiedler.

Cupido heard Fiedler and Bones talking.

'Captain Griessel will be there in five minutes,' said Fiedler eventually. 'He wants you just to keep an eye on Tyrone.'

★ ★ ★

Griessel called Nyathi and explained to him that Mbali, due to an unexpected confluence of events, was alone on a train where, just after Parow Station, she would be confronted by a Cobra who would want that card.

'Sir, if you could just wait for the train at Bellville – we have no other backup.'

'I will take Ulinda with me,' said Nyathi. 'How much time do we have?'

'Not more than ten minutes.'

No anxiety, no reproach, just: 'We'll be there.'

Beyond Maitland, Mbali sat with the memory card held between her fingers, wondering what disastrous data was stored on it. Information that was responsible for the death of at least nine people, and very nearly a tenth as well, an innocent young student.

She stowed the card carefully in a side pocket of her big handbag. She rolled the chewing gum between her fingers until it was one big ball again. She stuck it back precisely where it had been when she found it.

From her handbag she took a little bottle of waterless hand cleaner from Woolworths, and a tissue. She cleaned her fingers thoroughly.

Then, with both hands hidden in the darkness of the handbag, she took her Beretta pistol and made sure it was cocked.

She took her left hand out, but her right hand remained hidden in the depths of the bag, gripped around the pistol.

Benny Griessel had said that a Cobra would get on at Parow Station, and would come looking for the memory card.

And she would be ready for him.

Benny Griessel got off the train at Salt River and phoned Cupido.

'Where are you?'

'On the platform.'

'I can't see you.'

'Platform 11.'

'OK, I'm on the other side, I'm coming. Can you see Tyrone?'

'He is ten steps away from me. He's texting on his phone.'

'I'll be there directly.'

Griessel walked hurriedly down the stairs, heading for the other side of the railway line.

Bones would phone at any moment with news about the text that Tyrone was sending.

If the pickpocket was still here, that meant that he was going to receive the money here.

Good news, because he and Cupido were both here. One to catch the Cobra, and one to follow Tyrone and the money.

The ZTE rang, as he had expected.

'Cobra texted to say he has passed Maitland, then Tyrone answered with this: "When train stops at Salt River, wait until just before doors close again. Throw out money. Don't get out. Stay on train. Just throw out money bag. If money is good, I'll send card details."'

'Have they answered?'

'No . . . yes, just came in. Just "OK".'

'How long before that train comes in at Salt River?'

'Three minutes.'

Griessel began running. 'OK, I'll call you when I have news.'

Cupido saw Griessel running towards him, coat flapping, hair ruffled by the wind. He walked to meet him.

Griessel waited until he was beside his colleague and then explained quietly and breathlessly what was going to happen. 'I'm going to get on that train, Vaughn. You follow Tyrone and the money. If the Cobras are tracking his cellphone too, he's dead. Protect him.'

'Got it,' said Cupido.

Then Griessel walked away, towards the platform.

The money train was visible, a kilometre away.

Tyrone hid behind a pillar, his heart beating wildly. He had put the rucksack down on the concrete and now he looked up quickly to see if someone could see him, put his hand in the rucksack and pulled out the pistol. He pushed the pistol under the purple windcheater, closed the bag, swung it up onto his back.

It was the moment of truth, now.

Maybe they would try to shoot him.

Maybe they would just throw the money out.

Either way, he was as ready as he was ever going to be.

It's worth it, it's worth it, his sister's future . . .

He took the cellphone, typed the message in: *Card is in carriage 3, 3rd class, stuck in the middle of middle bench, table mountain side.*

He would send it when he was sure the money was correct.

The train came in.

He stood ready, behind the pillar, peering at the train.

It stopped.

A few people approached.

A few people got off.

A few people got on.

The train stood there.

The whistle blew.

His eyes scanned up and down, up and down.

A rush of air as the doors closed.

Where was the money?

Right at the back, the furthest from him, the rucksack bounced once, twice across the platform.

The train was leaving.

Tyrone waited.

No one else got off.

His eyes followed the train.

There through the glass, he saw Black Beanie, the man's eyes searching.

Instinctively, Tyrone ducked behind the pillar.

He waited.

The train was gone.

The rucksack lay there.

He looked around.

There was a tall coloured man in a coat, some distance away, with his back to Tyrone. Looked like he had a phone in his hand.

Tyrone waited.

The rucksack lay there.

The coloured man in the coat began to walk away.

Tyrone flew out from behind the pillar and ran to the rucksack.

He grabbed it, raced back to the pillar, opened it.
The money was there.
He sent the text.

58

Benny Griessel made a fatal error.

The chaos of the morning was to blame, the many threads that he had to hold on to and manipulate like a puppeteer, the adrenaline and crazy pace of the chase, the determination to bring the Cobras to book.

He should have stood still for a moment and thought, but he didn't.

Instinctively he shifted his service weapon into easy reach. And he stormed through the train carriage.

He had been standing at the window of the middle carriage, and saw where the rucksack was thrown out. Now he threaded his way between the people in the compartment, to get there, two carriages down. He didn't see the notice stuck in big cartoon strips above the door.

Travelling between coaches is illegal.
Do not board train when full.
Do not hold doors open when train is in motion.

Nobody stopped him when he went from the middle carriage to the next. He saw the Cobra, the one from the photo, with the black cap and the blue windcheater, on the other side of the last door. He put his hand on the Beretta on his hip, pressed the safety off, focused on the man who was staring intently out of the window.

Griessel was unaware of the middle-aged ticket inspector approaching, only noticed him when the man reached him and said, 'You can't travel between coaches.'

'I'm from the police,' said Griessel so as not to attract attention, especially not from the Cobra.

Griessel walked past the ticket inspector. The train was noisy and he didn't hear whether the man said anything in response. Griessel raised his left hand to open the door between the carriages.

The ticker inspector grabbed his right shoulder, to stop him. The man said, 'You can't go through there, it's against the rules.'

'I'm a policeman,' said Griessel, loudly and impatiently this time.

The Cobra saw the movement, turned his head, looked at him.

Griessel jerked the door open with his left hand, pulled out his service pistol.

The ticket inspector shoved Griessel's shoulder, pushing him off balance.

The Cobra was swift and practised. His right hand emerged from his windcheater, holding a pistol. He swung it towards Griessel as he moved forward. To the middle of the carriage.

The door began to close automatically again.

Time stood still. Griessel didn't know how thick the glass was, he would have to shoot before the door closed, before the Cobra could fire at him, there was no time to aim. He jerked his shoulder forwards, and pulled the trigger.

The deafening shot boomed through the train carriage. People screamed. Blood exploded in a fine spray around the Cobra's head and against the window behind him. The Cobra collapsed. The ticket inspector dived at Griessel and tried to wrench the pistol away from him.

Griessel aimed a punch at the man, the pistol was loaded and dangerous, what was the idiot doing? He hit the ticket inspector with an elbow somewhere in his face and the man fell. Griessel staggered forward, up to the Cobra.

The Cobra's lower cheekbone and nose was a bloody, gaping hole.

'*Fok!*' He wanted to know where David Adair was, he'd wanted to question the man.

The ticket inspector tackled Griessel, and both of them stumbled over the Cobra.

Griessel lost his temper, but he pressed the catch of the Beretta so the weapon was safe. Then he hit the ticket inspector angrily across the jaw with the pistol. The man fell down again. Griessel straightened up. He jammed the pistol against the ticket inspector's cheek. 'Are you *fokken* deaf? I'm a policeman.'

'Yes,' said the man, clearly confused.

'Yes, what?'

'Yes,' said the ticket inspector, 'I am a bit deaf.'

Only then Griessel did notice the discreet hearing aid in the man's ear.

Someone pulled the emergency cord so that Griessel completely lost his balance and fell over, on top of the Cobra's corpse.

Mbali sat and waited. She felt no fear. There was just a tingling of adrenaline in her veins.

Her hand was firmly on her service pistol, the barrel pointing straight ahead, even if it was deep in her cavernous handbag. Even though Bones had phoned her and said Benny Griessel asked that she should just watch the Cobra who came to fetch the memory card. At Bellville Station, Captain Zola Nyathi and Ulinda Radebe were waiting. Don't confront the Cobra. Identify him, watch him.

At Parow Station she looked out of the window, to see if she could spot a Cobra.

There were too many people getting in and out of her carriage.

Only once things had settled down, just before the door closed, did she become aware of him.

It was the one from the Waterfront. She knew it, because she recognised the baseball cap, the slender grace of his movement, the shape of his face, the *café au lait* complexion. It was the one they believed came from Mozambique, Joaquim Curado, currently travelling under the name of Hector Malot.

She admonished herself, inaudibly and in Zulu, to keep calm. Her heart began hammering in her chest, her hand perspired on the pistol butt.

He was the one who had shot five people.

The train pulled out of the station.

She watched him count the benches. He came over to her.

'Could you move?' he asked, and pointed at the empty seats on either side of her.

'No,' she said.

She looked into his eyes. She saw death.

She didn't look away.

He hesitated. He stooped, his hands fumbling under the bench to the left of her. He straightened up. He moved to her right side, bent and searched again. He rose, and stood in front of her. 'You will have to move. I lost something. I must find it.'

She sat, a female Buddha, deliberately motionless and stubborn. She sighed deeply, as if it were a great sacrifice. She shifted to her right, slowly.

He waited until she had the full weight of her body in the next seat. He bent down. He searched, until his fingers came to a stop.

She pulled the pistol out of her handbag in one smooth movement. She made sure it didn't hook on anything. His face was down near her thigh, while he was feeling about. He saw the movement too late. She pressed the muzzle of the pistol against the edge of the baseball cap, just above the man's temple. She said, 'If you make any movement, I will shoot you, because you are a killer. I am Captain Mbali Kaleni of the South African Police Services, and you are under arrest for the murder of five security officials at the Waterfront.'

He sat stock still, both hands still under the seat. She knew he had his hands on the chewing gum. Let him think the card was still there.

He said something, short and explosive, in a language she didn't understand. She knew it was a swearword.

Mbali banged the pistol muzzle hard against Joaquim Curado's temple. 'Profanity is the effort of a feeble brain to express itself forcibly,' she said. 'Don't do that again.'

She pulled the handcuffs out of the handbag with her left hand. She stood up carefully, without taking her eyes off the man or taking the pistol away from his head. The handbag slid down to the floor, but she left it. She pressed her knee and her considerable weight against Curado's back.

'Put your hands behind your back. Very slowly.'

He didn't listen.

She pressed harder with her weight, and her knee clamped him against the bench. She banged the pistol barrel hard against the back of his head.

He moved his hands behind him. She saw there was nothing in them. He would think the card was still there under the seat. She clicked the handcuffs first on his left wrist, changed grip and then on his right wrist.

'You are not all that dangerous,' she said, and bent to pick up her handbag. Time to report to her team leader, Benny Griessel.

Tyrone ran across the bridge at Salt River Station, past the coloured man with the coat that flapped like Batman's cloak in the wind. He must catch the train, to Bellville.

His shoes clattered down the stairs, to the platform.

The train wasn't there yet.

Relief.

He realised his grip on the money-rucksack was so tight that his fingers were cramping.

Relax, Ty, just relax. All that he could do now, was to get to the hospital. Extra insurance against an attack, but it shouldn't be necessary. No reason for them to harm Nadia, they had the card, the correct file on it. He had the money. Two point four fucking mill. His struggles were over, Nadia had a future.

The train came in. He walked, he had to sit down, he'd been on his feet since the crack of dawn, he was exhausted by all the worry, he just wanted to sit, just relax, enjoy the ride.

There were a lot of empty seats.

He chose the one at the back, at the end of the carriage.

He couldn't help himself. He pulled the rucksack open again. *Jirre*, that was a lot of money. He pushed his hand in, pulled out a bundle of notes.

Everything is legit.

The dude with the Batman coat came in through the intersecting door of the carriage and looked round. Tyrone zipped the rucksack closed, fastened the buckles. Batman headed towards him. Sat just one seat away. Cellphone in his hand.

Suspicious-looking motherfucker.

Tyrone put the rucksack on his lap.

The pistol was behind him now, in his belt, the butt pressed coldly against his ribs.

Was he one of *them*?

Or just a dude? Wouldn't it be really funny if he got robbed now?

He moved his hand very slowly, until he had hold of the pistol.

Nobody was going to rob him now.

Batman looked at him and smiled. '*Wa's jy op pad heen, my bru?*' Where are you going?

Tyrone was so relieved about the Flats Afrikaans, the smile, the fact that Batman might be a nice *ou*, over the dreadful tension that was broken, that he laughed.

'*Na my suster,*' he said. 'In Bellville.'

'Nice,' said Batman. The phone in his hand rang. 'Sorry,' he said, and answered: '*Jis*, Bones?'

59

Batman said 'OK.' and '*Jissis*' and 'Yes, everything is fine' into his cell-phone, and Tyrone tuned out and thought, can you believe it? He took a few deep breaths and exhaled. He felt light-headed, he wanted to laugh out loud. No, he wanted to dance, but that would all have to wait until he was dead sure the cops were looking after Nadia nicely. What he would do, he would phone them again, *sommer netnou* from Bellville, scare the bejaysus out of them: fifteen gangstas are on the way from the Plain to go and hurt that girlie in the hospital, get your SWAT team in, *manne*, call in the big guns, this is not child's play. All his plans had worked out so well, the whole lot, after all his worries. And now there was the small matter of what he was going to do with his share of the two point four. Nadia had six years of study, about fifty grand a year, let's make it sixty or seventy, let him *maar* let her have some luxuries too, some nice *goeters*. That's more than four hundred thousand bucks, leaves them with another two million. Buy her a little car, nothing fancy, just a little Peugeot or something.

How are you going to explain that to your sister, Ty, don't be stupid.

Not impossible. He could just say he got this *moerse* paint contract . . .

Batman said something.

'Sorry?' said Ty.

'It's not necessary, *jy wiet*.'

'*Ek versta' jou nie, my bru*.' I don't understand.

'You don't need to go to the hospital.'

Did he just say 'to the hospital' by mistake? Hadn't he told him Bellville?

'We've just caught the guy from the Waterfront. A bunch of Hawks are now on the way to the hospital, just to make sure. Your sister is safe. If I were you, I would just stay on the train.'

Tyrone grew ice cold.

'Who are you?' He moved his hand back to his pistol.

'My name is Vaughn Cupido. I'm a captain in the Directorate of Priority Crime Investigations of the Es A Pee Es. They call us the Hawks, pappie. We're the hot shit, the top cops, the main men. And if you have a weapon there under your jacket, my best advice is, forget it. They don't call me Crackshot McKenneth, the Pride of the Prairies, for nothing. I am Quick Draw McGraw, faster than a speeding bullet . . .'

'OK,' said Tyrone. 'I get the point.'

'So just relax.'

'I am relaxed.'

'Have you got a gun?' Cupido's voice was very calm, as if he were asking what he had had for breakfast.

It took a long time before Tyrone could get it out: '*Ja.*'

'Hand it over. Slowly. We really don't want anyone to get hurt.'

Tyrone sat frozen. The thought that he was going to lose everything, that it had all been for nothing, all the blood, the running, the terror, the worry, it made him feel paralysed.

Cupido looked at his watch. 'Time is running out. Just hand it over, everything will be OK.'

Tyrone lifted his hand slowly to his hip, pulled out the pistol reluctantly.

'Hold it like that so the *Hase* can't see it.'

'The *Hase*?'

'It's police-speak for the public. Slow and easy now.'

Tyrone passed the pistol over, low and unobtrusively. The cop dude took it.

'That's better, Tyrone. Tell me, where did you grow up?'

'Mitchells Plain.'

'Me too. What street?'

'Begonia.'

'I know Begonia. Hard times, *da*'.'

''S true.' What did the motherfucker want?

'I grew up in Blackbury Street. It's just other side Eisleben.'

'I know Blackbury.'

'How long have you been a pickpocket?'

Jirre. He knew everything. 'Since I was twelve.'

'Who taught you?'

'Uncle Solly. From Begonia Street.'

'Was he your real uncle?'

What kind of conversation was this? 'No. My foster father.'

'You and Nadia were orphans?'

'*Ja.* Daddy and Mommy died when I was three and she was one.'

'*Daai's* sad, my *bru.*'

'Uncle Solly was a good man.'

'But a pickpocket.'

'Damn fine pickpocket. And he had morals.'

'How much money is in the rucksack?'

That was a surprise. Such an ugly surprise that his body jerked with the shock of it.

He wanted to ask, 'How do you know about the money?'

But something else suddenly dawned on him: the Batman cop wanted a cut. Of course he wanted a cut. Or all of it. Everyone knew the cops were corrupt.

'What money?'

'The money in the photo that they sent to you. Did they hand it over?'

He kept quiet.

'Did they?' Cupido asked again.

'*Ja.*'

'How much?'

What did it help to lie. 'Two point four.'

'Million?'

'*Ja.*'

Cupido whistled softly. 'And it's all there?'

'I think so.'

'That's a lot of money.'

'How much do you want?'

Cupido laughed. 'If it wasn't such a *lekker* day, my bru, I would have bitchslapped you.'

Tyrone dared to look at the cop for the first time.

'*Ek sê*, it's a lot of money. A lot of responsibility.'

'It is.'

'Not many get such a chance. An *ou* who can put his sister through university. And make something of himself. Get out of Begonia Street.'

''S true.'

The cop put his hand in his coat pocket. Tyrone watched the movement. The hand emerged, holding a card.

'This is my business card. Take it.'

Tyrone took it.

'I'm getting off in Bellville just now. You are going to stay on the train. You are going to go all the way to Stellenbosch. Go and stay in your sister's flat, until you get your own place. Don't go back to that room in Schotsche Kloof. There's still people who might try to find you, for a week or two. So, lie low. If you have any trouble, call me. If you want to make absolutely sure the whole thing is over, call me.'

Tyrone nodded, dumbfounded.

'But no more pickpocketing. I am going to check the system. If you ever get arrested, if I see you on a CCTV camera, if you jaywalk, my *bru*, then I will come and bliksem you, and I will put you away, *versta' jy?*'

Tyrone nodded again.

'Make a life, Tyrone. Few people get the chance.'

'I will.'

Cupido put out a hand and squeezed Tyrone's shoulder. 'You're a brave *ou*. Very brave. Your sister is lucky to have you.'

And then the motherfucker stood up, smiled at him, and walked to the door of the railway carriage.

The train slowed. It stopped at Bellville. Tyrone watched Cupido walk away in his long swanky coat. The dude didn't look back, just stepped out when the doors opened. He followed Batman with his eyes, he watched the cocky walk, until he disappeared completely from view.

Tyrone sat there, staring, until the doors closed again, and the train left the station.

Then he shuddered, and began to cry.

He cried all the way to Muldersvlei, his tall, skinny, sore, tired body shaking uncontrollably.

60

They were questioning Joaquim Curado in a small office of the DPCI building in Bellville, away from the suspicious eyes of Criminal Intelligence, when Benny Griessel walked in.

There was blood on Griessel's jacket. His hair was even more dishevelled than usual, he was harried and stressed, but his eyes burned clear and full of fire.

'He won't say a word.' Cupido pointed at Curado, who sat like a sphinx at the table, still handcuffed.

'He doesn't have to talk,' said Griessel, 'but tell me first, who is with Nadia?'

'I've convinced the Bellville SC to send eight more people. They have every entrance covered,' said Zola Nyathi.

'OK. Thank you, sir.'

'How come he doesn't have to talk?' asked Cupido.

'Dave Fiedler has tracked the Cobra phone,' said Griessel. 'We have four other phone numbers. Two are registered with Orange France, and Dave can't do anything with them. The other two are Cell C, they must have bought them here. Dave has been plotting their location over the last twenty-four hours. I think David Adair is on a farm by the name of Hercules Pillar, near the R304.'

Griessel was watching Joaquim Curado closely. When he said the words 'Hercules Pillar', there was an infinitesimal movement of his head and eyes, and he knew that he was right.

'Dave said the place is advertised on the Internet: Rent a farmhouse, privacy and solitude, just twenty minutes from Cape Town. Here is the Internet address . . .'

They walked to Cupido's office, where they could look up the Hercules Pillar website.

'It's perfect,' said Mbali, because the old farmhouse, beautifully renovated and whitewashed, was situated on a hill. You would be able to see any intruders coming a kilometre away.

'We'll have to go in with speed and superior firepower,' said Nyathi. 'That is the only option.'

There were eight of them: Griessel and Cupido, Nyathi and Mbali, Radebe and Vusi Ndabeni, Frankie Fillander and Mooiwillem Liebenberg. Quietly, in pairs, each collected an assault rifle in the Hawks' weapon safe, then crept though the corridors to the car park.

They drove off in four cars.

On the N1, in the leading car, the Giraffe asked Mbali, 'What happened to the memory card?'

She tapped a chubby hand on her big black handbag.

'What are you going to do with it?'

She looked out of the window. She said, 'I'll keep it as a safeguard.'

'Against what?'

'Against people who want to harm our democracy, and the spirit of my father's struggle.'

Nyathi just nodded. He couldn't think of a better guardian for it.

In their car, second in the convoy, Griessel asked, 'What happened to Tyrone?'

'Canny coloured *daai*. He gave me the slip,' said Cupido.

'Yes,' said Griessel. 'We old dogs don't have the speed to keep up any more.'

Cupido's laugh was a little forced.

And Benny realised what must have really happened.

Their plan was simply to race up to the farmhouse on the hill: there was nowhere to hide, no room for surprise.

They would drive up to the farmhouse, park the four vehicles around it. Then they would give the Cobras a chance to come out before they stormed the house and began shooting.

The plan worked, up to a point.

When all the cars had come to a halt, when they had jumped out and found shelter, assault rifles cocked and aimed at the windows and doors behind the wide veranda of the big house, there was only silence. Just the cooing of a few doves, and a cow mooing somewhere.

Nyathi called out over the megaphone, 'You are surrounded. Please put down your weapons, and come out with your hands on your heads.'

They waited, the adrenaline pumping, fingers on triggers, heads shielded behind the safety of the vehicles' metal bodies.

No reaction. Only the afternoon hush, and the shadow of a fat white cloud that came and went.

Griessel looked at the bare ground outside the front door. There were the tracks of other vehicle tyres in the mud of last night's rain. The Cobras had parked in front of the door, with at least two vehicles. Maybe three.

Nyathi repeated the message, even louder.

Nothing happened.

'Sir, let me run to the door,' Cupido said.

'Wait,' said Nyathi.

They waited. The minutes crept by.

'OK, let's cover Vaughn,' said Nyathi. 'Wait for my signal.'

They stood up, lifted the barrels of the rifles over the roofs and bonnets of the cars, pointed them at the door and windows, where there was still no sign of life.

'Go!' yelled Nyathi.

Cupido, in his long, elegant coat, ran across the open yard to the front door, slightly crouched, as if that would somehow help. The automatic rifle in his hand made him look like a character from a 1930's film.

Only his footsteps were audible on the saturated ground.

He was safely at the door.

Silence.

'I hear something,' said Cupido. He knelt down in front of the door.

They waited, dead quiet.

'Yes, there's somebody in there.'

He shifted closer to the door.

'Someone is shouting for help,' he said. 'I think we should go in.'

They found David Patrick Adair in the master bedroom of the house. He was stretched out and tied to the bed, with cable ties and rope. He was unshaven, dirty, and smelly, but unharmed. His first words when Cupido walked in were, 'Are you the cavalry, or a different kind of trouble?'

'We are the Hawks,' said Cupido.

'I'm not sure that answers my question . . .'

Shouts from the other team members, as they declared the house safe, room by room.

'We are the South African Police Service,' said Cupido.

Nyathi and Mbali walked in, then Griessel and Fillander.

'And what a splendid representation of the Rainbow Nation you are,' said Adair, his nonchalant tone trying unsuccessfully to disguise his immense relief. 'You wouldn't happen to know if my student, the lovely Lillian Alvarez, is safe, would you?'

Adair politely requested a chance to shower. 'And, please God, let me brush my teeth.'

He was a tall, elegant man. Griessel saw that he wanted to preserve his dignity at all cost, but the trauma of the past days lay close to the surface.

They waited on the veranda to make sure the Cobras didn't make a surprise appearance. When Adair came out of the bathroom, Nyathi, Griessel, Mbali, and Cupido questioned him in the sitting room.

He said there were three of them during the abduction in Franschhoek. 'They were so terribly efficient. So utterly businesslike.'

They knew about Lillian Alvarez. That was how they found out precisely where he was, because they had tapped Alvarez's cellphone. And like a fool, he had phoned Alvarez last Friday night from the Franschhoek guesthouse.

'They also used her to convince me to hand over the data. They said they would kill her. And that I had to call her, to bring the memory card.'

'What was on the card?' asked Nyathi.

'A lot of data,' said Adair.

'What kind of data?'

'The monetary evil that men do.'

'Can you be more specific?'

'How much time do we have?'

'All the time we need.'

'Well, there is the data on possible terrorists. And possible spies. And possible organised crime money laundering. By organised crime, and by the banks. Damning evidence of dirty banking hands. Not murky little banks in banana republics. Continental, international banking colossi. And then there's the quite impressive and intimidatingly long list of corrupt government officials . . .'

'South African government officials?' asked Mbali.

'I'm afraid so. But let me hasten to add that the data also includes government officials from thirty-nine other countries. My own included. And the evidence is quite conclusive.'

'Can you tell us which South African government officials?'

'Quite a few. MPs. Ministers. Your president, I'm sorry to add.'

Mbali made a small despairing sound.

'That's how they got the SSA and CI involved,' said Nyathi.

'Who?' asked Adair.

'Your MI6 got our State Security Agency and Crime Intelligence Unit involved in the investigation, in the quest to find you.'

'I see. No stone unturned. How comforting. But yes, you might be right. I did mention the corrupt politicians list to my friends at MI6.'

'Who do the Cobras work for?' asked Griessel.

'The who?'

'The people who kidnapped you. Do they work for the CIA?' asked Cupido.

'Good heavens, no. They are working for the banks.'

61

They didn't believe him.

David Adair explained. He said he knew he would only get one chance to go fishing for all manner of evil in the SWIFT system with his extensive new protocol, because he had always been very open about his political and ethical standards. There were so many factions watching him, all waiting to see what he wanted to do with the system – and suspecting that he might be looking for ammunition for his crusades.

So he wrote the programming in such a way that he could slip in a digital Trojan horse afterwards, when everyone was satisfied that the protocol would not be damaging to them.

And the end result, when the data began coming in, was mind-boggling. There were the spying details, the corruption of politicians, the massive extent of large, well-respected international banks looking the other way and cooperating in the laundering of billions for organised crime. But what took him completely by surprise, was a conglomerate of international banks manipulating the financial system: to evade taxation, to fix rates, to tamper illegally with share prices and exchange rates, and to continue to trade in derivative instruments – indecipherable and complex derivatives, despite the huge risk it posed to the world economy.

Executives of banks and financial institutions enriched themselves on a massive scale, at the expense of common people. He was totally unprepared for the greed, the sheer extent of the machinations.

'The problem is, what does one do with such information? To make it public is an act of potential financial sabotage. The system, still very fragile after the meltdown, might well collapse. Or at least trigger a new international recession. The big losers won't be the banking fat cats, but the very people I had hoped to protect. The public. So, just after my dialogue with MI6, I made the mistake of calling the CEO of a very big international bank. Just to tell him that it might be a good idea to start winding down all the illegal and dangerous activities. Or run the risk of being exposed. Yes, it was blackmail, but the cause was good and just, I thought. Soon after, I became aware of a series of strange occurrences. I thought I was being followed, I was pretty sure someone had been in my office and my house. Perhaps to plant bugs? So I took a few precautions. I flew to Marseilles to get myself a false passport, and I put a considerable sum of money away in a new account under the false name—'

'Where would a university professor get a considerable sum of money from?' asked Cupido.

'The European Union has been rather generous in remunerating me for my work.'

'OK.'

'I packed a suitcase, just in case. And when I got home from Lillian's place last Monday night, and I saw that my home had been ransacked, I knew. And I ran.'

'But how do you know it was the banks?'

'I speak French,' said Adair. 'I understood what one of my abductors was saying over the phone to the people who hired them. There is only one conclusion.'

They concealed one vehicle behind a shed a hundred metres away from the farmyard. Cupido, Fillander, Mbali, and Ndabeni stayed behind, since the Cobras' luggage, a few firearms, and travel documents were still in the house.

Griessel and Nyathi took Adair to the city: he'd asked to be taken to Lillian Alvarez as quickly as possible.

Griessel sat in the back of the big Ford Territory, with his and Nyathi's assault rifles beside him on the seat. Adair sat in front beside Nyathi, who was behind the wheel.

On the R304 Nyathi said, 'You realise you are still in danger?'

'I do. But as soon as I've seen Lillian, I will rectify the matter. I will Skype the editor of the *Guardian*. He is a man of the utmost integrity, and I will make a full confession, and give him access to the data.'

'But the memory card is gone.'

'Good.'

'Wasn't the data on the memory card?'

'Of course it was. I was hoping against hope that, if I gave them the data in a tangible format, they would not kill me. But they would have, I'm sure. The data also lives in the cloud. Two or three places. They'll find it, eventually, I suppose. One always leaves tracks . . .'

On the N1, just before the Lucullus Street off-ramp, Adair said philosophically, 'Of course, one contemplates one's own demise, under these circumstances. And then you keep hoping that all the lies, all the deceit, will somehow be uncovered. That the truth will set us all free. But you know, it is such an imperfect world, and it is getting more imperfect every day. So, thank you . . .'

Griessel looked out of the window and thought about Mbali, who had also spoken about how liberating the truth could be. His mind was so filled with the question of secrets and lies that he was barely aware of the white Volkswagen Amarok double cab drawing up beside them.

Later he would not remember whether it was an odd movement, the sun reflecting on a gun barrel, or the vaguely familiar face of the man. Something suddenly made him focus, triggered the alarm in his head. In one move he grabbed the rifle on the seat next to him and shouted, 'Sir!'

It was too late.

The shots boomed beside them, the bullets punched through him, and through Nyathi. Shreds of fabric puffed from the headrests, the wind was suddenly loud in his ears, and a bloody mist, entire droplets, seemed to hang suspended in the interior of the car.

Griessel felt the exploding pain of bullet wounds, the terrible violence of lead slamming, tearing into his body.

Nyathi lost control of the Ford, the vehicle zigzagged across the road, skidded, overturned, and rolled. Griessel tried to hold on. Airbags exploded. He had his seat belt fastened, that was his only thought, he had his seat belt fastened, now he could tell Fritz it was proof that that was the right thing to do.

Just before everything went black, he saw the body of Zola Nyathi, still buckled into his seat, but strangely uncontrolled. Only the laws of physics in charge of his body now, tugging it back and forth. And he thought: how fragile a person's body is. Nyathi had always seemed so indestructible.

* * *

There was a moment when he recovered consciousness, as he was suspended upside down in the wreckage, watching his blood flow from his body and pooling on the roof of the Ford. A moment when he was aware of the man who rifled through his pockets, hastily and roughly, but thoroughly. The face was devoid of emotion. It was one of them, one of the men on the O. R. Tambo photos. The man's hands searched through all his pockets, coated in his blood.

A shot cracked, one last time, in the shattered space.

Then everything went quiet.

62

He saw Alexa beside the hospital bed, in the middle of the night. She was sleeping awkwardly in the chair. He tried to say something to her, but he was so very tired, he could scarcely open his mouth. His parched mouth.

He was awake. He was at Alexa's house, in the sitting room. His arm was gone. Completely. Alexa said don't worry, there are bass guitar players with only one arm. She puffed on a cigarette.

He dimly realised someone else was here too. Strange, it was daytime now. He opened his eyes. It was his daughter, Carla. She sat hunched over, her elbows on the bed, her face close to his, her expression intense, as if willing him not to go. He saw her mouth move, forming the word 'Papa', but he didn't hear it. He was drifting away from everything. But both his arms were here.

Fritz sat in the chair beside the hospital bed. His son, with a guitar. His son sang to him. It was so incredibly beautiful.

He had a conversation with Nyathi and Mbali. They spoke Zulu and Xhosa, and to his surprise so did he. Kaleni said, Isn't it wonderful?

Yes, said Nyathi.

What? Asked Griessel.

There's no corruption here, said Mbali. Look, Benny, none. It wasn't for nothing after all.

Cupido and Bones and Mbali stood beside his bed, their faces grim.

'Vaughn,' said Griessel.

'*Jissis*,' said Cupido and stood up, looked at him.

'This is a hospital. Watch your language,' said Mbali.

'Get a nurse, he's awake,' said Cupido.

And then Griessel was gone again.

They only told him Nyathi was dead after he had been awake for two days. Nyathi and David Adair.

'They thought you weren't going to make it, Benny,' said Alexa, her tears dripping on the sheet. She held his left hand tightly, the one on the arm that was still reasonably whole. 'They brought you back from the brink of death twice. They said you had no blood left. None.'

Two wounds in his right leg, one in his upper right arm, his right shoulder, his left wrist, two bullets through his ribs and his right lung. But everything would heal in time. There would be stiffness in the limbs, the surgeon said. For many years. He had been in a coma for sixteen days, they said. And he thought to himself, that was the easiest sixteen days off the bottle he had ever added to his tally.

Cloete came and sat with him. 'CNN, the BBC, Sky News and the *New York Times* are all asking for interviews, Benny. Are you up to it?'

'No.'

Superintendent Marie-Caroline Aubert phoned him from Lyon. She sympathised with the loss of his colleague. She congratulated him on the arrest of Curado. She said the one he shot dead was the only French citizen, one Romain Poite. The others that they identified were all Eastern Europeans, but also former members of the French Foreign Legion. 'We are trying to track them down, thanks to your good work.'

Jeanette Louw, the owner of Body Armour, came to sit with him too. He told her everything.

Alexa was there every day, in the morning, afternoon, and evening. Carla came to visit. Fritz. His colleagues. Doc Barkhuizen. His fellow Rust band members. And Lize Beekman, once. 'I'm sorry about your concert,' he said.

'It won't be the last one,' she said. 'Just get better.'

He had done a lot of thinking, in the hospital. When Alexa came to fetch him and take him to her house, his words were ready.

Tired and weak, he climbed into the double bed in Alexa's bedroom. Then he said, 'Come sit here, please. There is something I have to talk about.'

She sat down, concerned.

'I love you very much,' he said.

'And I love you, Benny.'

'Alexa, I didn't know what to say, because it's a difficult thing. But someone said: the truth makes us free . . .'

'What truth, Benny?'

'I can't . . . you know . . .' and all his planned words and phrases, practised in his mind, over and over, deserted him.

'What are you talking about?'

'Before this thing . . .' And he indicated the last of the bandages. 'I couldn't keep up. With the . . . sex. I'm too old and too fucked-up, Alexa. I can't do the thing every day any more. You are very sexy to me, my head wants to, but my . . .' He pointed at his groin.

'Your rascal,' she said.

'Yes. My rascal can't keep up. Not every day. Maybe every second day. We can try.'

He saw how her face crumpled. He saw her begin to cry, and he thought, *fok*, that was the wrong thing to say.

'I'll see a doctor,' he said.

She hugged him tightly. He felt the warmth of her breath, and her tears. 'I was so scared, Benny. I was never enough for Adam. I thought that was why he strayed. I just wanted to be enough for you.'

Adam, her late husband.

'You are more than enough for me,' he said. 'Just not every day.'

'Thank God,' she said.

And then he heard her vibrant, joyful laugh.

GLOSSARY

Ai – ah, oh; ow, ouch, mostly used a little despairingly.

Ag – Very similar to 'ai': ah!, oh!; alas, pooh!, mostly used with resignation.

Annerlike – Cape Flats Afrikaans for 'a different kind of' – often used in a negative way. (Cape Flats slang refers to the Afrikaans spoken on the Cape Flats, a vast area east of Cape Town, where the majority of 'Cape Coloured' people reside. 'Coloured people' refer to the descendants of Malaysian slaves in South Africa (forced migration by the Dutch East India Company), who inter-married with white farmers and local Khoi people – as opposed to Blacks (descendants of the Bantu people) and Whites (descendants of European settlers).

Appie – Diminutive of 'apprentice', someone who is learning a trade.

Baie – Afrikaans for 'A lot', or 'very'.

Bergie - Cape Flats Afrikaans for a homeless person, often a vagrant, living on the side of Table Mountain (berg = mountain).

Blerrie – Cape Flats slan for 'bloody'.

Bliksem – Mild profanity, used as an exclamation or adjective ('Damn!' or 'damned'), a verb (I will 'bliksem' you = I will hit you hard).

Blougatte – When trainee constables attend police college, they wear blue uniforms, and are called 'blue arses', or 'blougatte'. The nickname is also used to refer to lower, uniformed police ranks in uniform as a slightly derogatory term, as opposed to plain clothes police women and men.

Boetie – Diminutive of 'broer', which means 'brother'.

Bok – Afrikaans for 'goat' or 'deer', but used much more widely. 'Here's a middle-aged bok with a pretty young thing' refers to an Afrikaans idiom 'an old goat likes green leaves', meaning 'an older man likes younger women'. 'Bok' or the diminutive 'bokkie' is also used an as endearment for men or women.

Broe', daai's kwaai – Cape Flats Afrikaans for 'Brother, that's heavy'.

Coloured – See 'Annerlike' above.

Daai, daai's – Cape Flats Afrikaans for 'that' (daai) or 'that is' (daai's).

Daatlik – Cape Flats Afrikaans for 'immediately'.

Dagga – Afrikaans for cannabis.

Die Boer – Literally, 'The Farmer'. It is the name of a famous, intimate music theatre in Durbanville, a suburb of Cape Town.

Die rekening is agterstallig – Afrikaans for 'Your account is in arrears.'

Dis 'n lekker een die – Afrikaans for 'this is a good one'. 'Lekker' is word widely used for anything that is 'good', 'delicious', 'tasty'.

Dof – Afrikaans for 'faint', but also used to indicate a stupid person.

Donner – Mild Afrikaans expletive, literally meaning 'thunder'. Often used in the sense of "I am going to donner you' – I am going to hurt / hit you.

Doos – Afrikaans expletive, comparing someone to female genitalia. Closest English translation would be 'cunt'.

Dop – Afrikaans for 'a drink', referring to alcohol.

Drol – Afrikaans for 'turd'.

Dronkgat – Afrikaans for 'drunkard'. (Literally, 'a drunk arse'.)

Ek kom van die Pniel af – Cape Flats Afrikaans for 'I come from Pniel'. Pniel is a village near Stellenbosch.

Ek sê jou – Afrikaans for 'I am telling you.'

Ek versta' jou nie – Afrikaans for 'I don't understand you'. (Cape Flats vernacular.)

Ek vra ma net – Afrikaans for 'I am just asking.'

Ek wiet, ja – Cape Flats vernacular for 'I know, yes.'

Flippen – Mild expletive, used as an acceptable alternative for 'fucking'. (Afrikaans.)

Fokken – Afrikaans for 'fucking', as in 'that fucking guy . . .'

Gefok – Afrikaans for 'fucked', as in 'I am fucked.'

Fok weet – Afrikaans for 'fuck knows'.

Fokkit – Afrikaans for 'fuck it'.

Fokker – Afrikaans for 'fucker'.

Fokkol – Afrikaans for 'fuck all', meaning 'nothing'.

Goeters – Afrikaans for 'stuff'.

Gooi – Literally, Afrikaans for 'throw', but used as a slang verb substitute for, inter alia, 'sing for us', or 'tell me' …

Hase – Literally, Afrikaans for 'rabbits', but used here as the collective name by which members of the South African police refer to the public.

Helm – Literally, Afrikaans for 'helmet'. According to local superstition, when a baby is born with the placenta covering her / his head, it is believed the baby is born with the 'helm', and could have a special talent of foretelling the future, or 'see' or 'feel' evil.

"*Here is an example so long*" – 'So long' is a typical example of how Afrikaans had influenced South African English. 'Solank' (literally means 'in the mean time') became 'so long', and is widely used.

Hier's nou 'n ding – 'Now here's a thing.' (Afrikaans.)

Hierjy – A nobody, as in "I am not just some nobody". (Afrikaans.)

Hyahi – IsiZulu for 'No!'. (South Africa has 11 official languages: Afrikaans, English, IsiNdebele, IsiXhosa, IsiZulu, Sepedi, Sesotho, Setswana, SiSwati, Tshivenda, Xitsonga. Township slang transcends all 11.)

Jakob Regop – Afrikaans for the flower zinnia. Literally means 'Jacob standing at attention' sometimes Anglicized as 'Jacob Straight-up', it can also refer to an erect male sexual organ.

Jirre – Cape Flats slang for God, approximates 'Gawd'. (Afrikaans.)

Jissis – Jeez (as in harsher version of the exclamation Jesus!) (Afrikaans.)

Jy's – Abbreivates form of the Afrikaans 'jy is', meaning 'you are'.

Jy kannie net loep nie – 'You can't just walk away?' (Afrikaans.)

Jy wiet. Jy wietie – Cape Flats Afrikaans for 'You know'. Or: 'You don't know' = jy wietie.

Kaaps – Literally, 'from the Cape' or 'of the Cape', referring to anything from the Cape Town region, or the wider Western Cape Province. (South Africa has nine provinces (similar to the states of the USA): Gauteng, Limpopo, Mpumalanga, Northwest, Free State, KwaZulu-Natal, Northern Cape, Eastern Cape, and Western Cape.)

Kak – 'Shit'.

Knippies – Literally, 'knip' is Afrikaans for 'clasp', 'clip' or 'fastener'. Knippies would literally be the plural form, but used here as a nickname for the pickpocket Tyrone Kleinbooi, who uses a hair clip as distraction.

Kwaai – Mostly used in slang form to indicate coolness, it is an Afrikaans word with a very wide application. Literally meaning someone who is hot-tempered, bad-tempered, ill-natured, harsh or severe, it is also often used as an exclamation: 'Kwaai!' = "Cool!' (or 'Heavy!').

Kwaat – Cape Flats Afrikaans for 'angry'.

Lat ek een hier het – Afrikaans (Cape Flats vernacular) of: '… that I have one here.' "And it just so happens lat ek een hier het" means: "And it just so happens that I have one with me / right here with me".

Lekka, lekker – Afrikaans word widely used for anything that is 'good', 'delicious', 'tasty'. ('Lekka' is Cape Flats vernacular, 'lekker' is formal Afrikaans.)

Liewe ffff – Literally, 'dear ffff . . .' US English equivalent would be "Sweet fff…' as in someone just stopping short of saying 'sweet fuck'.

Lobola – (Or Labola, an isiZulu or isiXhosa word, sometimes translated as 'bride price'.) A traditional Southern African custom whereby the man pays the family of his fiancée for her hand in marriage. The custom is aimed at bringing the two families together, fostering mutual respect, and indicating that the man is capable of supporting his wife financially and emotionally. Traditionally paid in heads of cattle, but cash is now widely accepted. (Source: http:// en.wikipedia.org/wiki/Lobolo)

Los – Afrikaans for 'loose'.

Ma' – Abbreviated form of 'maar', meaning 'but'. (Afrikaans.)

Ma' nou weet hulle – 'But now they know.' (Afrikaans.)

Maaifoedie – Cape Flats Afrikaans for a scoundrel or rascal.

Maar – see 'Ma" above.

Middag, goeie middag – 'Afternoon, good afternoon.' (Afrikaans.)

Mkhonto we Sizwe – or Umkhonto weSizwe ("Spear of the Nation") or 'MK' as it was more commonly known, was the military wing of the African National Congress (ANC), launched on the 16th December 1961.

The African National Congress (ANC) is South Africa's governing party and has been in power since the transition to democracy in April 1994. The organisation was initially founded as the South African Native National Congress (SANNC) on 8 January 1912 in Bloemfontein, with the aim of fighting for the rights of black South

Africans. The organization was renamed the ANC in 1923. While the organization's early period was characterized by political inertia due to power struggles and lack of resources, increasing repression and the entrenchment of white minority rule galvanized the party. As a result of the establishment of apartheid, its aversion to dissent by black people and brutal crackdown of political activists, the ANC together with the SACP formed a military wing, uMkhonto we Sizwe (Spear of the Nation/ MK) in 1961. (Quoted from South African History Online: http://www.sahistory.org.za/topic/ umkhonto-wesizwe-mk and http://www.sahistory.org.za/organisations/african-national-congress-anc)

Moenie soe wies nie – Cape Flats vernacular for 'Don't be like that'.

Moenie worrie nie – Afrikaans slang for 'Don't worry'.

Moer in – 'Moer' is a wonderful, mildly vulgar Afrikaans expletive, and can be used in any conceivable way. Its origins lie in the Dutch word 'Moeder', meaning 'Mother'. 'Moer in'' means 'to be very angry', but you can also 'moer someone'' (to hit somebody), use it as an angry exclamation (Moer!, which approximates 'Damn!'), call something or someone 'moerse' (approximates 'great' or 'cool'), or use it as an adjective: I have a 'moerse' head ache – I have a huge head ache. 'Moer toe' means 'fucked up', or even 'dead'.

Mos – Widely used and applied Afrikaans adverb, mostly meaning 'indeed', or 'as you know'.

Nee, wat – Afrikaans expression approximating 'no, not really'.

Njaps, njapsed – Mild synonym for sexual intercourse.

Nogal – Afrikaans word with wide application, mostly meaning rather, quite, fairly . . .

Nooit – Never (Afrikaans).

Nou's dit – Now it is (Afrikaans).

Orraait – Afrikaans version of 'all right'.

Ou, Outjie – Guy. 'Outjie' is the diminutive form. (Afrikaans.)

Panados – A paracetemol pain killer in tablet form.

Poegaai – Cape Flats Afrikaans, meaning 'very tired'.

Rand value – Over the past two years, the value of the South African currency (Rand, or R) has fluctuated between 7 and 110 to the US$, 9 and 15 to the Euro, and 14 to 18 to the British pound.

Sê nou – 'Now tell', or 'do say'. (Afrikaans.)

Shebeens – A shebeen (Irish: síbín) was originally an illicit bar or club where excisable alcoholic beverages were sold without a licence. The term has spread far from its origins in Ireland, to Scotland, Canada, the United States, England, Zimbabwe, English-speaking Caribbean, Namibia and South Africa. In modern South Africa, many "shebeens" are now fully legal. The word derives from the Irish síbín, meaning 'illicit whiskey'. (Quoted from http://en.wikipedia.org/wiki/Shebeen)

Sien jy – 'Do you see?' (Afrikaans.)

Sisterjie – Diminutive of 'sister'. (Afrikaans.)

Sjoe – 'Wow'. (Afrikaans.) With wide, broad application.

Skelmpie – From the (Afrikaans) 'skelm' (noun) meaning rascal, or sly person, or 'skelm' (adverb), meaning dishonest, a 'skelmpie' is the common term for a lover out of wedlock.

Skep, pappie, skep – 'Skep' can mean 'scoop' (as in scoop up water from a well) or 'spoon' (as in spoon up, when eating soup, for instance). Vaughn Cupido uses it in the sense of the Afrikaans idiom 'you have to scoop when it rains', meaning you have to gather your hay while the sun shines. ('Pappie' is the Afrikaans for 'father', and is used in the sense of the African American slang 'dawg').

Slim kind – 'Clever child'.

Snotskoot – Literally, 'snot shot', as in 'I hit him a snot shot' – i.e. right on the nose, or 'hit him in such a way that the snot flew'.

Sommer netnou – 'Soon'.

Sussie – Another diminutive for 'sister'.

Tik – South African nickname for the drug methamphetamine.

Versta'jy – 'Do you understand?' (Cape Flats vernacular.)

Volkies – Derogatory reference to coloured farm workers.

Waterblommetjie stew – 'Waterblommetjie' literally means 'little water flower'. A plant growing in fresh water ponds in the Western Cape (translation 'water blister / hydatid / Cape pondweed / Cape hawthorn / Cape asparagus'), it is famous for its use in a stew with lamb.

Wiet jy – 'Do you know?' (Cape Flats vernacular.)

Read on for an excerpt from Deon Meyer's
next Bennie Griessel novel, *Icarus*

"Excellent . . . The richness of the characters,
especially the multifaceted Benny, elevates this
above most contemporary police procedurals."
—*Publishers Weekly* (starred review)

"Deon Meyer's South Africa is laid bare in *Icarus*;
it is as glittering and hard as the diamonds his
country is famous for . . . Meyer utilizes the
crime fiction genre as an apparatus to create
a multifaceted, unsparing picture of his country."
—*Independent* (UK)

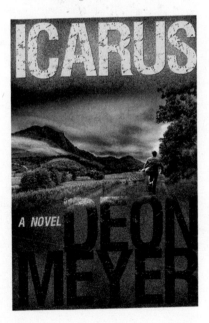

I

Heaven and earth conspired to expose Ernst Richter's corpse, the universe seemingly intent on reaching out a helping hand for justice.

First came the storm of 17 December, blowing in at just past eight in the morning. It was a rare one, but not extraordinary, borne in on a cut-off low pressure cell: a blue-black, billowing monster that thundered in from the Atlantic Ocean just north of Robben Island.

The massed clouds shot spectacular white forked tongues down to sea and land, dragging a dense curtain of rain behind them. In under half an hour 71mm had deluged Blouberg Strand and Parklands, Killarney Gardens and Zeezicht.

There was flood damage and traffic chaos. The mainstream and social media would breathlessly repeat the big G-word: *Global Warming*.

But with regard to the body it revealed, the earth's contribution was more modest; simply the contours of the veld beyond Blouberg – where the southeaster had randomly moulded the dunes like a blind sculptor – channelling the flood. It eroded the sand away around Ernst Richter's feet: one bare and tragic, while from the other a black sock dangled, comically, at half-mast.

The last link in the causal chain was fate that made twenty-nine-year-old cameraman Craig Bannister stop nearby at 11.17, beside Otto du Plessis Drive: the coast road between Blouberg and Melkbosstrand. He got out of his vehicle and gauged the weather. The worst of the wind had died down; the clouds were breaking up. He wanted to test his new radio-controlled plane, the DJI Phantom 2 Vision Plus with its stabilised high-resolution video camera. The Phantom, a so-called 'quadcopter', was a technological miracle in miniature. It was equipped with GPS, and a Wi-Fi network that allowed Bannister to connect his iPhone to the camera. He could see the video on his phone screen mere milliseconds after the Phantom recorded it up there in the sky.

Just after 11.31 Bannister frowned at the strange image and manoeuvred the Phantom to fly lower and closer. He let it hover, just one metre above the anomaly, until he was certain.

Sand, black plastic and feet: it was quite clear.

He said nothing. He looked up from the iPhone to determine exactly where the Phantom was hovering, and began to walk swiftly in that direction. It felt as though the video image was a fiction, like a TV drama, in which he could not believe. He followed a winding route, between shrubs, up and down the dunes. Only when he crested the last rise did he see it first-hand. He walked closer, leaving a solitary line of footprints in the rain-smoothed sand.

The feet protruded from beneath the thick black plastic that the body had apparently been rolled up in. The rest was still buried under the sand.

'Shit,' said Craig Bannister, prophetically.

He reached for his phone, which was still clamped to the radio control. Then he realised the Phantom was still hovering a metre above ground, busy recording everything on video. He let the quadcopter land and switched everything off. Then he made the call.

At 13.14, in the Ocean Basket on Kloof Street, Detective Captain Benny Griessel's phone rang. He checked the screen, and saw that it was Major Mbali Kaleni calling: his new commander at the Directorate of Priority Crime Investigations – also known as the DPCI, or 'the Hawks' – Violent Crimes Group. A possible chance of escape. He answered promptly, with a faint feeling of hope.

'Benny, I'm sorry to interrupt your lunch . . .'

'It's not a problem,' he said.

'I need you in Edgemead. Farmersfield Road. Vaughn is on his way too.'

'I'll be there in twenty minutes.'

'Please apologise to your family.' Because she knew about the 'special occasion' that his girlfriend Alexa Barnard had arranged.

'I will.'

He rang off. Alexa, Carla and the Van Eck boy had overheard the conversation. They were looking at him. His son Fritz still had his nose buried in his cellphone.

'*Ai*, Pappa,' said Carla, his daughter, with a mixture of understanding and disappointment.

Alexa took his hand, and squeezed it in sympathy.

'I'm sorry,' said Benny, and stood up. He felt the ache in his side and arm. Not as bad as it had been earlier that morning. 'I have to go to Edgemead.'

'Big murder?' asked the Van Eck boy. He was Carla's new 'friend', a Jesus lookalike with shoulder-length hair and sparse beard.

Griessel ignored him. He took out his wallet, then his credit card. He handed the card to Alexa. He was relieved when she nodded and took it. 'Just give me a kiss,' she said. 'My master detective.'

In the veld east of Otto du Plessis Drive they carefully unearthed the remains of Ernst Richter, as the wind marked the drama by blustering for a few minutes and then died down again, and the sun suddenly emerged from behind the clouds, at once warm and blindingly bright, reflecting off the undulating dunes and the still turbulent Atlantic Ocean.

The video unit of the SAPS made their recordings, while Forensics busied themselves carefully scooping up the sand around the body, and putting it in marked plastic bags.

Detective Adjutant Jamie Keyter of Table View was the man in charge. He had had the area within ten metres of the find cordoned off with crime-scene tape. He had ordered two uniforms to control the traffic on Otto du Plessis Drive, and keep the inquisitive away. With the suspicious, vaguely accusing tone he reserved for occasions such as this, he had interrogated Craig Bannister thoroughly.

'Why did you come and test your little aeroplane here, hey?'

'There's no law against it.'

'I know that. But why didn't you go to the place up there by the Vlei, where they fly the little aeroplanes?'

'That's for the radio control hobbyists.'

'So?'

'Look, I just got this thing. I'm a professional DOP. This is a—'

'What is a DOP?'

'A Director of Photography. I work on TV and film productions. This is the latest technology in aerial camera platforms: a drone, with an HD camera. I need to practise with it, without dodging a hundred little aeroplanes.'

'Do you have a licence for it?'

'A licence? Nobody needs a licence for a little drone.'

'So you just stopped here?'

'That's right.'

'Big coincidence.' Jamie Keyter at his ironic best.

'What are you saying?'

'I'm not saying anything. I'm asking.'

'Look, I drove until I found a spot with a nice view,' said Bannister with extreme patience. 'The road, the sea, the mountain – just take a look. That's pretty spectacular. I needed to practise flying the thing, but I wanted to test the camera too, on something worthwhile. Like this scenery.'

Jamie Keyter lifted his Ferrari sunglasses off his nose, to give Bannister the I-can-see-right-through-you look.

The man just stood there, waiting uneasily.

'So you have everything on video?' asked Keyter at last.

'Yes.'

'Show me.'

Together they watched the video on the cellphone. Twice. 'Okay,' Keyter said, and ordered Bannister to go and wait at his car. The adjutant replaced his Ferrari sunglasses on his nose. In a black polo golf shirt that displayed his bulging biceps and black Edgars chino trousers with black leather belt, hands on hips, he stared at the two feet protruding from under the black plastic.

He was pleased with himself. The feet, despite the post-mortem discolouration, were clearly those of a white man. That meant media attention.

Jamie Keyter loved media attention.

Benny Griessel, forty-six years old, rehabilitating alcoholic, six hundred and two days on the wagon, sat and stared through the windscreen of his car, stuck in the traffic jamming up Buitengracht.

Usually he hated December.

Usually he would curse this holidaymakers' madhouse with a muttered '*Jissis*'. Especially the *fokken* Gautengers who raced down to Cape Town as fast as they could in their shiny new BMWs, their fat wallets ready to blow all their Christmas bonuses with that 'We're gonna shake the Cape awake' attitude; and the entire population of the Cape's northern suburbs who abandoned their regular inhibitions and streamed down to the beaches in droves. Along with the hordes of Europeans fleeing the winter cold.

Usually he would brood resentfully on the consequences of this invasion. There was no parking, the traffic stank, prices doubled and crime stats went up at least 12 per cent, because everyone drank like a fish, which unleashed all the wrong demons.

Usually. But not this year: the oppression was in him and over him and around him, like a disconsolate cloud. Again. Still.

The momentary relief of his escape from the Ocean Basket had evaporated. On the way to the car the melancholy in Mbali's voice had registered with him – the muted dismay, accentuated by her attempt to disguise it. In stark contrast to the positivity she had tried to radiate over the past two months as group commander.

I need you in Edgemead. Farmersfield Road. Vaughn is on his way too.

Something bad was brewing. And he didn't have the strength for disaster any more.

So today the December madness and the snail's pace traffic wasn't so much a thorn in his flesh, but a blessing.

The Forensic team had exposed the full length of Ernst Richter's corpse.

Adjutant Jamie Keyter called the video team closer so they could record it: the thick black plastic rolled around the body, just not long enough to cover the feet, and the blood red rope with which it had been so thoroughly bound – up near the head, around the waist and down at the ankles.

Keyter had seen the newspaper photographer trying to take photos from Otto du Plessis drive with his long lens. That was why he stood with legs apart, hands on hips: the image of a detective in control of his crime scene. He kept an eye on the video team, until he was satisfied that the recording covered all the suitable angles.

'Okay,' he said. 'You come out.' Then, to Forensics, with a wave of the hand, 'Cut him open.'

The two forensic analysts chose the right tools from their kit, lifted the crime tape and knelt beside the victim. One carefully cut the cord loose. The other picked up the cord and packed it in an evidence bag.

Jamie Keyter ducked under the tape himself now and walked up to the victim. 'Let's unroll him.'

It took nearly ten minutes, as they had to work carefully and the single sheet of plastic seemed endless. The forensics men folded up every two metres of the plastic to limit contamination.

The uniforms, the video unit, the two detective constables, ambulance men all stepped closer, curious.

Finally the body was revealed.

'He hasn't been here long,' said one forensic analyst, as there were relatively few signs of decay, just a general darkening of the skin, the blueish-purple network of livor mortis visible on the feet and the underside of the neck, and the sand grains that clung to the body from head to toe. A lean man of average height, with thick, dark brown hair, dressed in a black T-shirt – with the words *I refuse to engage in a battle of wits with an unarmed person* in big white letters – and blue jeans.

'Maybe a week or so,' said the other, and thought the face seemed vaguely familiar, but he couldn't place it at that moment. He suppressed the impulse to say something.

It was the closest anyone came to identifying Ernst Richter at the scene of the crime.

'He's been strangled with something,' said the other forensic analyst, and pointed at the deep discolouration that circled the throat.

'Obviously,' said Jamie Keyter.